Historical Fiction
for Young Readers
(Grades 4–8)

Recent Titles in the
Children's and Young Adult Literature Reference Series
Catherine Barr, Series Editor

Books Kids Will Sit Still For 3: A Read-Aloud Guide
Judy Freeman

Classic Teenplots: A Booktalk Guide to Use with Readers Ages 12–18
John T. Gillespie and Corinne J. Naden

Best Books for Middle School and Junior High Readers: Grades 6–9. Supplement
to the First Edition
John T. Gillespie and Catherine Barr

Best Books for High School Readers: Grades 9–12. Supplement to the First Edition
John T. Gillespie and Catherine Barr

War and Peace: A Guide to Literature and New Media, Grades 4–8
Virginia A. Walter

Across Cultures: A Guide to Multicultural Literature for Children
Kathy East and Rebecca L. Thomas

Best Books for Children, Supplement to the 8th Edition: Preschool
through Grade 6
Catherine Barr and John T. Gillespie

Best Books for Boys: A Resource for Educators
Matthew D. Zbaracki

Beyond Picture Books: Subject Access to Best Books for Beginning Readers
Barbara Barstow, Judith Riggle, and Leslie Molnar

A to Zoo: Subject Access to Children's Picture Books. Supplement to the 7th
Edition
Carolyn W. Lima and Rebecca L. Thomas

Gentle Reads: Great Books to Warm Hearts and Lift Spirits, Grades 5–9
Deanna J. McDaniel

Best New Media, K–12: A Guide to Movies, Subscription Web Sites, and Educational
Software and Games
Catherine Barr

Historical Fiction for Young Readers (Grades 4–8)

An Introduction

JOHN T. GILLESPIE

Children's and Young Adult Literature Reference
Catherine Barr, Series Editor

LIBRARIES UNLIMITED

A Member of the Greenwood Publishing Group

Westport, Connecticut ✦ London

Library of Congress Cataloging-in-Publication Data

Gillespie, John Thomas, 1928–
  Historical fiction for young readers (grades 4–8) : an introduction / John T. Gillespie.
      p. cm. — (Children's and young adult literature reference)
  Includes bibliographical references and index.
  ISBN 978-1-59158-621-0 (alk. paper)
    1. Historical fiction—Juvenile literature—Bibliography. 2. History—Juvenile litera-
ture—Bibliography. 3. Children's literature—Bibliography. 4. Young adult literature—
Bibliography. 5. Children's libraries—Book lists. 6. Middle school libraries--Book lists.
7. Junior high school libraries—Book lists. 8. Readers' advisory services—United
States. I. Title.
  Z1037.G497 2008
  011.62—dc22   2008031343

British Library Cataloguing in Publication Data is available.

Library of Congress Catalog Card Number: 2008031343
ISBN: 978-1-59158-621-0

First published in 2008

Libraries Unlimited, 88 Post Road West, Westport, CT 06881
A Member of the Greenwood Publishing Group, Inc.
www.lu.com

Printed in the United States of America

The paper used in this book complies with the
Permanent Paper Standard issued by the National
Information Standards Organization (Z39.48–1984).

10 9 8 7 6 5 4 3 2 1

DEDICATION

To the wonderful staff of St. Vincent's Hospital in New York City,
particularly Drs. Michael Grasso and Paul Goldstein, for saving my body,
and to Terry Hirst for saving my spirit.

Contents

Preface

THE PURPOSE OF THIS BOOK IS TO INTRODUCE different facets of historical fiction written for young readers. The first three chapters give background information. The first introduces the genre, supplies general information on the structure of a novel, and gives criteria for evaluation. This is followed by specific criteria for historical fiction. The second gives a brief history of the historical novel in English for young readers beginning with the invention of printing and extending to important novelists writing today. The third supplies general techniques that can be used to promote and stimulate reading with youngsters.

Chapters four through eight give detailed information on 81 historical novels suitable for readers in grades four through eight. The primary purpose of this coverage is to introduce librarians and teachers to these books and, thus, give them the information to provide reading guidance to students mainly through either formal or informal booktalks or through the preparation of bibliographies. A further use would be for collection building.

These chapters are arranged geographically with subdivisions for important historical periods. In choosing these books, consideration was given to representing a wide array of subjects and interests at various reading levels and abilities within the grade-level range. However, the overriding criterion was the quality of the book. Emphasis was placed on recent titles, published from 1990 on. Newbery Medal winners were not included because this material can already be found in the author's *The Newbery/Printz Companion* (Libraries Unlimited, 2006), co-written with Corinne Naden. Before a title was considered for inclusion, it had to be recommended for purchase in either standard bibliographies or current reviewing periodicals, or both.

After the title, general bibliographic material, and suggested grade-level suitability, the detailed information on each title is divided into six sections.

1. Introduction. The author is introduced with brief, pertinent biographical information, mention of relevant other works (sequels and so forth) and significant information about the novel such as the identity of the narrator and time span.
2. Historical Background. Important historical events that are referred to in the novel are discussed. As well, actual living figures found in the books are identified and significant historical developments that followed the events in the novel are mentioned. This information is valuable in placing the novel in its correct setting and determining the significance of the events described. In addition, this orientation to the actual historical setting of the novel should help when introducing the book to potential readers.
3. Principal Characters. The important characters in the book are listed with brief material to identify each.
4. Plot Synopsis. The entire plot is retold, including incidents and characters. In each case, an attempt has been made to retain the mood and point of view of the author.
5. Passages for Booktalking. Key incidents suitable for retelling or reading aloud are indicated and the pagination for each is given.
6. Themes and Subjects. To facilitate the use of the book in various circumstances and different booktalking situations, the principal themes and subjects are mentioned in paragraph form followed by a list of secondary themes and subjects.

At the end of each of the five geographical chapters or sections thereof—, there is a list of "Additional Selections." These are other historical novels that explore the same geographical region or time period.

Each provides basic bibliographic material, a grade-level indication, and a brief annotation.

Following the body of the work, there are three indexes: the first two offer access by author and title to the five geographical chapters and the third is a subject index of key topics covered in the main titles.

It is hoped that this book will not be used as a substitute for reading the original novel, nor is it intended as a definitive work of literary criticism. It only represents a selection of books that have value in a variety of situations and the author's analysis of them.

In closing, the author would like to thank the staffs of the many libraries whose collections were consulted. The most used was the Children's Room of the Donnell Library, part of the New York Public Library system. Special thanks also to Barbara Ittner of Libraries Unlimited, to my editor Catherine Barr for her invaluable guidance and patience, and to Christine McNaull and Julia C. Miller for their careful editing and production work.

John T. Gillespie

CHAPTER 1

Introduction and Criteria
for Evaluating Historical Fiction

INTRODUCTION

The *Oxford Dictionary of Literary Terms* (Oxford, 2008) defines a historical novel as "a novel in which the action takes place during a specific historical period well before the time of writing (often one or two generations before, sometimes several generations), and in which some attempt is made to depict accurately the customs and mentality of the period." Author Jill Paton Walsh's definition is "A novel is a historical novel when it is wholly or partly about the public events and social conditions which are the material of history, regardless of the time at which it was written."

Like other types of fiction, young people mainly read historical novels for enjoyment; however, there are several additional reasons for reading this genre. Historical fiction gives young readers insight into the struggles, conflicts, and emotions—hope, fear, joy, and sometimes despair—of people who lived in the past. It enables children to experience, albeit in a secondhand fashion, daily life in ancient Rome, a covered wagon journey across the prairies, or the intrigues associated with the court of Elizabeth I. Young readers gain a sense of the continuity of life through historical fiction. History becomes a cumulative entity, a progressive flow, and by immersing themselves in it, young people can gain a sense of how we progressed to our present condition, how to evaluate the present in relation to the past, and how to determine their place in this continuum. They begin to realize that, though living conditions change, human nature remains the same.

On the other hand, the importance of and need for change is another lesson to be learned from historical fiction. Youngsters tend to live in the present. Historical fiction can bring perspective into their lives by showing them how people of their age lived in earlier times and how they solved problems, particularly those relating to reaching maturity, dealing with authority, and finding appropriate goals in life. Through historical fiction, a young reader should realize that life today is a result of the behavior of people in the past and that this behavior also has a role in determining the future.

Historical fiction points out not only the triumph of the human spirit but also the mistakes made by individuals and cultures in the past. Mistakes have produced personal tragedies and, at their worst, have determined the ultimate fate of whole cultures and civilizations.

An often-quoted adage states that those who are ignorant of history are doomed to repeat it. Here, historical fiction adds a different dimension to history than the one nonfiction provides. For example, textbooks can describe a battle, give statistics relating to it, and describe its effects, but there is no substitute for a novel in which this event becomes a first-hand experience in which the reader becomes personally involved. In superior historical fiction the reader experiences the horror, fear, carnage, brutality, heroism, squalor, and the sights and sounds of an event and it becomes a personal, memorable experience. In no other medium, is this total, special immersion possible.

GENERAL CRITERIA FOR EVALUATING FICTION

The elements of the novel that will be discussed in this section are plot, characterization, point of view, setting, theme, style and tone, and format.

Plot

Plot can be defined as "A series of events that tell the story." Everything that happens in a novel must have a purpose, and the sequence of these events must lead to a satisfying conclusion. For young readers, plot is the foremost element in a novel and preference is given to those that are fast-moving, interesting, and logical (but not necessarily, chronological). Though plots can give the impression of reality, the way an author manipulates these events should heighten reality and be more interesting. The author must choose incidents and events that will move the plot along and hold the interest of the reader.

The unessential and extraneous should be omitted. The degree to which the author can do this successfully determines the quality of the plotting.

Plots should be well constructed, should reflect the author's central purpose or theme, and be worthy of telling. Good pacing is essential to holding the interest of the reader. Beginnings are important, particularly with young readers who like instant immersion in the plot. Beginnings should create interest, usually through a bit of mystery or suspense, or an action sequence. Even the title and dust-jacket can create initial interest. The narrative can be structured in various ways. The most popular are linear plots, that is, plots that follow a chronological order. The timespan can vary—days, months, years, even generations—but young readers generally prefer a tight time span. A few use a reverse chronological approach, starting at the end (often the present) and working to the beginning (the past). Others combine these two structures and use a linear plot with glimpses into the past known as flashbacks. This device is used to inform the reader of events that occurred prior to the beginning of the novel. However, the overuse of this technique in a single novel can sometimes lead to confusion and lack of interest. The more sophisticated the readers, the most able they are to cope with time changes that flashbacks produce.

Another way of introducing background material on events or characters is through exposition. This is more direct than a flashback. For example, servants are often used at the beginnings of plays to give background material on the household. The subtlety with which a novelist can deliver this material is a test of writing prowess.

Some plots are episodic in nature—they consist of a series of separate incidents involving the same characters. Each of these incidents has a mini-plot with is own beginning, climax, and resolution. Many children's books about family situations, such as *Homer Price*, have episodic plots. Most plots, however, are progressive or cumulative in nature. That is, the plot contains the traditional beginning in which characters and situations are introduced, a middle in which these elements are developed, and an end where there is a climax and situations are resolved. Some plots progress on a rising straight line of dramatic incidents and progressive suspense while others, like the Little House books, essentially follow a flat straight line with a minimum of suspense but with a still interesting plot and conflicts.

Many novels also contain a subplot, a secondary sequence of events that is related to the main plot through locale, characters, or a defining incident. Subplots can add a sometimes important digression from the main plot, expand the central theme of the novel, and develop interesting secondary characters.

Some novels contain two main plots that are being developed simultaneously. These are often told in alternate chapters and are joined at the end—for example, a story in which two friends are separated and, after trying to find each other in a series of adventures, are reunited in the end.

Conflict, or the clash between forces or characters, is essential in the novel. There are various types of conflicts. The most common is person versus person, that is, protagonist versus antagonist. Usually the antagonist is known, but in most mystery stories the antagonist is not revealed until the ending. A novel in which there is sibling rivalry is a good example of person versus person conflict. Person versus self, in which a character tries to resolve an inner conflict or weakness, or accept a particular internal quality or condition, is also common. Many novels for young readers use this type of conflict to deal with themes of reaching maturity and self-acceptance. The conflict of person versus nature is popular with youngsters, as shown by the importance of survival novels, beginning with *Robinson Crusoe*. Most science fiction and fantasies contain another kind of conflict, person versus a superhuman force. In these novels the antagonist is superhuman and often represents the force of evil or darkness. One of the more interesting conflicts is person versus society. In these, an individual is at odds with the "system," particular social conditions, or a difficult social environment. Sometimes a novel can contain more than one conflict, for example, accepting the condition of being a slave (person versus society) while trying to adjust to an abusive father (person versus person).

There are many techniques that writers use to increase interest in the plot. Suspense is the creation of anticipation or tension in a situation and often includes purposefully delaying some revelation. When this appears at the end of chapters, it is called a cliffhanger, where the reader is left dangling awaiting the resolution of a situation. An example of a cliffhanger would be a chapter that ends with "When Sally opened the closet door, she stared in disbelief at the sight before her." Many important writers including Sir Walter Scott used this technique extensively, but its overuse can be frustrating to the reader and eventually counterproductive. Foreshadowing is a device that gives the reader an indication of events to come. An example would be: "Little did Sally realize the horror that lay in store when she answered that want ad."

Climax is defined as the moment when a conflict reaches particularly high intensity. There can be many climaxes within a novel, often increasing in intensity until the last, which usually produces a resolution, when a conflict is settled or decided. An anticlimax occurs when the author interrupts the growing tension with an occurrence that is often trivial in nature. Related to this is the term "denouement," which refers to the events that follow the climax, when the mystery is unraveled and misunderstandings are explained. An open-ended plot is one where the outcome is not completely decided and subsequent events remain uncertain. The opposite is a closed ending where all the conflicts are neatly resolved.

A number of pitfalls in plot construction can cause problems for readers. The overuse of coincidence can destroy a plot's believability. Dickens could get away with it, but he was an exception. The manipulation of an audience through sentimentality, tear-jerking situations and others that exploit emotions should be avoided. This is particularly prevalent in stories where animals are present. Here, anthropomorphism is also a danger. Some plots are so predictable and overworked that they become boring to readers in spite of otherwise good writing and others use sensationalism to disguise a lack of substance. Finally, slow-moving plots are generally not acceptable to young readers. They like their plots to move quickly without too many distractions such as lengthy descriptions. In this respect, they are like many adult readers.

Characterization

Although the plot is the most important element for young readers, the need for interesting, believable, well-rounded characters grows with the sophistication of the reader. There are various types of characters in fiction. Primary characters are those closest to plot developments, this is, those that play a large part in the story. These characters should be well-developed and rounded to an extent that the readers feel they know them. These characters are sometimes are so well-developed that one can predict their actions and attitudes. Consistency is important but unexpected actions are possible if they are made believable. Secondary characters are those that play small roles in the plot. They often are classified as flat characters, that is, those that are identified by one or two dominant qualities or traits. This is not necessarily a deficiency—many of Dickens's characters fall into this category. The number of rounded characters in a novel depends on the plot, but most plots have only a half dozen or fewer primary characters. In general, too many characters tend to confuse the plot and turn off young readers.

Dynamic characters are those that change. This change should result naturally from the plot and with cause. For example, a boy learns the value of sportsmanship and as a result his team wins the series. Sometimes the inability of a central character to change becomes the central conflict of the story. Static characters are those that do not change during the course of the action and it is usually necessary for them to do so.

Some authors begin with the central character and then place him or her into a situation that becomes the plot. There should be a unity of character and plot and characters should behave consistently. Character change can be made believable only through logical plot developments that could cause these changes. The sudden transformation of the evil landlord into a benevolent philanthropist in the last chapter will not work unless one believes in miracles. Readers like to discover elements of themselves or of other people they know in the novels they read. The process of identification with characters is important, particularly with youngsters.

Readers should feel that the author knows all about the characters, although it is not necessary to tell everything about a character at the beginning. Indeed the gradual revelation of the complexities of a character's traits or values can add a thrilling and dramatic dimension to a story. Character change through character growth is an important and valid theme in many young adult novels.

The desire on the part of the reader for depth of characterization depends on many factors: the age and maturity of the readers, amount of experience with reading, intellect, and the purpose of reading. If the need is for a light mystery, sophisticated character development is not necessary.

The use of stock characters or stereotypes is usually a sign of deficiency in character development. The mustache-twirling villain, the pure-as-gold heroine, the hard-drinking Irishman, and the blond-haired, incorruptible hero all remain boring stereotypes unless fleshed out with other believable characteristics.

Character can be revealed in many ways. Sometimes authors supply important details directly about characters by introducing them with descriptions of personality and character traits. Characters can also be made known by a description of appearance. Neatness of dress, an old-fashioned wardrobe, even physical features such as obesity or a handicap, can be clues to character traits. A character's actions define him or her, as do glimpses into their thoughts. The content of a character's speech and the speech patterns used can tell much about personality, education, attitudes, and social status. Characters should speak in a way consistent with their backgrounds, age, education, and sex. Dialogue in which others talk about the character is another method of revealing information, in which case material about both the speaker and the subject is disclosed. Whatever methods are used, they should be imaginative, interesting, and suited to the plot.

Point of View

Point of view is the perspective from which the story is seen or told. The point of view determines how the reader learns of the events and characters, their relative importance, value, and significance. One popular device is the first-person narrative in which the reader experiences everything through the thoughts of a single person. This device has many advantages. The story gains empathy, reality, intensity, sympathy, concentration, and immediacy through this simple focus on a single individual. The main disadvantage is related to its benefits, that is, the plot is limited to what a single character thinks and feels. Thus it is difficult to move the plot along when events outside the narrator's experience must be dealt with. It is also limited because the emotions and inner feelings of other characters cannot be expressed. In addition, the narrative is limited to the vocabulary, insights, and feelings of the narrator's age, experience, and personality. Sometimes the narrator is not the protagonist (Conrad uses this technique often). In that case, the narrator can comment on the action more objectively than the central character.

Authors also use more than a single-person narrative within a novel. With this technique, known as multiple points of view, the narration is shared by two or more characters. In this way, multiple viewpoints are provided without losing the personal attributes that are a good feature of the first-person narrative.

Some authors enter their characters' brains with the purpose of revealing only their thoughts in the most subjective manner possible. The result is the approach known as stream of consciousness. This device was used successfully by James Joyce.

An omniscient point of view uses a third-person voice for narration. With this device, the author knows all about the past, present, and future of the characters and is aware of all their motivations, characteristics, feelings, and actions. These are revealed in accordance with the author's purposes and plan. This device allows for greater freedom and flexibility but sacrifices the intensity of involvement of a first-person narrative.

A limited omniscience novel uses a third-person narrative but focuses on the viewpoint of one character. The Little House books are good examples of the use of this point of view. A related term is the "objective point of view" where the third-person is used but the author does not enter the minds of any of the characters. The narration, therefore, consists of simply describing the action, no inner thoughts are presented, no motives are explored, and no evaluative judgments are made. Writers including Ernest Hemingway and, more recently, Cormac McCarthy write using this point of view.

In conclusion, the point of view of a novel should be honest, consistent, and be the technique that best accomplishes the author's purpose.

Setting

The setting of a novel is the place and time in which it occurs, or its "where" and "when." The setting creates the framework for the plot, helps establish a desired mood, and forwards the central theme. Some genres, including historical fiction and fantasy, rely more on the setting than others. Regardless of genre, settings should be clear, appropriate, believable, and authentic. Settings can be wide, sometimes spanning long time periods and many places. They can achieve many purposes. They can establish a mood, be an antagonist, illuminate characters, and clarify conflict. Sometimes, as in allegories such as the Narnia books, the setting is used as a symbol.

Settings can be classified as one of two types: (1) general or broad or (2) specific or integral. In the first type, the setting is neither emphasized nor described at length, but is considered a backdrop for the action. Some settings—a farmyard, a summer camp, or a modern classroom—are immediately identifiable by readers and do not need to be expanded upon because the reader already is familiar with the setting and feels comfortable with it. Specific or integral settings are an essential part of the plot. Without a description of this setting, it would be impossible to achieve the author's purpose. For example, a novel that takes place during the Crusades or in prehistoric times becomes more meaningful and attractive through imaginative descriptions of these settings. Whether to emphasize the setting or not is the author's choice and depends on its importance in relation to other elements in the novel.

Theme

The theme of a novel answers the question "What is the basic truth behind the novel?" It is the novel's central idea and reveals the author's real purpose in writing the book. Themes should be worthy of exploring and suitable for the book's intended audience. Themes can be either explicit or implicit. Explicit themes are stated directly (for example, "The moral of this story is . . .") while implicit themes are revealed subtly and require the reader to extract them from the novel. Themes usually involve abstractions like revenge, betrayal, or love. Not all books have profound themes. Some novels are written entirely to entertain, like adventure stories whose themes are simply a conflict—good versus evil or humans versus nature. When the author is intent on proving a point, teaching a lesson, or preaching a sermon, the theme sometimes overrides the plot and the rules of good fiction writing are ignored. In these cases, the novel becomes didactic. This kind of moralizing was popular in the early days of children's literature but is frowned on today. Many of these lessons are best taught in a non-fiction format. A novel can contain more than one theme. Where there are multiple themes, one is usually the primary one and the others are secondary.

Many years ago G. Robert Carlsen, a young adult literature specialist, wrote an article (*Top of the News*, January 1965) in which he discussed themes popular with young readers and others that were not. Favored themes include those involving the search for a direction in life and books where decisions must be made that involve the protagonist's growth to maturity. Young people are also interested in novels that explore the social order, books that deal with characters facing economic problems, racial and other social injustices, and political tyranny. In these novels, these problems are brought to a personal level where an individual must take action to correct a particular situation. At this age, there is also a fascination with the bizarre, the offbeat, and the unusual in human experience. The great popularity of science fiction and fantasy demonstrates this. Lastly, the theme of transition is well-liked. In these novels, the central character makes decisions that define greater independence and progress. These landmarks might show the transition from childhood to adolescence or adolescence to adulthood. The important point is that positive growth has been shown. Unpopular themes include those that show life limitations, man's helplessness to change the social order, and resignation to the boundaries within which life can be lived. In short, youngsters like hopeful novels where change for the better is possible in a world where one can realize one's aspirations and destiny.

Style and Tone

Writing style refers to the way the author uses language: the choice of words, sentence structure, use of imagery, and rhythm. Jonathan Swift wrote, "Proper words in proper places make the true definition of style." An author's writing style can range from terse and direct to flamboyant and flowery. The important criterion is whether or not it is appropriate to the subject and accurately mirrors the book's theme, plot and characterization. Each author's writing style is unique. Many authors use imagery to heighten the impact and to appeal to the senses ("her dress was fire-engine red," for example). Others use figurative language such as personification, simile and metaphor, allusions, hyperbole, and wordplay. Some authors play with word sounds by using alliteration and onomatopoeia (words that sound like their meaning, such as swishing water), while others use word rhythms (as in Dr. Seuss's picture book *The Cat in the Hat*). Regardless of the nature of an author's style, one expects clarity, appropriateness, an absence of clichés, honesty, and imaginative use of words.

Tone refers to the author's attitude towards his or her subject. It could be, for example, a humorous, light-hearted approach, or one that is serious and emphasizes dramatic elements, or one that is satirical in nature. Obviously the tone should reflect the purpose of the author. In books written for young readers, be wary of signs of writing down to an audience. This form of condescension treats readers as though they lacked intelligent or maturity and should be avoided.

Format

Adult readers pay little attention to the format of a book but young readers do. For example, very thick books are often avoided (glaring exceptions include the Harry Potter books). The book's size, shape, and design should be appropriate to its audience. The use of high-quality illustrations can bring depth and clarity to the plot and its characters. An attractive book jacket does a great deal to attract readers (many people *do* judge a book by its cover). Typography, binding, and page layout are other factors in the format of a book.

SPECIFIC CRITERIA RELATING TO HISTORICAL FICTION

Historical novels, like those in other genres, should have well-paced plots, believable characters, authentic settings, and good use of dialogue. They should also contain elements for reader identification and valid themes. Here are some more-specific points.

Characterization

In relation to characters portrayed, there are three types of historical novels. In the first, all of the characters were real people; in the second, although the setting may be authentically in the past, all of the characters are fictional; and in the third, there is a mixture of both. If real characters are portrayed, it is essential that the writer depict them neither as plaster saints nor unredeemable villains, but as human beings with both faults and virtues. A historical hero should not have been "sanitized." Characters should not be stereotypes. Each character should exhibit personality traits with which readers can identify. Characters must act and hold beliefs and values in keeping with the times. This is particularly difficult when depicting the place of women in society or the types of civil liberties that commoners possessed.

Plots and Setting

Plots of historical novels should adhere to the basic criteria: logical structure, suitable pacing, be suspenseful, and contain plenty of action. The historical novel should also give an accurate, vivid picture of life during the period depicted. Details of everyday life, clothing, and food create local color and interest, but should be integrated into the plot and introduced when the timing is suitable. Overly long descriptions often distract the reader and ultimately result in boredom. The dialogue and conversations should give the flavor of the time but should not include excessive use of dialect or quaint expressions of the time that often can confuse the reader and require explanation. On the other hand, a moderate use of these can create local color and a feeling of authenticity. A balance is needed as there should be with the number of "thees" and "thous" used. The opposite problem arises if the speech is too modernized. In addition to producing anachronisms, the novel will lose validity.

Oversimplification of social problems and controversial issues is common when writing for children. It is tempting to simplify social conflicts and create black or white judgments. For example, although the practice of slavery was abhorrent, not all slave owners were incarnations of Simon Legree. Of course no author can be completely impartial but readers deserve honesty in the presentation of complex issues, including depicting various sides of a problem.

Themes

While the themes in historical novels should reflect their setting, they should also be relevant to today's society. Some examples of relevant themes are those that depict problems with changing values, the meaning of freedom, responsible behavior, and the conflict between good and evil. More so than with other genres, authors of historical novels often have particular messages to convey, perhaps an axe to grind, or a moral point to be stressed. Readers have become wary of this didacticism.

The opportunities to apply these criteria relating to plot, characterization, point of view, setting, style and tone, format, and themes increases with extended exposure to the wealth of reading pleasure found in historical novels. In time, one employs these criteria unconsciously. In any case, their use increases the depth and satisfaction one gets from reading.

CHAPTER 2

A Brief History of Historical Fiction for Young Readers in English

THE BEGINNINGS: FROM THE INVENTION OF PRINTING TO 1800

Although no historical fiction was written specifically for young people during this period, the groundwork was laid for important developments in this area in the next century. It is interesting to note that the first book published by William Caxton (1422–1491), the first printer in England, was a type of historical fiction: the *Recuyell of the Historyes of Troy* (1474), the story of the Trojan War recast in medieval settings. He was also responsible for publishing first editions of *The Fables of Aesop*, *Reynard the Fox*, and *Le Morte Darthur*. These and other popular folktales, such as those involving Robin Hood, Dick Whittington, the Arabian Nights, and St. George, later became available in cheap editions known as chapbooks and provided entertaining reading for both adults and children. Chapbooks were so named because they were sold by traveling salesmen known as chapmen. These slim volumes, cheap and poorly made, usually sold for a penny, and were typically 16 to 64 pages in length. In addition to bowdlerized folk and fairy tales, retellings of Bible stories were popular as were abridgements of three classics of the period discussed later: *The Pilgrim's Progress* (1678), *Robinson Crusoe* (1719), and *Gulliver's Travels* (1726). Chapbooks contained many illustrations—usually badly carved woodcuts recycled for economy's sake into different books regardless of their relevance to the subject matter. Though chapbooks were intended for an adult audience, children found this often-forbidden reading material attractive and appealing.

Books written for children during this period were of two types: books of instruction or books on moral instruction, religion, and manners. An example of the former is *A Little Book for Little Children* (1702), subtitled "wherein are set down, in a plain and pleasant Way, Directions for Spelling, and other remarkable Matters Adorn'd with Cuts." The alphabet section begins with the famous line "A was an Archer and shot at a frog" and ends with "Z was one Zeno the Great but he's dead." This book was popular on both sides of the Atlantic. A typical example of the second type, and a bestseller during the period, was a little book by a minister, James Janeway (1636–1672), *A Token for Children* (1671) which bears the subtitle "Being an Exact Account of the Conversion, Holy and Exemplary Lives and Joyful Deaths of Several Young Children." Of this book, John Rowe Townsend says, "The stories are of saintly children who died young in a rapture of prayer. This was clearly the highest fate the author could conceive for them. He exhorted his readers, 'If you love your parents, if you love your souls, if you would escape hellfire, and if you would go to Heaven when you die, do you go and do as these good children.' The Book was popular for many years and reprints continued into the nineteenth century." For the American market, several local case histories were added to the original thirteen. The purpose of these early children's books was entirely pedantic, with the aim of teaching the elements of writing, counting, and spelling, and of instilling proper Puritan behavioral patterns, religious beliefs, and a healthy fear of Hell.

The year 1744 was a milestone in the history of children's literature. In that year John Newbery (1713–1767) published the first book intended solely to amuse children. It was *A Little Pretty Pocket-Book*. Newbery was born in Berkshire and after learning the printing trade in Reading, moved to London and at the sign of the "Bible and Sun" in St. Paul's Churchyard began his illustrious publishing career. During his lifetime he published between twenty and thirty books for children, some of which included small toys in the packet. Newbery's most popular and enduring book was *The History of Little Goody-Two Shoes, Otherwise Called Mrs. Margery Two-Shoes*. The authorship has never been determined but many think it was Oliver Goldsmith, the author of *The Vicar of Wakefield* and a good friend of Mr. Newbery. The success of Newbery's publishing for children and the increased literacy in the younger population led other printers to publish books for children that to this day supply information but now also entertain and amuse.

The popularity of three great adventure stories of this period paved the way for the development of the historical novel in the 19th century and its expansion into books for children. The first was *The Pilgrim's Progress*, Part I of which was published in 1678 with Part II following in 1684. The writer, John Bunyan (1628–1688), a Protestant preacher, wrote much of it while in prison for his preaching and religious beliefs during the reign of Charles II. The book is a religious allegory in which, during the first part, the hero Christian embarks on a number of travels that test his faith and survival skills. In these travels he ventures into such areas as the Slough of Despond, the Valley of Humiliation, Doubting Castle, and Vanity Fair. In the second part, Christian's wife and children accompany him on a second pilgrimage. In these stories Bunyan drew on his own experience within his faith: his temptations, trials, and spiritual journeys to enlightenment and belief. The book was a great success and was published in ten editions during his life. Parts of it became popular in chapbooks where, in abridged formats, the adventurous and thrilling elements were stressed. These versions were particularly appealing to young readers.

Gulliver's Travels (1726) was also written by a cleric, the Irish Jonathan Swift (1667–1745) and consists of four parts, each of which tells of a different voyage by the narrator Lemuel Gulliver. Although it was intended as a social satire, many of its readers were too intrigued with the fantastic adventures of its hero in exotic lands peopled with bizarre characters to look beneath the surface narrative for hidden meanings. This is particularly true of youngsters and the first book, which recounts Gulliver's adventure when he is shipwrecked on the island of Lilliput and taken prisoner by the people, who are only 6 inches tall. Once again, the abridged chapbook editions were extremely popular.

The third was so popular that it spawned, in the next century, hundreds of imitations known as Robinsonnades. The book was *Robinson Crusoe* (1719) and the author, the English journalist and writer Daniel Defoe (1660–1731). Based on the actual experiences of a sailor, Alexander Selkirk, it tells how the hero, renamed Robinson Crusoe, is shipwrecked off South America and spends twenty-eight years on an island where his resourcefulness, courage, and inventiveness help him survive along with material he has salvaged from the ship. In the middle of his twenty-fourth year, he captures a savage who had visited the island earlier with his companions. He names him Friday after the day on which he was captured. The remainder of the story tells how he educates Friday and how he is eventually able to return to England. Although the book is often considered solely an adventure story, technically it is also one of the earliest historical novels because the events described occurred several years before the publication of the book. Two sequels were published but were not considered nearly as successful. Again, often in abridged formats, this story was read by and stirred the imaginations of young readers.

These three books and other adventure tales published during this time paved the way for exciting developments in the 19th century in the field of historical fiction for youth.

THE AGE OF THE GREAT ADVENTURE STORY (THE NINETEENTH CENTURY)

During the 19th century, literature for children flourished and developed in several different genres. There were the traditional books of instruction and information, now made more entertaining and accessible. Examples included, in America, the writings of Samuel Goodrich (1793–1860) and Jacob Abbott (1803–1879). The former, using the pen name of Peter Parley, wrote more than 150 slim books for children on subjects including history, geography, travel, science, and art. Using a chatty informal style (one book begins "Here I am! My name is Peter Parley! I am an old man but I have seen a great many things and had a great many adventures, and I love to talk about them"), he satisfied the curiosity of children in a painless way. At his death, about 7 million copies of his books had been sold and dozens of copy-cat writers flourished using similar techniques and subjects. Another prolific writer of sugar-coated nonfiction for young readers was Jacob Abbott, the author of nearly 200 titles. Twenty-eight of them made up the Rollo series, many of which described foreign countries using material that Abbott had gathered on his many trips to Europe. Stories of imagination and fantasy became increasingly popular. Some examples include: Lewis Carroll's *Alice's Adventures in Wonderland* (1865), George MacDonald's *At the Back of the North Wind* (1871), and Charles Kingsley's *The Water Babies*. Charles Kingsley (1819–1875) also wrote historical novels including *Westward Ho!*, a historical adventure set in Elizabethan times. The school story also flourished, as exemplified by Thomas Hughes's classic *Tom Brown's Schooldays* (1857), an autobiographical tale of a young boy attending the English public school Rugby in the 1830s when the headmaster was Dr. Arnold and the bully to be avoided was named Flashman. By century's end, the school story continued to thrive, an important exponent being Rudyard Kipling (1865–1936), whose *Stalky and Co.* (1899) consists of interrelated stories about three boys—Beetle, M'Turk, and Cockran, nicknamed Stalky—and their adventures in a boys' boarding school on the coast of Devon.

Domestic stories, aimed mainly at the young female audience, also thrived. In America, one of the great writers in this genre was Louisa May Alcott (1832–1888), whose novels about the March family, beginning with *Little Women* (1868), were extremely popular. At the turn of the century, the domestic drama continued to be successful and included such writers as Frances Hodgson Burnett (1849–1924) whose novels *Little Lord Fauntleroy* (1885) and *The Secret Garden* (1910) continue to attract readers today.

The boys' adventure story also developed and flourished in the 19th century. Because so many of them took place in the past and used historical subjects, it is almost impossible to separate these adventure stories from historical fiction. During the 19th century two writers of historical fiction for adults set the standards for all writers in the genre. They were Sir Walter Scott (1771–1832) in Britain and James Fenimore Cooper (1789–1851) in the United States. Scott derived much of his material from Scottish history and from medieval romances. He is best known for his series of thirty-two books known as the Waverley novels, which began with the publication of *Waverley* in 1814. Although most of his novels have a Scottish setting, some take place elsewhere. His first novel set in England, *Ivanhoe* (1820), a story of King Richard at the time of the Crusades, continues to be his most popular work. The series for which Cooper is best known is The Leatherstocking Tales, five novels that follow the career of Natty Bumppo from his youth in *The Deerslayer* (1841) to his death in *The Prairie* (1827). Natty is a white hunter and these stories deal with his adventures in the wilderness and with the Indians. The most popular of the series is *The Last of the Mohicans* (1826). During his prolific career, Cooper wrote more than 50 volumes. Both he and Scott had wide audiences for their books and this included a great number of young readers who enjoyed these tales of historical adventure.

British Writers (Nineteenth Century)

Captain Frederick Marryat (1792–1848) was an Englishman who, at age 13, went to sea in the British Navy and saw action around the world, including the West Indies and off the coast of North America and on one occasion nearly drowned when saving a shipmate. He resigned in 1830 and devoted his life to writing. One of his early works, *Mr. Midshipman Easy* (1836), although written for adults, proved to be very popular with younger readers, and so Marryat, encouraged by his own children, began writing novels for this audience. The first was written as a reaction to a Robinsonnade—*Swiss Family*

Robinson (1813), written by the Swiss pastor Johann Wyss (1743–1818), which tells the story of a Swiss family—a pastor, his wife, and four sons— shipwrecked on a tropical island. Although the book was popular in its English translation, Marryat was so annoyed at its inaccuracies that he wrote *Masterman Ready* (1834), also a story of a family marooned on an island. In this book, after being attacked by savages, they are saved by Master Ready, an old seafarer. This novel was one of the first historical adventures written specifically for young readers. It was followed by a frontier story about an immigrant English family, *The Settlers in Canada* (1844), and by his masterpiece, *Children of the New Forest* (1847), set in England during the civil war between the Royalists and the Roundheads. In it, four children, orphaned when their father dies fighting the Royalists, take refuge in the New Forest, where an old forester teaches them the ways of the forest and survival. One critic has called this book "the first enduring historical novel for children."

Another accomplished writer of historical fiction of the period was R. M. Ballantyne (1825–1894) who, at age 16, went to Canada as an agent for the Hudson's Bay Company and journeyed into the wilderness to trade with the Indians. Back in Britain, he wrote his first novel for children, *The Young Fur-Traders* (1856). Two years later he published his classic Robinsonnade, *The Coral Island* (1858). In it, young Ralph Rover and two companions are shipwrecked on a South Sea Island where they enjoy the lavish tropical paradise at first but later are nearly killed by a shark and encounter cannibals. Ralph is captured by pirates, escapes, returns to his companions, and eventually all three are rescued by missionaries.

Robert Louis Stevenson (1850–1894) was one of the youthful admirers of this hugely popular novel and it played a great part in the creation of *Treasure Island*. Stevenson was born in Edinburgh, an only child in a prosperous family. His father was an engineer who built lighthouses. Robert Louis had a sickly childhood and had difficulty establishing a professional aim in life. He finally turned to writing and first produced some volumes of essays before turning to fiction. While spending the summer with his wife and 12-year-old stepson in Braemar, Scotland, he and the boy amused themselves by creating a map of an island where there was buried treasure. This was the genesis of the novel that became Stevenson's first book for young readers and although he never took it seriously this became his most popular work. The author's revised sketch of the map still appears in reprints of the novel. After he began work on the book, he wrote to a friend, "Will you be surprised to learn that the book is about buccaneers, that it begins in the 'Admiral Benbow' public house, on the Devon coast, that it is about a map, and treasure, and a mutiny . . . and fine old Squire Trelawney, and a doctor, and a sea-cook with one leg." The book is narrated by young Jim Hawkins, who secures a map of a treasure buried on a far-off island by pirate Captain Flint. The voyage to the island with Squire Trelawney, Dr. Livesey, and a crew that includes a one-legged cook named Long John Silver; the subsequent mutiny by the crew; the eventual triumph of Jim and his friends; and the recovery of the treasure form the basic plot for the novel that many consider to be the greatest historical adventure story ever written for young readers. It was first serialized under the title *The Sea Cook* in *Young Folks* magazine and appeared in book form in 1883. Another of Stevenson's juvenile historical novels is *The Black Arrow* (1888), a tale of the War of the Roses that contains both a hero and a heroine. The author labeled it "a tale of tushery," that is, a novel of the *Ivanhoe* type. *Kidnapped* (1886), also by Stevenson, is a historical romance set in the Highlands involving young David Balfour, his wrongful kidnapping by his wicked uncle, and subsequent escape and adventures with Alan Breck, a Jacobite rebel. Although originally intended for adults, it also became a favorite with young readers. A sequel, *Catriona*, was published in 1893.

Another English writer of the Victorian Age associated with historical adventure is the prolific G. A. Henty (1832–1902). Henty came from a privileged English family and attended the best schools, including a time at Cambridge. He enlisted in the army and saw combat during the Crimean War. Later, as a foreign correspondent for a London newspaper, *The Standard*, he traveled throughout the world, visiting many exotic countries and witnessing many momentous events in history. He drew on this rich background of experience when he began writing action stories for boys. His first (actually written for his own children whose names are also the names of the children in the novel) was *Out of the Pampas or the Young Settlers* (1871), a story of a pioneering English family and their adventures in Argentina. With the success of this novel and his second, *The Young Franc-Tireurs* (1872), set in the Franco-Prussian War, Henty began a serious writing career while still continuing his newspaper work. At his height he was able to grind out three or four titles a year (he reckoned he could write one in twenty days). Gradually a formula was developed. The basic story involved a plucky young man in his mid- to late teens who, because of some domestic crisis, is forced to leave home and finds himself, through some quirk of fate, participating in an important historical event (usually a battle), and achieving an appropriate reward for some heroic accomplishment. During these adventures he is often accompanied by a loyal, submissive, comic sidekick. Typical titles are *Under Drake's Flag* (1883), *With Clive in India* (1884), and *With Wolfe at Quebec* (1896). His last novel, *With the Allies at Pekin*, was published posthumously in 1904. His output totaled about 200 books, 90 of them boys' adventure stories, most featuring the same stereotypic hero: a lad (his favorite term for such hero) who was attractive; excellent at sports; truthful and honest; loyal to family, God, and country; diligent and hard-working; and willing to defend at all costs the traditional ideals and values. A likable central character, plus a fast-moving plot, plenty of action, and authentic, interesting background details spelled a formula for popularity with the young male reading public. In many of the stories, British chauvinism is endorsed as well as the idea that Britain was justified in colonization because of such admirable qualities as intelligence, pluck, and superior fighting power. Although Henty did not consider girls to be part of his audience (he even began the introductions to each of his stories with "My dear lads"), many girls did read his books and the author corresponded with many of his female fans. He was enormously successful. It has been estimated that, by 1914, when his popularity began to wane, more than 25 million copies of his books had been sold.

American Writers (Nineteenth Century)

These British writers also had an avid readership in America, where they were joined by authors of historical adventures such as Henry Castlemon (Charles Austin Fosdick, 1842–1915) and Oliver Optic (William Taylor Adams, 1822–1897). As a youth, Castlemon ran away from his home in Buffalo, New York, joined the navy, and saw action on gunboats during the Civil War. Later he explored the American frontier where he climbed mountains, rode rapids, and had encounters with savage bears. He wrote about these experiences and others in a total of 58 volumes, many of them books in series like the Gunboat books. This series, begun in 1864, with the titles *Frank, the Young Naturalist* and *Frank on a Gun-Boat*, features the author's most popular hero, Frank Nelson, and reflects the writer's experiences during the Civil War. Other series like Go Ahead, Roughing It, Pony Express, and Rocky Mountain explore the opening up of the American West and the expansion of the frontier. About his books, he said, "Boys don't like fine writing. What they want is adventure and the more of it you can get into 250 pages of manuscript, the better fellow you are."

William Taylor Adams, who wrote under the pseudonym of Oliver Optic, was a New England teacher and later principal who wrote more than 125 books and 1,000 short stories for young readers. The books appeared mainly in a series format, usually with six books in a series. (Series books became a popular publishing format beginning in the 1860s.) In many of his series, the central characters were travelers. In such series as Yacht Club, Woodville, Army and Navy, Blue and Gold, and Young America Abroad, the author combined adventure with information about geography, science, and history. These books were often criticized for their sensationalism, far-fetched plots, and stilted language. Louisa May Alcott was a vocal critic calling them, "optical delusions." Nevertheless, their sales figures were phenomenal.

Howard Pyle (1853–1911) was a man of many talents and is highly regarded as both an author and illustrator. Born to Quaker parents in Wilmington, he studied art and began his career as an illustrator for a number of magazines. When some of his original illustrated stories were accepted by children's magazine, he began combining both of his talents. Some of his books are retellings of historical tales like *The Merry Adventures of Robin Hood* (1883) and *The Story of King Arthur and His Knights* (1903), some are collections of original or adapted fairy tales such as *The Wonder Clock* (1888), and still others are original historical fiction. His first, *Otto of the Silver Hand* (1888), is set in medieval Germany during the time of the robber barons and its hero is a boy who is heir to the Castle Drachenhausen. In the book he effectively contrasts the savagery of the period with its elements of gentleness. His second was *Men of Iron* (1892), which is set in England during the reign of Henry IV early in the 15th century. Its story concerns young Myles Farnsworth and his mission to reestablish the good name of his father, whose reputation had been tarnished because of his support of Richard II. A third of his historical novels is *The Story of Jack Ballister's Fortunes* (1895), a novel set in Colonial America with Blackbeard the pirate as one of its central characters. Critics continue to argue whether Pyle's most important contributions were his writing or his illustrations, although most would agree that, if only through his artwork and the school he founded, where such artists as N. C. Wyeth studied, he established an important place for himself in the history of children's literature.

Two other important writers of adventure stories should be mentioned even though their works are usually not historical in content. The first is Horatio Alger, Jr., and the second, Mark Twain. Horatio Alger, Jr. (1834–1899) is associated with a series of adventure novels with contemporary settings, each of which repeats with slight variations a "rags to riches" story. He wrote about a hundred books, many of them arranged in six-book series. His most commercially successful novel, and typical of his output, was *Ragged Dick* (1868). In it, the title character, Dick Hunter, begins as an illiterate, poor shoeshine boy in New York City, who will resort to stealing to survive but would never betray a friend. His courage and concern for others eventually pays off and he is offered a position in a bank. The book ends with him learning to read and write, becoming financially independent, and well on the road to success. Though his novels were never accepted by critics, they were popular with young readers, many of whom were inspired by their uplifting messages.

Mark Twain (Samuel Langhorne Clemens, 1835–1910) is one of the giants in American literature. Two of his many adventure novels, *The Adventures of Tom Sawyer* (1876) and *The Adventures of Huckleberry Finn* (1884), are enduring classics that continue to be popular with both adults and children. Though these could not be classified as historical fiction, Twain did write some novels in that genre. One that was intended for a juvenile audience was *The Prince and the Pauper* (1881), which tells of Prince Edward of England (later to be Edward VI) and his encounters with a look-alike street waif, Tom Canty. When they exchange clothes, Edward is thrown out of the place, and forced to roam through the English countryside where he encounters firsthand the poverty and misery that exists in his country. He reclaims his throne just as Tom is about to be crowned king. His second historical novel popular with young readers was *A Connecticut Yankee in King Arthur's Court* (1889), a fantasy in which a superintendent of a factory in Hartford suffers a blow on his head and is transported to the court of King Arthur where his Yankee know-how and ingenuity prove useful. Twain uses this situation to poke fun at chivalry and the Old World. In the end, another blow restores our hero to the present.

All of these writers laid the groundwork for the development of historical fiction for young readers as a separate, distinct literary form. Twentieth-century writers built on these beginnings and produced a flow of historical novels, many of which have become classics.

THE GOLDEN AGE (1900–1950)

During the first half of the 20th century, the historical novel for young readers came of age. It became a distinct genre rather than being a subsection of adventure literature. The number of titles published increased remarkably as did the number of authors who wrote historical fiction. New topics and new periods in history were explored, particularly in the area of America's past—frontier and pioneer life, for example. With this broadening in scope came other changes. There was a shift from portraying only boys as the central characters to including girls. In fact, by the end of this period, there were more heroines than heroes as the leading characters. There was also greater depth of characterization, although stereotypes still existed and the central character usually possessed conventional virtues and values, as before. Plots continued to be simple and straightforward but there was less emphasis on flamboyant heroic exploits and greater portrayal of everyday courage and virtue. Although plotting became more subtle, the central conflicts in most of these stories remained simplistic, that is, pure evil versus pure good. Although the range of subject matter broadened, many subjects continued to be either shunned or disregarded. Sex, for example, seldom reared its head, the injustice of slavery was ignored (in spite of *Uncle Tom's Cabin*), and minorities and their contributions to our culture were rarely portrayed.

In his writings, Rudyard Kipling (see coverage above) spanned two centuries. In addition to his school stories for young readers, he wrote many adult adventure stories such as *Kim* (1901), his masterpiece about a young waif growing up in the streets of Lahore. This novel also appealed to youngsters. His last two books for children were *Puck of Pock's Hill* (1906) and its sequel *Rewards and Fairies* (1910). In the first, two English youngsters, Dan and Una, conjure up the spirit of Puck from *A Midsummer's Night's Dream*, who takes them on a fantastic journey through time where they encounter people from the past and hear stories about such topics as the Roman invasion and the Norman Conquest and how English society evolved. Many of these narratives involved battles, and all glorify the armed forces and British nationalism. The second volume continues this variation on the historical novel with more stories of England's past.

American Writers (1900–1950)

Joseph Altsheler (1862–1919) was a Kentucky-born writer of popular boys' historical novels. He began as a journalist, before turning to writing full-time. He began writing novels in 1897 and in the next 21 years published 44 titles. In 1918 he was voted the most popular boys' writer in America by a committee from public libraries. Some of the events that became the backgrounds for his novels were the American Revolution, the struggle for Texas independence, the French and Indian Wars, and the Civil War. Some examples: *The Last of the Chiefs* (1909), *The Texas Star* (1912), and *The Guns of Bull Run* (1914). His most successful books deal with the opening up of the West and the exploration of the Rockies. Critics consider *The Young Trailers: A Story of Early Kentucky* (1907), part of the Young Trailer series to be his finest. It deals with the settling of the Ohio Valley.

An American author whose output spanned two centuries is John Bennett (1865–1956). He is best known for two historical novels he wrote for children. The first is *Master Skylark* (1997), which appeared originally as a serial in the famous children's magazine *St. Nicholas* and tells the story, set in Elizabethan England, of a Stratford singing boy who is kidnapped, taken to London, and eventually meets Shakespeare. It is noted for its accurate, enchanting portrayal of the sights and sounds of the period. The second, *Barnaby Lee* (1902), is a complex, rewarding story of the forced surrender to the British of New Amsterdam by Peter Stuyvesant.

Although he wrote principally for adults, the books of James Boyd (1888–1944) were also popular with young readers. After serving in World War I the author was forced into early retirement because of ill health and began writing. His first and most popular novel is *Drums* (1925), an exciting story of North Carolina in the early stages of the Revolution that has been called the best novel written about the American Revolution. Other historical novels by him include *Marching On* (1927) and *Long Hunt* (1930).

In the 1920s, two writers of historical fiction each won the Newbery Medal and a third won it in 1930 for a historical fantasy. They were: Charles B. Hawes (1889–1923), Eric P. Kelly (1884–1960), and Rachel Field (1894–1942).

With the untimely death of Charles Boardman Hawes at age 35, the world lost a great historical storyteller who, some say, could have rivaled Robert Louis Stevenson in his re-creation of the bold seafaring life of both buccaneers and honest seafaring men. He is known principally for three novels. The first is *The Great Quest* (1921), a Newbery Honor Book in 1922, which is the story of 20-year-old Joe Woods and his adventures aboard the brig called *Adventure*, which include narrowly avoiding being press-ganged in Havana. The second is *The Mutineers* (1923), which tells of a mutiny on a ship in which those in command are killed, but eventually the protagonists outwit the villains and regain control of the ship. This is essentially the same plot as the third, *The Dark Frigate* (1923), which garnered the author a posthumous Newbery Medal in 1924. It is set in England in the 17th century during the reign of Charles I and tells the story of 19-year-old Phil, who signs on to work on a frigate that is later boarded by pirates. In time Phil makes his escape and ultimately the pirates are brought to justice. Unfortunately these books, though filled with exiting adventure, lack the colorful characters, such as Long John Silver, found in Stevenson.

During World War I, Eric P. Kelly spent time in Poland working with a welfare organization. He learned the language and became fascinated with Polish culture and history. While teaching and studying in Krakow, he wrote *The Trumpeter of Krakow* (1928), winner of the 1929 Newbery Medal. Set in 15th-century Krakow, this story revolves around the Great Tarnov crystal, a gem of great value; a villain named Button Face who wants the crystal; and Andrew and his son Joseph who, at night, trumpet hourly the Polish Heynal from the tower of the Church of Our Lady Mary. This book forms the first of a highly praised trilogy. The others, also set in Poland, are *The Blacksmith of Vilno* (1930) and *The Golden Star of Halich* (1931).

While visiting an antique store in Greenwich Village in New York City, Rachel Field and her friend and illustrator, Dorothy Lathrop, discovered a wooden doll that was more than a hundred years old. Though it was too expensive for her to buy at the time, she couldn't forget the doll and it later became the inspiration for her 1929 novel *Hitty: Her First Hundred Years*, winner of the 1930 Newbery Medal. Incidentally, Hitty accompanied Rachel Field to the award ceremony. The episodic story presents a rich view of one hundred years of American history as seen through the eyes of Hitty, short for Mehitabel, a doll made from mountain-ash wood. Originally owned by 7-

year-old Phoebe Preble in rural New England at the beginning of the 19th century, the doll's adventures include traveling with the Prebles to India, being bought by a missionary and returning to America, meeting the poet John Greenleaf Whittier, spending time in a hayloft, seeing the States with a painter named Mr. Farley, being rescued by two boys after she is thrown into the river in New Orleans, and eventually being bought at auction by an antiquer and being placed in the window of his Greenwich Village shop. Hitty shows great spunk and charm as her lifestyles change, bringing conditions that she accepts with courage and strength. Rachel Field was multitalented: she illustrated books, wrote and published poetry and plays, and, in addition to her books for young readers, wrote four successful adult novels including *All This and Heaven Too* (1939). Two of the twelve other novels she wrote for youngsters are *Calico Bush* (1930), a Newbery Honor Book in 1932, and *Hepatica Hawks* (1932). *Calico Bush* takes places in the mid-18th century and tells the story of a young French girl who is a bound servant to a family that has settled in Maine and, in the second, the title character, Hepatica Hawks, is a 15-year-old who is six feet four and a quarter inches tall and whose family, in 1890, is part of a traveling circus called Joshua Pollack's "Famous Freaks and Fandangos." Rachel Field is particularly well known for her superb writing style, flawless plot structures, and strong, interesting female characters.

Two other female writers of historical fiction prominent in the late 1920s and later were Cornelia Meigs (1884–1971) and Caroline Dale Snedeker (1871–1956). Cornelia Meigs wrote one Newbery Medal winner (awarded in 1934) and three Newbery Honor Books (1922, 1929, and 1933). Three of these books are historical novels. Prior to these she had written many other historical novels, most notably *Master Simon's Garden* (1916), which broke new ground in its scope, covering three generations of New England history. The linking device is a garden originally planted by Simon Redpath and later cultivated by his descendents. The central message of the book is the importance of love and tolerance. In this, as in many of her other books, she is more interested in ideas than characters. The two historical novels that were Honor Books are *Clearing Weather* (1928), set in Massachusetts immediately after the American Revolution, which features an exciting trading voyage first to the West Indies, then around Cape Horn, and eventually to the Orient; and *Swift Rivers* (1932), an exciting tale of logging adventures in 1835 Minnesota. The Newbery Medal winner was a fictionalized biography of Louisa May Alcott, *Invincible Louisa: The Story of the Author of "Little Women"* (1933). From 1915 to 1961, she wrote about thirty books for children and was one of the most respected authors of her time. Her numerous accomplishments included editing and writing part of the monumental *A Critical History of Children's Literature* (1953, revised 1969).

As a child, Caroline Dale Snedeker fell in love with stories associated with ancient Greece and Rome and so, when she turned to writing novels for young people, these historical periods became her inspiration. Her first book, *The Coward of Thermopylae* (1911), later renamed *The Spartan*, tells of the famous battle, the hero who survived it, and of life in ancient Sparta. Others followed, including *The White Isle* (1940), the story of Lavinia, daughter of a Roman patrician family, who is exiled to Britain in the 2nd century. It creates a vivid picture of both Roman life and the early days of Christianity. Perhaps her most famous novel (it remained in print for more than fifty years) is set on the island of Nantucket in the early 19th century. *Downright Dencey* (1927), a Newbery Honor Book in 1928, has as its heroine a high-spirited, lovable Quaker girl whose innocent adventures make for heart-warming reading.

Several interesting writers of historical fiction emerged in the 1930s. Among them was Hildegarde Hoyt Swift (1890–1977), whose most famous novels are Newbery Honor Books of 1930 and 1933, respectively: *Little Black-nose* (1929), the fictionalized story of the first locomotive ever made for the New York Central Railroad; and a novel based on the life of Harriet Tubman, *The Railroad to Freedom* (1932).

Beginning in the 1930s both Erick Berry (1892–1977) and her husband Herbert Best (1894–1981) made important contributions to the field. Included in Erick Berry's output were collections of African folktales and novels such as *Honey of the Nile* (1937), a tale of ancient Egypt after the reign of Ikhnaton; the Newbery Honor Book of 1934, *The Winged Girl of Knossos* (1933), set in Bronze Age Crete; and *Sybil Ludington's Ride* (1952), based on a true incident of the American Revolution. Herbert Best wrote, among others, a 1931 Newbery Honor Book, *Garram the Hunter: A Boy of the Hill Tribes* (1930), an adventure tale set in precolonial Africa; *Border Iron* (1954), about a boy and his dog who help solve a border dispute between New York and Massachusetts in the 1750s; and *The Long Portage* (1948), a story set during the French and Indian Wars involving Rogers' Rangers.

Elizabeth Janet Gray (1902–1999), Agnes Dunforth Hewes (1874–1963), and Elsie Singmaster (1878–1959) also made important contributions during the period. Elizabeth Gray's books include *Maggie Macintosh* (1930), a 1931 Newbery Honor Book painting a vivid picture of Scottish immigrants who came to America before the Revolution; and *Beppy Marlowe* (1936), set in 18th-century London and then in Charles Town, South Carolina. Her best-known work is the 1943 Newbery Medal winner *Adam of the Road* (1942), which, through the adventures of 11-year-old Adam and his minstrel father, presents an authentic, fascinating picture of life in 13th-century England. Agnes D. Hewes was also a multi–Newbery Honor Book winner—in 1931, 1934, and 1937. Her first winner, *Spice and the Devil's Cave* (1930), is set in

Lisbon in the late 1490s and features such real-life characters as Vasco da Gama and Ferdinand Magellan; the second, *Glory of the Seas* (1933), combines adventures involving the clipper ships of the 1850s with the enforcement of the Fugitive Slave Act of 1850; and the third, *The Codfish Musket* (1936), is a complex story that involves young Dan Boit, historical figures like Lewis and Clark, and the opening up of the American frontier. Elsie Singmaster books include *A Boy at Gettysburg* (1924) and *Swords of Steel* (1933), which deals with the Civil War and the years preceding it as seen from the point of view of 12-year-old John Deane.

Three other giants of this period are Carol Ryrie Brink (1895–1981), Lois Lenski (1893–1974), and Kate Seredy (1899–1975). Carol Ryrie Brink is best known for *Caddie Woodlawn* (1936; Newbery Medal, 1936), a book so popular that it was reprinted thirty times in thirty years. Subtitled *A Frontier Story*, it chronicles a year in the life of 11-year-old Caddie, who is growing up on her family's farm in Wisconsin during the Civil War. Caddie has many harmless adventures running wild with her brothers, but there is some suspense when Indian-settler relations become tense and there is a threat from a raging forest fire. The book continues to attract young readers even today. Its sequel, *Magical Melons* (1944), an account of the further adventures of Caddie and her brothers, was never as popular. Two other titles by Carol Brink are *Baby Island* (1937), a Robinsonnade about two girls shipwrecked with a boatload of babies, and *Winter Cottage* (1968), in which a family tries to escape the hardships of the Great Depression by moving to the country.

During the forty-odd years that Lois Lenski was active in publishing, she wrote and illustrated about eighty of her own works for children and illustrated another fifty written by others. Apart from her numerous picture books featuring Mr. Small, she is best known for her regional and Round About America series that depicted children from different classes and different regions and times in the United States, such as *Strawberry Girl* (1945), which won the 1946 Newbery Medal. It focuses on the Boyer family, chiefly 10-year-old Bertie, whose family has moved into a frontier community in Florida's lake region in the early 1900s and is now having problems with their neighbors, the Slaters. Three of her historical novels are *Skipping Village* (1927), *A Girl of 1900* (1928), and her most popular, *Indian Captive: The Story of Mary Jemison* (1941), a Newbery Honor Book in 1942. This is a fictionalized biography of the first two years of Mary Jemison's life with the Seneca Indians beginning in 1758.

Hungarian-born Kate Seredy used the history and folklore of her country to create many of her works. For example, *The White Stag* (1937), winner of the 1938 Newbery Medal, is an old-style epic that tells the story of the founding of Hungary and the rise of Attila the Hun. Drawing on her own history,

Kate Seredy wrote *The Good Master* (1935), a Newbery Honor Book in 1936, that tells of a horse farm in the plains of Hungary where "the good master" lives with his son Jansci and rambunctious niece Kate. This story is continued in the Honor Book for 1940, *The Singing Tree* (1939), in which the family survives the horrors of World War I.

Perhaps the most beloved and most popular writer who wrote in the 1930s and early 1940s is Laura Ingalls Wilder (1867–1957) who was in her sixties when her daughter urged her to write down recollections of her life in frontier America during the 1870s and 1880s. These writings became known as the Little House books. The eight-book cycle begins with *Little House in the Big Woods* (1932), which tells of her childhood in a log cabin in Wisconsin. The second, *Farmer Boy* (1933), is the story of the youth of her future husband, Almanzo Wilder. Subsequent volumes tell of the family's move west by covered wagon (*Little House on the Prairie*, 1935), back east to Minnesota (*On the Banks of Plum Creek*, 1937), west again to Dakota Territory (*By the Shores of Silver Lake*, 1939), enduring a snow storm that isolates their village (*The Long Winter*, 1940), Laura's training as a school teacher (*Little Town on the Prairie*, 1941), and her teaching experience and marriage in the last of the series, *These Happy Golden Years* (1943). In 1971 a partially completed sequel, *The First Four Years* was published. Although none of these titles won the Newbery Medal, five were Honor Books. The books are particularly noteworthy for their touching honesty and sincerity. The harsh realities of frontier life are, however, not glossed over. For example, in *The Long Winter*, generally considered to be the best of series, the reader is not spared the details of their near-starvation ordeal. Like Laura, the heroine, the series "grows" with each volume, the last volume being at a higher reading level than the first. One critic has said, "Wilder belonged to the great age of children's literature . . . indeed, she was one of its brightest lights."

Another classic of children's literature was published in 1943, *Johnny Tremain*, the Newbery Medal winner of 1944 by Esther Forbes (1891–1967). This was only novel she wrote for young people and was an offshoot of the tremendous research she did for her Pulitzer Prize-winning biography *Paul Revere and the World He Lived In* (1941), in which she uncovered an incident about a horse boy who told Paul Revere of his discovery concerning the movement of British troops in Boston of 1775. This story, plus her interest in the lives of apprentices during the period, led to the creation of Johnny, a handicapped orphan who becomes a hero of the American Revolution. The likeability of this youngster and his growth to young manhood set against the drama of actual historical events make for a book that many consider to be the finest juvenile historical novel ever written.

Armstrong Sperry (1897–1976), Stephen Meader (1892–1977), and Walter D. Edmonds (1903–1998) wrote historical adventure stories that had appeal primarily for boys. Armstrong Sperry was first a book illustrator and later began a second career as a writer. The two greatest influences on his writings were the ethnology of the South Pacific, which he studied first-hand, and his love of the sea. His best-known work, *Call It Courage* (1940), won the Newbery Medal in 1941. Set in the distant past, it is the story of Mafatu, a 15-year-old Polynesian youth who has a fear of the sea and must conquer this phobia when he is engulfed in a storm at sea. During his adventures he also encounters a shark and a band of cannibals. *Black Falcon* (1949) tells how young Wade Thayer sails with Jean Lafitte in his raids against the English in 1814; *Danger to Windward* (1947) is a whaling story set just after the War of 1812; and *All Sails Set: A Romance of the Flying Cloud* (1935), a Newbery Honor Book for 1936, is a reminiscence by a 97-year-old sailor about his voyage on a clipper ship, the *Flying Cloud*, from New York to San Francisco and on to China. Like his other works, these books are accompanied by the author's brilliant illustrations.

Stephen Meader's writing career spanned almost fifty years and produced about as many books, many of them historical adventures such as *Who Rides in the Dark?* (1937), about a masked rider whose identity is finally discovered by a young stable boy, Daniel Drew, in New Hampshire after the War of 1812 and *Boy with a Pack* (1939), in which a young man in 1837 sets out from Connecticut with a trunk full of "notions" to sell. The latter was a Newbery Honor Book in 1940. Two others are *Guns for the Saratoga* (1955) about privateering during the Revolutionary War and *Phantom of the Blockade* (1962), which deals with life aboard a blockade runner during the Civil War.

Walter D. Edmonds is noted for his quality historical, well-researched novels for both adults (such as *Drums along the Mohawk*, 1936) and children. Examples of his children's books include *The Matchlock Gun* (1941), winner of the Newbery Medal in 1942, and *Bert Breen's Barn* (1975), which won the 1976 National Book Award. The former, handsomely illustrated by Paul Lantz, is set in the 1750s in British New York State and tells how 10-year-old Edward, during his father's absence, learns to load the family's Spanish gun and fires it, saving the family during an Indian attack. In the latter, Tom reclaims his family's lost reputation through his hard work and honesty. Two other excellent novels by this author are *Wilderness Clearing* (1944), the story of how the American Revolution affected settlers in the Mohawk Valley, and *Cadmus Henry* (1949), a tale of a young Confederate volunteer who is assigned to float over enemy lines in a balloon and report on their positions.

Alice Dalgliesh (1893–1979) was a prolific writer for children whose books included information books, picture books and some novels including historical fiction. In this category, her most noteworthy title is *The Courage of Sarah Noble* (1954; Newbery Honor Book, 1955), a simple pioneer story in which 8-year-old Sarah goes with her father on a dangerous journey into the Connecticut wilderness of 1707 to build a new family home.

Here are a few of this period's other authors of note. Ann Nolan Clark (1898–1995) is important for her sympathetic portrayal of Native Americans in her books. She is best known for the Newbery Medal (1953) winner *Secret of the Andes* (1952), in which a Peruvian boy helps an old Inca herder guard his flock of llamas and learns many of the sacred traditions of his ancestors. Doris Gates (1901–1987) wrote about a number of subjects including lumbering, classical mythology, and horse racing, but her major literary achievement is *Blue Willow* (1940; Newbery Honor Book, 1941), the poignant story of 10-year-old Janie Larkin, whose family, during the Depression, was forced to leave its farm in the Dust Bowl and become migrant workers in the San Joaquin Valley of California. Florence Crannell Means (1892–1977) broke new ground in historical fiction writing and became the first writer to specialize in works about ethnic minorities. Some examples: Navajos (*Tangled Waters*, 1935), Hopis (*Whispering Girl*, 1941), and African Americans (*Shuttered Windows*, 1938). She also wrote a number of stories about pioneers, such as *A Candle in the Mist* (1931).

Mary Montgomery, Rebel (1948), a fictionalized story of the Civil War; and *Pilgrim Kate* (1949), a novel about Pilgrims in Europe before leaving for the New World, are two examples of the excellent historical novels of Helen Dern Daringer (1892–1986). Enid LaMonte Meadowcroft (1898–1966) wrote a number of accessible novels about American history, such as *By Secret Railway* (1949), about a young slave and his trip on the Underground Railroad; *Silver for General Washington* (1944), the story of a brother and sister and their winter at Valley Forge; and *By Wagon and Flatboat* (1938), about two families who, in 1789, migrated from Pittsburgh to Losantiville (later Cincinnati). Eleanor M. Jewett's (1892–1955) most famous historical novel and a Newbery Honor Book for 1947 was *The Hidden Treasure of Glaston* (1946), the story of two boys in the 12th century who, during their work in a scriptorium, find lost pages of a book about the Holy Grail. Lastly, there was a series of books by Louis Andrews Kent, each featuring a young hero and a famous explorer, such as *He Went with Magellan* (1947) and *He Went with Columbus* (1940). Though formulaic and somewhat stilted in style, they were mainstays of library collections at the time.

British and Canadian Writers (1900–1950)

Two other English writers and one Canadian should also be discussed. The English authors are Geoffrey Trease (1909–1998) and C. Walter Hodges

(1909–2004) and the Canadian, Roderick Haig-Brown (1908–1976). Over a period of 70 years, Geoffrey Trease wrote about 120 books, many of them historical novels that often portray the struggle of oppressed lower classes against the wealthy, corrupt nobility. His leftist leanings are present in novels including his first, *Bows Against the Barons* (1934), which portrays Robin Hood's fight against the governing tyrants. In *Shadow of the Hawk* (1949), two young people set out in the 16th century to recover the manuscript of a Greek play; and in *Trumpets in the West* (1947), set in the time of James II, young Jack Norwood comes to London to study music with Purcell and soon is taking part in a struggle against dictatorship. Others show a wide use of locales: *The White Nights of St. Petersburg* (1967)—revolutionary Russia, *The Hills of Varna* (1948)—16th-century Albania, and *No Horns at Midnight* (1995)—Victorian England. C. Walter Hodges had no such axe to grind. Although he is best known as a book illustrator, his historical novels beginning with *Columbus Sails* (1939) gained a wide readership. Two of these published in the 1960s were about Alfred the Great. The first is *The Namesake* (1964), which tells of Alfred's early years, and the second, *The Marsh King* (1967), completes the story of Alfred's early wars. Roderick Haig-Brown's favorite milieu was the Canadian wilderness, the setting of many of his animal stories as well as his adventure and historical novels. His novels are somewhat old-fashioned in both their values and the purity of their coming-of-age central characters. One example is *The Whale People* (1962), set on the west coast of Canada and featuring a Nootka Indian teenager who must assume the role of tribal chief after the death of his father.

THE SILVER AGE (1950–1980)

During this period the historical novel continued to become more adult in approach and content. Characters, including the protagonists, became more complex and less stereotypical. There were more female leads, many of who displayed both negative and positive character traits. Historic characters were brought down from pedestals and treated as believable human beings, often to the point of irreverence. Witness the popularity of Jean Fritz's biographies with titles such as *What's the Big Idea, Ben Franklin?* (1976). There was greater attention to presenting controversial themes and subjects and, when these were introduced, there was more attention to covering various points on view on a subject. There was also greater experimentation in settings. For example, novels set in the Middle Ages were often told from the point of view of peasants rather than nobility. The use of wit and humor became more popular stylistic devices. In short, history became more accessible and less stodgy.

American Writers (1950–1980)

At the beginning of this period (the 1950s and 1960s), several important American writers emerged. Leading the list in terms of popularity are six names: Scott O'Dell (1898–1989), Jean Fritz (1915–), Robert Lawson (1892–1957), Elizabeth Speare (1908–1994), William Steele (1917–1979), and Leonard Wibberley (1915–1983). Scott O'Dell is one of the towering masters of historical fiction. He breathed new life into the historical novel in the latter half of the 20th century. He is particularly noted for his wonderful stories, memorable protagonists, and his excellent re-creations of historical places and times. He was over 60 when his first novel for young readers was published. It was the outstanding *Island of the Blue Dolphins* (1960), which won the Newbery Medal in 1961. Based on fact, this is the story of Karana, a young girl who is left behind on an island by her tribe and must, like Robinson Crusoe, survive on her own. This valiant, resourceful teenager conquers her loneliness and privation to emerge triumphantly from her ordeal. O'Dell's books often use a setting in the Southwest and explore various aspects of Spanish and Native American cultures. He wrote another twenty-five historical novels for young readers, three of which are Newbery Honor Books. Among these other works are *The King's Fifth* (1966; Newbery Honor Book, 1967), the story of a young cartographer in the time of Coronado and of a treasure hunt that misfires; and *Sing Down the Moon* (1970; Newbery Honor Book, 1971), which is narrated by a 15-year-old Navajo girl, Bright Morning, who tells of the inhuman treatment her people experienced at the hands of the U.S. Army during the 1860s. Other titles include *Zia* (1977), a sequel to *Island of the Blue Dolphins*; *The Black Pearl* (1967; Newbery Honor Book, 1968), an allegorical novel set in the Baja California part of Mexico and narrated by the son of a successful pearl dealer; and *Sarah Bishop* (1980), a novel set in Revolutionary New York and featured in the main body of this book.

In 1982 the author founded the Scott O'Dell Award for Historical Fiction (first presented in 1964), which is awarded annually to the author of the most distinguished work of historical fiction set in the New World.

Jean Fritz, whose memoir *Homesick: My Own Story* (1982; Newbery Honor Book, 1983) is about growing up in China during the late 1920s, is perhaps best known for a series of biographies of important figures in American history that have humorous titles such as *Who's That Stepping on Plymouth Rock?* (1975) and *Will You Sign Here, John Hancock?* (1976). She has also written numerous fine historical novels. Some examples: *Brady* (1960), set in Pennsylvania in the 1830s, the story of a young boy who discovers that his father, a minister, is a conductor on the Underground Railroad; *The Cabin Faces West* (1958), an affectionate tribute to the life of her great-great-grandmother who lived in Pennsylvania in the late 18th century; and *Early Thunder* (1967), set in Salem, Massachusetts, immediately before the American Revolution. As well as high literary quality, Jean Fritz brings an engaging sense of humor to her writing.

Robert Lawson, who was an accomplished illustrator and author, also brought humor and an innovative imagination to his work. He is the only person to have won both the Newbery and Caldecott Medals. As well as good feelings, his books exude a belief in the old-fashioned American virtues. *Ben and Me* (1939) is an early work that combines fantasy and history in the story of Amos, a poor church mouse, and how he makes himself invaluable to Ben Franklin. Following its success, Lawson wrote and illustrated similar books on Christopher Columbus (*I Discover Columbus*, 1941), Paul Revere (*Mr. Revere and I*, 1953), and Captain Kidd (*Captain Kidd's Cat*, 1956). *The Great Wheel* (1957; Newbery Honor Book, 1958), his last book, is a novel about the construction of the first Ferris wheel for the Chicago Exposition of 1893.

Elizabeth Speare, a New Englander, has an unusual success record in the field of children's literature. Of her four novels for young readers, two won Newbery Medals and a third was an Honor Book. Her first novel, *Calico Captive* (1957), based on Susanna Johnson's diary, tells of a family who are captured by Indians in 1754 and later bartered to the French. The novel concentrates on one of the prisoners, Susanna's younger sister, Miriam. Speare's first Newbery Medal came in 1959 for *The Witch of Blackbird Pond* (1958), which features 16-year-old Kit Tyler as the central character who arrives in Wethersfield, Connecticut, in April 1687, from Barbados, unable to cope not only with the climate but also with the strict Puritanism she encounters. Eventually this conflict leads to Kit being accused of witchcraft in a tense, tightly knit plot that features a vivacious, strong-willed heroine who is believably portrayed. Speare's second Newbery winner (1962), *The Bronze Bow* (1961), set in the Holy Land at the time of Jesus, features a young male protagonist, Daniel bar Jamin, who is torn between staying with his leader, Roth, an outlaw whose life is governed by violence and revenge, and following Jesus, who teaches love and forgiveness. *The Sign of the Beaver* (1983; Newbery Honor Book, 1984) is set in the Maine wilderness in 1768 and features 13-year-old Matthew who, when he must fend for himself in his parents' absence, is helped by members of the Beaver Indian tribe. Though only four in number, these novels have given Elizabeth Speare a lasting place in the genre of historical fiction because of their vivid characters, valid themes about upholding social justice, and well-constructed plots.

William Steele wrote about forty adventure-filled books principally for boys. Most are set in the Tennessee area during the early pioneering days and usually involve young protagonists who achieve maturity through overcoming adverse conditions. Some are notable for being written from the point of view of Native Americans. Among his best-known novels are *The Perilous Road* (1958; Newbery Honor Book, 1959), a Civil War novel that features an 11-year-old central character, Chris Brabson, who is growing up in the Tennessee mountains; *The Buffalo Knife* (1952), the story of a boy and his family's thousand-mile journey by flatboat down the Tennessee River in 1782; *The Man with the Silver Eyes* (1976), about an Indian boy who discovers he is half white; *The Lone Hunt* (1956), which tells of a youngster and his adventures hunting a buffalo; and *The Year of the Bloody Sevens* (1963), in which an 11-year-old boy travels through dangerous Indian territory to reach his father. Though his characterization is simplistic, William Steele wrote exciting stories filled with authentic detail.

Leonard Wibberley wrote both for young readers and adults. In the latter area, he is best known for his "mouse" books such as *The Mouse That Roared* (1959), a satire about a tiny European principality. His novels for young readers, many of them historical in nature, led the author Susan Cooper to name him "one of the best writers for children in the United States." His attraction to *Treasure Island* led him to write a sequel in 1972, called *Flint Island*. He is well known for his Treegate novels beginning with *John Treegate's Musket* (1959). It begins in 1769, and tells the story of Peter Treegate, son of American colonist John Treegate, and his conflicting emotions about which side to support in events prior to the Revolution. It ends with him taking down his father's musket and fighting for the Patriots. The three other volumes in this highly praised series are *Peter Treegate's War* (1960), *Sea Captain for Salem* (1961), and *Treegate's Raiders* (1962). Other important books by him are *Kevin O'Connor and the Light Brigade* (1957), which tells of a young man's adventures during the Crimean War, and a four-volume fictionalized biography of Thomas Jefferson. About his purpose in writing, he stated it is "not to instruct but to enrich that which is already known."

A number of other authors made significant contributions to the field of historical fiction during the 1950s and 1960s. Clyde Robert Bulla (1914–2007) wrote more than a hundred books, most of them for readers in the middle grades. Among his many historical novels are: *Squanto, Friend of the White Man* (1954), *John Billington, Friend of Squanto* (1956), and *Charlie's House* (1983), the story of a London waif sold as an indentured servant in America during colonial times. Marguerite De Angeli (1889–1987), Harold Keith (1907–1990), Marguerite Henry (1902–1997), and Irene Hunt (1907–2001) won Newbery Medals for their historical novels. Marguerite De Angeli's medal came in 1950 for *The Door in the Wall* (1949), a poignant story set in the England of Edward III that tells of Robin, a crippled boy who is haunted by fear, and how he accepts his handicap and triumphs over it. Two other novels by her are: *Thee, Hannah!* (1970), about a 9-year-old Quaker girl in pre-Civil War Philadelphia, and *Black Fox of Lorne* (1956; Newbery Honor Book, 1957), about twin Viking boys in the 10th century and how they avenge the death of their father. *Rifles for Watie* (1957; Newbery Medal, 1958) by Harold Keith is a coming-of-age story about 16-year-old Jeff, a Union soldier who is sent behind enemy lines as a spy. *Komantica* (1965), about a young Spaniard captured by Comanches in 1865, and *The Obstinate Land* (1977), set in 1983 during the Oklahoma land run into the Cherokee Strip, are two other novels by Harold Keith. Marguerite Henry and "horse stories" are inseparably linked in literature. Several of these were also historical novels. *King of the Wind* (1948; Newbery Medal, 1949) tells of an Arabian stallion in the early 18th century that survives cruel treatment and becomes one of the sires of the racehorse Man o' War. *Justin Morgan Had a Horse* (1945; Newbery Honor Book, 1946) is the story of a work horse that became the father of the Morgan horses, a famous family of American horses. In these and her other historical novels, Marguerite Henry is noted for her meticulous research and her vivid re-creation of the past. Irene Hunt wrote only eight novels, most of them historical. Perhaps her most lasting accomplishment was her first novel, *Across Five Aprils* (1964; Newbery Honor Book, 1965) (see Chapter 8), the touching story of the devastating effects of the Civil War on the Creighton family of southern Illinois as seen through the eyes of young Jethro Creighton. Her Newbery Medal winner of 1967 is the tender re-creation of rural American life in the first decades of the 20th century, *Up a Road Slowly* (1966). It is the story of the childhood of Julie Treling who, after the death of her mother, is raised by her strict but kindly teacher-aunt Cordelia. Two other of her historical novels that stress the importance of family life are *Trail of Apple Blossoms* (1968), a story about Johnny Appleseed, and *No Promises in the Wind* (1970), about a young man's difficult life during the Depression.

Another name associated with a Newbery Medal (but not for a historical novel) is Elizabeth Coatsworth (1893–1986), who wrote more than 90 books for children, many of them novels that take place in colonial or post-Revolutionary America. Noteworthy are her five Sally books beginning with *Away Goes Sally* (1934), about the moving of a house on skis from Massachusetts to Maine with the help of teams of oxen. *First Adventure* (1950) is an easy-read book about an 8-year-old boy who wanders away from his Plymouth settlement home and is taken in by Indians. Other pioneering stories are *Dancing Tom* (1938), *The Last Fort* (1953), and *Sword in the Wilderness* (1936). A sample of other locales and times the author has used include medieval Ireland (*The Wanderers*, 1972), and 18th-century Ethiopia (*The Princess and the Lion*, 1963).

Briefly here are a few other noteworthy authors of the period. Sydney Taylor (1904–1978) wrote lovingly about her Jewish American childhood in a series of novels set in turn-of-the-20th-century New York City beginning with *All-of-a-Kind Family* (1961). The Shakespearian scholar Marchette Chute (1909–) wrote two entertaining novels full of character and life: *The Innocent Wayfaring* (1943), about two young runaways in Chaucer's time, and *The Wonderful Winter* (1954), the story of a youthful nobleman who becomes part of Shakespeare's company of players. Gladys Malvern was a prolific author of romantic historical novels, many based on the lives of real people. Of doubtful literary quality (one critic called them "pleasantly diverting"), they were nevertheless very popular with girls. Some examples: *My Lady, My Love: The Story of Elizabeth of Valois* (1957), the story of a noble lady who travels to England to marry Richard II; *Your Kind Indulgence* (1949), set in New York at the time of the ratification of the Constitution in 1778; *Jonica's Island* (1960), the story of a 13-year-old girl who becomes an indentured servant in the New Amsterdam of 1660; and *Tamar* (1952), which involves the daughter of the ruler of Caperneum who falls in love with a Roman during the time when Jesus was preaching. Lastly, Marguerite Vance wrote a number of fictionalized biographies of famous ladies of history. Included are *Lady Jane Grey, Reluctant Queen* (1952), *Patsy Jefferson of Monticello* (1964), and *Elizabeth Tudor, Sovereign Lady* (1954).

During the 1970s and 1980s many new outstanding voices were heard in the field of American historical fiction, many of whom are continuing to make significant contributions today (some books by these authors are analyzed in the main body of this work). Four that come immediately to mind are Avi (1937–), Katherine Paterson (1932–), Mildred D. Taylor (1943–), and Laurence Yep (1947–). Avi (pen name of Avi Wortis), one of the most widely read and liked of present-day writers for young readers, is noted for his versatility and great range. He has written for different age groups from beginning readers to young adults on subjects that span a variety of times and places including several that deal with contemporary subjects. His first, *Captain Grey* (1977), is a robust adventure story about young Kevin Cartwright, who is the prisoner of a pirate king. Since then his novels have continued to grow in subtlety and depth of character creation and plotting. Many of his historical novels take place in America. Some examples: *The Fighting Ground* (1984) takes place over a 24-hour period during the American Revolution on a farm near Trenton where 13-year-old Jonathan experiences all its horror and death. In *The Man Who Was Poe* (1989), set in Providence, Rhode Island, in 1848, Poe decides to help find 11-year-old Edmund who has mysteriously disappeared. In *Night Journeys* (1979), set in New Jersey in 1768, Peter, who has been adopted by a strict Quaker family, thinks he can gain freedom by catching two runaway indentured servants and claiming the reward. Other novels set in the United States include *Barn* (1996), which takes place in the Oregon Territory of 1855; *The Secret School* (1996), which concerns an innocent deception by some grade-school students in 1924 Colorado; *Don't You Know There's a War On?* (2003), an exploration of the home front during World War II; and *Who Was that Masked Man, Anyway?* (1994), a satirical novel about life in the United States immediately before World War II. His recent novel *Iron Thunder* (2007), which tells about the building of the warship *Monitor* in 1862 and the battle with the *Merrimac*, was followed by *The Seer of Shadows* (2008), set in New York City in 1872 and involving a photographer who views the image of his client's dead daughter in his prints.

Many of his novels take place in England or on the high seas. The latter setting is used in *The Confessions of Charlotte Doyle* (1990; Newbery Honor Book, 1991), the story of a nightmarish Atlantic crossing filled with mutiny and murder as experienced by teenaged Charlotte as she journeys from England to Providence, Rhode Island, in 1832. The Atlantic is also the chief setting for *Beyond the Western Sea: Lord Kirkle's Money* (1998). The first part, *Beyond the Western Sea: The Escape from Home* (1997) takes place in the 19th century and tells how impoverished 15-year-old Maura and her young brother leave their wretched Irish village, meet up with the runaway son of their landlord, and go to Liverpool to find a ship to take them to the New World. In the second part, they make the harrowing voyage but find only hardship and deprivation when they land. The first two Crispin books—*Crispin: The Cross of Lead* (2002; Newbery Medal, 2003) and *Crispin: At the Edge of the World* (2004)—take place in England and France during and after the reign of Edward III while the Hundred Years War is in progress. They feature a young waif named Crispin who has been deprived of his birthright and is forced to flee from his home for survival. (A full description of these books is given in Chapter 4). Two others with English historical settings are *The Traitor's Gate* (2002) and *The Book Without Words* (2005). In all these novels he not only captures the essence of the settings and weaves convincing plots, but also frequently tells compelling coming-of-age stories.

Katherine Paterson is perhaps best known for her touching novels using contemporary settings and containing fascinating moral dilemmas—such as her Newbery-winning *Bridge to Terabithia* (1977; Newbery Medal, 1978) and *Jacob Have I Loved* (1980; Newbery Medal, 1981). She is represented in the body of this book by two novels: *The Master Puppeteer* (1975) found in Chapter 5 and *Bread and Roses, Too* (2006) analyzed in Chapter 8. The former is set in medieval Japan and the latter in the mill town of Lawrence, Massachusetts, during 1912. These two illustrate the range and variety in her historical novels. The author was born and spent her childhood in the Orient, the locale of her first three novels for young people. The first, *The Sign of the Chrysanthemum* (1973), is set in Samurai times in Japan and tells of a boy's search for his father; the second, *Of Nightingales that Weep* (1974), is the story of Takilo, who leaves home after her mother remarries and takes a position in the imperial court where she falls in love with a handsome warrior; and the third, *The Master Puppeteer* (1975) is about apprentices in the most prestigious puppet theater in ancient Japan. A fourth novel, *Rebels of the Heavenly Kingdom* (1983), is set in ancient China and tells of Wang Lee who is rescued from kidnappers and finds himself with a secret band intent on overthrowing the Manchu emperor.

The remainder of Katherine Paterson's historical novels take place in America. Two of them, *Bread and Roses, Too* (2006) and *Lyddie* (1991), explore the terrible working conditions in the mills of New England but at different times. Lyddie is a plucky young girl who is forced for economic reasons to work in the textile mills of Lowell, Massachusetts, during the 1840s. *Jeb, His Story* (1996) takes place in the mid-1850s in the days of slavery. Its hero is a young waif named Jeb who discovers that his father is a white master and his mother a black slave. When others hear this news, Jeb faces both prejudice and the threat of been caught by slave catchers. In *Preacher's Boy* (1988) we meet Robbie Hewitt, the son of the town's minister. The boy is growing up in a small Vermont town many years ago and tries but often fails to follow the example his father sets. Lastly, *Park's Quest* (1988) has a more contemporary setting. In it, 11-year-old Park is on a quest to find out about his father, who was killed in the Vietnam War. In her novels, the author exhibits an empathy and compassion toward her central characters. They manage to redeem themselves, but not without solving important ethical or moral problems such as adjusting to the death of a loved one, searching for identity, fighting for justice, or learning responsibility. She emphasizes that, through sacrifice and adherence to high principles, great things are possible.

Through the writings of Mildred D. Taylor readers have become acquainted with the saga of a valiant African American family, the Logans. The author spent her childhood in the North but her family often took trips to the old family homestead in Mississippi. There she heard many stories about the history of her family and of their friends and enemies. Other stories were told to her by her father whom she adored. Many stories involve family love and solidarity; others reveal the tragedy and destruction that racism can cause. From these stories emerged the saga of the unconquerable Logan family and gutsy, high-spirited Cassie. There are now eight stories in the series. A last volume is promised in which the family moves from Mississippi to Ohio. These books are briefly introduced in the chronological order of events described rather than the order of publication. The first is *The Land* (2001), which is based on the life of the author's great-grandfather whose name in the novel is Paul-Edward Logan, son of a plantation owner and an African-Indian slave woman. Through his narration the unfair double standards for blacks and whites that emerged after the Civil War are described, particularly when Paul-Edward leaves the plantation, moves to Mississippi, and encounters the racism that presents almost insurmountable problems when he tries to become a landowner. It is followed by *The Well: David's Story* (1995) told by Paul-Edward's son. This novella focuses on David (later to be Cassie's father). In the early 1900s, all wells but the Logans' dry up. David generously shares his water with others and the whites accept his offer but return his kindness with insults and scorn. David's brother fights back with unfortunate results. *Mississippi Bridge* (1990), the next, is the only one not narrated by a Logan. The story is told instead by a white boy and involves the injustice of ordering blacks off a bus to make places for whites. When the boy sympathizes with the oppressed, he is punished by his father. The fourth, *Song of the Trees* (1975), was the first to be published and is the first to feature Cassie. In it, Cassie, who gains comfort and beauty from the trees on their property, stands up to a white businessman who wants to chop them down for profit. The remaining four volumes are narrated by Cassie. *The Friendship* (1987) is set in 1933 Mississippi and tells of a confrontation between two friends when one, a black man, calls the other, a white, by his first name in public. The story shows that even close friendship cannot survive racism and peer pressure. It is followed by the two most popular volumes in the series: *Roll of Thunder, Hear My Cry* (1976) and *Let the Circle Be Unbroken* (1981). The time span covered is from 1935 through 1937. The first tells of a series of crises between the black sharecroppers and the white landowners, how Mr. Logan, a landowner, unsuccessfully tries to united his black friends and how T. J. Avery, the son of a family friend, gets involved with two trashy white boys and is circumstantially accused of murder. At the end Mr. Logan diverts a lynch mob out to get T. J. by burning his cotton fields. In the second, T. J. is tried, found guilty, and executed, and the family, including Cassie, endures terrible acts of racially based hatred but finds subtle ways of retaliating. At the end Cassie's brother, who has spent months away from home seeking work, returns and the family is reunited. The last volume, *The Road to Memphis* (1990), takes place in 1941. In it, Cassie is in her last year of high school in Jackson, Mississippi, when a series of disturbing events, including a pregnancy, a death, and upsetting news of the Pearl Harbor attack, cause problems for the Logan family. Mildred Taylor is a born storyteller who has created many memorable characters including Cassie. Although her novels are filled with many positive values including the importance of fighting injustice and the strength to be gained from family ties and traditional values, there is also an undercurrent of anger and antagonism throughout her books that reflects the iniquity of racism and the terrible effects it has on innocent people.

Laurence Yep represents another minority group, the Chinese Americans, and in his writing he not only explores their history and culture, but also relates the group to its roots and traditions in China. He is unique in his exploration of Chinese history for young readers and in reproducing the immigrant experience in America, the conflicts of cultures it often produces, and the process of growing up under these conditions. He writes in different genres. Many use contemporary settings and explore modern-day problems— *Thief of Hearts* (1995), for example; others are fantasies such as the series that begins with *Dragon of the Lost Sea* (1982), and still others are collections of folktales—*The Rainbow People* (1989), for example.

However, he has had his greatest success in his historical novels, particularly the Golden Mountain Chronicles (GMC), a series that describes various episodes in Chinese and Chinese American history. Historically, Golden Mountain was the name the Chinese gave to America. Arranged in chronological order rather than the years of publication, they begin with *The Serpent's Children: GMC, 1849* (1984) and its sequel *Mountain Light: GMC, 1855* (1985). The first of these tells of the fortunes of Cassia and her brother Foxfire, who are referred to as the serpent's children and are growing up in a China suffering from famine and violence. Their father is a rebel who is dedicated to ending the oppression of the Manchu rulers and the invading English. In the sequel the struggle continues, and Cassia and Squeaky Lau fall in love. To prove his love, Squeaky must seek his fortune in the Land of the Golden Mountain, America. In *Dragon's Gate: GMC, 1867* (1993; Newbery Honor Book, 1994), which covers a two-year period from 1865 to 1867, 14-year-old Otter is growing up in Manchu-dominated China when he is forced to flee to America. He works with his father and Uncle Foxfire under inhuman conditions in a railroad construction gang. After his father is seriously injured and Foxfire is killed in an accident, the Oriental workers strike and gain equal pay with the white workers. *The Traitor: GMC, 1885* (2003) has two teenage protagonists: one is a white outsider, Michael Purdy, and the other a Chinese American, Joseph Young, who is being exploited working in the mines under dangerous conditions. The time is 1885 and the setting, the town of Rock Springs in the Wyoming Territory. The fate of the boys intertwines in this novel whose background is one of the worst race riots in America's history. *Dragonwings: GMC, 1903* (1975; Newbery Honor Book 1976), tells the story of Moon Shadow, who is only 8 years old when he leaves China to join his father, Windrider. When his father is exiled for killing a man who has attacked his son, the two are banished from San Francisco's Chinatown. Their adventures culminate in Windrider's designing and flying a primitive airplane in September 1909 (a real-life event) and sending to China for Moon Shadow's mother. *Dragon Road: GMC, 1939* (formerly called *The Red Warrior* is scheduled for publication in the late fall of 2008). The remaining three titles have more contemporary settings. *Child of the Owl: GMC, 1960* (1977) tells how Casey, because of her father's illness, is sent to live with her grandmother in San Francisco's Chinatown in the 1960s. In spite of her initial resistance, she learns about her family's background, manages to eat Chinese food, and adjusts to a Chinese school. In *Sea Glass: GMC, 1970* (1979), a Chinese American boy is in conflict with his father who wants him to play sports. *Thief of Hearts: GMC, 1995* (1995) is completely contemporary in setting.

The *Star Fisher* (1991) and its sequel *Dream Soul* (2000) are based on events in the life of the author's grandmother who grew up in Clarksburg, West Virginia, a daughter of the only Chinese family in town. The time is the late 1920s and these stories tell of Joanie's struggle for acceptance and friendship and of her parents' gradual Americanization to the point where they even allow her to celebrate Christmas. Writing with his niece, Kathleen S. Yep, a historian, the author has recently published *The Dragon's Child: A Story of Angel Island* (2008), which is based on actual transcripts of the proceedings of his family passing the severe entrance requirements to proceed from Angel Island (the West Coast's equivalent of Ellis Island) into the United States. The story centers on a 10-year-old boy who is an outsider (he stutters and is left-handed) and who must accompany a father he doesn't know to America.

Lastly, Laurence Yep has written some entertaining historical mysteries such as *The Mark Twain Murders* (1982) and *The Tom Sawyer Files* (1984), both set in San Francisco when, supposedly, Mark Twain was a newspaper reporter and Tom Sawyer was a city firefighter. In summary, Laurence Yep has reconstructed Chinese American history in his books and brought to life the struggle, determination, and discrimination associated with this group's integration into American life. He shatters stereotypes, and gives readers a tantalizing glimpse into the traditions, morality, and thought of this rich culture.

Two sets of relatives also made great contributions to historical fiction at this time. The first is a team of brothers—James Lincoln Collier (1928–), a writer, and Christopher Collier (1930–), a historian; and the second, a father and son—Sid Fleischman (1920–) and Paul Fleischman (1952–) who, incidentally have never written together. James Lincoln Collier is a prolific author of nonfiction (with specializations in American history and jazz), as well as fiction. With his brother Christopher he has collaborated on several books including, at this writing, eight works of historical fiction for young readers. Their creative process involves Christopher choosing an interesting topic and, after doing extensive research, turning it over to James who does most of the writing. Their first book, *My Brother Sam Is Dead* (1974), was an immediate success, winning several prizes and becoming a Newbery Honor Book in 1975. It is set during Revolutionary times in Connecticut and describes the tragic effects of the war on the Meeker family, whose loyalties are divided. The action culminates in the execution of the teenaged Sam Meeker. In their second book, *The Bloody Country* (1976), a family tries to eke out a living in spite of floods, a massacre, and legal disputes in the area that later became Wilkes-Barre, Pennsylvania. *The Winter Hero* (1978) uses Shay's Rebellion of 1786 and 1787 as a backdrop for a story about 14-year-old Justin and his brother-in-law Peter, who join the men protesting unfair treatment of the farmers. The rebellion is squashed and Peter narrowly escapes being hanged, but Justin emerges as a hero. The next three—*Jump Ship to Freedom* (1981), *War Comes to Willy Freeman* (1983), and *Who Is Carrie?* (1984)—form the Arabus family saga. They are described in Chapter 8 under *Jump Ship to Freedom*.

In *The Clock* (1992), set in early 19th-century Connecticut, 15-year-old Annie is sent to work in a woolen mill by her debt-ridden father. There she encounters terrible working conditions, a villainous boss, and a tragic romance. Despite all these problems, Annie emerges triumphant. Lastly, *With Every Drop of Blood: A Novel of the Civil War* (1994) tells how a young southern soldier is captured by the Yankees and gradually begins to respect and admire his black soldier guard.

These novels combine authentic settings, solid plotting, and a mixture of real and factual characters. Their themes are on such ever-relevant subjects as divided loyalties, family conflicts, and right versus might. James Collier has also written many historical novels alone. Among them are *The Worst of Times: A Story of the Great Depression* (2001), in which poverty strikes young Petey's family and, after his beloved cousin becomes a labor organizer, real tragedy occurs. In *The Corn Raid: A Story of the Jamestown Settlement* (2000), 12-year-old Richard warns the nearby Indian settlement of a planned English raid. When his master discovers what he has done, he punishes him so severely that Richard swears he will escape. The "me" of *Billy and Me* (2004) is nicknamed Possum and he and his friend set out to the gold fields seeking their fortunes.

One only hopes that Sid Fleischman has as much fun writing his books as his readers have reading them. He is best known for his books of tall tales featuring the outlandish McBroom and for several ghost stories that often use historical settings. Don't expect a great deal of history in his historical novels; instead expect outrageous fast-moving plots, the most dastardly of villains, likable, often bumbling heroes, and unbelievable coincidences. His first novel was *Mr. Mysterious and Company* (1962), the story of a magician and his family touring the West in 1884. It was followed by *By the Great Horn Spoon!* (1963) about Jack and his aunt's butler, Faithful, who journey to the California gold fields as they try to restore Aunt Arabella's declining fortune; and *Chancy and the Grand Rascal* (1966), in which Chancy sets out to find the brothers and sisters from whom he was separated during the Civil War. Others are *Humbug Mountain* (1978), about a traveling frontier newspaperman and his family who foil some dangerous outlaws; *Jingo Django* (1971), in which a boy is apprenticed as a chimney sweep to a master who is looking for hidden treasure in Boston's chimneys; *Bandit's Moon* (1998), also set during the gold rush in California; and *Jim Ugly* (1992), a story set in 1894 that features Jack, a boy who sets out to find his supposedly dead father, accompanied by his father's dog, Jim Ugly. Sid Fleischman's crowning achievement is *The Whipping Boy* (1986; Newbery Medal, 1987), set in medieval times in which rightly named Prince Brat changes places with Jemmy, the boy who is hired to receive the prince's whippings for bad behavior. A more recent title, *The Giant Rat of Sumatra* (2005), is treated in Chapter 8. With its breathless adventures, boisterous characters, and nail-biting suspense, it can rightfully take an honored place with Sid Fleischman's other works.

The books of Paul Fleischman—son of Sid Fleischman—are more thoughtful, quieter, and more introspective. He has written in a variety of genres (plays, poetry, fantasy, picture books, historical fiction) and for different audiences. He has written four historical novels, each outstanding in its originality, his telling examination of human nature, and study of an interesting aspect of early American life. In *Path of the Pale Horse* (1983), set in Philadelphia during the yellow fever epidemic of 1793, Lep, a young physician's apprentice, and his master come to help and also to find Lep's sister who is visiting the city. *Saturnalia* (1990) is set in colonial times (December 1681) and examines the Puritans' attitudes toward Indians and servants. Through interconnected stories, the actions of masters and servants are examined both during the day and night during the celebration when, in Roman times, masters and servants switched places. In *Bull Run* (1993) sixteen characters, eight from the North and eight from the South, and representing different walks of life— such as a slave, an orphan, and a black man passing as white—all describe their experiences during Bull Run, the first major battle of the Civil War. Lastly, a moving story called *The Borning Room* (1991) is told in six poignant vignettes (and a brief epilogue) spanning a period of about seventy years before and after the Civil War. It chronicles the fortunes of the Lott family of Ohio through a series of events—some happy, some sad—that take place in the special room in their house known as "the borning room." Paul Fleischman's contributions to juvenile literature are many. In the historical novel specifically, he has brought innovations in subject, character, and plot structure, as well as an imaginative style.

Like Paul Fleischman, Paula Fox (1923–), Lois Lowry (1937–), and Patricia MacLachlan (1938–) have written in different genres for different audiences. The historical novels of Paula Fox are outstanding works that differ widely in settings and subjects but share the author's compassion and respect for humanity. The first is *The Slave Dancer* (1973; Newbery Medal, 1974), which is the story of 13-year-old Jessie Bollier who, because of his ability to play the fife, is kidnapped in 1840 from his New Orleans home and forced to provide the music used to exercise the slaves who are being transported from Africa to America. It is a harrowing story filled with cruelty and squalor that ends on a somewhat hopeful note when Jessie is able to help one of the slaves, a boy named Ras, escape via the Underground Railroad. The self-hatred that the crew feels emphasizes the novel's main theme that slavery diminishes both the oppressors and oppressed. The second, *One-Eyed Cat* (1984; Newbery Honor Book, 1985) is set in an upstate New York community during the Depression year of 1935 and tells of sensitive young Ned Wallis who is grow- ing up in the shadow of his saint-like father, the local minister. When Ned secretly disobeys his father's edict not to fire the air rifle he has received as a gift from an uncle, he has to face the guilt and consequences of his actions. In these novels Paula Fox shows rare insight into child psychology and writes convincingly of the character change and development of these protagonists.

Lois Lowry, in addition to creating vivid characters including Anastasia Krupnik and writing bone-chilling fantasies such as *The Giver* (1993; New- bery Medal, 1994), has written two very different novels set during World War II. The first, *Autumn Street* (1980), takes place on the home front in America. When her father leaves to serve in the armed forces, Elizabeth goes with her mother and sister to live in her grandmother's house where she meets the African American cook and her grandson Charles, with whom she becomes friendly. Soon she encounters the corrosive power of racism and must adjust to her grandmother's stroke and, later, the murder of Charles. In this coming-of- age novel, Elizabeth learns to cope with adult problems. *Number the Stars* (1989; Newbery Medal, 1990) is a powerful, suspenseful novel about the Nazi occupation of Denmark during World War II. In September 1943 when news arrives of the German plan to round up all Jews for deportation, the Danes rally to help them. This is the story of how the family of 10-year-old Annemarie Johansen helps Annemarie's Jewish friend Ellen Rosen and her family escape to Sweden. Although this is basically a story of sacrifice and heroism, the grim realities of the brutality and bloodshed of the period are not ignored.

Patricia MacLachlan's *Sarah, Plain and Tall* (1985; Newbery Medal, 1986) is the first of four novels about the Witting family. In it, Jacob Witting and his two children, Anna and Caleb, are living on a prairie farm. Some time after the death of his wife, Jacob applies for a mail-order bride and Sarah Elizabeth Wheaton arrives from Maine for a month-long trial period. The children and Sarah bond but they are afraid that this independent woman who stands plain and tall will not stay. Fortunately for both the family and the reader, Sarah decides to remain and the family is complete again. In *Skylark* (1994) drought threatens the future of the farm and Sarah, with Anna and Caleb, travel back to Sarah's original home in Maine to wait out the crisis, but the children are fearful that the reunion with their father will not take place. Caleb takes over the writing of the family chronicle from Anna in *Caleb's Story* (2001). The family life has become richer through the birth of a baby sister, Cassie, but everything changes when a mysterious stranger is found in the barn. Years pass and it is now Cassie's turn to be chronicler. She does this in *More Perfect Than the Moon* (2004). When she learns that her mother is going to have a baby, Cassie is filled with resentment and jealousy until her loving family brings her to acceptance and the realization that this should be a time of expectation and joy. Much of the beauty of these books lie in their simplicity, gentleness and what the author calls, "the heroics of common life."

During her life Patricia Beatty (1922–1991), wrote fifty books for young readers and an additional ten with her husband John Louis Beatty. She lived on an Indian reservation as a child and her first book was about Native American life before the coming of the missionaries. Many of her novels deal with important passages in American history. Some examples: *Jayhawker* (Morrow, 1985) is the story of Elijah, son of a Texas abolitionist, who becomes a spy and infiltrates Charles Quantrill's infamous Bushwhacker network; *Who Comes with Cannons?* (Morrow, 1992) in which danger comes to Truth Hopkins and her Quaker family who are pacifists during the Civil War. *Turn Homeward, Hannalee* (Morrow, 1984) (in Chapter 8) takes place during the last days of the Civil War during which Hannalee Reed, who was taken north to work, struggles to return to her family in the South. *Be Ever Hopeful, Hannalee* (Morrow, 1988) tells of the life of the Reed family after the war. In *Charlie Skedaddle* (Morrow, 1987), Charlie, a young Yankee soldier who has fled during his first battle, finds that this does not make him a coward forever, and *Sarah and Me and the Lady from the Sea* (Morrow, 1989) is set in Washington State in the 1890s and tells the story of the Kimball family.

This warm and nostalgic view of the past also infuses the historic novels of Robert Newton Peck (1928–) and Richard Peck (1934–). Robert Newton Peck has written more than sixty novels for young readers, about half of them historical in content. Many of them are excellent and one of them is a masterpiece: *A Day No Pigs Would Die* (1974), his first book published he was 44. It is largely autobiographical in nature (the narrator is named Rob Peck) and takes place in the late 1920s on a Vermont farm. The novel spans one year, beginning when Rob is 12. After a neighbor gives the boy a piglet for saving his cow while in labor, Rob spends all his time with his pet, Pinky, who becomes more precious than a human friend. When hard times come and there is no food on the Pecks' table, Rob's father, who is a both a farmer and the town butcher, slaughters Pinky although it breaks his heart. The title comes from the last episode in the book, the day of the death and burial of Rob's loving and saintly father. This book presents one of the most moving and tender pictures of family life in all young adult literature. Twenty-five years later, a sequel was published—*A Part of the Sky* (1987), a fine book but not as successful. In it, 13-year-old Rob must try to keep the family together during the Depression. The farm is eventually lost and Rob takes a job in a store. However, through faith and hard work the Pecks survive and Rob learns there are values more important than money. *Soup* (1974) is the first book in a series of about fifteen novels for the intermediate grades about the often-humorous exploits of Rob and his sidekick, Soup, in rural Vermont during the 1920s. There is also a series about Trig, Soup's counterpart, a young girl growing up in Vermont. Some of his other titles include *Rabbits and Redcoats* (1976), about two boys who participate in the capture by Ethan Allen and the Green Mountain Boys of Fort Ticonderoga in May 1775; *Millie's Boy* (1973), the story of a boy's search for his father after the murder of his mother, and of his life and escape from a work farm; and *The Horse Hunters* (1988), in which a 15-year-old boy travels more than 100 miles alone to take some wild horses to a rodeo in 1932 Florida. *Arley* (1989) is another of his better novels. In Jail-town, Florida, in 1927, young Arley Poole seems destined to follow in his father's footsteps as a field worker until a new schoolteacher, Miss Binnie Hoe, intervenes. This is followed by *Arley's Run* (1991). Three other titles: *Fawn* (1975), about an Indian boy at the Battle of Ticonderoga in 1758; *Eagle Fur* (1978), set in Canada in 1750; and *Cattle Ghost* (1999), set on a cattle ranch in Florida in the early 1900s and featuring a lonely boy and the brother he worships. At times Robert Newton Peck's plots can be predictable and his characters two-dimensional but at his best his books are humorous, warm-hearted, exciting tales that breathe life into American history and are as comforting as homespun.

Richard Peck is one of the best and most respected writers for young adults working today. He started with a number of books that explored modern social problems such as teenage suicide, but more recently has moved increasingly into historical fiction, much of it taking place in the Midwest during the Depression years. Prior to these titles, he wrote a series of delightful novels featuring the precocious heroine Blossom Culp (including *The Ghost Belonged to Me*, 1975), which take place in the small midwestern Mississippi valley town of Bluff City in 1913–1914. Because Blossom is gifted with second sight, which she uses frequently with amazing results, these novels could be classified as historical fantasies. More recently, he has published seven historical novels all dealing with events in the first half of the 20th century in the United States, beginning with *A Long Way from Chicago* (1998; Newbery

Honor Book, 1999), which chronicles the seven summer trips from 1929 to 1935 that Joey and young sister Mary Alice made to visit Grandma Dowdel in her sleepy Illinois town. Grandma Dowdel is an inspired creation. Eccentric, feisty, and unscrupulous, she also represents the Yankee virtues of decency and independence. In the sequel, *A Year Down Yonder* (2000; Newbery Medal, 2001), it is 1937 and Mary Alice, now 15, is sent to spend a year with Grandma while her father looks for work. The year is filled with short-term crises, and Mary Alice is alternately embarrassed, appalled, bemused, terrified, and pleased by her Grandma's eccentric but purposeful behavior. Suffice it to say that, at year's end, Mary Alice doesn't want to go home. There is a change of mood and setting in *The River Between Us* (2005), which begins in 1915 when young Howard visits his father's hometown and Grandma Tilly begins reminiscing. The scene then shifts to 1861 when Tilly is 15 and two mysterious ladies arrive in town. Tilly's twin brother falls for one of them before running off to war and being followed by the ladies. This is a taut, gripping mystery as well as a powerful account of the horrors of war. A gentler, mellower America is pictured in *Fair Weather* (2003), in which narrator 13-year-old Rosie, young Buster, older sister Lottie, and their Grandad can't contain themselves when they receive an invitation from Mama's sister to visit the 1893 World's Columbian Exposition in Chicago. For them, this becomes the adventure of a lifetime, and for the reader a humorous, delightful journey into the past. *On the Wings of Heroes* (2007), for middle-grade readers, describes small-town life in America during World War II. It is told from the perspective of young Davy Bowman, who has two heroes in his life: his father and older brother, Bill, who flies B-17s. The book is filled with authentic, appealing details of the period such as air raid drills and scrap metal drives plus a variety of well-drawn characters like Mr. Stonecypher who lost a son in a different war. Two additional charming, feel-good novels take place in rural Indiana in the early part of the last century. The first is *The Teacher's Funeral; A Comedy in Three Parts* (2004), described fully in Chapter 8, and the second, *Here Lies the Librarian* (2006), in which 14-year-old tomboy Pee Wee becomes enchanted with four ladies fresh from library school who come to town to reinstate library services after the local library is destroyed by a tornado. In a subplot, brother Jack is determined to win an upcoming automobile race. In these novels, Richard Peck has created a sub-genre that one critic has called "nostalgic fiction." They have many characteristics in common: enchanting characters, swift bright narratives, affection for the past, humor (often bordering on the slapstick), folksy settings, many touching moments, positive attitudes and themes, and a strong feel for language. On the basis of these novels, one understands why one critic said "no one does nostalgia like Peck."

The first three of Ann Rinaldi's (1934–) young adult novels had contemporary settings but with the fourth, *Time Enough for Drums* (1986), she turned to historical fiction. The story is set in Trenton, New Jersey, during Revolutionary times and tells of a young girl who experiences divided loyalties because her brother is fighting with the Patriots and her sister is married to a British officer. After the success of this novel, Rinaldi embarked on a career in historical fiction and, to date, has produced more than forty titles (she averages two a year). Most are aimed at young adults and have strong female protagonists. Almost twenty of these novels belong to the Great Episodes series, which highlights important events and personalities in American history. Some examples: *The Coffin Quilt: The Feud Between the Hatfields and the McCoys* (1999), which tells of the feud that begins in 1878 over the ownership of some pigs and escalates in 1882 when Roseanna McCoy runs off with Johnse Hatfield. The story is seen from the point of view of a sister, Fanny McCoy, who is caught in the middle. *Keep Smiling Through* (1999) uses the home front during World War II as its subject. In it, 10-year-old Kay Hennings must decide whether to tell the truth or do what she is told when she discovers that her German grandfather is unwittingly engaged in unpatriotic activities. A novel that is set in colonial times is *Hang a Thousand Trees with Ribbons: The Story of Phillis Whitney* (1996) (discussed in Chapter 8). An example of her contributions to the Dear America series for younger readers is *The Journal of Jasper Jonathan Pierce: A Pilgrim Boy* (2000), in which 14-year-old Jasper breaks with his group by becoming friends with the Nauset Indians. Aside from these series, Rinaldi has penned three books known as the Quilt Trilogy consisting of *A Stitch in Time* (1994), *Broken Days* (1995), and *The Blue Door* (1996). Together they tell of the fortunes of a shipping family in post-Revolutionary Salem. She has also written more than twenty stand-alone books. Some examples using events in American history as settings: *In My Father's House* (1993), which tells the story of a family from the first shot fired in the Civil War to their flight to Appomattox at war's end; *The Second Bend in the River*, concerning the romance between Shawnee Chief Tecumseh and Rebecca Galloway; and *Wolf by the Ears* (1991), the story of Harriet Hemmings, a slave at Monticello who was supposedly Jefferson's daughter. Another popular title is *The Last Silk Dress* (1988), a Civil War novel in which Susan Chilmark, a strong Confederate supporter, collects silk dresses to make a balloon to spy on the Yankees. The author has also written numerous novels that take place outside America. *Mutineer's Daughter* (2004), for example, is a fascinating tale about Mary, the daughter of Fletcher Christian (of the mutiny on the *Bounty*) by a Polynesian wife, and her stay at a boarding school in England where she hides her identity because her father has shamed the family name. *The Redheaded Princess* (2008) tells of the youth of Elizabeth I of England and the dangers and uncertainties that surrounded it, and *Nine Days a Queen: The Short Life and Reign of Lady Jane Grey* (2005) is a breathtaking story of the intrigue and pageantry surrounding Lady Jane's brief rule and her execution at age 16. These novels are well plotted and paced and written in a clean, clear writing style. The author is meticulous in accuracy and attention to minute details. Her themes are those that young adults, particularly girls, can relate to: family relationships, the important of forgiveness in life, and the power of love.

By comparison, the books by Gary Paulsen (1939–) have a stronger appeal for boys. He has written more than twenty books and as many magazine articles. Many of his most popular books for young readers are survival stories with contemporary settings, some of which also have coming-of-age themes. Representative of these are the four books that make up The Brian Saga, beginning with *Hatchet* (1987), which is a survival story about a boy trapped in a Canadian wilderness. Paulsen's first historical book for young readers was also an adventure story and involved survival in the Wild West of 1847–1849. It was *Mr. Tucket* (1969), which evolved into a five-book series. In the first, 14-year-old Francis Tucket is heading west on the Oregon Trail, with his family and a rifle he received for a birthday present, when he is captured by Pawnees. His subsequent adventures and courageous acts not only result in his freedom, but also the right to be called Mr. Tucket. In the last, *Tucket's Home* (2000), Francis and his adopted family, youngsters Lottie and Billy, are headed home to the Tucket family with a stash of gold they have discovered in a Spanish grave. The Tucket books are amusing, fast-paced adventures, but Paulsen has written many other historical novels on a serious note. For example, the three novels known as the Alida stories explore such themes as loneliness, family ties, responsibility, and the meaning of maturity, using a western setting around the time of World War II. In *The Cookcamp* (1991) a lonely 5-year-old boy is sent to spend a summer in a Canadian wilderness where his grandmother Alida is cooks for a crew of nine road builders. The boy spends a wonderful summer being the camp mascot, riding the tractor, and learning how to spit. This short lyrical work is followed by *The Quilt* (1999), another tender, poignant story. The boy is now a year older and again visiting his grandmother who is working on a quilt with other female members of the family. As they work they tell the boy stories of the past and present of the family—stories that are filled with love, courage, pain, and joy. In *Alida's Song* (2004) the boy, now 14, takes a job working on a farm where Grandmother Alida is again the cook. The boy is escaping a frightful home situation and, by summer's end, has regained his faith in himself and others. The two Nightjohn stories are also a reaffirmation of life as well as an indictment of slavery. In the first, *Nightjohn* (1993), the title character is an escaped slaved who returns to his plantation bloody but unbowed, determined to commit an illegal act (it is the 1850s)—he plans to empower his fellow slaves by teaching them to read and write. One of the slaves is a young girl named Sarny. She is the central character in the sequel, *Sarny* (1997), set in 1865. In it, Sarny escapes from the plantation to find her children who have been sold and taken from her. Two other notable titles are *The Winter Room* (1989; Newbery Honor Book, 1990), set on a Minnesota farm probably in the 1930s. It portrays a loving, close-knit, hard-working family and the amazing stories that Uncle David spins about his former life in Norway. The other is *Soldier's Heart* (1998), in which Charles Goddard enlists in the Northern army in 1861 when he is only 15. His tour of duty takes him from one battle to another. He emerges from the war sickened by what he has seen, but is now a man. It is interesting to note that this writer's style changes with the subject matter. The survival stories, for example, are written in a terse, staccato style, perhaps to echo the objectivity of nature. Many of his books portray the wonder and beauty of nature as well as its cruelty. The author also stresses traditional family values and the importance of family ties, although often the families portrayed are not supportive and even pitiless at times.

British Writers (1950–1980)

The period 1950 to 1980 was also a productive time for writers of historical fiction across the Atlantic. When one thinks of Roman Britain in fiction, the name that comes immediately to mind is Rosemary Sutcliff (1920–1992), one of the towering giants in historical fiction. She wrote about thirty-five novels, most which deal with British history. Her first was *The Chronicles of Robin Hood* (1950) and by her third, *Simon* (1953), about complex divided loyalties and set during the English Civil War, she had really hit her stride. Her fourth, *The Eagle of the Ninth* (1954) (analyzed in Chapter 4), is considered a classic. It is the story of a Roman, Marcus, a crippled former centurion, who travels north of Hadrian's Wall in search of information about his father's lost legion. Two others set in Roman Britain followed: *The Silver Branch* (1957) and *The Lantern Bearers* (1959), in which a Roman soldier decides to remain in Britain after the legions have gone. The author later returned to this setting for a short novel about the building of Hadrian's Wall, *The Bridge Builders* (1959), and *Frontier Wolf* (1980), in which Alexios Flavius, a relative of Marcus, is disgraced and sent to the far north of the British Isles in charge of a group of frontier scouts. In *The Mark of the Horse Lord* (1965), set in 2nd-century Britain, Phaedrus, a freed Roman gladiator, agrees to impersonate the Lord of the Horse People in northern Britain. Sutcliff is also well-known for her excellent trilogy based on Arthurian legends: *The Light Beyond the Forest: Quest for the Holy Grail* (1979), *The Sword and the Circle* (1981), and *The Road to Camlann* (1981). The following brief descriptions of some of her novels give some idea of the scope and variety of her work: *The Hound of Ulster* (1963) tells the story of Cuchulain, a hero of ancient Ireland; in *Flame-Colored Taffeta* (1985), set in 18th-century England, Damaris and her friends help a wounded smuggler; *The Shining Company* (1990) tells how a group of young warriors in A.D. 600 prepare to fight the invading Saxons; in *Blood Feud* (1977), Jestyn, a half Celtic–half Saxon boy is forced into slavery by the Vikings; *The Shield Ring* (1957) is the story of the Viking settlers' last stand against the Normans in the Lake District; and *Brother Dusty-Feet* (1952) is the story of strolling players in medieval England. Piece by piece, Sutcliff has created a picture of the making of Britain from prehistoric times to the 18th century. She does not romanticize history and her books are noted for their authenticity and for her realistic, non-sugar-coated description of events and social conditions. Many of her books are somber in tone and many deal with people who are outsiders— sometimes because of a physical condition, sometimes because of race or an act of fate—and the loneliness this condition brings. The deliverance and salvation of these people form strong, personal themes but, in summation, it is her ability to create convincing settings and narratives that completely absorbs the reader and makes her works memorable.

Several of Henry Treece's (1911–1966) twenty-five novels for young readers also use Roman Britain as settings. In *Legions of the Eagle* (1954), the conflict between the Celts and the Romans is explored through a Celtic boy's experience during the Roman invasion of A.D. 45. Three novels—*The Bronze Sword* (1966), *The Queen's Brooch* (1966), and *Red Queen, White Queen* (1966)—tell the story of Queen Boudicca and her valiant struggle against the Romans. What is considered his masterpiece is his first Viking trilogy—*Viking's Dawn* (1955), *The Road to Miklagard* (1957), and *Viking's Sunset* (1960)—which traces the adventures of young Viking Harald Sigurdsson from teenage to middle age in settings that range from Kiev to Vineland. In addition to a second Viking trilogy, Henry Treece wrote stories on such subjects as King Arthur, the Norman Conquest, and the Trojan War. One of his more unusual subjects was his desert-island survival story *The Further Adventures of Robinson Crusoe* (1958). His plots are fast-moving and dramatic and he does not shy away from the violence and ruthlessness that was common during these periods. Father-son relationships are stressed in many of his novels.

Cynthia Harnett (1893–1981) was tireless in the amount of research that went into her nearly twenty historical novels for young people. This is shown in the accurate details present in both her prose and the pictures she drew to illustrate her works. Her settings are always England. Four of her best works are: *The Great House* (1949), her beautifully illustrated first book for children that is set in the late 17th century and tells the story of the two children of a successful architect; *The Wool-Pack* (1951), a prize-winning novel about a wool merchant in the Cotswolds in the 16th century and his son who clears his father from charges of wrongdoing; *Ring Out Bow Bells* (1953), which is based on the real-life stories of George Washington's ancestors and the famous Dick Whittington; and *The Load of Unicorn* (1959), which describes the rivalry that existed between printers and professional handwriters in the days of the first British printer, Caxton. Her last novel, *The Writing on the Hearth* (1971), took ten years to research and tells the story of a 15th-century boy who longs to become an Oxford scholar. Her books are filled with details but also contain dialogue. They are more popular in the United Kingdom than in the United States.

Herbert Best (1894–1981) perhaps should be considered an American writer because, although he was born in England, he lived much of his adult life in the United States with his wife, who wrote under the pen name of Erick Berry (1923–1974) (see also the coverage earlier in this chapter). Drawing on his experience as a civil servant in Africa, he wrote several novels with this setting beginning with his first juvenile, *Garram the Hunter* (1930), an adventure story of a boy of the Hill tribes and his wonderful dog. Among his novels set in America are *Border Iron* (1954), in which a boy and his dog in the 1750s help solve a border dispute over iron ore mined in Massachusetts but smelted in New York, and *The Long Portage* (1948), about a boy who joins Rogers' Rangers during the French and Indian Wars. His wife's novels include *Harvest on the Hudson* (1945), set in the days of New Netherlands and including a voyage to the West Indies and an encounter with pirates, and *Sybil Ludington's Ride* (1952), based on a real event during the Revolution and featuring a 14-year-old heroine.

Three British authors who have continued in the footsteps of Charles Dickens are Leon Garfield (1921–1996), Joan Aiken (1924–2004), and Gillian Avery (1926–). Leon Garfield became a writer of young adult novels by accident. When his first novel *Jack Holborn* (1964) was submitted as an adult novel, his editor suggested that with a few changes it would be an excellent book for young readers. The novel deals with an orphan boy who stows away on a ship and encounters pirates, bloodcurdling deaths, and breathless adventures while solving the mystery of his long-lost mother. After the success of this novel, he continued to write for this audience but, ironically, his books are enjoyed by both audiences. *The Sound of Coaches* (1974) was, for example, a selection of an adult book club. His output totals about thirty books. The locale of many of his novels is London in the late 17th or 18th centuries. Often they deal with a youngster of humble origins who is thrust into incredible, suspenseful adventures that involve courage, danger, and intrigue. Leon Garfield has a strong sense of social justice and a dislike of cruelty and neglect. His novels show that the power of love can change people. He believes in personal redemption and the possibility of character change through sacrifice and enlightenment. Many themes also relate to the search for personal identity (for example, lost parents) and for social justice. All contain exuberant convoluted plots, high-speed adventure, fascinating characters, and cliff-hanging suspense. To give an idea of his subjects and themes, here is a brief description of a few popular titles. *Devil-in-the Fog* (1966) is the story of George Treet, a member of a band of traveling actors who discovers that Mr. Treet is not his real father, but when he goes to live with his real family he is aware of someone watching him in the fog. In *Smith* (1967), a 12-year-old pickpocket steals a document from a gentleman who is then murdered. After being taken in by a wealthy family, he is accused of the murder. *Black Jack* (1968) tells how a young apprentice in 18th-century England becomes involved with a hardened criminal and a girl who is supposedly crazy. In *The Empty Sleeve* (1988), Peter dreams of going to sea but instead is apprenticed to a locksmith, at least freeing Peter from his obnoxious, goody-goody brother. However, when the ghost of a former apprentice appears, Peter runs to his brother for help. In *The Sound of Coaches*, Sam, whose mother died when he was a baby, spends his childhood and youth searching for his real father. Garfield, like Joan Aiken, shares many writing qualities with Charles Dickens. All three authors possess vivid imaginations and incorporate wit and sardonic humor in their books. Their plots are well-paced and suspenseful and often use outlandish coincidence and plot twists, and their creation of characters is outstanding. Many of them are bizarre and eccentric but they are always memorable.

Joan Aiken wrote more than fifty books for children and young adults. For the latter audience, her best-known series is a sequence known variously as the James III books or the Wolves books after its first volume, *The Wolves of Willoughby Chase* (1963). These books could be considered historical fantasies because, although they appear to be set mainly in early Victorian England, they are set in an imaginary time when a Stuart, James III, is king and the Hanoverians are plotting to dethrone him and place their own candidate on the throne (none of the early Georges had yet reigned). As well, the geography of London is sometimes distorted, even to the point of inventing a canal district. The fantasy elements are deemphasized in several of these books. For example, *The Wolves of Willoughby Chase* is pure Victorian melodrama. When their parents go on a sea voyage, two girls are trapped in their remote English manor house by two villains, Miss Slighcarp and Mr. Grimshaw, who are intent on getting rid of the parents, disposing of the girls, and taking over the property. With the help of a poor neighborhood lad, Simon, the plot is foiled and justice triumphs. In the second volume, *Black Hearts in Battersea* (1964), Simon travels to London to study art and finds himself involved in a Hanoverian conspiracy against the king. Simon meets an outrageous Cockney waif, Dido Twite, who later becomes the unofficial heroine of the series. *Nightbirds on Nantucket* (1966), the third volume, features Dido who, after being shipwrecked, is saved by a whaling boat and uncovers a plot to assassinate King James by firing a long-distance canon across the Atlantic. In *The Cuckoo Tree* (1971), Dido, back home, foils another plot while she is tending a sick man in the countryside. Two other volumes in the series are *Midwinter Nightingale* (2003) and *The Witch of Clatteringshaws* (2005), published posthumously. In the former, James III has died and an ailing King Richard IV is on the throne. While Dido is kidnapped and held in a ramshackle manor house, Simon is tending to King Dick, discovers he is heir to the throne, and knows he must rescue Dido. In the last book, Simon becomes king but soon tires of the confining existence so decides that he, along with Dido, must discover a relative to take his place.

Joan Aiken also wrote a fascinating trilogy known as the Felix trilogy set in 19th-century Europe, chiefly in Spain, involving the life of the narrator, Felix de Cabezada. In the first, *Go Saddle the Sea* (1977), 12-year-old orphan Felix is disliked by his Spanish relations and is ignored by his unresponsive grandfather. When he receives a blood-stained envelope from his dead father, he sets off for England to locate his relatives there. In the second, *Bridle the Wind* (1983), Felix, now in England, is sent to a boarding school where he feels alone and trapped. He longs to return to Spain and escapes only to be shipwrecked off the coast of France. In the last, *Teeth of the Gale* (1988), 18-year-old Felix is back in Spain studying law at Salamanca and during this turbulent time in Spain's politics (1820) he becomes involved in complex political intrigues. At the end, he receives permission from his ailing grandfather to marry his childhood sweetheart.

Lastly, mention should be made of the terrific novel that most closely resembles Dickens in theme and plot. *Midnight Is a Place* (1971) is set in 1842 in the squalid factory town of Blastburn in Yorkshire and tells of the flight of two youngsters, a 13-year-old orphan named Lucas Bell and an 8-year-old girl, Anne-Marie. The author uses the familiar themes of coincidence, mistaken identity, and forgotten family secrets to produce a novel of suspense, melodrama, and unusual twists of plot. The plight of the factory workers and their dismal living conditions during the Industrial Revolution are memorably re-created. Aiken has left a legacy of novels whose chief purpose is to entertain. Along the way she has created imaginative plots filled with bizarre twists and many tongue-in-cheek situations. This wit also is seen in many of her characters. Their names alone—Dido Twite, Miss Slighcarp—express volumes. She is a wonderful storyteller and great fun to read.

Gillian Avery also wrote books that depict the lives of children in Victorian England, but her novels are more mild-mannered, placid, and less melodramatic; one might call them "domestic dramas." She wrote a cycle of novels set in Oxford in the 1870s. Her first book, *The Warden's Niece* (1957), introduces Maria who runs away from her boarding school to live with her great uncle, the head of an Oxford college. In time, he allows her to stay because he is impressed with her academic ability and her desire to become a professor of Greek. She even uncovers a piece of history relating to the English Civil War. Characters reappear in later works in the series—for example, Maria is featured once again in *The Italian Spring* (1964) in which she is taken on a trip to Italy by a bachelor cousin. Others in the series are: *Trespassers at Charlecote* (1958), *James Without Thomas* (1859), and *The Elephant War* (1960), whose story involves youngsters preventing the sale of the London Zoo's "Jumbo" to P. T. Barnum's circus. One of her best-liked books is *The Greatest Gresham* (1962), about sisters growing up in a London suburb in the 1890s who seek their father's approval by becoming great, but don't know how to accomplish this. Gillian Avery's novels present the gentler side of Victorian life but still supply details about its inconveniences such as drafty rooms and tight, hot clothing. Her stories are often told with humor, sometimes satiric, and always from the child's point of view.

Hester Burton (1913–2000) wrote eighteen thrilling historical adventures for young adults, each using a famous historical event as a background. Some examples: the English Civil War and the plague of 1665 (*Thomas*, 1969), the French Revolution (*The Rebel*, 1971), Drake's battle with the Spanish Armada (*When Beacons Blazed*, 1980), the effect of the Industrial Revolution on farmers (*No Beat of Drum*, 1966), and the Battle of Trafalgar (*Castors Away!*, 1962). Two of her novels deserve special praise. The first is *Time of Trial* (1969), which is set in 19th-century England and deals with the struggle for freedom of speech as seen through the eyes of 17-year-old Margaret Pargeter, the daughter of an idealistic bookseller. The second, *In Spite of All Terror* (1969), deals with a more contemporary subject, the first months of World War II (1939–1940) in Britain and their effect on a London schoolgirl, 15-year-old Liz Hawton, who is evacuated to a family in Oxfordshire. One son enlists and another, too young to sign up, participates with Liz and the father in the evacuation at Dunkirk. The subsequent Battle of Britain and the bombings of London are also integrated into this story of everyday courage and endurance. In all of Hester Burton's books, the description of these great events is secondary to the stories of the everyday people who experience them. By humanizing these events, her novels provide her readers a vicarious way of experiencing them.

Jill Paton Walsh (1937–) is a much-admired writer not only for her historical fiction but also for her novels with contemporary settings including the interrelated *Goldengrove* (1972) and *Unleaving* (1978), stories of love and loss.

Her historical novels cover a number of different settings and periods. *The Emperor's Winding Sheet* (1974) is set in Constantinople during the final days of the Byzantine Empire. It is seen through the eyes of an English boy named Piers who has become the servant of the new emperor, Constantine. The novel contains a graphic description of the sacking of Constantinople by the Turks. *A Parcel of Patterns* (1983) tells of the plague year 1665 when a stricken village in Derbyshire voluntarily cuts itself off from its neighbors to help prevent the spread of this pestilence. *The Dolphin Crossing* (1967) takes place during the early days of World War II and describes how two English boys take a small boat across the English Channel to help with the evacuation at Dunkirk. In *Fireweed* (1969), also set during World War II, an abused boy and girl flee their difficult family situations during the Blitz and live in air raid shelters and bombed-out buildings. As well as telling good stories with believable characters, Jill Paton Walsh is a master of creating atmosphere through vivid descriptions of her geographical backgrounds and historical periods.

Like Jill Paton Walsh, K. M. Peyton (Kathleen and her sometimes collaborator, husband, Michael) wrote both historical novels and those with contemporary settings. In the latter genre, she is best know for the excellent Pennington series about an English boy's journey through darkest adolescence and early manhood, and in the former, the Flambards trilogy, named after the decrepit old country house that is the setting of these stories that take place before, during, and after World War I, and trace the fortunes of a family from being old-fashioned, class-conscious landed gentry to a modern, more progressively democratic group who eschew fox hunting for the automobile. The titles are *Flambards* (1967), *The Edge of the Cloud* (1969), and *Flambards in Summer* (1969). In the first, orphaned Christina Parsons, comes to stay with her uncle, a crusty old-fashioned landowner, and his two sons, Mark and Will. Mark, the elder, would like to marry Christina but she prefers and marries Will, an airplane enthusiast. The second book deals with Will's dangerous life as an aviator and by the beginning of the third, he has been killed. In the third, Mark sells his share of Flambards to Christina, who becomes sole owner. Christina, who has borne a posthumous child by Will, continues to manage the estate with the help of a former stable boy, Dick. Twelve years after the publication of the trilogy, a fourth book appeared, *Flambards Divided* (1981), which is something of an anticlimax. In it, Christina's marriage to Dick is on the rocks when handsome Mark comes back from the war and their former romance is rekindled. In addition to a series of gripping love stories, this series traces the momentous changes that World War I brought to English society. Briefly, here are three other fine historical novels by K. M. Peyton: *The Maplin Bird* (1965) is set on the English coast and tells of two orphans in the 1850s who become involved with attractive Adam, who is smuggling brandy from France on a boat called *The Maplin Bird*; *Windfall* (1962), also set in the 19th century, is about a fisherman's son who, after gaining a reward for saving a man's life, loses both his father and the money; and *Thunder in the Sky* (1966), set at the beginning of World War I, in which an Essex boy named Sam suspects his brother of being a spy. The author is an acknowledged master of tight plot construction and attention-gaining situations.

Barbara Willard (1909–1994) was a prolific writer of books for both adults and children. She is best known for a series of eight historical novels for young readers published between 1970 and 1980 known as the Mantlemass series, after the name of the manor house in Ashdown Forest, Sussex, where much of the action takes place. The novels cover a period of about 150 years from the end of the War of the Roses (1495) to the English Civil War period (1642–1688), when the house was burned down. These stories involve two families, the Mallorys and the Medleys, and how they survive these chaotic times. The novels show how important historical events change the lives of people even though they are not directly involved. In the first book, *The Lark and the Laurel* (1970), a delicate London girl changes when she comes to live at Mantlemass and becomes involved with both the house and its inhabitants after the Battle of Bosworth Field. The third, *A Cold Wind Blowing* (1973), considered by some to be the best in the series, tells how the closing of the monasteries changed the lives of even the common folk. Two other titles are *The Spring of Broom* (1971) and *Harrow and Harvest* (1974). Most of these titles feature strong female characters, a sense of the importance of family, and a fine evocation of time and place.

Robert Westall (1929–1993) is best known for three historical novels centered around World War II. The most popular is *The Machine Gunners* (1975), in which 14-year-old Chas McGill retrieves a machine gun from a crashed German fighter plane and he and his friends decide to use it to deter other German airplanes. These adventures and the capture of a downed German airman form the basis of this exciting, believable adventure (a sequel is *Fathom Five*, 1977). The second is *Blitz Cat* (1989), in which a black cat named Lord Gort sets out to find his master who has left to fight in World War II. The third is *The Kingdom by the Sea* (1990), a thrilling story about a boy who has lost his family in World War II and who must survive alone with his dog or face being adopted by a disliked cousin. His travels and travails make up the plot. This and others of Robert Westall's works tell how young people grow during periods of violence and how this affects one's personality and attitudes.

Lastly mention should be made of the works of Erik Haugaard (1923–) who is Danish by birth but a world traveler and who has used his knowledge of countries including Norway, Japan, the United States, Great Britain, and

Italy in many of his historical novels. *A Messenger to Parliament* (1962) and its sequel *Cromwell's Boy* take place during England's Civil War; *The Boy and the Samurai* (1991) tells of a street waif who helps a samurai rescue his wife in violent 16th-century Japan; *Hakon of Rogen's Saga* (1962) and its sequel *A Slave's Tale* (1965) recount the adventures of an orphaned boy on a bleak Norwegian island at the end of the Viking period. Perhaps his best-known work is *The Little Fishes* (1967), set during World War II in Italy, which tells the story of the little fishes—the homeless, hapless victims of war. In Naples during 1943, a street urchin name Guido meets two other waifs, Anna and young brother Mario, and the three begin a journey through war-torn Italy looking for a benefactor. It is a grim story that verges on the despairing.

HISTORICAL FICTION FROM 1980 TO THE PRESENT

The past thirty years have seen the emergence of some excellent new writers in the field of historical fiction for young readers. Here, in alphabetical order, are a few of them. An asterisk indicates that there is fuller coverage on the author's work in the main body of the text. Additional authors are covered in the reading lists that follow each of these internal chapters. As one can see from these writers and their works discussed below, the future of this genre is in capable hands.

*Laurie Halse Anderson (1961–)

This young writer is best known, at time of printing, for her novels with contemporary settings, such as *Speak* (Farrar, 1999), but already she has two historical novels to her credit. The first, *Fever 1793* (Simon, 2000), is a gripping story about a family caught in Philadelphia during the yellow fever epidemic that ravaged the city. The second, *Chains* (Simon, 2008), is the story of a young black woman who was sold to a cruel Loyalist family at the start of the Revolution.

*Mary Louise Auch (1938–)

In addition to numerous delightful picture books illustrated by her husband, Mary Jane Auch has written a number of historical novels, notably a trilogy that began with *Journey to Nowhere* (Holt, 1997) about young Mem Nye and her pioneer family in Genesee County in western New York State. It was followed by *Frozen Summer* (Holt, 1998) and *The Road to Home* (Holt, 2000), which continue Mem's adventures. *Ashes of Roses* (Holt, 2002) is set in New

York City in 1891 and tells of the harsh, cruel life Irish immigrants endured as seen through the experiences of 16-year-old Rose.

*Gary Blackwood (1945–)

As well as a number of nonfiction books, such as *Gangsters* (Benchmark, 2001), Gary Blackwood has several historical novels to his credit. He is best known for his Shakespeare Stealer trilogy, which began with *Shakespeare's Stealer* (Dutton, 2003) and continued with *Shakespeare's Scribe* (Dutton, 2000) and *Shakespeare's Spy* (Dutton, 2003). These are narrated by a 14-year-old orphan named Widge who through various exciting incidents becomes part of Shakespeare's acting company and at one point becomes his secretary and at another, his spy. The author also writes books on alternate history of the "what if" type. In *The Year of the Hangman* (Turtleback, 2004), the author imagines what would have happened if the Patriots had lost the Revolution, and in *Second Sight* (Dutton, 2005), Lincoln's assassination is re-created with an unusual ending.

*Joseph Bruchac (1942–)

Joseph Bruchac, of Native American descent, is best known for his many books of Indian folklore and culture as well as a number of historical novels, such as *The Winter People* (Dial, 2002), which takes place in 1739 when an Indian settlement in present-day Quebec is brutally attacked by Rogers' Rangers because the inhabitants are loyal to the English. Others of his works include *The Arrow over the Door* (Dial, 1998), which takes place in New York State in 1777 and involves two boys—Sam, a Quaker, who is doubting his faith, and Stands Straight, an Abenaki youngster whose parents were killed by white men; *Crazy Horse's Vision* (Dial, 2000), about the Indian chieftain's early years; and *The Journey of Jesse Smoke* (Dial, 1994), the story of a Cherokee boy and the tragedy of the Trail of Tears.

*Jane I. Curry (1932–)

As well as being a master reteller of folktales, Jane I. Curry is a fine writer of historical novels, many involving time travel. In *Dark Shade* (Simon, 1998), Maggie and her quiet, withdrawn friend Kip travel back in time to 1758 during the French and Indian Wars and in *Moon Window* (Simon, 1996), the time traveling involves going to frontier New Hampshire in the 1700s. In *The Black Canary* (2005), biracial 13-year-old James is magically transported to Elizabeth I's England where he develops an amazing singing voice and in *A Stolen Life* (Simon, 1999), a young Scottish teenager is kidnapped and sent to America, where she has a number of adventures before returning home.

*Christopher Paul Curtis (1954–)

In the few years he has been writing, Christopher Paul Curtis already has three outstanding prize-winning historical novels to his credit. *The Watsons Go to Birmingham—1963* (Delacorte, 1995) tells of an automobile trip the Watson family takes from Flint to Birmingham and of the trauma caused by witnessing the death and destruction due to the bombing of a local church there. *Bud, Not Buddy* (Delacorte, 1999; Newbery Medal, 2000) is set in Depression-era Flint in 1936 and tells of the odyssey of a young black boy after he escapes from a cruel foster home, and *Elijah of Buxton* (Scholastic, 2007), is the story of an 11-year-old boy who, with his family, are members of the freed black community of Buxton in southern Ontario in 1859.

*Karen Cushman (1941–)

Karen Cushman has had major success with three delightfully wise but humorous novels set in the Middle Ages. The first, *Catherine, Called Birdy* (Clarion, 1994), is set in England in the 1290s and tells of Catherine, the birds she keeps as pets, and her disposal of unwanted suitors. The second, *The Midwife's Apprentice* (Clarion, 1995; Newbery Medal, 1996), is the story of Alyce, once known as Beetle, and her on-and-off career as an apprentice to the midwife, Jane. *Matilda Bone* (Clarion, 2000) features Matilda who in the 1330s is unceremoniously dumped at the cottage of Peg, a diamond-in-the-rough local bonesetter. Two historical novels that take place in America are *The Ballad of Lucy Whipple* (Clarion, 1986) and *Rodzina* (Clarion, 2003). In the first, California Morning Whipple (later Lucy) arrives with her mother at a mining camp in the Sierras during the gold rush, and gradually takes charge of her life and, in the second, young Rodzina, in an orphan train heading west in 1881, worries about her fate but hopes to live a better life.

Berlie Doherty (1943–)

Berlie Doherty, an English writer, is already a two-time winner of the Carnegie Medal. One was for *Granny Was a Buffer Girl* (Orchard, 1988), which consists of a series of linked stories that trace the history of a family. The past and present also mingle in *Children of Winter* (Mammoth, 1995). In Victorian England, a street urchin is forced to work on a London river barge until he escapes in *Street Child* (Scholastic, 1994). One of her outstanding novels with a contemporary setting is *Dear Nobody* (Hamish Hamilton, 1991), a poignant novel that consists of a series of letters written by a pregnant teenager to her unborn child.

Jennifer Donnelly (1963–)

This young novelist has three outstanding historical novels to her credit. *A Northern Light* (Harcourt, 2003) is a coming-of-age novel set against a story of a murder in the Adirondacks during the summer of 1906. *The Tea Rose* (St. Martin's, 2007) is the first of a projected trilogy. This story of the Finnegan family takes place in East London in 1888, where the gentry from high society and cutthroats mingle with exciting results. The second, *The Winter Rose* (Hyperion, 2008), continues the Finnegan family saga with the story of Charlie Finnegan—now Sid Malone—and a new female character, India Selwyn Jones.

*Louise Erdrich (1954–)

Louise Erdrich is best known for her stirring novels for adults which include *Love Medicine* (HarperCollins, 1984), *Beet Queen* (HarperCollins, 1986), and recently, *The Plague of Doves* (HarperCollins, 2008), but she has also written some outstanding books for young readers. *Grandmother's Pigeon* (Hyperion, 1996), a fantasy, and *The Range Eternal* (Hyperion, 2002) are picture books for the primary grades. In the latter, the author recalls her childhood in the mountains of North Dakota and the blue enamel stove in the kitchen that was the center of a number of family activities. The author, who has Native American roots, is also writing a series of books about her family's history. The first three have been published. *The Birchbark House* (Hyperion, 1999), set in the late 1840s, features the series heroine, Omakayas or Little Frog, an Ojibwa girl who is 7 years old in the first volume. It is divided into four parts and recounts the daily life of the tribe on an island on Lake Superior. In the second, *The Game of Silence* (HarperCollins, 2005), the tribe is forced from their homes by white men, and the third, *The Porcupine Year* (HarperCollins, 2008), continues the story in 1852 when Omakayas and her family search for a new home and in so doing face a freezing winter and near-starvation.

*Jamila Gavin (1941–)

Jamila Gavin's mother was English and her father was Indian. This duel heritage figures in her writing for young people. For example, she has written a fine trilogy of novels set both in India and in Britain. In the first, *The Wheel of Surya* (Egmont, 2001), set in India during World War II, a boy named Jaspal and his sister Marvinder are separated from their mother and decide to find their father who is working as a scholar in England. The second, *Eye of the Horse* (Egmont, 2001), and the third, *Track of the Wind* (Egmont, 2001), continue the story and, against historical events such as independence for India and the creation of Pakistan, the youngsters return to their homeland and are reunited with their mother. *The Blood Stone* (Farrar, 2003) takes place in 1630 and is set in Venice and the Near East in a story of intrigue, adventure, and mystery. Another of her novels is *Coram Boy* (Nick Hern, 2000), a Gothic thriller set in Dickensian England and featuring a villain who secretly murders the orphans under his care instead of taking them to orphanages.

*Patricia Giff (1935–)

Patricia Giff is perhaps best known for her trilogy whose central character is Nory Ryan. In the first book, *Nory Ryan's Song* (Delacorte, 2000), 12-year-old Nory and her family and friends are devastated by the potato famine that struck Ireland in 1845. After such travail, she, her young brother Patch, and her grandfather arrive in Galway hoping to get passage to New York. The second, *Maggie's Door* (Wendy Lamb Books, 2003), describes the horrendous passage over, the death of Grandpa, Nory's reunion on the ship with her sweetheart Sean, and their arrival in Brooklyn. In the final volume, *Water Street* (Wendy Lamb Books, 2006), 13-year-old Bird Mallon, the daughter of Nory and Sean, is attracted to a lonely boy who lives in their tenement. Three other historical novels by Patricia Giff are *Willow Run* (Random, 2005), which concerns Meggie who moves with her family from New York to Michigan where her father is employed during World War II; *All the Way Home* (Delacorte, 2001), about a polio epidemic in 1941 and how Mariel, a survivor, moves with her foster mother to Brooklyn; and *Lily's Crossing* (Delacorte, 1997), also set during World War II, which tells how a deceitful, rebellious girl harms the future of Albert, a refugee from Hungary.

*K. M. Grant

English-born K. M. (Katie) Grant loves both horses and telling stories, which explains why one of the central characters in *Blood Red Horse* (Walker, 2004), the first volume in her acclaimed de Granville trilogy, is Hosanna, the hero's stallion. The time is 1185 and Will de Granville, accompanied by his brother Gavin, his father, and faithful Hosanna embark on a Crusade with Richard the Lion-Hearted. In the Holy Land, Will's adventures include battles with the Saracens during which he temporarily loses ownership of Hosanna to a young Saracen, Kamil. In the second book, *Green Jasper* (Walker, 2006), Will and Gavin return from the Holy Land and must save the kidnapped Ellie, a girl they both love, from the villainous constable De Scabious. In the third, *Blaze of Silver* (Walker, 2007), Will sets out to deliver money necessary to free King Richard who is being held for ransom. In *How the Hangman Lost His Heart* (Walker, 2007), Alice's uncle, a supporter of Bonnie Prince Charlie, is executed. After he is drawn and quartered, the young girl, with the help of the hangman, Dan Skinslices, retrieves his head. K. M. Grant has embarked on a second trilogy, The Perfect Flame Books, which has begun with *Blue Flame* (Walker, 2008), set in 1199 about two lovers separated by their faiths.

*Karen Hesse (1954–)

As well as numerous picture books for young children, Karen Hesse has written several acclaimed historical novels for an older audience that vary widely in their settings. Her most famous is *Out of the Dust* (Scholastic, 1997). This Newbery Medal winner is a free-verse diary that covers two years (1935–1936) in the life of Billie Jo, who is growing up on a wretched farm in the Oklahoma panhandle, also known as the Dust Bowl. *Letters from Rifka* (Holt, 1992), based on her great-aunt's experiences, tells of the plight of a family of Russian Jews as they flee across Europe in 1919 to escape persecution at home. Boston at the time of the influenza epidemic that followed World War I, is the setting of *A Time of Angels* (Hyperion, 1995), and *Stowaway* (Simon, 2001) spans the years 1768 to 1771 as it tells of 11-year-old Nicholas Young who is a stowaway on the ship that carried Captain Cook on his fantastic adventures leading to the Pacific Ocean. Set in a small Vermont town in the 1920s, *Witness* (Scholastic, 2001) reveals various views on race as well as featuring a murder mystery and the Ku Klux Klan.

*Cynthia Kadohata (1956–)

Cynthia Kadohata is a relatively new writer of historical novels, with only three titles published thus far. All three are excellent and deserve the praise they have received. The first is *Kira-Kira* (Atheneum, 2004), which won the Newbery Medal for 2005. It is the story of Katie Takeshima and her family of hard-working Japanese Americans. For economic reasons the family moves to rural Georgia where her mother and father work in chicken processing plants. Their struggle for survival and the heartbreak of the death of Katie's older sister form the basis of this moving novel. Her second book for young readers is *Weedflower* (Atheneum, 2006), the story of the friendship between a Japanese American girl living in an internment camp during World War II and a Navajo boy who lives on a nearby reservation. *Cracker! The Best Dog in Vietnam* (Atheneum, 2007) is told from various viewpoints including that of a German Shepherd, Cracker, who has been trained to search for land mines, sniff out the enemy, and search for missing soldiers. This novel does not ignore the grizzly details of war's horrors.

Kathleen Karr (1946–)

Kathleen Karr has written more than two dozen books for young readers, many of them historical novels. *The Boxer* (Farrar, 2000) begins in the tough tenements of New York City in 1885 and tells of the rise in the boxing world of 15-year-old Johnny Woods. Set in New York City of the 1920s, *Playing with Fire* (Farrar, 2001) tells of a boy and his spiritualist mother, both of whom become involved in the world of the occult, and *It Ain't Always Easy* (Farrar, 1990) is the story of two orphans in the slums of New York in 1882. *The Great Turkey Walk* (Farrar, 1998) is a humorous adventure story set in 1860 in which 15-year-old Simon decides he can earn a fortune by walking 1,000 turkeys from Missouri to turkey-starved Denver. In *Spy in the Sky* (Hyperion, 1997), a book for younger readers (grades 2–4), an adventurous orphan is employed as balloonist Thaddeus Lowe's assistant during the Civil War, and *Born for Adventure* (Marshall Cavendish, 2007) tells how Tom Ormsby leaves London to join an expedition with Henry Morton Stanley in Africa to rescue a mysterious pasha.

*Iain Lawrence (1955–)

In addition to the popular High Seas Trilogy, which consists of *The Wreckers* (Delacorte, 1998), *The Smugglers* (Delacorte, 1999), and *The Buccaneers* (Delacorte, 2001) and is described in the body of this work, Iain Lawrence has written a second trilogy beginning with *The Convicts* (Delacorte, 2004) in which Tom Tin's father is sent to debtor's prison in London. While trying to determine why Mr. Goodfellow is an enemy of the family, Tom is unjustly convicted of murder and sentenced to Van Dieman's Land (Tasmania). In the second, *The Cannibals* (Delacorte, 2005), Tom and his fellow convict Midgely plot to escape from their prison ship as it approaches Australia even though the area where they land may house cannibals, and in the third, *The Castaways* (Delacorte, 2007), Tom and four convict escapees find an abandoned ship, help some castaways who conspire against them, and eventually sail home to England. Three other historical novels by this author are *B for Buster* (Delacorte, 2004), about a Canadian boy who joins the Air Force during World War II and sees action in Europe aboard a plane named B for Buster; *Lord of the Nutcracker Men* (Delacorte, 2001), set during World War I; and *German Summer* (Delacorte, 2006), the story of a family, the tragedy that affects them, and the dog that changes their lives during the year 1965.

Sonia Levitin (1934–)

Sonia Levitin and her family fled Nazi Germany and came to the United States in 1938. This was the subject of her first book for young adults, *Journey to America* (Atheneum, 1987). This was followed by *The Return* (Atheneum, 1987), the story of Desta, an Ethiopian Jewish girl and her long journey to join Operation Moses, the secret maneuver in 1984 to airlift Jews from the Sudan to freedom in Israel. *Escape from Egypt* (Little, Brown, 1994) tells of another Jewish exodus, the flight of the Hebrews from Egypt in biblical times.

It is told from the standpoint of Jesse, a Hebrew slave who becomes a follower of Moses. *Clem's Chances* (Scholastic, 2001) uses a different time and setting in its story about young Clem who sets out in the 1860s to find his father in the California gold fields.

*Michael Morpurgo (1943–)

Michael Morpurgo is an extremely prolific English writer of books for young readers, many of them historical novels. Two that take place during World War I are *War Horse* (Greenwillow, 1982) in which the war is seen from the perspective of the book's hero, a horse named Joey, and *Private Peaceful* (Scholastic, 2003), which details the slaughter and dislocation of war and how some overcome these disasters. *Joan of Arc* (Mammoth, 1998) is one of several fictionalized biographies of famous people written by Morpurgo. This volume is narrated by Eloise, who lives in the city of Orleans and tells of Joan's struggle to free France from England and of the turmoil this causes in her life. Mention of three of his other many historical novels follows. *Twist of Gold* (Mammoth, 1983) is the story of Sean and Annie, who flee Ireland during the potato famine to find their father in California. *The Wreck of the Zanzibar* (Mammoth, 1995) is set in the Scilly Islands during 1907 when a violent storm brings with it the revelation of a secret. *Alone on a Wide, Wide Sea* (Mammoth, 2007) is the story of orphaned Arthur Hobhouse who, after World War II, is sent from England to Australia where he endures maltreatment and forced labor.

Linda Sue Park (1960–)

Linda Sue Park is a Korean American who, in her writing for young people, explores her ethnic heritage. One of her earliest books is a picture book, *Seesaw Girl* (Clarion, 1989), which is set in 17th-century Korea and tells the story of Jade Blossom, a daughter in a wealthy family. Her first novel for older readers is *The Kite Fighters* (Clarion, 2000), which takes place in 15th-century Korea and tells how the young king asks Kee-sup to design a majestic kite for him and, when he does, the king eventually allows Kee-sup's younger brother to fly it. *A Single Shard* (Clarion, 2001; Newbery Medal, 2002), set in 12th-century Korea, is the story of an orphan, Tree-Ear, who works for a renowned potter named Min. Min has made some special pots for the emperor but, unfortunately, while Tree-Ear is transporting them to the royal court, he is attacked by thieves who break the precious pots. Sun-hee and her older brother Tae-yul are living in Korea in 1940 during the Japanese occupation and they are involved in a ban which makes it illegal to practice Korean customs and traditions; things change dramatically when World War II erupts in the exciting novel *When My Name Was Keoko* (Clarion, 2002).

*Michelle Paver (1960–)

Michelle Paver was born in Africa and now lives in England. In 2003, she began work on a six-book cycle called the Chronicles of Ancient Darkness, set in the prehistoric world of the New Stone Age. The first four titles have been published. *Wolf Brother* (Harper, 2005) introduces the hero of the series, a youth named Torak who, with his faithful dog, Wolf, is captured by the Raven tribe where he meets and is befriended by a girl named Renn. Later he and some Raven warriors embark on a journey to rid the tribe of the evil presence of the bear, during which Torak and Wolf become separated. In *Spirit Walker* (Tegen Books, 2006), the two are reunited and travel to find a cure for the plague that is destroying the tribe and also to locate the Soul Eaters, whom Torak has been chosen to vanquish. In *Soul Eater* (Tegen Books, 2007), Torak and Renn brave the blizzards in the north to rescue Wolf, who has been captured by unknown enemies; and in *Outcast* (Tegen Books, 2008), Torak, bearing the mark of the Soul Eaters, is cast out of the Raven clan, and without Wolf or Renn, is hunted by the Otter clan and must survive in the wilderness. Michelle Paver has written another historical trilogy called the Daughters of Eden trilogy, which is set on an exquisite plantation called Eden in colonial Jamaica after the slaves were freed. The books are *The Shadow Catcher* (Transworld, 2002), *Fever Hill* (Transworld, 2005), and *The Serpent's Tooth* (Transworld, 2006).

Philip Pullman (1946–)

Before he gained international fame for his fantasy trilogy His Dark Materials, the English writer Philip Pullman wrote another brilliant trilogy set in Victorian England and featuring the intrepid Sally Lockhart. These are the best adventure-mysteries in years and are filled with bloody murders, opium dens, cliff-hanging chapters, darkest villainy, colorful characters, and twisty plots. The first, *The Ruby in the Smoke* (Knopf, 1987), details the search for a fabulous ruby for which people would and do kill. In the second, *The Shadow in the North* (Knopf, 1988), Sally challenges the sinister power of the richest man in the world, and in the third, *The Tiger in the Well* (Knopf, 2000), evil is punished and justice triumphs.

*Graham Salisbury (1949–)

Graham Salisbury has written several contemporary adventure stories as well as historical novels set in his native Hawaii. In *Eye of the Emperor*, underage Japanese American Eddy Okubo, who has grown up in Hawaii, enlists after the attack on Pearl Harbor and gets involved in a bizarre experiment to train attack dogs that proves ultimately both insulting to his race and scientifically invalid. *Under the Blood-Red Sun* (Delacorte, 1994) also takes place in Hawaii immediately after the Pearl Harbor attack. Soon afterward, 13-year-old Tomikazu Nakaji witnesses the arrest and deportation of his Japanese American father and grandfather and the firing of his mother from her job because of her race. The welfare of his family now becomes his responsibility. Its sequel, *House of the Red Fish* (Wendy Lamb Books, 2006), takes place one year later in 1943, and Tomi still faces the prejudice of his fellow Hawaiians, who also fear another attack by the Japanese. He has hopes of raising his father's sunken fishing boat and using it to help his family finances. *Night of the Howling Dogs* (Wendy Lamb Books, 2007) is an adventure story that uses as background an actual event—a volcanic eruption in 1975. In the novel, Dylan's scout troop manages to avoid the lava flow and flees to a small beach below the volcano.

*Gary D. Schmidt (1957–)

Gary D. Schmidt, an English professor and part-time farmer in Michigan, has written several commendable historical novels. His most famous, *Lizzie Bright and the Buckminster Boy* (Clarion, 2004), was a Newbery Honor Book in 2005. It tells the poignant story of a minister's son and his friendship with a black girl whose family is squatting on an island off the coast of Maine in the early 20th century. *Straw into Gold* (Clarion, 2001) is a combination fantasy/historical novel that is set in the time of the Great Barons and tells a story that is a variation on the Rumpelstiltskin tale. In *Anson's Way* (Houghton, 1999), a young British subject, Anson Granville is sent to Ireland with his regiment in the mid-19th century as a drummer boy and witnesses the great injustices the English inflict on the Irish. *The Wednesday Wars* (Clarion, 2007) is set during the 1967–1968 school year when Holling Hoodhood, a seventh-grader, must spend his Wednesday afternoons alone with Mrs. Baker, one of his teachers, while his friends take religious instruction. In addition to personal problems, Holling and his friends are conflicted about the Vietnam War in this compelling novel.

*Michele Torrey

Michele Torrey, an American writer who lives in Auburn, Washington, is best known for her Doyle and Fossey Science Detective series for young readers and her Voyage of . . . trilogy for young adults. In the first volume, *Voyage of Ice* (Knopf, 2004), Nick joins his older brother Dexter aboard a whaler and finds that the glamorous adventure he dreamed about doesn't exist. The second, *Voyage of Plunder* (Knopf, 2005), tells how Daniel Markham is forced to join a pirate crew who board his father's ship, kill his dad, and force him to sail with them to the Red Sea, and in *Voyage of Midnight* (Knopf, 2006), orphan Philip finds a living relative, a seagoing uncle, who takes him aboard his ship as a surgeon's mate. Philip suddenly realizes he is on a slave ship and the voyage soon becomes a nightmare. Another historical novel by Michele Torrey is *To the Edge of the World* (Knopf, 2005), in which orphan Mateo becomes a cabin boy on a ship under Captain Ferdinand Magellan.

Lastly, here is a list of ten basic classics in historical fiction for young readers published before 1980.

Aiken, Joan. *The Wolves of Willoughby Chase* (1962)
Brink, Carol Ryrie. *Caddie Woodlawn* (1935)
Field, Rachel. *Hitty: Her First Hundred Years* (1929)
Fox, Paula. *The Slave Dancer* (1973)
O'Dell, Scott. *Island of the Blue Dolphins* (1960)
Paterson, Katherine. *The Master Puppeteer* (1976)
Speare, Elizabeth George. *The Witch of Blackbird Pond* (1958)
Stevenson, Robert Louis. *Treasure Island* (1883)
Sutcliff, Rosemary. *Eagle of the Ninth* (1954)
Wilder, Laura Ingalls. *The Long Winter* (1940)

BIBLIOGRAPHY

Many sources were used in writing this chapter. In addition to hundreds of Web sites, many books were consulted. Some of them are:

Carpenter, Humphrey, and Mari Prichard. *Oxford Companion to Children's Literature*. 1984, o.p.

Gillespie, John T., and Corinne J. Naden. *The Newbery/Printz Companion*. Libraries Unlimited, 2006.

Hunt, Peter, ed. *Children's Literature: An Illustrated History*. Oxford, 1995, o.p.

Meigs, Cornelia, et al. *A Critical History of Children's Literature*. Macmillan, o.p.

Thwaite, Mary F. *From Primer to Pleasure*. Library Association, 1972, o.p.

Townsend, John Rowe. *Written for Children*. Scarecrow, 2003.

Watson, Victor, ed. *The Cambridge Guide to Children's Books in English*. Cambridge, 2001.

CHAPTER 3

Bringing Young Readers and Books Together

ONE OF THE MOST IMPORTANT AND SATISFYING tasks for a librarian or teacher is to successfully match a reader with a book that he or she will enjoy. This chapter will outline some specific techniques that may help in this process. Many are designed primarily for the librarian but it is hoped that adaptations of these can also be used by classroom teachers and other professionals working with youngsters. There are four "Knows" that can help prepare a person for this undertaking. They are: "Know the community;" "Know the students;" "Know the literature and the existing collection;" and "Know how to build an effective collection."

In getting to know the community, one should collect general information on ethnic and religious backgrounds, age groupings, occupations, general economic status, cultural and recreational interests, and educational levels of the residents. Does the average child come from a family where basic reference materials and a computer are available? One should also be familiar with the community's other library collections, including their adequacy and accessibility, and with the availability of other cultural and recreational resources. Local religious and youth groups and community recreational centers and their programs also can influence a youngster's reading habits and interests.

One can get to know the students in two ways. First, by collecting general information on the grades and age levels served, on the students' basic interests and activities, their general reading ability, and their levels of emotional and social maturity. Second, a study of circulation records can reveal information about general reading interests and patterns. Ideally, this information can also be collected for each individual user and potential user of the library. This type of information is more easily collected in schools than in public libraries. Many schools conduct interest inventories on their students that provide information on interests and activities such as amount of TV watching, favorite shows, hours and nature of time spent on the computer, favorite hobbies and sports, part-time jobs, reading interests, nature and type of reading material, favorite books, and so forth. Others maintain reading records where children keep a simple diary of their reading experiences, books read, reactions, and so on. The best way to get to know students however, is through first-hand contact, where the librarian creates bonds of understanding and friendship through meetings and chats with the individual student.

To supply adequate reading guidance, one must also know the literature and the existing collection. Public librarians often have free time to acquaint themselves with individual titles and authors in the collections, but school librarians are usually too busy teaching classes and answering students' questions to sit and sample individual titles. If one is going to bring together the reader and the book, it is necessary, however, that the professional have a knowledge of both. Many librarians take home new books to read, or at least scan, in off hours. Sometimes, however, reading dust jackets and reviews, perusing standard bibliographies, or a general knowledge of other books by the same author will have to suffice. Librarians often keep their own "reading records" using cards on which general plot notes, pagination of key incidents, and their reactions are written down. This file can be helpful in preparing booktalks.

If a professional is in a new library position, there are ways of determining the adequacy of the existing collection beyond its general size. An examination of a shelf list and equipment inventory can determine areas that are stressed or slighted, currency of titles, and amount of duplication. Reading the shelves is another way to become familiar with the collection. Checking the holdings against a standard bibliography will determine the number of basic titles present.

With all of this background information, librarians can draw on their knowledge of different types of educational materials, their characteristics, strengths, and limitations, and their potential use in different situations—and on their knowledge of available bibliographic and reviewing tools—to make wise choices in selecting new acquisitions to build an effective collection that will meet patrons' needs. Knowledge of the curriculum and faculty are also important factors in determining the areas that should be stressed in collection development. A thorough understanding of the budget and the funds available for future purchases is also essential in determining priorities.

Armed with this knowledge, here are some basic techniques that can be used to stimulate reading.

1. Make the library attractive, including the use of displays

The library should be a friendly, cheerful place, one that conveys warmth and a feeling of hospitality. Bulletin boards and display cases can attract potential users to the library, publicize its services, and familiarize students with its collection. A few pointers on making displays: decide on a subject (specific, concrete subjects are best), select a caption (short and interest-grabbing), make a rough sketch showing placement of materials, provide good balance and a lack of clutter, make it neat (commercially manufactured letters are available, for example), and maintain a file of material and ideas. If highlighting specific books in the display, try to have additional copies (maybe paperback copies) available for circulation and try to change the display often.

2. Use current activities and interests

Whenever possible, try to connect the library to general activities of the school or community and the current interests and experiences of the students. For example, a student play, assembly program, a sports event, or a community issue can form the basis of a display, a reading list, or a library program. National holidays (e.g. birthdays of presidents) can be used to promote historical novels and nonfiction works. The library can be used to highlight student artwork, accomplishments, or hobbies. Short visits can be arranged to classrooms or to club meetings to introduce appropriate material to students and teachers. In schools, the school newspaper and public address system are two channels that can be used to promote the library. Some libraries publish their own newsletter with information about new acquisitions, special reading lists, recommendations from students, profiles of authors, and general library news.

3. Use student reactions and reviews

Student reading experiences can be used to help promote the library. Informal sharing periods—in which students are given the opportunity to talk about books they have or have not enjoyed—are popular. A computer file containing titles recommended by students arranged by the last name of the student is sometimes used. Displays or printed booklets containing brief reviews written by students can also promote reading. Many schools have also developed student booktalking teams that visit other classrooms, grades, and even other libraries and schools.

4. Give booktalks

Booktalks are an excellent way to stimulate reading. They can be informal or formal. The informal booktalk consists of the spontaneous introduction of books to a single person or a small group of students, often in reply to such questions as "Could you suggest some good books for me to read?" The formal booktalk is prepared and usually delivered to a large group like a class. Many result from a teacher's request relating to a specific curriculum unit; for example, a request to introduce some historical novels to a class that is studying the American Revolution. After the topic, the audience, and the setting have been determined, a decision on the number of titles to be introduced should be made. Many like to introduce several books via "quickie" minute-or-two teasers. Others prefer to introduce fewer titles (perhaps four or five) in greater depth. The books can be presented in many ways, including the description of a character, a situation and setting, or a conflict. Some people read short passages from the book, others paraphrase a situation in their own words. Some write out the talk beforehand, others simply prepare them mentally. A booktalk usually lasts about 15 minutes followed by a browsing time. Often other books on the same topic are put on display, and are mentioned briefly. Be sure to have enough copies to satisfy all potential readers. Duplicate paperback copies are useful in this situation. Brief annotated bibliographies are helpful for those who need additional guidance.

5. Use various formats to promote reading

Other media can be used to stimulate reading. For example, many of the novels that are discussed in the main body of this work are also available as audiobooks. Listening Library and Recorded Books are two firms that specialize in this area. Many titles have been filmed either for motion pictures or television and are available in DVD formats. These can be used in library programs or through regular circulation to interest young patrons in reading the books.

6. Schedule author visits

One important way to create an interest in books and reading is to schedule an author visit. To be successful, this requires thorough advance planning and an expenditure of money. For this reason, schools and libraries are often restricted to a single visit a year and therefore make it a gala occasion. Financial help is often provided by parent or library support groups. Sometimes more than one library or school shares both the program and the expense. Most authors' fees start at about $500. Fees vary with the services and time required and transportation involved. Try to work out a complete and accurate budget before making a definite commitment. Some tips: Because authors often plan their schedules a year in advance, pre-planning is essential. Authors can often be contacted through their publishers but increasingly they can be reached through their Web home pages, where they will give details of availability, costs, and programs offered. Try to find an author who is known and liked by your readers and be sure that a number of your students are prepared in advance by familiarizing them with both the author and his or her works. Decisions concerning the program expectations—will it be a formal lecture type before a large audience, small group chats, question-and-answer sessions, and/or writing workshops?—as well as the number of programs to be presented, locations, and audience(s) should be made in advance. These visits can be lots of fun and profitable for all the parties involved but, again, detailed preplanning is crucial for success.

7. Develop programs

Many libraries schedule regular programs aimed at young readers. These range from book discussion groups and reading programs to sponsoring talks by community leaders and other important local personalities. Group activities should be scheduled on a regular basis (perhaps once a month) and should be publicized thoroughly before each event. It is advisable to form a planning group or club council composed mainly of young people to make decisions on programs and increase potential interest. A prepared agenda should be drawn up before each meeting. As stated earlier, people and materials for programs may often be found in the community, with backup material in the library. When appropriate, mention could be made during the presentation of other library materials on the subject that are available and perhaps a bibliography of suggested readings could be distributed.

8. Consider holding a book fair

Book fairs are an excellent way of introducing books to young readers, stimulating reading, and developing home libraries, while incidentally making money for library projects. In planning a book fair, choosing a reputable book dealer is of primary importance. Some prepackaged book fairs concentrate on selling extraneous items such as pencils and drawing books and rely heavily on video games and books that are TV spin-offs and. Be sure that your book dealer allows for your input concerning the items for sale. Many bookstores and book fair companies are willing to meet the specific needs of a school or community. One source of reputable book fair dealers is the Web site http://www.commercialfreechildhood.org/bookfairs/. There are basically two types of fairs. In the first, a single copy of a book is displayed and the youngsters order from the display. In the second, multiple copies are available for purchase. The latter is preferable so that the excitement of purchasing a book is not lost. Whenever possible, only paperbacks should be sold to keep the price lower and allow for buying more books.

Some specific pointers:

a. Allow at least two months' preparation time.
b. Use a large space where books can be displayed properly.
c. Solicit the help of volunteers, perhaps from a parent or community organization.
d. Stimulate interest by distributing lists of books to be sold, holding poster contests or other contests like writing limericks or designing bookmarks about the fair. Special programs such as an author visit before or during the fair can help create a gala atmosphere.
e. Sell books that represent a wide range of interests and reading levels.
f. Although there will be some titles included "just for fun," be sure to include high-quality titles, like some Newbery winners.

9. Organize book clubs

Book clubs are usually associated with classrooms and are managed by teachers. Clubs not only stimulate reading and introduce books but also develop an interest in building home libraries. A name long associated with juvenile book clubs is Scholastic. The clubs geared to middle school and junior high school readers are the Arrow and TAB clubs.

———•◦•———

Finally, try to integrate the library into all the activities taking place in the community or in the school. With ingenuity, energy, imagination, patience, and hard work, programs can be developed that effectively stimulate and promote reading with young audiences. The rewards for creating such programs are boundless.

CHAPTER 4

Europe

PREHISTORIC LIFE AND ANCIENT HISTORY

BANKS, LYNNE REID. *Tiger, Tiger.* 2004, Delacorte, $15.95 (978-0-385-73240-6); pap. Dell, $5.99 (978-0-440-42044-6) (Grades 5–8)

Introduction

Lynne Reid Banks was born in England in 1929. To escape the horrors of World War II, she and her mother moved to Canada. After her return to Britain, she studied acting and appeared in repertory theater from 1949 through 1955. After turning to writing for a time, she spent ten years teaching English in a kibbutz in Israel before returning to Europe and her writing career. In the field of children's books she is best known for her many fantasies including a series of five stories beginning with *The Indian in the Cupboard* (pap. Harper, $5.99; 0380600129), which was published in 1985 and later made into a successful film. In it, 9-year-old Omri receives as birthday presents a cabinet once owned by his great-grandmother and a 3-inch high plastic Indian. When he places the Indian in the cupboard, the figure, whose name is Little Bear, comes to life. Omri builds his new friend a tiny longhouse and supplies him with a horse to ride, weapons, a bride, and a Texas cowboy named Boo-Hoo Boone.

Although the characters in *Tiger, Tiger* are fictional (including the emperor), the author suggests that the place and time of the novel are Rome in the late 3rd century A.D., about two hundred years before the Roman Empire fell. The action takes place over several months and is told from various points of view including the tigers' and, most frequently, Aurelia's.

Historical Background

Much of the action of the novel centers about the Colosseum in Rome and the "entertainments" supplied inside. Appropriately named because of its size, the Colosseum was built in A.D. 72 by Emperor Vespasian and inaugurated by Emperor Titus in A.D. 80 with one hundred days of games during which 9,000 animals—including leopards, lions, and bears—were killed. It is a four-tiered oval arena measuring 617 feet in length by 513 feet in width. The building accommodated more than 50,000 people. The top, fourth tier was enclosed and intended for women and paupers who sat on wooden seats. The next level down was for commoners and foreigners, and the second level for the middle classes and distinguished citizens. These people sat on marble seats. The front-row seats, also in marble, were reserved for senators, the Vestal Virgins, magistrates, priests, and the emperor and his family. Entrance was through 76 portals. Tickets indicated one's seat location. There were four additional entrances, two for the emperor and two for the gladiators. Atop the building was a colored awning called the velarium that was unfurled to protect the spectators from rain or excessive heat. The games began in the morning and lasted all day. After an impressive march past, the participants in the arena chanted, "Ave Caesar! Morituri te Salutamus!" (Hail Caesar! We who are about to die salute you!) In addition to the very popular gladiatorial combats (one is described in the novel), there were boxing matches, archery contests, circus acts, and competitions between charioteers. Probably the most popular and bloodiest combats were between starved animals and helpless men, usually condemned criminals or Christians. In A.D. 404, gladiatorial combats were banned and in the next century the killing of animals disappeared.

Two other terms of note: *Praetorian Guard* refers to the special bodyguards dedicated to guarding the emperor. This distinguished group was composed of the best, bravest, and most loyal of soldiers. Established around 275 B.C., the guard was abolished by Constantine in the 4th century. *The Vomitorium* was a passageway below or behind the seats in an amphitheater. Though not intended as a place for vomiting, these passageways were often used as such when people became physically sickened by the carnage in the arena.

Principal Characters

Aurelia, the 12-year-old daughter of the emperor
Julius Minimus, an animal trainer, a slave
Emperor Septimus, Aurelia's father
The Empress, Aurelia's mother
Marcus, Aurelia's 10-year-old cousin
Caius Lucius, an animal keeper at the Colosseum
Bella, Aurelia's old nurse

Rufus, a young simple-minded shepherd
Boots and Brute, two tigers

Plot Synopsis

It is late in the 3rd century A.D. and the emperor's scouts are scouring the far provinces to capture animals for the blood sports held in the Colosseum in Rome. One party in a far-off jungle snares a remarkable catch, two beautiful young tiger cubs. The cubs are easily captured and their mother killed. They are taken to the coast, placed in cages and made ready to be transported by sea to Italy. In the hold, the two cower together trying to understand this new environment of constant motion, strange noises from other captive animals, and the terrible smells of animal scat. In Rome the two are separated. The smaller more docile cub is sent to the city menagerie and the other to the Colosseum where, in the underground animal pens, he will be half starved, part of the training to become a ferocious man killer.

Meanwhile in the emperor's palace, Lady Aurelia, the 12-year-old daughter of the emperor, is asking her tutor about Christianity and why Christians are being persecuted. These thoughts are interrupted by the arrival of a handsome young slave, named Julius Minimus, who presents Aurelia with a gift from her father, the small tiger cub. She is enchanted with her new playmate even though Julius warns her that animals from the wild can be dangerous. Already the cub has been defanged and plans have been made to pull out his claws. Aurelia, a sensitive, thoughtful child, is horrified at the thought of this cruelty and so when Julius the next day brings the animal back from its night home in the menagerie, he has sewn leather protective coverings for the cub's feet. Now Aurelia knows what to name him: he must be Boots. Apart from visits from Julius and Boots, Aurelia lives in relative isolation. Her only friend and play-mate is Marcus, her spoiled 10-year-old cousin who is the son of a powerful senator. Marcus becomes jealous of the strong bonds of affection Aurelia has developed with both Julius and Boots.

Curious to find out about Boots's twin, Julius visits the cages under the Colosseum and talks with the animal keeper, Caius Lucius, a man who once courted Aurelia's nursemaid, Bella. Julius is told about the inhumane treatment of these animals and their eventual fate in the arena. He sees that Boots's brother, who is aptly named Brute, has become a savage, cold-blooded killer through starvation and constant taunts and prodding.

On the day that Brute is to debut in the arena, Marcus invites the sensitive, squeamish Aurelia to attend the games for the first time. She is repelled by the thought but her curiosity wins out and she reluctantly accepts. The imperial party—which includes the emperor, Aurelia, Julius, and Marcus and his father—is accompanied by the Praetorian Guard and makes a triumphal entrance. Aurelia becomes more and more horrified at the terrible sights of cruelty and carnage she witnesses. Julius is helpful in signaling when she should close her eyes. As a final tableau, Brute enters the arena and begins attacking a group of misbegotten "hunters." Having bitten and clawed several to death, he begins feasting on their entrails. At this point, smug little Marcus vomits. Humiliated, he hides at home for days unable to face Aurelia.

After about a month, Aurelia visits his home in the company of Julius, Boots, and several servants. Marcus, with the help of Aurelia, plays an innocent prank on Julius. While the slave is dozing, they lead Boots to a nearby storeroom. Julius panics when he awakens and finds the tiger is missing. Smiling at the success of their joke, they take Julius to the storeroom only to find the door open and Boots gone. Servants had come to the storeroom for supplies and, seeing the tiger, had fled in terror leaving the door open. Boots is now tasting freedom and wandering in the huge forest around Marcus's home. He is found by a simple-minded shepherd boy named Rufus, who takes the tiger's jewel-encrusted collar as a keepsake and removes the animal's boots. Now the tiger is able to hunt and feed himself. Julius searches in vain for the animal and finally he returns empty-handed to a furious emperor, who blames the boy's negligence for the incident and, in a fit of anger, condemns Julius to death in the Colosseum on the ides of July. Aurelia's pleas are fruitless and she begins to hate her cruel, unyielding father. She goes to the Tiber River one evening to pray to the gods for help and to make an offering of a precious bracelet. There on the bank among the reeds, she finds Boots who obeys her and accompanies her home. Instead of commuting Julius's sentence, the emperor decides the slave will now face two tigers in the arena—Boots and Brute.

As the day approaches, Aurelia persuades her maid Bella to visit her old flame Caius Lucius at the animal cages. In return for favors and money, Caius performs two good deeds. On the day of the contest, he feeds Brute and furnishes Julius with a spear. Having heard about Julius and the tigers, a bumper crowd fills the arena. Julius is brought in and he notices that among the emperor's party are a contrite Marcus and a seemingly heartbroken Aurelia. Boots is released first and, instead of attacking Julius, whom he recognizes as his kindly trainer, he places his paws around his shoulders and then lies by his side. With Brute it is different. Julius is forced to wound the animal before Brute acknowledges Julius as his master. With both animals at his feet, Julius turns to the emperor. The crowd roars support for the slave, and reluctantly Caesar gives the thumbs-up sign and declares Julius a free man. Julius gazes at Aurelia. Their eyes meet and he realizes the great, but impossible, love they share. Julius leads the animals out of the Colosseum and together the three walk out of the city.

In an epilogue, the author states that Julius found his way to a new life in the south, the animals were never recaptured, and that Aurelia later married her cousin Marcus. When their son later became emperor, Aurelia was granted her request that he change his name to Julius.

Passages for Booktalking

Some exciting passages are: the two cubs endure the trip to Rome (pp. 5–9); Aurelia receives her father's gift of the cub (pp. 19–28); the cub gets a name and learns to play (pp. 29–33); Aurelia's introduction to the Colosseum and Brute's first performance (pp. 83–92).

Themes and Subjects

This novel blends history with an examination of human emotions. The use and misuse of power are explored in the actions of both the emperor and Marcus. The themes of sacrifice and mercy are present in the behavior of other characters. The grandeur of ancient Rome is depicted accurately, as is the contrast between the culture and refinement of the upper classes and their barbaric pastimes. The emotions and feelings of the animals are described without anthropomorphism. The reader learns a great deal about the behavior of cats, both wild and domestic. Other subjects: Roman religion, government, the Colosseum, gladiatorial sports, Christianity, adventure stories, love stories, courage, friendship, and slavery.

DICKINSON, PETER. *A Bone from a Dry Sea.* Delacorte, 1992, $16 (978-0-385-30821-2); pap. Dell, $6.50 (978-0-440-21928-6) (Grades 6–10)

Introduction

Peter Dickinson was born in Africa in 1927 and spent his first seven years in Zambia, then known as Northern Rhodesia. He was educated at Eton and Cambridge and served in the British Army from 1946 to 1948. He wrote for the now defunct British humor magazine *Punch* before becoming a full-time freelance writer. After the death of his first wife, he married Robin McKinley, the famous writer of children's fantasies. Peter Dickinson is the author of highly acclaimed adult thriller-fantasies and a number of exciting, prize-winning books for young adults. An excellent companion to *A Bone from a Dry Sea* is his earlier science fiction novel *Eva* (Delacorte, 1989, $15.95; 0385297025). In this futuristic story, the brain of a young girl who has been horribly injured in the car accident that killed her parents is placed into the body of a female chimpanzee. Its central themes are humans' ruthless exploitation of all forms of life and the bonds that unite all forms of life, of which humanity is only a small part.

A Bone from a Dry Sea is told in two different time periods in alternating chapters. The first, *Then*, deals with prehistoric life some 6 million years ago and the second, *Now*, is set in the present and covers a period of only a few days. To avoid confusion, in this summary the chapters of each narrative are combined and told in two separate sections—"Then" and "Now." Both stories take place in the same geographical setting in Africa though time has changed the landscape considerably. Each has a female leading character—Li, a prehistoric youngster in the first, and Vinny, the daughter of a paleontologist, in the second.

Historical Background

One part of the novel (*Now*) deals with a paleontological dig in Africa. Paleontology, the study of prehistoric life through the collection and examination of both animal and plant fossils, has several specializations. Vinny's father, Sam, is a taphonomist. Taphonomy is a relatively new branch of paleontology that came into existence in the 1940s. It deals with the process of fossilization. It is generally believed that the dividing line between human and ape occurred between 6 million and 8 million years ago and that we are descended from apes that moved out of the dense forest into the grasslands or savannahs. This is the theory propounded in such books as Desmond Morris's *The Naked Ape* (1967). In the 1930s, Alister Hardy, an English marine biologist, began to notice the differences between humans and other land mammals and the similarities between them and aquatic animals. For example, the fat attached to human skin is like the blubber found in marine mammals. In a paper published in 1960 he suggested that humans had ancestors more aquatic than previously imagined. This theory, known as the Aquatic Ape theory, was initially dismissed but later championed by others including the Welsh-born science popularizer Elaine Morgan (Vinny has just finished reading one of her books in the *Now* section of the novel). This theory states that humans were already different from apes before they moved into the savannah. Because many features of human physiology are rare in other land mammals but common in aquatic ones, it is suggested that our earliest ancestors lived in a flooded, semi-aquatic habitat. Humans and aquatic mammals (swimmers like whales, walruses, and manatees, or wallowers like hippopotamuses and pigs) share some physical similarities: little body hair, subcutaneous fat deposits, enlarged sebaceous glands, psychic tears (weeping), and voluntary breath control. In *A Bone from a Dry Sea*, Peter Dickinson has accepted this theory and created a tribe of aquatic apes on the verge of humanity.

Principal Characters

Then

    Li, a prehistoric girl approaching physical maturity

    Ma-Ma, Li's mother

    Presh, Li's uncle, the tribal leader

    Greb, a bully

Now

    Vinny, an English teenager

    Sam, her father

    Dr. Joe Hamiska, the expedition's leader

    May Anna, a paleontologist

    Dr. Fred Wessler, another paleontologist

    Nikki Mako, an African artist and helper

    Dr. Watson Azikwe, an African paleontologist

    Jane Hamiska, Dr. Hamiska's wife

    Mr. Multan, Watson's uncle, a government dignitary

Plot Synopsis

Then

The time is about 6 million years ago and the place, a bay on the coast of Africa sheltered from the open ocean and surrounded by beaches and caves that can be used for refuge. The tribe is made up of man/apes on the brink of humanity. The have no language, except a few grunts and cries, no tools, no fire, and no homes other than caves and other natural shelters. Because they have no language, they have no names but, for convenience sake, the author has named them. Our central character is Li, a bright young female close to puberty. Her mother is Ma-Ma and her uncle, the leader of the tribe, is Presh. Li feels as much at home in water as on land and the webbing on her hands and feet help make her an excellent swimmer. One day while swimming she hears warning cries that a shark is nearby. Li, through clever and daring maneuvering, manages to beach the intruder, and the tribe claw and gnaw through its tough skin and enjoy a raw shark meat dinner. Inspired by watching a spider catch insects in its web, Li later fashions a primitive net of gourd fibers to catch ting shrimp for food. Soon the entire tribe is copying her invention and in awe of her ingenuity.

One day a dolphin approaches her when she is swimming and she is soon playing and dancing in the water with this friendly animal. Each day, the dolphin returns and they repeat this joyful routine. Li watches the birth of her mother's new baby in a water ritual practiced by the tribe's mothers. Later, when her Uncle Presh's authority is challenged by a bullying, surly young male named Greb, there is a fight during which Presh catches a foot in a rock fissure and breaks a leg. Again, Li shows her inventiveness by fashioning a primitive split to help the broken bone heal. With her mother and four other members of the tribe, she transports Presh to a cave and nurses him until he is able to walk again.

In the meantime, the dolphin and its companions prove to be the tribe's salvation. With Li's guidance, they force a shoal of fish into shallow water where the tribe members toss as many fish as possible onto the shore. Some are given back to the dolphins as food and the rest eaten by the tribe. After a few days, the dolphins return for a repeat performance to the benefit of both the tribe and the dolphins. Soon after Presh's recovery, Greb returns and murders Presh by crushing his skull with a rock. Greb is now the tribe leader and makes it apparent that he wants to mate with Li. In desperation, Li, her mother, and a few friends flee and, using vines as ropes, climb a steep cliff to a safe ledge above. They destroy the vines to make the ledge inaccessible.

Then nature intervenes in a terrible way. Under the ocean, the plates that carry the continents suddenly move, causing a giant tsunami. It crashes on shore killing Greb and the remaining members of the tribe and filling the bay with earth and sand. Li and her friends on the cliff survive. When they climb down, Li sees the body of her dolphin friend, another victim of the storm. Before moving on, Li returns to look at its skeleton. She takes its shoulder blade bone and, using a sharp stone, cuts a hole in it. She then ties the bone to her head with a strand of her hair. This ornament will be a lasting memorial to both her friend and her past.

Now

It is a scorching hot day when Vinny arrives at her father's encampment in Africa. Her father, Sam, is a paleontologist, specifically a taphonomist, working on a nearby dig under the direction of Dr. Joe Hamiska. The area is now a plain in one of the hottest, dreariest parts of Africa, but millions of years ago it was a sheltered bay. It is believed to be rich in hominid fossils. Since her parents' divorce eight years before, Vinny, a bright English teenager, has been living with her mother, her stepfather, and their two young sons. Vinny's mother was less than enthusiastic about her trip to Africa, but Vinny persisted because she hopes this adventure will bring her closer to her father. She quickly becomes acquainted with other members of the group including May Anna, a 30-ish paleontologist who has become very fond of her father; Nikki Mako, a black college student and fine artist; Dr. Fred Wessler, another paleontologist; and Jane Hamiska. Towering overall is the strong-willed, domineering Joe Hamiska, with whom Sam often has differences. The dig is situated in a country fraught with civil strife and Dr. Hamiska gained permission to explore the area only after he promised to make a black paleontologist named Watson

Azikwe part of the expedition. Dr. Azikwe is the nephew of Mr. Multan, the minister of the interior. Dr. Hamiska is very publicity-conscious, particularly when any discovery can be used to impress the backers of the expedition, the Craig Foundation in America.

Vinny fits in easily and begins helping on the dig. She often discusses with her father her readings on theories concerning evolution, including the Aquatic Ape premise, which Sam dismisses it as poppycock. When Vinny uncovers a fossilized toe bone of a 5-million-year-old humanoid, Dr. Hamiska is ecstatic and claims she is bringing the expedition much-needed luck. Sam decides to camp out at the dig with Vinny so they can avoid travel time and work longer hours. Vinny thinks it is exciting working closely with her gifted father, a distant but caring man. As the weather becomes more oppressive and the work more difficult, the clashes between Sam and Dr. Hamiska become more frequent. Because of a misunderstanding, Dr. Hamiska accuses Sam of hiding important bone finds. When Vinny uncovers another interesting bone specimen, he wants to photograph her with her find for the newspaper. He knows this will please the Craig people. Not wanting the publicity, she refuses. Dr. Hamiska, believing that Sam has planned this refusal to challenge his authority, dismisses him.

Vinny and Sam are preparing to leave the site when a helicopter arrives with Mr. Multan, the minister of the interior. He accuses Dr. Hamiska of violating the agreement with his government by digging outside the agreed parameters. He orders Dr. Hamiska to leave, takes over the dig in the country's name, and places his nephew, Dr. Azikwe, in charge. In a strange reversal of fortune, Dr. Azikwe asks Sam to rejoin the group and also makes an offer to retain May Anna. They both accept. While thinking about these strange developments, Vinny closely examines one of her bone discoveries. It is a scapula, perhaps that of a dolphin. She also notices that someone, ages ago, had bored a hole in it. She looks up and gazes at the plain that surrounds her. It had once been a sea that stretched out, like time, into the unfathomable distance.

Passages for Booktalking

From *Then*: the shark attack and Li's plans to catch him (pp. 3–7); Li swims with the dolphin (pp. 37–40); and Li witnesses the birth of Ma-Ma's new baby (pp. 53–55). From *Now*: Vinny meets Dr. Hamiska and sees May Anna at work (pp. 24–29) and Vinny and her father discuss the Aquatic Ape theory (pp. 44–45).

Themes and Subjects

The continuity of time is a central theme. The mysterious and awe-inspiring evolution of both man and the earth are explored and the Aquatic Ape theory applied in a real-life situation. Li's primitive but creative intelligence is well depicted as are the customs and social structure of a pre-Stone Age culture. The work of a paleontologist is presented with absorbing details and a good description of the intricate social relationships that working on a dig can produce. The contrast between the simple, straightforward society of primitive man and the complex social conventions and conflicts of our contemporaries is fascinating. Other subjects: Africa, mother-daughter and father-daughter relationships, courage, family life, dolphins, professional rivalry, and coming of age.

———•◦•———

LAWRENCE, CAROLINE.

The Thieves of Ostia: The Roman Mysteries Book I. Roaring Brook Press, 2002, $15.95 (978-0-7613-1582-7); pap. Puffin, $5.99 (978-0-14-240147-7) (Grades 4–7)

The Assassins of Rome: The Roman Mysteries Book IV. Roaring Brook Press, 2003, $15.95 (978-0-7613-1940-5); pap. Puffin, $5.99 (978-0-14-240214-6) (Grades 4–7)

Introduction

Caroline Lawrence was born in 1954 in England of American parents who moved back to Northern California shortly after her birth. She studied Classics at Berkeley and won a scholarship to Cambridge where she majored in Classical Art and Archaeology. Later, before taking up teaching and a writing career, she received a Masters degree in Hebrew and Jewish studies in London, where she continues to live with her husband, a graphic artist. The first of the Roman Mysteries series, which now numbers about 15 titles, was published in Britain in 2001. She averages two additions to the series each year. Set in ancient Rome, the series features four children: Flavia, a Roman girl of about 10 or 11; Nubia, an African slave girl who has been bought by Flavia; Jonathan, a Jewish-Christian boy; and Lupus, a street waif without a tongue.

In the second book in the series, *The Secrets of Vesuvius* (Roaring Brook Press, 2002, $15.95; 0761315837; pap. Puffin, $5.99; 0142401188), the four friends sail for the Bay of Naples to stay with Flavia's uncle near Pompeii. They rescue an admiral from a boating accident and he rewards them handsomely, presenting them with a riddle that could bring them great wealth. The riddle takes them to a blacksmith named Vulcan and, just as they are piecing together several clues, Mount Vesuvius erupts and they are forced to flee. The third volume, *The Pirates of Pompeii* (Roaring Brook Press, 2003, $15.95; 0761315845; pap. Puffin, $5.99; 0142402273), begins after the eruption when the four have found shelter in a refugee camp. They become suspicious when some children, including the daughter of powerful Publius Pollius Felix, are reported missing. Their investigation takes them to the home of a wealthy nobleman. Could he be behind these disappearances? This is another thrilling mystery in a consistently enthralling series. Instead of chapters, each novel is divided into numbered scrolls.

Historical Background

Each of the books contains a helpful appendix that defines and explains words such as *papyrus* and *atrium*. The first novel, *The Thieves of Ostia*, takes place during the last year of the reign of the Roman Emperor Vespasian (Titus Flavius Vespasianus), who lived from A.D. 9 to A.D. 79 and reigned from A.D. 69 to A.D. 79. He came from a poor family and made his way upward in the army through his outstanding ability. He served in Germany, Britain, in Africa under Nero, and in Judea. After a period of instability and inept rulers, Rome was ready for Vespasian. After being declared emperor, he began restoring the state and its finances. His reign is noted for its order and prosperity. The famous Colosseum in Rome was begun during his reign. Vespasian was succeeded by his son Titus and later by his second son, Domitian. Titus, the emperor in *The Assassins of Rome*, reigned for only three years (A.D. 79–81). Before become emperor he engaged in a number of military campaigns; the most noteworthy was the capture and destruction of Jerusalem in A.D. 70, which resulted in numerous Jewish captives being brought to Rome as slaves. During his reign, however, he was a benevolent ruler and pursued peace and conciliation throughout the empire. The Colosseum was completed under his rule, and two important disasters occurred. The first was the great fire of Rome and the second the eruption of Mount Vesuvius, which buried the cities of Pompeii and Herculaneum. The latter event was chronicled by Pliny the Elder (A.D. 23–79) who died of asphyxiation close to Pompeii after reporting the disaster. Pliny is best known for his 37-volume history of natural science.

The bringers of good luck to Flavia's family were the twin heroes of classical mythology, Castor and Pollux. Castor was a great horseman and Pollux a magnificent boxer. Both were great warriors and were noted for their devotion to each other.

At the time of these novels (A.D. 79), the town of Ostia was situated at the mouth of the Tiber River and served as the main seaport for Rome. The shoreline has changed since ancient times and the old city now lies inland and is called Old Ostia. Because of its many ruins, it is a popular tourist attraction. The present seaport town is called Ostia Lido.

Principal Characters in *The Thieves of Ostia*

Flavia Gemina, a girl of 10
Marcus Flavius Geminus, a shipowner and sea captain, her father
Mordecai ben Ezra, a doctor from Judaea
Jonathan, his son, about Flavia's age
Miriam, Jonathan's older sister
Venalicius, a slave dealer
Nubia, an African slave girl
Alma, Marcus's slave and cook
Caudex, Marcus's servant
Titus Cordius Atticus (Cordius), a wealthy merchant
Libertus, his ward
Publius Avitus Produlus (Avitus), a sailor
Julika Firma, his wife
Lupus, an 8-year-old mute waif
Hariola, a soothsayer
Marcus Artorius Bato, a magistrate

Plot Synopsis of *The Thieves of Ostia*

The time is June, A.D. 79, and the place is the house of the sea captain Marcus Flavius Geminus on Green Fountain Street in Ostia, an Italian seaport town at the mouth of the Tiber. Marcus's only child, a daughter of about 10 or 11 named Flavia has already gained a reputation as an accomplished amateur sleuth. Today she has a new puzzle, the disappearance of her father's amethyst signet ring. After seeing the imprint of a bird's foot on her father's papers, Flavia, who knows that magpies are attracted to bright objects, explores a bird's nest in a nearby oak tree and retrieves not only her father's ring but a valuable cache of other objects including a bejeweled earring. She is trapped in the tree by a pack of feral dogs until her screaming brings a young boy who frightens them off. He is soon joined by his father, and introductions are made. They are Flavia's new next-door neighbors: Dr. Mordecai ben Ezra and his son Jonathan, about Flavia's age. They take Flavia to their home where she meets the third member of the family, a beautiful slightly older daughter named Miriam.

Three days later, on Flavia's birthday, Captain Geminus agrees to take his daughter to the shop of a goldsmith friend to sell Flavia's little treasure trove. On the way, they pass a slave market that is run by the malevolent, one-eyed Venalicius. They see a beautiful African slave girl being paraded naked before potential buyers. Flavia is moved by the girl's plight. Coincidentally, the sum that the goldsmith gives her for her valuables matches the price asked for the slave girl. With her father's permission, she rushes back to the market to buy the girl only to learn from Venalicius, who has noted Flavia's interest, that the price has gone up. Marcus makes up the difference and they bring the shy and traumatized girl, whose name is Nubia, back to their home. Flavia sets about teaching Latin to her new friend. Although Nubia shuns human contact at first, she is a constant companion of the family watchdog, Scuto. Captain Geminus's ship has been chartered for a two-week buying expedition to Corinth by his patron and neighbor, the wealthy merchant Titus Cordius Atticus. Flavia will be left in the care of their two slaves, Alma and Caudex. The farewell party at the quay includes Jonathan and his family, Captain Geminus, Flavia, and Cordius and his beloved ward, a handsome young man named Libertus, who will remain behind. It has been rumored that on his return Cordius plans to adopt Libertus, a former slave, as his son.

Back at Dr. Mordecai's house, Jonathan and Flavia see blood on the doorstep and find inside the decapitated body of the family's watchdog, Bobas. Close by, they find a single gambling die. Jonathan tells Flavia that his family comes from Judaea and perhaps this is a hate crime. The two are shaken but determined to investigate and, along with Nubia and the dog Scuto, begin questioning neighbors. Libertus says he saw a man carrying a large leather bag running toward the large local graveyard. There, in addition to the pack of wild dogs that frightened Flavia, they spot a man sobbing convulsively beside a grave. When he sees Scuto, he turns on the group, throws pine cones at them, and screams that he hates dogs. Could this be the killer? They leave the grave-yard but later return and see a marker for Avita, who died at age 8. Back home, Flavia learns from the maid Alma, who knows the neighborhood gossip, that a girl died a few weeks ago after being bitten by a rabid dog. At Dr. Mordecai's home that evening, savage barking is again heard from the graveyard. The doc-tor investigates and kills two of the dogs with his bow and arrow. A scruffy 8-year-old urchin is rescued from a tree. After bathing the waif, the doctor and the young people question him and discover his tongue has been cut out. Through complicated miming, they discover his name is Lupus (Wolf) and that he is homeless. Flavia takes him home and finds that although he can't talk he is bright and observant.

The youngsters are now a group of four—Flavia, Jonathan, Nubia, and Lupus. Lupus, a skilled artist, draws a picture of the man he has seen weeping frequently at the cemetery, and Libertus confirms that this is the man he recently saw running from the area. The man is a sailor named Publius Avitus Proculus, married to Julia Firma. They are the parents of Avita, the young girl who died. The foursome visits Avitus's house, pretending to be friends of Avita. They are welcomed by Julia, who says her husband is crazed with grief over Avita's death. When Avitus arrives, he orders them out of his house. The youngsters try to find out more about Avitus at the waterfront, but are spotted by slave dealer Venalicius and his men, who chase them hoping to capture more new slaves. Through Jonathan's quick thinking, the four find refuge in a synagogue. There, Jonathan is greeted by a somewhat hostile rabbi and the boy later explains that his family members are no longer Jews; they have converted to the new religion of Christianity.

Because he knows the byways of Ostia, Lupus is sent off to follow Avitus. The sailor first visits a soothsayer, Haiola, who evidently is not able to console him because Avitus then visits a series of taverns to drown his sorrows with multiple flagons of wine. Hiding under a table at one tavern, Lupus overhears a youthful-sounding man promising to pay his gambling debts because there is a vast treasure "at the house of the sea captain Flavius Geminus."

Lupus follows Avitus to the harbor's lighthouse and, in horror, watches him commit suicide by jumping from its top level. While Lupus is away, Libertus's watchdog is killed and the young man blames Avitus. However, when Lupus returns with his story, Flavia knows that someone else must have killed the dogs. But who and why?

The heads of the dogs suddenly appear in Flavia's house and through the inadvertent help of Lupus, Flavia finds that Cordius has hidden much of his wealth in her father's house. She suddenly realizes who the culprit is. Flavia and Jonathan seek help from the magistrate, Marcus Artorius Bato, and that night the three lie in wait. Soon someone enters the house, headed for the storeroom where the treasure is hidden. Libertus is caught red-handed. He had orchestrated the dog killings in an effort to frighten Flavia and the neighbors into leaving the area and making it easier for him to commit a robbery or robberies to pay his gambling debts. As the trusted ward of Cordius, he knew where the treasure was hidden (the conversation overheard by Lupus confirmed this).

After the killer is apprehended, Captain Geminus's ship returns and there is a great reunion. Cordius is saddened by the news about Libertus but appreciative of the courage of Flavia and Co. The four adventurers are now ready for a new mystery.

Passages for Booktalking (pagination from paperback edition)

Flavia recovers her father's ring from the magpie's nest (pp. 2–6); Flavia visits the slave market and later buys Nubia (pp. 16–22); Flavia's birthday dinner (pp. 26–31); and Jonathan's dog is murdered and Flavia vows to find the killer (pp. 37–39).

Themes and Subjects

This is essentially a suspenseful, fast-moving adventure mystery with each scroll (chapter) ending in a cliff-hanger. The details of everyday life in Ancient

Rome are authentic, well-researched, and engrossing—an entertaining way to learn about an ancient civilization. The four adventurers are studies in contrast but each is intriguing in his or her own way. Each exhibits courage, ingenuity, and resolve in the fight for fairness and justice. Other subjects: class systems, slavery, Jews, Christianity, blacks, mutes, dogs, ships, mythology, friendship, religious prejudice, and family life.

Principal Characters in *The Assassins of Rome*

Flavia Gemina, a girl of 10
Mordecai ben Ezra, a Jewish doctor
Jonathan, his son, about Flavia's age
Miriam, Jonathan's older sister
Nubia, an African girl and former slave
Lupus, an 8-year-old mute
Caudex, a servant
Aristo, a Greek, the children's tutor
Marcus Artorius Bato, a magistrate
Simeon ben Jonah, Mordecai's brother-in-law
Susannah ben Jonah, Jonathan's mother
Feles, a carter
Huldan, his girlfriend
Sisyphus, the secretary of Senator Cornix
Bulbus, Senator Cornix's servant
Rizpah, an albino girl
Rachel, her mother
Celer, an architect
Emperor Titus

Plot Synopsis of *The Assassins of Rome*

After several adventures involving the eruption of Mount Vesuvius and its aftermath, our four heroes are back home in Ostia, a seaport town in Italy close to Rome. The four are Flavia Gemina, a 10-year-old girl whose only parent, her father, is currently away; her friend, a former slave named Nubia; their neighbor Jonathan, son of Dr. Mordecai ben Ezra, a Jewish doctor, and the doctor's ward, Lupus, an 8-year-old boy who is mute. It is Jonathan's birthday and the group is joined by Miriam, Jonathan's older sister. The smell of lemon blossom oil, one of Jonathan's presents, reminds Dr. Mordecai of Jerusalem, where the family lived before the city's destruction nine years before and of their exodus to Ostia when Jonathan was only one. This prompts Jonathan to ask about his mother, who stayed behind and supposedly died during the siege led by Titus, now the emperor. His father evades his questions and Jonathan becomes suspicious.

The party is interrupted by the arrival of Bato, the magistrate, who informs them that Simeon ben Jonah, the brother of Jonathan's mother, has secretly arrived from Corinth, Greece. Bato believes he is an assassin and warns the group that he could be dangerous.

Later that night Jonathan creeps downstairs to explore his mother's jewel box. He puts on one on her rings and, while trying unsuccessfully to remove it, he sees his father in his study talking about his mother with a stranger. The stranger mysteriously says that his sister, Susannah, stayed in Jerusalem because of Jonathan. The boy is discovered, and his father introduces the dark handsome stranger; it is Jonathan's Uncle Simeon. Although he is supposedly an assassin, Simeon says he is actually here to deliver a secret message to Emperor Titus. He spends a few days with the family, remaining in hiding from the police. Simeon's remark about his mother makes Jonathan believe that he was somehow responsible for her death.

Though a Christian, Dr. Mordecai still celebrates the Jewish holidays. When family and friends gather to celebrate the Jewish New Year, there is a misunderstanding and Lupus, thinking he has been insulted, runs away into the woods and becomes enmeshed in netting used to trap wild boars. That evening, while he is preparing to leave, Simeon tells Jonathan about his mission. Jonathan's mother is alive and is being held captive with other Jewish women brought from Jerusalem in the labyrinth-like Gold House of Nero in Rome. She has become Titus's confidante and friend, which has angered Titus's former mistress Berenice, who hopes to regain her former position with the Emperor. Now living in Corinth, Berenice has dispatched three assassins whose mission is to kill Susannah. Simeon hid his identity and was chosen as one of the three. He now hopes to reach Titus to warn him of the plot. Jonathan persuades Simeon to take him along and the next morning they quietly set off for Rome, 15 miles away.

Bato meanwhile visits Jonathan's home and finds evidence that Simeon has been there. He arrests Mordecai for harboring a criminal. After learning of Jonathan's departure, Flavia also leaves for Rome in the company of Nubia and servant Caudex. They ride with a carter named Feles, who tells them about the Jewish women being held in the imperial palaces in Rome. One of them is his girlfriend Huldah. Flavia plans to stay with her uncle in Rome, the Senator Cornix. He and his family are out of town but the trio are greeted by Sisyphus, a Greek slave who is her uncle's secretary, and Bulbus, a servant.

In the meantime, Lupus is freed from the boar trap by their tutor, Aristo, a Greek slave who discovered him while returning from a hunting trip. After communicating with Mordecai in prison, Lupus and Aristo ask Miriam to look after her father, and set out to join the others in Rome. At Senator Cornix's home, they are reunited with Flavia and Nubia. The group realizes that Nero's Golden House, where the Jewish women are being held, is probably the destination of Jonathan and Simeon, but they find it impossible to gain entrance, even though Sisyphus has secured plans of the structure from his friend, Celer, a Greek architect who worked on the building. They do learn that one of the two other assassins has been caught and executed.

In a different part of Rome, Jonathan and Simeon disguise themselves as court musicians to gain an audience with Titus. Their plan almost succeeds, but Simeon is recognized as one of the assassins from Corinth and Jonathan is branded on the shoulder as a slave of Titus. He passes out from the excruciating pain and wakes up in the cellar in the Golden House where he is cared for by a young albino slave girl, Rizpah, whose Jewish mother, Rachel, is also in the house. Rizpah introduces Jonathan to the many underground passages and tunnels and leads him to the room where his mother lives. There he witnesses a meeting between her and Titus and later presents himself to his mother, who recognizes her ring. Their meeting is an emotional one. Jonathan learns there were two Jonathans in her life, himself and a lover with whom she decided to stay in Jerusalem. The second Jonathan was killed during the siege. Jonathan realizes that his guilty feelings are unfounded.

Flavia and her friends, including Lupus, also disguise themselves as musicians, gain entrance to the Golden House to play at a gala musicale. During the performance, the astute Lupus notices that one of the female slaves is actually a man. He follows the slave, who is now brandishing a razor sharp dagger. When he enters the room where Susannah and Jonathan are talking. Lupus tackles the assassin, who chases Lupus across a high parapet before falling to his death below.

There is a wonderful reunion between Jonathan and his friends. When Titus learns of the plot and how it was foiled, he gives presents to the courageous youngsters and bestows an honorary citizenship on Jonathan. Both Mordecai and Simeon are freed and also praised. Susannah decides to remain with Titus in Rome. Though they are not lovers, their friendship is one that both treasure and do not wish to end. For the rest, they once again head back to Ostia, having accomplished another dangerous mission.

Passages for Booktalking

Some interesting episodes are: Jonathan explores his mother's jewel box and overhears an important conversation (pp. 14–17); Flavia arrives at her uncle's home in Rome (pp. 49–50 and 52–53); Sisyphus tells Flavia about Titus and Berenice (pp. 58–61); Lupus and Aristo visit Mordecai's prison (pp. 61–66).

Themes and Subjects

In addition to a convoluted puzzle, the reader is treated to a fascinating tour of ancient Rome including the Circus Maximus, the Coliseum, Nero's Golden House, and the Forum. Many actual historical events (such as the destruction of Jerusalem) are well integrated into the plot and everyday life in ancient Rome is effectively presented. Our four heroes, as usual, are an engaging, courageous group. Other subjects: Jewish life, Ostia, murder, suspense, friendship, courage, family life, marriage, mothers and fathers, slavery, and class structure.

----•·•----

PAVER, MICHELLE. *Wolf Brother (Book I of the Chronicles of Ancient Darkness).* Harper, 2005, $16.99 (978-0-06-072825-0); pap. $6.99 (978-0-06-072827-4) (Grades 5–9)

Introduction

This novel takes place about six thousand years ago and recounts the adventures of a Stone Age boy named Torak, and his pet, Wolf, during the life of one moon (about a month). Ms. Paver was born in Malawi, Africa, but has lived most of her life in England. Even before she could read, the author was fascinated by her parents' pictorial book on the Stone Age and by age 10, she had developed a keen interest in wolves and their behavior. Both of these elements form important parts of this breathtaking adventure story. To prepare for this writing project, Ms. Paver studied countless sources on prehistoric life and tried to experience the lives of Stone Age people by trekking through the forests of Finland and Lapland, sleeping on reindeer skins, and existing on such foods as lichens and wild berries. The authenticity of her work was shown when she was asked to create a *Wolf Brother* display case at Cambridge University's Museum of Archaeology and Anthropology. *Wolf Brother* is the first installment in what will be a six-volume cycle, the Chronicles of Ancient Darkness. In the next installment, *Spirit Walker* (Harper, 2006, $16.99, 0060728280; pap. $6.99, 0060728302), Torak misses his companion Wolf but settles in with the Raven clan. When a mysterious plague strikes, he seeks a cure with the Sea Clan, learns to Spirit Walk (change into another creature), and begins his search for the seven Soul Eaters he must vanquish. In *Soul Eater* (Harper, 2007, $16.99, 0060728310), the third novel in the series, Wolf is kidnapped by the Soul Eaters, forcing Torak and Renn to travel to the Arctic to rescue him. The fourth volume, *Outcast*, was recently published in Britain. Fans of the series, collectively known as The Clan, can be found at www.torak.info.

Historical Background

Although many elements of traditional fantasy are present in this book—such as the use of magic and the pursuit of a quest—the author has faithfully re-created the culture of New Stone Age people. There are many detailed descriptions of their living quarters, food, dress, arts, and religious beliefs and rites. The New Stone or Neolithic period was characterized by the use of stone tools for grinding, cutting, chopping, and hunting and by the existence of settled villages where (after the Chronicles) domesticated plants and animals were gradually introduced. At the time and place of the novel (6,000 B.C. in presumably northern Europe), the dominant cultures relied on hunting, fishing, and food-gathering for their livelihood. Food storage was essential. Meat could be frozen, cut up into strips, and dried outdoors or smoked above a fire. Meat including fish and birds was the main source of nourishment. Nothing of the animal was wasted—the bones were made into implements and utensils and the marrow was used as food. Depending on the climate, these people were nomadic, traveling on foot over vast areas and often moving to different camps at different seasons. The main social unit was the clan. Domestication of the dog for hunting and frightening off predators occurred at this time. Rites relating to death and burial differed among cultures. Other rituals involved birth, puberty, and marriage. Huts and tent-like homes were constructed as well as the beginning of more elaborate structures such as Stonehenge.

Principal Characters

Torak, a 12-year-old Stone Age boy
Fa (father), Torak's father, a member of the Seal Clan
Wolf, an orphaned wolf cub Torak adopts
Renn, a Raven Clan girl, slightly older than Torak
Hord, Renn's older brother, about 18 years old
Oslak, a Raven hunter and warrior
Fin-Kedinn, the leader of the Raven Clan
Sacunn, the mage (wise man) of the clan
Walker, a grotesque human wanderer

Plot Synopsis

As far back as he can remember, 12-year-old Torak has lived alone with his widowed Fa (father), in a shelter in the forest far from the members of his family's Wolf Clan. One day, the serenity of his life is shattered when a gigantic ferocious bear that has been terrorizing the area attacks, destroying their shelter and leaving Torak with a gash on an arm and his father mortally wounded. Realizing the bear may strike again and that death is approaching,

Fa orders Torak to flee. Torak reluctantly agrees. Before he leaves, his father tells him the bear must be possessed by a demon. Fa mysteriously adds that Torak can stop this slaughter by traveling north to the Mountain of the World Spirit, and he makes Torak swear he will undertake this journey. He adds that Torak will soon find a guide to help him.

Torak prepares his father for the Death Journey by painting sacred markings on his body, including a circle on his forehead to mark Nanuak, the world-soul. Overcome with sorrow, Torak then leaves, taking—as his father commands—his father's knife and the family's provisions. He soon finds he is not the only newly orphaned creature in the Forest. He discovers a wolf cub guarding the dead bodies of its parents and siblings. The two bond, and Torak names his new friend Wolf. By the cub's actions, Torak realizes that Wolf is the guide his father referred to. After several days without sighting any game and relying on his dwindling food supply, Torak has the good fortune to kill a roe buck with his bow and arrow. He uses every part of the animal including the meat, which he smokes. His preparations for his journey complete, he is suddenly confronted by three strangers who take him and Wolf prisoner.

The three are members of the Raven Clan. They are an adult warrior named Oslak; Hord, a handsome young man in his late teens; and Renn, Hord's younger sister. Torak is brought before Fin-Kedinn, the leader of the Raven Clan, who sentences Torak to death for poaching in the Clan's Forest. Torak manages to have the sentence modified: he will die, but only if he loses a contest between himself and the Clan's designate, Hord. In spite of the odds, Torak wins through his ingenuity and fast actions. Renn convinces the crowd that the stranger Torak is really the Listener cited in an old Clan prophecy, who has been sent to relieve the Clan of the bear's presence. Others point out that the prophecy also obtusely states that the Listener's "heart's blood" must be spilled. Torak is kept a prisoner while the elders, including Fin-Kedinn and Clan mage Sacunn, decide his fate.

However, with the help of Wolf, who nibbles through his rawhide handcuffs, and Renn, who believes in the boy's mission, he is able to escape with his two friends. Renn also believes in the rest of the prophecy, which states that the Listener must take to the Mountain three elements that are part of the life force Nanuak, In riddle form, they are "Deepest of all, the drowned sight; Oldest of all, the stone bite: Coldest of all, the darkest Light." The three set out on their quest for these elements and the journey to the Mountain of the World Spirit.

In a series of death-defying adventures they are able to collect the three elements. The first consists of two glowing blind eyes, unusual stones that Torak risks drowning to discover at the bottom of a deep, fast-moving river. After traveling through a dense fog, Wolf leads them to a valley where they encounter a ragged, evil-smelling old man known as the Walker, who talks in the third person. He directs Torak to a deep cave whose entrance is shaped like a mouth. Torak enters and inside finds a tooth-shaped rock, the second part of the Nanuak. After a narrow escape from the bear, who has been tracking them, Torak returns to Renn and Wolf. They travel into a desolate area of snow and ice. Torak falls into a deep hole but with the ingenious use of ice steps he carves in its wall, he is able to escape. Later, in a blinding snowstorm, he is separated from his friends and takes shelter in a deserted ice house. There, close to a frozen corpse, he discovers the third part of the Nanuak, an abandoned oil lamp. With the three parts safely hidden in a sealed pouch, the three set off on the final stage of their quest.

Torak notices that Wolf is becoming restless and often answers the howls of distant wolf packs. At the base of the Mountain, another setback occurs. They are accosted by members of the Raven Clan who have followed them from their camp. Some believe that an older, stronger Clan member, like Hord, should carry Nanuak up the mountain; others, including Renn, defend Torak's right to complete his mission. Alone with Fin-Kedinn, Torak learns much about his background. Torak's father was actually the mage, or wise man, of the Wolf Clan. He had become the sworn enemy of a group of seven mages from other clans who had begun to use their spiritual powers for evil purposes. It was one of them, disguised as a blind wanderer who was able to demonize the bear and send him on the rampage of destruction that killed Torak's Fa. The wicked mages are known as the Soul-Eaters and, should Torak survive, his mission in the future will be to kill them before they kill him.

With Wolf leading the way and the magic parts of the Nanuak in his hand, Torak climbs the narrow snow-encrusted path that leads to the peak. He calls on the World Spirit to hear his plea and kill the demon of the Forest. Suddenly he realizes he is being followed by Hord, who confronts Torak and demands the Nanuak so he can receive credit for the exorcism. He also confesses to Torak that he feels pangs of guilt because it was he who caught the bear and gave it to the wanderer for his evil purposes. Suddenly, the two discover that the bear is also on the trail and rapidly approaching them. Powerless, the two are awaiting death when there is a deafening roar and an avalanche of ice and snow descends, sending both Hord and the bear over the precipice to their deaths below. The World Spirit has spoken. Torak is safe but he realizes that Wolf is gone. The prophecy has been fulfilled. With the disappearance of Wolf, Torak, truly has lost his life's blood. Sorrowing but glad to be alive, Torak returns to Renn and the other members of the Clan.

Passages for Booktalking

Four interesting passages (the pagination is from the paperback edition) are: the bear strikes and Torak leaves his father (pp. 1–12); Torak butchers the deer (pp. 53–55); he is captured and he meets Renn (pp. 56–61); and a description of the Raven village (pp. 65–67).

Themes and Subjects

The author has successfully integrated a detailed, accurate portrait of New Stone Age life with exciting fantasy fiction. The information about prehistoric life, beliefs, and culture is fascinating. All the elements of good storytelling are present, including nail-biting suspense, cliff-hanging chapter endings, and believable characters. Torak's growth to maturity, his courage and loyalty, and his developing sense of responsibility are well presented, as is the interaction of people and nature. Other subjects: family life, friendship, pets, wolves, religion, and pursuit of a quest.

SUTCLIFF, ROSEMARY. *The Eagle of the Ninth.* Oxford, 1954, o.p.; pap. $13.84 (978-0-19-275392-2) (Grades 5–10)

Introduction

The historical novels of Rosemary Sutcliff (1920–1992) have become synonymous with superior quality in writing style, richness of detail, and an amazing ability to re-create the color, action, passion and living conditions of a particular period in British history. *The Eagle of the Ninth* was first published in 1954 and has now sold more than a million copies. The story takes place in 2nd-century Roman Britain and forms the first part of Sutcliff's Roman Trilogy. The second volume, *The Silver Branch* (Oxford, pap. $13.84, 0192755046), first published in 1959, also takes place in Roman Britain but about one hundred years after *Eagle*. Its story involves two friends, Justin and Flavius, who discover a plot to overthrow the emperor. They gather together a tattered band of men to do battle to save the emperor's life and attempt to unify Britain. Volume three, *The Lantern Bearers* (Farrar, pap. $6.95; 0374443025), also first published in 1959, is set in Britain in the twilight years of Roman civilization before Europe, including Britain, sinks into the Dark Ages. It is the story of Aquila, a Roman soldier who chooses to stay in Britain when the Romans leave. However, he and his sister are made slaves by the invading Saxons. Eventually, his sister marries one of the invaders. Aquila manages to escape and, through the help of friends, finds redemption and inner peace.

Historical Background

In order to prevent incursions into the recently occupied Gaul, Emperor Julius Caesar conducted successful military campaigns in Britain in 55–54 B.C., but the full-scale invasion of the island did not begin until the rule of Emperor Claudius in 54 A.D. The emperor himself visited England to receive the official surrender of some of the Celtic leaders. Thereafter, the conquest continued slowly both to the north and west. By 85 A.D. Rome controlled Britain south of the River Clyde in present-day Scotland. There were numerous revolts during the occupation, the most famous being that of Queen Boadicca in 61 A.D. Others were led by Druids hoping to preserve their religion and culture. In the second century A.D. (chiefly between 122 and 126 A.D.), Hadrian's Wall was constructed between Wallsend-on-Tyne and Bowness-on-Solway, the narrow part of Great Britain. The wall was about 74 miles long with fortified gateways every mile and observation towers every third of a mile. The actual boundary lines of Roman Britain varied and often included large areas of land north of the wall. As the barbarian invasions increased on the European mainland, Roman troops were gradually removed from England even though this area was also becoming a frequent target for Saxon raids. In the early 5th century, Rome withdrew its last officials.

A centurion was the captain of a century of foot soldiers in the ancient Roman army. A century originally consisted of one hundred men but later became a larger unit. A century was one-sixtieth of a legion.

Principal Characters

> Marcus Flavius Aquila, a brave young centurion in the Roman army stationed in Britain
> Cradoc, a Celtic hunter and leader
> Uncle Aquila, a brusque ex-army officer, Marcus's uncle
> Legate Claudius, a kindly high-ranking civil servant
> Esca, a native Briton who has been forced into slavery
> Kaeso, a Briton who has risen to the rank of magistrate
> Valaria, Kaeso's class-conscious wife
> Cattia (Camilla), Valaria's niece
> Guern the Hunter, a former member of the Ninth Legion
> Dergdian, a Highland chieftain
> Liathan, Dergdian's brother

Plot Synopsis

In Roman Britain in 117 A.D., the Ninth Roman Legion, named Hispana, disappears without a trace after marching into enemy territory north of Hadrian's Wall to quell an uprising of the Caledonian tribes. Gone with the soldiers is the legion's symbol of its glory, a prize standard that bears a shining eagle on top. Ten years later, the young son of the commander of the ill-fated Ninth, Marcus Flavius Aquila, arrives in Britain. He has completed his army training in his native Italy, has risen to the rank of centurion, and is now the commander of the Fourth Gaulish Auxiliaries of the Second Legion, marching to relieve the garrison currently stationed at Isca Dumnoniorum (present-day Exeter) in southwest Britain. Though young in years, Marcus displays remarkable maturity both in the decisions he makes and in the way he commands his troops.

After settling in, Marcus begins exploring the town outside the frontier fort. Some of the resident Britons have accepted the Roman occupation and try to copy the ways of their conquerors, while others, often led by Druid priests, plot insurrections to regain control of their land. Marcus's British guide outside the fort is a respected horse trainer and brave hunter named Cradoc. When Marcus wins a wager with Cradoc concerning maneuvering a team of chariot horses, he chooses as his prize one of Cradoc's spears. He notices that it has been freshly honed and decorated with new feathers, a signal to Marcus that the natives might be preparing an uprising. He strengthens the troop's vigilance. His hunch proves to be right. A few days later, the fort is attacked by Britons led by a fierce Druid and the traitorous Cradoc. Marcus is ready and signals a neighboring garrison, two or three marching days away, to send reinforcements. Marcus leaves the fort with some soldiers to clear a path for a returning troop of scouts to enter the fort. The operation is successful but Cradoc is killed in the fighting and Marcus suffers a serious leg wound. The reinforcements arrive and the siege is lifted.

Marcus, now acclaimed a hero, is forced to leave the service because of his crippling injury. He decides to recuperate at the home of his Uncle Aquila, a crusty retired Roman army officer who decided to remain in Britain in the town of Calleva (present-day Silchester, west of London) after his demobilization. There, Marcus and his uncle attend gladiatorial games. Marcus saves the life of a gallant slave, Esca, by exhorting the audience to give the thumbs-up signal when the slave is unfairly trapped by his adversary. Marcus then buys Esca, who is actually the son of a clan chieftain (in present-day Scotland). The two become fast friends and the distinction between master and slave almost disappears. On one occasion, Esca captures a tiny wolf cub and presents it to Marcus. The animal, Cub, becomes their constant companion. Marcus also meets a neighboring family that consists of Kaeso, a good natured magistrate; his wife, the overbearing Valaria; and their ward Cattia, a high-spirited, attractive 13-year-old girl. Both Kaeso and Valaria are Britons by birth but have assumed Roman ways and manners to climb the social ladder. Valaria even tries, without success, to change the young girl's name from Cattia to Camilla to become more Romanized. Marcus and Cattia soon become fond of each other. And under the guidance of his uncle's doctor, Marcus's health improves along with his ability to walk.

Uncle Aquila is visited by his old army companion, Legate Claudius, who reveals to Marcus that the eagle standard of his father's regiment, the Ninth, is believed to be in the hands of northern barbarians who desecrate it by using it during tribal ceremonies. Marcus is determined to retrieve this symbol of the legion's—and his father's—honor. After placing Cub in Cattia's care, Marcus and Esca cross Hadrian's Wall and enter the Highlands, home of the barbarians known as the Painted People. To avoid being identified as a Roman in this hostile country, Marcus assumes the identity of an eye-doctor named Demetrius of Alexandria and uses his rudimentary medical knowledge to good advantage. The two cross the land on a zigzag route hoping to unearth some information about the regiment and the fate of the Eagle. On the road, they meet many interesting people, including Guern the Hunter, who shares his home and provisions with them. Through clever detection, Marcus discovers that Guern once served in the Ninth Legion. Guern confesses that, after being severely wounded in battle, he deserted and assumed the identity of a native Briton. He also gives Marcus directions to the tribal area where the Eagle might be found. In this region the two adventurers encounter a tribe whose chieftain is named Dergdian. Marcus gains favor with the villagers when he cures Dergdian's son of an eye disorder. To show their appreciation, Dergdian and his fierce brother Liathan extend an invitation to witness a sacred ritual known as the Feast of New Spears, during which boys achieve adulthood by being presented with spears by their fathers. Marcus learns that this was one of the tribes that had surrounded and annihilated his father's regiment. He also learns that his father died a hero's death. At the height of the ceremony, the Eagle standard is unveiled, now sadly shorn of its wings. That night, when the feast has ended, Marcus and Esca secretly retrieve the Eagle and, with great stealth, leave the village. After several narrow escapes from the pursuing Highlanders, they finally reach the safety of Hadrian's Wall and eventually the home of Uncle Aquila. The Legate, Claudius, hears of their bravery and devotion to the Roman cause and secretly appeals to the Senate in Rome for suitable rewards. The result: Esca gains his freedom and is made a Roman citizen, and Marcus is awarded a tract of land either in Italy or Britain. He chooses the latter so he will be permanently in the land of his soon-to-be bride, Cattia.

Passages for Booktalking

Some interesting passages are: Marcus meets Cradoc and wins a wager (pp. 15–22); the battle in which Marcus is wounded and the patrol is saved (pp.

34–36); the gladiatorial game in which Esca is saved (pp. 55–59); and Marcus meets Cattia (pp. 74–81).

Themes and Subjects

Marcus emerges as a heroic figure of great stature; his nobility, high-mindedness, devotion to a cause, consideration for others, and his tenacity and bravery are well presented. The author has beautifully re-created a period in British history where Roman supremacy is being threatened and violence and anarchy are commonplace. The contrast between two cultures—Roman and barbarian—is well portrayed. The book contains many scenes of high adventure, suspense, and colorful atmosphere. Details on food, clothing, customs, and everyday life fill the pages and bring a sense of authenticity. Other subjects include slavery, friendship, young love, patriotism, courage, the importance of symbols, Scotland, Hadrian's Wall, and Roman civilization.

ADDITIONAL SELECTIONS

Blocklock, Dyan. *Pankration: The Ultimate Game* (Albert Whitman, 1999, pap. $5.95) (Grades 5–8)

In ancient Greece, two friends, separated by a shipwreck, are reunited at the Olympic Games during the Pankration, a sport that combines wrestling and boxing.

Carter, Dorothy. *His Majesty, Queen Hatshepsut* (HarperCollins, 1989, $16.89) (Grades 6–9)

The story of the daughter of Thutmose I who became the only female pharaoh of ancient Egypt.

Fletcher, Susan. *Alphabet of Dreams* (Simon, 2006, $16.95) (Grades 6–9)

Set in biblical times, this is the story of a Persian refugee, Mitta, whose life becomes entangled with a magus named Melchior, who eventually makes a momentous journey with two other magi to seek their new king.

Friesner, Ester. *Nobody's Princess* (Random, 2007, $16.99) (Grades 6–10)

This story tells of the childhood and youth of a strong, independent princess—Helen of Sparta—who later became known as Helen of Troy, the face that launched a thousand ships.

Lasky, Kathryn. *The Last Girls of Pompeii* (Viking, 2007, $15.99) (Grades 7–10)

Set in Pompeii immediately before the eruption of Vesuvius, this is the story of two outcast girls—Julia, born with a withered arm, and her slave Sura—and how they escape this historic disaster.

Lawrence, Caroline. *The Charioteer of Delphi* (Roaring Brook, 2007, $16.95) (Grades 5–8)

While visiting Rome, four young friends become involved in the intrigue and danger surrounding chariot races. This is number 12 in the Roman Mysteries series. See also the entry in this chapter under Lawrence.

Lester, Julius. *Pharaoh's Daughter: A Novel of Ancient Egypt* (Harcourt, 2000, $17) (Grades 6–9)

The grandeur of Ancient Egypt is re-created in this novel of young Moses and how he grew up in the court of the pharaoh.

McCaughrean, Geraldine. *Not the End of the World* (HarperCollins, 2005, $17.89) (Grades 6–10)

The harrowing but exciting story of what it was really like aboard Noah's Ark surrounded by terrified animals.

McLaren, Clemence. *Inside the Walls of Troy* (Simon, 1996, $17) (Grades 6–9)

The story of the Trojan War and the fall of Troy as seen through the eyes of two participants, Helen and Cassandra.

Miklowitz, Gloria D. *Masada: The Last Fortress* (Eerdmans, 1998, $16) (Grades 6–10)

The siege of Masada is re-created through the eyes of both a young Jewish man and a Roman commander.

Mitchell, Jack. *The Roman Conspiracy* (Tundra, 2005, pap. $8.95) (Grades 5–9)

Set in the days of the Roman Empire, this story involves young Aulus and his attempts to save his land from military pillagers.

Reynolds, Susan. *The First Marathon: The Legend of Pheidippides* (Whitman, 2006, $16.95) (Grades 2–4)

In a picture-book format, the story of the battle of Marathon and the role of the long-distance runner Pheidippides is retold.

Tomlinson, Theresa. *Voyage of the Snake Lady* (Eos, 2007, $17.89) (Grades 6–9)

Myrina, also known as the Snake Lady, and her Amazon followers escape from the clutches of the son of Achilles and find themselves in an unknown land in this novel that draws on Greek mythology.

Williams, Susan. *Wind Rider* (HarperCollins, 2006, $16.99) (Grades 6–8)

Some 6,000 years ago on the steppes of Central Asia, young Fern captures a foal she names Thunder and domesticates it much to the astonishment of the rest of the tribe.

Winterfield, Henry. *Detectives in Togas* (Harcourt, 1956, pap. $5.95) (Grades 5–8)

Set in ancient Rome, this is the story of six of the classmates of Caius, a boy who has been wrongfully accused of painting graffiti on a temple and breaking into his schoolroom.

MIDDLE AGES AND RENAISSANCE

AVI.

Crispin: The Cross of Lead. Hyperion, 2002, $15.99 (978-0-7868-0828-1) (Grades 5–9)

Crispin: At the Edge of the World. Hyperion, 2006, $16.99 (978-0-7868-5152-2) (Grades 5–9)

Introduction

These two novels form the first parts of a planned trilogy about the adventures of Crispin, a 13-year-old illiterate boy living in England in the mid-1370s. Avi (last name Wortis) was born in New York City in 1937. About his unusual penname, he says "my twin sister gave it to me when we were both about a year old. And it stuck." He has written more than 50 books for young readers, several of which have won prestigious awards including a Newbery Medal and two Newbery Honor Book designations. Although he has written in many genres, he is perhaps best known for his historical novels. For example, the 1991 Newbery Honor Book, *The True Confessions of Charlotte Doyle* (Orchard, 1990, $16.95, 053105893X), set in 1832, in which the young heroine, the sole passenger on the brig *Seahawk*, is returning to America after a stay in England when she discovers that the captain is a cruel, sadistic man whose crew is justifiably planning a mutiny. She allies herself with the crew and experiences many breathtaking adventures until, during a suspenseful chase on the ship's deck, the captain falls overboard and drowns.

Crispin: The Cross of Lead won the Newbery Medal in 2003 and its sequel received starred reviews in all the major book reviewing journals.

Historical Background

The setting of both novels is mainly England during the last days of the reign of Edward III (who was king from 1327 to 1377) and the first months of the reign of Richard II (who ruled from 1377 to 1399). Edward III was a magnetic, progressive ruler who is remembered principally for beginning the invasion of France (the English royalty believed that their Norman ancestry and land holdings on the continent gave them a right to the throne of France) that escalated into the conflict known as the Hundred Years War. Edward III was active in the war, as was his son Edward, known as the Black Prince. Edward III was famous for his many victories in France including the Battle of Poitiers in 1356. Toward the end of his reign Edward lost interest in the war and, after the Black Prince suffered ill health, he declared a truce in 1375. At the time of these novels there was technically peace between these countries but, as seen in the second book, coastal raids still took place and bands of renegade English soldiers roamed the French countryside. The Black Prince died in 1376, shortly before Edward III's death in 1377. The son of the Black Prince, Richard II, though only 9 years old came to the throne. During his minority, John of Gaunt, the Duke of Lancaster, was the most powerful nobleman and acted as the king's regent. The decline and fall of this young king is dramatized in Shakespeare's *Richard II*. Socially in England during this period, there was increasing unrest among the lower classes caused by the great injustices resulting from the feudal system and absentee landlords as well as the misuse of power by the Catholic Church hierarchy. This unrest, which is graphically presented in *The Cross of Lead*, culminated in the Peasants' Revolt of 1381, four years after the events of the two novels. It was led by Wat Tyler and John Ball, a priest, who is also a character in the first novel.

Principal Characters in *The Cross of Lead*

Crispin, also known as Asta's boy, the narrator, a 13-year-old illiterate waif
Asta, Crispin's mother
Lord Furnival, the area's absentee landlord
John Aycliffe, the lord's cruel bailiff
Father Quinel, Crispin's helpful parish priest
Bear, real name Orson Hagar, an itinerant juggler
Widow Daventry, an innkeeper in Great Wexly
John Ball, a priest who fights for the rights of peasants

Plot Synopsis of *The Cross of Lead* (edited from *The Newbery/Printz Companion*)

On a rainy, spring morning in 1377, two people huddle over a tiny shrouded body in the paupers' section of the graveyard in the small English village of Stromford. The village, surrounding land, and manor house are all owned by the absent Lord Furnival, who is believed to be fighting with King Edward III in France. In his absence, the property is managed by his cruel steward, John Aycliffe. The woman being buried without a coffin is an outcast peasant named Asta, and the two people at her graveside are the kindly village priest, Father Quinel, and Asta's illiterate 13-year-old son known only as "Asta's boy," who believes his father died of the plague. Now, he is totally alone except for Father Quinel.

Leaving the graveyard, the boy is accosted by Aycliffe who demands that the boy turn over his ox, the only valuable possession he owns, as a death tax. In the woods that evening the boy sees John Aycliffe receive an official-looking letter from a nobly dressed stranger.

The next day, he overhears two villagers discuss Aycliffe's public (and false) accusation that the boy is a thief. That evening, he seeks help from Father Quinel, who reveals that the boy's real name is Crispin and that the steward has declared him a wolf's head, or a subhuman creature that must be killed. Before promising to tell more the next night, the priest gives the boy his mother's cross of lead, which has writing on it that the boy cannot read. The next night Crispin discovers Father Quinel's body in the woods. His throat has been slit. Crispin now realizes that his life is in extreme danger and he must flee Stromford.

After wandering for several days and living off acorns and bitter roots, Crispin comes to a deserted village whose inhabitants have all died of the Plague. In the ruins of the village church, the boy discovers a mountain of a man with a huge red beard. He introduces himself as a traveling juggler and entertainer named Bear. At first Crispin is fearful of this giant, who openly speaks of the corruption and unjust practices of the clergy and landed gentry. But gradually the two become friends and intimate traveling companions.

Crispin tells Bear of his background and how Lord Furnival's steward tried to kill him. In turn, Bear teaches the boy the rudiments of juggling, singing, and playing the recorder. The two head for the city of Great Wexly, where Bear says he has some unfinished business. As they near the city, Crispin is horrified to see Aycliffe and his men in the distance, also traveling toward Great Wexly.

In the city, Crispin is overcome by the bustle, stench, and clamor of his new surroundings. Bear takes him to stay at the Green Man tavern, which is run by Bear's old friend Widow Daventry. Here they learn that Lord Furnival has died and, because he was childless, his widow will claim his fortune unless a rightful heir can be found.

The plot strands begin to coalesce. Crispin finds out that the writing on his mother's cross says "Crispin—Son of Furnival" and that he is the rightful heir to the Furnival lands and fortune. Bear discovers that Crispin's mother, a member of Lord Furnival's court, was abandoned by Furnival when she became pregnant, and that Aycliffe and Lady Furnival are plotting Crispin's death, fearful that he will learn his true origins.

The real reason for Bear's presence in Great Wexly is to help plot a revolt against the barons. His co-conspirators include John Ball, a priest who is also devoting his life to fighting for the rights of the common man. Unfortunately, a spy informs on the conspirators, and their meeting is raided by Aycliffe and his men.

Through Crispin's quick thinking, all escape except Bear, who is taken prisoner and held in Furnival's palace. Crispin devises an audacious plan. He scales a side wall and enters the palace through an outside balcony. But before he can reach Bear, he is trapped by Aycliffe. Crispin confronts the steward with his mother's cross and the truth of his parentage. The boy bargains with Aycliffe, promising to give up any claim to his family's wealth if Aycliffe will allow Crispin and Bear to leave the city unharmed. Aycliffe agrees, but as the two reach the city gates, Aycliffe treacherously commands his soldiers to kill Crispin. When they raise their swords to attack, Bear lifts Aycliffe and flings him onto the blades of the swords, impaling him fatally. In the ensuing confusion, Bear and Crispin make their escape from the city to freedom.

Passages for Booktalking in *The Cross of Lead*

Some important incidents: the burial of Asta and the introduction of the villain John Aycliffe (pp. 1–5): a description of peasant life (pp. 12–13); Crispin's escape from Aycliffe and the discovery of Father Quinel's body (pp. 45–48); and Crispin meets Bear (pp. 61–65).

Themes and Subjects in *The Cross of Lead*

This depiction of life in the villages and towns of 14th-century England accurately reveals the appalling conditions of the peasants' everyday life and the cruelty and exploitation they suffered at the hands of the nobles. All they could hope for was the happy afterlife promised them by the church. Avi portrays, with sympathy, the gallant few of the period who risked their lives for the principles of fairness and equality. One of these, John Ball, was a historical figure. Other important themes in this rip-roaring adventure story are courage, death, the role of the church, feudalism, friendship, villainy, royalty, importance of one's identity, devotion, class distinction, superstition, and family ties.

Principal Characters in *At the Edge of the World*

Crispin, a 13-year-old peasant boy who narrates the story
Bear (real name Orson Hagar), a traveling juggler who is also a revolutionary
Aude, a reclusive hag who is a herbologist and midwife
Troth, her young helper with a facial disfiguration
Benedicta, an innkeeper in Rye
Richard Dudley, a renegade British army officer in Brittany

Plot Synopsis of *At the Edge of the World*

At the Edge of the World begins where the story of *The Cross of Lead* left off. Although it is not necessary to have read the first part to understand the second part, knowledge of the first book will bring greater appreciation. Before reading the following summary, a reading of the plot synopsis of *The Cross of Lead* above is advised.

The spirits of young Crispin and his companion, a giant of a man nick-named Bear, are high as they flee from the city of Great Wexly and seek their freedom in the countryside. Their plans to resume their lives as itinerant jug-glers and entertainers, however, are short-lived. When the two stop at an ale-house for food and drink, the proprietor, a former archer and member of John Ball's radical brotherhood, recognizes Bear as a fellow member but he, along with others in the group, erroneously believes that Bear is the informer who caused the raid on the group's meeting in Great Wexly. While trying to escape the alehouse owner's wrath, Bear is shot through the left arm with an arrow. He and Crispin, however, manage to escape into the woods. Although Crispin is able to remove the arrow, Bear suffers severe loss of blood. The wound begins to fester and Bear's life is soon in danger. For days they hide in the woods, relying on Crispin's ability to snare small animals for food and the boy's innocent faith in God and the saints for moral support. Unexpectedly, they are discovered in their hideaway by a bizarre-looking pair. One is a bent, toothless old crone who is blind in one eye, and the other, a ragged silent young girl whose mouth is cleft and grotesquely ugly. The girl pathetically tries to hide her deformity by pulling her scraggly hair across her face. The hag's name is Aude and the girl's is Troth. Aude grudgingly agrees to help Bear, and Troth and Crispin drag the nearly unconscious man to her crude lean-to. There she prepares and applies several herbal poultices and pomades.

As Bear begins the slow process of recovery, Crispin learns more about his hosts. After being abandoned at birth by her parents because of her deformity, Troth was adopted by Aude, an outcast from the nearby village. Aude, who still practices her ancient pre-Christian religion, occasionally acts as midwife for the local villagers. Gradually Crispin gains the confidence of both of them and becomes very friendly with Troth, who confides in Crispin her thoughts and innermost feelings. One day Aude is summoned to the village by a peas-ant whose wife is having a difficult labor. Crispin accompanies Aude and Troth to the cottage. There, the bailiff of the town tries to prevent Aude from entering the peasant's cottage, claiming she is a pagan and an agent of the devil. Aude prevails but it is too late and the woman dies. Goaded on by the bailiff, the angry townspeople blame Aude, They attack her brutally and kill her. Then they turn on Crispin and Troth. Fortunately, the two elude the pursuing villagers and find their way back to Bear.

Hurriedly, the three gather up their meager belongings and flee. They make their way south to the (then) coastal town of Rye hoping to get passage to a safe area. The town is recovering from a raid by renegade French plunderers but they find rooms at an inn run by a friendly proprietor named Benedicta, and Bear earns their keep by working at odd jobs. When it is discovered that members of John Ball's brotherhood, including the archer who wounded Bear, are in town searching for them, the three quickly book passage on a cog (a single-masted ship) bound for Flanders with a cargo of wool. At sea, they encounter a raging storm. Crispin, Troth, and Bear survive by tying themselves to a deck railing, but all three members of the crew drown. In the morning, the cog drifts onto a rocky shore, and the three adventurers make it to dry land. They climb a rocky cliff to an open area overlooking the sea.

Within minutes, they are surrounded by mounted English soldiers led by a sword-wielding captain who identifies himself as Richard Dudley. He tells them they have landed in Brittany. Bear realizes this is a band of brigands—renegade English warriors known as a free company—who have ignored the truce between France and England and have stayed behind to terrorize and pillage the French countryside. Bear introduces himself as a former soldier, now a pilgrim, and Crispin and Troth as his children. Dudley spares their lives partly because he respects Bear's record of fighting with the Black Prince and partly because he has need of them, particularly Troth. After attacking, butchering, and looting a small village, Dudley outlines his audacious plan to seize an important treasure. King Edward has apparently left a treasure in the neighboring city of Bources to fund any future warfare. It is stored in a church fortified by an adjoining tower and guarded over by a garrison of English troops. Clandestine entrance into the church can by gained through a hole so tiny only a child can squeeze through it. Once inside, the intruder can easily open the main door. Richard plans to use little Troth for this purpose, holding Bear and Crispin as hostages to ensure her loyalty. Bear, already broken in body and spirit, is haltered and, like a captive beast, is placed in the custody of the men who will storm the church. Crispin is bound and left behind, guarded by the cook. Should Troth fail, Dudley plans on using Crispin as a substitute.

Crispin manages to free himself and kills the cook in hand-to-hand combat. He reaches the church through the small passageway and he and Troth open the main door for Dudley and his men. There are more soldiers in the tower than Dudley anticipated and a fierce battle ensues during which Dudley is knocked senseless and Bear, unarmed and defenseless, is severely wounded. In the ensuing turmoil and confusion, Crispin and Troth lead Bear away from the battle. He dies in their arms and the two grieving survivors bury him before setting out to find safety and salvation in some land as yet unknown.

Passages for Booktalking in *At the Edge of the World*

Some important passages: Crispin and Bear stop at the alehouse (pp. 6–10); Crispin removes the arrow (pp. 12–14); Crispin and Bear meet Aude and Troth (pp. 23–29); and Aude, Troth, and Crispin go to the village and the death of Aude (pp. 66–74).

Themes and Subjects in *At the Edge of the World*

As in *The Cross of Lead*, Avi has brilliantly re-created everyday life in medieval England. Far from a storybook land of dashing knights and damsels in distress, this is a setting filled with squalor, early death, intolerance, and cruelty. Superstition, ignorance, and blind faith—not reason, science, and knowledge—are predominant social forces. Crispin's transition from follower to leader is well developed. This growth of independence and maturity is coupled with his desire to learn and discover truth. Other themes are courage, villainy, family, friendship, devotion, sacrifice, religious faith, death, coming of age, the Hundred Years War, France, royalty, and feudalism.

————◆•◆————

CUSHMAN, KAREN. *Matilda Bone.* Clarion, 2000, $15 (978-0-395-88156-9); pap. Dell, $5.99 (978-0-440-41822-1)

Introduction

Karen Cushman (1941–) (see also *The Loud Silence of Francine Green* in Chapter 8) has written three novels set in the Middle Ages. The first, *Catherine, Called Birdy* (Clarion, 1994, $13.95; 0395681863) was a Newbery Honor Book for 1995. It tells the fascinating, often uproarious story of 14-year-old Birdy, so named because of the number of birds she has as pets, and the many wiles and schemes she devises to avoid marrying unsuitable mates. Told in a diary format from September 1290 through September 1291, the novel ends with Birdy finally settling on Stephen, a handsome lad and the first to gain her approval. The second, published the following year, was *The Midwife's Apprentice* (Clarion, 1995, $10.95; 0395692296) (see the complete plot summary in *The Newbery/Printz Companion*), the winner of the 1996 Newbery Medal. In it, Alyce, once known as Beetle, becomes an apprentice to midwife Jane but through a series of misunderstandings the two become alienated and Alyce leaves. Eventually circumstances change and Alyce is once again welcomed into Jane's home. Concerning her interest in medieval England, the author has said, "At 13 I was already reading English historical fiction and collecting things like a fifteenth-century illuminated manuscript." Therefore when it came to writing her first book with this setting she was already familiar with the period and "could read a lot of sources without having to learn another language." Although the settings and the historical era are important to the author, she says "It is the story and the character I seem to want to get involved with."

Matilda Bone takes place in a period of less than twelve months around the year 1330 during the reign of Edward III of England.

Historical Background

The Author's Note at the end of the novel gives an interesting, enlightening overview of medicine in the Middle Ages. Two important aspects are that religion and medicine were inseparable at the time and that there were four humors, blood, phlegm, yellow bile, and black bile that governed the well-being of the human body. Related to the first, there was a belief that God created everything and that there should be an acceptance of illness and suffering as part of God's will. For example, St. Augustine claimed that "health is a blessing from God." There arose in time a conflict between the scientific method and religious beliefs that claimed that illness came from evil and that prayer could be a major source of healing. The tension between faith and folk medicine was common and grew during the period. Medieval medicine was based on keeping a balance among the four humors through diet, medicines, and phlebotomy (bloodletting). It was believed that each organ within the human body had its own origin and that various organs were connected to specific veins. The dangers of bloodletting are obvious, including weakening of the body, infection, and accidental cutting of nerves or internal organs.

The novel takes place during the reign of the "young" king, Edward III (see also the entry for *Dogboy* and Avi's two *Crispin* novels in this chapter), probably around 1330. Edward was born in 1312. When he was 14 his father was murdered and he became king although power was in the hands of his mother Isabella (known as the She-Wolf of France) and her lover Roger Mortimer. Four years later, in 1330, Edward, barely 18, and his followers staged a coup. Mortimer was hanged and Isabella was placed under house arrest for her remaining years. Edward, who reigned until 1377, later invaded France and began the Hundred Years War. Three terms might need explanation. Red Peg is addicted to the game of *draughts*, an English term for checkers. Thus a draughtboard is a checkerboard and a draughtsman, a piece in the game of checkers. *Comfrey* is a rough hairy herb with blue flowers. Its root contains tannin and has been used medicinally for centuries. *Shambles* is an archaic term for a butcher's slaughterhouse.

Principal Characters

    Matilda Bone, a naïve 14-year-old girl
    Red Peg, the Bonesetter
    Father Leufredus, Matilda's former adviser
    Mr. Tom, Peg's husband
    Theobald the physician
    Margery Lewes, another physician
    Horanswith Leech, a bleeder

Nathaniel Cross, the apothecary
Sarah, his wife
Walter At-Water or Walter Mudd, the apothecary's assistant
Mother Uffa, a town resident
Grizzl Wimplewasher, a laundress
Matilda or Tildy, a kitchen maid
Fat Annet, Theobald's housekeeper
Hamish MacBroom, a Scottish resident of the town
Effie, his wife

Plot Synopsis

Matilda has been dumped unceremoniously by Father Leufredus at the house of Red Peg the Bonesetter on Blood and Bone Alley in Chipping Bagthorpe, an English town midway between Oxford and London. It is the early 1330s, and Matilda, whose mother disappeared after she was born and whose father died when she was 6, has been brought up in Lord Randall's manor some miles away under the care of the sanctimonious Father Leufredus. The priest has sheltered Matilda from reality and made her a God-fearing innocent who knows a great deal about the gory demises of hundreds of saints but nothing about everyday life. Now, the devoted Father has been called to London on business and has arranged for Matilda to leave the nest and become Red Peg's assistant.

Matilda gets a rude awaking when she meets Peg and enters her humble, dirt-floored cottage. Peg, an outspoken, no-nonsense type expects Matilda to shop, cook, and keep house, skills Matilda lacks to a remarkable degree. She gets off to bad start, staying on her straw pallet the first morning, not realizing she is responsible for making breakfast and, later being duped by a fishmonger into buying a rotten eel for dinner. But Red Peg, in spite of her exterior gruffness, is patient and she introduces Matilda to the science of bone setting. One day Matilda watches a distinguished-looking man identified as Master Theobald, the town's chief physician, as he disdainfully dismisses a woman who is following him asking for medical information. The same woman later visits Peg and Matilda learns she is Margery Lewes, the conscientious neighborhood physician who is always trying to improve her skills. Matilda watches Peg work on patients with bone problems and silently thinks she should use more prayer and less pushing and pulling. Kind-hearted Peg even treats the local animals, often for free. When grumpy Mother Uffa's cat breaks its leg, Peg promptly packs the leg with comfrey paste and binds it with cloth.

Matilda is unable to reconcile her religious beliefs with Peg's pagan practices and writes to Father Leufredus hoping he will rescue her. He never comes. When friend Grizzl Wimplewasher, a laundress, becomes sick, Peg sends Matilda to the local bloodletter, Horanswith Leech. Matilda accompanies him, with his pouch full of leeches to Grizzl's cottage, where Matilda is horrified to witness the practice of bleeding. One day, outside the magnificent house where Master Theobald lives, Matilda meets another Matilda, usually known as Tildy, an outspoken young kitchen maid who works for Theobald. She is terrorized by her boss, whom she calls Fat Annet. Matilda and Tildy become friends and share confidences. Tom, Peg's husband, returns home for a short visit. He is a larger-than-life character and Matilda finds him uncouth and ignorant, although he actually is a man of wisdom and great insight. Father Leufredus's lessons are unfortunately difficult to unlearn.

On an errand, Matilda meets a boy who will also become a friend. He is the charming Walter At-Water, the apprentice of the apothecary, Nathaniel Cross. Walter nicknames her Matilda Bone. Later she meets Mr. Cross and his wife Sarah, a couple who are loved and respected by all. Unfortunately, the apothecary's sight is failing fast and he is afraid he will have to give up his practice. Doctor Margery is called in and is shocked when Matilda suggests his sight might return if he repents his sins. Matilda gradually gains respect for Peg's knowledge and methods as she watches her treat Stephen Bybridge for muscle cramp and several brawlers injured in drunken fighting at the Shambles. Every day Peg sends Matilda to massage Sarah's aching legs and rub them with a special herbal lotion. Matilda's friendship with Sarah and Nathaniel deepens and she vows to help his fading eyesight. However, her ardent prayers don't seem to work and she uses Tildy to gain an audience with Theobald, the master physician. After collecting key important about Nathanial—including his birth date and month he first suffered this ailment—Theobald writes a prescription based primarily on astrology and quackery. He withholds the prescription when Matilda is unable to pay his 60 pence fee, more than Nathaniel makes in a month Fortunately Tildy is able to steal it, and Matilda brews the potion, which includes asses' dung. Not only does the medicine not work, its foul odor drives customers from Nathaniel's shop. In desperation, Matilda writes to professors at Oxford seeking their help. She gets a reply in which the professors tell about their work with lenses and suggest a visit. Matilda knows that at present, however, this is impossible.

Effie, the wife of burly Scotsman Hamish MacBroom suffers multiple injuries when the sign over the tailor's shop falls on her. After constant care from Doctor Margery, Peg, and Matilda, Effie pulls through but naïve Matilda continues to believe that Theobald might have hastened her recovery. In the spring, some six to eight months after Matilda's arrival, a second emergency occurs. In a fit of anger, Fat Annet pushes Tildy into a well, banging her head on the edge. Doctor Margery, Red Peg, and Matilda are called in and, once again, through constant care and—Matilda believes—through her prayers, Tildy regains her health. Slowly, Matilda begins to reconcile her faith with the seemingly antireligious practices of Peg and Margery. Although she doesn't want to be a bonesetter's helper forever, she owes a great deal to Red Peg for her kindness and support so, at least for the present, she will try to work out the conflicts that continue to disturb her while remaining at the humble dwelling on Blood and Bone Alley.

Passages for Booktalking

Some interesting passages: Matilda meets Red Peg and refuses her first meal (pp. 4–7); Peg teaches Matilda about bonesetting and they discuss Father Leufredus (pp. 15–19); Matilda shops and buys a rotten eel (pp. 23–26); Mother Uffa and her cat (pp. 37–39); and Matilda goes to Grizzl's home for bloodletting (pp. 44–48).

Themes and Subjects

This book re-creates artfully the details of medical practices during the Middle Ages, the role of religious faith, and the conflict between the two. The novel is filled with humorous situations and a variety of interesting characters. Matilda's simple, unyielding faith and the conflicts between this faith and reality make for an interesting clash of values. Other subjects: England, Edward III, friendship, devotion to a cause, superstition, astrology, maturation, cruelty, herbal medicine, bloodletting, and finding direction in life.

———•◦•———

GRANT, K. M. *Blood Red Horse.* Walker, 2004, $16.95 (978-0-8027-8960-0); pap. $7.95 (978-0-8027-7734-8) (Grades 5–9)

Introduction

The author, who was born in Lancashire, England, and now lives in Glasgow, Scotland, grew up with two loves—horses and telling stories. She and her sister used to make up stories to entertain each other, and her family always had horses. At age 14, she acquired a 5-year-old mare named Miss Muffet, who lived to be 30. The author says she was "the most loyal, steadfast, and brave horse I have ever known." With her shiny red coat she became the inspiration for Hosanna, William's mount in *Blood Red Horse.* This novel covers almost eight years, from the summer of 1185 to January of 1193. During this time, the hero, William, or Will, grows from a boy of 12 to a 20-year-old man. This is the first book in the De Granville trilogy.

In the second, *Green Jasper* (Walker, 2006, $16.95; 0802780733; pap. $7.95, 0802796273), brothers Will and Gavin have returned from the Third Crusade leaving King Richard behind in Europe. Gavin is preparing to marry

Ellie but on their wedding day the villainous constable De Scabious attacks the castle and carries Ellie off after announcing, incorrectly, that King Richard is dead and the new king, John, Richard's brother, has given him permission to marry Ellie. William sets out to save Ellie and is caught and imprisoned. Later, to save Will and Ellie, Gavin gives up his life. While in Eastern Europe, their Saracen friend Kamil prevents a plot by King John to assassinate King Richard, who is being held in a German prison.

In the third volume, *Blaze of Silver* (Walker, 2007, $16.95; 0802796257), Will has been chosen to collect and deliver part of the ransom money necessary to free King Richard. He sets out with his men and Ellie to deliver the money. But in the meantime, in Palestine, the fanatic Old Man of the Mountain has sent a spy, Amal, to Germany to persuade Kamil, Saladin's representative, to betray his leader, and steal the silver to forward the Saracen cause. During the seizure, most of Will's men are killed but eventually, through the quick thinking of Ellie, the villain Amal is unmasked and she and Will are united in marriage.

Historical Background

At the center of the novel's action are the Third Crusade and the historical personages King Richard I of England, known as the Lion Hearted or Coeur de Lion, and the Muslim leader Sultan Saladin. The Second Crusade (1147–1149) was a disaster for the West, but when Saladin conquered Jerusalem (also a holy city for the Muslims) after the battle of Hattin in 1187, Pope Gregory VIII called for a third crusade to free the holy places. This appeal was heeded by King Richard I of England and Philip II of France (who later became enemies). The crusade lasted from 1189 to 1192 and its important events included the lifting of the siege at Acre in 1191 by Richard and Philip and the establishment by Richard of his fortified home base at Jaffa. When the war reached a stalemate, a peace was declared by which a narrow coastal strip of land (all that was left of the Latin Kingdom of Jerusalem) was retained by the West as well as the right of free access to the Holy Sepulchre and other holy places in Jerusalem. Richard left the Holy Land in October 1192, thus ending the crusade.

Richard I (1157–1199) was king of England from 1189 to 1199, during which time he spent only six months in England, gathering money for his warlike pursuits. He was a son of Henry II (of *Becket* and *The Lion in Winter* fame) and Eleanor of Aquitaine. He had several armed skirmishes with his father and, after Henry's death became king only to leave England shortly after his coronation (1189) to begin the Third Crusade. Along the way, he captured Messina (Sicily) and Cyprus. On his homeward journey in 1192, he was captured and held for ransom, first by Leopold V of Austria and then by Holy

Roman Emperor Henry VI. Released in 1194, he returned to England to put down a revolt by his brother John and to collect money before returning to France to battle his former friend Philip II of France. Richard was killed in 1199. One historian said of him, "He was a bad son, a bad husband, a bad king, but a great and splendid soldier."

Sultan Saladin (1137?–1193) was a legendary Muslim warrior, great opponent of the Crusades, and Sultan of Egypt, who extended his empire both in the south and east capturing most of Syria and Palestine As well as being a warrior he was a builder of canals, mosques, and so forth. A wise, cultivated man who loved learning (he was a scholar and authority on the Sunni faith), he was also noted for his generosity and chivalry. The True Cross referred to in the novel was supposedly part of the cross on which Jesus was crucified. The relic was housed in various places through the ages, including Constantinople, before it was returned to Jerusalem. Housed in the Church of the Holy Sepulchre, it was captured during the Battle of Hattin in 1187 by Saladin but later disappeared.

Principal Characters

Ellie (Eleanor Theodora de Barre), a 10-year-old orphan
Will (William) de Granville, a 12-year-old boy
Gavin de Granville, his 16-year-old brother
Sir Thomas de Granville, their father
Mark, a groom to Gavin
Piers de Scabious, constable of the de Granville castle
Sir Percy, a family friend
Keeper John, in charge of the horses
Sir Walter de Strop, an old knight
Hal, a squire
Humphrey, a squire to Gavin
Adam Landless, Gavin's friend
Hosanna, a blood red horse
Brother Ranulf, a monk
Brother Andrew, another monk
Old Nurse, a family retainer
Richard I, King of England
Sultan Saladin, the renowned Saracen leader
Kamil ad-Din, his young apprentice
Baha ad-Din, Saladin's adviser
Abdul Raq, a follower of the Old Man of the Mountain
Rashid ed-Din Sinan, a fanatic, also known as the Old Man of the Mountain

Plot Synopsis

It is 1185 in the north of feudal England at Hartslove, the de Granville's castle. Sir Thomas de Granville lives here with his two sons, 12-year-old William, called Will, and his older brother, Gavin, age 16; and Sir Thomas's ward, 10-year-old Ellie, short for Eleanor Theodora de Barre. The first Sir Thomas came to England as a nobleman serving William the Conqueror in his invasion of 1066 and was granted this large estate as a reward. Among the present residents of the castle are friends Sir Percy and Sir Walter, an aging knight; Piers de Scabious, the castle's caretaker and constable; and Old Nurse, who cares primarily for Ellie. Mark and Humphrey are Gavin's groom and squire and Hal performs these functions for Will. The brothers' mother died during childbirth six years before, but the loss of mother and child is in part made up for by the presence of lively Ellie, an orphan whose mother also died in childbirth and whose father was killed in service to the king. In time, she will inherit a large fortune.

The boys are filled with dreams of knighthood and chivalry and Will is particularly excited because he is being allowed to choose his own horse. Accompanied by Hal and Sir Walter, Will goes to the compound where the horses are cared for by Keeper John. After carefully perusing the eligible horses, he surprises everyone by choosing a small but beautiful chestnut colored stallion, far from the Great Horse of everyone's expectations. Somehow the boy has bonded spiritually with this lovely animal named Hosanna and no amount of objections from his father or derision from his brother can change his mind. Hosanna proves his worth shortly thereafter when, in a mock tournament, Will bests Gavin on his much larger mount, Montlouis.

For the next two years, Sir Thomas and Gavin are absent much of the time on land-management business, and during this time Will cements two relationships, one with Ellie who has become his dear friend and the other with Hosanna. He and the horse become as one. Gavin has never been as affable or as outgoing as his brother and, when he returns, he is even more moody and distant. One day, when Montlouis is indisposed, Gavin, out of perversity, rides Hosanna on a hunting expedition. He drives the horse like a madman and the horse begins bleeding profusely from the nostrils. Will is distraught and administers constant care but Hosanna does not respond. After several months with no improvement, Sir Thomas tells Will he must give Hosanna to the local abbey and choose another horse. Abbot Hugh accepts the horse and Brother Ranulf and, to a lesser extent, Brother Andrew, both monks at the abbey, shower the horse with medicines and prayers, and a miracle occurs. Hosanna recovers and is returned to Will just as preparations are being made to accompany newly crowned King Richard on a crusade to free Jerusalem, recently occupied by the Saracens under Sultan Saladin.

During this time, Saladin has been gradually consolidating Muslim control of a great part of the Holy Land. He has taken Jerusalem and is now laying siege to the coastal port of Acre, held by the Crusaders. During these conquests, he has impressed both his allies and enemies with his sense of honor and his just, compassionate treatment of the vanquished peoples. One person who feels he is too lenient, however, is Saladin's beloved young protégé, Kamil ad-Din, a young man about Will's age. Kamil saw his own father murdered by a Christian knight and even though he achieves revenge by killing the knight's son, he is still filled with bitterness and hatred for the western invaders.

Before leaving for the Holy Land, Sir Thomas announces Gavin's betrothal to Ellie and Will's knighthood. The trip, particularly the weeks sailing the storm-tossed Mediterranean, is pure hell for the three de Granvilles and their servants Mark and Humphrey drown during the voyage. But Will, riding Hosanna, distinguishes himself in battle during the conquest of Cyprus. Arriving in the Holy Land, the Crusaders encamp outside the city of Acre, intending to relieve Saladin's siege. Sir Thomas, weakened by the voyage, develops a fever and dies despite his sons' constant care. Richard orders a giant banquet in his honor. Later, Acre falls to the Crusaders, and Richard, unable to negotiate a ransom for the captured Saracens, massacres them all. While the Crusaders march south to Jaffa, they are constantly harassed by Saracen troops led by Kamil, who foolishly provokes them into an attack in which the Saracens are defeated. Back at camp, Saladin and his adviser Baha ad-Din rebuke Kamil for being too impetuous. Later Kamil vindicates himself by attacking and killing many members of a foraging party of which Will and Gavin are members. The two brothers are spared but Gavin is badly wounded in the arm and Kamil takes Hosanna captive. He becomes as smitten with the horse as Will.

Kamil, who continues to believe Saladin is too compassionate, is secretly led by the traitorous Abdul Raq, to the mountain stronghold of Rahid ed-Din Sinan, a fanatical Muslim known as the Man of the Mountain, who believes all Westerners must die. Kamil falls under this militant's spell, and later agrees to lead Saladin into an ambush where he will be killed. At the last minute, however, Kamil has a change of heart and Saladin is saved.

Gavin's arm becomes infected and has to be amputated. He becomes so despondent that Will fears he will withdraw completely. Only Will's reassurance and his many displays of brotherly love save Gavin's life. The months of carnage drag on and finally Saladin asks for one last battle whose outcome will decide the war. Richard agrees, and Saladin graciously gives the Crusaders ten horses to even the odds. Will is overjoyed when he sees that one of them is Hosanna. The battle ends in a stalemate and Richard and Saladin, realizing that peace is imperative, sign an agreement allowing Christians access to the

Holy Places. Will is one of the first to enter Jerusalem and is privileged to view fragments of the True Cross. Soon he and Gavin board a ship heading for Europe and home. Of the four hundred Crusaders who left Hartslove, only fifteen are returning.

At the castle, Ellie is being held a virtual prisoner. The villainous constable Piers de Scabious has taken over after spreading a false rumor that all three of the de Granvilles have died in the Crusade. He unfairly accuses Ellie of having an affair with Brother Ranulf, the monk who has been secretly teaching her to read and write, and announces that he plans to marry Ellie. She refuses. Just when chances of escape seem hopeless, a miracle occurs. The brothers and Hosanna arrive home ready to start life anew. It is now 1193. They have weathered the Crusade and though now completely changed, they are confident that the future will be better.

Passages for Booktalking

Some interesting passages: Will chooses Hosanna (pp. 22–29); Hosanna proves his worth against Gavin's Montlouis (pp. 35–39); Gavin rides Hosanna and the aftermath (pp. 43–48); Saladin takes Jerusalem and Kamil thinks about his father's death (pp. 73–78) and has his revenge (pp. 78–80).

Themes and Subjects

This book effectively portrays the waste and futility of war particularly of war based on faith. Two contrasting Muslim personalities are presented: Saladin, who represents the benevolent, learned traditional Muslim; and the fanatical hate-filled Old Man of the Mountain, who leads a group of suicidal extremists. Impetuous young Kamil wavers between the two. The novel is also about maturing, particularly in the case of Will who "had gone away a youth, untried and untested . . . and had returned a full-fledged crusading knight." Other important subjects: friendship, loyalty, brotherly love, horses, the Crusades, King Richard I, Saladin, honor, chivalry, knighthood, battles, sieges, death, feudal England, Middle Ages, learning, monasteries, villainy, English history, Christianity, Islam, and the power of faith.

JINKS, CATHERINE. *Pagan's Crusade.* Candlewick, 2003, $15.99 (978-0-7636-2019-6); pap. Candlewick, $6.99 (978-0-7636-2584-9) (Grades 6–10)

Introduction

Australian author Catherine Jinks has written more than thirty books for young adults and children. Born in Brisbane, Queensland, in 1963, she majored in medieval history at the University of Sydney. During a short time spent in Nova Scotia, Canada, with her husband, she turned to full-time writing, before returning to her native land. *Pagan's Crusade* is the first in a four-book cycle about irrepressible, smart-alecky 16-year-old Pagan who is a squire to the pure and gallant Lord Roland. In the second book, *Pagan in Exile* (Candlewick, 2004, $16.99; 0763620203), the two return from the Holy Land to Lord Roland's family castle in France to recruit volunteers for another crusade. Lord Roland's family is brutish and ill-mannered, constantly at war among themselves and with their neighbors. Soon the two are also involved in a local squabble with the Church about a group of heretics. *Pagan's Vows* (Candlewick, 2004, $16.99; 0773620211) is set in the Abbey of Saint Martin, where Roland and Pagan have renounced violence and are taking vows to become monks. However, Pagan discovers that someone is stealing alms and that there is a bribery scheme to cover up a church official's pedophilia. The last book, *Pagan's Scribe* (Candlewick, 2005, $16.99; 0763629731), takes place twenty years later, in 1209. Pagan is now 39 and the Archdeacon of Carcassonne. He must contend with a marauding army of discontented Crusaders searching for heretics. The first three books in the series are narrated by Pagan and the last by Isidore, his bookish clerk. Each can be read separately but are more enjoyable if read in sequence. As the series progresses, the adult subject matter increases. *Pagan's Crusade* is divided into three time periods: May 1187, July 1187, and September 1187.

Historical Background

In the Middle Ages, the Knights Templar—or Order of the Temple—became a symbol of chivalry and purity because of both their monastic, disciplined way of life and their bravery on the battlefield. The order was founded during the Crusades and lasted for approximately two hundred years. Their distinctive garb was a white tunic emblazoned with a red cross. They were founded in about 1119 shortly after the First Crusade when a French nobleman gathered eight knights together to form a group whose purpose was to protect pilgrims traveling to the Holy Places in Palestine. Their headquarters was on Jerusalem's Temple Mount, supposedly where the Temple of Solomon once stood and the Ark of the Covenant was stored. There, a mosque was turned into a church called Templum Domini, and thus the order became the Knights Templar. The group was financed by gifts from the papacy and nobility and soon became a strong financial and military presence in the western world. In 1139, Pope Innocent II issued a papal bull that granted the group tax-free status, free passage anywhere, and the obligation to report only to the Pope. Well trained and well equipped, they became the elite fighting force of the day. They took vows never to retreat in battle unless such special circumstances prevailed, such as being outnumbered at least three to one. Gradually both their military and political functions declined. They ran afoul of Pope Clement V and in the early 14th century became a persecuted sect that was formally dissolved in 1314.

The Church of the Holy Sepulchre figures in the novel. It is located in the old walled city of Jerusalem, and was supposedly built on the site of Golgotha (Calvary) where Jesus was crucified and buried. Emperor Constantine had the first church built in the 4th century. This was destroyed by the Muslims and later rebuilt. The renovations of 1555 made the last major changes to the structure.

Sultan Saladin (1137–1193) is also an important character in *The Blood Red Horse* (also in this chapter). He was Sultan of Egypt and a great opponent of the Crusaders. He spread his conquests eastward to free the Muslim holy places from the Christians. He scored a great victory at the Battle of Hattin in 1187 and laid siege briefly to Jerusalem before it fell to his mighty military machine in the same year. He was noted as a great builder as well as a man of learning, nobility, and justice.

Principal Characters

Pagan Kidrouk, a 16-year-old squire
Rockhead or Sergeant Tibald, a soldier
Lord Roland Roucy de Bram, Pagan's knight
Brother Cavin, a monk in charge of the infirmary
Sergeant Bonetus, another soldier
Joselin, a scheming low-life
Berrold and Hamo, two more thugs
Heraclius, Patriarch of Jerusalem
Balian, Lord of Ibelin, leader of the Jerusalem forces
Malik al-Adin, the sultan's brother
Yusuf Salah ed-Din, or Saladin, the Sultan
Lord Felix, another defender of Jerusalem

Plot Synopsis

It is May 1187 in the fair city of Jerusalem, and 16-year-old Pagan Kidrouk has made a momentous decision. Actually, with half the low-lifes of Jerusalem—including members of the dreaded Silver Ring gang—after him for numerous shady deals and non-payment of gambling debts, he has no choice. Pagan is an orphan. He was raised and regularly abused by monks in a neighboring monastery until, at the age of 10, he escaped along with Joselin onto the streets of Jerusalem, where he has been living by his wits and his ability to read and write, an unusual talent at this time. Now facing terrible reprisals by his enemies, he seeks sanctuary by becoming a squire to one of the Knights Templar. Even his glib, witty banter, however, can't protect him from the no-nonsense orientation and arduous work schedule provided by Sergeant Tibald whom he nicknames Rockhead. Things improve when he is introduced to his knight and master, a French Templar named Lord Roland Roucy de Bram, a paragon of nobility and purity in both appearance and behavior. Pagan seeks in vain for any flaw in Lord Roland's character and comes to admire him so greatly that he secretly calls him Saint George.

Their first assignment is to protect a motley group of pilgrims, day trippers to the River Jordan, from roving brigands. The journey becomes, for Pagan, a comedy of errors particularly when the tour guide is revealed to be Pagan's former friend and world-renowned scam artist, Joselin, who at one point offers to sell his gullible clients a fragment of the Pillar of Salt that was Lot's wife. The pilgrims are dismayed to learn that they can only take back eight bottles each of the river water. This will cut into their profits when they return home. After saving several water-logged pilgrims from drowning and resisting Joselin's offer to make money by referring prospective customers to him, Pagan returns to Jerusalem with the rest of the group. Annoyed at Pagan's uncooperative attitude, Joselin leads him into an ambush where two thugs, Berrold and Hamo, begin beating him mercilessly for his unpaid debts. He is saved by the intervention of Lord Roland, his Knight in Shining Armor (one of Pagan's duties is to keep it shining). Pagan is taken to Brother Cavin's infirmary for treatment. Though risking dismissal, Pagan tells Lord Roland the full story of his unsavory past. With characteristic nobility, Lord Roland forgives the boy and vows, with God's help, to save Pagan from further temptations. Indeed, thinks Pagan, he is a saint in knight's clothing. However, Pagan notices a soupçon of a grin on Lord Roland's face after hearing one of his particularly witty and cutting remarks. Could his lordship's robes be hiding feet of clay? Probably not.

News reaches Jerusalem that many of the coastal cities in Palestine are falling to the invading army of infidels led by Sultan Saladin. Realizing that Jerusalem is next, high-level talks begin between the patriarch of the city; the commander of the troops, Lord Balian; and the leader of the Templars, Lord Roland. Preparations for a siege are made. A special prayer service is held at the Church of the Holy Sepulchre. Pagan is given the responsibility of policing the mob outside the church. An unhinged zealot arouses the crowd to violence and Pagan loses control. Once again, Lord Roland appears and restores order. Later Lord Roland learns that his superior, the Grand Master, whom he venerates, has broken the rules of the order by capitulating to the enemy during coastal fighting. This causes Lord Roland to question his faith in the Templars to the point of doubting his proclaimed purpose in life. Amazingly, Pagan is able to reassure him and restore his confidence.

The Saracens soon appear outside the city's gates. Their forces vastly out-number those of the Christians. A delegation led by Saladin's brother, Malik al-Adin, delivers an ultimatum: Surrender or every inhabitant will be slaugh-tered. Balian refuses and the fighting begins. The inhabitants of the city fight gallantly but their losses are enormous and the better-equipped invaders soon gain the upper hand and create a breach in the walls. With dwindling supplies and no hope of deliverance, the leaders, with the exception of Lord Felix, who has a martyr complex, decide to negotiate a peace with Saladin. During a tough bargaining session, the price of ransoming the citizens from slavery is hammered out. The agreed amounts range from a low of 1 dinar for a pauper to a high of 50 dinars for each knight. Unfortunately, there is not enough money in the city's treasury to rescue everyone and, in typical fashion, Lord Roland refuses to be ransomed in order to save as many as fifty other souls. Pagan pleads with him to change his mind, but Lord Roland is adamant. His great love for his master drives Pagan to desperation and he openly accuses Lord Roland of being stupid in sacrificing his life for a group of "scabby, snot-nosed" paupers. To silence Pagan, Lord Roland slaps him and immediately afterward begs Pagan's forgiveness.

Saladin permits another meeting with the conquered leaders to listen to their special petitions. After both the patriarch and Lord Balian get permis-sion to set more captives free without additional payment, Pagan boldly steps forward and, in spite of protests from Lord Roland, makes a special plea to save his master's life by recounting all of the good, unselfish works he has done. There is a long pause, and Saladin replies, "Your master is an enemy of the faith but Allah honors those who honor widows and orphans. Very well, I will grant this request." True to form, Lord Roland later accuses Pagan of dis-obedience and demands that he never try to save his life again. Pagan refuses with the words, "How can I? My Lord, have some mercy. Don't you under-stand? You're all I have left."

The two make plans to leave Palestine and go to Lord Roland's family castle in France. The journey to the ocean is slower than necessary because Lord Roland insists of taking care of refugees along the way.

Passages for Booktalking

Some amusing passages are: Pagan is indoctrinated by Rockhead (pp. 1–8); Pagan meets Lord Roland (pp. 11–19); the beginning of the pilgrimage to the River Jordan (pp. 49–59); and at the river (pp. 49–59).

Themes and Subjects

The opening chapters consist of picaresque incidents that resemble the zany, irreverent picture of the Middle Ages found in the musical *Spamalot* or many

Monty Python skits. The mood changes from the hilarious to the more serious as the siege progresses. Pagan's love and devotion for his master produce some poignant and moving episodes. His transformation from an irresponsible, sassy delinquent to a caring, brave squire is realistically portrayed. The contrast between Pagan's pragmatic, often jaundiced view, of the world and Lord's Roland's purity and idealism is sometimes humorous and sometimes touching. Authentic details of life in medieval times are well integrated into the plot. Some other subjects are: chivalry, pilgrimages, Crusades, knighthood, squires, Knights Templar, courage, death, sieges, warfare, Saracens, Saladin, religion, Jerusalem, humorous stories, adventure stories.

RUSSELL, CHRISTOPHER. *Dogboy.* Greenwillow, 2006, $15.99 (978-0-06-084116-4) (Grades 4–7)

Introduction

Russell Christopher was born on the Isle of Wight, an island off the south coast of England facing the port cities of Portsmouth and Southampton. The beaches, fields, and rocky coves of the island became his playground. After marriage and three children, he gave up trying to be a full-time writer and got a steady job as a postman. It was then, in 1975, that he sold his first script. Since then he has written for such British television shows as *EastEnders* and *A Touch of Frost*. His first book for young readers was *Dogboy* (titled *Brind and the Dogs of War* in the U.K.), the story of a kennel boy, Brind, who speaks to dogs, understands their behavior, and is able to lead them. Set against the background of the early part of the Hundred Years War, it is a tale of heroism and adventure. In the sequel *Hunted* (Greenwillow, 2007, $15.99; 0060841192), called *Plague Sorcerer* in the U.K., the Black Death sweeps across England, killing Lady Beatrice at Dowe Manor where Brind lives. An ambitious, ruthless monk accuses Brind and the young French servant Aurelie of being "agents of the Devil" and "plague bringers." A grief-stricken Sir Edmund Dowe throws Brind and Aurelie out and, along with the dog Glaive and puppy Gabion, they wander through hostile country until rescued by a beautiful outlaw named Chanterelle and her band. But further adventures await Brind and Company in their attempts to return to Dowe Manor. *Smugglers*, another historical adventure by the author, has not yet been published in the United States. It tells of a boy who is forced to become a smuggler to support his family. Mr. Russell has said that history is important because it is "where we come from that leads up to where we are today."

Historical Background

The Hundred Years War is the term used to link together a series of wars between France and England that actually lasted 116 years, from 1337 to 1453. Its origins date back to the Norman Conquest of England in 1066. After this successful invasion, the subsequent kings of England, through heredity and marriage, claimed to be the rulers of various parts of France and, sometimes, of the entire country. The first phase of the Hundred Years War is known as the Edwardian War (1337–1360). King Edward III of England (1312–1377) revived his claim to the throne of France through his mother Isabella, the daughter of Philip IV of France. After several skirmishes, fighting began in earnest when, on July 5, 1346, Edward, in the company of his 16-year-old son, known as the Black Prince, set sail from Portsmouth with 750 ships and 7,000 to 10,000 men (estimates vary) to conquer France. He marched through Normandy gaining a victory at the storming of Caen, and then met in full battle the French forces led by King Philip VI (1293–1350). Though greatly outnumbered (10,000 English to 20,000 French troops), Edward scored a brilliant victory at the Battle of Crecy. Unopposed, Edward laid siege to and later captured Calais in 1347. This economic and military base remained in the hands of the English until 1558, when it was lost during the reign of Mary Tudor. From 1348 through 1350 hostilities were disrupted by the Plague known as the Black Death, which reduced Europe's population by about a third. There were subsequent invasions, one led by the Black Prince and the other by Edward. At the end of this phase, Edward had added to his holdings in France but renounced his claim to the French throne. Later kings continued to consider themselves heirs to the French throne but, eventually, the presence and importance of the English in France declined particularly after the appearance of Joan of Arc (1412–1431). The wars ended with England holding only Calais. The title king of France was finally abandoned in 1801.

Principal Characters

Brind, a 12-year-old dogboy
Sir Edmund Dowe, lord of Dowe Manor
Tullo, Sir Edmund's ambitious servant
Hatton, the young carter at the manor
Lady Beatrice, Sir Edmund's wife
Philip, Sir Edmund's page
Glaive, the leader of Sir Edmund's pack of mastiffs
Sir Richard Baret, a handsome, arrogant knight
Aurelie, a 10-year-old French waif

Lucien de Peronne, a French knight
Earl of Arundel, Sir Edmund's liege lord
Captain Claret, master of the *The Gannet*

Plot Synopsis

Brind is being chased by a pack of howling mastiffs. He attempts to escape the dogs by climbing a cliff but falls. The dogs surround him and their leader begins licking his face. The running of the dogs has been successful and all, including Tullo, the servant who supervised the exercise, return to Sir Edmund Dowe's manor house where they live. The year is 1346, and Sir Edmund, a bumbling, good-natured but impoverished knight manages Dowe's Manor on a declining budget with the help of his wife, Lady Beatrice. His dwindling retinue includes the devious head servant, Tullo; his page, a gangling awkward boy of 13 named Philip; his carter, young Hatton; and the unusual dogboy Brind, who lives in the stable with Sir Edmund's pride and joy, the eighty mastiffs that are the prize pack in all of England.

Brind was found as a baby twelve years before. He was in the stable with a litter of puppies, and he has remained there ever since under the immediate control of Tullo who constantly mistreats him. Brind knows the sight, sound, and scent of the dogs and has an almost spiritual bond with them, particularly with the leader, Glaive, who obeys Brind like a slave.

Sir Edmund is summoned by his king, Edward, through his liege lord Sir Arundel to participate in a noble enterprise, the invasion of France. Despite the misgivings of Lady Beatrice, he collects his outmoded and rusty armor and weapons and, along with Tullo, Hatton, Philip, Brind, and a pack of forty male mastiffs, leaves for the coastal port of Portsmouth, where the troops are to assemble. While there, Tullo tries to impress the knights by baiting the mastiffs into showing their savagery but, to Tullo's annoyance, Brind intervenes and calms them. This episode is seen by Sir Richard Baret, a handsome, wealthy English knight. When they are unloading the cargo on the beach in France, the ropes used to transfer Sir Edmund's cart from the ship snap, and the wagon, Hatton, Brind, and the dogs plunge into the sea. Brind, who can't swim, grabs Glaive's collar and the dog carries him to shore where he is joined by the other dogs and Hatton. After they have established camp, Sir Edmund is visited by Sir Richard, who offers Sir Edmund a magnificent suit of armor in exchange for Brind. Though he is in dire need of armor that will truly protect him, Sir Edmund declines the offer.

Two days after taking the French city of Caen, the English encamp outside the village of Crecy. A fierce battle takes place and the English, though greatly outnumbered, score a glorious victory. During the battle, Sir Edmund calls for his mastiffs to enter the fray. The timing is wrong and all are killed except

Glaive, who is badly wounded and creeps off into the forest. At the end of the battle, Hatton is dead and Sir Edmund and Philip are missing. Tullo, who blames Brind for the loss of the dogs, assaults him brutally. That evening, Brind escapes into the forest to look for Glaive.

There he encounters a young French girl, aged 10, whose name is Aurelie. Along with her mother and two thousand other women and children, she has been cast out of Calais leaving only the men to withstand the forthcoming siege by Edward. She is hoping to find news about her father, a French soldier who fought at Crecy. Aurelie and Brind join forces but before long find themselves the prisoners of Sir Richard Baret and his followers. Sir Richard hopes that Aurelie will cook for his men and Brind will care for his deerhounds. That night the two are tied together, but Aurelie, who has stolen a knife from the kitchen, frees them. Before stealing away from the camp, they look into Sir Richard's cache of war spoils, where Aurelie discovers her father's brooch, a sign that he had been killed in the battle. Back in the forest, they find Glaive near death in a cave. He has an open, festering wound almost the entire length of his body. They nurse him for days surviving on nuts, berries, mushrooms, and fish caught in a local stream.

In the meantime, Sir Edmund, captured at Crecy, is living a luxurious life as the "prisoner" of the French knight Lucien de Peronne, who does all he can to make Sir Edmund welcome and comfortable. Philip the page is dispatched to England with the terms for Sir Edmund's ransom, although Sir Edmund knows his coffers will yield very little. Tullo discovers Brind, Aurelie, and Glaive in the forest and tries to take them prisoner. Philip happens on the scene and is killed defending Brind and his friends. Independently both Tullo and Brind discover the whereabouts of Sir Edmund from documents left by Philip. Brind and his friends escape from Tullo and get to Sir Edmund first. He welcomes the travelers to Lucien's hunting lodge. Tullo then arrives and concocts a fiendish plan. He blocks the exit doors and sets fire to the lodge. Quick-thinking Aurelie pushes her friends into the hearth, where all but Lucien survive the inferno. Thinking they are all dead, Tullo books passage to England where he plans to become the master of Dowe Manor. His role in the fire is revealed by an earthenware pot he accidentally left outside the lodge.

The survivors leave for Calais. Sir Edmund has an accident on the way and urges the others to go on ahead. At the siege camp, Brind is again claimed as a vassal by Sir Richard, but Sir Edmund makes a fortuitous appearance in time to save Brind, Aurelie, and his mastiff Glaive. Aurelie discovers her mother's grave outside Calais and after placing her father's brooch there decides that there is no future for her in France. She joins Sir Edmund when he gets permission to return to England with Brind and Glaive. They book passage on *The Gannet*, whose skipper is Captain Claret. The voyage is hellish and the ship sinks, but our heroes make it to shore. They arrive back at Dowe Manor in time to foil Tullo's plans to take over. While trying to escape, he falls into the dogs' pen and is killed. Brind returns to his life in the stables with the dogs, Aurelie becomes a surrogate daughter at Dowe Manor, and, one hopes, Sir Edmund and Lady Beatrice live happily ever after.

Passages for Booktalking

Brind is chased by the dogs (pp. 1–5); he saves the mastiffs from Tullo's baiting (pp. 25–28); the cart falls into the water (pp. 35–39); and Sir Edmund is visited by Sir Richard, who wants Brind (pp. 41–46).

Themes and Subjects

This is basically a suspenseful historical adventure filled with impossible coincidences and incredible escapes. The legendary splendor of the age of chivalry is somewhat tarnished in its presentation here but conditions in feudal England are realistically portrayed. Brind, for all of his singleness of purpose (he lives only for the dogs), is an engaging hero and Sir Edmund, a lovable albeit unpredictable knight. Other subjects: the Hundred Years War, France, England, courage, dogs, sea stories, adventure stories, knights and knighthood, the Battle of Crecy, arms and armor, and villainy.

ADDITIONAL SELECTIONS

Armstrong, Alan. *Raleigh's Page* (Random, 2007, $16.99) (Grades 4–7)
    In this adventure novel set in 1584 London, 11-year-old Andrew becomes a page to Sir Walter Raleigh rather than the carpenter's apprentice he hoped to become.

Armstrong, Alan. *Whittington* (Random, 2005, $14.95) (Grades 5–8)
    Told by an ancestor of Dick Whittington's cat, this is a tale of 14th-century derring-do and the adventures of Whittington and his feline companion.

Beaufrand, Mary Jane. *Primavera* (Little, 2008, $16.99) (Grades 7–10)
    Flora, a member of the outlawed Pazzi family in Renaissance Florence, must work undercover in a goldsmith's shop in fear that her family's enemies, the Medicis, will find her.

Cadnum, Michael. *The King's Arrow* (Viking, 2008, $16.99) (Grades 5–10)
    When an arrow shot by Walter Tirel, a Norman lord, goes astray and kills the king, he and his squire, Simon, must flee to France in this novel set in England after the Norman Conquest.

Chandler, Pauline. *Warrior Girl: A Novel of Joan of Arc* (Greenwillow, 2006, $17.99) (Grades 7–10)
    As told by a mute cousin and friend of Joan, this is the story of the young French girl who led her country to victory over the English and later became a martyr to her cause.

Finney, Patricia. *Feud* (Delacorte, 2006, $7.95) (Grades 4–7)
  As narrated by one of Queen Elizabeth I's maids of honor, this is a story of court life with all its diversions and intrigues.

Flanagan, John. *The Icebound Land* (Philomel, 2007, $16.99) (Grades 4–7)
  In this story set in the Middle Ages, Will, a ranger's apprentice, and the Princess Evanlyn are captured and made slaves but they hope for rescue by their friends the rangers and Horace, a young knight in training. This is part of the Ranger's Apprentice series.

Grove, Vicki. *Rhiannon* (Putnam, 2007, $18.99) (Grades 6–9)
  In 12th-century England, 14-year-old Rhia, whose family members are considered outcasts, must join the community to help a boy who is falsely convicted of murder.

Haahr, Berit. *The Minstrel's Tale* (Delacorte, 2000, $15.95) (Grades 6–9)
  In medieval England, the musically talented Judith runs away from her elderly husband to join a band of minstrels.

Holmes, Victoria. *The Horse from the Sea* (HarperCollins, 2005, $15.99) (Grades 5–8)
  In 1588 coastal Ireland during the war between England and Spain, Nora must decide whether or not to help a young Spanish sailor who has survived a shipwreck.

Lawlor, Laurie. *Dead Reckoning* (Simon, 2005, $15.95) (Grades 6–9)
  Fifteen-year-old Emmet Drake spends a wretched but exciting year as a page aboard the *Golden Hind*, the ship commanded by his cousin, Sir Francis Drake.

McDonnell, Kathleen. *1212: The Year of the Journey* (Second Story, 2007, pap. $9.95) (Grades 6–8)
  This is the story of three young people—Etienne, a young shepherd; Abel, a Jewish student; and Blanche, an orphan—as they embark on the Children's Crusade to the Holy Land.

Malone, Patricia. *Legend of Lady Ilena* (Random, 2002, $15.95) (Grades 6–9)
  Fifteen-year-old warrior Ilena has a series of adventures carrying out her father's dying wishes in this novel set in 6th-century Britain.

Morris, Gerald. *The Quest of the Fair Unknown* (Houghton, 2006, $16) (Grades 5–8)
  Set in Arthurian times, this novel tells of an innocent named Beaufils who, after his mother dies, sets out to find his father at Camelot.

Rinaldi, Ann. *The Redheaded Princess* (HarperCollins, 2008, $15.99) (Grades 6–9)
  Filled with intrigue and political treachery, this is the story of young Princess Elizabeth, who would later become one of England's greatest monarchs.

Schlitz, Laura Amy. *Good Masters! Sweet Ladies!* (Candlewick, 2007, $19.99) (Grades 5–9)
  This Newbery Medal winner consists of a number of brilliant monologues that depict various young people from different occupations and backgrounds and their lives in a manor house in medieval England.

Springer, Nancy. *Wild Boy: A Tale of Rowen Hood* (Putnam, 2004, $16.99) (Grades 3–6)

Young Rook, the wild boy of the Sherwood Forest outlaws that include Robin Hood and his daughter Rowen, finds the son of the wicked sheriff of Nottingham caught in a mantrap. Should he save him? This is part of an ongoing adventure series.

Thomas, Jane Rush. *The Counterfeit Princess* (Clarion, 2005, $15) (Grades 5–8)

A young English girl becomes involved in dangerous intrigue because she bears an uncanny resemblance to Princess, later Queen, Elizabeth.

Thomson, Sarah L. *The Secret of the Rose* (Greenwillow, 2006, $16.99) (Grades 6–8)

Set in England in 1592, this novel recounts the experiences of 14-year-old Rosalind and her younger brother when they flee to London after their father is arrested for being a Catholic.

Wright, Randall. *Hunchback* (Holt, 2004, $16.95) (Grades 6–9)

Fourteen-year-old Hodge, a hunchback orphan in medieval times, becomes a servant to royalty and gets involved in a series of intrigues and adventures.

SEVENTEENTH THROUGH NINETEENTH CENTURIES

BAJORIA, PAUL. *The Printer's Devil.* Little, Brown, 2005, $16.99 (978-0-316-01090-0); pap. $6.99 (978-0-316-10678-8) (Grades 6–9)

Introduction

The author, now in his 40s, is a successful producer of quiz programs on BBC radio. Regarding why he writes for young readers, he has said, "The magic of fiction is somehow broken once childhood is gone. . . . The ability to cast that spell for others has always seemed something special and enviable." He completed his first novel shortly after leaving university. It was rejected by publishers and filed away. Years later he reworked it and it became *The Printer's Devil*, his first published book. It takes place in London in the early part of the 19th century and involves a printer's apprentice (devil) named Mog Winter, who narrates this suspenseful yarn. The main action takes place over a six-day period. Each chapter is accompanied by an atmospheric illustration by Bret Bertholf. This is the first installment in a trilogy about Mog and Nick, twin orphans. In the second book, *The God of Mischief* (Little, Brown, 2007, $16.99; 0316010917), the two are sent to live with their closest living relative, Sir Septimus Clay, at his estate in the English countryside. Mysterious events occur including Nick's near-death from a falling gargoyle, Mog's narrow escape from decapitation by a malfunctioning dumb waiter, and the hanging of their governess. More secrets about their past are revealed but the two realize they must escape the manor house and the odd doings in the nearby town or be killed. The third volume, *The City of Spirits*, was published in the United Kingdom in late 2007 with American publication to follow. In it Mog and Nick Winter travel to Calcutta, India, where they were born and where the famous Winter diamond is housed. They find that the diamond has sinister powers and, while they pursue their quest, the two seem to be followed by the shadowy figure of DAMYATA.

Historical Background

Some terms and places referred to in the text may be unfamiliar to American readers. Fleet Street is named after the Fleet River, now the largest of London's subterranean rivers. At one time the river was exposed and there were commercial establishments on its banks. In time, it became the center of the printing trade (the famous printing pioneer Wynkyn de Worde established his printing shop on Fleet Street in 1500). However, the river became so polluted and such a disease carrier that is was gradually closed over, although parts were still exposed at the time of this novel.

Clerkenwell, where Mr. Cramplock's printing establishment was located, is now part of the Borough of Islington, north of the City. It is named after the Clerk's Well (in Farringdon) that functioned in the Middle Ages. Part of the well still exists.

Newgate Prison was situated on the corner of Newgate Street and the Old Bailey in the City of London. It served as a prison from 1188 to 1902.

The term *Bow Street Runners* refers to London's first professional constables or policemen. They were founded by the judge Henry Fielding, better known as the author of *Tom Jones*. Named because they were attached to the Bow Street magistrate's office (Number 4 Bow Street), they were paid from government funds. This became the model in the development of local police force organization for almost a century in England

A *bosun* is a boatswain, the ship's officer in charge of equipment and the crew; to *scarper* is British slang for to run away or to escape, probably originally from Cockney rhyming slang (Scapa Flow, to go). A watermark is a faint design made in the paper during manufacturing. Quality papermakers each had their own distinct watermark, which was visible only when the paper was held up to light.

Principal Characters

Mog Winter, the narrator, a 12-year-old printer's devil (apprentice)
Mr. Cramplock, Mog's employee, a printer in Clerkenwell
Lash, Mog's dog

Cockburn or Coben, an escaped convict
Mr. Flethick, a man who owes Mr. Cramplock money
Jiggs, Coben's accomplice
Tassie, a tavern owner
Nick, a street urchin
Pa or the Bosun, Nick's father
Ma (Mrs.) Muggerage, Nick's cruel keeper
Man from Calcutta, a mysterious stranger
Mr. Spintwice, a dwarf who is a jeweler
Mr. Fellman, a papermaker
Mr. Follyfeather, a Customs House employee
Cricklebone, a policeman one of the Bow Street Runners
DAMYATA, perhaps the Man from Calcutta
McAuchinleck, another policeman

Plot Synopsis

Mog Winter is a 12-year-old printer's devil at Mr. Cramplock's printing shop in Clerkenwell, London, in the early part of the 19th century. He is busy turning out copies of a poster for the Magistrates Office warning that a dangerous convict named Cockburn has escaped prison and is at large. The fierce face of the man on the posters sends shivers down Mog's back with each copy he takes from the press.

Mog knows little of his past except that his mother died giving birth on a ship bound to England from India. The only memento he has of her is a bangle he keeps in a tin can with a few other precious belongings. When he was still young, he was adopted out of an orphanage to become Mr. Cramplock's apprentice.

Mog is a hardworking, upstanding youngster with such delicate features that he is sometimes mistaken for a girl. His printing assignment is interrupted to perform two errands for Mr. Cramplock. The first is go to the Doll Head Tavern to purchase lunch from its kindly mistress, Tassie, and the second is to present a bill for printing service to Mr. Flethick at Corporation Row. Mog is accompanied on both calls by his faithful dog, Lash. At Flethick's house, Mog finds that he and his guests are smoking dope and are in a narcotic daze. While they babble incoherently about the Sun of Calcutta, Flethick takes the bill and contemptuously burns it, after warning Mog to be silent about what he has seen. On his way back to the shop, Mog passes a macabre-looking man with piercing eyes and a pointed mustache who glares at him. At Tassie's the next day, Mog learns that the *Sun of Calcutta* is a ship that just arrived from India. Mog decides to do some investigating.

At the dock he notices two shifty, menacing types exchanging money with a customs man before leaving on with a cart carrying a valuable-looking carved chest. Convinced that they are criminals who have used bribery to obtain the chest, Mog follows them. While on the trail, he is accosted by a man who mistakenly believes Mog to be someone named Nick whose Pa, the bosun of the *Sun of Calcutta*, is out to thrash him. After resuming the chase, Mog is suddenly hit by a brick. He regains consciousness in a squalid room, a prisoner of the two crooks, who call each other Coben and Jiggs. They interrogate him about a camel and a man from Calcutta. Getting no information from Mog, they lock him in the empty chest and leave. Hours later, he hears the chest being unlocked. He emerges to see the man with the pointed mustache. He believes this to be the Man from Calcutta but without waiting for explanations Mog races from the room, grabbing some papers from the table on his way.

Back at his room in Cramplock's shop, Mog peruses the papers. On one there is a list of names. Another is a receipt from the dishonest customs man, Mr. Follyfeather, written on paper with a strange watermark of a curled-up dog. The next day, before starting work, Mog again does some sleuthing. He sneaks onto the *Sun of Calcutta* and in Captain Shakeshere's cabin finds many documents about DAMYATA, whom Mog believes to be an Indian trader and somehow connected to these mysterious happenings. He traces Captain Shakeshere to the Three Friends Inn but gets no information from him. So he decides to visit the Bosun at the Lion's Mane Inn. In an underground chamber at the inn, he finds and frees a boy about his age called Nick, who is being held prisoner by the vicious Mrs. Muggerage, the mistress of Nick's father, the Bosun.

Nick's mother also died when he was very young, and he and Mog, two lookalikes, become immediate friends. In an old storeroom, Nick shows Mog hidden treasure from his father's latest voyage—a brass ornament shaped like a camel and about a foot tall. Promising to return, Mog takes off, narrowly missed by Mrs. Muggerage's flying meat cleaver. At Mr. Cramplock's, Mog finds that his room has been rifled and his tin box containing his mother's bangle and the papers he took while a prisoner are gone. He also accidentally discovers that the name of the escaped convict Cockburn is pronounced Coben. Mog realizes that he is in the middle of a dangerous, indeed deadly, game.

With Nick's help, Mog steals the camel and hides it in his room. However, because he sees the Man from Calcutta skulking about the building and often gets mysterious threatening notes, he decides to move the camel. Nick takes it to a jeweler friend, a dwarf named Mr. Spintwice, a benevolent man who consents to look after the ornament. Before hiding it, they discover that the body of the camel is filled with a white power that makes Mog dizzy when he accidentally breathes some. Mr. Spintwice substitutes flour for this powder and puts the camel away. Later, following a lead from a note he has received, Mog goes to the Three Friends Inn where he witnesses a conspiratorial meeting between Coben and a rich man referred to as His Lordship.

The plot becomes more complex when Jiggs, Coben's accomplice, is reported dead and Mr. Spintwice is robbed of the camel. With the help of Mr. Cramp-lock, Mog is able to trace the watermark of the curled-up dog to a crooked papermaker, Mr. Fellman. Again he investigates. At Fellman's mill, he hides in a barrel of a glue-like substance to avoid discovery and overhears a conversa-tion between Fellman and the customs man, Mr. Follyfeather, about forthcom-ing events involving Flethink and His Lordship. Back at Mr. Spintwice's, Mog realizes that the glue he is covered with is hardening. Despites great protesta-tions, Nick and Mr. Spintwice force Mog to take a bath. Then an amazing rev-elation is made. Mog is not a boy but a girl! It was easy to assume this identity after being dressed as a boy in the orphanage. Being a boy meant receiving greater privileges and opportunities than were available to a girl—like becom-ing a printer's devil. All swear to keep Mog's secret.

Soon, with the help of Cricklebone, a policeman, one of the Bow Street Runners, and the detective McAuchinleck, who often assumed the disguise of the Man from Calcutta, the plot unfolds. With the papers that he stole from Mog's room, when McAuchinleck was disguised as the Man from Calcutta, names of a large smuggling and dope trafficking ring are uncovered and soon a police net has captured and convicted many perpetrators including the leader, His Lordship, and the three F's—Fellman, Flethick, and Follyfeather. Newgate Prison suddenly has a number of new tenants. Coben, trapped in a bell tower, falls to his death and the Bosun, fleeing from the police with the camel, falls into the Thames and drowns. When, the contents of the tin box are returned to Mog, Nick sees the bangle and produces another one exactly the same that belonged to his mother. Mog and Nick realize that they are twins. They set out to discover more about their identity and such unanswered questions as the identity of DAMYATA.

Passages for Booktalking
Some exciting episodes are: Mog and the Cockburn poster (pp. 1–6); Mog presents the bill to Mr. Flethick (pp. 23–29); he first encounters the Man from Calcutta (pp. 29–31) and Mog is caught by Coben and Jiggs (pp. 57–64).

Themes and Subjects
In the true spirit of Joan Aiken and Leon Garfield, the author has created a rip-roaring, suspenseful thriller that races from one cliff-hanging adventure to

another. London of the early 19th century is well created without sparing details about its pollution and immorality. Although many in the novel are stock characters, both Mog and Nick are high-spirited, enterprising central characters who struggle for their rights and, at times, for survival. Other subjects are: printing, criminals and crime fighting, drugs, smuggling, India, courage, taverns, mystery stories, and twins.

BLACKWOOD, GARY. *Shakespeare's Scribe.* Dutton, 2000, $15.99 (978-0-525-46444-0); pap. Puffin, $6.96 (978-0-14-230066-4) (Grades 5–8)

Introduction

Born in 1945, Gary Blackwood is the author of many well-received novels as well as some distinguished nonfiction titles. Intrigued by Shakespeare and by the development of a "shorthand" in Elizabethan times by Dr. Timothy Bright, he wrote an unpublished adult novel that was later reworked for young readers as *Shakespeare's Stealer* (Dutton, $16.99, 2003; 0525458630; pap. Puffin 0141305959). Its popularity led to two sequels, *Shakespeare's Scribe* and *Shakespeare's Spy* (Dutton, 2003, $16.99; 0525471456; pap. Puffin, $6.99; 0142403113) (all three are available in an omnibus volume from Dutton, $14.99; 978-0525473206 under the title *Shakespeare Stealer Series*).

The first volume introduces the narrator Widge, who by 1601 has spent 14 years in a Yorkshire orphanage before being adopted by the unprincipled Dr. Timothy Bright, a minister who has invented a system of shorthand called "charactery." He teaches this to Widge for the purpose of stealing other pastors' sermons for his own use. Widge is later sold for ten pounds to Simon Bass, a London theatrical manager. He commissions Widge to attend performances of the Lord Chamberlain's Company, of which Shakespeare is a member, to copy the manuscript of *Hamlet* so that Bass's company can perform it without paying royalties. Widge is caught, but so convincingly pretends that he is simply stage-struck, that he is taken on as an acting apprentice.

The rest of the novels deal with Widge's career as he meets and works with many of the characters that figure in the next two volumes, including the villainous Nick, who continues to be a thorn in Widge's side. Adventures include unmasking Julia, an apprentice who is masquerading as a boy, and Widge's performance as Ophelia in *Hamlet*. In *Shakespeare's Spy*, Widge infiltrates a rival acting company, the Admiral's Men, to expose the person who has been stealing scripts of Shakespeare's latest play. He also begins to write his own plays to impress an older girl who turns out to be Shakespeare's daughter Judith. All three novels can be read separately but are best read consecutively.

Historical Background

Shakespeare worked and wrote with the Lord Chamberlain's Men at the Globe Theatre in London for most of his professional career. This group was founded in 1594 (the novel takes place in 1602) during Queen Elizabeth I's reign under the patronage of the Lord Chamberlain (then Baron Hunsdon), who was in charge of court entertainment. The key players were also shareholders (or "sharers") in the company. Together they shared artistic and financial decisions and divided up the profits. Some of their phenomenal success rests with the Burbage family—first the father James and later the sons, one of whom was Richard Burbage, an actor famous for playing Hamlet and Othello. Other sharers were Thomas Pope, who died in 1603, Augustine Phillips, Robert Armin, and John Heminges. The latter co-collected and edited the famous First Folio of Shakespeare's plays in 1623. With the advent of James I in 1603, the group became known as the King's Men. The organization was dissolved with the Puritan closing of the theaters in 1642.

This theatrical group acted in different venues until they had the Globe Theatre built in 1599 at Southwark, on the south bank of the Thames. It was destroyed by fire in 1613 when a cannon misfired during a performance. It was rebuilt, but later was closed by the Puritans in 1642 and, two years later, torn down to make room for tenements. A modern reconstruction of the Globe opened in 1997 less than 200 yards from the original site.

Spread by fleas, rodents, and human contact, the bubonic plague was a constant threat to the people of Europe from the 14th through the 17th centuries. In the great outbreaks of the 1340s between one third and one half of Europe's population perished. Symptoms included black patches on the skin as well as red bumps and growing weakness. Untreated, the infection caused death in one to six days.

Love's Labour's Won is a lost play by Shakespeare. Perhaps it is (as depicted in the novel) an earlier version of *All's Well That Ends Well*. This play is about an attractive low-born girl, Helena, who manages to get the nobleman Bertram to marry her. He imposes several conditions on his bride and Helena, through cunning and deceit, is able to achieve them and keep her husband.

Principal Characters

    Widge, the narrator, an orphaned apprentice actor
    Sam Crosse, another apprentice
    Sander Cooke, another apprentice and Widge's closest friend
    William Shakespeare, a sharer and principal playwright of the Lord
        Chamberlain's Men
    Mr. John Heminges, a sharer, actor, and company manager
    Mr. Pope, an actor, sharer, and keeper of an orphanage

Mr. Armin, clown, fencing master, and sharer
Mr. Burbage, a famous actor and sharer
Tetty, a girl who is an orphan at Mr. Pope's
Salathiel (Sal) Pavy, the new apprentice
Mr. Augustine Phillips, a sharer who specializes in villain roles
Mr. Ned Shakespeare, William's younger brother, an actor
Mistress MacGregor, a worker in an orphanage
Jamie Redshaw, a man who claims to be Widge's father

Plot Synopsis

In the spring of 1602 in Elizabethan London, 14-year-old Widge, an enterprising, spirited orphan, is celebrating the end of his first year as an apprentice with the Lord Chamberlain's Men, an acting company whose headquarters are at the Globe Theatre on the south bank of the Thames River. The shareholders or "sharers" in the company are all participating actors, writers, or managers. They include William Shakespeare, the principal playwright; Mr. Heminges, the stuttering company manager; and Mr. Pope, whose home is also the orphanage where Widge lives along with fellow apprentice Sander Cooke. The other apprentice, Sam Crosse, lodges with another sharer, Mr. Augustine Phillips, an actor whose specialty is villains.

One day a notice is posted on the theatre's door proclaiming that public performance will be banned until further notice because of an outbreak of the plague. Mr. Shakespeare proposes taking the company on the road until the crisis passes. This is agreed upon, though for various reasons some participants, including Mr. Pope and Mr. Burbage, a gifted actor, decide to stay home. Widge is unhappy that his best friend Sander also elects to stay to help Mr. Pope with the orphans. Before they leave, another apprentice is hired. He is Salathiel Pavy, a handsome youngster who has starred with the Children of the Royal Chapel company across the river at Blackfriars. Sal, unfortunately is an unfriendly, aloof youngster who remains distant from the rest of the group.

The traveling company consists of four sharers—Mr. Shakespeare, Mr. Heminges, Mr. Phillips, and Robert Armin, actor and fencing master—two hired men, and the three apprentices—Widge, Sam, and Sal. Widge says a touching farewell to Sander and to Tetty, a pathetic orphaned girl who is deathly afraid of the Black Plague. The company sets out and is soon joined by Ned Shakespeare, William's dissolute younger brother and an actor. At their first acting stop, Reading, the mayor greets them with the news that theatre performances have been banned for health reasons; however, he gives them 80 shillings for their trouble. They press on, with similar receptions in other towns.

When stopping at inns, Sam and Widge are aware that Sal refuses to sleep or bathe with the others. At Newbury, Mr. Heminges and company take a stand and decide to defy authorities and play outdoors on a makeshift stage. Constables arrive and a melee ensues in which the actors are roundly defeated. The worst injury—a broken right arm—is suffered by Mr. William Shakespeare. Widge, formerly a doctor's helper, is summoned and puts the arm in an improvised cast. Knowing that Widge is also master of a form of shorthand, the Bard requests that he become his scribe and write down the lines of his play in progress, *Love's Labours Won*. Widge is thrilled.

Sam is determined to learn why Sal demands such privacy. He spies on him while he is bathing and discovers that the boy has huge welts and scars on his back. Only later does Sal talk of the harsh punishments he suffered at his former school. His confession, however, does not make him any more cooperative or likable, but on the other hand his acting ability remains inspiring.

To add to existing problems, a rival theatrical company, the Earl of Pembroke's Men, is reported to be in the neighborhood and seem to be stirring up trouble against them, including trying to set their wagons on fire. Widge sees their leader, a churlish man with an eye patch, at one of their performances. Traveling north to avoid the plague, the company stops at York and Widge visits the orphanage, still managed by kindly Mistress MacGregor, where he lived as a child. The good woman gives Widge a crucifix she has found that belonged to his dead mother. It is inscribed "For Sarah." Encouraged by this, Widge begins visiting local taverns in his spare time hoping to find more news about his parents. In one, a former soldier named Jamie Redshaw, spins a story about his past that convinces Widge that he is his father. The trusting youngster brings Jamie Redshaw back to the company, where is given jobs as a handyman and collector of admission money.

On the road to Leeds, the company is accosted by a gang of five armed robbers. Quick-thinking Sam, who is riding in a covered wagon, covers his face with makeup resembling open sores. When he shows his face to the robbers they flee. For once, fear of the plague has helped the company! However, a letter from Sander in London brings bad news about the orphanage's poverty and the increased plague deaths. Widge also learns two disturbing bits of news: Sal has reported to Mr. Armin that Jamie is stealing from the money box, and both Ned Shakespeare and Jamie are sneaking out at night to gamble in local taverns. When the contents of the company's money box, including Widge's precious crucifix, are stolen, all eyes turn to Jamie Redshaw. Believing his father innocent, Widge helps him escape and, now in disgrace, the boy leaves the company to hitchhike back to London.

Along the way he has two important encounters. At a tavern, he notices a group of ruffians gambling. When their leader bets a crucifix instead of money, Widge realizes they are the robbers and then discovers they are actually a band of renegade actors, masquerading as Lord Pembroke's Men. They admit to using various nefarious methods to force Widge's group out of the territory. Widge also discovers that the leader with an eyepatch is the much-changed Nick, a villainous young man who was once an apprentice with Lord Chamberlain's Men. Widge manages to retrieve the crucifix and leaves. His second brief encounter, days later, is with Jamie Redshaw, who confesses that he stole small amounts of money from the company money box from time to time so that he could gamble. He also tells Widge that he is not his father, but fabricated the story to get a job with the company. Though disillusioned, Widge can't dislike this affable con man.

Back in London, Widge finds the city recovering from the ravages of the plague and Mr. Cooke's orphanage financially destitute. In an effort to help, Sander has taken a job gathering the bodies of plague victims. As a result he becomes infected and Widge witnesses the death of his beloved friend in the neighborhood pesthouse. When the Lord Chamberlain's Men return to London, misunderstandings are straightened out and Widge is welcomed back as an apprentice. Mr. Shakespeare has completed his new play, now called *All's Well That Ends Well*. Both Widge and Sal vie for the coveted role of Helena, the leading lady. To decide the matter, an acting competition is held and Widge wins. When he resumes his acting, Widge realizes that his real family consists of Mr. Shakespeare and the other members of this esteemed acting company.

Passages for Booktalking

Some interesting passages: Widge and Sander go talent-hunting at Blackfriars (pp. 12–15); Tetty talks about the plague (pp. 30–34); the fight at Newbury (pp. 58–62); and Widge takes dictation from William Shakespeare (pp. 72–77).

Themes and Subjects

Though one reviewer complained of some anachronisms, most agreed that the author has produced an accurate picture of life in Elizabethan England. The backstage details on acting, play writing, and stagecraft are fascinating. The author has skillfully integrated actual people and events into a fictional framework. Widge blossoms as a young man who survives both physical and spiritual hardships. He faces a number of moral questions and achieves increasingly mature responses. Some other subjects are family, friendship, the Black Plague, London, Elizabeth I, William Shakespeare, Lord Chamberlain's Men, "the show must go on," rivalry, villainy, orphans and orphanages, and the Globe Theatre.

COOPER, SUSAN. *Victory.* McElderry Books, 2006, $16.95 (978-1-4169-1477-8); pap. Aladdin, $6.99 (978-1-4169-1478-5) (Grades 4–8)

Introduction

Like the young heroine of *Victory*, Susan Cooper was born in England and later moved to the United States. The author was born in 1935 in Burnham, Buckinghamshire, about 20 miles from London. She remembers very well the bombings and the air raid shelters of World War II and is therefore knowledgeable about the effects of war. Her other home was in North Wales, where her grandmother was born. There, she became familiar with both English and Celtic myths and legends. She began writing as a young girl and, after receiving a Masters degree from Oxford, pursued a career in journalism. In 1963, she married an M.I.T. professor and moved to the United States, where she continued her interest in fiction writing. She is perhaps best known for her five-volume fantasy series The Dark Is Rising, named after the second book in the sequence. The plots are complex and deal, as the author has stated, with dualities in human nature such as forgiveness and revenge, love and hate, kindness and cruelty, and the epic struggle between good and evil.

Victory tells, in alternate chapters, two stories separated in time by more than two hundred years. The first story is set in the present and features Molly Jennings in a third-person narrative that extends over about four or five weeks. The second is told by another 11-year-old, Samuel Robbins, and covers a three-year period, from January 1803 to January 1806. For continuity, the sequence of chapters has sometimes been changed in the summary.

Historical Background

In the text and a brief Author's Note, Susan Cooper gives excellent background material, particularly about *HMS Victory*. The Napoleonic Wars were a continuation of the French Revolutionary Wars. They were a manifestation of Napoleon's desire to extend French influence and to control all of Europe. At the height of his power he and his allies did control most of continental Europe. His major enemies, known as the Coalition, were Great Britain, Russia, and the Ottoman Empire. In 1798–1799, he attempted to destroy British trade by conquering Egypt. He entered Cairo, but when his fleet was destroyed by Nelson in the Battle of the Nile he returned to Europe and there followed a period of peace from 1802 to 1803. Fearful that Napoleon was preparing an invasion, Britain resumed hostilities. There followed a long period of naval maneuvering, with the British trying to engage the French in battle.

Nelson succeeded in 1805 at the Battle of Trafalgar, named for the Spanish cape adjacent to the fighting. Napoleon now turned eastward and invaded Russia, where he suffered a crushing defeat at the hands of the Russian winter.

He was forced to retreat to France. In 1814, after the Coalition forces invaded France, Napoleon abdicated and was sent to the island of Elba. He escaped and reassembled his troops during a period known as the Hundred Days. His final defeat, which resulted in banishment to St. Helena, occurred at Waterloo in 1815. This battle brought honor to many, including the British Duke of Wellington.

Horatio Nelson is the most famous of all British naval heroes. He was born in Norfolk, England, on September 29, 1758, and died off Cape Trafalgar, Spain, on October 21, 1805. He entered the navy at age 12 and became a captain at 20. During the French Revolutionary and Napoleonic Wars, he served with distinction and became a vice admiral. He lost the sight of one eye in a battle to capture Corsica and, in a subsequent battle, lost his right arm. Though married, he had a prolonged affair with Emma, Lady Hamilton, with whom he had a child. After the end of the truce of 1802–1803, he gained command of the British Mediterranean fleet. He first blockaded the French fleet at Toulon, and when they escaped he chased them to the West Indies and back before a final confrontation off Cape Trafalgar in Spain on October 21, 1895. Before the battle he gave the famous signal, "England expects that every man will do his duty." He won a spectacular victory but died in action on the deck of his flagship, *HMS Victory*. Although, while dying, he uttered the words "Kiss me, Hardy" (Hardy was the captain of the *Victory*), his actual dying words were "drink, drink . . . fan, fan . . . rub, rub"—seeking relief from his thirst, heat, and the pain from his wound. After the battle, the heavily damaged *Victory* was towed to Gibraltar with Nelson's body preserved in a barrel of brandy. The body lay in state at Greenwich before the massive funeral (described vividly in the novel) and burial in St. Paul's Cathedral in London. There are many monuments to him throughout the world, the most famous being the column in Trafalgar Square in London.

HMS Victory is the only 18th-century ship of the line still in existence. She beautifully represents the skills and craftsmanship of shipbuilding in the mid-18th century. The vessel was launched at Chatham Dockyard in 1765, commissioned in 1778, and was in active service for the next 34 years. Her greatest glory was at the Battle of Trafalgar in 1805. At that time she was Nelson's flagship and her captain was Thomas Hardy (July 31, 1803–Jan. 13, 1806). In 1812, she was retired and for the next 110 years was moored in Portsmouth harbor. In 1922, she was moved to the Portsmouth Royal Naval Dockyard for restoration. In 1928, George V unveiled a tablet announcing completion, but work continues on the ship even today. It is open daily for visits and remains a popular tourist attraction.

Molly is reading *The Life of Horatio Lord Nelson* by Robert Southey (1774–1843). This was first published in 1813, only eight years after Nelson's death. It is extremely laudatory and can be downloaded free of charge from Project Gutenberg.

Principal Characters

I. Molly's story

    Molly Jennings, an 11-year-old English girl

    Kate Hibbert, her mother

    Carl Hibbert, her stepfather

    Russell Hibbert, her 16-year-old stepbrother

    Jack Parker, Russell's friend

    Alan Waterford, a bookseller

    Granny Blake, Molly's grandmother

    Grandad Blake, Molly's grandfather

II. Sam's story

    Samuel Robbins, an 11-year-old English boy

    Dick, his older brother

    Mam and Father, Sam's parents

    Uncle Charlie Davis, Mam's brother

    Joan, Charlie's wife

    Will, Charlie's co-worker

    Capt. Samuel Sutton, captain of the *HMS Victory*

    First Lieutenant Quilliam, an officer on board

    Mr. Smith, the ship's surgeon

    Charles Carroll, the ship's cook

    Stephen and Tommy, two of the cook's helpers

    William Pope, leader of the boys on board

    Lord Nelson, a vice admiral

    Oliver Pickin, a midshipman

    William Smith, the chief sail maker

    Andrew Scott and Jonathan Stead, his helpers

    Captain Hardy, later captain of *HMS Victory*

Plot Synopsis

In August 2006, 11-year-old Molly Jennings is a very unhappy girl. A few weeks ago her cozy, predictable life ended when she, along with her mother, Kate Hibbert, her stepfather, Carl Hibbert, and his son from a previous marriage, 16-year-old Russell, moved from their comfortable flat in London to a small town in Connecticut because Carl, an American businessman, has been transferred back to the States. Molly's father was killed in an airplane crash four years ago and her mother married Carl two years later. They now have a well-behaved, bouncing baby, Donald, who is about ready to crawl.

Molly loves both her new brother and her understanding mother dearly and Carl and Russell are far from the wicked step-relatives of storybook fame, but she is finding it difficult to adjust to America. She misses her friends terribly, most of all her Granny and Grandad, who live in the London suburb of High-gate. To add to her distress, she has a near-tragic boating accident on Long Island Sound, when she falls off Carl's sailboat and is fished out of the water by a quick-thinking Russell. To create a family diversion, Carl suggests a tour of Mystic Seaport, where several old sailing ships are on exhibit. At Mystic, heavy rains force the family into a quaint bookshop, Ships and the Sea, where they meet the ancient, amiable owner, Mr. Waterford, and Molly on impulse buys an old copy of Robert Southey's *Life of Nelson*.

Back home, Molly becomes so irritated at the glib, condescending remarks about England delivered by Russell's friend, Jack Parker, that she uncharacter-istically flings the book at him. She misses the target but damages the book. Later, when she and Russell examine it, they find the front binding has been split open revealing an envelope hidden under the front cover. In it are a small piece of a flag and two notes. The first, signed by an Emma Tenney, states that the fragment is part of Nelson's flag at Trafalgar and that it was saved by her father, Samuel Robbins, who served on Nelson's ship *HMS Victory* during the battle. The second is from Emma's grandson, who placed the flag and her note in the binding.

Molly becomes intrigued with the story of Nelson and feels a mystical one-ness between herself and these 200-year-old events. It is therefore not surpris-ing that, on a surprise visit to her grandparents in London, she asks Grandad if he will go with her to tour the *Victory*, which is open for visitors to the dry dock at Portsmouth. There, as their guide re-creates the events of the Battle of Trafalgar, Molly feels a strange force growing within her. She becomes separat-ed from Grandad, climbs into a narrow crawlspace, and remains there in a coma-like sleep until finally, four hours later, she is discovered by her frantic Grandad and taken home.

In January 1803, 11-year-old Samuel Robbins is also very unhappy. He is living with his large family in a hovel outside the manor house where Sam's abusive father works. Sam's life is one of drudgery, maltreatment, and near-starvation. His only consolation comes from his mother, who is battered regu-larly by her bullying husband. Mam's brother, Charlie Davis, pays a surprise visit to the Robbins and offers Sam a position as an apprentice in the rope-making factory where he works in the coastal city of Chatham. Sam's father agrees because he knows Sam will send money home and Mam also consents knowing this is a wonderful opportunity for her son.

At Chatham, Sam meets Charlie's amiable wife, Joan, and takes an exciting tour of the ropewalk, where all the riggings for the nearby shipyards are produced. He also meets Charlie's helper, Will. However, on the way home, the three are captured and knocked unconscious by press-gangers who kidnap able-bodied men for service in His Majesty's Navy. The kidnapped men are taken by rowboat to *HMS Victory* where, in spite of violent protests from Uncle Charlie, they are sworn into service by First Lieutenant Quilliam, a surrogate for Captain Samuel Sutton.

Will escapes but Charlie is sent to work with the rigging repair crew and Sam is consigned to the kitchen managed by the usually drunk and never kindly cook, Charles Carroll. His two other boy helpers are Stephen, a swaggering but friendly lad, and Tommy, a good-natured black boy. The living and working conditions are intolerable and Sam often longs for death. Discipline is severe and often unjust. For example, because of an imagined insubordinate action, the sadistic midshipman Pickin forces Sam to wear an iron bolt in his mouth, cutting his lips and preventing him from eating or drinking. After two days, William Pope, the leader of the boys on the ship, is able to remove it and helps nurse Sam back to health. On another occasion, Stephen is paddled so severely for a minor offense that his bottom is covered with bleeding wounds. Two bright moments occur when Sam has brief, accidental encounters with the stern but compassionate Admiral Nelson, who has made the *Victory* his flagship. Sam realizes how this great hero can inspire such love and devotion.

Gradually, life becomes easier for Sam. With the help of Uncle Charlie, he is transferred to the sail making and repairing unit where he works with a friendly group of men including the leader William Smith and his helpers Andrew Scott and Jonathan Steed. He also becomes a powder monkey, the boy who carries powder to the cannon crew to propel the shot. He is assigned to a single cannon on the lower deck and there he makes another batch of good friends. In time, Sam regards the 100-gun *Victory* as his home and his crewmates as his family.

Time passes. For two years, the British pursue the French fleet in and out of the Mediterranean and back and forth across the Atlantic. Finally the French are cornered at Cape Trafalgar on the coast of Spain and Sam at last sees action. The battle is bloodier, noisier, and more traumatic than Sam could ever have imagined. The decks are slippery with the blood of dozens of sailors and Sam sees his friend Stephen blown to bits. Sam has two fingers on his right hand shot off and is sent to see Mr. Smith, the chief surgeon. The hospital is filled with the dead and dying and Sam is devastated to see the corpse of his Uncle Charlie. After his hand is bandaged, Sam wanders on deck and witnesses another tragic event. Mortally wounded, Admiral Nelson dies in the arms of the new captain, Mr. Hardy.

Despite these losses, the battle is a great victory for the British. Later, Sam and other survivors are honored by being part of the funeral cortege that accompanies Nelson's body for burial in St. Paul's Cathedral in London. After the service, he receives a piece of the flag that flew over the *Victory*. He will treasure it for life and promises to bequeath it to his family. In the meantime, he must go back to sea and continue to serve as a proud member of His Majesty's Navy.

On her return to Connecticut, Molly seems happier in her new home and better adjusted to her stepfamily. She contacts Mr. Waterford and gets his permission to keep the book's hidden contents. He tells her that his research has shown that there was a ship's boy named Samuel Robbins aboard the *Victory* at Trafalgar. While Molly was away, Russell showed Carl the flag and notes and Carl has done some investigating into Emma Tenney, the signer of the first note. Then Carl announces his big surprise. Magnification shows that Tenney, in old-fashioned script, is actually Jennings. Further genealogical research reveals that Samuel Robbins was really Molly's many-times-over great-grandfather. Molly's obsessive interest in Nelson and his times was really an intuitive feeling that unified her family's past and present. The next time she is on Long Island Sound in Carl's boat, she murmurs, "I commit Sam's bit of Nelson to the deep," and lowers the fragment of flag into the water.

Passages for Booktalking

Molly falls overboard while boating with Carl and Russell (pp. 7–11) and she finds the bit of flag and the notes (pp. 46–50). Uncle Charlie visits the Robbins (pp. 22–26); Sam tours the ropeway (pp. 27–32); and he and Uncle Charlie are pressed into service on the *Victory* (pp. 32–38).

Themes and Subjects

The title of the book refers not only to the ship and the Battle of Trafalgar but also to Sam's triumph over the overwhelming obstacles in his life and to Molly's coming to terms with her new home and the death of her father. Both Molly and Sam struggle through doubts and fears to resolve their problems. The ties that keep families united are explored. Life in the British Navy of the early 19th century is so graphically and authentically presented that one feels like part of the crew. The battle scenes are also realistic and explicit in their gory details. Lord Nelson emerges as a great hero, as do both Molly and Sam in their own ways. Other subjects: Napoleonic Wars, antiquarian books and booksellers, Mystic Seaport, Battle of Trafalgar, stepfamilies, grandparents, London, Connecticut, courage, boats and ships, and sailing.

————•◦•————

CURRY, JANE LOUISE. *The Black Canary.* McElderry Books, 2005, $16.95 (978-0-689-86478-0) (Grades 5–8)

Introduction

Jane Louise Curry, born in 1932 in East Liverpool, Ohio, is a prolific writer of fantasy and time travel novels for young readers. She divides her time between a home in Southern California and one in London. Perhaps her best-known work is the Abaloc series of seven titles (eight if one counts the prequel *The Change Child*, published in 1969). Set in the magical landscape of the Ohio Valley, these books transcend time and incorporate contemporary, medieval, and prehistoric history and connect children to such elements as the mythology of Wales and the world of Indian legends.

The Black Canary takes place both in present-day London and, through the magic of time travel, in the London of 1600–1601 during the reign of Elizabeth I. Many of the streets and places referred to in the historical episodes still exist. Clerkenwell Close and Street are in the Borough of Islington north of Fleet Street and close to Farringdon tube station. The Saint Paul's Cathedral that James visits in 1600 is now referred to as Old St. Paul's. At this time it was in a state of extreme neglect. Many of its outbuildings were sold by the Crown and became shops chiefly for printers and booksellers (in the next century John Newbery established his business there). The old cathedral was destroyed in the Great Fire of London in 1666 and Sir Christopher Wren's masterpiece took its place.

Historical Background

Elizabeth I's reign was one of glory for England and for the arts. During her long rule, from 1558–1559 to her death in 1603, the seat of government and principal residence of the monarchy was Whitehall Palace, a massive group of buildings that covered about 23 acres on the Thames embankment in the Westminster area of London, east of Charing Cross. In 1698, all but Inigo Jones's Banqueting House was destroyed by fire.

Robert Devereaux, the Earl of Essex was the last of Elizabeth's "favorites." Hot-tempered and jealous, he failed disastrously in an ill-fated expedition to Ireland. On his return, he plotted against the queen, was discovered, and sent to the Tower where he was beheaded on February 25, 1601 (a few weeks after the end of the historic London passages in the novel). It is said that signing his death warrant broke Elizabeth's heart.

The Chapel Royal was a group of adults and children employed to serve the entertainment needs of the sovereign. The Children of the Chapel Royal served as choristers to the queen and took the female roles in plays that were performed. The choir achieved its greatest eminence under organists Thomas Tallis and William Byrd. The Master (Master Giles in the novel) had the right to press-gang children (usually from provincial choirs) to serve in the royal choir.

The playwright and poet Ben Jonson was Shakespeare's chief competitor. His play *Cynthia's Revels, or the Fountain of Self-Love* was first performed by boy actors of the Children of the Chapel Royal in 1600. The play is not considered one of his successes. Many other characters in the novel—such as Master Giles and Dr. Bull—are based on real people. During Elizabethan times the presence of blacks (referred to as blackamoors or Africans) in general society was still relatively rare. Although there were some incidents of intolerance, they were mainly accepted and served in wealthy households as honored servants or musicians.

Principal Characters

James Parrett, a biracial American boy almost 13 years old
Reenie, a talented black singer and James's mother
Phil Parrett, a white college professor and James's father
Thomas Clifton, James's fellow chorister
Jack Garland, an untrustworthy lad, also a chorister
Master Nathaniel Giles, the leader of the Children of the Chapel Royal
Plumed Hat, later named Tom Garland, Jack's older actor brother
Benjamin Jonson, poet and playwright
Mr. Moult, a teacher of Latin
Mrs. Moult, his wife
Dr. Bull, a music teacher

Plot Synopsis

James Parrett, now almost 13 years old, is growing up in a family dominated by music. His mother Reenie is a black singer noted as a soloist with early music ensembles, and his father, Phil, a white man, is a professor of music in their home town of Pittsburgh. Phil also makes duplicates of early instruments such as lutes. Both sets of grandparents are equally involved in various types of music. James, an intelligent, well-adjusted boy loves his family but at times feels overwhelmed, indeed suffocated, by the importance of music in his family's life. Although he outwardly accepts the situation (he even can read music), inwardly he is rebelling at his parents' desire that he pursue a career in music.

Reenie accepts a last-minute offer to become a soloist with Concentus, a musical group that specializes in Renaissance and Reformation music, on a

European tour that begins with several concerts in London. Phil makes arrangements to lease his Cousin Charles's apartment in Clerkenwell Close in the Old City of London while Charles is away. The three Parretts arrive and, while Reenie is rehearsing, Phil and James set out to explore London's sights. One night James is awakened by the sound of dripping water. He traces it to the basement, where he notices a shimmering light. Through the shimmer he sees another world of stairs leading to a bolted door that in turn leads to a well (the source of the sounds) and an enclosure of old buildings surrounded by a high wall. Thinking he's dreaming, he returns to bed. This experience haunts him and the following evening he again enters this strange world via the shimmer. This time he explores further before returning. Could these strange buildings, including a large church, and peculiarly dressed inhabitants be part of Clerkenwell Close but at a different period in time?

While Reenie prepares to leave for the continental tour, Phil and James explore Tate Modern and environs. On the Millennium Bridge, James again sees the shimmer. While taking a photo he loses his footing and falls into the Thames. His rescuers seem to be from a different era in speech and in dress. One kindly young man, whom he calls Plumed Hat because of his headgear, gets him some fresh clothes—breeches and a doublet—and takes him by coach to where James says is home, Clerkenwell. When Plumed Hat leaves, James makes a dive for the shimmer and the safety of his basement.

Through some strange time warp, James discovers that he is in London immediately before he and his parents arrived some two weeks before. Hoping to rectify this, he once again enters his newfound world. He explores the church entering through a back door. By piecing together bits of evidence on church notices, he determines that he is in Elizabethan London just before Christmas 1600, and that his previous visit was two months later probably in February 1601.

On the main thoroughfare, James meets a young boy named Thomas Clifton who is on his way to school. They stop to enjoy some street performers, one of whom is a skinny boy clad in a scarlet cloak trimmed in gold braid. While joining in on a song (that coincidentally Reenie had taught him), James learns from Thomas that the scarlet cloak is the uniform of boys who are part of the elite Children of the Chapel Royal, choristers to the queen. Suddenly the two boys are nabbed by two adults, dragged through the streets, and finally deposited in one of the halls of a large complex of buildings making up Chapel Royal. It turns out that the skinny boy, later identified as Jack Garland, and his companions are talent scouts looking for fresh material for the school. By royal decree, the master of the school, Nathaniel Giles, has the power to recruit any boy he feels has talent, and both James and Thomas have been selected.

At first the master has doubts about conscripting a foreign blackamoor but, realizing that Parrett is a fine English name, he consents. James doesn't know whether to be glad or distressed at the news. On his first day at school, James meets a variety of interesting people including the poet Benjamin Jonson, whose play *Cynthia's Revels* is being prepared for a royal performance; Dr. Bull, the music master; and Mr. Moult, a schoolteacher who marvels at James's lack of Latin. James makes one break for freedom but is caught by Jack Garland—a boy he has learned to distrust—brought back, and placed under close surveillance. In the next few days, James begins to enjoy the tight regime at the school. He gets an important non-speaking role in Mr. Jonson's play, and finds a new pleasure in singing with the choir. He is outfitted in the handsome school uniform and gets to share a room with Thomas and Jack at Mr. Moult's home. Mrs. Moult is an exceptionally fine cook.

James notices that every night while everyone is supposedly asleep Jack sneaks out for a few hours. Intrigued, James follows him and discovers that the boy is following the activities of a group of young actors from the Globe Theatre, one of whom is Jack's older brother, Tom, the Plumed Hat James met after his dowsing in the Thames. James also uses this freedom to try to reach the shimmer in Clerkenwell Close, but finds the church closed and the doors along the wall locked.

This routine is repeated until, one night, Jack confronts James. He explains that he is working secretly for one of Queen Elizabeth's spies and is fearful that his brother and his friends are part of a plot devised by the Earl of Essex against Queen Elizabeth. Jack has also followed James to Clerkenwell and is curious about his futile attempts to enter the Close. James remains silent. Thomas's parents use their influence and he is returned to his family, but James, without anyone to speak for him, remains at Chapel Royal. The performance of Jonson's play is canceled (much to Ben's disappointment) and an evening of music for Her Majesty is substituted. James is given some special solo music and is thrilled at this opportunity. When the choir is transported up the Thames by barge for a dress rehearsal in the magnificent Banqueting House of Whitehall Palace, he experiences for the first time the joy and exhilaration of producing music.

Not wishing to make his nefarious activities public, Jack asks James to convey a warning to his brother Tom that he must stop associating with the friends of Essex or face arrest. Tom heeds the warning. To repay this favor, Jack promises to help James get access into Clerkenwell Close. James is torn between performing before the queen and returning to his family. He chooses his family. Through his connections, Jack gets a copy of the key that opens one of the doors in the wall surrounding the Close and within minutes, James is back in the 21st century just in time to resume his exploration of London with his father. Only James is aware how much he really knows about this city.

Passages for Booktalking

Some important passages: James's first encounter with the portal to another time (pp. 9–19); James's adventure on the Millennium Bridge (pp. 56–60); he meets Thomas Clifton and both are kidnapped (pp. 100–108); and James is accepted as one of the Children of the Chapel Royal and meets Master Giles and Ben Jonson (pp. 115–123).

Themes and Subjects

It is refreshing to encounter a well-adjusted, intelligent biracial boy as the central character in a novel where neither prejudice nor discrimination is an important theme. James's acceptance of the importance of music in his life and the joy of creating music are important subjects. The color, excitement, and squalor of life in Elizabeth I's London are brilliantly re-created and the contrast between this and life in London under Elizabeth II is interestingly developed. Other themes and subjects: time travel, fantasy, plays and playwrights, Ben Jonson, music, songs and singing, schools, family life, biracialism, London past and present, Elizabeth I, courage, Earl of Essex, reaching maturity, and spies and spying.

GIFF, PATRICIA REILLY.

Nory Ryan's Song. Delacorte, 2000, $15.95 (978-0-385-32141-9); pap. Dell, $5.99 (978-0-440-41829-0) (Grades 4–8)

Maggie's Door. Wendy Lamb Books, 2003, $15.95 (978-0-385-32638-4); pap. $5.99 (978-0-440-41581-7) (Grades 4–8)

Introduction

Patricia Reilly Giff was born in 1935 in Brooklyn, New York, the Mecca that Nora Ryan and her friends and family seek in these novels when they are forced to leave Ireland during the terrible Potato Famine of the mid-1840s. The author has said that she spent all of her childhood with books in her hands and when she had exhausted the juvenile section of her local library, she was allowed into the adult section. She taught reading for many years and has also worked in publishing. She was in her 40s when she turned to writing. Most of her books deal with contemporary children and their problems. She is perhaps best known for the lighthearted Kids of the Polk Street School series, but a more serious novel, *Lily's Crossing* (Delacorte, 1997, $15.95; 0385321422) was a Newbery Honor Book. It tells of Lily, a deceitful, rebellious girl and the harm her lies cause Albert, a refugee from Hungary.

The story of the two principal characters in *Nory Ryan's Song* and *Maggie's Door*, Nora and Sean, is continued in a third volume, *Water Street* (Wendy Lamb Books, 2006, $15.95, 03857630683) set in 1875 in Brooklyn at the time of the building of the Brooklyn Bridge, then considered by many to be an architectural folly. Thirteen-year-old Bird Mallon, daughter of Nora and Sean, wants to become a healer like her mother. The story is narrated in alternate chapters by Bird and a new boy in her tenement, Thomas Neary. Because Thomas's father, a likable drunkard, is absent a great deal, the boy is "adopted" by the Mallons and a deep friendship grows between the two youngsters. The book presents an accurate picture of Irish immigrants' struggle in the 1870s. *Nory Ryan's Song* takes places over a few months probably in 1845 or 1846 in Ireland and is narrated by Nory. *Maggie's Door* begins where Nory's narrative ends. It covers a period of about two months and is told in the third person, from two different viewpoints—Nory's and her friend Sean's. The books can be read separately but have more impact if read together.

Historical Background

Although the official dates of the Irish Potato Famine were from 1845 through 1849, the economic, political, and social effects were felt for generations after. The cause was a potato blight that traveled from Mexico to Ireland. It turned the potato crop into a slimy, blackish mass that gave out a putrid odor. It is estimated that about 1 million people (about 12 percent of the population) died from starvation or famine-related diseases, and more than another million migrated, principally to Great Britain, the United States, Canada, and Australia.

After Cromwell's wars in Ireland in the late 1640s, much of the land taken from Irish Catholics was consolidated into large estates owned by English Protestants who were generally absentee landlords. The land rented out to the peasant tenant farmers was divided into small farm plots (more than half of the landholdings in 1845 consisted of less than 5 acres), which meant that the only crop that could support a family was the potato, which produced three times the yield of grain. The estates, on the other hand, exported huge amounts of cattle and other foodstuffs. Local taxes were increased because of the Poor Laws (legislation that made each parish responsible for handling poverty) and local farmers, unable to pay these levies, were often evicted. An estimated half million people lost their land during this period. All of these factors resulted in what has been termed the Irish Holocaust. The British Parliament was largely indifferent to the situation although many private organizations, such as the British Relief Association, helped. There are many monuments in the world to this catastrophe. One in Ennistymon, County Clare, is opposite a workhouse where 20,000 perished and a mass grave containing the remains of hundreds of children who were buried without coffins. In Lower Manhattan in New York City, there is an impressive Irish Hunger Memorial.

Concerning the mass emigration, often called the Irish Diaspora, many individuals—like Granda—never reached their destination. Hunger, disease, crowded conditions, and bad ventilation caused many deaths at sea. The death rate was so high that the vessels were called "coffin ships," and it is reported that there were so many sea burials that sharks followed the ships. Unfortunately, many Irish did not receive the reception in America that was afforded Nory and Sean. Almshouses were filled with Irish immigrants and many new arrivals were forced to beg in the streets. One Irish immigrant stated, "Our position in America is one of shame and poverty."

Granda refers to the conflict in which he served as the "War of 1798." It is more correctly known as the "Irish Rebellion of 1798." This was an uprising of an Irish republican group known as the United Irishmen, who rebelled against their English overseers. In the three-month conflict, 20,000 to 30,000 people were killed and the Irish were defeated.

The principal setting of the novels is the farmland close to the town of Ballilee and north of Galway, the principal port on Galway Bay in the southwest of Ireland, facing America. Some unusual words: *brack* is a hard cake made up of dried grain; *dulce* is dried salty seaweed, purple in color and chewed like gum (it is either loathed or loved); a *currack*, Irish for coracle, is a small boat not unlike a rowboat; and a *limpet* is an ocean mollusk with a broad foot that clings to rocks.

Principal Characters

Nora (Nory) Ryan, a 12-year-old Irish girl
Granda, her grandfather
Da, her father, a fisherman
Maggie, her oldest sister
Celia, her 14-year-old sister
Patch, her 3-year-old brother
Sean Mallon, a boy slightly older than Nory
Mrs. Mallon, his mother
Mary Mallon, a sister in Brooklyn
Francey (Francis) Mallon, Sean's oldest brother
Michael and Liam, Sean's older brothers
Anna Donnelly, a reclusive, elderly woman

Also in *Nory Ryan's Song*
>   Lord and Lady Cunningham, the local estate owners
>   Devlin, Lord Cunningham's bailiff

Also in *Maggie's Door*
>   Garvey, a friend of Sean on the *Samson*
>   The cook, the mean-spirited cook on the *Samson*
>   Mr. and Mrs. Casey, friends of Nory on the ship
>   Eliza, an Irish waif who becomes Nory's friend

Plot Synopsis of *Nory Ryan's Song*

For generations, 12-year-old Nory Ryan's family has eked out a meager living from their small plot of land close to the steep cliffs of Maidin Bay, a part of the larger Galway Bay in southwest Ireland. Besides herself, Nory's family consists of aged Granda; Da, a fisherman currently at sea; a young brother, 3-year-old Patch; and two older sisters, 14-year-old Celia, and Maggie, the eldest. Maggie is engaged to Francey, the eldest son of the neighboring Mallon family. Nory's Ma died giving birth to Patch.

They live on the brink of starvation and are constantly in fear of losing their pitiful thatched cottage with its dirt floor and shabby furniture to their English landowner, Lord Cunningham, and his bailiff Devlin. When Nory learns that her friend Cat Neely and her mother are being evicted for nonpayment of taxes, she runs to the house of Anna Donnelly, a reclusive herbalist who she knows has a coin that might save her friend. She borrows the coin but it is too late; the Neelys have already been forced off their property, leaving only their dog Maeve behind. To add to her gloom, Nory accidentally drops the coin down Patrick's Well and she is now beholden to Anna for the money.

Bittersweet news provides a distraction for Nory when her sister Maggie announces that she and her sweetheart Francey Mallon are marrying and going to America to live with Francey's oldest sister Mary in Brooklyn. Nory and her family, as well as the rest of the Mallons—Mrs. Mallon, Grandma, and Francey's brothers Michael, Liam, and Sean—also hope and pray that they will be able one day to leave the bleakness of their present situation for a new life in America.

Nory's best friend is the youngest Mallon, Sean. They have a close attachment and one day they poach for fish together in Lord Cunningham's stream, hoping to catch enough to feed both themselves and Maeve. They are discovered but manage to escape with one fish.

With terrible misgivings, Nory appears at Anna Donnelly's cottage to work off her debt. On the exterior Anna, a tiny wizened woman, appears gruff and bitter, but Nory later discovers that she is a caring, compassionate creature who has suffered many personal tragedies including the death of her only son while he was climbing the cliffs on Maidin Bay. Anna is a healer who makes a meager living prescribing herbal medicines to the locals. She begins teaching Nory, who is fascinated by the power of these simple medicines. Because the Ryans have no food to spare, Nory is forced to give Maeve to Anna, who enjoys the dog's company.

Disturbing news reaches the community—a potato plague is reported in the country and soon the air is filled with putrid odors. Within days their crops are stricken. First the stems and leaves and then the potatoes turn black and emit a terrible stench. Without potatoes, the community faces starvation. Everyone scours the beaches and rocks for mussels and almost inedible limpets but soon even the rocks are bare. Sean's older brothers, Michael and Liam, use the family's little boat to fish in the bay but bailiff Devlin confiscates it for back taxes. At this point the two boys decide they must leave, hoping to reach America and send for their mother, grandmother, and Sean. In desperation, Celia is forced to kill one of the family's three chickens for food. Later, news arrives that there is a package from America for the Ryans at the Post Office. Filled with anticipation, the family goes to retrieve it but they are told there is postage due. As they have no money, they must leave without the parcel. Celia is only laughed at when she applies for work at the Cunningham estate.

In time, the families become walking skeletons. When Devlin confiscates the Ryans' last chicken and their only pig, Granda decides on a bold plan. He and Celia will walk to the port of Galway to try to locate Da who, they hope, will have money from his fishing expedition. Nory stays behind with Patch. Though they receive some food from Anna, Devlin confiscates the old lady's only cow and pig as well as Maeve. Now the situation appears hopeless. Ever resourceful, Nory thinks of a money-making scheme. With Anna's help she completes work on Celia's knitted shawl and goes to the neighboring town of Ballilee to sell it. By coincidence, Lady Cunningham is taking tea at the town's hotel, sees the shawl and, through her servant, gives Nory three coins for it. With the money, Nory is able to by a few foodstuffs and pay the postage due on the parcel from America. Unfortunately, on the way home she is mugged by a horseman who steals both her food and the unopened parcel.

In the meantime, Sean has been working on a road-building gang but when his hands become blistered and infected he is laid off. His grandmother dies of plague-related diseases and now there is only his mother and himself left on the Mallon family plot of land. In desperation, Nory thinks of another way to get food. She persuades Sean to lower her by rope down the cliffs to collect eggs from the sea birds' nests. Nory succeeds, but they know that the slightest misstep could have meant death.

Sean's brothers have earned enough money in Galway to sail to America. Before leaving they send three boat tickets for their mother, Sean, and Granny. With Granny dead, there is a spare ticket. Although Sean begs Nory to use it, she asks if he will take Patch instead. She will remain behind until receiving news from Celia and Granda. Sean consents and, promising they will be reunited soon, the three leave on their little cart pulled by Sean. Anna and Nory receive an unexpected visit from Devlin. The lord is suffering from an unusual ailment and would like one of Anna's herbal remedies. Nory drives a hard bargain and Devlin gives in. In addition to food, Anna will get back her beloved Maeve. However meager the results, justice has been served.

One day a stranger arrives with two tickets to America from Nory's Da— one for her and one for the already departed Patch. She realizes that Granda and Celia must already have made contact. Soon, she hopes, the family will be reunited. Unable to persuade Anna to use the other ticket, Nory bids Anna a tearful goodbye and sets off by foot for Galway and, she hopes, Brooklyn, New York.

Passages in *Nory Ryan's Song* for Booktalking

Nory tries to save the Neelys (pp. 4–11); Nory and Sean are caught poaching in Lord Cunningham's stream (pp. 14–18); Maggie's wedding and departure (pp. 24–29); Nory talks to Anna and they are fearful of a potato blight (pp. 38–41).

Plot Synopsis of *Maggie's Door*

It is 1846 and southern Ireland in the midst of the potato famine and the oppressive occupation by English nobility. Nory Ryan, age 13, has left her dear friend Anna Donnelly, the herbalist, to walk to Galway, there to be reunited with her family: Granda, Da, and sister Celia for passage to America where her eldest sister Maggie is married and living in Brooklyn. Preceding her on the road by a few days is her beloved young brother, 4-year-old Patch, who is being taken by cart to Galway with Mrs. Mallon and her son Sean, Nory's boyfriend. Mrs. Mallon's son Francey is Maggie's husband, and both the Mallon and the Ryan families hope to escape the unbearable living conditions in Ireland for a new life at 416 Smith Street, Brooklyn.

Sean is pulling the cart containing Patch and his mother when he is stopped by an English landlord who seeks help because his horse has gone lame. Promised food in return, Sean leaves the cart to run to the manor house and get help. It takes hours to locate the manor and deliver his message but, thanks to a sympathetic cook, he is able to collect some valuable edibles. However, when he returns many hours later he finds the cart gone. After frantically searching the countryside, Sean sets off for Galway alone. Because his mother has the ship tickets, Sean must find a way to earn his own passage when he arrives in Galway. He signs on as a cook's assistant on the *Samson* bound from Liverpool to New York but he first must experience the excruciating experience of being ballast on the *Manchester* bound from Galway to Liverpool. Packed like sardines in the hold, he talks to the young man next to him, who is about his age and named Garvey. By coincidence, Garvey has also signed on the *Samson* as a cook's assistant. The two become friends.

Meanwhile, on the road, Nory finds that she is being watching from afar by a girl who is following her. When Nory cuts her foot badly and must stop to find a spider's web (Anna's prescription), the girl—a wild, savage-like creature—approaches cautiously. Nory shares her meager rations with the girl, and before the girl runs off she finds a board on the beach that Nory can use as a crutch. Nory sees a cart with a broken wheel half-hidden in a field and investigates. In the cart are Mrs. Mallon, Sean's mother, and her beloved Patch. Tired of waiting for her son, Mrs. Mallon decided to pull the cart herself and hid in the field when the wheel broke. The old lady decides she is too weak and discouraged to make the trip to Galway on foot and turns back to Maidin Bay. Nory, with her young brother on her back, resumes her walk to Galway.

The port is a mass of confusion bordering on chaos, with would-be travelers trying to find their ships and departure times. The wait has reduced many of them to begging for food. Finally Granda appears. He tells Nory that Da and Celia have already embarked. They discover that the ship *Samson* will soon be leaving from Liverpool. Unfortunately the tickets Da sent have expired and Nory must use the few coins Da left Granda for the passage, which will take forty days. Nory watches the waif she befriended on the road cleverly steal some of these coins when the ticketmaster is distracted and also buy a ticket for the *Samson*.

In one of the many waiting lines to which they are assigned, Nory, Granda, and Patch meet Mr. and Mrs. Casey, also bound for New York. On the trip to Liverpool, they become friends with the Caseys and with the wild girl, whose name is Eliza.

Conditions in steerage on the *Samson* are appalling. Food and water are scarce and the living conditions below deck are crowded and unsanitary. Sean works in the galley under the supervision of a sadistic, evil-tempered cook. Garvey, at least, has the privilege of occasionally going on deck to dole out the paltry rations to steerage passengers. On one occasion, Sean is allowed to deliver food to a family in cabin class. He is enthralled by their luxurious room and possessions—including the books that the mother, father, and young daughter are reading. He longs to be literate. Many of the steerage passengers were weak and sick on boarding the ship and, now with these terrible traveling conditions, all sorts of illnesses and diseases develop. Using herbs she has brought from Anna's, Nory is able to help some, including Eliza who recovers after suffering an almost fatal fever. Unfortunately, she can't help her aging Granda who, weakened by weeks of hunger and deprivation, gradually declines and dies. He is buried at sea and Nory, in a fit of despair, throws her remaining herbs overboard.

At one point the ship encounters a terrible storm and gigantic waves. In the galley, pots, pans, food, and provisions are strewn everywhere, and below decks the passengers are convinced they are facing a watery grave. Sean is able to save Elizabeth, the daughter of the rich parents, who has wandered onto the deck. When the cook later catches him away from his work checking on the girl in her cabin, he orders Sean back to the galley and, in a rage, begins pouring a kettle of hot water on him. To protect himself, the boy steps back, placing one arm and a hand on the sizzling hot stove. He is severely burned and Garvey, who has heard about the passenger who cures with herbs, seeks out Nory for help.

In these unfortunate circumstances, Nory and Sean are reunited. She applies a cast-like poultice of beeswax and mutton fat. Days later, Nory removes the plaster to reveal healthy new skin. At last they reach New York harbor, and the day she had dreamed of so many times arrives. On shore, Elizabeth approaches Sean and Nory with a reward from her parents, a gold coin that will allow them to ride in style to their destination. Nory says goodbye to the Caseys and to Eliza, and boards a carriage with Patch and Sean to ride royally to their new home, 416 Smith Street in Brooklyn where they are greeted by Maggie, Da, and Celia. Nory murmurs to her father, "We are here, Da, we are here."

Passages in *Maggie's Door* for Booktalking

Some interesting passages are: Sean leaves his cart to help the Englishman and get food (pp. 13–17); Nory cuts her foot and meets Eliza (pp. 20–23 and 35–38); Sean gets food from the cook but can't find the cart (pp. 25–33) and Sean travels by ship to Liverpool (pp. 51–54).

Themes and Subjects of Both Books

The story of the Ryan and Mallon families is a miniature history of the Irish people during this period, of their hardships, exploitation, courage, ingenuity, and endurance. Today's youngsters will be made aware of the terrible suffering and sacrifice some of our ancestors suffered to reach America. The author has created a realistic picture of both the Irish potato famine and the life on immigrant ships that is rich in grim details. Overriding this wretchedness are three precepts: the importance of the family as a unit, the love of the land they are leaving, and the hope for a new, better world. Both Nory and Sean are likable, courageous, and resourceful young people who, through their inner strength, are able to overcome incredible adversities. Other subjects: farming, the English occupation, herbal medicine, Brooklyn, ships and sea life, survival, starvation, feudalism, acceptance, friendship, and death.

———•◦•———

LAWRENCE, IAIN. *The Wreckers.* Delacorte, 1998, $15.95 (978-0-385-32535-6); pap. Dell, $5.95 (978-0-440-41545-9) (Grades 5–9)

Introduction

The author is well prepared to write swashbuckling sea stories because he has spent much of his life aboard a variety of ships and boats. At present, when not on his boat, he lives on a small island off Prince Rupert on the north coast of British Columbia. *The Wreckers*, his first book for young readers, is the first part of the High Seas Trilogy, each of which has young John Spencer as its hero and narrator. The second volume is *The Smugglers* (Delacorte, 1999. $15.95, 0385326637; pap. Dell, $5.95, 0440415961; condensed in *Teenplots*, Libraries Unlimited, 2003). In it, John is second-in-command of his father's newly acquired schooner, *Dragon*, and discovers that the captain is actually a smuggler intent on bringing barrels of illegal brandy from France to England and will stop at nothing, even murder, to accomplish his goals. In the last volume, *The Buccaneers* (Delacorte, 2001, $15.95, 0385327366; pap. Dell, $5.95, 044041671X), John, again aboard *Dragon*, encounters skullduggery, pirates, and hidden treasury in a Caribbean adventure that ends when, on the voyage home off the coast of Cornwall, the ship emerges from a fog and heads for the Tombstones, the same rocks that destroyed the *Isle of Skye* at the beginning of *The Wreckers*. Each book is rich in action, suspense, and atmosphere. They are bound to please young readers.

Historical Background

This story takes place on the stormy coast of Cornwall, England, over a period of four days in the year 1799. According to an author's note at the end of the book, at this time "there is no doubt that there were wreckers who profited by the plundering of unfortunate ships," and it is alleged that, in some cases, these shipwrecks were caused by people on the coast luring the ships onto rocks by false lantern signals.

In the book there is no mention of political or social events of the period but, except for insurrections in Ireland, this was a relatively peaceful time when England was between wars with France. George III (the monarch who reigned during the American Revolution) was still on the throne and in France the Reign of Terror was over and Napoleon was in his ascendancy.

Principal Characters

John Spencer, the narrator, age 14

Mr. Spencer, John's father and owner of the *Isle of Skye*

Cridge, the ship's mate

Caleb Stratton, the villainous leader of a gang of wreckers

Stumps, a legless scoundrel

Simon Mawgan, a wealthy estate owner

Mary, the orphan niece of Simon, about John's age

Parson Tweed, a seemingly benign prelate with a deadly secret life

Peter, Simon's son drowned in a shipwreck

The Widow, a deranged woman who lives in isolation on the moors

Plot Synopsis

One wild stormy night in 1799, the brig *Isle of Skye*, bound for London with a cargo of imports from Turkey, Italy, and Spain, is blown off course near the coast of Cornwall. Using the seemingly helpful shore beacons for directions, the captain suddenly realizes that he has been guided into a shoal of deadly rocks known as the Tombstones. On board as passengers are the ship's owner, Mr. Spencer, and his 14-year-old son John, who is experiencing his first sea voyage. The ship sinks after its bottom is ripped open on the rocks, and John is sucked into the sea.

The next morning he wakens on a sandy beach and sees the remains of the ship wedged between huge rocks and, around him, the bodies of dead crew members. In the distance, three men are approaching, stopping at each corpse. When they reach an old sailor, Cridge, who shows signs of life, instead of helping him they hold his head down until he drowns. John now realizes that these men engineered the shipwreck for its cargo and were now killing anyone who could give evidence against them. Terrified, he runs away with the wreckers in hot pursuit. Following a seaway into a small town called Pendennis, he dives into an abandoned blockhouse and there encounters a sinister legless man, known as Stumps, who moves on a trolley he pushes with his hands. John notices that Stumps is wearing a ring that belonged to his father.

Before he can question the man further, the three wreckers swoop down on them. Their leader, Caleb Stratton, is preparing to slit John's throat when a horse ridden by a large man in a billowing black cloak barrels into the group. The rider is Simon Mawgan, the lord of the large estate, Galilee, neighboring the town. He rescues John and takes him to his manor house. On the way, they meet Parson Tweed, the town minister, who appears kindly but has a sinister look. At Galilee, John meets Eli, Simon's brother, a strange shuffling man whose tongue has been cut out and who lives in the stable outside the mansion house. He also meets Mary, Simon's niece, a charming orphan girl about John's age. John and Mary immediately become close friends. Simon maintains that he and his villagers were not responsible for the sinking of the *Isle of Skye*. Although John doubts this, he is convinced that someone of importance in Pendennis is organizing the wreckers and his suspicions point to Simon.

The next day Mary tells John that he reminds Simon of his son Peter, who drowned in a shipwreck. Mary saddles two horses and the two explore the moors and the coastline around Galilee. Mary tells John about the area's history and John talks about Stumps and the hope he has of locating his father. They pass a deranged woman in a carriage, whom Mary calls the Widow because both her husband and her brother were drowned. The woman gives John the evil eye.

Back at Galilee, Simon tells John that a layer of sawdust has been found in the bottom on the wine casks on the *Isle of Skye* and that everyone in town believes Mr. Spencer was smuggling gold into the country in these barrels. John is left outraged but questioning.

That evening, another ship is seen to be in distress. While the townspeople of Pendennis gather on the cliffs to watch this drama (there are no misleading beacons, John notes), the boy and Mary sneak into Pendennis on horseback to search for John's father. They find him chained to the wall in a deserted brewery, a prisoner of the absent Stumps. After giving Mr. Spencer water and easing his discomfort, they leave to get tools to break his shackles. Outside the brewery, the two encounter Parson Tweed. John's suspicions are aroused and he doesn't tell the prelate about locating his father. Mary leaves to get the horses and John is surprised by Stumps, who has returned to check on his prisoner. Stumps tries to kill John, but incredibly Parson Tweed reappears and shoots Stumps. On their return to Galilee, Mary and John notice that the endangered ship has been freed and the townspeople are returning home.

The next night, John again returns to the village, this time equipped with a chisel and a hammer. While breaking the manacles, he is confronted by Mary, who has followed him into town, and Parson Tweed, who helps John free his father. Suddenly the parson aims two loaded pistols at the group demanding to know where Mr. Spencer has hidden the gold he believes is being smuggled into the country. John now knows the Parson Tweed is the power behind the gang of wreckers. With deadly aim, John throws a handspike at Tweed and kills him.

Later, back at Galilee, family secrets and other facts are divulged. Simon confesses that on one occasion, years ago, he condoned the use of false beacons. The wreck that resulted claimed the life of his wife, his son Peter, and Mary's parents who, unknown to him, were passengers on the ship. In order to prevent his brother Eli from revealing his part in the tragedy, Simon had his tongue cut out. Since then, Simon has tried to prevent the townspeople from engaging in wrecking. When Mr. Spencer is told about the smuggling accusation, he realizes that Spaniards tricked him by filling the casks with sawdust rather than premium wine.

John and his father are now free to leave. The next morning, after thanking Simon and Mary for their help, the two board a coach for London.

Passages for Booktalking

The book could be introduced using one of the following passages: the *Isle of Skye* is wrecked off the Cornish coast (p. 1–8); John wakes up in the sand and witnesses the murder of Cridge (pp. 10–14); John encounters Stumps (pp. 18–23); and John is saved from Caleb and his gang by Simon Mawgan (pp. 25–28).

Themes and Subjects

This is essentially an action-packed, suspenseful adventure story that leaves the reader breathless with its many plot twists. Among the subjects covered are life in 18th-century England, father-son relations, bravery, fighting for high principles, smuggling, sea stories, and friendship.

RICHARDSON, V. A. *The House of Windjammer.* Bloomsbury, 2003, $17.95 (978-1-58234-811-7); pap. $8.95 (978-1-58234-984-8) (Grades 5–9)

Introduction

V. A. Richardson was born in the northeast of England in the late 1960s. As a child, he loved nature and frequently roamed the Roman Wall near his home. He first wanted to be a designer and illustrator and later began writing and illustrating his own books. The inspiration for the Windjammer series came from a visit to Amsterdam and the Rijksmuseum where he saw Rembrandt's *The Night Watch*, in which a group of soldiers are pictured. The author says, "I started wondering where they were going and what it would be like when they got there. From that one idle thought came the Windjammer series." *The House of Windjammer* takes place in Amsterdam in 1636. In the next in the series, *The Moneylender's Daughter* (Bloomsbury, 2006, $17.95; 1582348855), our hero, young Adam Windjammer, is aboard the ship *Draco* bound for the New World to recapture the wealth and good name of his family's shipping company and investigate the whereabouts of the *Sirius*. After evading pirates and a Spanish warship, he discovers the wreckage of his uncle's ship. Disheartened, he returns home to Amsterdam. There he finds that Jade van Helsen, the daughter of his nemesis, the banker Hugo van Helsen, is willing to help him restore his family's previous position. But she is hampered by her efforts to extricate her father from shady business deals that are ruining him. She must also get out of a planned marriage engineered by her father. This leads to an action-filled sequel that brings Jade and Adam closer together.

Historical Background

The 17th century in the Netherlands is referred to as the Golden Age. Despite constant warfare, this was a period of extreme prosperity. Most of the inhabitants made their livelihood on the land, but overseas trade was responsible for the influx of great wealth into the country. The Dutch East India Company, founded in 1602, extended Dutch trading power throughout the Orient. With headquarters in Java, its commercial and political power extended into such areas as Ceylon, South Africa, and Japan. The accomplishments of its sister corporation, the Dutch West India Company, were more modest but involved settlements in the Caribbean Islands, and the establishment of the colony of New Netherlands (later New York and New Jersey), which was lost to the English on Sept. 8, 1664. The base for much of this trading and shipbuilding activity was Amsterdam, a canal city on the Amstel River about 15 miles east of the North Sea.

During this time, the Netherlands was also a center of culture. Painters such as Rembrandt (1606–1669) (who is mentioned in the novel), Vermeer, and Frans Hals became famous.

The production of tulip bulbs has long been an important Dutch industry. In the first half of the 17th century, tulips became so popular that financial speculation on various species grew out of control. Fantastic sums were paid for a single bulb. This "tulipmania" ended suddenly in the spring of 1637 when the High Court of Holland ruled all tulip bulbs worthless in an effort to restore order in the tulip trade.

Principal Characters

Adam Windjammer, the 15-year-old heir to the Windjammer shipping
    fortune
Hercules Windjammer, his father
Lucien Windjammer, his youngest uncle
Mary Windjammer, Adam's mother
Rose and Viola Windjammer, Adam's younger twin sisters
Augustus Windjammer, another uncle
Felecia, Augustus's wife
Willem and Angelica, Augustus's children
Gerrit, the trusted clerk of the Windjammer Company
Hugo van Helsen, an unscrupulous banker and moneylender

Jade van Helsen, his daughter
Saskia (or Minou), Jade's personal maid
Bartholomew de Leiden, a representative of the Dutch West India
    Company
Wolfie, an unprincipled street urchin
Abner Heems, a wicked preacher
Hobe, a shipwright

Plot Synopsis

In 1636 all four of the ships of the Amsterdam-based Windjammer Trading Company are on a trading expedition to New Amsterdam when they encounter a massive storm off the coast of America. The flagship of the small fleet, the *Sirius*, is commanded by the youngest of the three Windjammer brothers, Lucien. Although he tries valiantly to save his ship and the others, all are doomed. The only survivor is the cabin boy of the *Sirius*, Hobe.

Meanwhile in Amsterdam, Adam, the 15-year-old son of the company's commander and manager, Hercules Windjammer—Lucien's oldest brother— is gazing with pride and awe at the bow of the half-completed *Draco*, the newest addition to the Windjammer fleet. The Windjammers have been nautical traders for more than a hundred years and are proud of the company's uprightness and accomplishments.

On his way home Adam is accosted by a gang of young thieves led by a stuttering thug named Wolfie. Through quick thinking, Adam is able to elude them.

At home in the family's elegant mansion on the Herengracht canal, he hears a noisy crowd assembling outside. They are led by a haranguing, fanatical minister named Abner Heems, who claims the Windjammer family is sinful and doomed. News of the destruction of the fleet has arrived and the crowd is anxious about both possible survivors and future financial security. Hercules, an honest and honorable man, addresses the crowd and assures them that the *Draco* will be sent to investigate the tragedy and that the House of Windjammer will go on.

The crowd disperses, but at a meeting of the company's creditors later that day, Hercules and his faithful clerk Gerrit learn that the company faces immediate bankruptcy. Loyal friends such as Bartholomew de Leiden, an elderly gentleman who represents the Dutch West India Company, support Hercules, but the more powerful, greedy banker Hugo van Helsen threatens to foreclose on the debts owed to him. Hercules becomes so agitated that he suffers a heart attack and dies. Adam and his family are distraught at the loss of this gallant man. Adding hypocrisy to his other unsavory qualities, Hugo van Helsen attends the funeral with his daughter, Jade, a girl of Adam's age. She tries to comfort Adam but is rebuffed.

The fate of the company is now in question. Technically, under-age Adam is the heir. He is given his father's ring on a chain as a symbol of this power, but he knows nothing of business affairs. Mary, his mother, is efficient and knowledgeable but disqualified because she is a woman. The middle brother, Augustus, an ineffective, cowardly dilettante, is reluctantly consulted and agrees to work with Gerrit. Adam and his family are forced to cut back drastically, letting help go and eliminating luxuries.

While visiting the waterfront and the *Draco* one day, Adam sees Jade dressed in peasant clothes. When he is again attacked by Wolfie, Jade appears and—wielding a knife—saves him. Adam is intrigued by this strange girl who claims she ventures out alone, evading her maid Saskia, to find a way to escape from her father. One evening, while playing hide and seek with his young twin sisters, Rosa and Viola, Adam sees Gerrit enter the ledger room, take a casket from a concealed area, and remove its contents, including money bags and a black mask. Much later that night, the twins say they saw Gerrit burying something in the garden. Adam begins to distrust Gerrit but accompanies him to another meeting of creditors.

Outside the meeting the demented preacher Abner Heems stirs up the crowd against the Windjammers; inside, Hugo van Helsen delivers an ultimatum giving the Windjammers one week to pay or he will foreclose. In desperation, and at Augustus's insistence, Mary Windjammer signs a letter saying she will marry Hugo van Helsen to settle their financial differences. When Adam learns of this, he rushes to van Helsen's home, only to find his Uncle Augustus and Cousin Willem have preceded him. Hidden by Jade, the boy overhears his uncle propose a marriage—but between Jade and Willem. Hugo van Helsen is outraged. He shows Augustus a portrait of Jade painted by Rembrandt, a portrait he will send to England to find a wealthy merchant to be her husband.

Jade's feelings of helplessness increase. In a further confrontation with Wolfie, Adam forces some truths from the boy. He is in the employ of Abner Heems, who in turn is being paid to discredit the Windjammer family. A crowd of penniless Windjammer employees organize and decide to plunder the family's warehouse. They are led by unemployed *Draco* workers, including Hobe, a shipwright whose son was cabin boy on the *Sirius*. Augustus, Gerrit, and Adam confront the mob. Augustus flees in terror but Adam and Gerrit are quieting the protestors when a barrel on the floor above becomes dislodged and falls. Gerrit pushes Adam out of its path but is hit a glancing blow. Adam is convinced it is not an accident.

Before he dies, Gerrit, in a delirium, tells Adam that he has bought the Black Pearl and that Adam must find it and sell it to save the company. When Augustus hears of this incident, he is so shaken he leaves Holland with his family to resettle in New Amsterdam. Later, that night Adam catches Abner Deem ransacking the ledger room. The scoundrel unfortunately escapes.

Remembering that the twins saw Gerrit burying something in the garden, Adam digs on the spot but finds only a bulb. He discards it and the twins later plant it on their father's grave. Adam hopes to find clues to the whereabouts of the jewel, the Black Pearl, by reading Gerrit's diary. There he makes an astonishing discovery. The Black Pearl is a tulip bulb. Gerrit had joined in the tulip craze that gripped the country and invested in a rare, exotic bulb from a dealer named Ashmed the Turk. Adam retrieves what he thinks is the bulb from his father's grave and, with Jade, he goes to a tavern on the waterfront called the Trade Winds, where clandestine transactions take place.

Donning Gerrit's mask, he enters the secret back room but is taken prisoner by the tavern's proprietor and Abner Heems. Jade is also captured. The renegade preacher confesses to Adam that he had been in the employ of Hugo van Helsen but when he found out that Gerrit had bought the Black Pearl, he acted on his own and killed him hoping to find the bulb in the Windjammer house.

In another part of the tavern, Jade escapes from her captors and secretly contacts Adam. In a tense scene, Adam frees himself and Abner Heems is killed. However, the Black Pearl is lost. The seven days are up and Hugo van Helsen triumphs. The Windjammers lose their house and possessions but are taken in by kindly Bartholomew de Leider.

With support from friends there is enough money to complete work on the *Draco* and Adam makes plans to sail on its first voyage to fulfill his father's promises. In an encounter with Hugo van Helsen, he learns that Jade is to be sent to England to find a husband. Before leaving Amsterdam, Adam visits his father's' grave and sees the Black Pearl growing. He had mistaken bulbs. Unfortunately the tulip mania is over, and the Black Tulip is now only worth the beauty it brings to people's lives.

Passages for Booktalking

Four interesting passages are: the loss of the *Sirius* (pp. 11–17); Adam escapes from Wolfie (pp. 22–24); Hercules confronts the crows (pp. 31–35); Hugo van Helsen confronts Hercules and Hercules suffers a heart attack (pp. 43–48).

Themes and Subjects

In spite of a formulaic plot and stock characters, this is an exciting, suspenseful tale that is a satisfying read. Particularly memorable are the scenes of life in 17th-century Amsterdam. All is portrayed—from the wealthy mansions of the merchant class to squalid life in the slums, including the far-from-romantic stench and filth of the canals. Adam progresses from an obedient, submissive son to a responsible, decision-making young man. Other subjects include the tulip trade, ships and sailing, adventure stories, mystery stories, the Dutch trading industry, loans and banking, courage, crime and criminals, murder, family life, loyalty, and friendship.

SPRINGER, NANCY. *The Case of the Missing Marquess.* Philomel, 2006, $10.99 (978-0-399-24304-2) (Grades 5–8)

Introduction

Shortly after she graduated from Gettysburg College in 1970, Nancy Springer began her writing career. Since then, she has published more than forty novels for children, young adults, and adults. Her works for juveniles include contemporary realism, mystery and crime, historical fiction, and fantasy. In the last category, she has two excellent novels based on Arthurian legends, and in historical fiction, she has produced a series of stories featuring Rowan Hood, Robin Hood's daughter. Her works for young readers have won many awards including two Edgars (Edgar Allan Poe Awards). Two of these are awarded each year by the Mystery Writers of America for the best mysteries, one for the best book for children and the other for young adults. The award consists of a citation and a ceramic bust of Poe. Ms. Springer's most recent series is set in late Victorian England and features Enola Holmes, the much younger sister of Sherlock Holmes. The first installment is *The Case of the Missing Marquess*, and the second, which can be read separately, is *The Case of the Left-Handed Lady* (Philomel, 2007, $12.99; 039924517). In it, Enola starts her own detective agency in London and, while continuing to avoid her two older brothers who want to send her to boarding school, she uses her great powers of detection to locate Miss Cecily, a young lady of privilege. The novel ends with a surprise reunion.

Historical Background

The novel is set in rural England and in London in 1888. At this time London was a city of contrasts. The wealthy middle and upper classes had established themselves in the affluent, fashionable "suburbs" in the western parts of the city while the poor became increasingly crowded in the filthy slums in the East End. Here the streets were often littered with garbage and even excrement, the water was polluted, and rats were omnipresent. In the 1860s John Ruskin said, "That great foul city of London—rattling, growling, smoking—a ghastly heap of fermenting brickwork, pouring out poison at every pore." However, Samuel Johnson also said, "When a man is tired of London, he is tired of life." The great fogs described in the book were caused by the pollution created by burning coal.

As every reader knows, the creator of Sherlock Holmes was Sir Arthur Conan Doyle (1859–1930). *A Study in Scarlet* (ascribed to Holmes in the novel) was the first of four novels and four collections of short stories to feature the famous detective. It was published as a book in 1888 after appearing the previous year in serial form. In addition to Holmes and Watson, Doyle introduced the character of Inspector Lestrode, a Scotland Yard detective. Named for an acquaintance from Doyle's student days in Edinburgh, Lestrode appears in several Holmes mysteries. At one point Holmes refers to him as "the best of the professionals."

Principal Characters

Enola Holmes, the 14-year-old heroine and narrator
Mrs. Holmes, Enola's strong-willed mother, mistress of Ferndell Hall
Mr. and Mrs. Lane, servants at Ferndell Hall
Mycroft Holmes, Enola's older bachelor brother
Sherlock Holmes, Enola's other older bachelor brother
Viscount Tewksbury of Basilwether Hall, a 12-year-old boy
Inspector Lestrade, a detective at Scotland Yard
Madame Laelia, a pompous clairvoyant specializing in finding lost things
    and people
Cutter, a London lowlife
Squeaky, his accomplice
Mrs. Culhane, the proprietor of a used clothing store

Plot Synopsis

A brief preface dated August 1888 describes a furtive woman dressed completely in black skulking through the filthy streets of the East End of London hunting for something and unaware that she, too, is being hunted.

The story begins one month earlier at the large estate of Ferndell in southern England, where Enola (the backward spelling of alone) Holmes has just received an unwanted fourteenth birthday present. Her mother, an independent, self-willed lady, has disappeared without trace or explanation. She has, however, left Enola three presents: a drawing kit, a book about flowers, and a small homemade booklet containing ciphers or word puzzles. Enola is an intelligent, self-reliant girl who could be described as a bit sassy. She is upset by her mother's disappearance but, even with the help of the indulgent servants Mr. and Mrs. Lane, is unable to come up with any clues. In desperation, she wires her two much-older bothers, Mycroft and Sherlock, asking for help. They arrive by train the following morning, and Enola bicycles to meet them.

Her mother had been alienated from her sons for some time, partly because of the humiliation of having Enola so late in life. (Remember, this is Victorian England.) The girl has not seen her brothers for ten years but she is particularly proud of her detective brother Sherlock whose novel *A Study in Scarlet* has just been published.

The brothers are a study in contrasting personalities. Mycroft, a well-dressed, monocled gentleman, seven years older than Sherlock, is stuffy, overbearing, and quite obnoxious. Sherlock, though equally fastidious, is much more approachable and understanding. Unfortunately, after a few days without any further discoveries, Sherlock returns to London.

By English law Mycroft became the master of Ferndell on his father's death and is therefore responsible for its upkeep. It appears that Mrs. Holmes sent false expense accounts to him listing nonexistent servants, education expenses for Enola, home improvements, and care of the estate. Enola wonders what she did with all the money. In spite of Enola's violent objections, Mycroft makes arrangements to send the girl to a finishing school. He also summons a seamstress to produce a new wardrobe for her.

Meantime, Enola, forever inquisitive and resourceful, is inspired to look into the book of ciphers her mother gave her for a possible message. The ciphers yield clues to where she hid money in her room—behind paintings, in bed knobs, and so forth. Soon Enola has retrieved a small fortune and devised a plan. On the day she is to leave for private school, she cleverly hides the money and many personal items in articles of clothing (such as her bustle), and escapes by bicycling to a railroad station. She changes into her mother's widow's garb, including a thick black veil to hide her face, and buys a ticket to London. In London, she hopes to remain anonymous and to find her mother by placing cryptic messages in newspapers.

While waiting for the train, she reads a glaring newspaper headline about the kidnapping of 12-year-old Lord Tewksbury of nearby Basilwether Park. A picture shows the boy with long curls and a velvet suit, looking exactly like Lord Fauntleroy. She has time to spare, and, intrigued, she visits the estate. After some sleuthing she finds the boy's secret tree-house. Along with mounds of hair and discarded clothing, she discovers several books about ships and life at sea. Enola deduces in true Holmesian fashion that the young boy, fed up with his pampered life, has staged his kidnapping and is now in London seeking a cabin boy's position. Enola confides this information to the detective in charge of the investigation, Inspector Lestrade, who is within earshot of Madame Laelia, a clairvoyant who has volunteered her services to locate the boy.

After boarding the train to London, Enola is horrified to see a ghastly face staring at her through the compartment window. An old crone in the compartment, trying to be helpful, suggests going to Culhane's Used Clothing Emporium when it is time to get rid of her mourning costume.

That night, alone in the filthy streets of East London, Enola is accosted by the man whose hideous face she had seen on the train. He demands to know where the young Tewksbury is and drags her into the hold of a small, deserted ship. There she finds a boy whom she recognizes as young Lord Tewksbury. He soon reveals an impudent and superior nature, but is no match for Enola's quick wit and sharp tongue. The assistant of her assailant had found him and brought them to the ship.

The two villains discuss the situation and the ransom they hope to collect as they tie up their prisoners. The assistant's name is Squeaky and the big bruiser who, in disguise, was Madame Laelia, is identified as Cutter. Slowly and painfully Enola uses the sharp edge of a corset stay to cut through her ropes. Then she frees the young, somewhat chastened, lord. Together they make a wild dash for freedom and with Squeaky and Cutter in hot pursuit set off through the slums of East London. After several near-captures, they bribe a shopkeeper to hide them. By coincidence, the shopkeeper is Mrs. Culhane, proprietor of Culhane's Used Clothing Emporium. For a price, she shelters the two fugitives and sells them different sets of clothes. The next day, Enola accompanies Lord Tewksbury to the police station where he will turn himself in. She sees Inspector Lestgrade talking with her brother Sherlock and decides she must leave the boy to face the inspector by himself. She makes a hurried retreat.

Later she rents an office, planning to use this as the headquarters of a detective agency she hopes to start using the assumed name of Ivy Meshle (an anagram of Holmes). She also learns that Cutter and Squeaky have been captured. Using the characteristics of flowers revealed in the book her mother gave as directives, she composes a cryptic message directed to her mother. In time an equally cryptic message appears in the paper. When decoded, it states that her mother is "blooming in the sun." Although she continues to wonder why her mother didn't take her with her, Enola is looking forward to an exciting future.

Passages for Booktalking
The short preface about Enola roaming the deserted streets of London is found on pp. 1–4. Other interesting passages are: Enola meets her brothers at the station (pp. 31–38); the brothers theorize about their mother's disappearance (pp. 47–51); and Enola solves the first cipher (pp. 73–81).

Themes and Subjects
In addition to a cracking good mystery story filled with action and suspense, the author gives an accurate picture of Victorian social life, mores, and

hypocrisy. Victorian prudery is depicted in often uproarious detail. The unfairness of class segregation and the unequal treatment of women are well presented. The seamy side of London life—including the filth, crime, and squalor—is well portrayed. Enola is a courageous, spunky heroine who grows in maturity and stature as the novel progresses. The ciphers and their solutions are fascinating. Other subjects: Arthur Conan Doyle, Sherlock Holmes, inheritances, dress and clothing, detectives, justice, and sex discrimination.

TURNBULL, ANN. *Forged in the Fire.* Candlewick, 2007, $16.95 (978-0-7636-3144-4) (Grades 6–10)

Introduction

Ann Turnbull (1943–) is a distinguished English writer of books for children and young adults, many of which take place in Shropshire, the county in England where she lives. Her two Quaker novels, *No Shame, No Fear* (Candlewick, 2004, $15.99; 0763625051) and its sequel *Forged in the Fire*, take place in England from 1662 through 1667. According to the author, "The inspiration for these stories began years ago when I first learned about the early Quakers and was struck by their vitality, faith and courage in face of relentless persecution. They rejected the formal structure of the established church, had no priests, met in fields or barns or in each other's homes and refused to pay church tithes." *No Shame, No Fear,* a story of passion and persecution, begins in 1662 after the Civil War in which Cromwell was defeated. The Stuart monarchy (Charles II) and the authority of the Church of England have been restored and dissenting religious groups are being persecuted. Susanna Thorn, a 15-year-old Quaker girl has left her country home to work in the town of Hemsbury, Shropshire, in a print shop run by Mary Faulkner. William Haywood, the 17-year-old son of a wealthy merchant, has returned to Hemsbury after three years studying at Oxford and meets Susanna. He is attracted not only to Susanna but also to her faith and in defiance of his father's strict decrees he becomes a Quaker. Will and Susanna, together with their friends, experience incredible harassment, beatings, arrests, imprisonment in squalid conditions, disease, and public humiliation. Though deeply in love, the two decide to wait three years before marriage. Will, now disowned by his father, goes to London to work in the book trade while Susanna remains behind and continues to work in Mary's shop. This book and its sequel are narrated in alternating chapters by Will and Susanna. Some realistic language and adult situations make *Forged in the Fire* suitable for mature readers in grades 6 and up.

Historical Background

The Society of Friends or Quakers is a religious sect founded in England in 1648 by George Fox and his followers. They believe that "god is in every man" and that there is no need for a formal religious structure. This belief in human goodness led them to refuse to take oaths of allegiance, to condemn war, and to resist the power of the existing church and state. After the monarchy was restored in 1660, several parliamentary acts were passed to reestablish the power of the Church of England. The Quaker Act of 1662 made it treason to refuse to take the Oath of Allegiance and to hold any religious meetings other than those of the established church. These regulations were reinforced by the Conventicle Act of 1664.

The infamous Newgate Prison (where Will is held) was situated within the City of London. Founded in 1158, it was noted for its squalid conditions and was rebuilt many times—including after the Great Fire of 1666—before its closure in 1912. Among famous prisoners held there were Daniel Defoe, Ben Jonson, and William Penn, the Quaker who founded Pennsylvania (in 1681, Charles II granted Penn a land charter in the New World).

Will almost dies from ague, an early English word for malaria, which caused extreme fever, shivering, sweating, and often death. Shakespeare mentions the ague in several plays. The Great Fire of London began on Sunday, September 2, and continued through Wednesday, September 5, 1666, when a decrease in winds and the firebreaks from gunpowder shot from the Tower of London halted its spread. About 14,000 structures were consumed, including Old St. Paul's Cathedral. The fire was confined to the original City of London and did not spread to Westminster, now called the West End. The novel begins in Shropshire, a county in the extreme west of England, bordering on Wales.

Principal Characters

Susanna Thorn, an 18-year-old Quaker girl
Mary Faulkner, the owner of a print shop
William Haywood, Susanna's 20-year-old fiancé
Nat Lacon, Mary's former apprentice and Susanna and Will's close friend
Henry Haywood, Will's father
Judith Minton and Daniel Kite, a married couple, friends of Susanna's
James Martell, a London bookseller and Will's employer
Cecily Martell, his wife
Amos Bligh, another London printer and Nat's employer
Rachel Chaney, a London Quaker
Vincent and Tabitha Chaney, Rachel's husband and daughter
John Turner, Will's friend
Francis Palmer, an 18-year-old Friend

Edmund Ramsey, a wealthy Quaker merchant in London
Catherine Ramsey, his attractive 17-year-old daughter
Jane and Dorothy Ramsey, Catherine's younger sisters
Alice Betts, Susanna's Shropshire friend

Plot Synopsis

It is June 1665 in the town of Hensbury in Shropshire, England and 18-year-old Susanna Thorn is awaiting news from her fiancé, William Haywood, about his return to Hensbury and their forthcoming marriage. Will is currently working in a printer's shop run by James Martell close to Old St. Paul's in the City of London. After falling in love as teenagers, Susanna and Will agreed to test their love by staying apart for three years. The time is almost up and both are eager to be reunited and get married. They are ardent Quakers and both have suffered severe persecution, particularly Will, who has been disowned by his wealthy father, Henry Haywood, because of his conversion. Susanna is happy working in a printer's shop operated by fellow Quaker and mentor Mary Faulkner, but she is anxious to be with Will. Susanna spends time visiting with Friends Judith and Daniel Kite, a young married couple who hope to escape the persecutions by emigrating to Massachusetts. She also visits her family in the countryside and receives as a gift a homemade shift to wear on her wedding night.

In the meantime, Will is alarmed at the growing signs of a plague epidemic in London. He and his roommate, Nat Lacon, another printer's apprentice from Hensbury now working for Amos Bligh in London, notice the increase in blood-red signs on doorways, indicating the plague. Will and Nat had planned to travel to Hensbury with two aged gentlemen, the Leighton brothers. By the time the Leightons are ready to leave, the plague is so rampant that certificates for legal departure from the city are impossible to obtain, particularly for dissidents. Will and Nat are stranded in London.

Will's Quaker friend John Turner tells him that a group of 50 Quakers, held prisoner in Newgate Prison, are to be transported to a ship that is anchored in the Thames, the *Black Spread-Eagle*, for eventual shipment to Jamaica. Will joins a group of family members and colleagues on small boats that cruise alongside the prisoners' barge to express support. One of the supporters is Rachel Chaney, whose husband Richard, a friend of Will's, is in the prisoners' barge. Will and the group are sickened by the cruel, inhuman treatment the prisoners receive. Back on shore, Will speaks imprudently to a bullying prison official and, as a result, he and his two companions, John Turner and Francis Palmer, are seized and taken to Newgate Prison. In the prison they are surrounded by unbelievable squalor, filth, and human misery. The three are found guilty of unlawful congregation and fined five pounds each, which they refuse to pay on principle.

Back in prison, cases of plague are reported. Within days Francis dies, followed by John. Will feels guilty knowing he was the cause of their initial incarceration. Will also falls ill, not with the plague, but a severe case of the ague. He suffers from bouts of fever, sweating, and shivering. He is visited by his employer, James Martell, and his wife Cecily. They realize that Will is near death and appeal to Edmund Ramsey, a wealthy Quaker merchant, who pays Will's fine and brings him to his house to recover. While there, Will learns that the entire Martell family has died of the plague. Will regains his health rapidly and finds work as the organizer of Mr. Ramsey's impressive library while also getting to know the Ramsey family, including Catherine, Mr. Ramsey's charming and beautiful 17-year-old daughter.

The plague is subsiding and Susanna, anxious to see Will, decides to travel to London with a group of Quakers led by Alice Betts. When Susanna enters the luxurious Ramsey house she sees Will and Catherine gazing at one anther as they play duets on the virginal. Suspecting the worst, a jealous Susanna flees before Will can offer an explanation. A period of misunderstanding and estrangement ensues. Susanna, unable and unwilling to believe Will's innocence, refuses to see him. She takes lodging with Rachel Chaney and seeks the friendship of her old Hensbury friend Nat, who is attracted to Susanna but still values Will's friendship. While Susanna is at the Chaneys', Rachel learns that her husband has died on the *Black Spread-Eagle*. When Will's job ends, he leaves the Ramseys and, now with only casual employment, thinks it is an unsuitable time to contact Susanna. When a long-lost letter to Susanna from Will arrives, telling her about Newgate, the Ramseys, and his undying love, Susanna relents and a joyous reunion takes place. They consummate their love in Will's humble lodging and make plans for a London wedding.

Nine days later, on Susanna's nineteenth birthday, they are married and move into a charming two-room flat atop a building in the City next to a steeple-house (church) called Mary Aldermary. As a present, Mr. Ramsey buys Mr. Martell's bookshop and hires Will to be the manager. Susanna leaves her job with Amos Bligh to be Will's assistant. Within months their joy is complete when Susanna realizes that she is pregnant. She writes Will's father telling him of the marriage and that she is expecting. However, on September 2, tragedy strikes London in the form of a huge fire that sweeps through the old city. Will and Susanna try to save their book stock by burying it a nearby crypt, part of Old St. Paul's. When the fire becomes dangerously close, Will orders Susanna to accompany other Quaker refugees out of the city to fields in the farming area of Islington. With Nat's help, Will continues the salvage operation. Susanna leaves reluctantly and spends a sleepless night anxiously awaiting news of her husband.

The next morning, out of the smoke and haze, Susanna is astonished to see Will's father, Henry Haywood, emerge. He has come to London, anxious for a reconciliation with his son and daughter-in-law particularly now that he will soon be a grandfather. The two spend several fretful hours but miraculously both Will and Nat arrive unharmed. The stock, however, was lost when the crypt collapsed. Will at first refuses his father's offer of money to start over, but at Susanna's urging and, in the true spirit of reconciliation, he finally accepts. In a letter to friend Judith Kite, now in Massachusetts, dated six months later (February 1667), Susanna reports on the birth of a son, Josiah, and says that Will is recovering his losses and is working for Ned in Ned's new book store. In closing, she says, "We have come through persecution, plague, and fire, and will live and work in the truth."

Passages for Booktalking

Some interesting passages are: Will writes to Susanna about marriage (pp. 1–3); Susanna visits her parents and receives a wedding present (pp. 12–15); plague-ridden London (pp. 25–30); Will and friends on the Thames supporting the prisoners (pp. 53–58); and Will is sent to Newgate Prison (pp. 58–61).

Themes and Subjects

The author has created a masterful picture of London life during the Restoration when first the plague and then the Great Fire of 1666 occurred. The reader is treated to authentic details of the time—housing and lodgings, businesses and commerce, food and cooking, sanitation and health, class differences, the labor market and the apprenticeship system, family life, prisons, town and city life, publishing and book selling, and clothing. Two themes are paramount: the beauty and fulfillment in true love (this is essentially a moving love story) and the power, consolation, and dedication involved in religious faith. Other subjects are the nature of the Quaker religion, jealousy, marriage, friendship, Charles II, Newgate Prison, London, religious persecution, superstition, human depravity, and the nature of hope.

ADDITIONAL SELECTIONS

Avi. *The Traitor's Gate* (Atheneum, 2007, $17.99) (Grades 5–8)

Narrator John Huffam, age 14, investigates the real reason for his father being sent to a debtor's prison in this adventure story set in the Dickensian London of 1849.

Bradley, Kimberly Brubaker. *The Lacemaker and the Princess* (Simon, 2007, $16.99) (Grades 6–8)
In this novel set in Versailles when Marie Antoinette held sway, 11-year-old Isabelle is leading a double life; during the day she is a lacemaker and after hours she is the friend of the young Princess Marie Therese.

Buckley-Archer, Linda. *Gideon the Cutpurse: Being the First Part of the Gideon Trilogy* (Simon, 2006, $17.95) (Grades 4–8)
Two children befriend an honorable thief and encounter the villainous Tar Man when they find themselves in 18th-century London.

Bunce, Elizabeth C. *A Curse as Dark as Gold* (Scholastic, 2008, $17.99) (Grades 6–10)
After the death of their father, sisters Charlotte and Rosie take over the management of a mill that has been cursed in this novel that takes place during the early days of the Industrial Revolution in England.

Downswell, Paul. *Battle Fleet* (Bloomsbury, 2008, $16.95) (Grades 5–8)
Seafaring Sam, the hero of *Powder Monkey* (Bloomsbury, 2005, $16.95) and *Prison Ship* (Bloomsbury, 2006, $16.95), returns to war to aid Nelson at Trafalgar and later attend the Admiral's funeral in London.

Forsyth, Kate. *The Gypsy Crown* (Hyperion, 2008, $16.88) (Grades 6–9)
In this exciting adventure story set in 17th-century England, the Puritan fervor targets the Gypsies and results in the Rom (Gypsy) families of cousins Emilia and Luka being caught in a web of prejudice and persecution.

Frost, Helen. *The Braid* (Farrar, 2006, $16) (Grades 7–10)
When her family is evicted from their landholding in 19th-century Scotland, Sarah's family, including her sister Jeannie, sails for Canada; but Sarah, age 15, hides and flees to the north to be with relatives on an island in the Outer Hebrides.

Golding, Julia. *The Diamond of Drury Lane* (Roaring Brook, 2008, $12.50) (Grades 7–10)
Set in early eighteenth-century London, this is the story of Catherine Royal, her home in the Drury Lane theater, and the diamond she believes is hidden there.

Grant, K. M. *How the Hangman Lost His Heart* (Walker, 2007, $16.95) (Grades 5–8)
After the Battle of Culloden in 1746, Alice's Royalist uncle is captured, drawn, quartered, and beheaded, and Alice and her hangman friend Dan Skinslicer decide to save her uncle's head and his dignity.

Hearn, Julie. *The Minister's Daughter* (Atheneum, 2005, $16.95) (Grades 7–10)
In 17th-century England an unmarried Puritan minister's daughter, with the cooperation of her sister and father, goes to extreme lengths to disguise the fact that she is pregnant.

Hesse, Karen. *Stowaway* (Simon, 2000, $17.95) (Grades 5–8)
An 11-year-old boy tells of his adventurous life as a stowaway during Captain Cook's two-and-one-half year voyage around the world beginning in 1768.

Higgins, F. E. *The Black Book of Secrets* (Feiwal and Friends, 2007, $14.95) (Grades 4–6)

Set roughly in Dickensian England, this is the story of a waif named Ludlow who escapes his avaricious parents by fleeing to a small town controlled by a wicked landowner where he begins working for a secret pawnbroker.

Ibbotson, Eva. *The Star of Kazan* (Dutton, 2004, $16) (Grades 4–8)

Set in the days of the Austro-Hungarian Empire, this is the story of 12-year-old Annika and her adventures with her aristocratic mother.

Lawrence, Iain. *The Castaways* (Delacorte, 2007, $15.99) (Grades 5–8)

In this sequel to *The Convicts* (Delacorte, 2005, $15.99) and *The Cannibals* (Delacorte, 2005, $15.99), Tom Tin and his crew again take to the high seas and Mr. Goodfellow continues his acts of villainy.

Meyer, Carolyn. *In Mozart's Shadow* (Harcourt, 2008, $17) (Grades 7–12)

This novel, told from the viewpoint of Mozart's older but also talented sister, tells what it was like growing up in the shadow of this great composer.

Molloy, Michael. *Peter Raven Under Fire* (Scholastic, 2005, $16.95) (Grades 6–9)

This is a fast-paced adventure featuring Peter Raven, age 13, who is a midshipman during the Napoleonic Wars.

Morgan, Nicola. *The Highwayman's Footsteps* (Candlestick, 2007, $16.77) (Grades 7–10)

Inspired by the Alfred Noyes poem *The Highwayman*, this novel of daring adventure features a feisty heroine, a rebellious hero, and lots of thrilling historical action.

Peacock, Shane. *Eye of the Crow* (Tundra, 2007, $19.95) (Grades 6–10)

In 1867 London, 13-year-old Sherlock Holmes, a pauper, helps an Arab youth who has been wrongfully accused of murder.

Pennington, Kate. *Brief Candle* (Hodder, 2005, pap. $12.50) (Grades 6–8)

In this novel set in Yorkshire that features the Bronte family, Emily helps two hapless lovers.

Rabin, Staton. *Betsy and the Emperor* (Simon, 2004, $16.95) (Grades 6–9)

On the island of St. Helena in the South Atlantic, 14-year-old Betsy develops a friendship with the exiled Napoleon Bonaparte.

Springer, Nancy. *The Case of the Left-Handed Lady* (Philomel, 2007, $12.99) (Grades 6–9)

Fourteen-year-old Enola Holmes, the young sister of Sherlock, begins her own detective agency in 19th-century London. See also in this section *The Missing Marquess*.

Sturtevant, Katherine. *A True and Playful Narrative* (Farrar, 2006, $17) (Grades 7–10)

Sixteen-year-old Meg Moore, growing up in 17th-century England, is dismayed when her request comes true that her suitor be captured by Barbary pirates so she that she can write about the experience.

Updale, Eleanor. *Montmorency's Revenge* (Orchard, 2007, $16.99) (Grades 7–10)
In this, the fourth volume in this Victorian spy thriller series, Montmorency and his friends seek revenge for the murder by an anarchist of George Fox-Selwyn as reported in the third volume, *Montmorency and the Assassin* (Orchard, 2006, $16.88).

Wallace, Karen. *The Unrivalled Spangles* (Atheneum, 2006, $16.95) (Grades 7–10)
Fourteen-year-old Lucy, part of a famous equestrian act in her father's circus, falls in love with the son of the owner of a rival circus in this novel set in 19th-century England.

Yolen, Jane, and Robert J. Harris. *The Rogues* (Philomel, 2007, $18.99) (Grades 6–10)
In Scotland in the late 1790s, Roddy and his family are dispossessed from their land in the Scottish Highlands and the boy later sets out to locate a precious jewel belonging to his mother. This is the fourth volume in the series known as the Scottish Quartet.

TWENTIETH CENTURY

BRADLEY, KIMBERLY BRUBAKER. *For Freedom: The Story of a French Spy.* Delacorte, 2003, $15.95 (978-0-385-72961-1); pap. Dell, $5.50 (978-0-440-41831-3) (Grades 6–9)

Introduction
Kimberley Brubaker Bradley, who was born in Fort Wayne, Indiana, in 1967, majored in chemistry at college and spent some time as a research chemist. After marrying her longtime sweetheart and beginning to raise a family, she turned to writing for young readers. Her books are written for different age levels and in different genres.

One of her historical novels is *Weaver's Daughter* (Delacorte, 2000, $15.95; 0385327692), winner of the Bank Street College of Education Children's Book of the Year. Written for a younger audience (grades 4–6), it tells the story of 10-year-old Lizzie Baker, living in the Southwest Territory (now Tennessee) in the 1790s. She suffers from acute asthma and only survives because of the intervention of a slave-owning southern family who take her to their home in Charleston, South Carolina.

For Freedom takes place over a four-year period from May 1940 through June 1944, principally in the French coastal town of Cherbourg in Normandy. Suzanne, the heroine and narrator, ages from 13 to 17 during the course of the novel. The story is based on the true experiences of Suzanne David, who was a spy for the French Resistance during World War II. In 1945 she married an

American soldier, gave up her singing career, and moved to the United States. Much later, the author conducted the interviews with Suzanne that became the basis for this book.

Historical Background

Cherbourg (renamed Cherbourg-Octerville in 2000 when two cities merged) is a city on the English Channel in Normandy in northwestern France. Its artificial harbor is the largest in the world. Its harbor was partially destroyed by bombs and floating mines during the Battle of Normandy in 1944. The city was liberated from the Germans by the Battle of Cherbourg on June 26–27, 1944, after June 6 invasion of France known as D-Day. This was the largest seaborne invasion in history, with 3 million troops eventually crossing the English Channel in Operation Overlord. Omaha Beach was the bloodiest of the landing areas and involved American troops. There were more than 2,400 casualties on the first day of fighting.

The inland city of St. Lo (where Suzanne sings) was the scene of major conflict in the Battle of Normandy, which left 95 percent of the city destroyed. The wartime Resistance movement in France played an important part in the invasion by alerting the Allies of German activities, troop movements, and arsenals.

Suzanne's singing breakthrough occurs in an operetta, not an opera. It is *White Horse Inn*, in which a waiter woos the owner of the inn, a woman who is more interested in her guests than her swain. Premiering in 1930, it became an instant international success. It was *The Sound of Music* of its time. The operas in which Suzanne sings (*Carmen*, for example) are all well known and contain important roles for the soprano voice.

Principal Characters

Suzanne David, the narrator, a 13-year-old girl
Madame David, or Maman, Suzanne's mother
Monsieur David, or Papa, Suzanne's father, a railroad dispatcher
Pierre, her 14-year-old brother
Etienne, a cripple, her 16-year-old brother
Madame Montagne, a neighbor
Madame Marcelle, Suzanne's music teacher
Yvette Giveau, Suzanne's best friend
Dr. Leclerc, the family doctor

Plot Synopsis

For the first few months of World War II, life proceeds normally for 13-year-old Suzanne David and her family. She is growing up in the French coastal town of Cherbourg in Normandy with her loving family: Maman, Papa, a railroad dispatcher, and two brothers, 14-year-old Pierre and 16-year-old Etienne who is crippled by a back injury. Both boys attend a monastery school. Suzanne is a fine, obedient student at a private academy for girls. In addition to her regular school work, she studies voice privately with Madame Marcelle, who thinks she shows great promise as a singer.

On May 29, 1940, some eight months after France declared war on Germany, life changes dramatically for Suzanne. She and her best friend Yvette obtain permission from their teacher to study at the beach. They stop at the Place Napoleon, in downtown Cherbourg, to greet their neighbor, the very pregnant Madame Montagne. Suddenly German planes swarm overhead and soon bombs explode in the square. The shrapnel from one decapitates Madame Montagne and rips open her stomach, killing her exposed unborn child. Suzanne and Yvette are so shocked that they scarcely realize they have also suffered shrapnel wounds. Suzanne is taken to Dr. Leclerc and gallantly endures the painful procedure of having the shards of metal removed. When Suzanne returns to school the next day Yvette is not there. Yvette is so traumatized by the bombing that she cannot speak and wanders around as if in a coma. Suzanne visits her but cannot arouse any reaction.

Shortly after summer recess begins, the Germans arrive in Cherbourg. Within days, soldiers smash into the family's house to confiscate it for barracks. The Davids are given only half an hour to clear out. In that short time, they gather up as much personal goods as possible and move into the street. A kindly neighbor houses them in her basement until, three weeks later, Papa finds a tiny apartment overlooking a cemetery. Their new home is so small that Suzanne must sleep in a closet! Nevertheless life goes on and Suzanne continues her voice lessons and her fruitless visits to Yvette. Food and clothing shortages are severe, everyday life becomes more difficult, and Suzanne notices that Jewish families and the few blacks in Cherbourg are suddenly disappearing.

In December 1941, the Davids are encouraged by news of Pearl Harbor and America's entry into the war. They find out that the Germans have abandoned their home but return to a house left completely stripped and filthy. At least they have their home back. To celebrate, Papa somehow obtains a steak, which is stolen by an intruding cat. The steak is rescued and the cat, Niki, becomes part of the household. Suzanne stars in the operetta *White Horse Inn* and later plays Mimi in *La Boheme* in Cherbourg and neighboring towns including St. Lo. In the spring of 1943 Suzanne cuts herself badly in a kitchen accident and must see Dr. Leclerc. During subsequent visits for stitch removal and therapy, she and the doctor develop a mutual affection and trust. The doctor drops several telling hints and soon Suzanne realizes that he is an important member of the Resistance. He asks her if she will be a message carrier for the movement, cautioning her that no one, not even her family, must know about these activities. She consents, happy to be part of the war effort, and becomes spy number 22 in the Cherbourg underground.

Her first assignment is to deliver a message to number 7 in a local café. In spite of a severe case of nerves, she delivers the message, which she had hidden in her hair. During the run of *Carmen*, in which young Suzanne appears for the first time, she is still busy delivering messages. Before each assignation, she prays to Jesus and Mary for strength.

The strain begins to show, but her parents think it is caused by the stress of performing. Suzanne must make a trip to St. Lo with Madame Marcelle and decides to combine this with delivery of a secret message. As the two get off the bus, Suzanne, who again has the message tucked in her hair, realizes she has forgotten her identification papers and some German soldiers are approaching. Thinking quickly, she grabs Madame Marcelle and pulls her behind a haystack where they are forced to spend the night until the soldiers move on. This narrow escape encourages Suzanne to seek a better hiding place for her messages. She lifts the insole covering of one of her shoes and drills a hole in the sole big enough to hide a crumpled message.

As rumors about a possible Normandy invasion increase, the number of messages she delivers also increases. Her parents become alarmed by her many absences and she is running out of excuses—rehearsals, costume fittings, and so forth. The tension is relieved somewhat when Suzanne is asked to sing in *Rigoletto* with the Cherbourg Opera Co. at the Palace Garnier in Paris. The performance is a thrilling success but Suzanne seriously strains her vocal chords and Dr. Leclerc forbids her to sing until the condition improves.

The message deliveries and the danger, however, don't stop. One day, a group of German soldiers burst into the salon when she is having her hair cut. Her hairdresser places her arm around one of the soldiers and, as Suzanne is arrested, murmurs an apology.

Someone has informed on the spies. She is dragged off to the city jail and questioned for hours without being given food or water. She courageously admits to nothing. The next day a miracle occurs. There is a great commotion and the Germans leave hastily. It is June 6, 1944—D-Day—and the Allies are landing on the nearby Normandy beaches. Suzanne and another prisoner, number 14, are the only surviving spies. The others including Dr. Leclerc and his family have been shot. Suzanne returns to her family and confesses all. A huge feast is prepared for her and everyone toasts the gallant young lady who is both a spy and a hero.

(In an epilogue, the author tells how Suzanne met and married a GI, gave up her singing career, and moved to America to raise a family. The hairdresser and other collaborators were punished, and it appears that Yvette did not recover.)

Passages for Booktalking

There are many fine passages to read: bombs fall on Cherbourg (pp. 1–9); the David family is forced out of its house (pp. 323–327); life in the new apartment (pp. 43–46); and the family returns to their house (pp. 77–82).

Themes and Subjects

This book gives a vivid picture of the horrors of war, the terrible ordeal of living through the Nazi occupation during World War II and how ordinary people react to these hardships. This is also a tale that combines suspense and excitement with details of everyday life within a caring family. Suzanne is a gallant, heroic character who places devotion to freedom and her country before her own life. Her growing courage, acceptance of enormous responsibilities, and rapid maturation are effectively portrayed. Some addition subjects: France, D-Day, Cherbourg, friendship, loyalty, spies and spying, family life, Nazi Germany, French Resistance, Nazi occupation, school life, death, homes, singing, and opera.

DAHLBERG, MAURINE F. *Escape to West Berlin.* Farrar, Straus, 2004, $16 (978-0-374-30959-6) (Grades 4–8)

Introduction

Maurine Dahlberg was born in 1951 in Fulton, Missouri. She has always had an interest in both literature and music. She is an editor for a Navy research institute, has studied the piano, and plays the piccolo and flute in a concert band. She is married and now lives in Springfield, Virginia. Her first historical novel, *Play to the Angels* (Farrar, Straus, 2000, o.p.), takes place in Vienna in February 1938. Its central character is 12-year-old Greta Radky who, in spite of lack of support from her mother, is pursuing her ambition to be a concert pianist like her brother Kurt, who died almost a year before. She meets a brilliant but secretive piano teacher who agrees to take her as a pupil. She practices diligently for her first concert which, by coincidence is the day Hitler's troops invade Austria. It is then that she learns about her teacher's past. He is Karl von Engelhart, a renowned German pianist who has sacrificed his money and career to help Jewish artists escape from Nazi Germany. Greta helps him flee to Prague and she maintains her resolve, in spite of the Nazis, to achieve a career in music. Ms. Dahlberg's most recent novel is *The Story of Jonas* (Farrar, Straus, 2007, $16; 0374372644), about a 13-year-old slave who accompanies his master's son to the goldfields in Kansas in 1859.

Escape to West Berlin takes place over a period of about a month beginning in July 1961 in East Berlin. The narrator is 13-year-old Heidi Klenk.

Historical Background

Toward the end of World War II, the Battle of Berlin resulted on May 2, 1945, with the unconditional surrender of the German army to Russian troops. Later, under the Potsdam Agreement, Berlin and Germany were divided into four sectors: the French, British, American, and Russian. In 1949, as a result of the Cold War, the three western areas in both the city and country were combined and the Federal Republic of Germany was created with its capital in Bonn. The German Democratic Republic (East Germany) was established in the Russian sector. Because of the repressive Communist regime in the East and deteriorating economic conditions, increasing numbers of East Germans sought refuge in the West. Soviet leaders in Moscow pressed the East German political leadership under Walter Ulbricht to build up their border defenses. Even Stalin called the situation "intolerable" and stated that "The demarcation line between East and West Germany should be considered a border-not any border, but a dangerous one." The situation worsened as more people defected. However, on June 15, 1961 (a month before the novel begins), Ulbricht stated that "No one has the intention of erecting a wall."

Under increased pressure, the East Germans capitulated and after closing the border and laying down miles of barbed wire as a barrier, construction of the Berlin Wall began on August 13, 1961. Eventually, it divided East and West Berlin and completely surrounded West Berlin. Additionally, the whole length of the border between East and West Germany was closed with chain fences, walls, minefields, and wire. It is estimated that as many as 200 people died trying to cross the wall in Berlin during the 28 years of its existence. After weeks of unrest during the collapse of the Soviet Union and its satellites, the East German government announced on November 9, 1989, that East Germans could enter West Berlin. Soon parts of the wall were chipped away, often by souvenir hunters, and eventually construction equipment destroyed the rest of it. The reunification of Germany was announced on October 3, 1990.

There are many references in the novel to Herr Ulbricht. Walter Ulbricht (1893–1973) was a German Communist who became a leader of the German Democratic Republic (East Germany) after its foundation in 1949. He rose to the position of chairman in 1953 and thus became the unquestioned leader of both the Communist Party in Germany and the country. A confirmed Stalinist, he formulated a central economic policy. But after Russian leadership was seized by Leonid Brezhnev, he fell into disfavor and was forced to resign in 1971. He died on August 1, 1973.

Principal Characters

Heidi Klenk, a 13-year-old East German girl, the narrator
Mutter Anne-Marie Klenk, her mother
Vater Karl Klenk, her father
Opa Fritz, her step-grandfather
Oma Sophie, her grandmother
Heinrich Sterns, an auto repair shop owner
The Weppelmanns, the Klenks' neighbors
Aunt Adelheide, Heidi's aunt in the West
Petra Hansen, Heidi's best friend
Ulrike Eisenstein, an unlikable girl
Herr Brecht, the Klenks' building supervisor
Hans and Emmy Bauer, a West Berlin couple

Plot Synopsis

It is late July 1961 in East Berlin and only two days until Heidi Klenk's thirteenth birthday. Instead of the joy that the occasion should bring, Heidi is feeling a growing sense of unease and apprehension, and now comes a major disappointment. Every August, she and her loving parents, Mutter and Vater, visit with Oma Sophie, her grandmother, and Opa Fritz, her step-grandfather, on the family farm close to Leipzig. Because Mutter is about due to give birth, this year's vacation has been canceled. Although Heidi begs to make the journey by herself, her parents worry about her traveling this distance alone and reluctantly refuse.

Heidi's general sense of anxiety and apprehension stems from the living conditions in East Berlin. Supposedly this is a "worker's paradise," but the situation is really one of economic depression and political harassment, where the slightest remark that might appear critical of the system or its leaders could have serious repercussions. Heidi tries to be loyal to the party and believe the propaganda she hears every day. She engages, for example, in proper communal activities—such as belonging to the Pioneers, the party's youth group for girls—but she secretly breaks some rules, listening, for example, to forbidden Western pop music on her radio. She keeps the volume low so that her neighbors, the Weppelmanns, can't hear the music and possibly report her. Heidi is relaxed with both her parents and her best friend, Petra Hansen, but must always be careful of her speech when girls like Ulrike Eisenstein, a dedicated patriot and obsessive achiever, are present.

Heidi is a well-adjusted, good-natured girl who unfortunately has developed an unfortunate phobia. While attending a Pioneer outing to a lake,

Heidi, an excellent swimmer, disobeyed the rules and swam out so far she almost drowned. Since then she has refused to go near water, even to the neighborhood swimming pool. The situation at home is also of growing concern. Her father, an expert mechanic, commutes daily to his job in the auto shop run by Heinrich Sterns in West Berlin. Because of the increased number of defections to the West and the growing government opposition to border crossings, Vater Klenk is under pressure to find a job in the East even though the pay is poorer and working conditions far inferior.

These worries are momentarily forgotten on Heidi's birthday. She spends the day with Petra visiting the zoo in West Berlin and has a lovely dinner that evening with her parents at the restaurant on the top of the Radio Tower. She receives a lovely pendant from Petra and a pair of American blue jeans from her Aunt Adelheide, who now lives in the West. The harassment against her father, however, increases. His name appears on a list of "border crossing warmongers" posted in the subway station. A group of neighbors visit and demand he resign his job, and their building superintendent, Herr Brecht, delivers an ultimatum that either Vater find a new job in East Berlin in two weeks or the family will be evicted. Heidi notices that her parents begin talking together in whispers. One morning, shortly thereafter, they tell her they have made plans for the three of them to defect to West Berlin in four days's time. At first Heidi is in a state of disbelief, but she later recognizes the need for this move to freedom. The families of Herr Sterns and of Vater's coworker Hans Bauer have found an apartment for them and will help with goods and furniture.

While giving the impression that life is continuing as usual, preparations are being made to leave when an unforeseen crisis arises. Opa Fritz dies suddenly and Vater must attend the funeral. Their departure is delayed by a further emergency—Mutter feels that the baby is about to be born. So their plans change again. Mutter and Vater will leave for the West immediately and Heidi will follow after she attends her step-grandfather's funeral, at which she will try to persuade her grandmother to accompany her to the West. Her parents succeed in making the crossing, and Heidi travels south. After the funeral Oma Sophie is told of the plan and, although it means leaving the farm and years of fond memories, she agrees to accompany Heidi back to Berlin and eventually across the border.

Unfortunately, in Heidi's absence, Herr Albricht, the German Communist leader, has closed the border and ordered miles of barbed wire to be laid around East Berlin prior to the building of a great wall. Heidi and Oma Sophie are denied permission to cross at a border checkpoint in Berlin in spite of Oma's show of great indignation. But at a section of unguarded barbed wire some Westerners help Oma through the barrier. Before Heidi can join her, some East German guards turn up and Heidi escapes back into East Berlin. Alone, Heidi turns to Petra for help. Petra asks her father, a Communist official, about areas where escape is still possible. He mentions that some adventurous souls are managing to leave by swimming across the Teltow Canal that divides East and West Berlin. He says there aren't enough guards to patrol its entire length. The following evening, Petra and Heidi meet and Petra gives Heidi her gym shorts and useful advice on making a safe crossing. Heidi, petrified as the thought of swimming again, nevertheless realizes she has no other choice. That night she slips silently into the canal and, though she has never believed in religion, utters a silent prayer before beginning the swim. She notices people waving flashlights on the shore. Could she, in the darkness, have turned around and be swimming back to the East? In spite of her misgivings, she continues and discovers when she reaches the other side exhausted that they are well-wishers who are shouting "Welcome to West Berlin." They treat her like a heroine and take her to her family for a joyous reunion. She is looking forward to sharing a bedroom with beloved Oma Sophie and helping to care for the new addition to the family, a healthy baby brother named Franz Dieter Klenk.

Passages for Booktalking
Some interesting passages: Heidi's home life and conditions in East Berlin (pp. 5–19); Heidi listens to Elvis and overhears her parents whispering (pp. 16–18); she visits Petra and remembers her swimming disaster (pp. 27–31); and Heidi's birthday and a warning (pp. 49–54).

Themes and Subjects
Daily life under a totalitarian regime, with its oppression and harassment, is well portrayed as is how the fear of authority can change one. Heidi's character, on the borderline of maturity, is well defined—at times she is peevish and pouting and on other occasions she assumes responsibilities and makes decisions that are wise beyond her years. The plot is well-paced with plenty of action and suspense. Intergenerational ties and allegiances are important elements in the story. It is interesting to trace the story with a map of Berlin at hand and locate the place names mentioned, like Alexanderplatz, the Zoo, Friedrichstrasse, and Tiergarten. Other subjects include: East and West Berlin. Germany, Communism, the Cold War, Berlin Wall, courage, grandparents, defection, Pioneers Youth Group, friendship, swimming, patriotism, informants, death, and sacrifice.

------·•·------

HESSE, KAREN. *Letters from Rifka.* Holt, 1992 (978-0-8050-1964-3); pap. Puffin, $6.99 (978-0-14-036391-3) (Grades 4–8)

Introduction

Karen Hesse was born in Baltimore in 1952. As a youngster, she was frequently ill and, as a result, had a lonely childhood. After college, she held many book-related jobs and was a librarian, book reviewer, and freelance editor before turning to full-time writing. In addition to several picture books, she has written a number of books for older children including some historical novels. Perhaps her most famous is the Newbery Medal winner *Out of the Dust* (Scholastic, 1997, $15.95, 0590360809; condensed in *The Newbery/Printz Companion*). It is told through a series of free-verse diary entries that cover two years (1934–1935) in the life of Billie Jo who is growing up on a wretched farm in the Oklahoma Panhandle. In addition to family problems including her mother's death, the young girl is confronted with a neverending battle against drought and a relentless series of dust storms.

The story of *Letters from Rifka* is based on the true experiences of the author's great-aunt. It is told through a series of twenty-odd letters written between September 2, 1919, and October 22, 1920, by a 12- (later 13-) year-old Jewish girl to her crippled older cousin, Tovah, who has given Rifka a volume of Pushkin's poems as a gift. In the blank pages in this volume, Rifka writes these letters recounting her journey from Russia to America. She hopes eventually to send the book back to her beloved cousin as a chronicle of her adventures as an immigrant. Each letter is preceded by a brief poetic quote from Pushkin.

Historical Background

In this novel there are many references to the continual persecution of Jews in Russia. In its extreme, this took the form of organized raids called pogroms on Jewish communities. The word "pogrom" is Yiddish for "devastation" and now refers to massacres of helpless people, specifically those directed against Russian Jews. During these pogroms, thousands of innocent people were killed and their property confiscated. In 1881, when Jews were wrongfully blamed for the assassination of Czar Alexander II, there was an outbreak of ferocious attacks in which whole communities were destroyed. The following year, Czar Alexander III passed legislation that further limited the civil liberties of the

Jews. Quotas were placed on the number of Jews allowed into secondary schools and entry, for Jews, into most professions was forbidden.

After the Russian Revolution, in spite of the Communist espousal of equality for all, persecutions continued. The period 1919 through 1921 was one of continued violence and barbarous pogroms targeting Jews. This persecution led to a massive emigration of Jews from Russia.

More than 2 million Jews left Russian between 1880 and 1920. Of these, more than 1.5 million came to the United States. For most of them, the point of entry was Ellis Island, in New York City's harbor. This 27-acre piece of land was named after Samuel Ellis, a colonial landowner. It became government property in 1808, and served as a fort and arsenal until 1892 when it was turned into a federal immigration station. By the time it closed in 1954, more than 12 million people had been processed in this institution. Each immigrant had to pass a health examination. Those who had health problems (like Rifka), were either sent home or detained on the island until fully recovered, sometimes a period of several months. More than 5,000 prospective immigrants died on Ellis Island while being treated. About 2 percent of all entrants were sent back to their native countries for reasons that included contagious diseases, criminal background, and insanity. The island is now part of the Statue of Liberty National Monument administered by the National Park Service. It is a popular tourist site, attracting more than 3 million visitors each year. The main building houses a fascinating museum. Legally, the island is divided in two—part is in the state of New York and the other part in New Jersey.

Principal Characters

Rifka Nebrot, a 12-year-old Jewish girl
Mama and Papa Nebrot, her parents
Tovah, Rifka's disabled cousin
Uncle Avrum, Rifka's wealthy uncle
Nathan, Rifka's brother who joined the army
Saul, her 16-year-old brother
Isaac, Reuben, and Asher, her three older brothers in America
Gaston and Marie, a couple who care for Rifka in Antwerp
Gizelle, Rifka's friend in Antwerp
Sister Katrina, a nun who tends to Rifka during her illness
Pieter, a 17-year-old sailor
Nurse Bowen, a nurse on Ellis Island
Ilya, a 7-year-old Russian immigrant
Mr. Fargate, an immigration officer
Dr. Askin, a medic on Ellis Island

Plot Synopsis

It is September 1919 in the village of Berdichev in Ukrainian Russia, and the Jewish Nebrot family is facing a major crisis. Rifka, age 12, is the youngest of the six Nebrot children. Her three oldest brothers—Isaac, Reuben and Asher—left home before she was born to find a new life in America. They promised to send money home to enable the rest of the family to join them. The family currently consists of Mama and Papa, Rifka, and her two remaining brothers—Nathan, a sensitive, kind-hearted young man who joined the army, and Saul, age 16, who seems to delight in pestering his young sister. Persecution of the Jews is increasing in intensity in Russia, particularly in the army. Nathan, unable to endure the cruelties inflicted on him, has deserted and returned home. Knowing that discovery of Nathan's whereabouts will result in his death and reprisals on the family, Mama and Papa decide on a bold move. Although they have no papers, they will escape via freight train to Poland, contact their sons for money, and book passage from Belgium to America. They are so secretive about these plans that only rich Uncle Avrum is included in the plotting. Not even Rifka's best friend, her cousin Tovah, is told, although Rifka is determined to write letters to this dearest companion recounting her experiences on the blank pages of a book of poems by Pushkin that Tovah has given her.

That night, the family hides in boxcars and Rifka, who is blond and speaks Russian without a Yiddish accent, is posted in the freight yards to divert any soldiers who might search the train for stowaways. Though almost petrified with fear, she is able to distract two soldiers with her idle chatter. Uncle Avrum arrives and invents a story, telling the soldiers that his factory has been robbed. They leave to investigate and Rifka climbs aboard the already-moving train.

After experiencing the humiliation of being stripped naked and examined by a depraved Polish doctor at the border, they enter Poland, where another calamity occurs. In the town of Motziv, where the family has relatives, Rifka is stricken with typhus. To avoid being separated from the family, her illness is kept secret and she is treated at home. But just as she is beginning to recover, Mama, Papa, and Nathan fall ill and are sent to the hospital. Rifka is cared for by Saul, who has also taken a full-time job to help pay the family's expenses. During this period, Rifka realizes that her brother possesses a generous, sacrificing nature that has emerged only because of this family crisis. Miraculously, everyone survives and the family heads for Warsaw to pick up the money for their steamship tickets.

On the crowded, stinking train to Warsaw, Rifka befriends a young mother who is nursing a child. Rifka volunteers to comb out the tangles in the woman's hair, and, in the process, discovers that the woman's scalp is covered with sores. This act of kindness has dire results. Rifka develops a severe case of ringworm and the ship's doctor will not issue her a ticket. Her parents consult a female representative of the Hebrew Immigrant Aid Society, who makes arrangements for Rifka to get treatments in Antwerp while the rest of the family proceeds to America without her. Because the treatment will take several months, this is the only logical solution but Rifka and the rest of the family are heartbroken at the separation and Rifka is fearful of traveling to the United States by herself. As farewell presents, Mama gives her daughter her gold locket and Papa, his tallis, a precious prayer shawl.

In Antwerp, Rifka stays at the home of a friendly couple, Gaston and Marie, and receives daily treatments involving soap and special intense lights from kindly Sister Katrina in a nearby convent. Rifka loses all her hair, learns both Flemish and English, has her thirteenth birthday, makes friends with a girl named Gizelle, comes to love Belgian food, particularly ice cream and chocolates, and has a series of small adventures such as relying on a good-natured milkman to escort her home after she gets lost. Almost a year after leaving Russia, she finally receives medical permission to leave Belgium and books passage on a small ship bound for New York City, where her reunited family is now living.

On board, she forms a tender relationship with Pieter, a 17-year-old sailor who gives her her first romantic kiss. The ship encounters a storm so severe that the ship is disabled and one sailor is lost at sea. Rifka learns that this was Pieter, and she is heartbroken. The ship is towed into New York harbor and the passengers are sent to Ellis Island for immigration screening. Mr. Fargate, one of the officers, is not convinced that this bald Jewish girl is free of ringworm and she is sent by the resident physician, Dr. Askin, to the hospital for contagious diseases on the island. There, she is befriended by Nurse Bowen, who helps her with her English and allows Rifka to help with her chores. Because she is now immune, Rifka is allowed to care for a Polish baby with typhus. She also gets to know a pathetic Russian orphan, 7-year-old Ilya who has been so traumatized by his recent experiences that he refuses to eat or speak. The authorities believe he is simple-minded and plan to return him to Russia. Rifka works with him, persuades him to eat and speak to her in Russian, and together they study English and read from her Russian book of Pushkin poems. Rifka soon realizes that Ilya is actually a very bright youngster.

Rifka is visited first by her brother Saul, who is amazed at how mature she has become, and then by her beloved mother. Mama, Papa, and Nathan have been forced to take sweatshop jobs but are beginning to adjust to life in America. Rifka is shattered when the Polish baby dies but she continues to make progress with bringing Ilya back to normal. After three weeks of confinement,

Rifka and Ilya are scheduled to appear before the admission board. Ilya goes first and once again refuses to speak. Rifka intervenes and gets him not only to read Pushkin before the group but also to quote a poem in English that she has written. Ilya is allowed to stay and is turned over to the welcoming arms of an uncle who has promised to care for him. When it is Rifka's turn, she is apprehensive because her scalp has begun to itch again and she is afraid the ringworm has returned. However the examination shows the itchiness is caused by the growth of new hair, and Rifka is released to a joyful family, some of whom she is meeting for the first time. Her new life is just beginning.

Passages for Booktalking (using pagination in paperback edition)

Some interesting excerpts from the letters: Rifka distracts the soldiers (pp. 7–14); the family is stripped at the Polish border (pp. 16–20); the family catches typhus (pp. 22–25); and Rifka helps the Polish girl with ringworm (pp. 35–38).

Themes and Subjects

At times this narrative seems like an anxiety dream with one catastrophe following another. However in this case the dream has a happy ending. Anti-Semitism in Russia is vividly portrayed as are the details and particulars of the immigrant experience. Jewish life and the importance of family are key themes. Rifka emerges not only as a loving, caring person but also as a resourceful, courageous woman who matures through overcoming impossible obstacles. Other subjects are diseases, medical treatments, immigration, Jews, brothers, Russia, Poland, Belgium, ships, sea stories, death, friendship, loyalty, perseverance, Ellis Island, prejudice, and determination.

MORPURGO, MICHAEL. *War Horse.* Greenwillow, 1982, $10.95 (978-0-688-02296-9); Scholastic (reissue), 2007, $16.99 (978-0-439-79663-7) (Grades 4–7)

Introduction

English-born Michael Morpurgo has written more than a hundred books chiefly for children. He was born in 1943 and after graduating from the University of London took a teaching job in a primary school in Kent where he found his calling as a writer after making up stories to tell his pupils. He now describes himself as "oldish, married with three children, and a grandfather six times over." In 1975 he and his wife founded the charity Farms for City Children, which provides inner-city and urban children the opportunity to spend a week on a working farm. There are now three participating farms and more than 50,000 children have been involved in the program. The initial inspiration for *War Horse* came when the author saw an old painting of a cavalry charge in World War I in which two of the horses were caught in barbed wire. Later, in a pub, he talked to an old war veteran who told him of the great contributions horses made to the war effort and how, at the end of the war, they were sold to French butchers for meat. During the 2007–2008 season at the National Theatre in London, a dramatization of the book caused a sensation with life-size puppets coming to life and galloping across the stage.

War Horse takes place over a period of about six years starting two years before the outbreak of World War I and through the four years of the war. It is told in the first person by the book's hero, a horse named Joey.

Historical Background

World War I is sometimes called the Great War or the First World War. It was also often referred to as "the war to end all wars," which proved to be a misnomer. The precipitating cause was the assassination of the heir to the Austro-Hungarian Empire, Archduke Franz Ferdinand, by a Serbian student in Sarajevo, Serbia. When Serbia appeared unwilling to punish the perpetrators properly and accede to other Austrian demands, Austria declared war on Serbia. Because the Allies had agreements on the security of Serbia, they also declared war. The Allies were the British Empire, France, Russia (until 1917), Italy (from 1915), and the United States (from 1917). The opposing powers were Germany, the Austro-Hungarian Empire, and the Ottoman Empire. Underlying and long-stating causes were as an intense arms race between Germany and Britain, the "saber-rattling" by all the nations involved, rivalry for trade and colonies, and a deep-seated animosity between the Germans and French. The war began in August 1914 and lasted until November 11, 1918 (the eleventh hour of the eleventh day of the eleventh month).

The war was fought principally on two fronts, the Western and Eastern. The Western Front (roughly Belgium and France) is the principal locale of the story. After a period when both sides maneuvered for position, the combatants settled into warfare using an intricate system of trenches stretching for about 475 miles. Between the opposing sides there was a small area known as no-man's land. It has been estimated that about 20 million military and civilian deaths occurred during the war plus 40 million casualties. Horses also played an important role in the hostilities. The author says, "They were used as cavalry horses, and for pulling guns and ambulances. They were essential to the armies of both sides." More than 2 million horses died in this conflict.

Principal Characters

Joey, a horse
Albert Narracott, a 13-year-old boy
Mr. Narracott, a farmer, Albert's father
Mrs. Narracott, his mother
Zoey, another horse
Captain Nicholls, a cavalry officer
Corporal Samuel Perkins, Joey's trainer
Captain Jamie Steward, a friend of Captain Nicholls
Topthorn, Captain Steward's horse
Trooper Jamie Warren, a cavalryman
Herr Hauptmann, a German officer
Amelie, a 13-year-old French girl
Grandfather, Amelie's grandfather
Heinie and Coco, two horses
Friedrich, a kindly German master
A Welshman
David, Albert's army buddy
Major Martin, a veterinarian

Plot Synopsis

When he is less than 6 months old, Joey and his mother, a fine working farm horse, are taken to a horse sale where they are auctioned off. Joey is a beautiful reddish brown colt with a black tail and mane. His markings are also distinctive—a white cross on his forehead and four white socks above his hooves. He is heartbroken at being separated from his mother and having a new owner—a drunken farmer named Narracott who, on a wager, bought Joey for 3 guineas rather than the livestock he originally intended to buy. Dragged back to the Narracott farm, he is greeted by Albert, the farmer's 13-year-old son, and placed in a stall next to a friendly work horse named Zoey. Albert's mother makes excuses for her husband's erratic behavior, particularly when he is drinking, and tries to keep peace in the family, but Albert hates his father's cruel streak and his dictatorial ways. It is 1912 in Devon, England, and news of international tensions is ever-present. Talk of war is constant. For the next two years, Albert spends all of his spare time caring for Joey, and a bond that surpasses the closeness of any human friendship develops between them. During one of his drunken rages Albert's father attacks Joey, who responds by kicking the farmer in self defense. The next day, a vengeful Mr. Narracott threatens to sell Joey unless Albert trains him to be a plough horse like Zoey. Both Albert and Joey capitulate, and soon Joey is ploughing the fields. From then on, Albert scarcely speaks to his father.

War comes and with it increased financial burdens on the farm. One day, while Albert is busy with his farm chores, his father takes Joey into the village and sells him to a cavalry officer named Captain Nicholls for 40 pounds. Distraught at the news, Albert tries to enlist to be with Joey but is refused because he is only 15. He vows, however, that somehow and somewhere he and his horse will be reunited. In the army, Joey ceases to be a farm horse and becomes a cavalry mount. His trainer is Corporal Samuel Perkins, a stern, unyielding man whom Joey dislikes. Captain Nicholls, who is an experienced horseman and an amateur artist, comes regularly to ride Joey and to sketch him. During maneuvers, Joey becomes acquainted with Captain Nicholls's best friend, Captain Jamie Steward, and his beautiful sleek mount named Topthorn.

After the Channel crossing to France and making camp, Joey and Topthorn, now stable mates, gradually become accustomed to the sound of gunfire in the distance. The first battle comes and, during the charge, his beloved Captain Nicholls is killed by machine gun fire and Joey is brought back to camp riderless. He is placed under the care of Trooper Warren, but in the next battle both Warren and Steward are trapped behind enemy lines and taken prisoner. Joey and Topthorn are placed in the care of a German officer, Herr Hauptmann, who uses them to pull ambulance carts that carry the wounded to camp hospitals. The two horses are billeted in a stable of a farm occupied by an old man and his young granddaughter Amelie. The girl's parents were killed during the first week of the war and she welcomes the chance to lavish her love and attention on the two horses. For many months the horses enjoy this attention every day after fulfilling their duties pulling ambulances. During the winter, the frail, wispy Amelie is stricken with pneumonia but she recovers in the spring and, when not needed on the front, Joey and Topthorn are used as farm animals by Amelie's grandfather.

This idyllic interlude ends when German officers take the two horses away to haul cannons and other arms to the front. Now life for Joey and Topthorn becomes a living hell. Food is scarce and during the winter they spend their days and nights in freezing mud. They are used as part of a team of four that includes two work horses, Heinie and little Coco. The underfeeding, exposure, and hard work take their toll. Topthorn shows signs of decline but improves somewhat during the following spring and summer, particularly after they are placed under the care of a soldier nicknamed mad old Friedrich. Friedrich, who often talks to himself, is however far from mad—he alone realizes the stupidity and terrible waste of war. In spite of Friedrich's care, Topthorn dies and both Friedrich and Joey are heartbroken.

In a disconsolate mood, Joey wanders aimlessly and finds himself at the front in the nightmare zone known as no-man's land. Miraculously, when the German and British soldiers in the trenches see him, they stop shooting. Waving a white flag, a German soldier emerges from his trench to help Joey, whose legs have been ripped and torn by barbed wire. The soldier is joined by a Welshman from the other side. In a spirit of camaraderie, they flip a coin to see who will take custody of the injured horse. The Welshman wins and leads Joey to the safety of the animal hospital behind the lines. Here, two young members of the Veterinary Corps begin cleaning up the blood- and mud-soaked horse. An overjoyed Joey recognizes a voice. It is Albert, his first master! The other, a lad named David, is the first to recognize Joey's tell-tale markings as they have been described to him.

There is a wonderful reunion between a still-incredulous Albert and his beloved Joey. Joey develops tetanus from his wounds and the commanding officer, Major Martin, feels Joey should be put down. He relents when both Joey and David plead for his life. For weeks they nurse him and feed him liquids after his jaw becomes locked. Miraculously he recovers only to face another difficult crisis. The war has ended and surviving horses are to be kept in France and sold at public auction. All the soldiers generously contribute money to bid for Joey, but it is not enough to beat the bid of a French butcher who plans to kill Joey for meat. Unexpectedly, at the last minute, an old man outbids the butcher and gains possession of Joey. It is Amelie's grandfather. The young girl has died and he wants to keep Joey, whom his granddaughter adored. However, when he hears Albert's story, he realizes that Joey rightfully belongs to him. Albert and Joey sail for England and home on the next troopship.

Passages for Booktalking
Joey is separated from his mother but finds a friend in Albert (pp. 1–6); Joey kicks Mr. Narracott and later learns to plough (pp. 8–13); he is sold to Captain Nicholls and Albert is inconsolable (pp. 21–27); his first battle and the death of Captain Nicholls (pp. 40–43).

Themes and Subjects
On p. 88 Friedrich states one of the main themes of this novel, "How can one man kill another and not really know the reason why he does it, except that the other man wears a different color uniform and speaks a different language." This book portrays the senseless brutality of war plus its waste, futility, and horror. The companionship, loyalty, and compassion that can exist in animal/human and animal/animal relationships are touchingly described. Joey's instincts and traits are described without undue anthropomorphism. Other subjects are: World War I, England, France, battles, death, horses, cruelty to animals, courage, kindness, heroism, survival, decency, and friendship.

———•◦•———

SACHS, MARILYN.

A Pocket Full of Seeds. Doubleday, 1973, o.p.; pap. Backinprint, 2005, $10.95 (978-0-595-33846-7) (Grades 4–8)

Lost in America. Roaring Brook Press, 2005, $16.95 (978-1-59643-040-2) (Grades 5–8)

Introduction

Marilyn Sachs, the prolific author of many books for children and young adults, was born in New York City on December 18, 1927, and received degrees from both Hunter College and Columbia University. She lived in New York when the heroine of *Lost in America*, Nicole Nieman, also lived in the Big Apple. This explains the book's wealth of detail—often amusing—about life in the city during the late 1940s. The two books are based on the real life of Fanny Kreiger, a French-Jewish girl who lost her family at the Auschwitz concentration camp in Poland. At the end of World War II, Fanny left Europe and came to New York City. Much later when both Marilyn and Fanny married and relocated to San Francisco, the two met and became close friends. Subsequently Marilyn decided to tell Fanny's story in a two-part novel format. Other details of their friendship and the lot of other real-life characters are given in an Afterword in *Lost in America.*

A Pocket Full of Seeds covers about six years in the life of Nicole, from May 1938 through February 1944 or from age 8 through 14, and *Lost in America* continues the story for four more years, from June 1944 through August 1948, ending when Nicole is 18. The books form a continuous narrative but can be read separately.

Historical Background

Great Britain and France declared war on Germany on September 3, 1939, thus beginning World War II. In May 1940 Germany invaded the Low Countries and subsequently France. The following month Italy entered the war on the German side and invaded France in the south. France was ignominiously defeated and forced to sign a peace agreement, at Compiègne, in which the northern three-fifths of the country became German-occupied territory and the remainder, with headquarters at Vichy, became a puppet government under the leadership of Marshal Pétain. Some, like Mlle Legrand in the novels, regarded Pétain as a hero but most felt he was a traitor (after the war, he was tried for war crimes and his death sentence later commuted to life imprisonment). When Anglo-American forces invaded North Africa, Hitler rescinded the peace agreement. German troops entered unoccupied France in November of 1942 and occupied Aix-les-Bains in June 1943. The deportation of Jews to concentration camps began soon thereafter. In August 1944, the Allies made successful landings on the French Mediterranean coast and liberated the south of France. The city of Aix-les-Bains, the setting of these two novels, was part of Vichy France. It is a spa town in southeastern France close to the Swiss and Italian borders. As well as popular hot sulfur baths, it boasts an attractive beach on Bourget Lake, France's largest lake.

In *Lost in America*, the author has successfully portrayed life in New York City in the late 1940s, including Jewish life on the Grand Concourse in the Bronx. Unfortunately, many of the department stores mentioned, such as Alexander's, and popular restaurants—the Automat, Chock Full o'Nuts, Schrafft's, and Toffenetti's, for example—no longer exist. In the story, the heroine attends a Broadway musical, *High Button Shoes*. It opened on October 9, 1947, and ran for 737 performances. It featured such songs as "I Still Get Jealous" and "Papa, Won't You Dance with Me?"

Principal Characters in *A Pocket Full of Seeds*

Nicole Nieman, the narrator, a sensitive, outspoken French girl, age 8
Jacqueline Nieman, Nicole's 4-year-old sister
Henrietta Nieman (Maman), Nicole's mother
David Nieman (Papa), Nicole's father
Mr. and Mrs. Durand, the family with whom Nicole and Jacqueline board
Lucie Fiori, Nicole's unfriendly classmate
Françoise Rosten, Nicole's friend
Mr. and Mrs. Rosten, Françoise's parents
Mlle Legrand, the headmistress at Nicole's school
Berthe and Isaac, Polish refugees who are Maman's cousins

Plot Synopsis of *A Pocket Full of Seeds*

In a prefatory chapter set in the French town of Aix-les-Bains in February 1944, Nicole Nieman, the Jewish girl who narrates the story, is a live-in student at a private school whose stern headmistress is Mlle Legrand. It is World War II and the Germans have occupied the town. Food is scarce and Nicole is lonely and despondent, relying on the friendship of her fellow students for comfort. Her family was taken away by the Nazis three months before and she does not know what has happened to them. In spite of her uncertainty and apprehension about her future, Nicole takes time to help and give needed leadership to other students.

The principal narrative begins in Aix-les-Bains about six years earlier, in May of 1938 when Nicole is 8 and her young sister Jacqueline, only 4. The two girls are living with the Durand family in the countryside until their loving, hard-working parents, who are in the garment trade, can afford both a larger apartment and the time away from work to reunite the family. At the Durands', the girls have been brought up as Christians even though their parents are non-practicing Jews.

At last, the happy time comes for the two girls to move in with their parents. Nicole is a bright girl whose honesty and outspokenness often verge on the tactless. This trait sometimes gets her into trouble both at home and school, like the time she tells Mme Thibault, one of her mother's clients, that she is too fat to wear bright colors. In spite of her bossiness, a quality that Nicole denies, she has many friends in her class, whose teacher is the severe Mlle Legrand. Among her friends is Françoise Rosten, whose parents belong to one of the few wealthy Jewish families in town. Nicole tries hard but fails to become friendly with attractive classmate Lucie Fiore, who one day in class calls Nicole "a dirty Jew." Nicole reports this incident to her parents and Maman goes to school the next day and, through Mlle Legrand's intervention, gets a tearful Lucie to apologize publicly.

At Christmas time the families in town celebrate with opulent dinners. When Maman discovers she hasn't enough dishes for the occasion, Nicole not only arranges to borrow a set from the Rostens but also invites them to dinner. Along with the other guests Françoise and her family have a grand time at the gala feast.

War comes and Nicole's father enlists in the army. When France surrenders and Aix-les-Bains becomes part of Vichy France, Papa is demobilized and returns home. Refugees from the German-occupied part of France soon stream across the border. Among them are Berthe and Isaac, Maman's cousins, who have fled from Paris and live for a time with the Niemans.

As the German vise tightens around the beleaguered Vichy government, financial problems beset the people, including the Niemans, who are forced to trade their possessions for food. Acts of anti-Semitism increase and Maman and Papa Nieman respond by becoming more proudly and openly Jewish. They celebrate, for example, their first Passover seder. Mysteriously, Lucie Fiori and her family suddenly disappear. Nicole later discovers that Mr. Fiori, an Italian Socialist agitator, had fled Italy with his family after Mussolini gained power, and settled in Aix-les-Bains. Someone informed on Mr. Fiori and he and his family have been kidnapped and sent back to Italy where they probably will face death.

The Germans occupy Aix-les-Bains in June of 1943, and many of the Jewish families begin clandestine preparations to flee to the safety of nearby Switzerland. Maman wants the family to travel to the border town of Annemasse and then pay a guide to sneak them out of France. But Papa, who is confident the war will end soon, refuses. When this appears unlikely, Papa becomes despondent and despairing. He begins staying out late drinking and playing cards in the local tavern. At last he consents to his wife's escape plan. He will go to Switzerland alone and send for the rest of the family when he has made plans for them to cross the border safely and enter an internment camp.

Nicole accompanies him to the train station but at the last minute he can't face leaving his family, and decides not to board the train. Back home, her parents embrace and kiss. Maman never mentions going to Switzerland again.

A few days later, the Rostens tell the Niemans that they too have decided to risk leaving the country to seek refuge in Switzerland. The Rostens pack nothing, leaving all their precious belongings and household treasures behind. As a parting gift, Mrs. Rosten gives her hosts a beautiful cut-glass pitcher. Nicole and Françoise are so reluctant to part that both sets of parents agree that the girls should spend their last night together at the Rostens' house. The next day, after the Rostens have left, Nicole returns home. The apartment is deserted and the cut-glass pitcher lies shattered on the kitchen floor. A neighbor rushes in and tells Nicole that the Germans raided the apartment during the night, took away her parents and Jacqueline, and are now looking for her. She must flee.

Nicole seeks help from neighbors but they are too fearful of reprisals. She bicycles out of town to the Durands, with whom she and Jacqueline had stayed for many years, but reluctantly they too tell her she cannot stay. She drags herself back into town and, half a block from the school, is found by Mlle Legrand who becomes her unlikely savior, offering to give her shelter and hide her in the school.

Passages for Booktalking in *A Pocket Full of Seeds*

Some interesting passages, with pagination from the out-of-print Puffin paperback, are: life at the Durands (pp. 15–20); Nicole and family move into the apartment (pp. 23–27); Lucie calls Nicole a "dirty Jew" and Maman protests (pp. 45–52); and Christmas with the Rostens (pp. 53–57).

Themes and Subjects in *A Pocket Full of Seeds*

This first-person narrative becomes more real and poignant when one realizes that it is based on fact. Various levels of anti-Semitism, including that of young Lucie, are presented. The despair and helplessness of being trapped during the Holocaust are well depicted as is the irrational hatred and discrimination that fostered a holocaust. Nicole's maturation and coming of age are important themes. Other subjects are the love, solidarity, and loyalty that exist in families, good parenting, friendship, Jews, Holocaust, death, France, Vichy France, Nazis, World War II, prejudice, and religious holidays and practices.

Principal Characters in *Lost in America*

Nicole Nieman, an orphaned French teenager

Mlle Le Grand (spelled Legrand in *A Pocket Full of Seeds*), headmistress of Nicole's school

Rosette (Rose) Segal, Nicole's Jewish classmate

Sophie Nieman/Raymonde, Nicole's aunt

Louise, Sophie's friend

Mme Marchand, the new headmistress

Jake, Nicole's American cousin

Harriet, Jake's wife

Evvie, Jake's daughter

Simone Leniger, Nicole's friend, another French refugee

Mr. Dupuis, Nicole's boss at Air France

Alan Bernstein, Simone's date and later Nicole's friend

Jerry, Alan's friend

Mrs. Walker, Nicole and Simone's landlady

Plot Synopsis of *Lost in America*

Nicole Nieman, a 14-year-old French Jew, remembers the fateful morning in November 1943 when she returned to her family's apartment after a sleepover at her friend Françoise's house to find that her family had been rounded up by the occupying German soldiers and deported to an unknown destination. Alone in her hometown of Aix-les-Bains, France, she is rescued by the stern headmistress of her school, Mlle Le Grand and, along with another Jewish girl, Rosette Segal, is sequestered in the school with other live-in gentile students. Nicole is waiting for her family—Maman, Papa, and young sister Jacqueline—to return but she has received no news of their whereabouts.

After the Allied invasion along the Mediterranean coast of France, the Germans prepare for combat and issue an order closing all schools and demanding that students be sent home. Nicole, without any family, has no place to go until she remembers an aunt, estranged from her family, who left Aix-les-Bains and relocated to the town of Gap in the north of Provence. With financial help from Mlle Le Grand and, ironically, a friendly German soldier, Nicole is able to purchase a ticket and make the arduous journey south to Gap. There, Nicole finds her aunt's whereabouts with the aid of a kindly postman. Her aunt, who has changed her name from Nieman to Raymonde to conceal her Jewishness, and her friend Louise share a little home to which Nicole is welcomed. Within days the Americans liberate the town and soon Nicole is back in Aix-les-Bains living with her aunt in the family's old apartment.

Nicole does not approve of her aunt's wanton ways and when she invites her boyfriend to move in Nicole decides to move out. She returns as a boarder to her old school, now under the leadership of kindly Mme Marchand. Nicole is briefly reunited with her friend Rosette before Rosette and her family emigrate to the United States.

Nicole is visited at the school by a sickly old man with devastating news about her family. All three were sent to Auschwitz, where Maman and Jacqueline were gassed. Papa was evacuated when the Russians approached the camp but died on the way to freedom. With nothing left to keep her in France, Nicole makes arrangements in September 1947 to emigrate to New York City and live with a distant cousin and his family.

Jake, the cousin, is a kindly but ineffective man who lives under the thumb of his bossy, greedy wife, Harriet, and of his unfriendly daughter, Evvie. Nicole is overcome by the wonders of New York—the subway system, elevators, luxurious clothing, banana splits—and the bustle of life on the Grand Concourse in the Bronx where the apartment is situated. Harriet quickly makes it clear that Nicole must get a job and pay for her room and board.

Within days, Nicole rekindles her friendship with Rosette (now named Rose) Segal, whose family has prospered in New York and has taken a summer rental in Coney Island near the beach and boardwalk. Nicole also finds a job selling chocolates at La Chocolaterie, where her French-accented English adds class to the establishment. Within a few months rival chocolate shops open in the neighborhood and the La Chocolaterie closes, leaving Nicole ten pounds heavier (from feeding her chocolate habit) but without a job. Nicole meets another lonely Jewish girl from France, Simone Leniger, and they soon become fast friends. Nicole applies in person for a job at Air France coincidentally on the day that one of the officers, gruff Mr. Dupuis, a Hitler look-alike, has fired his assistant. Through a combination of innate charm and brazen deception (she dishonestly claims that she can type), Nicole lands the job. When Mr. Dupuis discovers the deception, Nicole promises to master the necessary skills after hours and her new boss capitulates.

Rose becomes infatuated with a bright but reserved young man, Alan Bernstein, and arranges with a friend of Alan's, Jerry, to double-date with Nicole. Nicole is thrilled and frightened at the thought of her first date, but Rose reassures her and together they shop for a new outfit for Nicole. The evening is a qualified success (they attend an enjoyable Broadway musical *High Button Shoes*) and soon afterward the two girls switch partners. Rose and Jerry date and Nicole inherits, for a time, the attentions of Alan. However, the boy proves to be too intellectual and somber and Nicole, somewhat sadder and wiser, tactfully ends the relationship.

Simone and Nicole make fine progress at their respective jobs. As they become more savvy at mastering life in New York, the two decide to pool resources and rent an apartment. Through Simone's boss, they hear about a one-room apartment that is available in Flatbush. The owner, a World War II widow named Mrs. Walker, is a caring, attentive music teacher, but the rent is a little steep for the girls' budgets. When Mrs. Walker reduces it from $75 to $70 a month, they decide to take it. It has many advantages including convenience to transportation and shopping and access to a lovely, small garden that the girls promise to tend. Ill-prepared as they are, the girls excitedly begin to round up the necessary furniture and household equipment.

Harriet explodes when Nicole says she is leaving but, out of earshot of his wife, Jake offers Nicole an old sofa and some folding chairs. For her first year in America Nicole felt lost but now, for the first time, she begins thinking of it as home.

Passages for Booktalking in *Lost in America*

Some interesting passages: Nicole is ordered out of school and Mlle Le Grand helps (pp. 18–21); Nicole travels to Gap (pp. 22–26); the Americans arrive (pp. 30–34); Nicole learns about the fate of her family and decides to go to America (pp. 47–50).

Themes and Subjects in *Lost in America*

This novel begins with a description in personal terms of the last days of the German occupation of France and the appalling legacy of the Holocaust. By contrast, the vibrant, energetic life of postwar New York City is vividly re-created as are the sometimes bewildering adjustments that face a foreigner who is thrust into this environment. This is basically the story of a plucky, intelligent girl who overcomes tremendous odds including the loss of her family, and creates, through imagination, courage, and stamina, a new life for herself. Her adjustments to America and her growing independence are well portrayed as are her enhanced self-confidence and belief in her own worth and importance. Other subjects: World War II, France, Jews, religious prejudice, friendship, boy-girl relationships, death, family life, independence, and cultural differences.

SPINELLI, JERRY. *Milkweed.* Knopf, 2003, $15.95 (978-0-375-81374-0); pap. Dell, $6.99 (978-0-439-67695-3) (Grades 5–9)

Introduction

Jerry Spinelli (1941–) has written a string of highly regarded books for young readers since his first novels appeared in the early 1980s. He tells of his youth in the entertaining *Knots in My Yo-yo String: The Autobiography of a Kid* (Knopf, 1998, $16.99; 0679987916), which includes an account of the ten years he spent living in Norristown, Pa., and describes his family, friends, pastimes, and events during this period (the late 1940s and 1950s). He also relates how these experiences served as a preparation for his later career as an author. Perhaps his most famous book is *Maniac Magee* (Little, 1990, $15.45; 0316807222; pap. Harper, $3.95; 0064471519), winner of the 1991 Newbery Medal and condensed in *The Newbery/Printz Companion.*

The central character in *Maniac Magee* is described by the author as "the kid as legendary hero." He is an orphan who fights for the rights of others while seeking for himself security, a family, and a home. Misha, the hero and narrator of *Milkweed* reminds one of Maniac because he, too, is a naïve innocent orphan battling for survival and the well-being of others. The body of the novel takes place in Warsaw, Poland, over a period of about three years, from September 1939, the beginning of the Nazi invasion and occupation, to the summer of 1942 when large numbers of Jews were removed from the Warsaw ghetto and sent to concentration camps. The novel is divided into sections according to the season but no specific years are given. An "epilogue" of several short chapters brings Misha's story to the present.

Historical Background

Perhaps no country in Europe has had a sadder history than Poland. For centuries it was invaded and occupied by neighbors including Russia, Sweden, and various German states. It regained its independence in 1918 after World War I, but on Sept. 1, 1939, Hitler's armed forces began another invasion with troops numbering about 1,700,000, precipitating a declaration of war against Germany by France and Britain on Sept. 3. The poorly equipped Polish army of approximately 700,000 surrendered Warsaw on Sept. 27 after facing a second invasion from the east by Russian troops. The combination of aerial and ground bombardments almost completely destroyed the city. Mass arrests and public executions became common during the German occupation, the chief target being the Jews. About half a million Jews were rounded up and marched into the already crowded ghetto, where they lived in horrible conditions. Thousands died of disease and starvation or by execution. In 1942 the deportations began and between July and by October of that year more than

300,000 had been sent to Treblinka, a concentration camp, where they were killed. This is where the Warsaw narrative in *Milkweed* ends.

For a short period the deportations stopped but when they began again in April 1943, the remaining Jews in the ghetto revolted in one of the most gallant acts of World War II bravery. Amazingly the fighting lasted for one month. About 7,000 Jews died and the remaining 30,000 were sent to the death camps. The Germans then reduced the Warsaw ghetto to rubble. In the summer of 1944, believing Russian troops would soon liberate Warsaw, the residents again rose in revolt. The Russians, however, did not appear and 200,000 Poles died in the rebellion. On Jan. 15, 1945, Soviet troops entered Warsaw but not before the retreating Germans had destroyed what was left of the city.

Principal Characters

Stopthief, later Misha Pilsudski, the narrator, a homeless waif in Warsaw
Uri, an older, redheaded Jewish boy who befriends Misha
Kube, Olek, Fendi, and Enos, members of a Jewish street gang in Warsaw
Dr. Kovczak, the kindly administrator of an orphanage
Janina Milgrom, an 8-year-old Jewish girl
Mr. Milgrom, a pharmacist and Janina's father
Mrs. Milgrom, Janina's grouchy mother
Uncle Shepsel, Janina's eccentric uncle
Buffo, the hated flop (ghetto policeman), nicknamed Fatman

Plot Synopsis

He knows himself only by the name he most often hears himself called, Stopthief. He is a homeless waif, probably about 8 years old, without memory, living in Warsaw by stealing his daily bread. He is a naïve, innocent, curious as a cat, and, in spite of his dire circumstances, a kind and compassionate youngster. It is the fall of 1939, and the sounds of German bombardments are getting closer to the city every day. One day Stopthief is saved from pursuers he has robbed by an older Jewish boy named Uri who takes him to a deserted stable where he meets other members of a gang made up of homeless Jewish boys. Among them are Kube, the clown of the group; one-armed Olek; Fendi, who enjoys smoking cigars; and grim-faced Enos. Together they engage in many foraging escapades, one resulting in an exciting ride on a conductor-less streetcar. Uri, the loner of the group, later takes Stopthief to live in his cellar hangout. Uri is a wily, clever lad who has a talent of adjusting to difficult situations and is also given to mysterious disappearances. But he is protective of Stopthief and teaches him the tricks of being streetwise. He also supplies the boy with a name and a fictitious background. He dubs him Misha Pilsudski and says he is a gypsy lad who was separated from his family when the Germans bombed their caravan and who wandered into the streets of Warsaw. The boy is thrilled with his new identity.

Meanwhile after days of heavy bombing, the Germans, nicknamed the Jackboots, arrive and take over Warsaw. At first Misha admires these strong, disciplined soldiers but after witnessing their ruthless behavior toward civilians, particularly Jews, he changes his mind.

One day, while stealing tomatoes from a garden, Misha sees a girl staring at him from her back window. When he returns for more loot, she introduces herself as Janina, and invites him to her seventh birthday party the next day. The party is a fiasco because Misha grabs the cake and runs, thinking the lit candles might cause great damage. In spite of this incident, his friendship with Janina thrives. When food shortages hit Warsaw, Misha begins sharing the treasures he steals. He gives some to Janina and her parents, Mr. and Mrs. Milgrom, and others to a Jewish orphanage run by the kindly Dr. Kovczak.

Misha sees increased anti-Semitic acts of violence, brutality, and murder. Eventually the Jackboots round up the city's Jewish population and march them to the city's ghetto, around which a stone wall has been built. Janina and her parents, with Dr. Kovczak and the orphans, are among the detainees forced into cramped quarters with intolerable sanitary conditions and dwindling food supplies. Misha joins the group and proudly wears the blue-and-white arm band proclaiming he is a Jew even though in his new identity he is a gypsy. Soon the street gang is also rounded up and sent to the ghetto. Food becomes so scarce that even rats are roasted and eaten.

One day, Misha discovers a small crack in the wall that he can squeeze through. Soon he is living a double life. During the day he is with the Milgroms, who share a squalid single room with Uncle Shepsel, and at night he roams the streets of Warsaw looking for food and other supplies to smuggle into the ghetto. Again he divides his booty between the Milgroms and Dr. Korczak. Though Mr. Milgrom and Janina can tolerate the deplorable conditions, Mrs. Milgrom withdraws and ceases to communicate. Meanwhile the eccentric Uncle Shepsel is studying to be a Lutheran, hoping this will help him escape further persecution. One night, outside the wall in the area nicknamed Heaven, Misha encounters the cunning Uri who, with his red hair, is passing as a gentile.

Against Misha's protests, Janina joins him in his nocturnal forays. The punishment for smuggling is death, and one night Janina and Misha see the body of one-armed Olek dangling from a street lamp with the sign "I am a smuggler" hanging from his chest.

In addition to the Jackboot soldiers, the streets of the ghetto are patrolled by flops, Jewish ghetto policemen. Particularly vicious is Buffo, nicknamed Fatman, who seems determined to nab Misha.

Carts travel through the streets gathering up dead bodies, but in spite of these and other horrors, there are occasional bright moments. For example, one day Misha and Janina see from an alleyway a sky full of milkweed puffs floating heavenward like magical parachutes.

Mrs. Milgrom dies about the time the train deportations begin. None of the inmates knows the destination of these deportations—some think it is their own village, others correctly fear the worst. Misha is determined to leave with his beloved Janina and Mr. Milgrom, but he is confronted by Uri, now a Nazi soldier, who shoots him to prevent him boarding the train. The injury results in the loss of an ear but ultimately Misha's survival.

In a few brief chapters that serve as an epilogue, Misha's fate is outlined. He leaves Warsaw and, in a daze, roams the countryside. He is taken in by a farmer and spends the rest of the war years living with the pigs. After the war, he wanders back to Warsaw. The ghetto is gone and the city is a pile of rubble. In the ruins, he encounters a skeleton of a man whom he recognizes as Buffo the Fatman. The former flop seems to be unaware of his surroundings. Unable or unwilling to recognize Misha, he shuffles off and is lost in the crowd.

Eventually Misha finds his way to America but is so scarred by his experiences and his memories that he is unable to fit in. He takes odd jobs, changes his last name to Milgrom in honor of his beloved Janina, and gets married. However, his pregnant wife leaves him, unable to cope with his erratic behavior. Many years later, he is tracked down by his daughter, who offers him a place to stay. She also gives him something more precious. At Misha's request, she names her daughter Wendy Janina.

Passages for Booktalking

Some interesting passages: Uri takes Stopthief to his basement home (pp. 9–12); the streetcar adventure (pp. 12–15); Stopthief receives a new identity from Uri (pp. 29–31); Misha is invited to Janina's birthday party (pp. 32–35); and the milkweed episode that gives the book its title (pp. 142–143).

Themes and Subjects

This is a harrowing tale that remains with the readers long after its reading. In human terms it brings to life the horror, bestiality, and heroism of the Holocaust. In the heartbreak and misery of Misha's life, there is also a story of hope, innocence, naivety, and survival. The author calls Misha "a little kid with a big heart, trapped in a walled-in nightmare." It is also a story of courage and endurance. Other subjects are the Holocaust, ghettos, Warsaw, Poland, World War II, Jews, and religious prejudice.

------•◦•------

TOKSVIG, SANDI. *Hitler's Canary.* Roaring Brook Press, 2005, $16.95 (978-0-596-43247-8) (Grades 5–8)

Introduction

Sandi Toksvig was born in 1958 in Copenhagen, Denmark. Her father was a foreign correspondent for a Danish television network so she spent much of her youth abroad. She studied law and anthropology at Cambridge where she began her comedy career performing and writing skits for revues. She is currently an important radio and television personality in the United Kingdom. In 2007, she was named Political Humorist of the Year on Channel 4 as well as Radio Broadcaster of the Year. She has written widely in different genres for both adults and children—in addition to many novels, she has recently written travel guides to France and Spain.

Hitler's Canary is currently her most popular book for young readers. It is based loosely on her father's life and family during the World War II Nazi occupation of Denmark beginning in 1940. As in the novel, her grandmother was an actress and her grandfather a painter. Her grandmother was given an award for her work in the Danish Resistance including, as in the novel, mutilating her legs to distract the Germans from discovering Jews hidden in the family's apartment. The novel is narrated by Bamse Skovlund who ages from 10 to 13 during the novel. The setting of the novel is Copenhagen and the time period from April 1940 to October 1943. Instead of chapters, the novel is divided, like a play, into three acts, each with several scenes.

Historical Background

The author gives a lot of background material on internal conditions in Denmark during the Nazi occupation. This is complemented by Program Notes and Author Notes at the end of the book.

The following material is adapted from the article "Rescue of the Danish Jews" on the web site www.auschwitz.dk/Denmark.htm. On April 9, 1940, Germany attacked Denmark, and from then until 1945 Denmark was under German occupation. At first it was a "soft" occupation. King Christian X remained in Denmark, the Danish government continued to rule, and many Danish agricultural products were shipped to Germany. Most Danes were anti-German and resented the occupation and soon an effective resistance movement was organized and acts of sabotage increased. By 1943 crippling labor strikes and bombings of military targets and businesses run by collaborators were common. The Germans tightened their grip. In 1941 the Germans began their "Final Solution" for European Jews. At the infamous Wannsee Conference in January 1942, details of the mass murder plans were outlined. At first, Denmark was exempted and the 7,500 Jews there were not required to wear the yellow star. However, as acts of defiance increased, a state of emergency was declared and by August 1943 the Nazis felt they could move against the Jews. News of a projected deportation leaked out, and in Copenhagen on September 29, two days before the projected sweep, Rabbi Marcus Melchior, implored his congregation and all Danish Jews to go into hiding. All strata of Danish society—from farmers and fishermen to clergymen and professionals—cooperated and offered protection. One outstanding refuge was the Bispebjerg Hospital in Copenhagen, which housed hundreds of Jews with the cooperation of the entire staff. The best avenue of escape was by boat across the narrow straits to neutral Sweden. Every kind of craft was commandeered, from the tiniest of fishing boats to coastal freighters. In some cases, the Germans turned a blind eye to these rescue operations. During the ten days of ferrying, from the Rosh Hashanah to Yom Kippur holidays in 1943, more than 7,000 Jews and almost 700 dissenters escaped. Only 481 Jews were captured and sent to the Nazi prison at Theresienstadt, which was not a death camp. Danish officials successfully persuaded Adolf Eichmann and Werner Best of the SS, Hitler's chief in Denmark, not to send them to the extermination camps in Poland. Every month Danish citizens sent packages of food, vitamins, and clothing with the result that almost all of the Jews survived the camp experience and returned home at the end of the war in 1945. Unlike returning Jews in other countries, these refugees found that their homes, pets, and gardens had been cared for by their neighbors. About 99 percent of the Danish Jewish population survived the Holocaust.

Principal Characters

Bamse Skovlund, a Danish boy of 10
Marie Skovlund, Bamse's mother, an actress
Thomas, her dresser
Orlando, Bamse's 16-year-old brother
Masha, his 14-year-old sister
Anton Beilin, Bamse's best friend, a Jewish boy
Mr. and Mrs. Beilin, Anton's parents
Gilda, Anton's little sister
Mrs. Jensen, a neighbor whose cow is Bess
Uncle Johann, Mr. Skovlund's brother

Sallie Besiakov, a Jewish hat maker
Boris, a young German soldier
Mr. and Mrs. Isak, a Jewish couple

Plot Synopsis

Until the German invasion of Denmark in April 1940, 10-year-old Bamse (Danish for teddy bear) Skovlund has lived in a make-believe world. As far back as he can remember, his second home has been the theater in Copenhagen where his mother, Marie Skovlund, the most famous actress in all Denmark, has starred in a variety of plays and where his father, an artist noted for his political cartoons, has been a part-time set designer. Even his brother, 16-year-old Orlando, and his sister, 14-year-old Masha, were named after characters in *Twelfth Night* and *The Three Sisters*. Marie's gay dresser and makeup expert, Thomas, is so important in both her theatrical and everyday life (these actually often merge into one) that he has become part of the family. Bamse's real home is a large flat in a fashionable residential neighborhood in Copenhagen. His best friend, 10-year-old Anton Beilin, lives upstairs with his parents, Mr. and Mrs. Beilin and younger sister, Gilda. The Beilins are Jewish and Anton always wears his yarmulke underneath his school cap. Next door Mrs. Jensen lives with her cow, Bess, who grazes in the garden at the back of their apartments.

Although outwardly life is proceeding as usual, there is a feeling of unease and apprehension everywhere, particularly among Jews including Anton and his family, who are aware of Hitler's anti-Semitic campaign. Innocent acts of defiance become commonplace and the occupying Germans react with increased hostility. The only family member unaffected by the occupation is Marie, who, with Thomas, lives entirely in a theatrical never-never-land, spending her spare time buying hats from her favorite hat maker, Sallie Besiakov, another Jew.

However, Orlando, who works part-time as a grocery store delivery boy, is becoming more aggressively hostile toward the Germans, particularly after being stopped on his delivery bike by a German guard. One night at diner an argument begins about how the Danes are too accepting of the occupation. Orlando has heard on the BBC that the Danes are being called Hitler's canaries because they "sit in a cage and sing any tune he wants." When Orlando begins spending time away from home, Anton is convinced that he is working in the resistance movement. Almost three years pass and conditions in Denmark continue to deteriorate. Anxious to express their own defiance, one day Anton and Bamse cautiously approach a German traffic guard who is shielded to the waist by sandbags, and pin a note on a sandbag for motorists to read that says, "Attention! This soldier is not wearing trousers."

Orlando, who has confessed to the boys that he is a resistance fighter, offers them a more dangerous assignment. While Anton stands guard, Bamse will distract the German soldiers drinking at a popular downtown café, La Tosca, and Orlando will steal a pistol from one of holsters they hang in the vestibule before entering the main dining room. The operation is successful although there is a tight moment when Anton is also invited in to chat and Bamse is afraid they will ask him to remove his school cap. This doesn't happen and Orlando is able to steal the gun.

It is summer vacation, and the boys have time to become active resistance workers. As well as passing on messages, they copy news items from forbidden BBC news programs which they listen to on an illicit radio set. They deliver these to printing offices for publication in forbidden newspapers. It is dangerous but important. In the midst of all these underground activities, Bamse discovers that his sister, Masha, now 16, has a secret boyfriend—a handsome young German soldier. Bamse tells no one about this. Family harmony is disturbed when Uncle Johann comes to stay and alienates everyone by spouting collaborationist and anti-Semitic remarks. At the point where Bamse is beginning to hate his uncle, Father tells how Johann saved his life years before by dragging him out of a burning barn.

Tensions escalate in Denmark and there is more violence. Sallie's hat shop is raided and destroyed by an anti-Jewish Danish youth group and Bamse and Anton engage in more dangerous missions, going to the train station and taping copies of the illegal newsletter under a railway car bound for Sweden. One evening two momentous events occur. Father, on a tip from Bamse, catches Masha in the garden with her soldier boyfriend, Boris, and news comes that Orlando has been arrested. Marie is devastated by the news and becomes reclusive and morose. Eager for revenge, Bamse and Anton use bomb-making equipment found in Orlando's room to fashion two bombs that they plant on a bridge. Unfortunately both the bombs and the plot fizzle. After some months, Orlando manages to escape and hides in a local hospital. Bamse delivers civilian clothes to his room and Orlando escapes into the night.

News comes that the Germans are about to round up all Jews for deportation and that patriotic Danes should hide them and help them escape. While Uncle Johann is absent, the family uses Father's expertise in set designing and constructs a false wall in their living room. Behind it, they hide the four Beilins and a neighboring Jewish couple, Mr. and Mrs. Isak. The SS guards are approaching the building when Uncle Johann returns. Afraid he will blab, Father knocks Uncle Johann out and drags him behind the false wall. In the meantime, Marie deliberately slashes her legs and covers them with makeup to look like an infection. "Nurse" Thomas, in drag, is tending to her when the Germans arrive. They recognize Marie as a famous actress and she gives a per-

formance that would outdo Camille. After showing concern about the infection on her legs, they are about to leave when Uncle Johann groans audibly.
Quick-thinking Masha claims it is only Bess, Mrs. Jensen's cow, and the soldiers leave.

All six Jews are taken to the docks to board a boat. At the dockside, Bamse
sees Orlando helping with the rescue mission. While the six are in hiding
awaiting their boat, young Gilda runs into the road to retrieve a teddy bear she
has dropped. She is grabbed by the German police. To save the others,
Thomas gallantly rushes to her side saying they are only a party of two. Both
are taken away by the guards but the rest make a successful escape to Sweden.
Gilda survives her stay in a concentration camp and, at the end of the war, the
Beilin family returns. Unfortunately, Thomas dies in the camp. After the war,
the Skovlund family is also reunited, sadder, wiser, and with hundreds of
remarkable memories.

Passages for Booktalking

Orlando, on his delivery bike, is stopped by a German guard (pp. 39–41);
Anton and Bamse play a prank on the traffic guard (pp. 51–54); the caper at
La Tosca (pp. 57–61); Uncle Johann and the Jewish question (pp. 67–71).

Themes and Subjects

The rescue of the Danish Jews is an inspiring story from a terrible time in
human history. The author shows all the excitement and drama of the resistance movement in Denmark as well as brining everyday life during the occupation to life. Both Anton and Bamse are courageous, ingenious boys who
engage the reader with their dedication and their gallantry. Bamse's frequent
use of sardonic humor enlivens the plot. Other subjects are: Nazi Germany,
collaborators, concentration camps, anti-Semitism, friendship, family life,
actors and acting, theaters, Copenhagen, resistance movements, World War II,
and escapes.

ADDITIONAL SELECTIONS

Bartoletti, Susan Campbell. *The Boy Who Dared* (Scholastic, 2007, $16.99) (Grades
6–12)

This is a fictionalized biography of Helmuth Hubener, the brave German youth
who was executed for his anti-Nazi activities.

Benchley, Nathaniel. *Bright Candles: A Novel of the Danish Resistance* (HarperCollins,
1972, $13.95)

This is the now-classic novel about the people who courageously fought against the
Nazi occupation of Denmark during World War II.

Casanova. Mary. *The Kingfish Code* (Houghton, 2007, $16) (Grades 4–7)

During the Nazi occupation of Norway during World War II, young Marit, who has been sent to live with her grandfather, helps a young resistance fighter who has been wounded.

Crisp, Marty. *White Star: A Dog on the Titanic* (Holiday, 2004, $16.95) (Grades 4–6)

After living with his grandparents in England for six years, Sam Harris, age 12, is returning to America on the *Titanic,* where he helps in the kennels and befriends the captain's dog.

Durbin, William. *The Winter War* (Random, 2008, $15.88) (Grades 6–9)

In 1939 after Russia invaded his native Finland, Marco, in spite of a crippled leg, plays an important role in the guerrilla resistance movement by running messages, preparing bombs, and, later, by rescuing a dear friend.

Fine, Anne. *Frozen Billy* (Farrar, 2006, $16) (Grades 5–9)

When both her parents disappear, young Clarrie must keep the family together even when her younger brother Will becomes part of Uncle Len's music hall act.

Glatshteyn, Yankev. *Emil and Karl* (Roaring Brook, 2006, $16.95) (Grades 5–8)

In Nazi-occupied Vienna, Emil who is Jewish and Karl who is not are brought together when the Germans destroy both their families.

Graber, Janet. *Resistance* (Marshall Cavendish, 2005, $15.95) (Grades 6–10)

In World War II France, 15-year-old Marianne is living with a secret—she and her mother are nursing an English serviceman in their woodshed; things become more complicated when a German soldier is billeted in their house.

Hartnett, Sonya. *The Silver Donkey* (Candlewick, 2006, $15.99) (Grades 5–8)

During World War I, 10-year-old Marcelle and 8-year-old Coco discover a British soldier, a deserter, close to their French village and after feeding him they help to smuggle him home across the Channel.

Holmes, Victoria. *Heart of Fire* (HarperCollins, 2006, $15.99) (Grades 5–8)

When Maddie's older brother returns to the family's English estate after serving in World War I, he is troubled by a secret that Maddie is determined to discover.

Houston, Kimberley. *The Book of Jude* (Front Street, 2008, $17.95) (Grades 6–9)

About the time of the fall of the Berlin Wall, Jude and her family move from New York to Prague and the cultural shock produces severe mental problems for the teenager.

Hull, Nancy L. *On Rough Seas* (Clarion, 2008, $16) (Grades 6–9)

This is the story of the evacuation of Dunkirk during World War II as experienced by a young, part-time galley boy working on a boat harbored in Dover.

Isaacs, Anne. *Torn Thread* (Scholastic, 2000, $15.95) (Grades 5–8)

In a story of courage and survival, two girls—12-year-old Eva and her older sister Rachael—endure the horrors of a Nazi work camp during World War II.

Morpurgo, Michael. *The Mozart Question* (Candlewick, 2008, $15.99) (Grades 6–9)
Paolo Levi discovers why his father never plays Mozart on his violin in this novel about a Nazi death camp survivor who had been forced to play his violin to calm prisoners as they were marched to the ovens.

Morpurgo, Michael. *Private Peaceful* (Scholastic, 2004, $16.95) (Grades 7–10)
The horrors of World War I are revealed through the experiences of a young British soldier in the trenches.

Napoli, Donna Jo. *Fire in the Hills* (Dutton, 2006, $16.99) (Grades 5–8)
In this sequel to *Stones in the Water* (Dutton, 1997, $16.99), 14-year-old Roberto, who has escaped from a Nazi prison camp and is journeying to Venice, is persuaded to join the Italian resistance movement.

Orlev, Uri. *Run, Boy, Run* (Houghton, 2003, $15) (Grades 5–8)
After escaping from the Warsaw Ghetto during World War II, 8-year-old Srulik Frydman must survive in the hostile Polish countryside.

Parker, Marjorie Hodgson. *David and the Mighty Eighth* (Bright Sky, 2007, $17.95) (Grades 4–7)
During World War II, an English boy who has been evacuated from London to the countryside becomes friendly with an American airman stationed nearby.

Pausewang, Gudrun. *Dark Hours* (Annick, 2006, $21.95) (Grades 5–8)
In the days immediately after the end of World War II in Germany, refugee Gisel, age 15, becomes separated from her mother and now must find food and shelter for both herself and her younger siblings.

Pausewang, Gudrun. *Traitor* (Carolrhoda, 2006, $16.95) (Grades 7–10)
In Germany in 1944, Anna finds a fugitive Russian soldier hiding in a barn and, although it means possible execution if she is found out, she decides to help him.

Riordan, James. *Escape from War* (Kingfisher, 2005, pap. $6.95) (Grades 4–6)
In parallel stories, Frank, an English schoolboy, and Hannah, a German Jewish refugee, tell how each survives the hardships and dangers of World War II.

Roy, Jennifer. *Yellow Star* (Marshall Cavendish, 2006, $16.95) (Grades 5–8)
Based on a true story of the World War II Holocaust in Lodz, Poland, this is the story of one of the children who survived.

Sedgwick, Marcus. *The Foreshadowing* (Lamb/Random, 2006, $16.95) (Grades 6–10)
In the fall of 1915, during World War I, 17-year-old Alexandra (Sasha) poses as a nurse at the front and the terrible sights she witnesses are made more severe by her uncanny gift to foresee the imminent deaths of others.

Selznick, Brian. *The Invention of Hugo Cabret* (Scholastic, 2007, $22.99) (Grades 5 and up)
In this prize winning mostly graphic novel set in Paris in 1931, young Hugo has a series of adventures with such characters as an automaton that draws pictures and a stage magician based on the real-life French filmmaker George Melies.

Spillebeen, Geert. *Kipling's Choice* (Houghton, 2005, $16) (Grades 7–10)
    This is a powerful fictionalized account of how Rudyard Kipling engineered getting his son into the British armed forces during World War I and how the young man was killed during his first battle.

Whelan, Gerard. *The Guns of Easter* (O'Brien, 2000, pap. $7.95) (Grades 6–9)
    In Ireland at the beginning of the 20th century, 12-year-old Jimmy Conway witnesses the growing political violence around him. Continued in *A Winter of Spies* (O'Brien, 2002, pap. $6.95).

Whelan, Gloria. *Parade of Shadows* (HarperCollins, 2007, $15.99) (Grades 6–10)
    Set in the Middle East in 1907, this novel of intrigue and danger during the days of the dying Ottoman Empire features Julia, the daughter of an American diplomat.

Wolf, Joan M. *Someone Named Eva* (Clarion, 2007, $16) (Grades 6–9)
    In 1942 in occupied Czechoslovakia, blond, blue-eyed, 11-year-old Milada, is seized by the Nazis, sent to Germany, renamed Eva, and adopted by a wealthy German family.

CHAPTER 5

Asia and Oceania

COMPESTINE, YING CHANG. *Revolution Is Not a Dinner Party.*
Holt, 2007, $16.95 (978-0-8050-8207-4) (Grades 5–9)

Introduction

In an "Author's Note" at the end of this novel, the author states, "Although this is a work of fiction, many of the scenes and characters in the book are based on or inspired by real places, actual events, and people from my childhood." Like the Ling of the novel, Ying Chang Compestine was born in Wuhan, China, to parents who were both doctors. From an early age, she showed an interest in writing. At age 8, as a result of a referral from one of her teachers, an article that Ying wrote was published in a magazine. The family suffered many hardships including the imprisonment of her father during the Cultural Revolution of the 1970s. Following this upheaval, the universities reopened after being closed for ten years, and Ying, after two years of intense studying, passed the entrance exams, gaining a degree in English literature. After serving as an interpreter for the government, she came to the United States in 1981 and earned a Master's degree in sociology from the University of Colorado. Since her marriage and parenthood, she has devoted her time to two passions: writing and food. She has written several children's books about Chinese food (e.g., noodles) and cultural artifacts (e.g., kites and paper).

Revolution Is Not a Dinner Party is Compestine's first novel. The title comes from Chairman Mao's *Little Red Book*, "A revolution is not a dinner party, [it] is an insurrection, an act of violence by which one class overthrows another." The action takes place over a period of four years from the summer of 1972 to the fall of 1976. This book, which has often been compared with *The Diary of Anne Frank*, covers the life of the narrator, Ling, from nearly 9 years old to almost her 13th birthday. The photograph on the dust jacket and the frontispiece is that of the author as a young girl.

Historical Background

Mao Zedong, also known as Mao Tse Tung or Chairman Mao (1893–1976), was one of the organizers of the Chinese Communist Party in 1931 and later became the founder of the People's Republic of China in 1949. During 1934–1935, he led the Red Army on the Long March (6,000 miles) to reorganize and fight the rival Kuomintang faction whose leader was Chiang Kaishek. Emerging victorious from the long civil war that coincided with battles against Japanese forces during World War II, Mao's first actions after founding the republic were land reforms. During this upheaval anyone associated with the old regime was targeted, with the result that over a million people died. Mao's first Five Year Plan was a success but the second, begun in 1958 and known as the Great Leap Forward, was a failure. Large farm communes were established but the implementation of unscientific farming methods and the diverting of farm labor to industry, caused a drop in agricultural production. This, coupled with drought and floods, brought death to millions (probably as many as 15 million). In an attempt to establish revolutionary ideals and maintain his power, Mao, along with his wife Jiang Qing (1914–1991) began the Cultural Revolution in 1966, the purpose of which was to suppress "bourgeois" elements in society. It became a reign of terror during which art objects from former times were destroyed, and citizens were imprisoned, relocated, or murdered on the flimsiest of evidence (usually fabricated). Millions of lives were ruined. To enforce these Spartan ideas, power was given to the Red Guards, groups of young people, often teenagers, who set up their own makeshift tribunals. After Mao's death in 1976 at age 82, a power struggle for control of China began. Eventually, in a bloodless coup, Mao's opponents, the reformers, gained control and the Cultural Revolution came to an end.

Jiang Qing, Mao's fourth wife, was the deputy director of the Cultural Revolution. Once a famous actress, she abandoned the stage, became involved in Communist politics, and married Mao after the Long March. She formed the notorious Gang of Four, who advised Mao in his declining years. After his death, the "gang" members were arrested and brought to trial and she was sentenced to death. This was later changed to life imprisonment. She committed suicide in 1991 at age 77.

Quotations from Chairman Mao (known in the West as *The Little Red Book*) is an anthology of pithy excerpts from Mao's speeches, poems, and publications. It is estimated that, during the Cultural Revolution, there were 900 million copies in print in China. It became the bible of the Revolution and was the curriculum of compulsory study groups in schools. Every citizen was required to own, read, and carry a copy at all times. Failure to produce a copy when challenged would lead to beatings, or imprisonment, or both. The contents are divided by topic into 33 chapters. The 427 quotes cover such topics as the Revolutionary Communist Party, proper methods of thinking and working, and class and class struggle.

Principal Characters

Ling Chang, a Chinese girl, almost 9 at the beginning of the story
Dr. Chang, her father
Dr. Xiong, her mother
Dr. Wong, an upstairs neighbor
Mrs. Wong, his wife
Niu, their son
Yo, a bullying classmate
Gao, another obnoxious classmate, son of Comrade Sin
Comrade Sin, a Communist leader
Comrade Li, chief political official at the hospital
Ji, a liberal writer

Plot Synopsis

In the summer of 1972 in the central Chinese city of Wuhan, situated at the confluence of the Han and Yangtze rivers, Ling Chang, almost 9 years old, is enjoying growing up in an apartment compound connected to the city hospital where both of her parents work. Her father, Dr. Chang, is a highly respected surgeon who showers love and attention on his only child to the point of allowing her, in moments of play, to tie his hair into tiny ponytails. Ling's mother, Dr. Xiong, a practitioner of traditional medicine, is less indulgent but, in her restrained and stern way, also exhibits a caring nature. Dr. Chang and Dr. Wong—who lives upstairs with his wife and 12-year-old son Niu—both studied medicine in the United States and have fond memories of their lives there. Voicing thoughts favorable to America, however, is becoming more dangerous every day as Chairman Mao's Cultural Revolution—a repressive, barbaric program intended to erase all evidence of pre-Communist traditions and values (now labeled bourgeois)—gains a foothold.

One day, without warning, part of the Changs' apartment is commandeered as living quarters for the bossy, self-important Comrade Li, the new political officer at the hospital and leader of the Red Guards, who is charged with teaching Chairman Mao's ideas and enforcing the principles stated in his Book of Quotations. Ill-mannered and crude, Comrade Li soon becomes a fearful presence in their lives. Ling often escapes upstairs to the Wongs' apartment. Although Dr. Wong tends to be gruff and unapproachable, Mrs. Wong, a delightful, caring woman, showers Ling with gifts of food and clothes, and Niu, their son, acts as an older brother toward her. At school, Ling, a fine student, begins to experience problems. She has skipped a grade, and on her first day in fifth grade, she happily wears a pretty red and white dress to school. Her classmates, who are clad in the plain grey of the Young Pioneers uniform, accuse her of anti-Revolutionary behavior and ostracize her. Particularly obnoxious are gang leaders Yo, a girl who considers Ling's long hair subversive, and a rabbit-faced boy called Gao, whose father, Comrade Sin, helps oversee the Cultural Revolution in the district. Ling resents these acts of cruelty and injustice but, after trying unsuccessfully to oppose them, retreats into silence.

Weeks later, Dr. Wong suddenly disappears, and Comrade Li explains that he was an enemy of the state. Later, Red Guards raid and pillage the apartment of the heartbroken Mrs. Wong. In time, more doctors disappear and whole families are sent to labor camps. Coincidentally, on Ling's 10th birthday, Comrade Li orders all the residents of the complex to attend a meeting in the slogan-plastered courtyard. Here he denounces Mrs. Wong and Niu. Though endangering his life, Dr. Chang speaks in their defense and gains their release. Ling is proud of her father and his great courage but, in time, the Red Guards send Mrs. Wong to a labor camp, and confiscate their apartment. Niu moves in with the Changs, but their apartment is also raided and many of their possessions destroyed. Later, Niu and his high school classmates are sent to the countryside for "re-education." There, Niu is caught trying to escape and undergoes severe brainwashing to instill correct party doctrines.

Meanwhile, the Changs dream of escaping to America and freedom. However, Dr. Chang is relieved of his medical duties and forced to become a janitor in the hospital. On her 11th birthday, Ling and her father are wandering on the banks of the Han River when they see a man wading into the water beyond his depth. Father saves him. He is Ji, a revolutionary writer whose persecution has driven him to attempt suicide. After feeding him, Dr. Chang makes him promise to continue to live and hope for a better time. Later that winter, the apartment is once again stormed by Red Guards, this time led by a "reformed" Niu. The Red Guards drag Dr. Chang away—destination, unknown.

Hardships increase for Ling and her mother. Food is scarce and the apartment has no heat. At one point, Ling is convinced that her mother is contemplating suicide. Conditions are also terrible at school. Mornings and afternoons are spent chanting the sayings of Chairman Mao. Because she defiantly refuses to cut her beautiful pigtails, Ling is attacked by classmates led by Gao. She lashes out, swinging her schoolbag and wounding Gao in the face. Intimidated, the gang lets her escape and Gao doesn't return to school for several days. One night, Ling is awakened by her mother. Her father is in the hospital, operating on Comrade Sin. Dr. Chang, it seems, has been held in the city jail all these months and has been summoned by seriously ill Sin, who doesn't trust any of the remaining half-trained medics. Ling sneaks off to the hospital to get a glimpse of her father. Unfortunately she is caught by guards and thrown into a room with a filthy mattress. After her release the next day, her mother discovers she has head lice and must have her head shaved. At last Ling has lost the battle to save her pigtails.

Chairman Mao dies, and for weeks the city is engulfed in mourning. Hours of weeping and wailing are compulsory in the school. Through Niu, whose conscience is obviously troubling him, a note is delivered to Ling and her mother. Dr. Chang is well and has been returned to the city jail. Gao, now recovered from his wounds, uses his father's influence to get Comrade Li to call a public meeting to demand an apology from Ling for her assault. At first, Ling is defiant but, realizing that her mother's life could be in danger if she persists, grudgingly acquiesces and says "I apologize to Gao" and under her breath "for being so ugly."

Suddenly troops arrive on the scene. The counterrevolutionaries have taken power. Both Comrade Li and Comrade Sin are arrested. Father is released from jail and reunited with his family. Somehow, the Changs have survived this terrible ordeal and begin preparing for a future that, they hope, will include America.

Passages for Booktalking
Ling braids her father's hair and discusses family relationships (pp. 9–17); Comrade Li moves in (pp. 19–22); Mrs. Wong spoils Ling (pp. 39–51); and Ling's first day in the fifth grade (pp. 59–61).

Themes and Subjects
The author has said, "I hope that my book can inspire others to overcome their personal obstacles." Let us hope that none of her readers ever experience the hardships faced by the Chang family. This is the story of totalitarianism gone wild, where an entire nation is brought to its knees by power-mad fanatics. Yet within this atmosphere of terror and mistrust, some individuals dare to stand up for truth and humanity. In spite of the horror, hardships, and insecurity of life during the Cultural Revolution, the spirit of hope, courage, and human dignity survive in the lives of Dr. Chang and his family. Ling is a girl of outstanding bravery and valor who, in spite of her age, fights for the ideals of justice and individualism her father has taught her. Other subjects: Cultural Revolution, Chinese history, Chairman Mao, death, prison camps, tyranny, freedom, education, brain washing, and Chinese culture.

GAVIN, JAMILA. *The Blood Stone.* 2003, Farrar, Straus, $18 (978-0-374-30846-9) (Grades 6–9)

Introduction

Jamila Gavin was born at Mussoorie in the foothills of the Indian Himalayas on August 8, 1941. Her father was Indian and her mother English. At age 12 she moved to England where she majored in music at college but eventually found writing was her most important interest. Many of her books use India as a backdrop, including a trilogy of novels for young people that feature modern Indian history as a subject, with discussion of independence from Britain and the creation of Pakistan. These novels (unfortunately out of print in this country) are *The Wheel of Surya*, *The Eye of the Horse*, and *The Track of the Wind*. Another of her popular novels is *Coram Boy* (Nick Horn, 2000, $18.95; 185459843). Set in England in the middle of the 18th century, a time when children born out of wedlock were secretly disposed of, this is the story of one unwanted child who was fortunate enough to be placed in the orphanage founded by the benevolent Captain Thomas Coram. It is also the story of the families the boy never knew and of the terrible villainy perpatrated by a man who secretly murders many of these children instead of delivering them to orphanages. *Coram Boy* was adapted into a musical and, after playing in London, had a brief run on Broadway.

The Blood Stone takes place principally in three locales: Venice, the court of Shah Jahan at Agra, and the area around Kabul in present-day Afghanistan. The time period is about two years, roughly 1630 and 1631. Throughout the text, there are quotes from Homer's *Odyssey*, and the adventures of Odysseus parallel those of the young hero, Filippo. As a preface, there is a helpful map of Filippo's journey. Because of the tragic stories that often surround diamonds, they are referred to in this book as blood stones.

Historical Background

Several Mogul emperors are referred to in the text (and two are important characters in the plot). Beginning in the 12th century, the Moguls, from the north, regularly raided and occupied parts of India. Gradually more of north and central India became part of their empire. The conquering Moguls were Muslim and the conquered Indians were Hindu. The reign of Babur and the following five emperors ushered in a golden age for India, particularly in the arts and architecture. After them, the fall of the Mogul Empire was fast and dramatic. These important emperors and the dates of their reigns are:

Babur (1527–1530)
Humayun (1530–1556)
Akbar (1556–1605)
Jehangir (1605–1627)
Shah Jahan (1627–1658)
Aurangzeb (1658–1707)

Babur, a descendant of Genghis Khan, successfully extended Mogul rule but his successor, Humayan, had difficulty maintaining these gains (he was forced by the Hindus to spend fifteen years in exile). At his death, from falling down a flight of steep stairs, he had, however, managed to recapture the throne. Humayan's son, Akbar, was the greatest of these emperors. Not only was he an outstanding warrior, he was also a man of learning, wisdom, and fairness. For example, instead of trying to subdue the Hindus, who were in the majority, he integrated them into his administration. During his reign, the city of Fatehpu Sikri was built and abandoned. Jehangir was an important builder of tombs and mosques but preferred Kashmir to Delhi or Agra. Besides his sadism, he is noted for his love of alcohol and women. Shah Jahan spent more time in Agra and Delhi. He is best known for the opulent buildings he constructed, which included the Red Fort and the huge Royal Mosque in Delhi, and the Pearl Mosque in the Agra Fort. His masterpiece was the Taj Mahal in Agra, a tribute to his beloved wife, Mumtaz Mahal, who died in 1631 giving birth to their fourteenth child. Both to gain power and to prevent bankruptcy from his father's uncontrolled building sprees, his son Aurangzeb usurped power after murdering his brothers and their sons. For the last seven years of his life, Shah Jahan was held prisoner in a room in the royal palace that overlooked the distant Taj Mahal. In contrast to his father, Aurangzeb was dull, frugal, and a religious zealot. He alienated the Hindus by building mosques on their temple sites. After a series of insignificant leaders, the power of the Moguls ended when they were defeated by the British at the battle of Plessey in 1757. This defeat signaled the birth of a new power in India—the British Raj.

Principal Characters

Filippo Veroneo, a 12-year-old Venetian boy
Elisabetta (Betta), Filippo's oldest sister
Carlo, Filippo's older brother
Giuseppe, Filippo's other brother
Sofia and Gabriella, Filippo's other older sisters
Teodora Veroneo, Filippo's mother
Andreas Georgilis, Filippo's best friend
Stefino Georgilis, Andreas's father

Bernardo Pagliarin, Elisabetta's husband
Antonio Rodriguez, a mysterious stranger
Federigo and Matteo, Bernardo's sons
Sadiqui Igbal Khan, a Muslim from India
Abdul Mir, an Afghani warlord
Grand Vizier, councilor to the emperor
Prince Murad Bhakhsh, youngest son of Shah Jahan
Aurangzeb, another of Shah Jahan's sons
Mumtaz Mahal, wife of Shah Jahan
Noor (Marianne) Wallace, a palace girl
Captain Robert Wallace, Noor's father

Plot Synopsis

The year is about A.D. 1630. Filippo Veroneo is the youngest of six children born in Venice to the jeweler Geronimo Veroneo and his devoted wife, Teodora. Filippo has three sisters—Elisabetta (Betta), the eldest in the family, Sofia, and Gabriella—as well as two brothers, Carlo and Giuseppe (Beppo). Filippo has never seen his father because he was born a few months after Geronimo left on a jewel-buying expedition to Hindustan (India). That was twelve years ago and, although most people think Geronimo must be dead, Teodora has never given up hope. Before he left, Geronimo married Elisabetta, then only 14, to a wealthy merchant, Bernardo Pagliarin. He also named Bernardo the family guardian. Because Bernardo has proven to be an unscrupulous, greedy scoundrel, Carlo, the eldest son, who takes care of the family jewelry-making business, is now engaged in a court fight to become the legal head of the family. Filippo's best friend is Andreas Georgilis, a Greek boy whose father, Stefino, a fisherman, is planning an expedition to Crete. Filippo wishes he could join them and get away from his overbearing guardian.

One day, Bernardo, who already is hiding near-bankruptcy because of the loss of a fleet at sea, receives disturbing news from a mysterious stranger named Antonio Rodriguez, who emits a strange spicy smell like cinnamon. Rodriguez, who just returned from Hindustan, tells Bernardo that Geronimo, his very dear friend, is still alive. Wishing to keep this news a secret, Bernardo has Rodriguez followed, but the wily ruffian eludes capture. Fearing the family will hear this news, Bernardo plans to marry off the two remaining daughters quickly and to seize as much of the Veroneo fortune as possible. He and an appraiser visit the family and see, in a portrait of Geronimo, that he is holding a large pendant whose centerpiece is a magnificent diamond known as the Ocean of the Moon.

Teodora confesses that she owns the pendant but refuses to produce it even when her daughter Betta is sent by her deceitful husband to discover its whereabouts. One night, Carlo is almost strangled in a dark alley but is saved by a stranger who disappears, leaving only a cinnamon-like odor. While crossing town to deliver drawings of jewelry settings to a customer, Filippo and his ailing brother Giuseppe are accosted by a gang of hooligans led by Federigo and Matteo, Bernardo's sons from a previous marriage. During the melee, Giuseppe is stabbed to death, and the designs are thrown in a canal. Filippo almost drowns trying to retrieve them, but a stranger who smells of cinnamon extends a pole that saves his life. Before he can thank him, the stranger disappears. While the family is in deep mourning for Giuseppe, another stranger appears. He introduces himself as Sadiqui Igbal Khan, a Muslim who has returned from the East via Mecca, where he made a pilgrimage. He informs the family that he and Geronimo were held prisoners by a warlord named Abdul Mir in a fort outside Kabul. Signor Khan was released on the condition that he collect ransom money from the Veroneo family and return with it to free their father.

With some misgivings, the family decides to trust the man. Filippo will accompany Signor Khan with the family's only valuable asset, the Ocean of the Moon. After dismantling the pendant, the diamond is sewn into Filippo's skull by a skilled Jewish surgeon and a fake stone is placed in a pouch around his neck. To confuse Bernardo and would-be pursuers, the boy travels to Crete with Andreas and his father and there meets up with Signor Khan. However, danger follows them. Andreas is mistaken for Filippo and shanghaied onto a ship. He escapes overboard into the sea where some dolphins gently nudge him to the shore of an island where he is befriended by a lonely old hag. Meantime, Filippo and Signor Khan share many adventures. By sea, they voyage to Damascus and then travel overland, through desert sandstorms and a bandit attack during which the fake diamond is stolen, to Basra. There they board another ship for Surat on the coast of India and then go overland to the magical city of Agra, home of the Mogul emperor, Shah Jahan. In Agra, Filippo and Signor Khan stay in the opulent home of the Grand Vizier to the emperor, a friend of Signor Khan.

One day, Filippo climbs the wall that surrounds the house to witness a parade. The emperor's young son, Prince Murad, is riding on an elephant. Filippo is spotted by the boy's guards, who mistake him for a spy and drag him to the royal palace. There he is held prisoner and treated as a playmate and curiosity by the young prince, whose older brother, Aurangzeb, reveals himself to be a threatening menace eager to usurp power from his father. Aurangzeb scornfully dismisses Filippo's request to see the emperor and present him with the diamond, hoping to get gold in exchange for the ransom.

Filippo becomes aware that someone is watching him through the tiles in his room. Finally, the spy appears. It is a beautiful young girl named Noor, also called Marianne, the daughter of a deceased Indian mother and Captain Robert Wallace, an administrator of the British East India Company who is a resident of the palace. They form a close friendship and, when the pains in Filippo's head caused by the diamond become unbearable, Noor takes Filippo to her father, who surgically removes it. Filippo reassembles the pendant and, through Noor's clever manipulations, presents it to the emperor in the presence of the Grand Vizier, Signor Khan, and the vengeful Aurangzeb. The plan works. Filippo is given five thousand gold coins for the ransom and another five thousand that are to be held in the palace for his return journey to Venice.

Signor Khan and Filippo set out again, but before they reach Kabul their caravan is ambushed by Aurangzeb's men, the ransom money is stolen, and Signor Khan is murdered. Filippo is once again saved by the appearance of Rodriguez, who reveals that he has devoted his life to helping the family of his dear friend Geronimo. Filippo confronts the warlord Abdul Mir without the ransom. However, he is able to get permission to take his father, now a broken, mortally sick man, away with him. On the road back to Agra, his father dies and Filippo is heartbroken. He and Rodriguez return to Agra, a city now in mourning for the dead wife of Shah Jahan, Mumtaz Mahal. They return to Venice where they learn that Carlo had been goaded into killing Bernardo but was freed when Bernardo's evil deeds were revealed. The Veroneo family is reunited and, in time, Filippo marries Andreas's young sister. Andreas has not returned and is presumed dead. Years later, Filippo goes to Agra with brother Carlo. Together they spend time with Noor and visit Mumtaz's magnificent tomb, the Taj Mahal. All these experiences remind Filippo of the father he scarcely knew.

Passages for Booktalking
Some interesting passages are: Rodriguez is introduced and escapes from Bernardo's men (pp. 36–40); Geronimo cuts the diamond, the Ocean of the Moon (pp. 47–51); Giuseppe and Filippo are attacked (pp. 64–72); and Signor Khan arrives (pp. 87–92).

Themes and Subjects
The reader is introduced first to the Mediterranean world of the early 17th century and then given a picture of exotic Muslim India during the reign of the Mogul emperors. It is also a tale of darkest villainy, convoluted intrigue, and intricate, unpredictable plotting. Devotion to family and the strength of father-son love are important themes as is the struggle for fairness and justice. The author's prose frequently borders on the poetic. Other subjects include: Venice, ships and shipping, jewels and jewelry making, epic adventure stories,

suspense, Agra, Afghanistan, ransoms, Odysseus, sea stories, deserts, friendship, murder, and diamonds.

———•◦•———

HAUSMAN, GERALD, AND LORETTA HAUSMAN. *Escape from Botany Bay: The True Story of Mary Bryant.* Orchard, 2003, $16.95 (978-0-439-40327-6)

Introduction

Gerald Hausman was born in Baltimore, Maryland, in 1945 to a family interested in storytelling. He graduated from college in New Mexico and, while there, married his wife Loretta. He has spent most of his life writing and teaching. He and his wife left New Mexico temporarily while Gerald taught creative writing in various schools in New England, but in the late 1970s moved back and remained there until moving, in 1994, to the town of Bokeelia, Florida, located on an island on the west coast close to Fort Myers. As well as being a renowned storyteller, Gerald Hausman has developed many creative writing programs, including one in Jamaica that lasted from 1986 through 1993. His keen interest in the folklore and mythology of various native populations, including the Navajo, has led to many books written with his wife that are retellings of these stories. Together they now have published more than 50 adult and juvenile titles. A recent fictional biography is *A Mind with Wings: The Story of Henry David Thoreau* (Random, 2006, $15.95; 1590302281), which is the life story of the great American thinker and writer. Told in brief anecdotal chapters, it contains material on Thoreau's work helping the family's pencil business, his overnight stay in a jail because he would not compromise his principles, and, of course, his two-year stay in Walden Woods.

Escape from Botany Bay is told in the first person by Mary Bryant. It takes place over a period of almost eight years, from January 1786, when Mary was caught by the police for stealing, until her final release in London in November 1793.

Historical Background

Many historical names and geographical places figure in this story. Mary was born in the town of Fowey (rhymes with "boy") in Cornwall in southwest England. The town is situated on the southern coast at the mouth of the Fowey River and is associated with Daphne Du Maurier and Kenneth Grahame, the author of *The Wind in the Willows*, both of whom had houses there. Fowey is about 30 miles east of the city of Plymouth, Devon, where Mary was arrested. Plymouth is also on the coast, at the mouths of the Plym and Tamar rivers. It is famous as the port from which the Pilgrims began their journey on the *Mayflower*, and it was from here that Sir Francis Drake embarked with his fleet to defeat the Spanish Armada. In Plymouth, Mary was held in Exeter Castle, a Norman stone fortress in the center of town whose construction began in 1068. In the 18th century, its interior buildings were destroyed to build the Assize County Courts that are featured in the story.

New Holland was the historical name for Australia. It was named this in 1644 by the Dutch explorer Abel Tasman (of Tasmania fame) and was not renamed until more than 150 years later, when, in 1804, the explorer and cartographer Matthew Flinders recommended changing the name to Australia, from Terra Australis (Southern Land). The name became official in 1824.

The coastal area in the southeast had already been discovered and named New South Wales by Captain Cook during his voyage of 1770.

The First Fleet was the name of the flotilla of eleven ships carrying convicts that left England under the command of Captain Arthur Phillip, whose purpose was to found an English colony in New South Wales. From 1788 to 1792, Captain Phillip was the governor of the colony. The colonists first landed at Botany Bay, close to present-day Sydney, but found this site unsuitable because of poor soil and lack of fresh water. They moved to Sydney Cove at Port Jackson, north of Botany Bay, on January 26, 1788. In spite of the move the colony was always known in England as the Botany Bay settlement. Botany Bay was named by Captain Cook because of the great quantity of plants found there (he had originally called it Stingray Bay for obvious reasons). Sydney Cove was named after Lord Sydney who issued the charter authorizing Captain Phillip to establish a colony in New South Wales.

Mary and her friends land at Kupang in Timor, an island in the Malay Archipelago in southeast Asia. At the time of the novel Timor was controlled by the Dutch. It is now divided into West Timor, which is part of Indonesia, and East Timor or Timor-Leste, an independent nation since 2002. Timor is due east of Java and about 400 miles north, across the Timor Sea, of the northern tip of Australia. Kupang (also spelt Koupang), in West Timor, is the port where Captain William Bligh of the *Bounty* landed two years before Mary. This event is referred to in the novel many times.

Captain Bligh took command of the *Bounty* in 1787. After a difficult voyage from England, the ship reached Tahiti to load a cargo of breadfruit trees. After leaving Tahiti there was a mutiny led by Fletcher Christian. Bligh and eighteen of his crew were cast adrift in a 23-foot launch with meager food and water. Fearful of landing and encountering hostile natives, they pressed on and completed in 47 days a seemingly impossible journey of more than 3,600 miles to Timor. After a period of recovery, they were returned to England. In the meantime, Fletcher Christian took a native bride and settled on Pitcairn Island.

Mary and her companions were sent from Kupang to Batavia. From 1619 to 1942 this was the name given to the largest city and capital of Indonesia. Its current name is Jakarta. It is situated on the northern coast of Java.

Back in London, Mary was incarcerated in Newgate Prison, which was situated close to the courts known as the Old Bailey in the old city of London. The first prison was built in 1188 on the orders of Henry II. It was rebuilt many times and, in 1783, the public gallows of the city were moved to the yard outside the prison. Public executions did not end until 1868. Other famous personalities housed in Newgate Prison include Daniel Defoe, Ben Jonson, William (Captain) Kidd, and William Penn. The Old Bailey continues to be an important criminal court in England.

Mary is eventually rescued from Newgate with the help of James Boswell (1740–1785), a well-known lawyer, diarist, and author of the period. Although he practiced law primarily in his native Scotland, he spent about one month a year in London, principally in the company of Dr. Samuel Johnson, London's famous man of letters. From these encounters came Boswell's masterpiece, *The Life of Johnson*, published in 1791, considered by many to be the greatest biography ever written. Boswell was notoriously promiscuous although there has never been evidence linking him and Mary Bryant sexually.

The important facts of Mary Bryant's life are covered in this novel. She was born in Fowey, Cornwall, in 1765 or 1767 (sources differ), and later left home to find work in Plymouth, where she was arrested for petty thievery. In 1787, she was sent to Australia (New Holland) aboard the *Charlotte*, the name she gave to the baby she bore during the voyage. The father was probably one of the convicts (not the sailor Tench as in the novel). She married William Bryant, a convicted smuggler, and had a baby with him. At the colony, he was caught selling fish on the side, and was given 100 lashes. On March 28, 1791, Mary, her family, and seven other convicts escaped and completed a 3,000-mile journey to Kupang in Timor in 66 days. Back in prison in London, she was championed by the lawyer James Boswell. Nothing is known of her life afterward, but her amazing story has been the subject of plays, a television movie, and several books.

Principal Characters

    Mary Broad Bryant, a 19-year-old girl in 1784
    Catherine Fryer, her friend
    Mary Haydon, another friend
    Watkin Tench, a marine
    Will Bryant, a smuggler

Captain Phillip, head of the expedition
Captain Gilbert, master of the Charlotte
Dr. John White, the ship surgeon
Charlotte, Mary's daughter
Emmanuel, her son
Captain Smith, an officer sympathetic to Mary's escape plans
William Allen, William Morton, James Martin, Sam Bond, Nat Lilley,
     James Cox, and Sam Broom, the seven convicts who join the Bryants on
     their voyage
Timotheus Wanjon, Dutch governor of Timor
Captain John Parker, captain of the Gorgon
James Boswell, a Scottish lawyer

Plot Synopsis

Poverty and hopelessness often produce desperate behavior. Nineteen-year-old Mary Broad, on the brink of starvation, is in such a situation. It is January 1786 and Mary, who has left her home in Fowey, Cornwall, hoping to find work in nearby Plymouth, now finds herself destitute along with her equally impoverished friends, Catherine Fryer and Mary Haydon. The three attempt to rob a wealthy-looking woman, whose screams attract the police. The three are captured: Mary's net gain, a silk bonnet. For this and a few shillings, the three are locked up in Exeter Castle. Instead of receiving the customary death penalty, they are sentenced to seven years of penal transportation and are transferred to a prison ship, the *Dunkirk*, anchored in nearby Devonport. Living conditions there are appalling. The cramped quarters, between decks, allow each prisoner, already in chains, a space of only 9 feet by 20 inches. Mary's body soon burns with lice and her hair is covered with nits. Fortunately, she is befriended by a marine named Watkin Tench. Periodically, he sneaks food to her and unlocks her manacles so she can secretly walk freely on deck. He even gives her a clean dress. To express her thanks, Mary gives him the only thing she owns, her body. The convicts spend nine months living in these miserable conditions. They then discover they are to be sent to New Holland (Australia) to found a colony and they are transferred to a seaworthy ship, the *Charlotte*. Among the male convicts, Mary sees a convicted smuggler named Will Bryant, whom she recognizes as someone she met four years before through her father's shady dealings. She is immediately attracted to this dark, handsome man.

Four grueling months pass before they set sail along with other ships, collectively known as the First Fleet, each vessel carrying a cargo of convicts. Captain Phillip leads the expedition and Captain Gilbert is the captain of the *Charlotte*. The first stop for supplies is Tenerife in the Canary Islands. Mr. Tench continues to help Mary with little kindnesses but she is horrified to witness two public floggings, the first of a convict captured during an escape attempt, and the second of a man who was caught "coining," making counterfeit silver coins from melted-down teaspoons. Before the *Charlotte* reaches their second stop, Rio de Janeiro, Mary realizes she is pregnant. Mr. Tench refuses to marry her because he is already engaged to a girl in England. Time passes. Occasionally, Mary encounters Will Bryant and a mutual attraction develops. After a brief stay at Cape Town, Mary, with the help of the ship's surgeon, Dr. John White, gives birth to a baby girl during a violent storm. She names her Charlotte after the ship, the baby's first home.

Finally, in January 1788, the bedraggled assemblage of 627 souls (48 died during the voyage) arrives in Botany Bay, and begins constructing shelters in an area known as Port Jackson. Captain Phillip, now Governor Phillip, later names the place Sydney. The exhausting, arduous daily life is made easier for Mary when Will proposes marriage. Will's seafaring skills result in a promotion to chief of the colony's fishing enterprises and, as a further reward, Governor Phillip allows the newly married couple to move into one of the new single-family dwellings. Still, colony life is difficult with most living near starvation. One night, during a violent gale, some of the convicts run riot, raping and pillaging. Governor Phillip restores order and imposes martial law. Months later, Will is accused of stealing fish and, in addition to losing their home, he is sentenced to 100 lashes. While Mary tends to his torn flesh, the two vow that somehow they will escape from Botany Bay. In April 1789, Mary gives birth to a son and names him Emmanuel, meaning hope.

Slowly their plans for escape take shape. With caution, others are brought into the scheme and, with the help of sympathetic Captain Smith, they secure a chart, compass, and quadrant. One dark night, they steal out to the cutter used for fishing and take off. In addition to the four Bryants, there are seven others, all convicts: James Martin, Sam Bond, Nat Lilley, James Cox, Sam Broom, William Allen and William Morton. They sail north between land and the Great Barrier Reef, stopping occasionally for water and to forage for food. The trip is grueling and plagued by crises. Mary is always level-headed and reliable, as in the day she saves the boat from a shark attack. On another occasion she quiets hostile natives by singing a nursery song. After seven weeks and several thousands of miles, they reach the port of Koupang on the island of Timor and are greeted by the Dutch governor, Timotheus Wanjon. James Martin, an able liar, convinces the governor that they are the only survivors of a ship that sank during a gale and, as a result, the group is treated to great hospitality. This deceit ends abruptly after two months when, Will, in a drunken stupor, blabs the truth to his newfound drinking buddies. The group is taken prisoner and sent in chains to Batavia on the island of Java. There, both Will and baby Emmanuel become sick and die. James Cox jumps ship during the trip and Sam Bond also dies. The surviving seven board *HMS Gorgon*, bound for London under the command of Captain John Parker. Charlotte dies during the voyage and, in London, Mary and the five remaining convicts are sent to Newgate Prison.

News of Mary's heroism and courage has preceded her and there is a public outcry for her release. Her savior appears in the form of a plump, ruddy-faced Scottish lawyer, James Boswell, who is intrigued by her case and committed to saving her. The process is long but his devotion never wavers. The appeal takes one year and then suddenly, in May 1793, seven and a half years after her initial arrest, Mary becomes a free woman. Later, her companions are also freed. Mr. Boswell bestows on her a small stipend, and Mary fulfils her longstanding dream of returning to her home in Fowey, Cornwall, to begin a new life.

Passages for Booktalking
Some interesting passages are: the robbery and Mary's capture (pp. 2–5); Mary sees Will Bryant and remembers who he is (pp. 25–27); their wedding (pp. 77–80); Will's problems fishing for the colony (pp. 84–87) and Will is tried and flogged (pp. 95–99).

Themes and Subjects
In Queen Victoria's time Gilbert and Sullivan wrote about the necessity that "the punishment fit the crime." This was certainly not true of 18th-century England where the judicial system was seldom judicious. The inhumanity and corruption associated with the courts of this time are realistically portrayed. Mary emerges as a courageous, resourceful, and loyal young woman who stands up for her rights and those of her family and friends. Her story is of one of sacrifice and survival that tells of a woman facing and conquering a series of physical and emotional problems. Other subjects: Australia, New South Wales, Sydney, Southeast Asia, Cornwall, Plymouth, London convicts, theft, friendship, families, marriage, children, love, ships and shipping, prisons, Newgate Prison, death, disease, flogging, ocean journeys, escapes, and liberty.

McCAUGHREAN, GERALDINE. *The Kite Rider.* Harper, 2002, $6.99; pap. $5.99 (978-0-06-441091-5) (Grades 5–9)

Introduction
Geraldine McCaughrean (pronounced McCorkran) was born in London, England, in 1951. After trying her hand at teaching, she gravitated to publishing, where she was an editor before becoming an author. With more than 140

books to her credit, she must be one of the most prolific writers working today. Most of her titles are retellings or adaptations of classic stories such as *The Canterbury Tales, The Faerie Queene, The Odyssey, El Cid,* and *One Thousand and One Nights.* She is also the prize-winning author of many works of original fiction for young readers.

For example, the novel *A Pack of Lies* (Oxford, 2001, $12.27; 0192752030) won the 1999 Guardian Children's Fiction Award and the 1998 Carnegie Medal. The latter is the most prestigious award presented to an author of children's books in the United Kingdom. Subtitled *Twelve Stories in One,* the novel deals with Ailsa, who does not trust M. C. C. Berkshire, the man who helps her mother in her antique shop, because he spins fantastic stories about antiques with settings as varied as Ireland and ancient China. Although Ailsa is convinced they are a pack of lies, his stories do sell the antiques.

The Kite Rider, which is set in 13th-century China at the time of Kublai Khan, also won several British literary prizes for children's fiction. Ms. McCaughrean currently lives in a village outside London with her husband, a retired merchant seaman.

Historical Background

The Mongol Empire was established by the bloodthirsty tyrant Genghis Khan (1167–1227). He waged several successful campaigns in western Asia and Europe and began a full-scale invasion of China. This was continued by his successors, including the fifth of the great Mongol Khans, Kublai Khan (1212–1294), who was responsible for the complete defeat of the Sung dynasty. Although the Chinese tried from time to time to oust the invaders, these gallant rebellions proved abortive. Under Kublai Khan the Mongol Empire expanded south and east as far as Burma and Java. In 1284 (1281 in the novel) Kublai Khan (who reigned from 1279 to 1294) sent a great armada with 150,000 men to invade Japan. A sudden typhoon (called the "divine wind" or Kamikaze in Japanese history) destroyed the ships and the invaders were either killed or taken prisoner. Kublai Khan was much more progressive and liberal than his predecessors. He promoted the arts and practiced religious tolerance, but made Buddhism the state religion. He also encouraged foreign visitors. Marco Polo and his trader relatives first visited China in 1260 and returned in 1275 to stay until 1292. Marco Polo is not mentioned in *The Kite Rider* but the author has drawn freely from his memoirs, *The Travels of Marco Polo,* in which, for example, he mentions that the Chinese used kites to test the wind. At the same time, the Japanese invented man-carrying kites that were used for scouting purposes. The author has combined both practices in this novel. In time, the Mongols lost power and withdrew. The victorious Chinese founded the Ming dynasty, which remained in power for almost three hundred years.

Principal Characters

    Great-uncle Gou Bo, the unscrupulous head of the Gou family
    Great-aunt Mo, his browbeaten wife
    Gou Pei, a deckhand, nephew of Bo
    Qing'an, Pei's wife
    Haoyou, Pei's 12-year-old son (later know as Qiqi)
    Wawa, Pei's two-year-old daughter
    Mipeng, Haoyou's second cousin, a young widow purported to be a medium
    Di Chou, an evil first mate on Pei's ship
    Miao Jie, aka "the Great Miao," master of the Jade Circus
    Bukhur, a Mongol bird catcher and member of the circus
    Khutulin, Bukhur's daughter
    Chiggis, an unfortunate Mongol boy
    Kublai Khan, the ruler of China aka Cathay

Plot Synopsis

In 1280, in the Chinese port city of Dagu on the Yellow Sea, 12-year-old Haoyou has accompanied his beloved father, Pei, a deckhand and member of the Gou family, to his ship to say goodbye and witness his departure. In order to pacify the Mongols who are occupying China, Pei's ship was recently renamed the *Chabi*, honoring the name of Kublai Khan's favorite wife.

Without provocation, the barbarous first mate, Di Chou, flings Pei down a hatchway. A horrified Haoyou learns that a human kite rider will be used to test the fitness of the winds for traveling. Within minutes he sees that his terrified father has been strapped to a hatch cover and hoisted into the sky. Pei dies of a heart attack and Haoyou, desolate at his loss, rushes home to his mother, Qing'an, and two-year-old sister Wawa. Di Chou, it turns out, had an ulterior motive for disposing of Pei. He is lusting after the uncommonly beautiful and virtuous Qing'an and now approaches, with money, the head of the Gou family, Great Uncle Bo, seeking her hand in marriage. Bo, who is married to browbeaten Great Aunt Mo, looks like on overstuffed Buddha, but is actually an unscrupulous villain who takes advantage of his family position. He now assembles the family to hear the words of a medium, Mipeng, a young distant relative, recently widowed, who has been coached to promote this marriage. Instead, Mipeng, an independent, feisty, and highly principled girl, adopts an otherworldly voice, condemns the marriage, and suggests that Haoyou support the family by kite making.

Haoyou, an expert kite maker, begins work and, within two months, the house is filled with gorgeous kites ready for sale. But the house catches fire one evening and all of Haoyou's handiwork goes up in flames. Di Chou has struck again, and once more presses for marriage with the impoverished widow. Bo makes arrangements for the wedding, but Mipeng, who has taken pity on the naive, innocent Haoyou, hatches a scheme. On the eve of the wedding, the two get Di Chou dead drunk in a local tavern and transport him to a ship that is ready to sail. The shanghaiing of Di Chou hits a snag, however, when the captain refuses to sail until he gets a favorable report from a kite rider. In desperation, Haoyou volunteers and is sent aloft. Though frightened beyond words, Haoyou is exhilarated by this nearly religious experience in the sky. The omens are favorable and ship sails, taking Di Chou with it.

Haoyou's ascent has been witnessed by Miao Jie, or "The Great Miao," owner of the Jade Circus, who contacts Bo wanting to hire the boy for one of his acts. Realizing that this could be a new source of revenue, Bo agrees, and Haoyou, along with Mipeng, joins the circus on a trip up river, destination: Dadu City (Beijing), home of Kublai Khan. Miao is a wonderful boss—fair, just, and somewhat aristocratic in mien. Both Haoyou and Mipeng love the world of roustabouts, jugglers, acrobats, elephants and other assorted animals, and Chinese and Mongols working together harmoniously. As Haoyou adjusts to the danger of kite riding, he becomes fonder of the kind Miao, now his second father. In each of the towns and cities they visit, Haoyou gets a different nickname, his favorite being Qiqi, "up-in-the-air." He continues to send money home to his Great-uncle Bo, even though Mipeng reveals some horrible truths about the man. Bo has been fired from his warehouse job for stealing and will stop at nothing to feed his insatiable gambling habit.

One day Khutulin, the baby daughter of the bird catcher—a Mongol named Bukhur—is reported missing. Without hesitation, Haoyou mounts his kite and finds the child stranded in a rice paddy. She is saved, but Haoyou crashes and sustains many injuries, including a pierced eye and a dislocated shoulder.

In Dadu, the circus is well received but the troop presses on to Xanadu where the Khan is spending the summer. Bo appears with his wife in tow, hoping to make some money out of Haoyou's growing renown as a kite rider. Through some clever public relations work, the Jade Circus is invited to perform for Kublai Khan. An agitated Miao makes a confession to Mipeng and Haoyou. He is actually a member of the Sung family, the rulers before Kublai Khan's invasion. Miao was a witness to his father's murder. The Khan, not wishing to spill royal blood on the ground had his father wrapped in a carpet before sending his horsemen to trample him to death. Before his death, his father made Miao promise to kill the Khan if the opportunity arose. At the performance Miao has this chance but, realizing the entire circus would suffer reprisals, he forgoes the opportunity.

Meanwhile Bo, eager for some fast money, bets with some violent Mongols that Haoyou can outlast any kite rider they can find. Haoyou, still bound by his filial obligations, consents to the flight. The Mongol's rider, a hapless lad named Chiggis, is killed in the ensuing no-holds-barred competition and Haoyou, in a damaged kite, falls to earth on a sacred shrine belonging to the Khan. He escapes death through a plea for leniency by Bukhur, who cites his daughter's rescue as proof of Haoyou's worth. The Khan makes Haoyou an unwilling member of his entourage.

By accident, Haoyou reveals Miao's origins to Bo. At first Bo tries to bribe Miao to be silent. When that fails, he tries to curry favor with the Khan by telling him that an enemy, a Sung family member, is in his midst. Everyone is summoned for the verdict. A carpet is brought out and Miao is commanded to lie on it. Soon he is joined by Mipeng, then Haoyou, and the entire staff of the Jade Circus. The Khan is so moved that he grants Miao amnesty. Later, Haoyou is able to make his escape from the Khan's legions during a severe storm spawned by a typhoon in the China Sea. After a month of wandering and begging, he arrives back in his hometown of Dagu. Great-uncle Bo, still absent on the road, has forced Qing'an into backbreaking servitude to feed herself and little Wawa. Haoyou at last recognizes his uncle for the greedy, selfish, dishonest villain that he is. While trying to help his mother, Haoyou is confronted by Di Chou, who is intent on revenge. By clever trickery, Haoyou engineers Di Chou's arrest for robbery. Luckily, the circus comes to town and Mipeng finds Haoyou. She is now married to Miao and they are expecting their first child. Soon, Haoyou and his mother and sister join the Jade Circus on their great red-sailed junk. He even persuades Great-aunt Mo to join them. Leaving a penniless, but not contrite, Bo on shore, the group heads to new ports to perform while Haoyou has dreams of resuming his kite-making career.

Passages for Booktalking

Some interesting passages are: the role of the kite rider and the death of Pei (pp. 3–10); Di Chou consults with Great-uncle Bo about the marriage (pp. 23–25); Mipeng, as a medium, condemns the marriage but proposes that Haoyou become a kite maker (pp. 25–32); and Haoyou's first flight (pp. 68–77).

Themes and Subjects

Both Miao and Haoyou are wrestling with the same problem: obedience to parents and one's obligation to family authority versus one's sense of right and justice. The separate resolutions to these problems make for a good story.

Haoyou is a Candide-like character—guileless, innocent, and full of trust and good will for everyone. His eye-opening journey to maturity is well presented. The author has made Chinese history during the reign of Kublai Khan come alive with all its barbarity, exoticism, ignorance, and superstition. We learn about the dual society (i.e. Chinese vs. Mongol or Cathay vs. Tartary), the people's dress, family ties, responsibilities, beliefs, occupations, sports, and recreations. Other themes are marriage, courage, adventure stories, codes of behavior, racism, prejudice, villainy, individualism, and murder.

PATERSON, KATHERINE. *The Master Puppeteer.* Harper, 1976, o.p.; pap. $5.99 (978-0-06-440281-1) (Grades 4–8)

Introduction

Katherine Paterson was born in China in 1932 to missionary parents who originally hailed from the American South. At the outbreak of World War II, they relocated to North Carolina, where she spent her childhood. As an adult she became a missionary to Japan, where she spent four years. Drawing on her knowledge of the history and the culture of Japan, she has written three novels using this setting, including her first two for young readers. The first of these is *Sign of the Chrysanthemum* (pap. Harper, $5.99; 0064402320). It is set in 12th-century Japan and tells of Muna, who has never known his samurai father but, according to his mother, will recognize him by the sign of the chrysanthemum. He travels to the capital of Japan and there becomes the servant of a great swordsman while continuing the quest for his father. The second, also set in feudal Japan, is *Of Nightingales that Weep* (pap. Harper, $6.99; 0064402827). In it, Takiko, whose samurai father has been killed, finds it impossible to get along with her new stepfather, a strange country potter. Therefore she accepts a position at the royal Japanese court, where her beauty and ability to sing like a nightingale make her popular, particularly with a handsome warrior who is revealed to be an enemy spy.

The Master Puppeteer takes place in famine-stricken Osaka during the 18th century. It has been charmingly illustrated with full-page black-and-white drawings by Haru Wells.

Historical Background

The classic art of Japanese puppetry emerged more than 300 years ago although earlier forms developed centuries before. The first important traditional puppet theater was founded in Osaka (the setting of the novel) in 1684. Osaka is an ancient Japanese city situated on the southwest coast of Honshu

Island. Today the generic term *Bunraku* refers to all types of Japanese puppetry, but the official title is *ningyo-joruri*, the first word meaning puppet and the second referring to chanted narration. At one time there were hundreds of such companies in Japan but this number has dwindled considerably. The National Buraku Theater is still situated in Osaka but the company makes many annual tours, particularly to Tokyo. There are three types of puppeteers (most puppets are about half life size and are controlled by sticks). The main puppeteer uses his right hand to control the right arm, head, and face of the puppet; the left-hand puppeteer controls the left hand; and the third controls the feet and legs. To become a main puppeteer usually involves about twenty years of training (ten in each of the second and third positions). Puppeteers wear black costumes and head masks so as not to be seen by the audience. Of great importance in a performance is the role of the chanter who narrates the story and takes all the parts, modifying his voice to create different characters. Some chanters have hundreds of stories in their repertories. Also important is the samisen player. A samisen is a musical instrument resembling a three-stringed banjo. Most of the plots involve the conflict of social obligations versus personal needs and emotions.

Principal Characters

Jiro, a 13-year-old Japanese boy
Hanji, a puppet maker and Jiro's father
Isako, Jiro's cranky mother
Saburo, a notorious robber
Yoshida, the master puppeteer of the Hanaza theater
Yoshida Kinshi, Yoshida's son, now in his later teens
Mochida, a puppeteer who operates the left hands
Okada, the revered reciter who is now blind
Wada, an apprentice puppeteer who is jealous of Jiro
Minoru, another apprentice with a dripping nose
Teniji, a good-natured apprentice with a bad stutter
Kawada, the senior foot operating puppeteer
Taro, son of Jiro's neighbor
Tozo, a young samisen player who is the servant of Okada

Plot Synopsis

Severe drought conditions in 18th-century Japan have brought misery and near-starvation to the citizens of Osaka. With food prices rising beyond belief, the only people to profit from these dire conditions are the rice merchants, who become richer every day by raising prices. The homeless are dead and dying in the streets and gangs of peasants roam through the city at night robbing and plundering. The only ray of hope for the peasants are the stories that circulate about the daring Robin Hood-like character, Saburo, whose followers assume audacious disguises and rob the rich to give to the poor. The identity of this gallant scoundrel remains a secret and a price has been placed on his head.

The dedicated puppet-maker Hanji has, with the help of his son, completed work on a new puppet for Yoshida, the revered, tyrannical puppet master of the prestigious Hanaza theater. Jiro's mother, Isako, an ill-tempered woman worn down by years of poverty, hopes that the sale of the puppet will bring much-needed money to the household. Hanji and Jiro deliver the puppet to Yoshida and both are intimidated by the overpowering presence of this great artist. Jiro embarrasses his father by accepting Yoshida's offer of food and wolfing it down. Yoshida, however, is amused and offers Jiro an apprenticeship in his theater, which Hanji refuses. After the money from the puppet's sale has been spent, Jiro realizes that his family would fare better with one less mouth to feed. Over his parents' objections, he steals off and gains acceptance from Yoshida to the apprenticeship program.

At the theater, he meets a number of fascinating, dedicated people. Among them are Okada, the ancient revered reciter, or chanter, who is now blind but has committed hundreds of scripts to memory. Before becoming blind, Okada was master of his own theater and had employed Yoshida, who still regards him as a god. Other puppeteers include Mochida and Kawada, each specializing in moving a particular part of the puppet's body. The apprentices are led by Yoshida Kinshi, an older, high-spirited boy, son of the Master and continually at odds with his father who does not believe in sparing the rod for the slightest infraction. Kinshi becomes Jiro's close friend and protector. The three other apprentices are Wada, a conscientious, intelligent lad; Minoru, a fat boy with a runny nose; and tiny Teniji who is afflicted with a nervous stutter. Slowly Jiro becomes acquainted with the routines and classes. He witnesses several performances and is filled with admiration and reverence for the completely black-costumed puppeteers and their dedication to their art.

Worried because he has not heard from his parents, Jiro receives permission to visit his home. He finds it empty and Taro, a neighbor's son, explains that Hanji became ill and Jiro's parents have moved temporarily to Kyoto.

When Kawada, a foot operator, suddenly becomes ill, Yoshida grudgingly allows his son to fill in and Kinshi fortunately triumphs. The apprentices secretly celebrate with rice wine. They are discovered by Yoshida, who mercilessly beats his son. Kinshi has been regularly borrowing scripts without permission from his father's house for the boys to study. With Kinshi still in pain, Jiro volunteers to steal the next one. In Yoshida's house, he is surprised to find a costume used in one of the sorties made by the robber Saburo. Okada, the blind chanter, has written a new play about a robber, much like Saburo, that is going into rehearsal. The apprentices are eager to study the script and Jiro, with the help of Tozo, a young samisen player and guardian of Okada, gains an audience with the old man, who graciously lends Jiro a copy. Jiro's admiration and respect for this man grows.

At New Year's, Taro visits the theater and tells Jiro that his mother has returned. Jiro steals out one night to visit her, carrying a gift of food that Kinshi has stolen from the kitchen. His mother, as ungrateful and ill-spirited as ever, tells him that his father is still in Kyoto. In the dead of night, Jiro starts out for the theater. He is accosted in the streets by a ruffian but saved by Yoshida, who mysteriously appears but warns the boy not to speak of the incident.

The new play is cast and both Kinshi and Jiro are given parts as foot operators, making Wada very jealous. In spite of its subject, the audience, made up chiefly of wealthy merchants, proclaims the play a success. But when Saburo issues a proclamation demanding a performance for non-paying peasants and Yoshida complies, the authorities close the play down, forcing the puppeteers to schedule a revival of an older play. Attacks by night rioters become more violent and one night, after learning from Isako that the Hanaza theater has food, they assemble before the stage door and begin pounding and demanding food. Jiro recognizes his mother's voice among the protesters. Yoshida vehemently decrees that the doors remain shut and by morning the demonstrators have dispersed. Kinshi is horrified at his father's seeming callousness and begins staying out nights with the mob. Jiro is frightened that the boy will be killed, but he has nowhere to turn for help.

One day, while practicing his movements in an old storeroom, Jiro discovers a section where Yoshida's memorabilia are stored and sees a samurai sword that had been stolen from an official by Saburo. Now convinced that Yoshida is Saburo, he seeks an audience with Okada, hoping the old man will intervene to bring Yoshida and Kinshi, both fighters for the same cause, together. Okada's behavior when confronted with the sword leads Jiro to a surprising conclusion: Okada is actually Saburo, and Yoshida is the faithful disciple who carries out his decisions. Severe rioting is reported in the streets and Jiro, fearful for both Kinshi and Isako's well-being, ventures out into the night. Swept up in the angry crowd, he is rescued by a man in a fireman's uniform. It is his father, who confesses to returning secretly to Osaka to become one of Saburo's men. Jiro returns to the rioters and discovers Kinshi and his mother together in the streets. Before escaping the police, Kinshi had one hand chopped off. After several misadventures, the three return to the Hanaza theater, where a reconciliation takes place. Isako will become a worker at the theater and Kinshi, now unable to be a puppeteer, is taken on as a protege of Okada, the chanter. Secrets about Saburo are buried and Jiro looks forward to a prosperous life on the way to becoming a master puppeteer.

Passages for Booktalking

Some interesting passages are: Jiro goes to a public bath with his father and hears about Saburo (pp. 5–7); Hanji and Jiro deliver a puppet to the puppet master Yoshida (pp. 12–16); Jiro takes the initiative and seeks admission to the puppet theater (pp. 23–29); and Jiro meets with his fellow apprentices and talks with Yoshida (pp. 31–36).

Themes and Subjects

Ms. Paterson supplies wonderful details on how a 19th-century Japanese puppet theater was operated, with material on costuming, performance, structure, and the complexities and significance of each puppet's movements and actions. The importance of traditions and the respect for the past is underlined. Teamwork and cooperation between the players are also stressed. Yoshida emphasizes that adherence to the last detail of the script is all-important. Father-parent relationships are explored and contrasted in the family problems of both Jiro and Kinshi. Respect for elders and other traditional Japanese cultural traits are introduced. Jiro's conflict between family obligations and loyalty to his new friends is an important theme, as is the fact that dedication, hard work, and sacrifice are necessary components for success. Other subjects are Osaka, Japanese history, class struggle, famine, friendship, and courage.

RUBY, LOIS. *Shanghai Shadows.* Holiday House, 2006, $16.95 (978-0-8234-1960-9) (Grades 6–10)

Introduction

Lois Ruby (1942–) grew up mainly in San Francisco, where she haunted the San Francisco Public Library for reading material. Later she began writing her own. She met her future husband on her first day at the University of California at Berkeley where she received a Bachelor's degree with a major in English. Later she earned a Master's degree in Library Science, and still later became a young-adult librarian at the Dallas Public Library. Her first book was published about 30 years ago. Regarding the writing process, she states that she begins with hundreds of books and notes surrounding her for quick reference. First drafts of chapters are written out in longhand and then transferred to the computer for revision. She has written a number of novels dealing with contemporary problems such as child abuse and teenage pregnancy, as well as a body of historical fiction, including *Journey to Jamestown* (Kingfisher, 2005, pap. $7.95; 0753457962), which is for a younger audience (grades 4-6). In this story told from two different viewpoints, the reader meets 13-year-old Elias, an apprentice to a barber-surgeon. The youngster has left England for a new life in the Jamestown Colony. His enthusiasm for healing others is shared by a Pamunkee Indian girl named Sacahocan, who is studying to become a medicine woman. The two form a strong friendship and share some exciting adventures.

Shanghai Shadows was inspired by the author's curiosity about the experiences of the many European Jews who fled the Nazi regime in the late 1930s and, by necessity, were forced to go to Shanghai, a city then occupied by the Japanese. The story covers a six-year period, from 1939 through 1945, and describes the experiences of the narrator, Ilse Shpann, from age 11 to 17.

Historical Background

In March 1938 an event known as the Anschluss occurred, during which German troops invaded Austria and annexed it as part of the Third Reich. Reports of the Jewish persecution in Germany caused many Austrian Jews to seek refuge elsewhere. Denied entry into a number of countries, many were forced to journey to China, specifically to Shanghai, which contained a separate International Settlement and a French Concession. Shanghai, one of the world's busiest seaports, is located on the banks of the Yangtze River delta in East China. In the mid-1930s, Japan, using Manchuria as a springboard, had invaded a China torn by civil war. The battle for Shanghai, in 1937, resulted in occupation of the entire city by the Japanese with the exception of the international zones. By 1939, Japan controlled large chunks of China including the cities of Nanking and Canton and the coastal areas. When the waves of Jewish immigrants arrived circa 1939 they were helped considerably by the well-established Sephardic Jewish community. But, in time, the Japanese were pressured by their Nazi allies to be more aggressive toward the European Jews. The Japanese then required all Jewish refugees, the "stateless" ones, to move to Hongkew, a tiny already-crowded district in the city. The day after Pearl Harbor, the international settlements were taken over and, later, the residents sent to internment camps. Disease, famine, and inhumane living conditions claimed the lives of many foreign nationals and refugees. One zone that was exempt was the Polish Jewish yeshiva, or seminary, of about 400 people who had arrived through the efforts of Japanese diplomat Chiune Sugihara. Called "the Japanese Schindler," he was the Japanese Consul General in Lithuania in 1940 when the consulate was deluged with requests for exit visas from Jews frantic to escape Hitler. Ordered to leave his position, he defied his country's policy and wrote about two thousand visas only stopping when his train pulled out of the station.

Principal Characters

Ilse Shpann, an 11-year-old Austrian Jew, the narrator
Erich, her 13-year-old brother
Jacob Shpann, her father
Frieda Shpann, her mother
Tanya Mogelevsky, Ilse's best friend
Mrs. Mogelevsky, Tanya's mother
Liu, a street urchin
Dovid Ruzevich, a struggling Jewish artist
Gerhardt, Rolf, and Madame Liang, members of REACT, a resistance organization
M. O. (Michael O'Halloran), a benefactor
Reb Chaim, a rabbi
Shlomo Liebovitz, a rabbinical student
Mr. and Mrs. Kawashima, neighbors
Mr. Hsu, a professional letter writer

Plot Synopsis

Hitler's occupation of Austria in 1938 brought great changes to the comfortable middle-class Shpann family of Viennese Jews. Forced to flee with only a few of their precious possessions and without visas, they were denied entry to many other countries. In August 1939, they land in Japanese-occupied Shanghai, ill-prepared to start life over. The family consists of Mr. and Mrs. Shpann (Jacob and Frieda), son Erich, age 13, and daughter Ilse, who is 11. While awaiting processing, Ilse notices a clever young pickpocket, a miserable street urchin plying his trade. Their guide identifies him as a stray named Liu. Shanghai is teeming with refugees, and the only accommodation available in the unoccupied international section is a one room walkup with three closets, each of which becomes a bedroom. The seven families in the house share the kitchen and bathroom facilities. Almost immediately Ilse meets and becomes friends with one of her neighbors, a girl her age named Tanya Mogelevsky, a refugee from the Ukraine who lives with her mother and a pesky cat named Moishe. Later Ilse learns that Mrs. Mogelevsky, who has survived traumatic war experiences, supplements her meager income by "entertaining" Japanese soldiers. Because Mr. Shpann is a music teacher, a special place in their apartment is found for The Violin.

The young people gradually adjust to their new cramped and dismal lifestyle and continue to marvel at their multicultural exotic surroundings, which often include glimpses of Liu racing through the streets of the Chinese quarter called Hongkew. Ilse is an outspoken, idealistic girl and her brother is more realistic and a bit cynical, but both are devoted to their parents and each other. Mrs. Shpann, who spent her college years in the United States, is proficient in English and begins taking in students. One of these is a Pole in his late teens named Dovid Ruzevish, who has lost his entire family in the Holocaust. A brilliant artist, he escaped Europe via Lithuania with the help of the Japanese diplomat Chiune Sugihara. Ilse is deeply attracted to this sad, talented man and they gradually develop a close friendship.

Months stretch into years. One bright light in their lives is the occasional package containing food, clothes, and money from the United States, courtesy of a person whose signature is only M.O. The kids fantasize that these gifts are from an American school chum of their mother's and nickname the donor Molly O'Toole. After Pearl Harbor, the entire city is occupied and daily life steadily becomes more difficult. Erich begins staying out for long stretches and suddenly appears with an old motorbike that they call Peaches. Now he is able to hire himself out as a delivery boy and earn a little extra money. Intrigued by his frequent disappearances, Ilse follows him one day to a warehouse area and discovers that he is secretly part of an Underground Resistance movement known as REACT. Ilse meets two high-ranking members, Gerhardt and Rolf, and is sworn to secrecy about Erich's activities, many of which involve relaying messages. This explains the organization's gift of Peaches. In time, Ilse requests her own assignment. Her first notification is a letter from a mysterious Madame Liang, who, in code, instructs her to warn neighbors that the Japanese will shortly confiscate all short-wave radios and that they should be hidden. She completes the mission successfully and eagerly awaits the next, which is to enter the swank Shanghai Club in the fashionable Bund Road area and, disguised as a messenger, enter the men's room and break the floats in the toilets. A minor inconvenience and embarrassment for the Japanese but a major triumph for Ilse!

One day, a notice is posted stating that all stateless persons—i.e., the Jewish refugees—must relocate to the Hongkew area, an overcrowded square mile filled with squalid tenements. Before the move, Ilse is involved in another operation for REACT, tailing a woman known as "Beehive," believed to be a double agent. Although Ilse plays her part successfully and Beehive is exposed, another member of the group is caught and murdered by the Japanese. Without financial resources, the Shpanns are forced to move to a single room in a Hongkew tenement where sheets are used as makeshift room dividers. They derive some comfort from their new, supportive neighbors, an elderly Japanese couple called Mr. and Mrs. Kawashima, and, for Ilse, from her continuing friendship with Tanya and her deepening relationship with Dovid. As a single man, Dovid is forced to live like a prisoner in dismal barracks. This proves too much for his sensitive nature and, after bidding Ilse a moving farewell, he flees the city. A brokenhearted Ilse never hears from him again.

Barbed wire appears around the Hongkew enclave and exit permits are only granted erratically by the head guard, Kanoh Ghoya, a toad-like official who calls himself "King of the Jews." One day, Reb Chaim, the head of the well-established and well-respected Mirrer Yeshiva, calls on Mr. Shpann with a proposal. He would like Ilse to marry one of his students, Shlomo Liebovitz. This way she could escape ghetto life and also marry a fine young man. Ilse is horrified at the thought and her understanding father accedes to her wishes and refuses the offer. Soon, Shlomo transfers his attentions to a more receptive listener, Tanya.

Further misfortunes face the family. When foreign nationals are rounded up for transfer to internment camps, Mrs. Shpann's name appears on the alien list and her darkest secret is revealed. While a student in America she married her tutor, Michael O'Halloran (the M.O. of the letters). She returned to Austria before getting a divorce and is therefore considered an American alien. She is taken away to a nearby camp and, except for one monthly letter, has no contact with her family. By selling a few remaining valuables and with the combined help of the local letter-writer, Mr. Hsu, and ragamuffin Liu, Ilse is able to smuggle some money to her mother. Erich suddenly disappears and Ilse and her father appeal to the Kawashimas for help. Through contacts, they trace him to the Ward Road jail. Father sells them The Violin, their last treasure, to obtain bribe money for Ilse to enter the prison. She finds Erich ill and half-starved. Ilse is able to persuade the authorities to free Erich who is suffering from typhus. For weeks Erich hovers between life and death. Finally, after the fever breaks, he recovers.

It is now 1945 and the war is ending. Before peace is declared, the American Air Force bombs Shanghai severely but the Shpanns survive and are reunited when the Japanese troops surrender. Mr. O'Halloran has agreed to sponsor their immigration to the United States, where Mrs. Shpann will get a divorce and remarry her second husband of over twenty years. Before leaving, Mr. Kawashima is able to return the violin, Erich gives Peaches to Liu, and Tanya makes plans to marry her rabbi. Before they board the ship, Liu presents Ilse with a present. It is one of Dovid's pictures. He had entrusted it to Liu to be given to her only when she left Shanghai. For the Shpanns, Shanghai will soon be only a dot on the horizon, a waystation to a better world.

Passages for Booktalking

Some interesting episodes: the family lands in Shanghai and see their new quarters (pp. 8–12); the young people explore the Hongkew district (pp.

17–21); Mother takes in English students including Dovid (pp. 28–30); Madame Liang and the short-wave radios (pp. 72–75); and Ilse and the toilets (pp. 79–83).

Themes and Subjects

The author explores an aspect of World War II history that is often overlooked. The deplorable conditions in the Shanghai ghetto and the internment camps are vividly and unsparingly depicted. The misery that humans are capable of inflicting on others is presented well as are the courage, determination, and resourcefulness of the survivors. The importance and solidarity of the family unit is explored. During the six years of the story, Ilse is transformed from a self-centered child to a responsible, caring young woman. Other subjects include; the Chinese-Japanese War (1937–1945), internment camps, Jewish religion, Holocaust, survival, resistance movements, Shanghai, cultural differences, Pearl Harbor, marriage, and divorce.

ADDITIONAL SELECTIONS

Dubosarsky, Ursula. *The Red Shoe* (Roaring Brook, 2007, $16.95) (Grades 6–9)
  In the fall of 1954 in a suburb of Sydney, Australia, three young sisters become neighbors of Australia's defecting Soviet ambassador, who is in hiding.

Garland, Sherri. *Song of the Buffalo Boy* (Harcourt, 1992, pap. $6) (Grades 7–10)
  Seventeen-year-old Loi, part American and part Vietnamese, flees from the prejudice of her small Vietnamese village to Ho Chi Minh City, where she wonders about finding her father in America.

Gratz, Alan. *Samurai Shortstop* (Dial, 2006. $15.99) (Grades 7–11)
  Growing up in Tokyo in the 1890s, young Toyo must make a difficult choice between adhering to the traditional ways of the samurai or following his new love, baseball.

Ho, Minfong. *The Clay Marble* (Houghton, 1991, $12) (Grades 5–9)
  After fleeing from her Cambodian home in the 1980s, 12-year-old Dara is separated from her family during an attack on her refugee camp.

Hong, Chen Jiang. *Little Eagle* (Enchanted Lion, 2007, $16.95) (Grades 3–5)
  Using a large picture-book format, this story set in 15th-century China tells how an orphaned boy learns the art of kung fu from his master and later helps defeat a gang of bullies.

Hoobler, Dorothy, and Thomas Hoobler. *A Samurai Never Fears Death* (Philomel, 2007, $12.99) (Grades 6–9)
  Set in 18th-century Japan, this is the story of 16-year-old Seiko who, like his father, becomes a samurai. This is part of a series.

Kadohata, Cynthia. *Cracker! The Best Dog in Vietnam* (Atheneum, 2007, $16.99) (Grades 5–8)

Cracker, a German shepherd, trains as a war dog with his master Rick and, after they are shipped out together, the two experience the boredom, excitement, and terror of the Vietnam War.

Mah, Adeline Yen. *Chinese Cinderella and the Secret Dragon Society* (HarperCollins, 2005, $16.89) (Grades 5–8)

During the Japanese occupation of Shanghai during World War II, 12-year-old Ye Xian joins a kung fu group hoping to help the Americans.

Napoli, Donna Jo. *Bound* (Atheneum, 2004, $16.95) (Grades 7–12)

Set in China during the Ming period, this is a Cinderella story about Xing Xing, who is a slave to her cruel stepmother and stepsister who has been crippled by incorrect foot binding.

Newton, Robert. *Runner* (Knopf, 2007, $15.99) (Grades 7–10)

In 1919 Australia, in order to help himself and his mother survive the poverty of their slum neighborhood, 15-year-old Charlie turns to working for the mob.

Sheth, Kashmira. *Keeping Corner* (Hyperion, 2007, $15.99) (Grades 7–12)

India's fight for independence is experienced by 12-year-old Leela, who has been forced into a year of isolation after the death of her husband.

Venkatraman, Padma. *Climbing the Stairs* (Putnam, 2008, $16.99) (Grades 6–9)

During World War II in India, 15-year-old Vidya, who is growing up in a progressive household in Bombay, must adjust to more traditional, old-fashioned ways when she and her family move to her grandfather's house in Madras, in the south.

Whelan, Gloria. *Goodbye, Vietnam* (Turtleback, 1992, pap. $11.65) (Grades 5–8)

After an incredible journey fleeing with her family from war-torn Vietnam, Mai finally reaches Hong Kong and the hope of a new life.

Whitesel, Cheryl Aylward. *Blue Fingers: A Ninja's Tale* (Clarion, 2004, $15) (Grades 5–8)

In 16th-century Japan, 12-year-old Koji is training to become a ninja warrior.

Wulffson, Don. *The Golden Rat* (Bloomsbury, 2007, $16.95) (Grades 6–9)

This story, set in 12th-century China, tells how 16-year-old Baolui fights the corruption in his community after he has been accused of being responsible for his stepmother's death.

CHAPTER 6

Africa

KURTZ, JANE. *The Storyteller's Beads.* Harcourt, 1998, $16 (978-0-15-201074-4) (Grades 5–8)

Introduction

Jane Kurtz was born in Portland, Oregon, but moved to Ethiopia at age 2 with her missionary parents, who raised their five daughters and one son in a remote village. In fourth grade, she went to a boarding school in Addis Ababa. The family returned to the United States in the late 1970s, but they have maintained an interest in their adopted country, and one sister and brother returned there to teach. Jane attended college in the United States, married, and raised three children. The first of her now more than two dozen books for young readers was a picture book published in 1994, *Fire on the Mountain* (pap. Aladdin, $7.99; 0689878963). It is a retelling of an Ethiopian folktale about a clever shepherd boy who wins a bet by surviving a night on a frigid mountain and eventually collects his reward from the rich man who wants to cheat him.

The Storyteller's Beads, which takes place over a period of about two months, is set in northern Ethiopia and, later, in the Sudan. It is a third-person narrative told from the perspective of two girls—Sahay, of the Christian Kemant people, and Rahel, an Ethiopian Jew. The inspiration for the character Sahay, came when the author thought, "What if a girl, growing up in a sheltered Kemant community, was suddenly thrown into the wide world and found that the same prejudice she'd been taught . . . was directed unthinkingly towards her." When the author read about a blind girl who had walked to the Sudan with her hand on her brother's shoulder, the character of Rahel came into being.

Historical Background

The author supplies some interesting background facts in a valuable After-word. Here is some basic information on Ethiopia, once called Abyssinia. It is located in the area known as the Horn of Africa and, following the independence of Eritrea in 1993, it has been landlocked. In addition to Eritrea, it borders on the Sudan on the west, Kenya on the south, Djibouti on the northeast, and Somalia on the east. Its population is now about 75 million (it was 34 million at the time of the novel). It is the third-poorest nation in the world and the average life expectancy is only 41 years. There are about 80 ethnic groups in the country. English is the most-spoken foreign language (high school instruction is given in English). Christians make up about 60 percent of the population and Muslims about 33 percent. There is a small group of Jews in the north but most migrated to Israel in the 1980s and 1990s (see below). The early 20th-century history of Ethiopia was dominated by Haile Selassie, who became emperor in 1930. The Italians occupied the country from 1936 to 1941, when it was liberated by British and Ethiopian forces. Haile Selassie returned to power and annexed Eritrea in 1952, which provoked a series of wars for independence that continued into the time of the novel. The emperor's reputation suffered because of severe famines, border wars, and charges of mismanagement. He was deposed in 1974 by a Soviet-sponsored coup and a one-party communist regime was installed under the leadership of Mengistu Haile Mariam. During his regime, millions died unnecessarily in Ethiopia. His Red Terror, which began in 1978 and was directed at political adversaries resulted in more than half a million deaths. A later "relocation" project, a form of genocide, resulted in another 1.5 million deaths (this was the fate of Sahay's family). In the 1980s, the time of the novel, an additional million died from starvation. Mengistu was president from 1987 to 1991, when, after an uprising against the communist regime, he fled to Zimbabwe where he is still sheltered by Robert Mugabe. He was convicted of genocide in absentia in 2007.

During Mengistu's rule, many Ethiopian Jews, called Beta-Israel, fled to refugee camps in the Sudan. It is estimated that about 4,000 died on the trek. In a cooperative effort involving Israel, the American CIA, and the American Embassy in Khartoum, an airlift was organized to take these Jews to Israel. Operation Moses, begun in 1984, transported about 8,000 Jews until the Arab countries persuaded the Sudan to stop the airlift. The following year, through the influence of Vice President George H. W. Bush, the remaining 800 were transported during Operation Joshua and, after Mengistu's fall in 1991, the transportation of Ethiopian Jews to Israel was resumed in Operation Solomon.

The illiteracy rate is extremely high in Ethiopia. About 99 percent of schools have no libraries and 60 percent of the population over age 15 cannot read. The Kurtz family, including Jane, has been active in a nonprofit organization called Ethiopia Reads, whose purpose is to bringing literacy-related resources to the country. They have created libraries and reading centers throughout the nation. In 2003, for example, they opened the first free children's library—the Shola Children's Library in Addis Ababa. The history of this organization, like *The Storyteller's Beads*, makes for an inspiring story.

Principal Characters

Sahay, an Ethiopian girl, about 11 years old
Uncle, Sahay's only living relative
Rahel, a young Beta-Israel girl
Mother and Father, her parents
Dawit, her brother

Plot Synopsis

In 1984, Ethiopia is in a state of chaos and misery. A catastrophic famine has bought the population to the brink of starvation, a futile war to prevent Eritrean succession has meant indiscriminate press-ganging of young boys and men into the army, and the repressive communist regime conducts massacres, sometimes of whole towns and villages, to prevent rebellion. Young Sahay, who is of the Kemant people of northern Ethiopia, has not been spared such horror. She is haunted by the memory of the slaughter of her family by government forces wishing to take over their land. Only she and her uncle have miraculously been spared. Although it is forbidden to leave the country, her uncle believes their only hope of survival is to leave their village and begin a trek across the highlands into the Sudan, more than a hundred miles away.

Sahay hurriedly packs a small supply of chickpeas and, with her dead father's walking stick in hand leaves with her uncle. Sahay is a timid, fearful girl. Childish superstition has made her fear and loath the Falasha, a derogatory name for Ethiopian Jews or Beta-Israel, even though she has never met one. She believes they are *budas* possessed of evil spirits and able to turn themselves into hyenas and attack people.

After several days trekking in the wilderness, the two are half-starved and extremely tired. On the outskirts of a village, Sahay approaches a group of children playing outdoors. She hopes that they will give her food but instead, seeing that she is from a different people, they call her *buda* and pelt her with stones.

Deep in the mountains, they join some other refugees also bound for the Sudan who have the services of a guide. The band now numbers about 30. With great stealth, they travel only by night to avoid detection by roaming bandits or by militia who would force them back. Although Sahay welcomes the company, she is dismayed to learn that some of the group are Falasha, one of whom is a blind girl about her age who wears a beaded necklace.

A few days before this, in a village close to Sahay's, a family is planning an exodus. It is Rahel's family—her mother, father, grandmother, and older brother Dawit. They are Beta-Israels who hope to escape the terrible prejudice and hardships they are experiencing by fleeing to the Sudan and eventually getting to Jerusalem in the promised land of Israel. Rahel was blinded by a childhood illness but she is without self-pity and is amazingly independent in both action and feelings. She is a fine flute player and is particularly devoted to her grandmother, who tells her many traditional stories from the Bible. Because Grandmother wants to remain behind, she has Rahel memorize these stories to take with her to her new home. Each bead on the necklace that Grandmother gives Rahel represents a different story. Rahel persuades Grandmother to join them, but before they can leave the family finds out not only that their plan has been discovered but also that Dawit is about to be conscripted. In a rapid change of plans, Dawit and Rahel leave quickly, hoping the others can join them later. With her arm on his shoulder, Dawit leads her away from their village to the spot where they will meet some fellow refugees and a guide who will lead them through the highlands to the border.

On a particular dusty part of the journey, Dawit give a young non-Beta-Israel girl about Rahel's age a drink of his water. Sahay is horrified when she realizes she has drunk Falasha water. In the mountains, walking becomes difficult, and possessions must be discarded to lighten their loads. Rahel stubbornly refuses to give up her flute. When the group is attacked by bandits, most of the refugees hide in a cave. In the morning, Sahay realizes she has slept next to Rahel but has not been bewitched. Unfortunately, they discover that their guide was killed in the gunfire. One member, who has traveled the route before, volunteers to take his place.

Leaving the mountains, they enter the grasslands where walking is easier but where they are completely exposed. They are spotted by a band of soldiers who surround them. They allow the women and children to proceed but the men, including Dawit and Sahay's uncle, are detained, eventually to serve in the army in the Eritrean war. Rahel and Sahay, who are now without their guardians, slowly begin to rely on one another. The tattered remnants of the group finally cross the border and reach the refugee camp, Umm Rekuba.

Conditions in the huge camp are appalling. There is little food and disease is rampant. Everyone is living in misery and despair and each day the death toll rises. Rahel is taken to the part of the camp where the Beta-Israels live, separating the girls. Every day, Sahay crawls to the spot where new refugees arrive hoping in vain to see her uncle. Days pass. Near starvation and afraid of dying alone, Sahay seeks out Rahel and begs to live with her and the other Falasha. Rahel agrees.

Throughout this terrible ordeal, Rahel has maintained her belief that she, like Moses and his followers, will complete an *aliyah*, the journey to the Promised Land. And to keep up her spirits she amuses herself and others by playing traditional melodies on her flute. Rahel receives word that plans are being made to smuggle the Beta-Israel out of the camp and transport them to Jerusalem. The orphans and the sick and old are to go first, that night. The signal will be a tapping on their mud hut. Sahay thinks this will mean parting with her friend but the ingenious Rahel has her own plan. She has told the authorities that Sahay is a Beta-Israel and that she must accompany her as her guide. Sahay is pleased but wary about becoming an honorary Beta-Israel. She swears never to use the word Falasha again. The plan works, and that evening, after hearing the tapping, they are shepherded to a waiting airplane that whisks them off, first to Brussels, and then to Jerusalem. As they step off the plane, Rahel, who still has her grandmother's beads around her neck, lifts her flute to her lips and plays a new song, the music of a new land.

Passages for Booktalking

Sahay and her uncle leave their farm (pp. 5–8); Rahel visits the market with her grandmother and hears plans for their departure (pp. 21–25); Sahay is accused of being a *buda* (pp. 45–48); and Grandmother's stories and her beads (pp. 49–52).

Themes and Subjects

Author Nancy Farmer has said of this book, "How can anyone comprehend a million deaths (from famine)? Jane Kurtz has made the tragedy devastatingly real with her superb adventure of two courageous girls who overcome prejudices taught to them before birth." Kurtz has also created a brilliant picture of the Ethiopian countryside and the everyday life of people living primitively (though in the 1980s) without modern comforts. The contrast between the timid, fearful Sahay and the independent, forceful (though handicapped) Rahel is fascinating, and the maturation of both through adversity is well presented. Other subjects: famine, dictatorships, Jewish history, Operation Moses, the Sudan, refugee camps, death, friendship, blindness, handicaps, courage, family relationships, tolerance, prejudice, Bible tales, and music.

STOLZ, JOELLE. *The Shadows of Ghadames.* Delacorte, 2004, $15.95 (978-0-385-73194-2); pap. Dell, $5.99 (978-0-440-41939-6) (Grades 5–9)

Introduction

This novel was translated from the French (title *Les Ombres de Ghadames*) by Catherine Temerson. Joelle Stolz is a French journalist who lives in Vienna and reports for the newspaper *Le Monde* and for Radio France Internationale. Her articles have covered many subjects such as the place of woman in African societies particularly Nigeria, reparations for victims of Nazi oppression in Austria during World War II, and the merits of Nobel Prize winners for literature. This is her first book for young readers. It won for its publisher, Delacorte, the Mildred L. Batchelder Award in 2005. This annual award is given to "an American publisher for the children's book considered to be the most outstanding of those books originally published in a foreign country and subsequently published in English in the United States." The award, which is administered by the Association for Library Service to Children of the American Library Association, was established in 1966 and named after a former director of the association. The 2008 winner is *Brave Story* (VIZ Media, $23.99, 2007; 1421511967), written originally in Japanese by Miyuki Miyabe. This massive book (843 pages), with appeal for all ages, tells the story of 10-year-old Wataru Mitani who faces many personal problems, including his father's disappearance, his parents' probable divorce, and his mother's suicide attempt. To sort out his life and save his parents' marriage, he enters the fantasy world of Vision, where he encounters many creatures who both help and hinder his quest.

   The Shadows of Ghadames takes place in the Libyan city of Ghadames over a period of about a month during the late 19th century. It is told in the first person by Malika, a young girl who is almost 12 years old.

Historical Background

This story takes place in the city of Ghadames, sometimes spelled Ghadamis. It is situated in west Libya on a sizable oasis in the Sahara Desert close to the borders with Algeria and Tunisia. In former times it was an important center on the trade routes from Tripoli to West Africa. The town was once held by the Romans, but was captured by the Arabs in the 7th century. In 1830, it became a territory controlled by the Bey of Tripoli. Italy occupied it in 1921, followed by the French in 1943. After World War II all of Libya gained its independence.

   Two other cities, Tripoli and Kano, are mentioned in the text. Tripoli is situated on a bay on the southern coast of the Mediterranean Sea close to the Tunisian border, about 300 miles north of Ghadames. It was founded by the

Phoenicians in the 7th century B.C. and in the 2nd century B.C. became a Roman colony. It was captured by the Muslims in the 8th century. In the early 19th century, the United States engaged in two wars, known as the Barbary Wars, against Algiers, Tripoli, and Tunis, known collective as the Barbary States. The cause was the harassing activities and unlawful boarding of U.S. merchant ships by the notorious Barbary pirates.

In 1911, Italy assumed control of Tripoli from the Ottoman Empire. After World War II, Tripoli became the capital of Libya. It is the largest city in Libya with a population of approximately 1.75 million.

Kano is several hundred miles south of Ghadames. It is now the administrative center of Kano State in Nigeria. The British captured it in 1903 and made it part of Nigeria. Today, with a population of almost 4 million, most of whom are Muslim, it is the third-largest city in Nigeria.

Islam is the religion of Libya. In many Islamic countries (certainly at the time of he novel), there was a distinct division of gender roles. A woman's place was in the privacy of the home and a man's in the public area of everyday work and commerce. Women relied on men for their economic well-being and therefore according to the Muslim holy book, the Qur'an, this justified the dominance of the male over the female. The Qur'an limits the number of wives per husband to four. Women were confined to being housekeepers, wives, and mothers. Children were taught always to respect their mothers. When children approached the time to consider marriage (around the age of 12), they were separated and no longer played together. The boys were allowed the freedom of the streets but the girls were confined to home and restricted, except for close friends and relatives, to female society.

According to the Qur'an, both males and females should dress and behave in a modest fashion, but there is a wide difference in what is considered correct dress for females particularly when it comes to covering the head and face. The most extreme garment, still worn in parts of Afghanistan, for example, is the burka, which conceals even the eyes, allowing the wearer to see through tiny slits in the cloth. In more liberal countries, only head coverings called hijah (an ancient term for veil) are worn and in still others, no head coverings are worn. At the time of the novel, women covered their heads and wore facial veils in public.

Several Muslim holidays are referred to in the text. The most important is Ramadan, which occurs annually during the ninth month of the Islamic calendar. During this time, a fast is observed during daylight hours. Eating is permitted only before dawn and after sunset. This also applies to sexual activity. Purity of mind and body is stressed as are self-discipline and sacrifice. Pregnant women, children, the elderly, and sick are exempt from fasting. Reading of the Qur'an, is encouraged. Ramadan ends with Eid-ul-Fitr, a holiday with feasting, giving to the poor, putting on fancy dress, and visiting family and friends.

Principal Characters

Malika, an 11-year-old girl (soon to be 12)
Meriem, her mother
Mahmud, her father
Bilkisu, Mahmud's second wife
Jasin, Bilkisu's son, age 12
Ladi, a servant
Abdelkarin, a religious dissident
Aishatou, a witch-nurse
Uncle, Mahmud's brother

Plot Synopsis

Dawn is rising over the Islamic city of Ghadames in North Africa. It is more than one hundred years ago in the late 19th century. Malika, now almost 12 years old, is awakened early by her father's second wife, Bilkisu, to say goodbye to Mahmud, her father, who is leaving on a month-long trading expedition to Tripoli, about one hundred miles to the north. Malika's mother, Meriem, Mahmud's first wife, is a caring woman but always aware of conventions and propriety, whereas Bilkisu is more daring and almost like a sister to Malika. Jasin, Bilkisu's 12-year-old son is also aroused from his sleep to say goodbye to his father. Mahmud loves both his children equally and promises to bring them presents on his return. He is a devoted, high-principled man who, for example, won't own slaves because he finds slavery abhorrent. In Tripoli, he will sell ivory goods and handiwork that he bought in Kano in the south and, with this money, purchase the luxuries available in Tripoli. Jasin accompanies his father through the streets to the city gates; Malika and Bilkisu also go to the edge of the city but via the city's flat rooftops, the only areas where men are forbidden and women may walk freely.

After the departure of their beloved father, life continues normally. The family servant, Ladi, arrives and Jasin and Malika engage in a rooftop race. Through a highly risky maneuver, Malika wins and, as a prize, Jasin gives her a board and stylus, useless for Malika because her mother thinks it is pointless for girls to learn to read or write. That night, Malika is awakened by a commotion in the streets followed by a silence that is interrupted by loud moaning. She and Bilkisu hesitantly go into the street to investigate and find a young man unconscious and bleeding from a severe head wound. He has obviously hit his head on one of the alleyway's low-hanging beams. They drag him inside and hide him in a shed on the property. After dressing the wound, they go to bed. In the morning, Bilkisu tells Meriem and Ladi what has happened and, amazingly, they agree that the young man should be saved. The four women carry the still unconscious fugitive upstairs and hide him in the pantry on the roof.

They send for nurse Aishatou, a forbidding woman whom Malika thinks is a witch. Aishatou agrees to keep their secret, and applies poultices and powders to the wound. To ensure that Jasin will not interfere and also to enforce an Islamic practice, Bilkisu tells her son that as he is now 12 he is too old to mix with the women and girls on the rooftops. She makes arrangements for him to begin working days at his uncle's store. After Jasin's first day at work, his uncle visits Mahmud's home and reports that the boy has done very well. Through discreet questions, the women learn from Uncle that a former resident of the city named Abdelkarim, who has joined an objectionable religious sect, returned to Ghadames last night. He has alienated many with his preaching and, while resisting an attempt to expel him from the city, eluded his pursuers in a chase through the city streets. This is the man they rescued.

Shortly afterward, Abdelkarim regains consciousness. He questions the propriety of bringing him into a household when the husband is absent and instead of showing gratitude, he initially is offended and reclusive. But a lecture from Bilkisu about proper attitudes has an impact and he gradually warms up to his caregivers, particularly toward Malika, who has spent more time looking after him than any of the others. He volunteers to teach her to read and write Arabic. Although Meriem, her mother, thinks literacy is unnecessary for women, she gives her consent and lessons begins using the board and stylus Malika won from Jasin.

Realizing that Malika will soon be of marriageable age and, therefore facing isolation on the rooftops with only the company of women, Bilkisu gets permission from Meriem to take Malika first to the women's baths and then for a visit to the palm grove where the harvest festival, Arous, is taking place. It is a magical day for Malika. She dreads the time when these simple pleasures will be denied her. When Bilkisu tells her about her former life in the city of Kano, many miles away in southwest Libya, it arouses in Malika a yearning to travel, a desire she knows can never be fulfilled. Days pass. Aishatou continues her visits to tend to Abdelkarim and, while ministering to his wound, finds time to read Meriem's fortune in coffee dregs. Both the patient's recovery and Malika's lessons are progressing well. Malika is an avid student and quickly masters the 26 letters of the Arabic alphabet and begins writing in the Arabic style from the right to the left of the slate.

When news comes that Mahmud's caravans are only two or three days away, hurried plans are made to smuggle Abdelkarim out of town. Fortunately, a women's festival is going to be held outside the city walls the following evening. By joining the women, Abdelkarim can leave the city and escape to a neighboring town. At first he objects to the indignity of disguising himself as a woman but when he realizes the convenience of escaping by simply hiding his body and his face, with its ample beard and mustache, with a robe and veil, he accepts the idea. That night, Malika together with Bilkisu, Meriem and an unknown fourth person, join the women's procession and leave the city. While the others observe the rituals, Malika and Abdelkarin linger behind. When the coast is clear, he murmurs a goodbye before slipping into the darkness.

As expected, Lord Mahmud arrives a day later. The women realize that ignorance is bliss and decide not to tell him about their rescue operation. The trading mission was a great success and everyone is overjoyed at the reunion with this wise, affectionate man. As promised, he brings gifts. Jasin receives a handsome dagger with a horn handle, Meriem is given a new invention—a kerosene lamp, and Bilkisu, a beautifully illustrated book on foreign lands. Malika receives a wondrous gift, a telescope that will enable her, though confined to the rooftops, to visit the stars. In addition, at Meriem's bidding (no less) Mahmud is making arrangements for a teacher to give Malika lessons in reading and writing. Though physical confinement is near, Malika now knows she has avenues of escape.

Passages for Booktalking

Malika says goodbye to her father (pp. 6–10); Jasin and Malika race on the rooftop (pp. 14–17); Malika and Bilkisu rescue the fugitive (pp. 21–25); and Aishatou comes to nurse Abdelkarim.

Themes and Subjects

The author has created a vivid picture of a traditional Muslim community observing conventions and beliefs similar to those still practiced in many areas today. Though the status of women is one of subservience, obedience, and restriction, hope for the future and gradual change is personified in the characters of Bilkisu and Malika, who obey the laws but seek self-fulfillment. Both are independent, strong, and resourceful women. The sights, sounds, and even smells of desert city life are colorfully reproduced. Other subjects: Libya, desert life, Islam, Ghadames, Tripoli, Kano, Nigeria, polygamy, family life, Islamic festivals, trade and traders, Arabic language and writing, doctoring, telescopes, and 19th-century life.

WHELAN, GLORIA. *Listening for Lions.* HarperCollins, 2005, $16.95 (978-0-06-058174-9); pap. $5.99 (978-0-06-058176-3) (Grades 5–8)

Introduction

Gloria Whelan (1923–) was born in Detroit, Michigan. When she was 9 years old she suffered from rheumatic heart disease and was confined to bed for a period during which her only escape was reading. She read and reread many books, but her favorite was *Little Women*. After graduating from the University of Michigan she worked in a number of positions involving children's welfare. She confesses that she was always a writer, even making up stories before she could write. For more than 30 years she has lived with her husband and family in a cabin on a small lake in the woods of North Michigan. It was after her move from the city that she began writing seriously. She has dozens of books to her credit in various genres for both adults and young readers. For young readers her books include a trilogy set on Mackinac Island years ago and a four-book series set in Communist Russia.

Whelan won the National Book Award for *Homeless Bird* (HarperCollins, 2000, o.p.; pap, $5.99, 0064408191). Set in India, it tells the story of 13-year-old Koly, whose arranged marriage ends when her sickly husband dies, leaving her to find a new life. The author spends months and months researching each novel until she "could walk around in those countries and feel at home." A great nature lover, she also says that much of the wildlife that surrounds her is present in her books. "There are (for example) herons and eagles in my books about India, Africa, and China only their plumage is a little different."

Listening for Lions is narrated by Rachel Sheridan, covers a period of about ten years beginning in 1919, and is set in both Africa and England.

Historical Background

About one third of the novel takes place in British East Africa, now known as Kenya—named after its most famous landmark, Mount Kenya. The setting is an inland bush hospital not far from Nairobi, which is about 300 miles by rail from the coastal city of Mombasa. British influence in the area began in 1888 when the British East Africa Company was chartered and began administering a sizable stretch of coastline. British influence gradually expanded inland and, in an agreement with their German competitors, the British established a "sphere of influence" across the future Kenya. After 1890 this included Uganda as well. When the company began to fail in 1895, the British proclaimed the land the

British East Africa Protectorate, with the establishment of the Uganda Protectorate following in 1896. In 1920, the protectorate became the Kenya Colony.

During the early part of the 20th century, the interior highlands (the setting of the novel) were settled by British and other European farmers, many of whom became wealthy from crops of coffee, tea, and sisal. From 1952 to 1959, Kenya was in a state of emergency because of the Mau Mau rebellions against British rule. The first direct elections for Africans took place in 1957 and Kenya became totally independent at the end of 1963.

The Spanish influenza epidemic of 1918–1919 was a worldwide catastrophe that killed more people than died in World War I. It was first identified in America and soon spread abroad where it was responsible for between 20 million and 40 million deaths. Seventeen million died in India, about half a million in the United States and 200,000 in the United Kingdom. It is considered the most devastating epidemic ever to occur. Fortunately, it ended as suddenly and unexpectedly as it began.

Principal Characters

Rachel Sheridan, a 13-year-old girl and the narrator
Dr. Sheridan, her father
Mrs. Sheridan, her mother
Kanoro, their servant
Ngigi, his son
Mr. and Mrs. Pritchard, the Sheridans' neighbors
Valerie Pritchard, their daughter
Mr. Grumbloch, Mr. Pritchard Sr.'s solicitor
Mr. Hobart Pritchard, Valerie's grandfather
Burker, Ellie, Duggen, and Mrs. Nessel, servants at Stagsway

Plot Synopsis

The only home that 13-year-old Rachel Sheridan has ever known is the small rural hospital compound known as Tumaini, in the southwestern part of the British East Africa Protectorate (soon to be renamed Kenya), where her father is a missionary doctor and her mother teaches the native children. Both her parents are orphans who grew up in England and met through socials held by their respective orphanages. After Mr. Sheridan completed medical school, they married and, through the Mission Society, volunteered to work in Africa where Rachel was born.

Their only white neighbors are the unpleasant Pritchards, who live a few miles away. Mr. Pritchard, an English transplant, runs a sisal plantation. They have one daughter, the equally unpleasant Valerie, who is about Rachel's ago and who has pretty ginger hair.

The Sheridans have been totally accepted by the native Kikuyu population, although the other tribe in the area, the Masai, is more stand-offish. Valerie loves her servant/guardian Kanoro and often visits his family on their little farm and plays with his young son Ngigi. Rachel also adores her family, the work they do, and her surroundings. She knows and is devoted to the myriad animals and plants around her and looks forward every night to listening to her lullaby, the roar of the lions.

This idyllic situation comes to an abrupt end in 1919 when the flu epidemic that has decimated other lands arrives in Africa. The hospital is overcrowded with the sick and dying and her parents spend night and day there. First her mother dies, then the Pritchards arrive with mortally ill Valerie. Shortly after her death, Dr. Sheridan also dies, and Rachel witnesses the burial of both parents within a few days' time.

She is alone with no one to turn to when the Pritchards arrive and take her to their home. She sleeps in Valerie's room, but refuses Mrs. Pritchard's suggestion that she wear her late daughter's clothes. Although outwardly solicitous toward Valerie, the Pritchards are actually very unpleasant and secretive. On her third day at their house, they reveal a plan in which Rachel will play a vital part. Mr. Pritchard's only brother was killed in the war and he is now the heir to a great fortune and the grand estate of Stagsway in England. The Pritchards have heard that the ailing Mr. Pritchard, Sr., an avid birder, plans to leave his entire fortune to the Royal Bird Society. The Pritchards ask Rachel to assume Valerie's identity and go to England to cheer the elderly Pritchard during what they claim will be his dying days. (Actually they hope that Rachel, with her charming, wholesome personality, will be able to persuade him to change the will.)

Feeling completely helpless and under great pressure, Rachel agrees, and Valerie is buried next to Mr. and Mrs. Sheridan as Rachel Sheridan. A few days later, Rachel, now Valerie Pritchard, boards a ship bound for Southampton at the island port of Mombasa. Her escort for the voyage is a governess named Miss Limplinger, who makes a hasty retreat when they dock at Southampton and she is paid by Mr. Pritchard, Sr.'s solicitor, Mr. Reginald Grumbloch, who meets the ship. As he and "Valerie" chat, he voices disbelief that this is the same girl who writes whiny, begging letters to her grandfather complaining about being in Africa.

Rachel is overwhelmed by the vastness and beauty of Stagsway and the immense grounds surrounding the mansion. She meets a number of the servants—Burker, the ancient butler; Duggan the gardener; Mrs. Nessel, the cook; and her own maid, Ellie. Although everyone makes her welcome, Rachel feels guilty about the deception and longs to be back in Africa. Soon she is taken to meet the grandfather, and is impressed at how affable but frail he is.

In no time they are talking enthusiastically about birds, African and English, and Grandfather confides to "Valerie" that he has seen a new species of thrush on his property that he is trying to have registered with the Royal Bird Society. Like Mr. Grumbloch, he voices disbelief that this "Valerie" could be the same girl who wrote him those complaining letters.

The old man and Rachel get along famously and he is amazed that she really loves Africa and enjoys talking about it. Not wishing to reveal her identity, she claims that the adventures and observations that "Valerie" talks about are actually the experiences of her dear friend Rachel Sheridan, the daughter of a missionary doctor in the area. Grandfather also confides the reason he is not leaving the estate to her "father." Pritchard, Jr., was a wastrel whose high life and gambling debts broke his mother's heart and caused her death. Grandfather has never forgiven him and refuses to reward his shameful conduct with an inheritance.

Because Grandfather can't venture out of doors, "Valerie" becomes his surrogate nature observer and bird watcher. She even spots the elusive thrush he calls *Hylocichla guttata pritchardi*. Complications arise when Mr. and Mrs. Pritchard arrive and, in an ugly scene during which Grandfather tells them that they are not welcome at Stagsway, demand that Rachel join them in London. In London, Rachel, unable to continue the deception, goes to Mr. Grumbloch's office and blurts out the truth. To her amazement, he tells her that both he and Mr. Pritchard had been suspicious of her identity from the start. Later they obtained photographs of the family sent to the Mission Society by her father and this confirmed their belief that she was really Rachel Sheridan. She returns to Stagsway for a joyous reunion.

Grandfather grudgingly gives the younger Pritchards a small endowment so they can remain in England and he initiates legal proceedings to adopt Rachel. Within months she officially becomes Rachel Pritchard. She excels at the preparatory school she attends, and, at college, chooses a program that will lead to a medical degree, a rarity for women at this time. Unfortunately Grandfather dies but leaves her a sizable fortune and, as promised, bequeaths Stagsway to the Royal Bird Society. Rachel graduates with honors and applies to the Mission Society to be assigned to the deserted hospital at Tumaini. After she promises to donate funds to restore the buildings and equipment, they agree. She returns to Kenya and the old property. It has been ten years since she left. She is greeted by someone she at first thinks is her beloved Kanoro, but she is mistaken. It is his son, Ngigi, now a fine young man. Kanoro and family are still alive and also bring her greetings. Together they will build a new hospital and, in memory of her parents, she will again name it Tumaini, the Swahili word for hope.

Passages for Booktalking

Among interesting passages are: Rachel's life and pleasures at Tumaini (pp. 9–14); the death of Rachel's mother (pp. 23–26); Valerie Pritchard is brought to the hospital and dies (pp. 26–32); and the Pritchards propose that Rachel impersonate Valerie (pp. 49–55).

Themes and Subjects

The plot is Dickensian in nature with its hidden identities, intricate deceptions, and setting in a drafty country mansion. The dramatic splendor of Africa and its wildlife forms a perfect contrast to the serene, quiet English countryside with its tiny birds and lovely delicate flowers. Both are described lovingly. The simple dignity and loyalty of the Kikuyu natives are beautifully depicted. Rachel is a courageous, high-principled girl with whom readers will identity easily. Other subjects: deception, villainy, inheritances, England, Kenya, the influenza epidemic, mansions, wealth, servants, the 1920s, doctors, women's rights, bird watching, nature lovers, family life, and friendship.

WULF, LINDA PRESS. *The Night of the Burning: Devorah's Story.*
Farrar, Straus, 2006, $16 (978-0-384-36419-6) (Grades 5–8)

Introduction

The author grew up in Johannesburg, South Africa, while it was still under apartheid, a system of enforced separation of races. As a youngster, she read voraciously including classics by Louisa May Alcott, L. M. Montgomery, and Frances Hodgson Burnett. In college, she helped tutor teenage black students whose high schools were closed after the racial riots of 1976. Disillusioned with the government and fearful of the future, she left South Africa. After some time in Toronto, Canada, as an editor and freelance writer, she moved to Israel where she met and married her husband, a fellow South African. They now live in Berkeley, California.

The Night of the Burning, Ms. Wulf's first book, was rejected by publishers seventeen times and required four rewrites before it was accepted for publication. It is based on the true story of Devorah Lehrman, the mother of the author's husband, who was one of two hundred refugee Jewish orphans brought from Europe to South Africa in 1921 by the philanthropist Isaac Ochberg. The book covers a period of about nine years from 1915 to 1924 during which time Devorah, the narrator, grows from a 5-year-old child to a girl in her early teens. The first half of the book is told in alternating chapters that tell of life in the Warsaw orphanage with flashbacks to Devorah's years before that. For clarity, these two narratives are consolidated into one in the synopsis.

Historical Background

The author has supplied excellent supplementary material both at the beginning and end of the novel, including brief biographies of the real Devorah Lehrman and Isaac Ochberg and a glossary of Hebrew and Yiddish terms such as Shabbes, the Sabbath day that begins at sundown on Friday and extends until nightfall on Saturday. The word *pogrom* is a Russian one meaning attack. Historically it has come to mean violent attacks on Jewish people in the Russian Empire carried out by local populations, usually with the cooperation and even participation of local police including the Cossacks. The pogroms became particularly severe during the Russian Revolution and the Civil War that followed, from roughly 1917 into the early 1920s. During that time it has been estimated that 70,000 to 250,000 Jews were killed and thousands of children, like Devorah and her sister, were orphaned.

In 1920 a maverick South African businessman originally from the Ukraine—Isaac Ochberg (1878–1937)—received permission from the government led by Jan Smuts to bring 200 of these orphaned Jewish children to South Africa. Jan Smuts (1830–1950) was a forward-looking man who believed in racial integration. Unfortunately, apartheid was implemented just before his death. To complete his rescue operation, Ochberg donated funds and collected more from South African Jews. In 1921 he traveled to Europe and single-handedly supervised the project. Today he is also known in South Africa for the many scholarships that are awarded in his name.

The king and queen who visit the orphans in London are King George V and Queen Mary, the grandparents of the present queen. George V (1865–1936), the first British monarch of the House of Windsor, reigned from 1910 to 1936.

Principal Characters

Devorah Lehrman, a young Jewish girl and the narrator
Nechama (Naomi) Lehrman, Devorah's younger sister
Bzalel, Papa Lehrman, Devorah's father, a peddler
Chanah, Mama Lehrman, Devorah's mother
Uncle Pinchas, Devorah's uncle
Aunt Friedka, Devorah's aunt
Panya Truda, a Christian neighbor
Alexander Bobrow, the director of an orphanage in Pinsk
Isaac Ochberg, a South African philanthropist
Madame Engel, a restaurant owner in Warsaw

Mr. and Mrs. Stein, the couple who adopt Nechama
Mr. and Mrs. Kagan, the couple who adopt Devorah
Elizabeth, the Kagans' maid
Monica Meisner, Devorah's friend
Heather Smith, a spiteful classmate

Plot Synopsis

The Lehrmans, a kosher Jewish family, live in the predominantly Jewish peasant community of Domachevo, in Russian-dominated Poland. As well as Papa, a hard-working peddler, and Mama, there are 5-year-old Devorah and her darling young sister, Nechama, who is 2. Although money and possessions are scarce, the Lehrman household is filled with love and faith. Papa's twin brother Uncle Pinchas and his wife Aunt Friedka, who are childless, live nearby. There are about a thousand Jews in the community and only about a hundred Christian Poles. There is little intermingling and there are often signs of deep-rooted hostility from the Christian minority.

It is 1915 and World War I is raging—in which Russia is fighting against Germany. One day, when Papa is off selling his goods, the community's peace is shattered by a raid by Czarist troops rounding up men for the army. Although he tries to hide in a trunk, Uncle Pinchas is seized and taken away. Later, an official letter arrives demanding that Papa also report but, with one family member already conscripted, he is granted an exemption by the authorities. Everyday life—helping with chores, listening to Papa's stories from the Torah, and playing with neighborhood children—continues. The highlight of every week is the Shabbes (Sabbath) ceremony and the mid-day meal that follows.

Because it is forbidden to light a fire on this holy day, a Christian neighbor, Panya Truda, keeps the cholent, a vegetable stew, warm for them but Devorah has to run the gauntlet of taunts and insults from the Christian children when she goes to pick it up.

After a year in the army, Uncle Pinchas is brought back, a broken man near death from poison gas attacks in the trenches. After the peace agreement in 1917 and the subsequent Russian Revolution and Civil War, there is increased instability and deprivation. Without money, no one can buy Papa's goods. He sells his horse and cart and later the family goat. Uncle Pinchas dies, and the never-ending stress causes Papa to become sick and he too dies. A few months later, typhoid strikes and Mama passes away. Orphaned, Devorah and Nechama are cared for by Aunt Friedka until an even greater tragedy occurs. In August 1920, a pogrom led by locals aided by Cossacks is directed at the Jews. Devorah notices that some of the looters are her Christian neighbors. The synagogue and other buildings are burned, their contents destroyed or plundered. Many are killed, including Aunt Friedka who is murdered while

trying to save the children. After the Night of the Burning the sisters are rescued by their neighbor Panya Truda, who hides them in a cart and takes them
to an orphanage in Pinsk.

Although Devorah is well liked there, especially by the director, kindly Dr.
Bobrow, Devorah's heart is full of hurt, loneliness, and sorrow. She is a conscientious, serious young girl who is very protective of her bight, vivacious young
sister Nechama. One day the orphanage is abuzz with the news that a visitor
from South Africa, Mr. Ochberg, will take some of them back to his homeland, a land of great opportunity. He meets with Devorah and offers to take
both her and Nechama. At first, Devorah is hesitant but Nechama is so anxious to go that she agrees, pleased when she learns that Mr. Bobrow will
accompany them. On their railroad trip to Warsaw, two of the orphans who
have eye infections have to be hidden from the health inspectors lest they be
sent back.

The orphans wait in Warsaw for weeks until the rest of the group—a total
of 200—arrive. Devorah impresses everyone by making useful garments such
as aprons from discarded flour sacks. Some of the children are allowed to eat,
during off-hours, at the posh restaurant owned by Madame Engel. Devorah
becomes her favorite and the young girl spends hours in her company before
the group leaves by ship, first for Danzig (now Gdansk) and then on to London, where the youngsters are honored by a visit from the king and queen of
England. Devorah is disappointed to see they are really just ordinary people
like herself.

After seventeen days at sea, the group arrives in Cape Town and the children are housed in a big beautiful orphanage. Time passes. The girls go to
school, enjoy visits from Daddy Ochberg, learn English, and adopt the ways of
their hosts. One day, the two sisters are called into the Matron's office and she
informs them that a wealthy couple, Mr. and Mrs. Stein, want to adopt
Nechama. Devorah is devastated at the separation but Nechama, now
renamed Naomi, thrives in the sumptuous surroundings. Devorah's turn
comes soon, and she is adopted into the comfortable but much less affluent
household of Mr. and Mrs. Kagan. Both the Kagans are well-meaning and
attentive but Devorah clings to the memories of her Mama and Papa and,
though obedient and responsive, remains aloof. She enjoys talking to their
black maid, Elizabeth, and befriends a charming young girl, Monica Meisner, a
fellow student in her high school. Together they manage to overlook the anti-
Semitic slurs of their hostile classmate Heather Smith.

Months pass, and one day Naomi visits Devorah at the Kagans'. Surrounded by wealth and new possessions, Naomi has become snobbish and spoiled.
When she claims that Mrs. Kagan is low-class and vulgar, Devorah defends
her foster mother. After Naomi leaves, Devorah finds Mrs. Kagan in tears. She

has overheard the conversation and is crying not because of the insults as Devorah first thinks, but because she is touched by Devorah's defense. Devorah suddenly realizes how deeply she feels for Mrs. Kagan and meekly asks her if she might call her Mummy in the future.

Passages for Booktalking

Two interesting passages before the pogrom are: Uncle Pinchas is conscripted into the army (pp. 15–17); and a Shabbes and picking up the stew (pp. 43–46). Three later episodes are Devorah meets Isaac Ochberg (pp. 44–48); Madame Engel's restaurant (pp. 59–61) and a visit from the king and queen of England (pp. 91–93).

Themes and Subjects

This is a masterful portrayal of the effects of traumatic experiences on a young girl and how, in time, she learns to accept and live with the past. It is a story of heartbreak, of human savagery, and ultimately of hope. The complex relationships between and among Jews and non-Jews are well portrayed. Both the depths of human depravity on one hand and the strength in sacrifice and altruism on the other are well conveyed. Anti-Semitism in various ugly forms is presented. Relations between the two sisters and between the girls and their adoptive parents are sympathetically and often poignantly depicted. The strength of family ties and the rituals and beliefs connected with the Jewish faith are important themes. Other subjects: Poland, Russian Revolution, World War I, South Africa, race relations, pogroms, death, adoption, orphanages, and personal growth and maturation.

ADDITIONAL SELECTIONS

Burns, Khephra. *Mansa Musa: The Lion of Mali* (Harcourt, 2001, $18) (Grades 4–7)

In this lavishly illustrated book, Mansa Musa journeys from his rural village to become the king of Mali.

Grifalconi, Ann. *The Village That Vanished* (Dial, 2002, $16.99) (Grades 2–5)

African villagers escape slavers by dismantling their village piece by piece.

Jansen, Hanna. *Over a Thousand Hills I Walk with You* (Carolrhoda, 2006, $16.50) (Grades 6–10)

This fictionalized biography tells the story of 8-year-old Jeanne, the only member of her family to escape the 1994 genocide in Rwanda.

Karr, Kathleen. *Born for Adventure* (Marshall Cavendish, 2007, $16.99) (Grades 6–9)

Tom Ormsby longs for adventure and he finds it when he joins Henry Morton Stanley's expedition to Africa in 1887.

Kurtz, Jane. *Under the Hyena's Foot* (Pleasant, 2003, $15.95) (Grades 5–8)
In 19th-century Ethiopia, 12-year-old Saba discovers that she is a member of the ruling family.

McKissack, Patricia. *Nzingha: Warrior Queen of Matamba* (Scholastic, 1999, pap. $10.95) (Grades 5–8)
This is the story of the 17th-century African queen Nzingha who, in present-day Angola, resisted Portuguese slave traders.

Marie, D. *Tea for Ashan* (Creative, 1989, $12.95) (Grades 3–6)
In Africa, years ago, Kumasi sees his best friend taken captive by slave traders.

Rubalcaba, Jill. *A Place in the Sun* (Clarion, 1997, $13.95) (Grades 3–6)
Set in the 13th century, this novel describes the fate of a boy who is exiled to the gold mines of Nubia.

Wein, Elizabeth E. *The Lion Hunter (The Mark of Solomon)* (Viking, 2007, $16.99) (Grades 6–9)
This novel, first in a proposed series, takes place in 6th-century Africa in the kingdom of Aksum (ancient Ethiopia) and features 12-year-old Telemakos, who suffers both physically and emotionally when he loses an arm to one of the emperor's pet lions. The second volume is *The Empty Kingdom* (Viking, 2008, $16.99).

Williams, Mary. *Brothers in Hope: The Story of the Lost Boys of Sudan* (Lee and Low, 2005, $17.95) (Grades 3–5)
Garang, a Sudanese boy, flees to Ethiopia and then Kenya hoping to find a way to reach America.

CHAPTER 7

Latin America and Canada

BRUCHAC, JOSEPH. *The Winter People.* Dial, 2002, o.p.; pap. Puffin, $5.99 (978-0-14-240229-0) (Grades 5–9)

Introduction

Joseph Bruchac was born in 1942 in Saratoga Springs, New York. He is partially of Abenaki descent (the Native American people featured in this novel). He attended both Cornell and Syracuse universities and later received a doctorate from Union Graduate School. In his writing, he is best known for his use of Native American lore and culture. In *The Continuum Encyclopedia of Children's Literature* (Continuum, 2001), Janelle B. Mathis writes, "Bruchac's Native American heritage and his interest in its history, culture, and literature are the essence of his writing. He focuses on Native American wisdom, spirituality, relationships with the natural world, and its practical connections to contemporary society. His stories are rich combinations of his own heritage and his literary style with which he creates characters with multidimensional attributes interacting within authentic contexts."

The Winter People takes place over a period of a few weeks in the fall of 1759. The setting is first a small Indian village in present-day Quebec and later the area in northern Vermont and New York State where Saxso, the book's hero, journeys seeking his abducted family. A map of this journey is given before the table of contents. The book is narrated by 14-year-old Saxso.

Historical Background

In an Author's Note at the end of the novel, Bruchac supplies rich, authentic details on the facts behind the novel. Particularly fascinating is the background material on Chief Joseph-Louis Gill and on Suzanne Johnson, a white woman who was captured and later adopted by the Abenaki. After being ransomed by her people, she wrote a true-life account of her experiences in the best-selling book *A Narrative of Mrs. Johnson's Captivity Among the French and Indians.* The Abenaki (sometimes spelled Abnaki) Indians are members of the Algonquian family. Named by the French, the name translates roughly as "living at the sunrise."

The Abenaki originally lived in northern New England, but after a series of bloody conflicts with English settlers, they moved into Canada to what is now the province of Quebec, where they received protection from the French. They lived in villages and subsisted by hunting, fishing, and growing crops such as corn. Although they eventually constructed wooden structures for habitation, they lived at first in cone-shaped huts made of mats and bark. Their word for these homes was "wigwam," a name that has been incorporated into English.

The French and Indian Wars (1754–1763) were the last of a series of wars the British and the French fought for supremacy in the North America. At first the struggle was a series of disasters for the British, but in 1759 (the year of the novel) the tide turned. In July, the British captured Fort Carillon, which then became Fort Ticonderoga. And on September 13, British soldiers under General James Wolfe scaled the cliffs above Quebec and won a decisive battle over the forces of General Montcalm. Montreal fell a year later, and the entire province of New France surrendered in September 1760. By the Treaties of Fontainebleau and Paris, France relinquished all claims to territory in North America.

Robert Rogers (1731–1795) was a military leader for the English. He was born in Methuen, Massachusetts, and as a youngster moved with his family to the New Hampshire frontier, where he began service as a military scout. During the French and Indian Wars he raised and commanded several military units known collectively as Rogers' Rangers, and was appointed official leader of these groups in 1758. In 1759, he led a small band of his Rangers on a daring raid of the village of St. Francis, home of a group of Abenaki Indians. In 1760, the French forts on the Great Lakes surrendered to him. Because of his many exploits, he became a popular hero but when it was discovered that he was trading illicitly with the Indians, he suffered public humiliation. During his life he set out on many expeditions to find a Northwest Passage and, as a fierce supporter of the English, he sided with the Loyalists during the American Revolution. He was imprisoned briefly as a Loyalist spy but he escaped and rejoined the Loyalist forces. After the Revolution, he moved to England, where it is believed he died in a debtor's prison.

Principal Characters

Saxso, a 14-year-old Abenaki Indian
Mother, Saxso's mother
Katrin, his 8-year-old sister
Marie-Jeanne, his 11-year-old sister
Antoine Gill and Piel, Saxso's friends
Beaver Tail, Saxso's grandfather
The Worrier, an Indian wise man
Father Roubaud, the town's priest
Pierre Ktsi Awasos, Saxso's uncle
Chief Joseph-Louis Gill, chief of the Abenaki
Simon Obomsawin, a village resident
Malian, his daughter
Robert Rogers, leader of the English raiders

Plot Synopsis

It is the late fall of 1759 in the small Abenaki village of St. Francis, situated on the St. Francis River close to its mouth on the St. Lawrence River almost midway between Montreal and Quebec City. The conflicts (known collectively as the French and Indian Wars) between the French and the English have resumed and the peace-loving Abenaki, who traditionally have been allies of the French, fear an attack by roving bands of British raiders known as the Bostoniak. Saxso, whose father was killed in battle more than a year ago, is now head of his family, which consists of his mother, and his two younger sisters, 11-year-old Marie-Jeanne and 8-year-old Katrin. Saxso and his family are well-loved and respected by the rest of the tribe, and the boy numbers among his closest friends Piel and Antoine, who was the the son the of their Chief Joseph-Louis Gill and also the boyfriend of Marie-Jeanne. As a youngster, Saxso learned much of the tribe's accumulated wisdom and lore, as well as its troubled history with the English, the "Winter People," from his great-grandfather Beaver Tail. He also learned English from Mrs. Susannah Johnson, who spent some time as a captive of the Indians.

On the fateful day that changes Saxso's life forever, many of the village leaders—including Chief Joseph-Louis Gill, Saxso's uncle Pierre Ktsi Awasos, and the local priest, Father Roubaud—are away on various missions. It is the fall harvest festival and, that evening, most of the residents have already assembled at the Council Hall for the festivities when Saxso leaves his house to join them. On his way, he hears a voice coming from a bush. He recognizes it as that of Samadagwis, a Mahigan who lived in the village for a time before moving back south and joining the Bostoniak Rangers. Out of loyalty to his former friends, Samadagwis warns Saxso that a band of Bostoniak Rangers under Robert Rogers is poised to attack the village. Saxso rushes to the only remaining wigwam in the village (the rest of the buildings have already been converted to wooden structures). There the tribal wise man, the Worrier, lives. The old man has recently had a premonition about an impending attack and now his fears appear to be justified. Together the two warn their tribesman, some of whom stay to defend their village, while others, like Saxso lead their families to safety in the forest. On the way, Simon Obomsawin realizes he has left his youngest daughter, Malian, behind. The attack has begun but Saxso valiantly volunteers to accompany Simon back to the village. When they return along with Malian, Saxso cannot find his family. While shepherding refugees to the other side of the St. Francis River, he is wounded in the shoulder and loses consciousness.

When he wakens, the attack is over. He and the Worrier return to find that almost the entire village is a smoldering ruin. About thirty people, mainly woman and children, have perished. Saxso wonders if two of the charred corpses could be those of his friends Piel and Antoine. Before leaving, the Rangers shot Samadagwis for his treachery and left him to die. A villager mercifully put him out of his misery with a hatchet blow. Bodies of the dead and dying are everywhere and, although many of the tribe have survived the attack, others, including Saxso's family, are missing, presumably captured by the retreating Rangers. The tribal leaders return and Chief Gill and Saxso's uncle organize separate rescue parties, each intent on rescuing captives and avenging themselves on the Rangers and their leader, Rogers, whom they call the White Devil.

Saxso, who blames himself for his family's fate, decides that when he has recovered from his wounds he will mount his own rescue mission. Before his Uncle Pierre leaves, he gives Saxso a beautiful canoe as well as valuable advice on surviving alone in the woods. Energized by his sense of purpose and by the justice of his cause, Saxso sets off. His loneliness is eased by the beauty and grandeur of the natural wonders he sees. After a few days, he encounters Chief Gill's party, returning with discouraging news. The chief has learned that his family including his son, Antoine, has been killed and eaten by the group of Rangers entrusted by Rogers to care for them.

Undaunted, Saxso presses on. The trail south is now overland, so Saxso hides his canoe and heads toward Lake Champlain on foot. On the trail, he sees signs that people have recently passed that way. His spirits rise further when he sees tiny branches of trees tied into knots, a sign his tribe uses to indicate directions. One evening he sees below him an encampment with five Rangers, four Stockbridge Indians, and eight captives. Among the captives he identifies his mother and two sisters. The following morning he rushes ahead, trying to put some distance between himself and the Rangers so that he can find a place to stage a rescue. To alert his mother to his presence, he leaves a trail of tied tree branches. She gets the message and soon places herself and her daughters about 40 paces ahead of the others. When Saxso spots a part of the trail so narrow that the party must walk in single file, he puts his plan into action. After his family passes, he dislodges some large boulders, sending them cascading onto the trail. In the ensuing confusion Saxso and his family escape, but not before he is wounded by a Ranger's bullet. His mother's curative powers give Saxso the strength to guide them to his canoe and eventually back to their village, where the process of rebuilding has already begun.

Amid all the sorrow, there is some unexpected happiness, particularly for Saxso's sister Marie-Jeanne. A tattered and weary refugee arrives one day. It is Antoine, the chief's son, who has managed to escape. Reconstruction of the village proceeds and the Worrier tells Saxso, "We are always within the eye of the Creator, and we find that each is connected to the other. Only those who live with winter in their hearts cannot see those connections. We must not hate these Winter People. Pity them and keep the summer in your heart."

Passages for Booktalking

Some interesting passages: The Worrier warns the community about an attack on the village (pp. 19–24); the warning from the bush (pp. 7–9); Beaver Tail tells Saxso about the arrival of the Bostoniak (pp. 10–13); Saxso returns to his village after the attack (pp. 53–56); and the death of Samadagwis (pp. 57–61).

Themes and Subjects

This is a heartbreaking, suspenseful novel about the fate of the Abenaki at the hands of the English raiders. The author's detailed description of the everyday life of these Native Americans and their innate nobility and dignity makes for fascinating reading. The book is filled with material on the lore and beliefs of a people who manage a happy compromise between their traditional beliefs and the new religion of Christianity. The unity of man and nature is stressed, and the positive belief that we should be thankful for the gifts that nature bestows is emphasized. Saxso's courage and determination are well portrayed, as is his healthy relationship with nature and his growing maturation. Some other subjects: Canada, New England, New York State, Rogers' Rangers, the French and Indian Wars, family ties, escapes, journeys, Native Americans, Abenaki, and the raid on St. Francis.

CURTIS, CHRISTOPHER PAUL. *Elijah of Buxton.* Scholastic, 2007, $16.99 (978-0-439-02344-3) (Grades 4–8)

Introduction

Christopher Paul Curtis was born in Flint, Michigan, in 1954. His odyssey to becoming an award-winning black writer is a fascinating one. Unable to complete his college degree for financial reasons, he worked for ten years on the assembly line of the Fisher Body Works. With his wife's help and encouragement, he took a year off to write, using a table in the children's room of his local public library as a desk. He wrote everything in longhand (and he still does), and at night his young son transcribed it onto a computer. The result was his first novel for young people *The Watsons Go to Birmingham—1963* (Delacorte, 1995, $15.95; 0385321759), a Newbery Honor Book for 1996. It tells of the automobile trip the Watson family takes from Flint to Birmingham, Alabama, and of the trauma they experience from witnessing the death and destruction caused by the firebombing of a church there. The author's advice to young writers includes "Do it everyday. Stay in practice. At first it seems hard but your mind is so fantastic, it learns how to make it easier."

Of *Elijah of Buxton*, Mr. Curtis said, "This novel came to me in a way that was different from any other. From the word 'go,' Elijah and I became close friends. When I'd go to the library to write, it was as if he were anxiously awaiting me, waiting to tell about his life, his worries, his adventures." The novel won the Scott O'Dell Historical Fiction Award, the Coretta Scott King Award, and was a Newbery Honor Book in 2008. It takes place over a period of a month or so in 1859, just prior to the outbreak of the Civil War. The setting is Buxton, the freed black community in present-day southern Ontario, and the narrator is 11-year-old Elijah Freeman.

Historical Background

In an Author's Note after the text, Mr. Curtis gives a brief history of Buxton and its inhabitants. After the American Revolution, eastern Canada (except the Maritimes) was divided into two geographical and political parts to reflect the differences between the English- and French-speaking areas. One was Upper Canada and the other Lower Canada. The Act Against Slavery was passed by the Upper Canada Parliament on July 9, 1793. With the Act of Union of 1840, these two areas were joined into the United Province of Canada and renamed Canada West and Canada East. Buxton was in Canada West. Under the British North America Act of 1867, there was a further name change and Canada West became Ontario and Canada East, Quebec.

The Reverend William King (1812–1895) was born in Londonderry, Ireland, and educated in Scotland. He emigrated to the United States and worked in a Louisiana college but later returned to his homeland and, after studying theology, was sent to Canada as a missionary. Acting on his hatred of slavery, he brought fifteen American slaves to Canada in 1849, freed them, and, along with six escaped slaves, founded the Elgin or Buxton Settlement on a 3-mile-by-6-mile tract of land he purchased in southern Ontario about six miles from Lake Erie and the same distance from the city of Chatham. This western peninsula of Ontario also contained the city of Windsor, opposite Detroit on the American side, and became a mecca for fugitive slaves eager to find freedom in Canada. The King land was divided into 50-acre lots and sold to fugitive and former slaves for $2.50 per acre with 10-year loans. Writing about the settlement in the *Journal of Negro History*, Fred Landon said, "The Buxton or Elgin Association Settlement, in Kent county, western Ontario, was in many respects the most important attempt made before the Civil War to found a Negro refugee colony in Canada. In population, material wealth and general organization it was outstanding, and the firm foundation upon which it was established is shown by the fact that today, about a century and a half after emancipation, it is still a prosperous and distinctly Negro settlement." During the Civil War about 70 men from the settlement served in the Union forces. After the war, many families returned to the United States. At its peak, its population was about 2,000. Today it numbers about 100. Now known as North Buxton, the town contains an interesting Buxton National Historic Site and Museum.

The term "paddy-rollers" is used in this novel and refers to men who were hired by masters to chase, capture, and return runaway slaves. They were known for the inhumane tactics they used. After the Civil War, the term referred to gangs of white vigilantes who terrorized black communities. They later evolved into the Ku Klux Klan.

Principal Characters

Elijah (Eli or Lijah) Freeman, an 11-year-old black boy
Spencer Freeman (Pa), Elijah's father
Sarah Freeman (Ma), Elijah's mother
Cooter Bixby, Elijah's friend
Right Reverend Deacon Doctor Zephariah Connerly III, a man known as the Preacher
Mr. Leroy, a friendly resident of Buxton
Mrs. Holton, another resident
Mr. Segee, a stable owner
Mr. Travis, Elijah's classroom and Sunday school teacher
Charles Mondial Vaughn, a carnival owner
Madame Sabbar, a carnival attraction

MaWee, a black boy attached to the carnival
Emma Collins, Elijah's classmate
Mr. Highgate, a neighbor in Buxton
Benjamin Alston, an American free black
Mrs. Chloe and Mr. Kamau, two slaves
Hope Too-mah-ee-mee, their child

Plot Synopsis

Eleven-year-old Elijah Freeman is the only child and the pride and joy of his loving parents, Sarah and Spencer Freeman or, to him, Ma and Pa. The year is 1859, and Elijah is growing up and attending school in the free black community of Buxton situated in present-day Ontario, Canada, close to the city of Chatham, and near the Windsor-Detroit border. Most of the inhabitants are escaped slaves, many of whom arrived via the Underground Railroad. Elijah has the honor of being the first free baby born in the settlement, but he has been told that he distinguished himself during the ceremony to mark the occasion by vomiting all over guest speaker Frederick Douglass.

Elijah is a well-liked, respectful boy who is very sensitive (Ma calls him fragile). Though easily moved to tears, he is not above playing practical jokes on people with his friend Cooter Bixby. For example, knowing his mother's fear of frogs, he plants a huge "toady-frog" in her knitting basket and hoots with glee when she is terrified at its discovery. However, revenge is sweet, and Ma hides a snake, Elijah's greatest phobia, in the cookie jar just before he decides to taste a delicious sugar cookie.

Elijah is naïve and overly trusting of others, and often believes the tall stories that the smooth-talking, flim-flam artist known as the Preacher tells him, including the one about the existence of hoop snakes. Elijah possesses a rare talent and can throw stones with incredible accuracy and power. He can float a horsefly on the water and then hit a fish when it surfaces to eat the fly. One day, this form of fishing and other feats of accurate stone-throwing are witnessed by the Preacher, who is impressed by Elijah's amazing gift and by the possibilities of exploiting it. The Preacher's real name is Zephariah Connerly. He lives outside the settlement, rides a white horse, and sports what Elijah calls a "mystery pistol," both of which people believe to be stolen. After cheating Elijah out of some of his fish, he mysteriously makes Elijah swear that he will participate in a future act to help the settlement.

Meanwhile, there is great excitement at school. One day, before school begins, the pupils notice an agitated Mr. Travis, their teacher, writing "Familiarity Breeds Contempt" on the blackboard. Cooter, with his limited vocabulary, translates this as "Family Breeding Contest." But Cooter's great expectations for a lesson in sex education are shattered when classmate Emma

Collins explains the phrase and Mr. Travis applies its meaning by punishing Cooter severely for behaving in a disrespectful manner when they met the previous day on the street.

Elijah often helps a workman, Mr. Leroy, to remove stumps from Mrs. Holton's property. Mr. Leroy is saving his money to buy freedom for his wife and two children, and Mrs. Holton, an escaped slave, pays his wages from a large sum of money her husband gave her before he was caught and sent back into slavery. On their way home from Mrs. Holton's, Elijah is chattering away about his friends and says "Me and all 'em other nigg—." Before he can finish the word, Mr. Leroy slaps him across the face and tells him that no matter who speaks that word, it is an outrageous insult to their race and should never be spoken. Elijah realizes he has learned a valuable lesson.

The Preacher reappears and explains that part of his proposition involves attending the last night of a traveling American carnival in nearby Chatham. Elijah is thrilled and sneaks out that night to meet the Preacher. One of the popular acts they witness is Madame Sabbar and her amazing feats of accuracy with her slingshot; another is a demonstration of hypnotism by the carnival's owner, Sir Charles M. Vaughn. After closing time, Elijah, at the Preacher's bidding, demonstrates his throwing prowess. Sir Charles is so impressed that he offers Elijah a job. He is not too enthusiastic, however, about also hiring the Preacher. When a nappy-haired black boy named MaWee arrives and reveals that he is Sir Charles's slave, the Preacher's attitude suddenly changes. He grabs Elijah and marches him home. The next day, there is a new pupil at school. It is MaWee. After leaving Elijah, the Preacher had returned to the carnival. Mounted on his white stallion and waving his revolver, he kidnapped the boy and brought him to freedom in Buxton.

Other incidents impress on Elijah the blessing known as freedom. On a picnic to Lake Erie, he overhears his mother tell Mrs. Holton about being punished by her mother, Elijah's grandmother, for her failure to try to escape to Canada when she was taken to Detroit on vacation as a companion for her master's daughter. When the opportunity arose again the next year, she obeyed her mother even though it meant never seeing her family again. Elijah also helps welcome into the community a new family of escaped slaves and takes pride in sounding the settlement's Freedom Bell in their honor. Mrs. Holton gets news that, after being captured, her husband was beaten to death by his master for stealing the money he had given his wife. Elijah helps write a tribute that is engraved on a wooden slab by Mr. Leroy. To show her appreciation, Mrs. Holton gives Mr. Leroy enough money to buy his family out of slavery.

The Preacher volunteers to take the money across the border to a man who will negotiate the family's release. Pa, suspicious of the Preacher's motives, suggests that an honest neighbor, Mr. Highgate, accompany him. A few days later, a badly wounded Mr. Highgate returns. The Preacher, eager to feed his gambling habit, shot him, left him for dead, and took the money. Luckily, a kindly freed black man named Benjamin Alston found him and arranged to get him home. Mr. Leroy, already ailing and infirm, is incensed at the news and persuades Elijah to sneak away and accompany him across the border to retrieve the money. They locate Benjamin Alston, who tells them that the Preacher won (probably by cheating) a game of dice with some of the local blacks and, last heard of, was heading for a game with some white folks in a nearby stable. Before they reach the stable, Mr. Leroy dies of a heart attack and Elijah has to enter the stable alone. He silences a ferocious guard dog with a powerful toss of one of his rock missiles. Inside, he is confronted with a horrible sight. The Preacher, stripped naked, has been tied up and murdered. Close by, there are several pitiable blacks chained to the stable's cement wall. All are shackled both by hand and foot, except for the one woman in the group. She has a baby to carry and only her feet are in chains. In halting speech, she introduces herself as Chloe and her husband as Kamau. It is their child she is holding. All six are escaped slaves who have been taken by four paddy-rollers, men who profit from recapturing fugitive slaves. They are to be shipped out in the morning.

As Elijah talks to her, he realizes he is powerless to help them. In desperation, he remembers his mother's past and how her freedom was so important to her mother. He knows he must try to bring the baby back to Buxton. Chloe agrees to give up the baby she has called Hope and the African name Too-mah-ee-mee. That evening he says a tearful farewell to the slaves and returns to Buxton with Hope in his tote sack. Another soul has been given the precious gift of freedom.

Passages for Booktalking
Some interesting passages are: the Preacher tells Elijah and Cooter about hoop snakes (pp. 1–8); Elijah puts a frog into his mother's sewing basket (pp. 12–15) and Ma gets even with a snake in the cookie jar (pp. 18–21); baby Elijah vomits on Frederick Douglass (pp. 23–27); and collecting horseflies for stone fishing (pp. 30–34).

Themes and Subjects
Elijah is a beguiling, admirable character who may be vulnerable and sensitive but can muster courage and strength beyond his years to fight for the principles in which he believes. Although this story tells of the inhumane barbarism of slavery, it also emphasizes the virtue of hope and the necessity of freedom for an individual to live happily and productively. The book also supplies a graphic portrait of a community of freed slaves living in a harmonious, pro-

ductive environment but still aware of the responsibility to welcome new residents and the need to help others seeking freedom. Other subjects: Buxton, Ontario, Canada West, Detroit, pre-Civil War America, Frederick Douglass, family ties, friendship, sacrifice, schooling, farming, fishing, carnivals, trickery, gambling, kidnapping, and adventure.

EBOCH, CHRIS. *The Well of Sacrifice.* Clarion, 1999, $18 (978-0-395-90374-2) (Grades 5–8)

Introduction

Chris Eboch comes from a writing family. Both her parents write articles and books and her brother, Doug Eboch, is an important Hollywood screen writer. Chris Eboch first developed a love of history and ancient civilization when she and her parents moved to Saudi Arabia when she was five. She visited many different places, including India and Afghanistan. They later lived in Colorado and then Alaska. She has a Master's degree in writing and publishing and has considerable experience writing freelance magazine articles. This is her first novel, but she has also written several nonfiction books for young people including easy science books, biographies, and two titles in the Modern Nations of the World series. Closely related to the subject matter of this novel is *Life Among the Maya* (Lucent, 2005, $28.50; 159018162X), part of the Way People Live series. Of this, one reviewer said, "the author's lively, well-researched narrative details the structure of the culture." This is also true of *The Well of Sacrifice*, which was inspired by the author's visit to Yucatan, where she saw a limestone sinkhole into which the Maya threw sacrificial victims. The setting of the novel is Guatemala during the Golden Age of Mayan civilization, specifically the 9th century, or the end of the Classic Period in Mayan history. The action takes place over a three-year period during which the narrator and heroine, Eveningstar Macaw, changes from a girl of 11 to a young woman of 14. The text is enhanced by several full-page illustrations by Bryn Barnard.

Historical Background

The author gives good background information in an "Author's Note" following the text. The Maya are Central American Indians who occupy an area consisting roughly of the Yucatan peninsula and southeastern highlands in Mexico, Guatemala, Belize, and western Honduras. Today, they number about 2 million people and still maintain many aspects of their ancient culture. It is believed that their civilization began about 1000 B.C., among nomadic tribes in the area. There are three epochs in Mayan history: Pre-Classic, Classic, and Post-Classic (which ended with Spanish domination). The Classic Period, from 300 to 900 A.D., is considered the Golden Age of Mayan culture. The novel takes place during this era in the 9th century. At this time the population (estimated at about 14 million) was organized into many separate city-states. The government of each was closely tied to their religion. At the head was a hereditary ruler. The leading priest was a close second in terms of power (Great Skull Zero in the novel). He and his associates were not only the administrators but also the important scholars, astronomers, mathematicians, and warriors. Below them came the majority of the people, who were farmers, laborers, and artisans. Lastly there were the slaves, who were criminals and prisoners of war. The common people lived in wattle-and-daub huts with thatched roofs, but the socially elite had much grander quarters built of stone. The Maya were master builders and architects. Their magnificent ceremonial buildings (temples, palaces, and so forth) were grouped around central plazas. These structures were often built on a pyramidal design and achieved a beauty of design not equaled by any other American Indian group. They also surpassed their contemporaries at mastering abstract knowledge—writing, mathematics, astronomy, accurate measurement of time, and the development of calendars. To record numbers, the Maya used a system of bars and dots with a bar representing five and a dot, one.

The Maya were the only people in America to develop an original writing system. It is estimated that it consisted of as many as 850 characters and until the 1970s remained undeciphered. They produced books, but almost all of them were destroyed by the Spanish. Of the 10,000 texts still in existence, most are on stone monuments and pottery and have been translated in the last few decades. The Mayan religion was closely related to the cycle of nature. They worshipped a number of gods—some good, such as Chac, the god of corn; others bad, such as Ah Puch, the god of death. The Mayan high priest had the responsibility of studying and interpreting the cycles of nature and the disposition of the gods. He was also empowered with the gift of prophecy. People engaged in blood-letting as part of religious rituals, as well as the practice of making human sacrifices. Usually the victim was held while his chest was opened and his heart removed. Toward the end of the Classic Period there was a time when a number of the centers of culture such as Palenque and Piedras Negras were mysteriously abandoned. There have been many theories about these population changes, some suggesting environmental problems (soil exhaustion, droughts, climate change, and so forth), and others positing disease, overpopulation, or (as in the novel) revolts against the rulers.

Principal Characters

Eveningstar Macaw, an 11-year-old Mayan girl
Feather Dawn, her 12-year-old sister
Smoke Shell, her brother, about 20
Blue Quetzal, her mother
Eighteen Rabbit, her father
Small, a Savage about Eveningstar's age
King Flint Sky God, their ruler
Great Skull Zero, the high priest
Smoking Squirrel, a priest and interpreter
Double Bird, later Smoke Shell's wife
Six Sky Monkey, Feather Dawn's husband

Plot Synopsis

The Mayan city-state to which Eveningstar's family belongs has been facing repeated raids by roaming bands of Indians known as the Savages. It is the 9th century in Guatemala, the Mayan civilization is at its peak, and, other than news of these incursions, life for the 11-year-old girl is peaceful and happy. Her father, Eighteen Rabbit, is a successful trader, mainly in pottery, and her mother is a respected, sought-after healer who uses roots and herbs to effect amazing cures. Eveningstar has an older sister, Feather Dawn, now 12, who has recently experienced the religious rites of passage into adulthood. She also has a much-admired brother, Smoke Shell, who is about 20 and in military training.

One steamy spring day, Eveningstar is in the neighboring jungle collecting plants for her mother when she sees a group of Savages approaching. She seems to have found a fine hiding place but unfortunately is spotted by a young Savage. The boy, whom Eveningstar dubs Small, realizes her fear and doesn't reveal her presence to the others. When she feels out of danger, she rushes into the city to the communal house where Smoke Shell resides. After she tells him about the Savages, he collects a large group of his men and gives chase. Several uneventful days pass, during which Eveningstar tries unsuccessfully to learn weaving from her bossy sister. The warriors return triumphant with a large group of Savage prisoners. Eveningstar sees Small among them and, to show her thanks, begs for and gains his release and an assignment to her household as a slave.

There is a great celebration and Smoke Shell is honored for his outstanding leadership role in killing and capturing so many Savages. The high priest, Great Skull Zero, is restrained in his praise, thinking the young man should have got official approval before setting out, but King Flint Sky God objects and honors Smoke Shell by making his family members of the noble class. As well as receiving land and a house in the nobility compound, they are given special privileges such as seats in a restricted area of the ball-court during the victory celebrations. There they witness a sacred ball game between the Maya and some of the conquered Savages, followed by the sacrifice of eight prisoners by removing their hearts and the ceremonial blood-letting of the king. During these events, Eveningstar sits next to a kindly old priest and interpreter named Smoking Squirrel. To pass the time, he tells her a Mayan legend, the story of the Hero Twins.

Time passes and the family becomes accustomed to its new status. Small learns the Mayan language and soon is a treasured part of the household. When she is 12, Eveningstar attends the Rite of Passage ceremony and later hears reports that the king's health is declining. A few months after Eveningstar turns 13, Smoke Shell marries a beautiful maiden named Double Bird, and later Feather Dawn is also married, to a handsome warrior called Six Sky Monkey. Then King Flint Sky God dies. Because the king had no children, Great Skull Zero assumes his responsibilities until a successor can be chosen. Before the funeral Great Skull Zero announces that the gods have decreed that the king's body must be accompanied to the underworld by the bodies of six Mayan warriors. When the names of the six are read out, they include Smoke Shell and Six Sky Monkey. All six are placed in confinement.

Eveningstar and others are convinced that Great Skull Zero is killing these young men to eliminate competition in the struggle for succession. With the help of Small, Eveningstar gains access to the funeral temple where her brother is being kept, but before she can speak to him, Great Skull Zero knocks her out with a blow to the head. When she awakens, she sees before her six bodies, including that of Smoke Shell, all wrapped in shrouds. Great Skull Zero has prevailed! Trapped in the sealed burial chamber, Eveningstar uses her knife to loosen one of the limestone blocks. In the meantime, Small has alerted Eveningstar's mother to her whereabouts and, with their help, she escapes and she and Small flee to the countryside.

Eveningstar spends her fourteenth birthday there, acting as a healer to poor farmers. But after several months, she decides she must return home. There, she finds that Great Skull Zero is continuing his reign of terror, sending any who oppose him to their deaths by flinging them over the sharp limestone cliff that leads into the Well of Sacrifice. Supposedly, the innocent survive, but so far none has returned. The tyrant also has made plans to marry Feather Dawn, Eveningstar's sister. When Great Skull Zero comes to claim Feather Dawn, he discovers Eveningstar and she is imprisoned. Using great ingenuity, she manages to escape only to be caught again. Once more she tricks her guards and flees for her life. Great Skull Zero threatens to kill her family unless she surrenders. Given no choice, she gives herself up. Great Skull Zero announces publicly that the gods have decreed that she be thrown into the Well of Sacrifice. After several religious rituals, two priests hurl her over the cliff and into the water far below. Miraculously, she survives the fall and, using all her strength, slowly climbs back up the limestone cliff to freedom.

She plans to appear the next day at the public nuptials of Great Skull Zero and Feather Dawn to announce that the gods have shown their anger at Great Skull Zero by allowing her to escape from the well. Dressed in fine robes she has obtained at one of the temples, she appears in the midst of the dignitaries attending the wedding. Before she can speak, Great Skull Zero lunges at her with his knife. Small steps between them and is stabbed in the shoulder and, within seconds, her loyal old friend Smoking Squirrel, who has been standing nearby, draws his knife and kills Great Skull Zero. Sickened by the continual injustice and tyranny, he has decided to take action and save both Eveningstar and his beloved city. Small survives and is given his freedom by Eveningstar's parents as well as a new name, Shield. All the family members and many other residents decide to leave the city and find homes elsewhere. As they prepare to depart, Eveningstar looks into Shield's eyes and realizes that wherever the gods take them, she must go with him.

Passages for Booktalking

Some exciting passages: Eveningstar narrowly escapes from the Savages in the jungle (pp. 6–11); Eveningstar and Smoke Shell visit the king and Smoke Shell relates his exploits and is honored (pp. 30–36); Smoking Squirrel tells the legend of the Hero Twins (pp. 39–40); and the sacrifice of the Savages and the blood-letting of the king (pp. 50–60).

Themes and Subjects

Although many of Eveningstar's escapades may border on the improbable, this is still a fast-paced suspenseful adventure story that is a real page-turner. Particularly interesting are the details of everyday life of the ancient Maya. Their religious beliefs and ceremonies are graphically described, sometimes testing the staying power of the squeamish. Eveningstar is a likable narrator and heroine. She shows great courage, devotion to her family, and belief in justice. Other subjects: Guatemala, religion, human sacrifice, jungles, family life, warfare, royalty, city-states, class struggle, tyranny, and heroism.

IBBOTSON, EVA. *Journey to the River Sea.* Dutton, 2002, $17.99 (978-0-525-46739-7); pap. Puffin, $6.99 (978-0-14-250184-9) (Grades 4–8)

Introduction

The author was born Maria Wiesner to Jewish parents in Austria in 1925. Her family left Vienna in 1933 when she was 8 years old. Her parents separated and she moved first to Edinburgh with her father, a scientist, and later to London. She is now a well-known and prize-winning writer alternating between adult and juvenile fiction. Many of her novels for young readers are fantasies. *Which Witch?* (Dutton, 1999, $15.99; 0525461647) features the wizard Arriman the Awful, who dreads the thought of marriage but must ensure an heir to the throne of darkness. The witches of a local coven compete in a contest to be chosen as his bride, each trying to outdo the others with the blackest trick.

Journey to the River Sea, which takes place chiefly around Manaus in Brazil, was written to honor her husband, a naturalist, who died just before she began the novel. Commenting on the research needed to write it, Ms. Ibbotson says, "I read books, looked at pictures, watched films and videos of wildlife, talked to travelers, and tried to learn some Portuguese. There was a lot of historical research to do on the rubber boom, which brought settlers to the Amazon at the turn of the century. . . . Usually I go to the places I write about, but Manaus has changed so much that I decided to keep it in my head." The novel, a third-person narrative, takes place over several months beginning in the autumn of 1910. The story is enhanced by a number of black-and-white drawings by Kevin Hawkes.

Historical Background

Manaus is a city in northern Brazil on the Negro River about six miles north of the confluence of the Negro, whose waters are black, and the Solimoes, better known as the Amazon. The city is named after an Indian tribe, the Manaos (Mother of God), that once lived in the area. Around the city, situated near the equator, is the largest and most diversified tropical rainforest in the world. More than one third of all species live here. The temperature varies little from month to month, averaging in the low 90s with periods of heavy rainfall. The city's boom time was between 1890 and 1920, when it was the center of the world's rubber trade. Huge fortunes were amassed and architects and artisans from around the world were imported to turn this backwater settlement into "the Paris of the Tropics." Among its treasures is the opera house, the Teatro Amazonas, which took fifteen years to build and was opened in 1896. It is decorated with elaborate crystal chandeliers and beautiful banisters and frescoes, and seats 640. Its construction was the subject of Werner Herzog's 1982 film *Fitzcarraldo*.

Until the late 1920s, Brazil had a virtual monopoly on the production of rubber, and efforts were made to prevent the exportation of seedlings of the latex-producing trees. Rubber comes from a milky substance (latex) found in many plants but harvested chiefly from the sap of the Para rubber tree. Efforts to prevent the growth of rubber plantations elsewhere failed, and soon other countries—notably Indonesia, Singapore, and Malaysia—became leaders in the rubber trade, the latter eventually becoming the world's largest producer of natural rubber. Contributing to the decline of Manaus was the development in the 1930s of synthetic rubber in both Germany and the United States.

Manaus is still a bustling river port and gateway to the Amazon rainforest. It became the capital of the state of Amazonas in 1856. Belem, the Brazilian port at the mouth of the Amazon, is the Portuguese word for Bethlehem. Now the capital of the state of Para, it, too, was an important port during the heyday of the rubber trade.

In the novel, Clovis portrays Fauntleroy. *Little Lord Fauntleroy* was a sentimental novel by Frances Hodgson Burnett, who also wrote *A Little Princess* and *The Secret Garden*. The author was born in England but lived most of her life in America. The story originally appeared in serial form in 1885 and in book form the year after. It is the story of a Brooklyn boy who is found to be the heir to an English earldom. He and his mother, whom he calls "Dearest," are summoned to England, where the boy wins over the heart of his crusty, selfish grandfather, the old Earl. There were many stage versions (the author won a copyright case over illegal play adaptations in 1888) and films based on the novel, including a silent version starring Mary Pickford as Cedric and the classic 1930 film with Freddie Bartholomew as the heir and Mickey Rooney in a bit part.

Principal Characters

Maia Fielding, an English orphan of about 12 or 13
Mr. Murray, her guardian
Miss Minton, her governess
Clifford Carter, her second cousin
Mrs. Carter, his wife
Beatrice and Gwendolyn, their twin daughters
Clovis King (Jimmy Bates), an actor of Maia's age
The Goodleys, a family of actors
Furo, a boatman for the Carters
Mr. Trapwood and Mr. Low, two English private investigators
Prof. Glastonberry, curator of the local Natural History Museum
Finn Taverner, a boy of Maia's age, the son of the naturalist Bernard Taverner

Plot Synopsis

Maia, a girl on the brink of adolescence, has been living in a private school in London since her parents, archaeologists, were killed in a train accident in Egypt. The heir to a sizable fortune, she believes she has no living relatives until one day her cautious and caring guardian, Mr. Murray, announces he has found a second cousin, Clifford Carter, who lives with his wife and twin daughters, Beatrice and Gwendolyn, on a rubber plantation close to the city of Manaus in northern Brazil. Not only do they send greetings to Maia but also an offer that she come to live with them. Although her classmates think only of alligators and piranhas, Maia romantically dreams that her new home will be filled with both exotic flora and fauna and mysterious adventures.

Mr. Murray hires Miss Minton as her governess and the two soon board a steamship, the *Cardinal*, bound first for the port city of Belem and then on to Manaus. Miss Minton is something of an enigma. She seems stern and distant but Maia becomes aware of a sweet, caring person inside. Perhaps because of her many hardships and rebuffs, she has created a protective wall around herself. Maia, an inquisitive, daring youngster soon makes friends with Clovis King, the youngest member of a down-and-out acting troupe, the Pilgrim Players, that consists of Mr. and Mrs. Goodley, their assorted relatives, and Clovis, whose real name is Jimmy Bates. Clovis is an orphan of Maia's age who, at the urging of Mrs. Bates, his loving foster mother, has left home to seek his fortune on the stage. He longs to return to England, particularly now that the onset of puberty means his days as a juvenile in such plays as *Little Lord Fauntleroy* are numbered. The Pilgrim Players leave the ship at Belem for a two-week engagement before continuing on to Manaus to play at its fabled opera house. Maia promises to attend the performances there.

At Manaus, she and Miss Minton are ferried upstream to the Carter rubber plantation in the Carters' private boat, navigated by a native named Furo. The Carter family does not live up to Maia's expectations. Mr. Carter seems preoccupied and anxious to return to cataloging his collection of glass eyes. Mrs. Carter is obsessed with hermetically sealing the mansion to prevent any bugs from intruding. And the twins are a nasty, snobbish, and extremely unfriendly. Miss Minton later discovers that, through mismanagement, the plantation is bankrupt and that Maia's invitation stemmed from the promise of a healthy stipend.

Maia longs to mingle with the natives in the compound and to become acquainted with their families, customs, and food. The Carters remain aloof and forbid contact with these "inferiors," but Miss Minton finds ways for Maia to escape occasionally. One diversion is trips to Manaus for dancing and music lessons. The first dancing class, however, is interrupted by the unexpected arrival of two blustering Englishmen whom Maia immediately dubs "the crows." They are private detectives—Mr. Trapwood and Mr. Low—who have been sent from England to locate the young son of a recently deceased naturalist, Bernard Taverner, and bring him back to England.

Later, while the twins shop, Maia and Miss Minton learn more from Prof. Glastonberry, the curator of the local Natural History Museum. Mr. Taverner, it seems, who died four months ago in a boating accident, was a dedicated nature lover and collector who made a living selling exotic specimens and medicines to English markets.

On the opening night of the Pilgrim Players' performance, Maia finds that the Carters have not included her in their theater party to see Clovis as Cedric, young Fauntleroy. Not to be outmaneuvered, she hitches a ride into town in a dugout canoe paddled by a strange young native boy her age whose name she doesn't know. With the help of one of the Goodleys, she gets a last-minute front row seat. Disaster strikes when, in a highly emotional scene, Clovis's voice breaks and he suddenly becomes a basso profundo. Led by the giggling of the twins, the audience breaks out into derisive laughter and the curtain comes down. Clovis is inconsolable.

A few days later, Furo, the boatman, takes Maia to a secret lagoon where she has been summoned to meet the "native" boy who ferried her to Manaus. Now out of disguise, the boy introduces himself as Finn Taverner, the missing son of the famous naturalist. As a youngster, his father had been constantly bullied by his older brother and sister and scorned by his father because of his studious pursuits. At the age of 16, he left the wealth and privilege of his palatial home to find peace and study nature in the Amazon rainforest. He later married a woman from the peaceful Xanti tribe, who died giving birth to Finn. With the death of his uncle and father, Finn has become the heir to Westwood, a large estate in England and Messrs. Trapwood and Low, "the crows," have been sent to bring him back. Finn, however, wants to stay in his tropical paradise and become a part of the Xanti tribe.

At this point, Miss Minton makes an interesting confession. As a young girl, she worked at Westwood and was friendly with young Bernard. After many years, she had planned to join him in Brazil. When news of his death reached England she became Maia's governess to fulfill her dream of coming to Manaus.

When Maia brings the humiliated Clovis to stay with Finn, the three hatch a brilliant scheme. Clovis will get his wish to return to England by assuming the identity of Finn. With the help of Prof. Glastonberry, who hides Clovis in the basement of the museum and helps engineer a last minute "discovery" of their quarry by the crows, Clovis boards the ship bound for England and Westwood.

Soon afterward, Maia's stay in Brazil also comes to an abrupt end when Mrs. Carter accidentally sets fire to their home. Luckily all escape but the house is destroyed. Mrs. Carter and the twins, now impoverished, decide to return to England and become the charges of a wealthy, overbearing relative—Lady Parsons—who treats them like indentured servants. Mr. Carter stays behind to face charges of embezzling bank funds. Maia and Miss Minton, accompanied by Finn—who feels obliged to check on Clovis—also sail back to England where they find that Clovis has settled nicely into the Taverner household. Maia, Miss Minton, and Finn, however, feel like strangers in England and long to be back in the rainforest. So with Mr. Murray's financial help, Maia and her friends make plans to return to the land they now call home.

Passages for Booktalking

Maia is told about her relatives in Brazil (pp. 5–7) and is introduced to Miss Minton (pp. 14–16); on board the *Cardinal*, Maia meets Clovis and the Goodleys and hears of their theatrical plans (pp. 19–23); and Maia encounters the Carters and their restricted lifestyle (pp. 32–39).

Themes and Subjects

All four of the principal characters are interesting individuals but Maia remains outstanding. She is obedient without being subservient, curious, resourceful, courageous, imaginative, and self-possessed. As well as a tale of wrongdoing being punished, this is a tale of identity: lost, stolen, usurped, and gained. The portrayal of the color, variety, and uniqueness of the flora and fauna of the Amazon is vivid and fascinating. The sympathetic picture of the natives and their lifestyle and the contrast between this and the constricted, artificial life of the European settlers adds an interesting dimension. Other subjects: rubber plantations, naturalists, nature study, manor life, families, twins, orphans, actors and acting, Brazil, Manaus, rivers, native culture, adventure stories, and sea stories.

SCHWARTZ, VIRGINIA FRANCES. *Messenger.* Holiday House, 2002, $17.95 (978-0-8234-1716-2); pap. Fitzhenry and Whiteside, $9.95 (978-1-55041-946-7) (Grades 5–9)

Introduction

Virginia Frances Schwartz was born on December 14, 1950, on a farm in Stoney Creek, Ontario (the site of Frank's farm in the novel). She came from a poor family of Croatian descent and attended a strict Catholic elementary school nearby before being bused to Hamilton to attend high school. She attended McMaster University for one year but graduated from a Lutheran college in Ontario. Her first marriage ended after one year when her husband was killed in a car accident. She moved to New York to study nursing and has remained there ever since. After she drifted into teaching, she was chosen by New York's Board of Education to attend Columbia University's Writing Program. There, she learned not only how to write but also how to teach writing, her present full-time job. The two greatest influences on her writing, she claims, are the rural setting of her childhood, which stirred her imagination, and the close proximity of a public library whose contents she devoured. She has remarried and become involved in yoga, meditation, and vegetarianism. Another well-received historical novel by her is *If I Just Had Two Wings* (Fitzhenry and Whiteside, 2001, $15.95; 0773733027) in which a 13-year-old slave girl in Alabama dreams of freedom. After she befriends Liney, a 19-year-old fellow slave with two children, she discovers clues to the Underground Railroad in the songs she hears and soon the four set out on what, they hope, is a road to freedom.

Messenger takes place over a period of fifteen years from 1923 to 1938 in different locations in Ontario, Canada. It is based on the lives of the author's mother (Frances Jr.) and her grandmother (Frances or Ma). It is told in the first person by Frances Jr.

Historical Background

The novel takes place principally in three Ontario communities: Cobalt, Schumacher, and Hamilton. Cobalt, in Northern Ontario, is situated about 300 miles due north of Toronto, close to the Quebec border. Today it is a sleepy ghost town with a population of slightly more than 1,000, but at one time it was a bustling mining boomtown. In 1903, a pair of railway lumber scouts discovered a vein of silver and overnight the area became one of the richest silver-producing areas in the world. The population rose from 100 in 1903 to 10,000 in 1909. By 1911, there were more than a hundred mines operating in the area. Because the ore was close to the surface, men with limited capital and experience could enter the field easily. At present prices, it is estimated that the mines produced a total of $2 billion worth of silver. The fortunes made from Cobalt's silver exceeded those from Klondike gold. The railroad station built in 1909 was considered the most elegant in Ontario. The number of people who became millionaires from these mines rivaled the number of miners killed in accidents often caused by unsafe working conditions. Many Croatians were part of the work force in the heyday of Cobalt.

With the stock market crash of 1929, the demand for silver declined and with it, the fortunes of the town. There are no mines currently operating in the area. In 2001, Cobalt was designated "Ontario's Most Historic Town." The Mining Museum there contains the world's finest collection of native silver, as well as artifacts and old photographs. The Heritage Silver Trail, about four miles long, takes visitors on a self-guided tour of important mining sites, and it is possible to visit one of the underground mines. The famous railway station now houses a military museum.

Miners often moved north from Cobalt to the Timmins-Kirkland Lake area, where gold had been discovered. Schumacher, once known as Aura Lake, is a community in the Timmins area, about 100 miles north of Cobalt. It was named after a Danish pharmacologist named Frederick W. Schumacher, who had formed his own patent medicine company when he heard of the great gold discoveries in the Porcupine Camp (later Timmins) area. Several important mines had already been established in the area when he arrived, hired his own prospectors, and bought a large tract of land where he established his mine. People flocked into the area and soon the town of Schumacher had a population of 4,000. Because so many were Croatians, it was sometimes called Little Zagreb. Its fortunes also declined during and after the Great Depression.

Hamilton, with a present population of more than 500,000, is the third-largest city in Ontario and the ninth-largest in Canada. It is situated about halfway between Toronto and Niagara Falls, about an hour's drive away from each. Once nicknamed "Steel Town," it was, in pre-World War II Canada, the blast furnace capital of the country with great industrial smelting plants that produced iron and steel, machinery, and miscellaneous steel products. These plants also produced incredible air pollution that blanketed the city and made both breathing and sight difficult. In many ways, its history can be compared to that of Detroit because both cities have declined after periods of great productivity and importance.

Principal Characters

Phillip (Pa) Chopp, a miner
Frances (Ma) Chopp, his wife
Phillip, their older son
William, their younger son
Frances, their daughter
Auntie Tracey, Ma's sister
Uncle Matt, Tracey's husband
Helen and Paul, their children
Aunt Annie, another sister of Ma's
Uncle Jack, her husband
Aunt Elsie, another of Ma's sisters
Joseph Severenski, a cousin of Ma's
Mike and Peter Slivac, second cousins
Vinka, Joseph Severenski's wife

Novenka, Joe and Vinka's daughter
Johan Michich, an Austrian immigrant
Frank Stampfl, Johan's friend
Dr. Agro, the family's doctor

Plot Synopsis

When jobs open up in the nickel mines of Cobalt, Ontario, Phillip and Frances Chopp, a young married couple, decide to leave their Croatian settlement in Calumet, Michigan, and move north to Canada. Others in the family have preceded them to Canada. Frances's sister Tracey already lives in the town of Cobalt with her husband, Matt, also a mine worker, and their two children, Paul, age 8, and Helen, age 5. Another sister, Annie, and her husband Jack own a farm in Simcoe, in southern Ontario, close to Hamilton.

It is now October 1923, and the Chopps are living in primitive cabin above a mine shaft on the outskirts of town with their two, soon to be three, children, 6-year-old Phillip and 2-year-old William. The couple love each other deeply and although life is difficult and exhausting (miners work 11-hour days), the two have created a loving, close-knit family with hopes for a better future. Frances is tiny in stature, scarcely 5 feet, but makes up for it with enormous strength of character and a cast-iron determination. Suddenly, tragedy strikes the Chopp family. Phillip is killed in a mine cave-in. His crushed body is brought home and he is dressed in the suit in which he was married, before being buried on a hillside in the local cemetery. Frances is so devastated by the loss that she gives birth a month early to a girl whom she also names Frances, with the nickname Baby. Ironically, shortly after the funeral she receives a letter from Phillip's sister in Croatia, warning him not to go into the mines because of a premonition she has experienced. Though friends advise Ma (Frances) to move back to Calumet, she decides to remain in Cobalt and forge a life for her family with the small stipend she receives monthly from the mine owners for each child, as well as a promised settlement of $1,000. She supplements this income by baking bread for the locals, and by growing a wide variety of fruits and vegetables in her garden. She also receives occasional food packages from her youngest sister, Elsie, in Calumet. Ma's first attempt at gardening is almost ruined by a marauding groundhog. Armed with the family shotgun, Ma solves that problem and shortly after, the family is treated (?) to a groundhog stew.

Timee is buried on a hillside in the local cemetery. She bakes bread and sells it locally and playtime passes and Frances Jr. develops into a perceptive young child. She notices that Ma never talks about their father yet always dresses in black, her mourning clothes. Three strangers arrive from Croatia to work in the mines. They are: Ma's first cousin, Joseph Severenski, and two second cousins, Mike and Peter Slivac. Joe has left a wife, Vinka, and a young daughter, Novenka, behind, hoping he will soon earn enough to send for them and leave his present worker's quarters.

The Chopps's hand-to-mouth existence continues until Joe makes an interesting proposal. He suggests a move north to the mining town of Schumacher, which has prospered since the discovery of gold. Using his savings and part of Ma's settlement money, they could buy a boarding house. Ma would manage it while he and the cousins work in the mines. At first, Ma hesitates. Her main reason, she confesses much later, is that she does not want to leave her husband's grave. But, again much later, she recalls having a dream in which Phillip came to her and told her to move.

After a farewell to Aunt Tracey, Uncle Matt, and family, the Chopps move to Schumacher, into one of the tall, skinny boardinghouses situated in a dismal, unattractive row of buildings. As soon as news of Ma's cooking spreads, the place fills up with miners and lumberjacks. The boarders eat and, sometimes, sleep, in shifts, but the family maintains separate quarters and a different time for meals. There is usually little contact between the boarders and the youngsters.

One night, however, William sneaks into the living room to watch a group talking and spitting tobacco juice into the spittoons from long distances with amazing accuracy. A brawny lumberjack named Grizzly Bear catches William and embarrasses him by making him also use a spittoon. Months later, William gets his revenge by over-peppering Grizzly's soup so he can't stop sneezing.

Ma works night and day even though two young girls, Erin and Maureen, are hired to help. She has little time for her children and Frances, who would like to know about her father and their marriage, feels this absence of family time very keenly. When Uncle Matt suffers a debilitating mine accident in Cobalt, Aunt Annie makes a surprising suggestion: that they all move south to Hamilton, where jobs are available in the steel mills (much safer than the mines) and where she has found a huge house that could also be used for boarders. Again they move. The new household includes not only Ma and Aunt Tracey and their families, but also Joe's family—wife Vinka and daughter Novenka—who have arrived from Croatia. The house, unfortunately, is situated across from the city dump and the air is filled with both the stench of garbage and the suffocating fumes of the steel mills. Hoards of rats add to the problem but soon the house is full of family and boarders.

The blended families live harmoniously together and some fun is added to their lives by a visit from Aunt Elsie, the much-married, effervescent sister from Calumet. Besides cooking and cleaning during the day, Ma takes a night job in a laundry. She eventually become so run down that she catches pneumonia and is at death's door until the doctor administers a new drug that saves her life. Frances, now 10, helps nurse her mother, and during this period she learns more about her father, whom she often feels visits her in her thoughts and dreams like a messenger bringing her peace and hope.

The family becomes fond of a young boarder from Austria, Johan Michich. When he dies in an auto accident, his friend Frank Stampfl arrives from Austria, first to collect Johan's things and then to visit, particularly with Ma, who has recovered and given up the laundry job. Their friendship grows into a romance. Soon Frank acquires a plot of land in nearby Stoney Creek with the hopes of becoming a fruit farmer. The family and neighbors help with the planting and the building of a house. Frances has become a teenager, happily riding her bike around the area, often with her pet dog, a stray she has named Poochie. She, too, adores Frank and looks forward to moving with her mother from the boarding house to the farm.

Before the marriage, Ma, with Frances and Frank, travels to Cobalt. It is twelve years since they left and Cobalt has become a ghost town. They visit the cemetery and while Frank cuts the heavy grass that has grown unchecked in their absence, mother and daughter look at the grave, united in their loss and their love. Young Frances thinks, "Pa was not there in the ground anymore. He had moved on, like us."

Passages for Booktalking

Pa is killed and laid out (pp. 3–8); the settlement with the mine and the decision to stay in Cobalt (pp. 20–22); the letter from Croatia (pp. 23–24); and planting the garden and the groundhog incident (pp. 41-46).

Themes and Subjects

This story of resilience, fortitude, and survival is told in deceptively simple but elegant prose that is often poetic. Ma's story is both heart-breaking and inspiring and the growth and maturation of the sensitive, generous Frances is also moving. The book accurately describes the hardscrabble life during the Great Depression, particularly that of new immigrants. Details of Croatian beliefs, superstitions, and culture are well integrated into the story. The mystical ability to communicate with the dead and be influenced by them and the visions that these experiences produce are believably portrayed. The joys and problems involved in extended, intergenerational family life are important elements in the story. Other subjects include: Canada, Ontario, mines and mining, boarding houses, silver and gold, death, mining accidents, steel mills, brothers and sisters, and family devotion and solidarity.

ADDITIONAL SELECTIONS

Canada

Burtinshaw, Julie. *The Freedom of Jenny* (Raincoast, 2006, pap. $7.95) (Grades 5–8)
Jenny and her family, all recently freed slaves, journey to a wild British Columbia island to establish a homestead in this tale based on fact.

Crook, Connie Brummel. *The Perilous Year* (Fitzhenry and Whiteside, 2003, pap. $7.95) (Grades 5–7)
Eleven-year-old twins Alex and Ryan have many adventures, including an encounter with pirates, in this adventure story set in 18th-century Canada.

Doyle, Brian. *Pure Spring* (Groundwood, 2007, $16.99) (Grades 6–10)
In this sequel to *Boy O'Boy* (Groundwood, 2004, $16.99), 15-year-old Martin O'Day lies about his age to get a job and is blackmailed as a result.

Duble, Kathleen Bonner. *Quest* (Simon, 2008, $16.99) (Grades 5–8)
The story of Henry Hudson's ill-fated last voyage to find a northwest passage to the Orient is told from several points of view, including that of the explorer and his son John.

Horrocks, Anita. *Almost Eden* (Tundra, 2006, pap. $9.95) (Grades 5–8)
Elsie, age 12, who is growing up in a Mennonite community on the Canadian prairies in the 1960s, questions her faith when her loving mother falls deeper into depression.

Hunter, Bernice Thurman. *The Girls They Left Behind* (Fitzhenry and Whiteside, 2005, pap. $9.95) (Grades 7–10)
Life on the home front during World War II is revealed in this story of 17-year-old Beryl living in Toronto in 1943.

Joselyn, Marthe. *Mabel Riley: A Reliable Tale of Humdrum, Peril, and Romance* (Candlewick, 2004, $15.99) (Grades 5–9)
In diary form, this story tells of a 14-year-old girl who in the year 1901 accompanies her teacher sister to Stratford, Ontario.

Major, Kevin. *Ann and Sea* (Groundwood, 2003, $16.95) (Grades 5–9)
This story based on fact recounts a shipwreck off the coast of Newfoundland in the 19th century and the romance that develops between a girl and the young sailor she has rescued.

Slade, Arthur. *Megiddo's Shadow* (Random House, 2006, $17.99) (Grades 5–9)
When his brother is killed in World War I, Edward, a farm boy from Saskatchewan, enlists and experiences the horrors of war.

Taylor, Joanne. *There You Are: A Novel* (Tundra, 2004, pap. $8.95) (Grades 4–7)
On post-World War II Cape Breton Island, 12-year-old Jeannie lives in a remote community and longs for a friend.

Trottier, Maxine. *Sister of the Wolf* (Kids Can, 2004, $16.95) (Grades 6–9)
This novel set in Quebec in the early 18th century tells how Cecile, the daughter of a fur trader, buys an Indian slave to save him from abuse.

Latin America

Belpré, Pura. *Firefly Summer* (Pinata, 1996, pap. $9.95) (Grades 5–8)
This gently story depicts family and community life in rural Puerto Rico as experienced by young Teresa Rodrigo at the turn of the last century.

Danticat, Edwidge. *Anacaona* (Scholastic, 2005, $10.95) (Grades 5–8)
The effects of the coming of the white man on a Native American culture are described in this novel about Anacaona, a royal maiden living in 15th-century Haiti.

Engle, Margarita. *The Poet Slave of Cuba: A Biography of Juan Francisco Mansano* (Holt, 2006, $16.95) (Grades 6–10)
Told in free verse, this is the true story of the boyhood of a 19th-century Cuban slave and how, after learning to read and write, he began to write poetry.

Flores-Gulbis, Enrique. *Raining Sardines* (Roaring Brook, 2007, $16.99) (Grades 6–9)

Two boys growing up in pre-revolutionary Cuba are determined to rescue some wild horses slated for destruction by a rich landowner.

Kirwan, Anna. *Lady of Palenque, Flower of Bacal* (Scholastic, 2004, $10.95) (Grades 6–9)
Set at the time of Mayan supremacy in Latin America, this novel involves a spoiled princess and her hazardous journey to the land where she will marry the king of Xuchpi.

Lattimore, Deborah N. *The Flame of Peace: A Tale of the Aztecs* (HarperCollins, 1987, pap. $7.95) (Grades 4–6)
Told with folktale-like elements, this story also reveals fascinating information about the lifestyle of the Aztecs.

Mikaelsen, Ben. *Tree Girl* (HarperTempest, 2004, $16.99) (Grades 7–10)
This first-person account by a Mayan teenager tells of the horrors of the civil war fought in Guatemala.

Vande Grikek, Susan. *A Gift for Ampato* (Groundwood, 1999, $14.95) (Grades 5–8)
Set in the days of the ancient Incas, this story tells about a young girl, Tinto, who has been chosen as a human sacrifice to the gods.

Whelan, Gloria. *The Disappeared* (Dial, 2008, $16.99) (Grades 7–12)
In 1976 in Argentina during a time of terror and oppression, police enter Silvia's home in Buenos Aires and drag off her beloved older brother, for whom she is willing to sacrifice everything.

CHAPTER 8

United States

DISCOVERY AND COLONIAL PERIOD

CURRY, JANE LOUISE. *A Stolen Life.* McElderry, 1999, $16 (978-0-689-82732-7); pap. Scholastic, $4.50 (978-0-439-48908-9) (Grades 5–8)

Introduction

Jane Louise Curry was born on a farm in East Liverpool, Ohio, on September 24, 1932. As a child she enjoyed both reading and writing. At age nine she began writing fairy-tale plays and in junior and senior high school wrote stories and articles for school newspapers and also enjoyed acting in school productions. Later she acted in professional summer theaters and studied acting and creative writing in college. After a stint as an art teacher, she earned a master's degree in English at the University of California at Los Angeles and later a Ph.D. in English from Stanford University. While studying on a Fulbright grant in London, she began working with a group of Girl Guides and told them American Indian folktales. She was encouraged to write these down and from this came her first book, *Down from the Lonely Mountain* (Harcourt, Brace, 1967, o.p.). She has since written about forty more books for young readers in a number of different genres: fantasy, adventure, time travel, historical fiction, and stories of Native Americans (see *The Black Canary* in Chapter 4). She once said, "I find great satisfaction in involving children in other places, people and times," and her advice for young writers is, "Read, read, read. That's the way to get to know what makes a good story. Then, when you write stories or draw pictures to go with stories, put in details, the more the better—that will help to make your story or pictures come alive for your audience."

A Stolen Life covers almost three years, from late 1748 to 1750, in the life of Jamesina (Jamie) Mackenzie and takes place principally in Scotland, on the Atlantic ocean, and in Virginia. It is a third-person narrative and, although the opening chapters may be a bit confusing, the plot gradually becomes more focused and ultimately very rewarding.

Historical Background

This novel takes place during the reign of George II (1683–1760) and his wife, Queen Caroline. His reign lasted from 1727 to October 1760. Allegiance to the Stuart family's claim to the British throne remained strong in different areas during this period, particularly in the Scottish Highlands, where loyalty to Charles Edward Stuart, known as Bonnie Prince Charles or the Young Pretender, was common. In an ill-advised move, Charles, who was born in Rome and brought up speaking French, decided to restore the Stuart line by sailing from France and landing on the west coast of Scotland in July 1745 with only a few companions (promised French aid did not materialize). At first, with the support of the Highlanders, he gained many successes and invaded England but when his English followers, the Jacobites, failed to materialize, he was forced to retreat. He and his troops suffered a calamitous defeat at Culloden, near Inverness, on April 16, 1746. He became a fugitive and fled across the Highlands, finally escaping on a French frigate to France in October. The English dealt unmercifully with the Pretender's defeated forces. A few of the survivors, like Jamesina's father in the novel, also fled to France. Charles died without children and, with his death, the Stuart claim to the throne essentially ended.

The practice of having indentured servants in the American colonies was prevalent during the 17th and 18th centuries. It has been estimated that between one-half and two-thirds of all immigrants to America during colonial times came as indentured servants. In some colonies, 75 percent of the population was indentured. Unlike slavery (which existed alongside the indenture system for a time but later became more widespread in the South) it was a source of short-term labor. Tobacco growing is a labor-intensive business and in such states as Virginia indentured laborers were common.

Terms of indenture varied: for some it was four to seven years; minors' terms ended when they reached twenty-one. The servant received passage, lodging, board, and "freedom dues" on completion of his or her service. These dues often consisted of a tract of land, a year's worth of corn, arms, a cow, and new clothes. To encourage the importation of indentured servants, plantation owners were often given inducements such as 50 acres of land per servant. The cost of a servant varied with skills and talents. Most servants without any particular qualifications sold themselves to an agent or sea captain who would receive his money from the buyer of the servant when the ship landed. Criminals could often choose to be indentured rather than face the death penalty or a prison sentence. Debtors could also choose to be indentured and churches sometimes indentured orphans rather than trying to feed them. At times, entire families, facing starvation, would become indentured even though it meant separation.

Conditions on the ships carrying these servants were appalling. Many died before reaching America. Treatment on the plantations was also often cruel and inhumane. Because of the arduous work and terrible living conditions, many servants died before completing the terms of their contracts. Indentured servants were not allowed to marry or have children. As the demand for cheap labor increased in the colonies, so did the price of indentured servants. The result was that more and more plantation owners bought African slaves instead. This shift to owning slaves rather than hiring indentured servants continued into the 19th century.

In *A Stolen Life*, Jamesina is the victim of "spiriters," brigands who kidnapped children and smuggled them onto ships to be transported to America and sold as indentured servants. This practice was unlawful and punishable by prison terms. If a servant could prove that he or she had been forced into service by spiriters, his or her freedom would be restored.

The French and Indian Wars lasted from 1754 to 1763 and were part of what Europeans call the Seven Years' War. The Cherokee Indians were one group of Native Americans involved in the conflict. At one time the Cherokee Nation spread across eight states from Virginia and West Virginia in the north to Alabama and Georgia in the south. Itsati, near present-day Vonore in Tennessee, was the largest of the Overhill Cherokee towns. Ocomostata (Aganstata) (1710–1783), the great Cherokee warrior, was once a resident of this town. Today, the site is under the waters of the Tellico Reservoir, which was created by Tellico Dam. Most Cherokees were forcefully removed to the west, principally to present-day Oklahoma, in the 1830s.

Principal Characters
SCOTLAND
> Jamesina Mackenzie, a Highland girl
> Allan Graeme, Jamesina's uncle by marriage
> Aunt Mairi, Allan's wife
> Murdo (Murdock Mackenzie of Grudidh), Jamesina's father
> Dougal, Hector Macrae's grandson
> Roderick Mackenzie (Big Rorie), Jamesina's grandfather
> Rorie, Jamesina's youngest brother

Kenneth, Davie, and Donald, her other brothers

ON THE *SPARROWHAWK*
    Captain Lumsden, the ship's captain
    Crookie, the cook's young helper
    Mr. Reece, the first mate
    Shrankie (Peter Cochran), an 8-year-old boy
    Attercap (Archie Gordon), a 15-year-old indentured servant
    Justice and Mrs. Moon, passengers

VIRGINIA
    Colonel Robert Leslie, a plantation owner
    Chal (Chalmers) Leslie, his son
    Mrs. Caroline Leslie, the Colonel's wife
    Adelaide Leslie, her daughter
    Mr. Mollison, the plantation manager
    Royal, a slave
    Mariyaama, another slave
    Biggs and Mrs. Biggs, two formerly indentured servants
    Nanychi, a Cherokee woman
    Tsulu, her husband

Plot Synopsis

It is October 1758 in the coastal Highlands of Scotland, and proud, independent Jamesina Mackenzie is awaiting word about her family. Her mother is dead and she has not seen her father, Mackenzie of Grudidh (nicknamed Murdo), and her youngest brother, Rorie, for four years since their defeat serving in Bonnie Prince Charlie's forces at the battle of Culloden and their flight from the troops of King George II to safety in France. Her three oldest brothers—Kenneth, Davie, and Donald—are fighting the French and the Indians with the Seventy-seventh Highlanders, part of Montgomery's Rifles, in the New World, presumably in Quebec. Jamesina's father was a prosperous farmer. In his absence, the land and Jamesina have been cared for by faithful, trustworthy Allan Graeme, and his wife, Mairi, Jamesina's aunt. News arrives that Murdo and his son, still fugitives from the Redcoats, have been seen in Scotland. To avoid suspicion, Jamesina is sent, as planned, to visit with her grandfather Roderick (called Big Rorie) and his family. She is accompanied by a boy she has known all her life, devoted Dougal, old Hector Macrae's grandson. Dougal is infatuated with the indifferent Jamesina and has promised to fulfill a family pledge to protect and defend her during her father's absence.

During Halloween celebrations at Big Rorie's, news comes that Jamesina's father and brother have been murdered by the Redcoats. Fearful that the English might also seek out Jamesina, it is decided that she must be disguised as a boy and go to live with the Macraes as Dougal's "brother." She is beginning to adjust to her new life as "Jamie" when another calamity strikes. While she and Dougal are playing on the beach, they are surprised by spiriters. Dougal is struck on the head and left for dead, but Jamie is dragged to a waiting rowboat and taken to a ship, the *Sparrowhawk*, which is bound first for Glasgow then Virginia. Still masquerading as a boy, Jamie meets some of her fellow captives held belowdecks including a pathetic 8-year-old, Shrankie, and 15-year-old Attercap (whose real name is Archie Gordon). Each has a horrendous story of abduction and imprisonment.

Jamie's ruse is discovered and she is sent to a more comfortable passenger cabin where she joins eleven other girls. At Glasgow, regular passengers, including Justice Moon and his wife, come on board, but Jamie's hopes of telling someone in authority of her illegal abduction are thwarted when she and the others are denied access to the passengers. Her only news of the ship's progress comes from Mr. Reece, the first mate, and Crookie, the young cook's apprentice. The trip across the Atlantic is horrendous, and three boys and one girl die. At Virginia, the captives are taken to Richmond, where they are sold to plantation owners. Jamie, who has become sullen and uncooperative, is in the last "batch" of captives along with Attercap and Shrankie. The three are bought for fifteen pounds by the foppish Chal Leslie, son of Colonel Robert Leslie, who owns the Shaw tobacco plantation.

On the plantation, Jamie meets the penny-pinching mistress, Caroline Leslie; her daughter, Adelaide; and the estate manager, Mr. Mollison; but becomes most friendly with some of the slaves including the cook, Mariyaama, and the aptly named chief footman, Royal. Months pass. Shrankie, who had been in fragile health, dies, and an apathetic Colonel Leslie says a short prayer before the coffin is lowered into the ground. Although Jamie's living conditions could be much worse, she broods over the injustice of her situation and plans to somehow get word to Justice Moon in Richmond about her status in time for the spring assizes. Prince points out to her that her situation is much better than that of a slave, who has no hope of freedom. Nevertheless, he helps her with her plan to write letters to Justice Moon. But the Colonel has other plans for Jamie and Attercap. Realizing that they were kidnapped by spiriters and that he could be liable as an accessory, the Colonel decides to dispose of the two by making them part of the freedom dues owed to Mr. Biggs, one of his indentured servants, who plans on moving west with his wife.

The Biggs's two grown sons await them at a log cabin they have constructed on the 50-acre plot that is also part of the freedom package. Jamie and Attercap are bound, put in the Biggs's wagon, and taken to their property. At the cabin, the Biggs--a detestable couple whom the two captives instantly dislike—are greeted by their sons, who are accompanied by two beautiful horses that they claim to have found. With their hands still tied, Jamie and Attercap are hoisted into the cabin's loft. That night, Cherokees attack, seeking revenge for the theft of their horses. The Biggs family is massacred but Jamie and Attercap are spared because of their innocence. They are placed under the care of a Cherokee woman named Nanychi and her warrior husband Tsulu and taken by their captors on long treks inland: first to the Cherokee town of Itsati and later to other encampments, always avoiding the English army base at Fort St. George.

Both captives are impressed with the Cherokee mores and cultural rituals. The maneuvering of the Indians is in preparation for a battle with the English, some of whom, Jamie learns, wear kilts—meaning they must be Highlanders. When fighting appears imminent, Nanychi thoughtfully suggests that Jamie and Attercap leave the area and seek safety. As they wander in the forest, they are met by Dougal Macrae. After recovering from his wound, he remained faithful to his family oath to protect Jamesina and followed her to Virginia. Unable to find her, he continued west to her brothers' regiment, which had returned south after serving in Quebec. Jamesina is soon reunited with her three brothers, including Kenneth, who was wounded in the skirmish. Both she and Attercap receive their freedom. Attercap decides to stay in Virginia and seek his fortune but Jamesina, now fifteen, and Dougal and Kenneth board a ship bound for Scotland and their beloved Highlands.

Passages for Booktalking
Jamesina is caught by spiriters (pp. 33–35); how the spiriters operate (pp. 49–53); life aboard the *Sparrowhawk* including a storm (pp. 68–73); the auction and sale of Jamesina to the Leslies of Shaw Plantation (pp. 87–91).

Themes and Subjects
The reader is introduced to three different lifestyles and cultures. The first is that of the rugged, fiercely independent, highly principled Scottish Highlanders. The second is the self-indulgent, artificial life on a colonial tobacco plantation, where prosperity comes from exploiting others; and the last is the Cherokee, portrayed as an industrious, ethical people who were used by the settlers. The author has also created a number of fascinating characters including the high-spirited, resourceful Jamesina, who gains maturity through adversity. Other subjects: indentured servants, slavery, Virginia, Bonnie Prince Charlie, George II, ships, "spiriting," death, friendship, family life, loyalty, perseverance, frontier life, the French and Indian Wars, and tobacco.

DURRANT, LYNDA. *The Beaded Moccasins: The Story of Mary Campbell.* Clarion, 1998, $15 (978-0-395-85398-6); pap. Dell, $5.99 (978-0-440-41591-6) (Grades 5–9)

Introduction

Lynda Durrant was born on December 17, 1954, in Cleveland. After a move to Virginia, her family returned to Ohio when the author was entering the first grade. She has both bachelor's and master's degrees and is married with one child. She lives on a horse farm near Bath, Ohio, where she teaches remedial reading, and enjoys swimming, skiing, and riding a horse named Irish. She has written six historical novels for young readers. Many are fictionalized biographies and deal with the hardships and struggles of frontier life for both the white pioneers and the American Indians. Durrant's later novel, *My Last Skirt: The Story of Jennie Hodgers, Union Soldier* (Clarion, 2006, $16; 0618574905), is based on the real-life adventures of a woman who spent her life as a man. Jennie Hodgers was an Irish immigrant who wore pants when farming in Ireland and continued the disguise in America, where she found more job opportunities and better pay as a man than as a woman. To increase her wages, Jennie volunteered for the Union Army during the Civil War. She served three years in combat including the 18-month siege of Vicksburg. She was the only woman on either side to receive a war pension and continued the deception for more than fifty years. This fascinating book is a suitable companion to *The Beaded Moccasins*, the first-person narrative of another courageous woman, Mary Campbell. This novel takes place chiefly in frontier Ohio over a period of two years, from mid-1759 through 1761.

Historical Background

In a six-page Afterword, the author supplies interesting factual information about the Delaware Indians, Mary Campbell, and the political situation in the 1750s. The Delaware Indians are more correctly called the Lenape, a word meaning "the people." They originally lived along the Delaware River in what is today New Jersey and Pennsylvania. They were large-scale farmers who used flint, stone, wood, and bone tools. They were also excellent hunters and fishermen.

In 1737 the "Walking Purchase" occurred between the Lenape and the relatives and agents of William Penn, who had returned to England. The white men falsely told the Indians that the Indians' ancestors had deeded to the Penns all the land that could be covered by a day-and-a-half walk. Wishing to comply with the treaty, the Lenape agreed but were tricked out of their land when the Penns hired three runners who were able to "walk" 55 miles. Thus began the westward migration of the Lenape. Later, the Easton Treaty between the Lenape and the British promised the Indians land farther west and resulted in another move. They migrated first to Ohio (Oya Hohing in the book), then to Indiana, Missouri, Kansas, and finally to the Indian Territory, which later became Oklahoma.

The return of white settlers held in Ohio by the Lenape and other tribes was engineered by Colonel Henry Bouquet, who had led a large force of soldiers into the territory in 1763–1764 and relieved the siege of Fort Pitt, the fort that was situated at present-day Pittsburgh. The Lenape, together with other tribes, were defeated at the Battle of Bushy Run. In October 1764, meetings were held with the Indian leaders at Fort Pitt. Facing destruction if they did not comply, the Indians released sixty former captives including Mary Campbell, who was in her late teens. She had spent six years with the Lenape. After her release, she returned to Pennsylvania, married Joseph Wilford in 1770, and had several children before her death in 1801.

During the Revolutionary War, the Lenape signed a treaty with the future United States government to supply warriors and scouts in exchange for food and supplies, and Fort Pitt became the headquarters of the western theater of the war. Recently parts of the fort have been excavated and restored and are on display in the Fort Pitt Museum.

Principal Characters

Mary Campbell, a 12-year-old girl
Dougal, Mary's brother
Mr. and Mrs. Campbell, her parents
Mrs. Stewart, a neighbor
Sammy Stewart, her 2-year-old son
Netawatwees Sachem, the leader of the Turtle clan
Smallpox Scars, one of Mary's kidnappers
Meriem, Mary's Lenape mother
Coquetakeghton or White Eyes, her Lenape father
Chickadee, Meriem's young daughter
Francois Sequin, a French-Canadian fur trader
Kolachuisen or Beautiful Bluebird, Mary's friend

Plot Synopsis

Mary Caroline Campbell is unhappy with her situation and her family—her mother, father, and older brother Dougal. Her father, in his desire to go "westering," has moved them from their comfortable civilized existence in Fairfield,

Connecticut, to the backwoods of Pennsylvania, where they are homesteading in a crude log cabin far from dear friends and family. To add to Mary's frustration, her mother assigns Mary arduous chores while Dougal leads a privileged life simply because he is a boy. On her twelfth birthday, May 11, 1759, while her father is out hunting with his neighbor Mr. Stewart, Mary receives a beautiful hand-sewn dress with a lacy store-bought chemise. Although it should be a special day for her, her mother uncharitably orders her to churn the butter. Mary rebels and, in her finery, runs away to the meadow to dwell on her unhappiness. She suddenly realizes she is not alone. She is seized and handcuffed with rope by a group of five Indians, who also take captive her neighbor, Mrs. Stewart, and Mrs. Stewart's 2-year-old son Sammy. Mary begs in vain to be released and sees in the distance the family home consumed by flames. The leader of the group, an older man who speaks English, commands the captives to walk. Sammy cries continuously and becomes a burden. On the second day, one of the Indians, whom Mary has nicknamed Smallpox Scars because of the pockmarks on his face takes Sammy into the woods and returns with a bloody blond scalp in his hand. Mrs. Stewart goes berserk and runs into the woods to bury her child. In the meantime, a shocked and disbelieving Mary checks the other scalps the Indians carry and is relieved that she doesn't recognize any of them. The old man tells Mary that they are members of a tribe of Delaware Indians called the Lenape, and that she is to become the daughter of the sachem, or chief, to take the place of his granddaughter who recently died.

After several days of hiking, the group reaches Mary's new home, an encampment of about two hundred Lenape on the banks of the Allegheny River. She meets her adoptive family: the sachem's daughter Meriem, who is to be Mary's new "mother;" Meriem's husband Coquetakeghton or White Eyes, and their cute young daughter whom Mary calls Chickadee. Mary is surprised to learn that the leader of her kidnappers, Netawatwees Sachem, is now her grandfather. Before Mary can adjust to her new surroundings, the group begins packing their belongings for a migration west to Oya Hohing, where the white men have promised them land and peace. They walk for several weeks under unbelievably harsh conditions. It takes ten weeks to reach Fort Pitt and, while passing the fort, Mary dreams of a possible escape. She is given a heavy backpack of cornmeal to carry. Soon every bone and muscle in her body aches and, although the straps on the backpack cause bleeding wounds, she endures the pain and hardship. Her birthday dress and chemise are in tatters, so she must put on the buckskin clothes that the others wear.

She becomes, however, increasingly fond of her new family and learns their language in order to communicate with them. Meriem is particularly kind and understanding and one day gives Mary a pair of lovely beaded moccasins that once belonged to her deceased daughter. Mary decides to save them for special occasions. She makes a new friend, a girl her age named Kolachuisan (Beautiful Bluebird) and they both play with adorable little Chickadee. Finally, the Delaware reach their destination and their new home. The clan moves into their winter quarters, a large cave on the side of a cliff overlooking the Cuyahoga River. It is a harsh winter, food is meager and unappetizing, and life in the cave uncomfortable and confining. Mary is amazed every morning to see the 8-year-old boys of the clan marched down to the Cuyahoga where they dunk in the icy water through holes cut in the ice. The purpose of the ritual is to produce strength and fortitude. Mary decides she, too, must build her strength by jumping in one of the ice holes. She does but is trapped under the ice. Fortunately White Eyes has followed her and saves her from drowning. Although everyone admires her courage, she is scolded for her foolhardiness.

As spring approaches, Grandfather Sachem, accompanied by Mary, her father, and two other braves, hike to sell their furs at the trading post on Lac du Chat (Lake Erie) operated by French-Canadian fur trader Francois Sequin. On the way, they share a cave one night with a hibernating bear and her two cubs. Sequin's post is a shambles and he is dirty, disheveled, and generally repulsive. However, he is honest and the group returns with much-needed cloth, kettles, and gunpowder. In the summer, the clan moves outdoors to the plain above the cliff where they build their wigwams and plant crops of corn, pumpkin, squash, and beans. While Mary is becoming assimilated into the clan, Mrs. Stewart remains aloof and alienated. Mary's new grandfather, at the end of his patience and sensing the group's growing hostility toward Mrs. Stewart, sells her to Sequin to be his bride. Mary is aghast but realizes that this fate is better than possible death by a disaffected tribe. Her new grandfather is often severe and forbidding but Mary grows to admire and respect his knowledge and wisdom. At times, he enthralls her by telling tribal folktales.

A few weeks later, Mary and others revisit Sequin and find that Mrs. Stewart, now Mrs. Sequin, has transformed the house into a clean, attractive dwelling, and has also transformed her new husband, who is now attired in a shirt and tie. Before harvest time, a deluge arrives with rains so heavy that the earth around the plants begins to wash away. The tribe feverishly tries to build canals to drain off the water. No one works harder than Mary, who digs in the earth with such ferocity that her hands bleed. Everyone is in awe of her great contribution. When the rains end, most of the plants are saved and replanted. To show their appreciation, the tribe agrees with Netawatness Sachem to formally admit Mary into the tribe. She beams with pride when she is named "Woman-Who-Has-Saved-the-Corn."

In a postscript, the author tells that after six years in captivity, Mary was returned to her parents. It is said that she left the Delaware with reluctance. Mrs. Stewart also left Ohio and returned to her husband.

Passages for Booktalking

Mary and Mrs. Stewart are captured (pp. 19–25); Sammy is murdered and Mary checks the scalps (pp. 28–33); Netawatwees Sachem tells Mary a folktale (pp. 73–76); the 8-year-olds' trial by ice (pp. 76–79); and Mary receives a doll from Mrs. Stewart (pp. 78–79).

Themes and Subjects.

Mary's search for identity and her true self is made difficult by living in two cultures, but she is able slowly to reconcile both and emerge a mature person. Her transformation from a petulant child to a responsible, unselfish young woman is well portrayed. Her thoughts comparing the comforts and friendships of Connecticut life with the spartan but honest life of the Indians are interesting and although she is ashamed of her former childish behavior, she becomes mature enough to understand and forgive herself. The everyday life and beliefs of the Delaware are accurately portrayed, as is Mary's struggle to understand the values of her new family. Other subjects include: Pennsylvania, folklore, family stories, scalping, death, fur trading, Ohio, Lake Erie, marriage, agriculture, colonial times, relations between the Native Americans and the settlers, the French and Indian Wars, frontier life, captivity stories, and cultural differences.

PETRY, ANN. *Tituba of Salem Village.* Harper, 1964, o.p.; pap. $6.95 (978-0-06-440403-7) (Grades 6–9)

Introduction

Ann Petry (1908–1997) was born and died in the same charming coastal Connecticut town of Old Saybrook. Her parents, both African Americans, were successful middle-class professionals: her father was a pharmacist and her mother, a chiropodist and shop owner. Only once as a child did Petry experience racial prejudice when at age four she was attacked by a gang of white children, who were later punished. Although she was encouraged in school to become a writer, she became a pharmacist. After she married and moved to New York, she observed the hardship and discrimination experienced by many blacks in America. She began writing articles for newspapers and magazines. She wrote her most famous novel for adults in 1946. It was called *The Street* and with it she gained critical and popular success. Petry has been compared to Richard Wright, another writer of realistic fiction depicting the black community. Her writing for a younger audience first gained recognition with her 1955 biography of Harriet Tubman. Petry always had a special interest in slavery, believing that school textbooks did not give "an adequate or accurate picture of the history of slavery in the United States."

Tituba of Salem Village appeared in 1964. It begins in 1688, when Tituba of the title is 29, and ends with her release from a Boston prison in 1693.

Historical Background

The historic city of Salem in eastern Massachusetts is situated on Massachusetts Bay about 15 miles northeast of Boston. It is noted for being the center of the notorious witch trials of 1692. The problems began when 9-year-old Betsey Parris—whose father was the Reverend Samuel Parris—and her cousin, 11-year-old Abigail Williams, began having seizures during which they screamed, grunted, rolled on the floor, and contorted themselves into strange positions. They also complained about being pinched and physically abused by their housekeeper, a slave named Tituba. Then other girls began to exhibit similar bizarre behavior. Clergy members and concerned citizens investigated and three people were arrested for "infecting" the girls. They were Tituba, a poor beggar named Sarah Good, and social outcast Sarah Osborne, who had married her indentured servant and rarely went to church. All three were sent to prison in Boston. The hysteria increased and resulted in more accusations. More than one hundred and fifty people were arrested and imprisoned. Of these, nineteen (fourteen women and five men) were hanged and one, an 80-year-old man, was crushed to death with stones. Having been excommunicated by their churches, the executed were buried in unmarked graves.

At this time, the Puritans believed that invisible beings lived among humans and influenced their lives. Preachers spoke about the devil and his demons, who were capable of possessing the bodies of living humans. In addition, the life of a Puritan was filled with what we today would call repression and superstition. Toys and games were discouraged; women were subservient to men and thought to be easily led into sin by the devil. Much of the evidence used against accused witches was "spectral," that is, invisible to all but the accuser. Because it was believed that the devil could assume a person's shape only with that person's consent, testimony about these apparitions was considered proof that the accused was in league with Satan. Witches could be identified by using a "witch cake," which is described in the novel. Another method of proving guilt was the "touch test." An accused witch describes this test: "We were blindfolded, and our hands were laid upon the afflicted persons, they being in their fits. Some led us and laid our hands upon them, and then they said they were well and that we were guilty of afflicting them whereupon we were seized as prisoners." Gradually, the hysteria subsided and reason was restored. In May of 1693, all prisoners accused of witchcraft were pardoned.

The true life story of Tituba is clouded in controversy. Most believe that she was not an African slave but originally from an Arawak village in Venezuela and therefore an Indian. As a child she was captured and sold as a slave in Barbados, where she was bought by merchant trader Samuel Parris (who later became a minister) and brought to Boston in 1686 with another slave named John. In 1689, she married John and moved with Parris and his family to Salem. After Betsey, Parris's daughter, began having fits and witchcraft was suspected, Tituba was beaten into a confession. She provided evidence against the other two women accused alongside her and was sent to prison. Later she rescinded her confession. After thirteen months in prison she was released when an unknown person paid the seven-pound debt for her upkeep. It is unknown what happened to her under her new master. Tituba is also a character in Arthur Miller's play *The Crucible.*

In the novel, a number of the female characters are "bound girls," another name for indentured servants. Unlike slaves, indentured servants were usually white and were kept in service for only a specific period of time: usually seven years or, in the case of children, until the age of twenty-one. Their owners were bound to give these servants food, clothing, and shelter. Adults often became indentured in order to gain passage to America. Children became indentured to escape orphanages or after being sold into servitude by their parents for passage money or other needs.

The city of Salem is also the birthplace of Nathaniel Hawthorne; the home of Nathaniel Bowditch, the famous navigator; and the location of the House of Seven Gables.

Principal Characters

Tituba, a slave woman
John Indian, her husband
Susanna Endicott, their mistress
Reverend Samuel Parris, John and Tituba's later owner
Mistress Parris, Samuel's sickly wife
Betsey, the Parris's daughter
Abigail, the Parris's spiteful niece
Pim, a stowaway
Samuel Conklin, a Boston weaver
Goodwife Mary Sibley, a Salem resident
Sergeant Thomas and Mistress Anne Putnam, a prominent Salem couple
Anne Putnam, Jr., their daughter
Mercy Lewis, the Putnams' bound girl
Goody Good, a homeless beggar
Dorkas, her daughter

Deacon Ingersoll, a townsperson
Mary Walcott, Mary Warren, Elizabeth Hubbard, local girls
Gammer Osburne, an old lady
Justices John Hathorne and Jonathan Corwin, judges

Plot Synopsis

It is 1688 in the city of Bridgetown on the island of Barbados, where 19-year-old Tituba and John, her husband of ten years, are slaves in the amiable household of their widowed mistress, Susanna Endicott. Their agreeable, secure lifestyle comes to an abrupt end one November day when Mistress Endicott informs them that, because of financial difficulties (later revealed to be gambling debts), she has sold both of them to the Reverend Samuel Parris, who is sailing that day for Boston to seek a church appointment.

Besides an ailing, compassionate wife, the Parris household also consists of an impressionable, fragile daughter—5-year-old Betsey—and their mean-spirited, troublemaking niece, Abigail, age 8. Reverend Parris is a dour, solitary man who makes a real show of his religiosity. While on the ship, Tituba discovers a teenaged stowaway named Pim. She helps feed him but spiteful Abigail reveals his hiding place. Much later Tituba learns that, as punishment, he has been indentured to a tavern keeper named Ingersoll in Salem, Massachusetts. In Boston, Reverend Parris unsuccessfully looks for a parish and, to make ends meet, rents out John to a tavern keeper and Tituba to their neighbor Samuel Conklin. While working in the Conklin household Tituba learns to be an expert spinner of thread. John is disturbed after witnessing the hanging of an old woman for witchcraft. They spend a miserably cold winter in Boston.

During the following spring and summer Reverend Parris completes negotiations with representatives of Salem Village, a community about 15 miles away, and accepts an appointment there even though the terms of the contract are not as generous as he had expected. At the dilapidated parsonage, they are greeted by Goodwife Sibley, who helps Tituba put the sickly Mrs. Parris to bed. The house is in great disrepair, the garden overgrown, and the well poisoned, but Tituba conscientiously begins to correct matters. One day they are visited by an unkempt, rancid-smelling beggar named Goody Good and her 4-year-old waif-like daughter, Dorkas. Reverend Parris, characteristically, turns them away.

In exchange for a cow and a mare, John is hired out to Deacon Ingersoll, owner of the local inn and tavern where Pim now works. With Mrs. Parris ill upstairs and the parson out visiting parishioners or preparing hellfire-and-brimstone sermons in his room, Abigail feels free to invite her new friends over. Among them are the bound girl of Nathaniel and Anne Putnam, Mercy

Lewis; the Putnams' daughter, Anne, Jr.; Elizabeth Hubbard; and another bound girl, Mary Warren. They are a flighty, hysterical lot and, under Abigail's bidding, try to induce trances in Betsey, who is impressionable and open to suggestion. In turn, they begin feigning being possessed. Mercy secures a pack of tarot cards from her boyfriend Pim and, against her better judgment, Tituba begins telling the girls' fortunes, a skill she learned from Mistress Endicott in the Bahamas. One of these sessions is interrupted by the arrival of Goody Good who demands a reading. Tituba sees her imminent death in the cards and tells her so. Mercy is persuaded by Pim to run away with him. He helps her assume a disguise as a boy by cutting off her beautiful golden tresses. At the last minute she decides to stay and, to save herself from telling the truth, claims that the devil cut her hair. She also begins having violent seizures, often timed to escape work or punishment. Soon all the girls are having these fits including Abigail, who is clearly using them to spite Tituba and to get attention. The girls begin accusing Tituba of being the power behind these bewitchings.

Soon everything Tituba does becomes suspect. When she innocently talks to a stray cat she has befriended she is accused of consorting with the devil. Even the fact that her garden has progressed phenomenally under her care is seen as a sign that witchcraft is at work. Her unusual ability at the spinning wheel is also questioned. The girls' fits, particularly Abigail's, become more extreme and vicious, and the alarm and unease of the townspeople grows. One day, Goody Sibley visits Tituba while several of the girls are present. She proposes to bake a "witch cake" made of urine and flour whose purpose is to identify if a witch is present. After the cake is baked, the first person to enter the house is a witch. Tituba, who had stepped out of the house during the baking to escape the smoke, is the first to enter, followed by Goody Good, who has come for another reading; and Gammer Osburne, a sickly woman who wants to buy some medicinal herbs from Tituba. Immediately the girls fall into fits and begin shrieking that all three are guilty of witchcraft.

Reverend Parris returns and, horrified that his house has been used for these demonic rituals, sends everyone home. He beats Tituba mercilessly until she confesses to being a witch to stop the torture. To prove that he is right, he makes Tituba perform a "touch test" on Abigail. He makes her touch Abigail during one of her fits and sees that the touch returns Abigail to normal. He fails to suspect that Abigail is maliciously using this ruse to spite Tituba. The girls often say they have seen the devil and he is in the guise of a big black man. Fearful that John will become another target, Tituba persuades him to have public fits to avert suspicion. Within days a public trial is conveyed under the direction of Justices John Hathorne and Jonathan Corwin from Boston. Tituba, Goody Good, and Gammer Osburne are accused of witchcraft and

Tituba's forced confession is held up as evidence. The "bewitched" girls provide stellar performances, each outdoing the other, and all three women are found guilty and sent to prison in Boston, where Goody Good is hanged and Gammer Osburne dies of natural causes. Tituba alone survives, and thirteen months later when the hysteria has subsided is released from prison when Samuel Conklin pays her debtor's fees. Later he also buys John and the couple is reunited. Now that the ordeal is over they hope for a better life.

Passages for Booktalking
Some interesting incidents are: Tituba and John leave the household of Mistress Endicott (pp. 1–6); Tituba discovers the stowaway Pim on the ship (pp. 15–19); John witnesses the hanging of witch Glover (pp. 61–62); and Goody Good pays the Parris household a visit (pp. 73–76).

Themes and Subjects
The use of fear and manipulation to gain power and create hysteria is impressively portrayed, as is the plight of the innocents who are the victims of this deception and trickery. The author's painstaking research and forceful presentation re-create daily life in the Massachusetts colony, the Puritan mind-set, and the fate of slaves and indentured servants at this time. Tituba emerges as a simple, well-meaning innocent who is unable to comprehend the evil that surrounds her. Other subjects include: Salem Village, witchcraft, superstition, death, Boston, the colonial period, religion, trials, justice, prisons, marriage, love, and slavery.

RINALDI, ANN. *Hang a Thousand Trees with Ribbons: The Story of Phillis Wheatley.* Harcourt, 1996, o.p.; pap. $6.95 (978-0-15-205393-2) (Grades 6–10)

Introduction
Ann Rinaldi, born in 1934, is the author of more than forty admired novels for young readers. Many of them, such as *Hang a Thousand Trees with Ribbons*, are part of the Great Episodes series, which is set in America during the colonial and revolutionary periods. Rinaldi's novels are known for their authenticity, expert plotting, and fine characterization. When she first began writing for young adults, Rinaldi produced several novels that dealt with contemporary problems. Then her 14-year-old son became part of a historical reenactment group and she developed an interest in American history. Of her writing, Rinaldi has said, "I write young adult novels because I like writing

them. But, as with my first book, I don't write for young people, I just write . . . real life . . . goes into my books. I draw all my characters fully, give my adults as many problems and as much dimension as the young protagonist . . . I give my readers good writing, literary writing."

Hang a Thousand Trees with Ribbons covers fourteen years in the life of the poet and slave Phillis Wheatley, from her abduction from Africa in 1761 at age 7 to the year 1775, when she met George Washington at age 21. (Historians differ by a year or two on the dates of her birth and death.) The story is told as a first-person narrative by Phillis. Part of it is told in flashbacks. For clarity, the plot is discussed chronologically below. The title of the book comes from something John Wheatley, Phillis's owner and benefactor, says to her. When he gives Phillis a document that grants her freedom, he says, "Do you know what I have just done? I have hung a thousand trees with ribbons."

Historical Background

In an excellent 11-page Author's Note following the story, Rinaldi separates fact from fiction in her novel and tells what happened to Phillis after the story ends in 1775. Tragically, Phillis died in 1784, at the age of only 30 and extremely poor. Phillis Wheatley had a number of "firsts" to her credit. She wrote the first full-length book published by an African American poet, she was the first African American to earn a living from writing, and she was the first African American writer encouraged and financed by a group of female sponsors. John Wheatley said of her childhood accomplishments, "Phillis was brought from Africa to America in the Year 1761, between Seven and Eight Years of Age. Without any Assistance for School Education, and by only what she was taught in the Family, she, in sixteen Months Time from her Arrival, attained the English Language, to which she was an utter Stranger before, to such a Degree, as to read any of the most difficult Parts of the Sacred Writings, to the great Astonishment of all who heard her." She wrote her first poem, "On Messrs. Hussey and Coffin," at the age of 12. With the publication of this and other poems in newspapers her renown grew. When skeptics doubted that a slave could write such poetry, Phillis appeared before a distinguished group of Boston citizens to prove she was indeed the author. With her eventual vindication she challenged the popular belief that African Americans were intellectually inferior to whites.

Her first and only published book of poetry, *Poems of Various Subjects, Religious and Moral*, appeared in 1773 when she was 19 or 20. It consisted of thirty-nine poems. Many are elegies, others reflect upon pious Christian sentiments, and many allude to mythology and ancient history. They are written in rhyming couplets and seldom make reference to the author's African American status. One exception is the eight-line verse, "On Being Brought from Africa to America," which begins, "'Twas mercy brought me from my Pagan land/Taught my benighted soul to understand" and ends, "Remember, Christians, Negroes black as Cain/May be refin'd and join th' angelic train." With this publication, Phillis became the most famous African American in the world, but this fame was not lasting. After deaths in the Wheatley family, she married a free black man named John Peters. He proved to be a ne'er-do-well who left her after a time in debtor's prison. Phillis had three children, two of whom died young. After being reduced to abject poverty while vainly hoping to see a second book of poems published, she and her third child died of malnutrition in a Boston boarding house and were buried in an unmarked grave.

Principal Characters
> Phillis Wheatley, originally named Keziah
> Obour Tanner, Phillis's friend
> Captain Quinn, captain of the slave ship *Phillis*
> Kunkle, the cruel first mate
> Mrs. Susanna Wheatley, Phillis's owner's wife
> Mr. John Wheatley, Phillis's owner
> Nathaniel Wheatley, Mr. Wheatley's son
> Mary Wheatley, Nathaniel's twin sister
> Aunt Cumsee, the Wheatleys' old servant
> Sulie, a mean, sour serving girl
> Reverend Lathrop, pastor of the Old North Church
> Cary Mae, Cumsee's sister
> Mary Enderby, a London beauty
> Aaron Lopez, a trader in slaves
> John Hancock, an influential Bostonian
> George Washington, a patriot
> John Peters, a free black man

Plot Synopsis
The time is early 1761 and the place Gambia (now Senegal) in West Africa. Keziah is only 7 years old and her idyllic life as the daughter of a great hunter on the Senegal River in Gambia comes to an abrupt end. Disobeying her mother, who fears black slavers, Keziah ventures outdoors to play with her friend Obour. The two are immediately captured and, when Keziah's mother intervenes, she too is seized. Keziah is sold for 72 cowie shells—the legal tender in this part of Africa—to Captain Quinn, the captain of the slave vessel *Phillis*, which is bound for Boston. The ocean voyage is pure hell. When it is discovered that Keziah's mother has a sore on her body, she is thrown over-

board by first mate Kunkle, who fears the spread of disease among the human cargo. When her mother vainly clings to the ship's rope, Kunkle cuts the rope and Keziah sees her mother drown. Traumatized, the young girl begins starving herself until her friend Obour, through trickery, persuades her to eat.

In Boston the girls are separately brought to auction. Obour is bought by the Tanner family from Newport, Rhode Island, and Keziah by the Wheatley family of Boston for two British pounds. Mr. Wheatley immediately names her Phillis after the dreadful ship that transported her to America. Mr. Wheatley is a wealthy, progressive trader and his family consists of his equally liberal-minded wife, Susanna, and their children, twins Nathaniel and Mary, who are ten years older than Phillis. Their servants, all black slaves, include a kindly older woman, Aunt Cumsee, the serving girl Sulie—whom Phillis soon discovers to be spiteful and jealous—and Prince, their carriage driver and handyman. Soon, Phillis astounds everyone in her new family with her intelligence and quick mind, and they realize that they own a most unusual youngster.

At first Mary is primarily responsible for Phillis but when she begins treating Phillis as a submissive plaything, Nathaniel intervenes and, along with his mother, becomes Phillis's primary teacher and an often harsh taskmaster. Phillis adores Nathaniel who, she finds, is as strong-willed and opinionated as she. One subject that causes conflict is Phillis's belief that she should be free. Nathaniel, who thinks this would be harmful for her, disagrees. He also believes that she should act like her white family. When he sees Phillis performing a water ceremony that her mother practiced, he becomes furious and forbids her to carry out any of the old rituals. When Reverend Lathrop of the Old North Church becomes Nathaniel's tutor, Phillis attends the sessions and soon become proficient not only in English, but also in Latin and Greek.

Time passes: Aunt Cumsee survives an attack of smallpox, Nathaniel makes a successful debut in business, and Mary marries the Reverend Lathrop and moves to Providence. In the colonies there is open hostility to new taxes and a growing desire for independence. At the age of 12, Phillis writes her first poem and is allowed to adopt an attractive new hairstyle. The latter is more important than the former to Phillis, but not to the Wheatleys. Soon they are spreading the word about their wonder child, and with each poem she becomes more famous and more of a celebrity. She begins to give readings at the Wheatley home and, one night, is outraged when Nathaniel forces her to give a private reading for Aaron Lopez, a customer of Nathaniel's and a prominent slave-trader. Soon there is talk of a book publication. Many prominent Bostonians, skeptical that any black could produce a work of art, form a tribunal to question her. Accompanied by Nathaniel, Phillis triumphantly parries questions from such notables as John Hancock, all of whom emerge from the meeting in awe of this young genius. Phillis's love for Nathaniel grows even though she knows dreams of a relationship are futile. Plans are made for a London publication, where financial support from wealthy sponsors has been promised.

Nathaniel, who has financial dealings in England, plans a trip and offers to take Phillis along. Before leaving, the Wheatleys visit Rhode Island where Phillis has a joyful reunion with Obour, who has settled comfortably into the Tanner household as a semi-privileged member but still a slave. In June of 1773, when Phillis is 19, she and Nathaniel arrive in London. She soon becomes the toast of the town and a sought-after guest. She is enchanted with the sights of the city and enthralled by meeting such dignitaries as Benjamin Franklin but disturbed when she learns that Nathaniel is courting a girl named Mary Enderby. A gala is planned with important society figures in attendance, many of whom are eager to help the budding writer. At the event, Phillis resents having to be polite to Aaron Lopez's sister and, when Nathaniel arrives with the beautiful blond Mary Enderby on his arm, she is flooded with such jealousy that she leaves without excusing herself. That night, back at the hotel, there is an ugly confrontation between Phillis and Nathaniel, who accuses her of being selfish, confused, and immature. The question of freedom is again discussed and, after giving her a paper asking his father to grant Phillis her freedom, Nathaniel makes arrangements for Phillis to return alone to America. They part as virtual enemies.

Upon her return, Phillis is amazed by the changes in the Wheatley residence in only five months. Prince has left to join a freedom group, Aunt Cumsee has sickened and gone to live with her sister, Cary Mae, and bossy Sulie has taken over management of the house. Both Mr. and Mrs. Wheatley are ailing and require Phillis's constant attention. Under these circumstances, Phillis doesn't give Mr. Wheatley Nathaniel's letter, but one day Mr. Wheatley spontaneously signs papers releasing her from slavery. Although touched, she does not feel the spirit of joy she anticipated. In quick succession both Aunt Cumsee and Mrs. Wheatley die but Phillis's sorrow is somewhat eased when cartons of her books arrive from London. She begins distributing them for sale among booksellers and friends. Later, she is flattered by the attention she receives from a free black greengrocer named John Peters. Nathaniel, now happily married, returns for a visit in 1775 and, sensing that revolutionary Boston is a dangerous place, has Phillis take Mr. Wheatley to Providence for a stay with Mary. Later, Phillis writes a poem in praise of George Washington. The general is so impressed that he requests a meeting with Phillis. They spend a fine afternoon together. Could this be the pinnacle of her success?

Passages for Booktalking

Some interesting passages: a conversation with John Hancock on why Phillis writes (pp. 20–24); Phillis's mother is thrown overboard from the slave ship (pp. 37–40); the slave auction during which Phillis is bought and named (pp. 45–51); and reactions to her first poem (pp. 142–146).

Themes and Subjects

Phillis is portrayed as a complex character: outwardly amiable, respectful and demure, and inwardly independent and opinionated—a self-willed person of artistic temperament who cannot accept any social status but that of a free, independent woman. The character of Nathaniel, a proper Bostonian, provides an interesting contrast in values and social standards. The horrors of slavery and its corrosive effects on both the oppressors and the oppressed are well presented. Phillis represents the conflict faced by a black girl conditioned to live in a white society. Other subjects include Boston, the American Revolution, family relations, love, social classes, colonial America, education, poetry, England, fidelity, and courage.

SCHWABACH, KAREN. *A Pickpocket's Tale.* Random House, 2006, $15.95 (978-0-375-83380-9); pap. Dell, $5.99 (978-0-375-83379-3) (Grades 5–8)

Introduction

Karen Schwabach was born in Gilbertsville, New York, and received an undergraduate degree in English from Antioch College in Ohio. She later attended the State University of New York at Albany and graduated with a degree in teaching English to speakers of other languages (TESOL). She taught for eight years in Alaska as part of a TESOL program. She lives in Winston-Salem and is a professor of teacher's education at Salem College, the oldest women's college in the United States. *A Pickpocket's Tale* is her first novel. In 2002, it won the Sydney Taylor Manuscript Award from the Association of Jewish Libraries. This annual award of $1,000 is named after the beloved writer of the All-of-a-Kind Family series and given to the best fiction manuscript by an unpublished author that has universal Jewish appeal for readers aged eight to eleven. In her acceptance speech, she said, "I chose to set [*A Pickpocket's Tale*] in New York City in the year 1730 because nothing important happened then. So I could just concentrate on the story . . . One problem I had writing the story was, I'm not Jewish." After studying books on Judaism, she finally had to rely on her Jewish friends for help in correctly portraying Jewish characters and Jewish family life. The story takes place over several months in two locations—London and New York City. It is told from the viewpoint of Molly Abraham, a feisty ten-year-old. Molly and several other characters speak in the London underworld slang of the period called Flash or Flash-cant. The author has included a useful glossary of terms at the end of the book.

Historical Background

The author supplies valuable background information in an afterword, "How Much of This Is True?" which includes a map of New York City in 1730.

The practice of indenturing servants during colonial times and the differences between slavery and indenturing are discussed earlier in this chapter in the historical background section on Jane Louise Curry's novel *A Stolen Life*.

The first Jews to arrive in New York (then known as New Amsterdam) came in 1654. They were twenty-three Jews of Spanish and Portuguese origin from Recife, Brazil. Peter Stuyvesant, then the governor of the city, wanted to deny them entry, but his decision was overturned by his council. These Sephardic Jews were later joined by some Ashkenazim, Jews from central and eastern Europe. During colonial times the Jewish population in New York remained small, numbering only slightly more than two hundred in 1730. Most of them, like Mr. Bell in the novel, were merchants. Jews generally did not have political rights in the colonies, but the exception was New York. One of the first Jewish settlers, Asher Levy, gained civil rights for Jews in New Amsterdam and, when the British peacefully took over and renamed the town New York in 1664, these rights and the tolerance established by the Dutch were retained. In 1727, Jews could become naturalized and, in 1740, Jews became full citizens. Jews and Christians in colonial America worked together, ate together, and attended one another's celebrations. At first, Jews in New York attended religious services in rented quarters but in 1730 their first synagogue was built on Mill Street (now South William Street). This building plays an important part in the novel. Congregation Shearith Israel, as it is still called, was the only Jewish congregation in New York from 1654 until 1825. The population of New York in 1730 was about 8,000, 1,200 of whom were slaves. Only a few residents were Jewish. Today the New York metropolitan area has the largest Jewish population outside Israel and there are more Jews in New York City than there are in Jerusalem. About 12 percent of New Yorkers claim Jewish descent.

Principal Characters

Molly Abraham, an aggressive 10-year-old street urchin
Mr. Mendez, a Jewish philanthropist
Mr. Lopez, his partner
Mrs. Wilkes, a street person
Hesper Crudge, a mean-spirited girl
Darby Mattock, captain of the *Good Intention*

Ephraim Bell, a Jewish merchant
Hannah Bell, his wife
Rachel, their 3-year-old daughter
David, their son, about 14
Arabella, their black slave
Adah Grip, a cranky neighbor
Rene Duguay, a sea captain
Christy, a young slave
Dr. Alvarez, the family doctor

Plot Synopsis

The year is 1730 and the place, London. Since her mother's death two years earlier, 10-year-old Molly Abraham has been living a hand-to-mouth existence as a street pickpocket. Her luck suddenly runs out when, shortly after successfully filching a watch from a wealthy gentleman, she is nabbed by her victim and a constable. Molly is certain that someone has squealed on her for a reward, but is unable to investigate. After her arrest she is sent to Newgate Prison and sentenced to serve a term as an indentured servant in Virginia. Suffering similar sentences are Mrs. Wilkes, known as "Liftin' Lizzie," a tough, case-hardened petty thief; and Hesper Crudge, a mean-spirited girl about Molly's age, also a street urchin. Molly is a bright, resourceful girl who has learned, through bitter experience, to care about the well-being of only one person: herself.

Before boarding the ship the *Good Intention*, Molly is visited by two gentlemen, Mr. Mendez and Mr. Lopez, who are important members of the Jewish synagogue where Molly's mother occasionally attended services. They remind Molly that she is Jewish (a status that Molly has completely ignored) and, in a gesture of great philanthropy, give her keeper money so Molly will be given extra rations and remain unchained on the ship. They also promise to make arrangements for her situation in the New World. On the ship, Molly is impressed with the tough but sensible justice administered by captain Darby Mattock and continues both her tentative friendship with Mrs. Wilkes and her dislike of Hesper Crudge. Instead of continuing on to Virginia, all three are auctioned off when the ship anchors in New York harbor. After a fair amount of haggling, Molly is bought by a prosperous Jewish merchant and shopkeeper named Mr. Bell. She realizes that her purchase is part of Mr. Mendez's promise of help.

Molly is taken to the comfortable Bell household and meets the other members of the family: Mrs. Bell, an understanding, hard-working housewife; their darling 3-year-old daughter, Rachel; and their bright, agreeable son, 14-year-old David. She also meets their black slave, the caring Arabella, and a dislikable neighbor, Adah Grip. The Bells welcome Molly and shower her with patience and kindness, two virtues that emotionally deprived Molly finds hard to understand and accept. Mrs. Bell begins teaching her to read and to use table manners, and instructs her and Arabella in the rules of running a kosher Jewish kitchen. From Arabella, Molly learns the difference between a slave and an indentured servant. Secretly, Molly plans to somehow return to London, the place she regards as her real home.

The Bells are a religious family. Mr. Bell and David attend synagogue twice daily and, on the Sabbath, Mrs. Bell takes Molly to services where they sit in the women's balcony. Molly is particularly impressed by the Torah scrolls and their coverings topped by crowns of silver. At one service, she overhears Adah Grip bad-mouthing her because of her unsavory past. Later, Rachel convinces Molly go to the market at the port so she can see her "sweetheart man," a peddler of ribbons and trinkets. Reluctantly, Molly agrees. On the way she notices Hesper Crudge, again up to crime in the streets.

At the market, when Molly stops to talk to a sea captain named Rene Duguay about the cost of a passage back to England, she and Rachel become separated. When she can't find the girl, Molly panics. Mrs. Wilkes happens by. While Molly continues her search, Mrs. Wilkes rushes to the synagogue to tell the Bells of the disaster. Soon the entire congregation arrives and almost immediately Rachel is located wandering on one of the ships and returned to her parents. On the way home, Molly feels so disgraced and embarrassed by her carelessness that she runs away. She soon becomes lost in a wooded area but is found by David, who after calming and reassuring her, takes Molly home.

Although custom requires that Molly be punished for her negligence and for running away, the Bells are lenient. In spite of this Molly continues to remain aloof and thinks about escaping to London. Molly devises a plan to get enough money for her passage. She will steal the silver from the Torah casings in the synagogue and sell it. An expert lock-picker, she fashions a key-like device from a kitchen spoon and makes preparations to commit the robbery one night when everyone is asleep. But during a trial run she is aware that someone is following her.

Arabella has a dear friend, a young slave girl named Christy who is owned by a sadistic neighbor. Christy arrives at the Bells so beaten and bruised that she loses consciousness. With their typical generosity, Mr. and Mrs. Bell takes Christy in and send for their physician, Dr. Alvarez. Molly is forced to postpone her robbery plans while she helps nurse Christy back to health. Meanwhile, Arabella secretly plans to spirit Christy out of New York to be adopted by Mohawk Indians. Molly accidentally discovers the plan and volunteers to help. On the appointed night, the three realize that someone is spying on them. Molly investigates and, without being seen, recognizes Hesper Crudge in the shadows. She has been following Molly, sensing correctly that the synagogue was Molly's target for a robbery.

Molly decides to act as a decoy so that Christy can escape unseen. Molly leaves the house knowing that Hesper will follow her. She goes to the synagogue where, after gaining entrance by using her jimmying device, she confronts Hesper. During their conversation, Hesper confesses that she was the one who squealed on Molly in London. Their talk is interrupted by the arrival of passers-by who realize that someone has illegally entered the synagogue. The two girls escape but in her haste Molly leaves her moccasins behind. Now, alone and wandering the streets, Molly has time to sort out the tangled mess she calls her life. She discovers that she really belongs with the Bells and, regardless of the consequences, she decides to return to their house, the place she now wants to call her home.

Passages for Booktalking

Molly gets caught by the constable in London (pp. 27–31); Mr. Bell bargains for Molly in New York (pp. 45–50); Molly talks about her background and her mother (pp. 50–55); Molly meets the Bells (pp. 57–60) and takes her first bath (pp. 60–66).

Themes and Subjects

Molly's story tells of the gradual transformation of a girl who is battered—both emotionally and physically—by society. She grows from a hardened street urchin into a person who can reach out to help others and accept unconditional love. The novel contains a wonderful description of the life of street people and their jargon in early 18th-century London during the reign of George II. Life in colonial New York—relatively peaceful and uncomplicated—is also well-portrayed. Jewish life and customs of the period are accurately depicted, as are the lives of slaves and indentured servants. Some other subjects: pickpockets, crime and punishment, sailing ships, street slang, maturation, family love and devotion, and friendship.

ADDITIONAL SELECTIONS

Carbone, Elisa. *Blood on the River* (Viking, 2007, $16.99) (Grades 5–8)
> Told from the standpoint of Samuel Collier, an orphan and page to Captain John Smith, this novel about the founding of James Town includes an accurate picture of Indian life at the time.

Duble, Kathleen Bonner. *The Sacrifice* (Simon, 2005, $15.99) (Grades 6–9)
This novel set in Salem in 1692 concerns two young sisters who are accused of witchcraft and consorting with the devil.

Duey, Kathleen. *Silence and Lily, 1773* (Dutton, 2007, $15.99) (Grades 3–6)
Silence, who in 1773 is growing up in Boston, part of a wealthy family, resents the fact that she is often forbidden to ride her beloved horse, Lily.

Durrant, Lynda. *Turtle Clan Journey* (Clarion, 1999, $15.) (Grades 5–9)
In this sequel to *Echohawk* (Clarion, 1997, $15), Jonathan leaves the Indians who raised him and is forced to go to Albany to live with an aunt he doesn't know.

Greene, Jacqueline D. *Out of Many Waters* (Walker, 1988, $16.95) (Grades 6–8)
This novel based on fact tells how a group of Jews from Brazil landed in New Amsterdam and formed the first Jewish congregation in America.

Harrah, Madge. *My Brother, My Enemy* (Simon, 1997, $15) (Grades 5–7)
Set during Bacon's Rebellion of 1676, this story involves a 14-year-old boy whose family is killed when Indians attack their cabin.

Hermes, Patricia. *Salem Witch* (Kingfisher, 2006, pap. $7.95) (Grades 5–8)
Two teenage friends develop differing viewpoints during the witch trials in 17th-century Salem.

Karr, Kathleen. *Worlds Apart* (Marshall Cavendish, 2005, $15.95) (Grades 4–7)
In 1670 South Carolina, Christopher, a teenage settler, forms a friendship with Asha-po, a Sewee Indian.

Keehn, Sally M. *I Am Regina* (Putnam, 1991, $17.99) (Grades 6–9)
Based on fact, this is the story of a white girl who becomes so adjusted to Indian ways after her capture at age 10 that she can't remember her earlier life when she is released nine years later.

Kimmel, Eric. *Blackbeard's Last Fight* (Farrar, 2006, $17) (Grades 3–5)
Vivid illustrations accompany this story set in the early 1700s about a cabin boy who witnesses the capture and execution of the fearsome pirate Blackbeard.

Kudlinski, Kathleen V. *My Lady Pocahontas* (Marshall Cavendish, 2006, $16.95) (Grades 7–10)
This is a novelized biography of the strong, vital daughter of a powerful Powhatan chief who lived during the time when whites were establishing Jamestown.

Lasky, Kathryn. *A Journey to the New World: The Diary of Remember Patience Whipple* (Scholastic, 1996, pap. $10.95) (Grades 4–6)
Using diary entries, 12-year-old Mem Whipple describes her voyage on the *Mayflower* and her first year in the New World.

Rinaldi, Ann. *The Color of Fire* (Hyperion, 2005, $15.99) (Grades 7–10)
Based on fact, this novel set in 18th-century New York, looks at the consequences when false accusations against black people cause an eruption of violence.

Schwartz, Virginia Frances. *Initiation* (Fitzhenry and Whiteside, 2003, $16.95) (Grades 5–8)
Set on the West Coast of North America in the 15th century, this is the story of two Kwakiuti twins who are preparing to face adult responsibilities.

Stainer, L. M. *The Lion's Cub* (Chicken Soup Press, 1998, $9.95) (Grades 5–8)
This story, a continuation of *The Lion's Roar* (Chicken Soup Press, 1997, $9.95), tells what happened to the settlers of the lost colony of Roanoke and describes their friendly relations with the neighboring Indians.

Torrey, Michele. *Voyage of Plunder* (Knopf, 2005, $15.95) (Grades 6–10)
In this tale set in the late 17th century, the ship taking young Bostonian David Markam to Jamaica is captured by pirates led by the notorious Josiah Black (see also *Voyage of Midnight* in main text).

Wyss, Thelma Hatch. *Bear Dancer: The Story of a Ute Girl* (Simon, 2005, $15.95) (Grades 4–7)
Based on fact, this historical novel tells how Elk Girl's life is turned around when she is captured by a rival tribe.

REVOLUTION AND AFTER (1776–1821)

ANDERSON, LAURIE HALSE. *Fever 1793.* Simon, 2000, $16 (978-0-689-83858-3) (Grades 6–10).

Introduction

Laurie Halse (rhymes with "waltz") Anderson was born on October 23, 1961, in Potsdam in upstate New York. She was an avid reader and claims that she read practically every book in her school library. Historical fiction was her favorite genre in elementary school, and science fiction and fantasy her first choice as a teenager. She spent her senior year in high school on a pig farm in Denmark. In 1993 she began research and making drafts on the novel that would later become *Fever 1793*. This work was interrupted by the writing and publication of her first novel for young adults, *Speak* (Farrar, 1999, $17; 0374371520), the story of how high school student Melina is ostracized by her classmates after calling the police when trouble breaks out at a party. What she is unable to tell her friends is that she was raped by an upper-classman that terrible night. The same high school is used as a setting and some of the same characters appear in a later novel *Catalyst* (Viking, 2002, $17.95, 0670035661), which features a driven teenager whose goal is to gain admission to M. I. T.

Fever 1793 is narrated by its heroine, Mattie Cook, and is set in Philadelphia and environs over a four-month period from mid-August through mid-December 1793, or roughly the time during which the yellow fever epidemic ravaged the city.

Historical Background

The author gives valuable background information in an eight-page appendix. This includes information on yellow fever, Dr. Benjamin Rush and the medical practices of the day, coffeehouses, the Free African Society, the portraitist Charles Willson Peale, Stephen Girard and his balloon, and famous personages of the day, including George Washington. In 1793 Philadelphia was the largest city and capital of the newly constituted United States of America. Yellow fever, also known as Yellow Jack and the American Plague, was later discovered to be a viral infection spread by the bite of infected mosquitoes. There is still no cure for it although a vaccine has been developed. Today, treatment consists of rest, fresh air, and plenty of liquids.

In Philadelphia, the summer of 1793 was exceptionally hot and dry—perfect conditions for breeding mosquitoes. The plague killed about 5,000 inhabitants or about 10 percent of the city's population. About one half of the total population, including George Washington and Alexander Hamilton, left the city for the safety of the countryside. The fever began in July and raged through late November when cold weather killed the mosquitoes. Controversy surrounded the treatment of patients. Dr. Benjamin Rush, a signer of the Constitution and a prominent physician favored bloodletting, a practice looked down on by a progressive group of doctors including a number of French-American doctors who favored rest and fresh air.

The hospital at Bush Hill, outside Philadelphia, is featured in the novel. It was founded in a converted mansion by Stephen Girard, a wealthy banker and philanthropist. Born in France, he became a sailor at an early age and, as a result of his maritime exploits during the Revolution, settled in a seaport, Philadelphia.

Other outbreaks of yellow fever occurred in Haiti in 1802; Norfolk, Virginia, in 1855; and in Memphis, Tennessee, in 1878, an epidemic that claimed the lives of more than 20,000 people in the Mississippi Valley. The men most closely associated with triumph over this disease are Carlos Finlay and Dr. Walter Reed (1851–1902). The former, a Cuban scientist, first proposed in 1881 that the fever was transmitted by mosquitoes and not human contact. Reed conducted research that proved Finlay to be right. This research involved working with human volunteers who were infected with the virus. Several of these volunteers gave their lives in this scientific study but their sacrifice saved many others. In the epidemic of 1905 in New Orleans the destruction of mosquitoes' breeding areas reduced the death toll considerably, with similar results during the building of the Panama Canal. Outbreaks of yellow fever still occur in areas of Africa and South America although they are becoming less frequent now that the vaccine is widely distributed.

Principal Characters

Matilda Cook, the 14-year-old heroine
Lucille Cook, her mother
Captain William Farnsworth Cook, her grandfather
Polly, a serving girl in Cook's coffeehouse
Eliza, the black cook in the coffeehouse
Pernilla Ogilvie, a Philadelphia society matron
Edward, Colette, and Jeannine, her children
Nathaniel Benson, an apprentice to the painter Mr. Peale
Mrs. Bridget Flagg, a nurse
Nell, an orphan
Joseph, a cooper, Eliza's brother
Robert and William, Joseph's twin sons
Mother Smith, a black woman who works with the sick

Plot Synopsis

During the long hot summer of 1793 in Philadelphia, the mosquitoes are particularly numerous and pesky. But it is not the mosquito bites that are 14-year-old Matilda (Mattie) Cook's chief annoyance; it is the endless harangues from her strong-willed mother about chores being done correctly and promptly. Mattie's mother, however, is usually justified in her strictness. Mattie tends to procrastinate and avoid her responsibilities. Since her husband's death at age 35, eight years ago, Mrs. Cook has successfully managed the busy Cook's Coffeehouse in the bustling capital of the United States with a minimum of help. As well as Mattie, there is Eliza, the cook, a freed slave whose husband is dead; Mattie's grandfather, Captain William Farnsworth Cook, an ailing, good-natured old man who revels in his past glories fighting alongside George Washington in the Revolutionary War; and a young serving girl, Polly who, for some unaccountable reason, has not turned up to work today. Rumors that a pestilence is spreading in the city become real later that day when news arrives that Polly fell ill the night before and died within a few hours. Discussion among Grandfather Cook and his cronies at the coffeehouse turns to the increase in cases of yellow fever and its possible causes and recommended treatments. In a week's time the death count has risen sharply and many townspeople, including George Washington and Alexander Hamilton, are reported to be leaving town to seek safety in the countryside. Mrs. Cook is even considering sending Mattie and Grandfather to stay with friends, the Ludingtons, on their farm.

One chore Mattie enjoys is going to market to buy provisions, partly because she often meets her friend of many years, Nathaniel Benson, a handsome young man who is an apprentice to the well-known painter Charles Willson Peale. Mrs. Cook, however, does not encourage this budding romance because she believes Mattie should marry into higher society. With this in mind, she engineers a visit for tea with one of Philadelphia's pillars of society, Mrs. Pernilla Ogilvie, and her daughters Colette and Jeannine. Mrs. Ogilvie also has a son Edward, a most eligible candidate for marriage. The visit is a disaster, however. Mattie, who is a self-willed, plucky young lady, bridles at the Ogilvies' condescending attitude. The outing ends abruptly when Colette passes out, another victim of the plague.

When Grandfather develops a bad cough and Mrs. Cook shows symptoms of the fever, she decides she must send Mattie and Grandfather out of town. The faithful, dependable Eliza volunteers to stay with the ailing Mrs. Cook while Mattie and Grandfather—ever the gallant, courteous army officer—leave on a hired wagon. Unfortunately they are scarcely out of town when they are stopped by residents who mistake Grandfather's persistent cough as a sign of yellow fever and forbid them to enter this rural area. The cart driver leaves them stranded in the countryside with no belongings or food. For two days, the two walk toward Philadelphia, subsisting on the berries that Mattie gathers. Weakened by all these hardships, Mattie develops the fever and passes out. She awakens in the Bush Hill hospital where she receives excellent care from a group of progressive French doctors and a kindly nurse, Mrs. Flagg. After recovering, she and Grandfather travel by cart back to the city where they find the coffeehouse deserted and the place wrecked by looters. Fortunately, the strongbox was not discovered, but her mother's and Eliza's whereabouts remain unknown. The two restore order but robbers break in a few nights later. Grandfather frightens them off with his shotgun, but the emotional strain proves too much for him. He suffers a heart attack and dies, and a heartbroken Mattie sees him buried in a common grave along with fever victims.

On her way back from this makeshift funeral, Mattie comes across an orphaned waif named Nell and takes her back to the shelter of the coffeehouse. Later, Mattie is able to track down Eliza who tells Mattie that her mother recovered and left several days before for the Ludington farm. Eliza, who lives with her newly widowed brother Joseph, a cooper, and his two children, twins named Robert and William, has been busy tending to the sick and dying through the Free African Society. Mattie and Nell move in with Eliza. Mattie cares for the children while Eliza, with her mentor, Mother Smith, makes the rounds helping the stricken. However, when both Robert and

William develop the fever, Eliza and Mattie move the children to the coffee-house. Here Mattie cares for the boys with the methods used in Bush Hill, which did not include bloodletting. The boys recover.

The first frost arrives and with it an end to the contagion. Mattie and Eliza reopen the coffeehouse, with Mattie insisting that she and Eliza become equal partners. There is a sudden return of refugees, including Washington and Hamilton, to the city. In one of the groups, Mattie sees her mother. There is a joyful reunion, but Mrs. Cook's health has been so broken by illness and worry that she will be unable to resume management of the coffeehouse. Secretly, Mattie is pleased because she knows that she and Eliza can bring new life to the business. Her newfound happiness is made complete, when Nathaniel reappears. He has spent the plague months sequestered with the Peale family. The two young people resume their friendship, which now appears to be blossoming into courtship. Phoenix-like, the city and its gallant inhabitants have been reborn.

Passages for Booktalking
Introducing Cook's Coffeehouse and the death of Polly (pp. 7–13); customers at the coffeehouse discuss yellow fever (pp. 18–23); Mattie goes to the market and meets Nathaniel Benson (pp. 27–33); and Mattie and her mother visit the Ogilvies (pp. 46–53).

Themes and Subjects
The author has brilliantly re-created the sights and sounds of life in the busy post-Revolution city of Philadelphia. The plague and how adversity can bring out the best and worst in people are important subjects. Mattie's transformation from a willful, immature youngster to a responsible, determined young lady is well handled. As well as a tale of hardship and struggle, it is a story of survival and growth. The life and contributions of freed black citizens is an interesting additional theme. Other subjects: post-Revolution Philadelphia, medical practices, yellow fever, George Washington, death, grandfathers, family stories, and coffeehouses.

AUCH, MARY JANE. *Journey to Nowhere.* Holt, 1997, $16.95 (978-0-8050-4922-0); pap. Dell, $4.99 (978-0-440-41491-9) (Grades 4–8)

Introduction
As a child, Mary Jane Auch wrote and illustrated many books in a comic book style. This interest in drawing led after college to work in the design field.

Seeking a change, she returned to college and entered the Occupational Therapy Program at Columbia University. She worked for many years as a therapist
in Hartford, Connecticut (not far from where this book begins). She married
the artist Herm Auch in 1967, and now has two grown children. After taking
a children's literature writing course with the noted author Natalie Babbitt, she
turned to writing and has achieved great success with both contemporary and
historical fiction.

Journey to Nowhere takes place over a period of about six months in 1815. It
is the first volume of a trilogy about young Mem Nye and her pioneer family
in Genesee County in western New York State. In the second book, *Frozen
Summer* (Holt, 1998, $15.99; 0805049237; pap. Dell. $4.99; 0440416248),
Mem's family has settled into their log cabin and planted their first farm crop.
However, severe early frosts destroy the plants and, under the strain and stress
of the situation and the problems of caring for a newborn baby, Mem's mother's delicate mental state collapses and she sinks into a terrible depression. One
stormy night she and her baby disappear and Mem sets out to find them. The
third installment is *The Road to Home* (Holt, 2000, $15.99; 0805049215; pap.
Dell $4.99; 0440418054). After her mother's death, Mem, now 13, wants to
return to Connecticut and to her mother's family. Her father reluctantly agrees
but when they stop in Rome, New York, and he gets a job on the Erie Canal, it
appears he will not leave. Mem sets out with her brother Joshua and the baby
in a futile effort to complete the journey alone. In Mem, the narrator, the
author has created a courageous, likable figure whom youngsters will enjoy
meeting.

Historical Background

A useful map of the Nye family's journey is included in the book. Most of
their trip is on a toll road called the Seneca Turnpike. It runs east to west on a
route roughly parallel to the present-day New York Thruway. The Turnpike
originally extended for about 160 miles from Utica west to Canandaigua (it is
now called Route 5). The family crosses Cayuga Lake, the longest of New
York's Finger Lakes, by way of the famous mile-long wooden Cayuga Bridge.
Built in 1800, it was then the longest bridge in the Western Hemisphere. It
linked the east with the developing west. During the War of 1812, armies
marched over this bridge. In time, other bridges took its place but with the
growing competition from canal and railroad transportation, all of them disappeared. The family's destination was Genesee Country (*genesee* is an Indian
word meaning "beautiful valley"), which had been founded in 1802. It is located midway between today's Buffalo and Rochester, New York. In its early days,
great farmland settlements were established, usually around taverns. Originally it comprised virtually all of western New York State. But from 1806

through 1841 separate countries were formed. The Nyes' farmland would be situated in today's Wayne County, close to the shores of Lake Ontario. In the text there are references to Mr. Madison's War. This is a derisive name for the War of 1812 (1812–1815) fought during the presidency of James Madison, which was from 1809 to 1817. One contemporary critic of the war said it was "commanded in folly . . . carried on with madness and will end in ruin." In 1814, British troops landed in Pultneyville on the shores of Lake Ontario in Genesee Country, where they were allowed to purchase supplies. There was a dispute and in the subsequent shooting some citizens were killed before the British fled.

Principal Characters

Mem, short for Remembrance, Nye, the narrator, an 11-year-old girl
Papa Jeremiah Nye, her father
Mama Aurelia Nye, her mother
Joshua, Mem's 4-year-old brother
Grandma, Mem's grandmother
Graves, the head of a group of drovers
Artemus Ware, a wanderer
Emos Hatch, his friend
Belle Lanson, a tavern keeper
Rose and Sally, her helpers
Daniel Root, his wife, and sons Ira and Orrin, the Nyes' saviors
George and Rebecca Pierce, friendly neighbors
Mercy, age 16, and Hannah, age 11, their daughters
Eliza Crandell, Mercy's friend

Plot Synopsis

It's the spring of 1815, and the only member of the Nye family who is enthusiastic about the planned move from Hartland, their northern Connecticut home, to the wilderness of Genesee Country in western New York State, is Papa Nye. Mama is apprehensive about leaving her friends, disposing of her possessions, and trekking into the unknown backwoods, as are her children, 11-year-old Mem (short for Remembrance) and 4-year-old Joshua. But Papa had traveled into this area last autumn and, impressed with what he knew would make excellent farmland, purchased a large tract of land covered with thick virgin forest.

Mama and the children go along with his decision and begin packing what little can be held in a single covered wagon and disposing of the rest. Mem is particularly distressed when she learns that her pet horse, Colonel, must be sold to help pay for a pair of oxen. At the huge farewell party attended by family and friends, Mem's maternal Grandma gives her a locket that contains a lock of her hair and of the hair of Mem's great-grandmother, both named Remembrance. To these Grandma adds a lock of Mem's hair. Three generations in a single gold locket on a chain that Mem swears always to wear around her neck. There are tearful goodbyes as the Nyes depart on their heavily loaded wagon followed by their tethered cow, Chloe and pregnant pig, Sophie.

Their first stop is at the Red Lion, a tavern across the Massachusetts border in East Otis. In the tavern is a group of uncouth, drunken drovers who are leading a flock of turkeys to market. Their leader is the foul-smelling Graves, who forces his presence on the Nye family. In the middle of the night, Mem, Joshua, and Mama leave their beds to visit the outdoor privy and, there they are accosted by the whiskey-sodden drovers. Papa is aroused by the commotion, and the resulting fight stops only when the tavern keeper arrives with his gun. In bed later that night Mem realizes that in the future she must learn to take care of herself. As a symbol of her resolve she cuts off her braids, to the great displeasure of her parents.

The next morning, amid driving rain and deafening thunder, the Nyes leave the tavern. Mem discovers that her locket is missing, and silently slips off the wagon to retrieve it. As she finds the locket, Graves emerges from the tavern. Mem runs into the woods and gets completely lost. She spends the night in a hollow tree truck and witnesses a mountain lion stalk and kill its prey, a large deer. The following morning, she returns to the turnpike road and meets an odd, disheveled woodsman named Artemus Ware. With his bow and arrow, Artemus kills a rabbit and roasts it over a campfire for himself and Mem. Unfortunately, Artemus is bitten by a rattlesnake and Mem is sent on a trek to summon his friend Emos Hatch. She finds Emos who, before taking Artemus to his house for attention, directs Mem to the nearest tavern where she hopes to get news of her family. The tavern is run by tough but sympathetic Belle Lanson, who feeds Mem the customers' leftovers and lets her sleep in a narrow bed with her two hired servants, Rose and Sally. The accommodations are so uncomfortable that Mem decides to set out, even though it's the middle of the night, for the Red Lion, some 9 miles back. There she is reunited with her frantic family.

They resume their journey into New York State. Papa decides to try the shorter Great Western Turnpike rather than the more-traveled Seneca Turnpike. It is a bad choice. The road is rutted and the river is swollen by the heavy rains. They have problems while crossing a decaying bridge and some of the furniture falls into the river. In an effort to save her belongings, Mama jumps into the river and is swept away by the current, as is Papa when he tries to save her. Mem's screams alert a settler, Daniel Root, and his sons Ira and Orrin, who fish Mama and Papa out of the torrent. After recovering and enjoying the

fine food of Mrs. Root, our travelers press on, this time using the more northern Seneca Turnpike. The turnpike trip is relatively uneventful except for an
encounter with friendly Oneida Indians and crossing the awe-inspiring mile-
long bridge across Cayuga Lake.

After they leave the turnpike and head north, Papa finds his beautiful
wooded tract of land close to Pultneyville and the shores of Lake Ontario.
Papa builds a shelter while starting to chop trees for a log cabin. Their first few
days are fraught with almost fatal accidents. Mem is nearly crushed by a huge
tree that her father is felling, and Joshua also narrowly escapes disaster in
another logging mishap. Sophie the pig is mauled by a bear and must be shot.
The family has a pork dinner that evening. Under all this stress and strain,
Mama's resolve cracks and she demands that Papa take the family back to
Connecticut.

Help and hope arrive in the form of a neighbor, George Pierce. He not only
supplies valuable advice to Papa on clearing the land and planting crops, but
also volunteers to bring his family and those of neighbors to participate in an
old-fashioned two-day cabin raising. The Nyes are delighted but Mama makes
one stipulation, no liquor. Mama makes elaborate preparations but no one
appears on the appointed day. Again there is gloom and doom. However,
everyone arrives the next day; the delay was caused by a house fire. Mr. and
Mrs. Pierce bring with them their four strapping sons, two daughters, and several other families all eager to help. After the timbers are put into place everyone participates in chinking the spaces between the logs. Mem is delighted to
meet Hannah, the Pierces' 11-year-old daughter. They become immediate
friends and Mem is able to help Hannah turn the tables on her domineering
older sister Mercy and Mercy's obnoxious friend, Eliza Crandell. When the
cabin is finished there is a boisterous family-style hoe-down. Mama tactfully
doesn't ask about the contents of the men's cups. After the jolly gang leaves and
the family begins moving into the cabin, Mama asks Mem, "Do you feel happy
now?" and Mem replies, "Oh, yes. And I feel safe, Mama. I feel as if we're come
home."

Passages for Booktalking
Some memorable incidents: Grandma gives Mem the locket (pp. 18–20);
friends and family bid the Nyes goodbye (pp. 20–23); in the tavern with the
drovers (pp. 27–32); the fight at the privy (pp. 33–37); and Mem declares her
independence (pp. 37–39).

Themes and Subjects
The hardships and tribulations of homesteaders in the American West are
vividly brought to life. Details of everyday life in the early 19th century are fas-

cinating and bring a sense of reality to every turn of the plot. Mem's journey to maturity is effectively portrayed, as is the loving family dealing with hardships that challenge their mutual trust and loyalty. Other subjects: upper New York State, War of 1812, turnpikes, taverns, friendship, courage, pioneer life, cooperation, neighborliness, and sacrifice.

COLLIER, JAMES LINCOLN, AND CHRISTOPHER COLLIER.
Jump Ship to Freedom. Delacorte, 1981, o.p.; pap. Dell. $5.99 (978-0-440-44323-0) (Grades 4–8)

Introduction
James Lincoln Collier, born in 1928, is a professional writer who has written many excellent books for young readers but is probably best known as the author of several historical novels written in collaboration with his brother Christopher (1930–), a professor of history whose area of specialization is the same period as this novel, the American Revolution and its aftermath. Christopher does the initial research, both brothers discuss the characters, and James does the detailed plotting and writing. *Jump Ship to Freedom* is the second in sequence (but the first to be published) of a trilogy, the Arabus Family Saga, that tells the story of blacks during the American Revolution and their relationship to the emerging Constitution. *Jump Ship to Freedom* takes place during the summer of 1787 and is narrated by its 14-year-old black hero, Daniel Arabus. The first book, *War Comes to Willy Freeman* (pap. Dell, $6.50; 0440495040), is the story of a 13-year-old black girl named Willy (short for Wilhelmina), who has seen her father murdered by the Redcoats during the Revolution and her mother taken as a prisoner to New York City. Disguised as a boy, she goes to the city and finds work and a haven at Fraunces Tavern. But here, even with the help of Sam Fraunces, she faces many dangers including being discovered and returned to slavery. In the third volume, *Who Is Carrie?* (Delacorte, 1984 $12; 0375895035), Carrie (called Nosy in *Jump Ship to Freedom*) is a kitchen slave at Fraunces Tavern. She knows nothing of her background, not even her last name. After meeting Daniel Arabus and hearing of his quest for freedom for himself and his mother, Carrie decides she must explore her own identity. When she learns who her parents are, she believes she should not be a slave. Though powerless, she never gives up hope. In this trilogy, the authors seek authenticity in the speech and behavior of their characters. This results in the frequent use of the offensive word *nigger*. This should not deter anyone from recommending these books, but one might wish to discuss this usage in its historical context with young readers beforehand.

Historical Background

In a concluding section, "How Much of This Book Is True?," the authors try to separate fact from fiction. For example, William Samuel Johnson was a real character but Peter Fatherscreft is a composite of several influential Quaker anti-slavery politicians of the day. These pages also give valuable information about the Constitutional Convention of 1787 and its problems and accomplishments. In 1786, the young country was facing many crises including near-bankruptcy. It was necessary for delegates to meet "to devise such further provisions as shall appear to them necessary to render the constitution of the Federal Government adequate to the exigencies of the Union." The Constitutional Convention, also known as the Philadelphia Convention, was held between May 25 and September 17, 1787. Among the delegates were James Madison and Alexander Hamilton. William Samuel Johnson was one of three delegates from Connecticut. George Washington presided over this convention during which the U.S. Constitution was drafted. As a result of the Great Compromise, the membership in the House of Representatives would be by population and that of the Senate would be two senators per state. Another compromise was reached regarding slavery. Ten states had already banned the continuation of the slave trade, but three southern states vowed to leave the Convention if the ban was extended to all states. The result: Congress could ban the slave trade but not before twenty years had passed. For population statistics, a slave was considered three-fifths of a person.

Fraunces Tavern is currently a restaurant and museum situated in Lower Manhattan on the corner of Pearl and Broad Streets. In spite of several renovations through the years, it is still considered the oldest building in Manhattan. Originally a private home, it was bought by Samuel Fraunces in 1762 and turned into a popular tavern. In the pre-Revolutionary War years, it was a meeting place for the Sons of Liberty and it was here that Washington bade farewell to his officers in the Continental Army. When the war was almost over, it became the official meeting place at different times for the withdrawing British and the incoming American forces and, when the Americans captured the city, it was the site of a massive victory banquet. It remains a popular tourist attraction today.

Principal Characters

Daniel Arabus, a 14-year-old slave
Mum, his mother
Mrs. Ivers, a nasty, grasping woman
Captain Ivers, her equally cruel, heartless husband
Birdsey Brooks, the Ivers's nephew
Big Tom, Captain Ivers's vicious mate

Black Sam Fraunces, a tavern keeper in New York
Nosy (real name Carrie), a black girl, a kitchen slave at Fraunces Tavern
Mr. Fatherscreft, an elderly Quaker and influential politician

Plot Synopsis

It is June 1787 in the seaport of Stratford, Connecticut, and Daniel Arabus, a 14-year-old black slave in the household of vindictive Mrs. Ivers and her cruel husband Captain Ivers, is about to correct an injustice. His father, Jack, fought valiantly and had a distinguished career in the Revolutionary War as a substitute soldier for his master, Captain Ivers. For this, Jack was promised his freedom after the war. Ivers, a thorough scoundrel, reneged on his promise but Jack won the ensuing court case. He also earned 600 dollars in soldiers' notes, but the fledgling Congress has not yet authorized their payment. In the meantime, Jack has gone to sea to make money to buy freedom for his son and his wife. Only a few weeks ago, Mum and Daniel received news that Jack has drowned at sea.

Pretending to take the soldiers' notes for safekeeping, Mrs. Ivers has hidden them in the family Bible in her bedroom, and Daniel wants them back. One evening, to distract Mrs. Ivers, he builds a smoky fire in the living room. When Mrs. Ivers rushes in to extinguish the blaze, Daniel sneaks into her bedroom and retrieves the notes. He and his mother hide them in the hayloft in the cowshed.

The next day Daniel goes to the docks to help load Captain Ivers's brig, the *Junius Brutus*, before it sails. He is joined by his friend and long-time companion, Birdsey Brooks, Captain Ivers's nephew, who also helps loads the ship. Birdsey will be traveling with his uncle and, though Daniel loathes and fears the Captain, he is envious of Birdsey's opportunity to go to sea. Captain Ivers appears. He has discovered that the soldiers' notes are missing and beats Daniel brutally. He demands to know where they are hidden but Daniel remains silent. Getting nowhere with the interrogation, Ivers informs Daniel that he, too, will be part of the crew at the next sailing. Daniel hides the notes in the bundle of extra clothes that he takes aboard the ship. He believes the *Junius Brutus* is bound for New York, where he hopes to contact Samuel Fraunces, tavern keeper and friend of his father, and get the notes to William Samuel Johnson, a Connecticut government legislator currently in New York. Daniel hopes Mr. Johnson will help him cash the notes. On board, he immediately runs afoul of a mean-spirited, ugly black sailor named Big Tom who is a confidant of the Captain.

Daniel hides the notes in a cherrywood chest of drawers, part of the cargo in the hold. Among other chores, Daniel and Birdsey trim or sometimes furl the sails, a dizzying job that involves climbing the rigging. To his dismay,

Daniel discovers that the ship's destination is not New York but St. Eustatia in the West Indies. While eavesdropping on a conversation between the Captain and Birdsey, he also learns that he is to be sold as a slave to work on the plantations. This upsetting news is momentarily forgotten when the ship experiences a typhoon-like storm. It is so intense and prolonged that Daniel is certain the ship will sink. The captain, forever aware of his profits, refuses to lessen the danger by jettisoning the deck cargo. Before the storm diminishes, Birdsey has been swept overboard and the main mast breaks and crashes into the sea.

The *Junius Brutus* limps into the New York harbor. Afraid Daniel will try to escape, Captain Ivers locks him in his cabin. Daniel sets the cabin on fire and in the ensuing confusion jumps overboard and swims to Bedloe's Island. From there, with the help of a man with a rowboat, he travels to the lower tip of Manhattan. In the city, he asks directions of a sassy 10-year-old black girl pushing a barrow load of oysters. Because she asks as many questions as she answers, he dubs her Nosy although her real name is Carrie. Daniel is pleased to learn that the girl works as a kitchen slave at Fraunces Tavern.

There he meets the friendly owner, Mr. Samuel Fraunces, who offers him shelter and later introduces him to Mr. Fatherscreft, a resident of the inn who is a Quaker and an important New York politician. Mr. Fatherscreft immediately befriends Daniel but is so frail and sickly that Daniel fears for his life.

Daniel is determined to rescue his notes from the cherrywood chest. He finds out where the *Junius Brutus* is docked. The cargo, including the chest, is on the dock. That night, he and Nosy carry out a daring robbery. Daniel deliberately shows his face to the guard, Big Tom, who takes off after him, leaving Nosy alone with the cargo. She opens the chest and grabs the notes. Daniel again avoids capture by jumping into the water and swimming to safety.

After Captain Ivers and Big Tom trace him to Fraunces Tavern and he experiences another narrow escape, Daniel realizes he must leave New York. An opportunity arises when ailing Mr. Fatherscreft asks Daniel to accompany him to Philadelphia where he will attend the Constitutional Convention. However, by the time they reach Trenton, Mr. Fatherscreft can scarcely breathe. Realizing death is near, he entrusts Daniel with a message to be delivered only to William Samuel Johnson. It is that, to save the fragile union, New York is reluctantly willing to compromise on the immediate banning of the slave trade. Daniel promises to deliver the message even though he knows that passage of this legislation, along with its provision concerning the return of escaped slaves, will diminish his chances of eventual freedom.

Mr. Fatherscreft dies and Daniel continues on to Philadelphia partly by foot and partly in a stolen rowboat. He appears at the Convention headquarters and, in spite of confrontations with guards, he is led into the presence of

Alexander Hamilton and George Washington. He convinces them that he has an important message from Mr. Fatherscreft that must be given in person to Mr. Johnson. Eventually, he is able to delivers his message and the legislative roadblock is broken. In time, Connecticut passes laws prohibiting the sale of slaves out of the state and, still later, Congress authorizes payment of the soldiers' notes. With this money, Daniel buys freedom for himself and his mother and together they move into a humble lean-to, their own home at last. His mother takes a position, as a free woman, in Mr. Johnson's household and Daniel, now rid of the Ivers family, decides to dedicate his new life to the sea, and try to be as fine a sailor as his father was.

Passages for Booktalking
Daniel retrieves his father's army money (pp. 12–19); he works loading the ship and is beaten up by Captain Ivers (pp. 21–27); Daniel meets Big Tom and assumes duties on the ship (pp. 31–36); the beginning of the storm (pp. 55–62).

Themes and Subjects
During the novel, Daniel matures from a boy who feels inferior because of his race to a proud, independent young man capable of making adult decisions and assuming great responsibilities. The novel also presents a revealing, often shocking, picture of post-Revolution America from a black slave's point of view. The authors have crafted an intriguing mixture of fact and fiction while showing how fragile the union of the states was after the Revolution. The sights and activities of New York City in the 1780s are accurately depicted. Other subjects: Connecticut, Fraunces Tavern, slavery, Constitutional Convention, Philadelphia, sea stories, courage, escapes, the Constitution, George Washington, Alexander Hamilton, family relationships, brutality, and freedom.

ELLIOTT, L. M. *Give Me Liberty.* Harper, 2006, $16.99 (978-0-06-074421-2) (Grades 5–8)

Introduction
Give Me Liberty takes place in and around Williamsburg, Virginia, over a period of a year and a half (May 1774 through December 1775). Virginia is the birthplace and present home of the author, Laura Malone Elliott. Before turning to fiction writing, she practiced journalism and worked for 18 years at *Washington Magazine.* Another of her books set in Virginia is the Civil War novel *Annie, Between the States* (Harper, 2004, o.p.; pap. $6.99; 0060012137),

which tells the story of teenage Annie, whose brother fights on the Confederate side but who falls in love with a wounded Yankee soldier. In this exciting, realistic story, she eventually spends six months in a prison in Washington for hiding Confederate soldiers and for passing on illegal war-related documents. The author, who plays both flute and piano, claims that music influences her writing and gives it a feeling of pace and rhythm. She reads everything she writes to test it for sound quality.

Music also plays an important role in *Give Me Liberty*. Much of the plot revolves about the fact that both leading characters play musical instruments. Each of the eight parts of the novel is introduced by the lyrics of a song or ballad of the period.

Historical Background

The novel begins in Virginia shortly after the Boston Tea Party and contains appearances by many of the Southern leaders of the time including the patriots Patrick Henry, Thomas Jefferson, James Monroe (later the fifth president), and Peyton Randolph, who is called "the most revered man in Williamsburg." Lord Dunmore, the colonial governor and official king's representative in the capital, Williamsburg, also plays an important part in the events. In an interesting Afterword, the author points out that many of the secondary characters are also based on real-life characters.

The novel's climax occurs at the Battle of Great Bridge, about 12 miles from Norfolk, on December 9, 1775. It has been called "the second Bunker Hill." It ended the rule of the British crown in Virginia. Lord Dunmore defeated the rebels at Kemp's Landing (now Kempsville) and moved south 10 miles to the tiny village of Great Bridge close to Norfolk. To bolster the number of his troops, he promised freedom to any slave who volunteered. On the north (Norfolk) side of the bridge, he built a stockade and fortified the causeway with two 12-pound cannons. Late in November the rebels marched south and by December 2 the Second Virginia Regiment and five companies of the Culpepper Minutemen arrived at Great Bridge. A figure at this point in the novel is one of the Minutemen, John Marshall (1755–1835), who grew up on the Virginia frontier and later helped shape American constitutional law by become the longest-serving chief justice of the Supreme Court. Dunmore engaged the Patriots in a surprise attack but, misinformed about the strength of the opposition, suffered a critical defeat in the half-hour battle with 102 of his men killed (only one American was injured). In a complete rout, the British retreated to Norfolk and eventually Dunmore and the Tory families were evacuated to Dunmore's ship, the *Otter*, where he spent the last part of his term as governor. Royal authority in the Virginia Colony was at an end and six months later, on July 4, 1776, the Declaration of Independence was issued.

Principal Characters

Nathaniel Dunn, a 13-year-old indentured servant
Mr. Owen, a cruel blacksmith
Moses, a 16-year-old slave
Basil Wilkinson, an elderly music teacher
Edan Maguire, a carriage maker and blacksmith
Ben, Edan's 16-year-old apprentice
Mrs. Maguire, Edan's long-suffering wife
John Hunter, an indentured servant
Obadjah Puryer, Edan's journeyman
Thomas Jefferson, a Patriot and landowner
Lord Dunmore, British governor of Virginia
John Marshall, an American army officer
Jeremiah, an arrogant hooligan

Plot Synopsis

In 1774, 11-year-old Nathaniel Dunn, together with his mother and saddle-maker father, emigrated from England to the Colony of Virginia. During the voyage, his mother died and, upon arrival, his distraught father, indentured Nathaniel to a tobacco plantation owner to pay for the boy's passage and took off to seek his fortune on the frontier. Now, two years later, Nathaniel is once again up for sale. His owner, facing mounting gambling debts, has put the plantation and its contents, including Nathaniel and his dear friend Moses, a slave, on the block. Nathaniel, with eight more years of indenture still owing, is bought by Mr. Owen, a cruel, mean-tempered blacksmith, for eight pounds ten shillings. Moses's fate remains unknown.

During the auction, Owen cuffs Nathaniel's ears for no real reason. To get even, Nathaniel recommends that Owen buy the horse River Fox, aka Vixen, a gorgeous but rebellious animal that only Nathaniel can tame. When Owen is thrown and almost trampled to death by Vixen, he rightly blames Nathaniel and begins giving him a terrible life-threatening thrashing. Nathaniel is rescued by an elderly musician and schoolteacher named Basil Wilkinson, who sells part of his valuable book collection to raise the ten pounds to buy Nathaniel from Owen. On their way to Basil's home in Williamsburg, the old man explains that he boards with Edan Maguire, a carriage maker, and his kindly wife, while making his living as a tutor and music teacher. Nathaniel shows him his only worldly possession—a flute his father gave him—and Basil promises to give him free instruction.

Nathaniel becomes an indentured apprentice to Mr. Maguire, a sullen foul-tempered man, but he shares Basil's room and dines with the family. Edan's other helpers are Ben, an attractive hot-headed apprentice aged 16; John Hunter, an indentured servant; and Obadjah Puryer, the journeyman. Williamsburg is a town dangerously divided politically. Many—such as Thomas Jefferson and Patrick Henry—espouse rebellion to guarantee their rights; some, like Speaker Peyton Randolph, seek compromises; and others, including the governor, Lord Dunmore, want to preserve British rule at any cost. Basil and Ben, who has become Nathaniel's close friend, are Patriots but Edan, who fears he is losing trade because of his political beliefs, is a staunch Tory. One day, in a fit of drunken self-pity, Edan terrorizes his helpers and partially destroys a phaeton (carriage) they have been working on.

That night, John Hunter runs away and the next day Nathaniel is sent to the office of the *Virginia Gazette* to have a "Wanted with Reward" advertisement printed. He alters the text provided by Mrs. Maguire, leaving out details that might entrap John. At the newspaper he encounters beautiful 12-year-old Maria Rind, daughter of the recently deceased owners. While exploring the pressroom, Nathaniel reads an item reporting the escape and capture of a slave named Moses who is now being held in the Williamsburg jail. Nathaniel visits his old friend in jail before he is to be sent back to his master and a painful flogging. Nathaniel is overwhelmed by his friend's indomitable courage.

As the political situation continues to deteriorate, Lord Dunmore's threats and edicts against the Patriots become more virulent and oppressive. One evening Nathaniel is accosted in the Maguire barn by Moses and a fellow slave. Moses is a runaway again and they need two pounds to make their way to the Chesapeake, where they will gain freedom by joining the Loyalist forces. Desperate to help his old friend, Nathaniel steals the money from Basil's money-box but is too ashamed to tell the old man what he has done. Basil discovers the loss and, suspecting Nathaniel, banishes him to live in the barn. One day, on an errand in the *Gazette* office, Nathaniel is enjoying another pleasant visit with Maria Rind when a flustered Thomas Jefferson appears, wanting to place an ad about a horse that ran away. Nathaniel realizes that the animal is the untamable Vixen. After finding and calming her, the boy returns the horse to Mr. Jefferson, who gives him a four pound reward. Nathaniel puts the money into Basil's money-box. When the old man discovers it, Nathaniel is reinstated into his good graces.

Increasingly intent on joining the Yankee army, Ben decides to rob the deserted town's armament magazine and steal some muskets. He is accompanied by a gang of young zealots included a surly, unpleasant boy named Jeremiah and a reluctant Nathaniel. Unfortunately, the British have booby-trapped the entrance. When they open the door a spring gun fires, wounding

Nathaniel slightly in the shoulder and ripping one of Ben's hands to shreds. Realizing that his soldiering and apprentice days are over, Ben reluctantly retires to the family farm.

When serious fighting erupts, Basil, in spite of his advanced age, is accepted into the Virginia Regiment with Nathaniel accompanying him as a fifer. Army life is tough, both for Basil, whose age shows, and for Nathaniel, who is constantly harassed by an older, jealous drummer—the boorish Jeremiah who was part of Ben's former gang. In an act of friendship and appreciation, Basil grants Nathaniel his freedom. When Jeremiah is caught stealing food from a neighboring farm, he is sentenced to a flogging that is to be administered by his equals, the other fifers, including Nathaniel. Nathaniel, however, refuses to be part of this cruel punishment and is therefore sentenced to the same flogging as Jeremiah. After the first blow has been stuck, a figure emerges to defend the two young men. It is John Marshall, an officer in the Culpepper Minutemen. He addresses the military tribunal eloquently, begging for leniency. Both Jeremiah and Nathaniel are released.

Throughout these incidents, Nathaniel notices that one of the Minutemen is paying particular attention to him. The man is ugly, with severe pock marks and a long scar on his forehead from a partial scalping by Indians. In time, the man identifies himself. He is Nathaniel's father. After explaining his reasons for abandoning his son, he offers Nathaniel a place in his frontier home after the Revolution. Nathaniel tactfully refuses, wishing to remain with his dear friend Basil.

At the little town of Great Bridge, 12 miles from Norfolk, the two armies encamp on either side of an inlet. A short but decisive battle takes place on December 9, 1775. Though the battle is brief, the British suffer many casualties. Basil and Nathaniel, along with their comrades, emerge victorious and ready to press on to assure that Virginia receives the freedom it deserves.

Passages for Booktalking

Some interesting incidents: Owen encounters Vixen (pp. 14–22); Owen attacks Nathaniel, who is saved by Basil (pp. 29–41); Basil explains the political situation in Williamsburg (pp. 59–66); and Nathaniel, Basil, and Mrs. Maguire play music together (pp. 117–122).

Themes and Subjects

The author has created an amazingly accurate picture of life in Colonial Williamsburg through vivid description of occupations, everyday life, social niceties, and recreational pursuits. The political situation is simply but truthfully described. Historical figures are appropriately introduced and form a natural part of the story. The issue of "freedom for whom" in the Revolution and the continued existence of slavery produce valid confusion and questions for Nathaniel. The boy grows to maturity both intellectually and emotionally during the novel. Other subjects: Virginia, Revolutionary War, loyalty, friendship, conflicting values, freedom, slavery, Battle of Great Bridge, courage, music, and self-determination.

KETCHUM, LIZA. *Where the Great Hawk Flies.* Clarion, 2005, $16 (978-0-618-40085-0) (Grades 4–8)

Introduction

Liza Ketchum grew up in rural Vermont with few neighboring children to play with. As a result, she developed, with the encouragement of her parents, a great interest in books and reading. As a little girl, she began composing stories, many featuring her toys as characters. At Sarah Lawrence College, she took courses in both writing and education and, while still in college, conducted her first writing workshop for children. After living in England for a number of years she moved back to Vermont, opened a preschool, and raised a family. On a family car trip from Vermont to California, she visited sites on the Oregon Trail and places associated with the works of Laura Ingalls Wilder. From these experiences, she fashioned a diary of a young girl on a wagon train west, which developed into her first published book for young people, the historical novel *West Against the Wind* (Backinprint.com, 2000, $15.95; 0595092004), first published in 1987. It is set in 1850 and tells of Abigail Parker's journey from Missouri to meet her father in gold rush California.

Where the Great Hawk Flies mixes fact and fiction. Two of the author's relatives (many generations ago) were Joseph Griswold, who lived in Randolph, Vermont, and his wife, a Pequot Indian noted for her doctoring prowess. Months of research and writing resulted in a rich, exciting novel that contains many authentic details of events during and after the American Revolution. Further details and explanations are given in the Author's Note. The novel takes place over a period of a few weeks beginning in October 1782 and is narrated alternately by two young protagonists, Daniel Tucker and Hiram Coombs. The text includes three evocative, lyrical poems.

Historical Background

The Author's Note and concluding section on Pequot Indians and their language provide fascinating details. The town of Royalton (Griswold in the novel) is located in the White River Valley in the heart of the Green Mountains of Vermont. The area was originally chartered by King George III and rechartered by the Independent Republic of Vermont in 1781 (Vermont did not become a state until 1791). During the Revolution, on October 16, 1780, the infamous Royalton Raid took place. A handful of British soldiers and about 300 Mohawk (part of the Caughnawaga group) Indians from Canada, led by Lieutenant Houghton, attacked several settlements in an effort to terrorize the settlers and drive them from their land. This was intended to prevent them from assisting the Patriots in a possible invasion of Quebec City and Montreal. Historically this is considered the last and most fierce of the Indian raids. Simultaneously, similar raids were conducted in the Mohawk River Valley and Lake George region of New York State. In the Vermont raid, houses were plundered and burned and food stocks were destroyed. Four (some accounts say two) settlers were killed, and 26 were taken prisoner (like Hiram's uncle) and transported to Quebec. A militia of Patriots caught up with the raiders but, fearing for the lives of the prisoners, allowed the invaders to escape. One of the captives, Zadock Steele, wrote an account of his captivity. He was first held by the Indians in Canada and later placed in a British prison on an island in the St. Lawrence, where he endured brutal living conditions for two years. In 1782, not realizing that the Revolution was over, he and some other prisoners dug a 22-foot tunnel and swam dangerous river rapids to escape. They wandered for 22 days in the wilderness before reaching an American settlement. Meanwhile, in Quebec, the rest of the prisoners had been released.

The raiders are identified as Caughnawaga Indians, a group of the Mohawk Indians which was part of the Iroquois Confederation. Many of the Caughnawaga came under the influence of priests of the French Canadian missions and converted to Christianity. They became separated from the rest of the pagan Iroquois and first settled in La Prairie close to Montreal. They became known as the "Praying Indians" or the "French Mohawks." The Iroquois tried to reintegrate them with little success. Later many sympathized with the Patriots but others fell under the influence of the British command and participated in the Royalton Raid. It is estimated that about 13,000 Indians fought with the British during the Revolution, the largest contingent—of about 1,500 men—from the Iroquois Confederation.

Daniel's mother, Kate, belongs to the Pequot nation, originally a group that resided in southeastern Connecticut. It is believed that at one time the Pequot and the Mehagan tribes were one and that they later separated. The Pequot were an agrarian people who raised such crops as corn, beans, squash, and tobacco. They also hunted and fished. Living in wigwams or longhouses, they had a tight social structure governed by a tribal council led by a sachem. After the white man came, their numbers were decimated by disease and the hardship caused by being forced from their lands. In the 19th century, they were sent to reservations. Today, there are about 1,000 Pequot in the United States. The Mashantucket Pequot in Connecticut became entrepreneurs on their land and opened a bingo parlor in 1986 that evolved into the profitable Fox-woods Resort Casino. From these revenues, they opened a Mashantucket Museum and Research Center dedicated to the study of the Pequot people and traditions.

Daniel is given a wampum belt. Wampum were strings of white shell beads collected from the North Atlantic. The belt that contained these shells gradually became the symbols of power and status within the tribe. Because the Indians had no currency, these were used as a medium of exchange when the white men came.

A favorite dish of the Tuckers is pompion, a name used by English settlers for different kinds of squash, principally pumpkin.

Principal Characters

Daniel Tucker, a 13-year-old part-Indian boy
Rhoda Tucker, his sister, who is nearly 7
Kate Tucker, his mother, a Pequot
Caleb Tucker, his English father
Hiram Coombs, an 11-year-old boy
Hannah Coombs, his mother
Isaac Coombs, his father
Daniel's Grandfather
Uncle Abner, Hiram's uncle
The Ellis family, neighbors of the Tuckers
Mr. Chase, the blacksmith
Mr. Sykes, the cooper

Plot Synopsis

It is October 1782, two years after the conclusion of the Revolution, in the tiny settlement of Griswold in rural Vermont. Two houses—one well-kept and thriving with substantial outbuildings and stock, and the other dilapidated and in need of repair—are on adjacent plots separated by a few acres of wooded land and a stream that marks the border line between properties. The first houses the Tucker family—Caleb, the father, a studious industrious farmer born in England, and his wife Kate, a Pequot with a rich knowledge of native medicines who tends to the doctoring needs of the community. They have two children—Daniel, who is celebrating his 13th birthday, and his engaging 7-year-old sister Rhoda. Both children have inherited their mother's complexion and facial features so that they look like Indians rather than half-breeds.

Kate and Caleb met when Caleb injured himself in the Connecticut woods, fell into a stream, and was rescued by the Pequot. They took him into their community and he was nursed back to health by Kate and her grandfather, the tribe's revered medicine man. Kate and Caleb fell in love and, in spite of Grandfather's initial objections, married and moved to Vermont to settle and raise a family.

The newly arrived Coombs family—Isaac, his wife Hannah, and their 11-year old son Hiram—lives in the second house. They have come from Connecticut to open the first general store in the settlement. They were promised a substantial house but instead found an unsafe, unfurnished structure with a dirt floor and leaky roof. It had been abandoned two years ago after the raid in 1780, when a pack of ferocious Canadian Indians under British leadership destroyed their homes. Mrs. Coombs, who is eight months pregnant, is ordinarily an ill-spirited woman and under these circumstances, has become more peevish and shrewish, blaming her husband for their misfortune. The two families have not met nor do they know that each survived the raid two years before. Kate and her children survived by hiding in a cave, guided there, Kate maintains, by a large hawk. Caleb was away fighting in the militia. The Coombs also survived by hiding, but the horrors of the raid are indelibly imprinted in Hiram's. He saw his wounded Uncle Abner carried off by the British and as a result both Hiram and his mother have developed a fanatical hatred of all Indians. After the raid, the Tuckers rebuilt their home but the Coombs family retreated to Connecticut to live with Hannah's relatives.

Daniel's 13th birthday begins poorly. He loses a big trout caught in the weir his mother taught him to make. And when he looks at a young blond boy across the stream, the boy inexplicably runs off in a panic. The boy is actually his new neighbor, Hiram Coombs, who has run home to warn his folks that there are wild Indians in the area. Mr. Tucker decides to help his new neighbors settle in and Daniel follows him to lend a hand. On the way, he successfully catches the elusive trout and leaves it in the bushes to be picked up on his way home for a splendid birthday dinner. At the Coombs's house, the traumatized Hiram runs away again. He does not want to mess with no "injun." Mrs. Coombs, who also behaves coolly toward the boy, rejects Mr. Tucker's suggestion that his wife, an expert midwife but an Indian, help during the imminent birthing process. Daniel is further outraged, when at lunch break, they eat the trout he caught earlier. Hiram had found it in the woods but makes up a story that he caught it himself. After a day of work, both Mr. Tucker and Daniel leave the Coombs's home somewhat disgruntled despite apologies from the well-meaning Mr. Coombs for the inhospitable behavior of his wife and son.

The Tuckers then receive an unexpected visitor—Kate's ancient and ailing father—who has traveled from Connecticut on his spindly mare to visit the family. The old man is the powwaw of his tribe, the possessor of great spiritual powers, and he begins imparting this knowledge to both Daniel and his responsive sister Rhoda. The day ends when Daniel receives gifts for his birthday, including a treasured wampum belt from Grandfather, a doeskin pouch from his mother, and a knife and sheaf from Dad.

Meanwhile, the Coombs are also receiving a visitor. Uncle Abner, more dead than alive, arrives after escaping from a Quebec prison and wandering in the wilderness for 22 days. From his suffering and pain, he has become deranged and obsessive in his hatred of Indians.

When Grandfather begins building a teepee, Hiram visits the Tucker property and even deigns to help in the process. However, after the teepee is complete, someone destroys it. Daniel does some sleuthing and, with the help of the family dog, Jody, follows boot prints to the Coombs property and confronts the culprit, Uncle Abner. A chase ensues and, through Daniel's clever maneuvering, a posse of outraged locals—including members of the Ellis family and Mr. Chase, the blacksmith—trap him in a root cellar. Mr. Tucker generously gives Abner some money and he is run out of town.

Days later, Mrs. Coombs goes into labor. The Ellis ladies are called to help. When it appears that Mrs. Coombs is bleeding to death, the ladies summon Kate Tucker in spite of Hannah's protests. Miraculously, Kate and Grandfather, using native medications, save both the mother and her twin babies, a boy and a girl.

The teepee is rebuilt, but Grandfather suffers multiple seizures and dies. This loss devastates both Daniel and Rhoda and, in a traditional show of grief, Kate cuts her hair and covers her face with ashes. Daniel is sent to his friend Mr. Sykes, the cooper, to have a coffin built and, after a simple service, Grandfather is buried on the property with three large stones covering the grave. Gradually the loss is accepted and life goes on. Relations between the Coombs and Tuckers families improve: Hiram and Daniel begin building a canoe together and, in a sign of appreciation, Mrs. Coombs names her girl Lila Kate. Daniel begins an apprenticeship with Mr. Sykes, and Rhoda continues in her grandfather's footsteps, studying the mysteries and oneness of all nature.

Passages for Booktalking

Four interesting passages are: Daniel loses his fish and encounters Hiram (pp. 9–12); Hiram reacts to seeing Daniel, and the Coombs family is introduced (pp. 13–18); Daniel catches the fish, and begins working with the Coombs family (pp. 32–37); and Grandfather arrives (pp. 47–50).

Themes and Subjects

This is a story of prejudice and the hatred it produces being gradually over-come through knowledge, understanding, and love. The roots of this prejudice are realistically portrayed. Daniel, a boy of two races, adjusts to living in these two worlds, embracing his dual ancestry, and accepting as his friend a boy sworn to be his enemy because of this heritage. The subtle growth of both Daniel and Hiram is expertly depicted. Details of pioneering and frontier life in the 18th century are accurate as is the depiction of Pequot lore, beliefs, and folktales. Other subjects: Vermont, Connecticut, American Revolution, farm-ing, family life, babies, neighborliness, grandfathers, crafts, medicine, friend-ship, birth, and death.

O'DELL, SCOTT. *Sarah Bishop.* Houghton, 1980 o.p.; pap. Scholastic, $5.99 (978-0-590-44651-8) (Grades 5–8)

Introduction

Scott O'Dell (1898–1989) is known as one of the foremost writers of histori-cal fiction for young readers. In a writing career that spanned more than forty years, he published more than two dozen novels for juveniles, most dealing with North American and Hispanic-American subjects. Many have won major literary awards including his first book for youngsters, *Island of the Blue Dolphins* (Houghton, 1960, $13.45, 0395069629; condensed in *The New-bery/Printz Companion*), which won the Newbery Medal in 1961. This novel, like *Sarah Bishop*, features as its central character a strong-willed heroine who overcomes great odds.

Sarah Bishop takes place over roughly a year's time—from the events imme-diately preceding the Battle of Long Island (or Battle of Brooklyn Heights) in August 1776 through the following summer. It is based on the life of Sarah Bishop, who was born in England, moved with her family to Long Island shortly before the Revolution and later fled to the wilderness of Westchester County directly north of New York City.

The author helped establish the Scott O'Dell Award for Historical Fiction, given annually to the author of a distinguished work of historical fiction writ-ten by an American, set in the New World, and published in English by a U.S. publisher. In addition to prestige, the award carries a $5,000 prize. The first award was given in 1984.

Historical Background

Many of the events in the novel involve the Battle of Long Island, also known as the Battle of Brooklyn Heights, and its aftermath. After the Declaration of Independence was ratified in Philadelphia on July 4, 1776, George Washington, expecting an attack on New York by the British, moved his troops to western Long Island and Manhattan. Meanwhile, the British, under Lieutenant General Sir William Howe, concentrated their ships and forces on Staten Island and on the night of August 27, 1776, invaded Brooklyn with 22,000 men including 9,000 Hessian mercenaries. The Americans were led jointly by Washington and Major General Israel Putnam. The outnumbered Americans suffered great losses. During the night of August 30, 1776, having lost the battle, the American troops retreated to Manhattan and, later, after another loss at the Battle of White Plains in Westchester County, retreated further to New Jersey. The British occupied the New York City area until 1783. On September 21, 1776, a mysterious fire broke out in downtown New York City and destroyed nearly a quarter of the city's buildings. The British blamed the rebels (including Sarah Bishop in the novel) of setting the Great Fire of New York. After this, Sarah sought refuge on the mainland north of the Bronx in the wilderness of northern Westchester County close to the Connecticut border. Long Pond, where she lived in a cave, is still referred to by its Indian name, Waccabuc.

Principal Characters

Sarah Bishop, the spunky 15-year-old heroine and narrator
James Bishop, Sarah's Loyalist father
Mr. Purdy, a mill owner with rebel sympathies
Chad Bishop, Sarah's older brother
David Whitlock, Chad's friend
Old Lady Ryder, a secret Loyalist sympathizer
Jim Quarme, a Revolutionary thug
Ben Birdsall, the ruthless leader of rebel hoodlums
Mr. and Mrs. Pennywells, owners of a local tavern
Captain Cunningham, a cold-hearted British officer
Sam Goshen, a lascivious depraved troublemaker
Thomas Morton, a Quaker shopowner in Ridgeford
Isaac Morton, his son
The Longknifes, an Indian couple who befriend Sarah

Plot Synopsis

Fifteen-year-old Sarah Bishop remembers growing up on a farm in England before her family was dispossessed during hard times. Her father relocated the Bishops to land he purchased on Long Island across the East River from Manhattan. Since her mother's death most of the household chores have fallen on Sarah's shoulders while her father tends to the new farm and supplements their small income by being a general handyman to neighbors like Old Lady Ryder, whose clock he is currently repairing. Also in the household is Sarah's beloved older brother Chad, who also helps his father on the farm as well as working at the local hotel/tavern, the Lion and Lamb. It is August 1776 and, like the rest of the American colonies, the Bishop household is full of dissent. Mr. Bishop is a fierce and outspoken Loyalist (he even had a portrait of King George above his bed until Chad secretly burned it), while Chad and many of his young contemporaries are caught up with revolutionary fervor. Many of these youthful firebrands congregate at Purdy's mill, including Jim Quarme and Ben Birdsall, members of the Skinners, a gang that terrorizes sympathizers of King George.

On a trip to the mill, Sarah is warned by Mr. Purdy that her father should be more careful about voicing his Loyalist sympathies. Sarah and her father become more isolated when, a few days later, Chad and his friend David Whitlock announce they have joined the militia and leave for Brooklyn Fort. Not all the townspeople, however, are rebels. The Bishops learn that Old Lady Ryder has secretly been sabotaging Mr. Purdy's mill machinery as part of her war effort. Soon, the harassment begins in earnest. Sarah and her father emerge from church one Sunday to find that their horses, along with those of five other Loyalist families, have been stolen. Everyone is convinced it is the work of Birdsall and his gang.

One evening three weeks later, while Sarah and her father are reading the Bible together, they are visited by Bill Birdsall and a group that includes Jim Quarme. After setting fire to the farm and outbuildings, they tie Sarah to a tree and drag off Mr. Bishop. He later stumbles back to the charred ruins of his farm, tarred and feathered. He dies within hours and Sarah, with only the clothes on her back and a copy of the Bible, a gift from a neighbor, sets off to the Lion and Lamb hoping to get a job. Mr. and Mrs. Pennywell, the owners and Chad's former employers, give Sarah a job as their baker.

Sarah is frantic for news about her brother. After the Battle of Brooklyn Heights, the British occupy the area and, with the help of an officer, Sarah gets a note that must be delivered to Captain Cunningham, the officer in charge of prisoners. Over the protests of the Pennywells, she sets out for New York City. There she discovers that Chad is being held as a prisoner of war. Determined to get permission to visit him, she decides to contact Cunningham. She finds lodging in a disreputable flophouse, but in the middle of the night, this building and several others are destroyed by a raging fire. The following morning, lucky to have escaped death, Sarah wanders through smoke-filled streets to Captain Cunningham's headquarters. He proves to be a mean-spirited, sadistic man who, after revealing that her brother is on a prison ship called the *Scorpion*, accuses her, on circumstantial evidence, of setting the previous evening's disastrous fire. Though she is now under arrest, a kindly officer agrees to accompany her to the prison where she learns from David Whitlock, also a prisoner, that Chad died that morning.

Sarah manages to elude her captors and get back to the Pennywells on Long Island. With their help, she makes her way to the mainland ferry and, for protection, buys a musket from the ferryman. On shore close to White Plains in Westchester County, she hears the sounds of battle and presses northward. She hitches a ride on a cart driven by a man named Sam Goshen who makes sexual advances toward her. Holding him at bay with her musket, she takes his horse and, promising to leave it at the next town, Ridgeford, rides off. In town, she uses the last of her money to buy provisions and an ax from the local general store operated by Thomas Morton and his friendly but timid son, Isaac. From their generous use of "thees" and "thous" Sarah determines they must be Quakers. Heading north, in dense wilderness near the edge of Lake Waccabuc, also known as Long Pond, Sarah discovers a large cave and makes it her home. She ousts the current residents, hundreds of bats, except for a pure white one that she names Gabriel of Waccabuc.

It is now autumn, and Sarah begins to make preparations for the long winter by gathering wood, smoking trout from the lake, and insulating her cave. She is befriended by a family of wandering Indians, the Longknifes, who help her build a dugout canoe. One day she discovers a man near the lake whose leg has been caught in his bear trap. It is Sam Goshen and, despite her feelings of revulsion and apprehension, she nurses him back to health before ordering him back to his home in Ridgeford. Because of these extreme vicissitudes, Sarah begins to question her religious beliefs. To gain money for more provisions, Sarah goes to Ridgeford and works for a few days in the local tavern. In town, she becomes reacquainted with Isaac Morton, who takes an interest in her and offers her help. Spring comes and with it Sarah suffers an additional tribulation-the bite of a copperhead snake. She gradually recovers and decides to accept an invitation, conveyed by the Longknifes, from Isaac Morton to attend a Meeting in town. Her contact with the townspeople, however, turns ugly when, because of a plant-withering drought and Sam Goshen's fabricated stories about Sarah's relationship with a white bat, she is accused of witchcraft. Luckily, through the intervention of Isaac and the arrival of a huge rainstorm, the charges are dropped. Again with Isaac's help, Sarah is gradually accepted by the people of Ridgeford and also regains some of her faith. Nevertheless, she fiercely resolves to remain independent and remain in her cave home with Gabriel.

Passages for Booktalking

Here are a few interesting passages: Sarah visits Mr. Purdy's mill and receives a warning (pp. 8–13); Chad tells his father about enlisting (pp. 21–26); at church, Mr. Bishop's horses are stolen (pp. 29–33); and Mr. Bishop is murdered (pp. 38–43).

Themes and Subjects

This novel examines the American Revolution from several points of view, principally the fate of the Loyalists who remained faithful to King George. More important is the depiction of the senseless brutality and barbarism that war brings regardless of the cause (the evil of both Birdsall the rebel and Cunningham the Loyalist, for example). Bigotry, superstition, and intolerance are depicted in the behavior of the Ridgeford residents. Sarah is a strong-willed heroine who triumphs through courage, determination, and persistence while maintaining feelings of compassion and humanity toward others. This novel contains an excellent depiction of survival over adverse conditions. The struggle to retain faith when faced with injustice and undeserved affliction is well presented. Other subjects include: the American Revolution, the Battle of Brooklyn Heights, the Battle of White Plains, everyday colonial life, death, family life, Quakers, religion, and Native Americans.

TORREY, MICHELE. *Voyage of Midnight.* Knopf, 2006, $15.95 (978-0-375-82382-4) (Grades 6–9)

Introduction

The author was born in Wenatchee, Washington, the apple capital of the United States, but spent her youth in France, England, and Germany. In the fifth grade she wrote a story that was printed in her class newspaper and, from that moment, knew she wanted to be a writer. She is best known for her Doyle and Fossey, Science Detectives series as well as her Chronicles of Courage "Voyage" historical adventure stories, of which this is number three. The first book, *Voyage of Ice* (Knopf, 2004, $15.95; 00375823816; pap. Dell, $5.99; 0440418860), portrays the grim realities of the whaling industry. Nick, age 15, and his older brother Dexter decide to follow the example of their late father, a whaling captain, and go to sea. Nick signs on to the *Sea Hawk* but finds this life, with its hardships and brutality, is not for him. After a failed attempt to desert, however, he finds himself back on the ship and sailing through ice-filled Arctic waters. A shipwreck occurs and Nick and his companions must survive in this hostile frozen environment. In the second volume, a pirate story titled *Voyage of Plunder* (Knopf, 2005, $15.95, 0375823822; pap. Dell, $5.99; 0440418879), 14-year-old Daniel's father remarries and the boy's life changes completely. The old family friends, including Josiah Black, no longer visit and Father later decides to move the family from Baltimore to Jamaica. On the way, pirates, led by the same Josiah Black, board their vessel, murder Daniel's father, and force the boy into a life of piracy. When all the pirates are captured, they are condemned to death, but Josiah, who is actually Daniel's biological father, saves him.

The main action of *Voyage of Midnight* takes place on the Atlantic Ocean on a slave ship during several months in 1821. As well as a suspenseful nautical story, it is a heart-wrenching chronicle of the slave trade.

Historical Background

In an intriguing Author's Note at the end of the novel, Ms. Torrey describes the three major narratives that were used as a basis for this book. There was, was, for example, an actual case where a young man worked on a slaver on which all but one of the crew went blind from eye infections. It has been esti-mated that between 12 million and 16 million slaves left Africa during the transatlantic slave trade. About the same number died before being herded onto the ships and, of course many died during the voyage. More than half of the survivors were sent to South America, another 40 percent to the Carib-bean, and about 5 percent were transported to what became the United States.

Reference is made in the novel to several pieces of anti-slavery legislation. In 1807, the British Parliament passed the Abolition of Slavery Act, which made it unlawful for any British subject to capture or transport slaves. If caught, the captain of a slave ship was fined a hundred pounds per slave. But when slave ships were in danger of capture, the human cargo was often thrown into the sea. (In 1833, the British passed the Slavery Abolition Act, which gave free-dom to all the slaves in the British Empire.) In 1808, the United States passed a law similar to the British one of 1807 but it was not often enforced. On May 15, 1820, the United States Law on Slave Trade declared that the trading of slaves by a U.S. citizen was comparable to piracy and, in some cases, punish-able by death. Because the United States was lax in enforcing its anti-slavery laws and because of its lack of cooperation with other nations, the slave trade continued well into the 19th century.

Among the ailments that afflict the crew and slaves in the story are oph-thalmia and the bloody flux. The first is an inflammation of the eyeball, a form of bacterial conjunctivitis. In its milder form this highly contagious condition is often called pinkeye; but untreated it can cause severe eye problems including temporary or permanent blindness. The bloody flux or flux is an old term for dysentery, an inflammation of the intestines, usually caused by an infection from water or food containing harmful microorganisms. Symptoms include diarrhea, fever, and general weakness.

As well as a bibliography, at the end of the book there is a glossary of nautical terms like bo'sun and binnacle, very useful for land lubbers.

Principal Characters

Philip Arthur Higgins, the young hero and narrator of the story
Isaac Smythe, or Captain Towne, Philip's uncle and captain of the
Formidable
Master Crump, a workhouse director
Mr. Gallagher, a chemist
Mrs. Gallagher, his wife
Jonas Drinkwater, the ship's medic
Billy Dorsett, also called Billy the Vermin, the cabin boy
Jack Numbly, the first mate
McGuire, the second mate
Pea Soup, or Oji, Philip's slave
Ikoro, a slave leader
Cookie, the Cook

Plot Synopsis

English lad Philip Arthur Higgins never knew his father, a sailor who drowned at sea before he was born, and scarcely remembers his mother, who died when he was only four and a half years old. After her death, Philip was sent to the Magford workhouse under the cruel supervision of the cane-wielding Master Crump. At ten, he worked for a cushion maker until he caught his hand in a roller and was sent back to Master Crump's to recuperate. Relief from this dismal existence appears in the form of a tall, handsome man, Isaac Smythe, who is Philip's uncle, the brother of Philip's mother. Before ending a brief visit, he promises to help Philip, but a year passes before money arrives to bring Philip to New Orleans to live with Mr. Smythe. In September 1818 he boards the *Hope*. After a violent crossing, he arrives, alone and penniless, first in Baltimore and then in New Orleans. No one is at the port to meet Philip. However, a kindly man with a warm Irish brogue named Mr. Gallagher, who is waiting for his own young nephew, begins chatting with him. When Mr. Gallagher learns that his nephew has died at sea, he asks Philip if he would like to take his place and come live with him and his wife. Philip agrees and immediately fits comfortably into the Gallagher household. Mr. Gallagher is a chemist and Philip begins to learn this profession while also attending a local Catholic school. Mr. and Mrs. Gallagher treat Philip as they would their own son.

Two years pass and one day Philip spots his uncle in a tavern. Philip is once again impressed by the man's demeanor, sophistication and obvious wealth. His uncle reintroduces himself and uses his real name, Isaac Towne. He is the captain of the vessel *Formidable*. When the Captain learns that Philip has a knowledge of drugs and medicine, he invites him to become the surgeon's mate on his ship sailing in one week. Philip is thrilled at the prospect and gets reluctant consent from the Gallaghers. On board, he meets the truly motley crew including Jonas Drinkwater, the affable but alcoholic ship's doctor; the weasel-like cabin boy, Billy Dorsett; and various crew members including the first mate Jack Numbly and second mate McGuire. Philip is surprised to learn that the ship is bound for Africa for a cargo of slaves. Although the transporting of slaves is illegal according to legislation passed in both Britain and the United States, Philip's uncle persuasively explains to him that slavery is a necessary evil and that saving these unfortunates from a different kind of slavery in Africa and giving them an opportunity to lead a Christian life in America is actually an act of benevolence. The ship stops in Havana first and there Philip receives as a gift his own slave, a young man named Pea Soup who has recently arrived from Africa.

In Africa, on the coast of the Gulf of Guinea, the ship moves upstream on the River Bonny to a settlement where a large group of slaves are being held prisoner for sale. The captain shrewdly examines each one to weed out the weak and infirm. After final choices are made, branding begins. This inhuman practice involves branding each slave between the shoulders with a hot iron that bears the ship's name. Uncle forces Philip to be part of the ritual but when Philip tries to brand one of the slaves—Ikoro, a fierce and admired specimen of African manhood—the slave turns on Philip, grabs the iron, and brands the boy on the chest. As punishment for this action, the slave is branded by a reluctant but suffering Philip without any of the soothing oil that lessens the pain.

With a cargo of 244 men and 124 women and children, the ship is heading into open water when two warships, one English and the other American, are spotted. The captain hastily backtracks into the Bonny River. That night Philip sees Pea Soup climbing out on the bowsprit, dagger in hand, intent on sabotage. Philip crawls out after him, almost falling into the shark-filled waters below (see dust jacket cover). Although he saves the ship from harm and has Pea Soup placed in temporary confinement, Philip will never forget the hatred he saw in the young slave's eyes.

The *Formidable* eludes its pursuers and once again sails into Atlantic waters, where the slaves are allowed on deck for short periods while Billy Dorsett plays the fiddle to make them dance. Both Jonas and Philip are disturbed when a number of slaves show severe eye infections, but this concern is momentarily forgotten when the ship crosses the equator and Father Neptune (Jonas in disguise) and the other veteran sailors reveal the rites of the crossing. Jonas, a constant imbiber, dies suddenly and Philip is appointed the ship's surgeon.

Pea Soup is released and is seen acting suspiciously. One day the slaves, led by Ikoro, stage a rebellion armed with weapons, Philip realizes, that were smuggled to them by Pea Soup. The revolt is squashed but six crew members and sixteen slaves are killed. In retaliation, the captain has six slaves executed, including Ikoro. Philip discovers that Ikoro is Pea Soup's father and sympathizes with the boy, who for some reason saved him during the revolt.

Conditions in the hold are hellish and the slaves exist with little food and water and live in their own waste. When a baby is born, Captain Towne throws it overboard. Philip realizes that slavery is not a necessary evil but instead pure evil. He begins to loath the man he once admired. Along with other diseases, the eye infection spreads and in a short time several of the slaves become blind. Soon the infection affects the crew and within days everyone on board is blind. Somehow, even after the death of Cookie the cook, enough food and water are dispensed by the sightless crew to ward off starvation, although the death rate among the slaves rises.

During this ordeal, Philip becomes fast friends with Pea Soup, whose real name is Oji. Philip frees him. For his work helping the sick slaves, Philip is given the name Ikeotuonye, "the strength of one person." Miraculously Philip regains his sight and hatches a plan with the still-blind Oji. Using the navigational skills his uncle taught him, Philip turns the boat around and heads for Africa. Through a series of clever deceptions, the plan works until the ship nears the coast of Africa and the blind captain realizes from the direction of the sun's rays that the ship is off course. When the treacherous cabin boy, who has also regained his sight, confirms this, Philip confesses in order to save the life of another newborn child the captain has discovered.

While trying to escape the crew, Philip climbs the shrouds—the ropes that stretch to the mastheads—pursued by Billy and other crew members. Philip loses his footing and falls into the water but is a saved by crew members of the American naval vessel that the *Formidable* eluded some months before. The Americans board the ship and arrest the captain and crew. Philip and Oji have triumphed. Their precious cargo is released to freedom. In an epilogue, Philip reports on the eventual fate of those on the *Formidable*: Captain Towne, permanently blind, spends years in prison before retiring to Cuba; Oji, also blind, returns to his village; and Philip Arthur Higgins, later to become Dr. Higgins, returns to the open arms of the Gallaghers.

Passages for Booktalking

Philip's uncle appears and disappears and Philip gets passage to New Orleans (pp. 3–7); Philip's arrival in New Orleans and welcome into the Gallagher household (pp. 10–15); Philip finds his uncle and says goodbye to the Gallaghers (pp. 19–24); Uncle explains his position on slavery (pp. 36–40) and the branding incident (pp. 48–54).

Themes and Subjects

As the series title suggests this is truly a "chronicle of courage." The horrors of slavery in general and the slave trade in particular are graphically portrayed using often-shocking but truthful details. A boy's discovery of his idol's true nature and coping with the subsequent disillusionment is an important theme, as is his painful journey to discovering the terrible evil of slavery. The debasement and dehumanization associated with both the slaves and the slave traders is powerfully presented. Philip's journey to manhood and maturity is also an important theme. Other subjects: Africans, friendship, disease, conjunctivitis, death, medicine, ships, sea stories, adventure stories, families, and survival.

ADDITIONAL SELECTIONS

Carlow, Drew. *Attack of the Turtle* (Eerdmans, 2007, $16) (Grades 4–6)
    During the American Revolution 14-year-old Nate conquers his fear of water to work on the *Turtle*, the first submarine used in naval warfare.

Demas, Corinne. *If Ever I Return Again* (HarperCollins, 2000, $15.89) (Grades 5–8)
    Twelve-year-old Celia describes life aboard a whaling ship in letters to her cousin.

Durrant, Lynda. *Betty Zane, the Rose of Fort Henry* (Clarion, 2000, $15) (Grades 5–8)
    Toward the end of the Revolutionary War, Betsy sets out alone from Philadelphia to rejoin her five brothers in western Virginia.

Ernst, Kathleen. *Betrayal at Cross Creek* (Pleasant, 2004, $10.95) (Grades 5–9)
    During the Revolutionary War, a young Scottish refugee and her grandparents are torn apart by conflicting loyalties.

Gaeddert, Louann. *Breaking Free* (Atheneum, 1994, $16) (Grades 5–8)
    In 1800 in upstate New York, young Richard becomes so upset at seeing slaves on his uncle's farm that he decides to help one escape.

Giblin, James Cross. *The Boy Who Saved Cleveland* (Holt, 2006, $15.95) (Grades 3–6)
    Set in 1798 in the city of Cleveland, this is the story of 10-year-old Seth Doan and how he helped the settlers during an outbreak of malaria.

Jones, Elizabeth McDavid. *Traitor in Williamsburg* (American Girl, 2008, pap. $6.95) (Grades 3–5)
It is 1776 in Williamsburg, Virginia, and Felicity and Elizabeth set out to reveal who is accusing their friend's father of having Loyalist sympathies.

Lunn, Janet. *The Hollow Tree* (Viking, 2000, $15.99) (Grades 5–9)
Torn between her sympathy for both the Rebels and Tories, Phoebe decides to join the refugees heading for Canada and safety.

McCully, Emily Arnold. *The Escape of Oney Judge: Martha Washington's Slave Finds Freedom* (Farrar, 2006, $16) (Grades 2–4)
Even though she is well treated by her mistress, Martha Washington, Oney seeks personal freedom and runs away.

Meyer, L. A. *Curse of the Blue Tattoo: Being an Account of the Misadventures of Jacky Faber, Midshipman and Fine Lady* (Harcourt, 2004, $17) (Grades 6–9)
In this sequel to *Bloody Jack* (Harcourt, 2002, $17), also set in the early 19th century, tomboy Jacky Faber is enrolled in a girl's finishing school in Boston with disastrous but hilarious results.

Pearsall, Shelley. *Crooked River* (Knopf, 2005, $15.95) (Grades 4–6)
In 1812, 13-year-old Rebecca Carver and her older sister return to their Ohio home and find their father is holding a Native American prisoner because he supposedly killed a trapper.

Roop, Pete, and Connie Roop. *An Eye for an Eye: A Story of the Revolutionary War* (Jamestown, 2000, pap. $5.95) (Grades 5–9)
During the Revolutionary War, Samantha, disguised as a boy, sets out to contact her brother who is a prisoner of the British.

Shaik, Fatima. *Melitte* (Dial, 1997, $15.99) (Grades 6–9)
In the late 18th century, Melitte is living a miserable life as a slave in Louisiana.

Wait, Lea. *Stopping to Home* (Simon, 2001, $16) (Grades 4–7)
In this story set in early 19th-century Maine, 11-year-old Abbie takes a job as a housemaid after her mother dies of smallpox.

Wisler, G. Clifton. *Kings Mountain* (HarperCollins, 2002, $15.89) (Grades 5–8)
When 14-year-old Francis goes to South Carolina to work in her grandmother's tavern, she becomes involved in the intrigue and danger of the Revolutionary War.

THE GROWTH OF THE NATION AND WESTWARD MOVEMENT (1821–1861)

AYRES, KATHERINE. *North by Night: A Story of the Underground Railroad.* Delacorte, 1998, o.p.; Dell, pap. $4.99 (978-0-440-22747-2) (Grades 5–8)

Introduction

Before she learned how to write, Katherine Ayres was making up stories to tell. Many years later she became a successful author of books for children and young adults in addition to being, at various times, a grade school teacher, an elementary school principal, and a professor of creative writing. She is also a homemaker, mother, and grandmother. Her first two novels were set in Ohio. The first, *Family Tree* (Dell, pap. $4.99, 0440411939), features Tyler Stoudt, a young girl who is convinced she will flunk sixth grade because the year's class project is to develop one's family tree and she has only her father. Later, however, she discovers his Amish upbringing and secrets of her family's past. The second is *North by Night*, whose central character is Lucinda (Lucy) Spencer. In a sequel, *Stealing South: A Story of the Underground Railroad* (Dell, pap. $4.99; 0440418011), Lucy's younger brother Will, now age 16, decides to leave his Ohio home and become a peddler. His family ties to the Underground Railroad convince him to help Noah, a runaway slave, to free his brother and sister in the South. While there he gains the trust and confidence of some generous slave owners and agrees to take six boys and an elderly woman to the slave market. Conscience prevails and instead he takes them, along with Noah's sister, north to freedom.

North by Night is set principally in the small northern Ohio town of Atwater and consists of Lucy's journal entries and letters to and from her over a period of about three months, from January through March of 1851. The author has included a preface that supplies valuable background information.

Historical Background

It has been estimated that more than 70,000 blacks escaped slavery via the Underground Railroad, an intricate web of people and places that provided food, shelter, and transportation to runaways whose destination was usually Canada. The idea was conceived by Reverend Charles Torrey, who first elicited aid from cooperative white people. He died in a Maryland Penitentiary after helping 400 slaves to freedom. Much of the terminology of this system came from the railroads—shelters were called "stations," the leaders were "conductors" or "station managers," and financial supporters were "stockholders." A journey might take several weeks because traveling was done in darkness either on foot or in wagons (many equipped with false bottoms to hide their human cargo) and only 10 to 20 miles could be covered each night. The Ohio land routes usually ended around Cleveland where boats transported the runaways across Lake Erie to an area in present-day Ontario between Windsor and Toronto. Workers on the railroad were sometimes freed slaves or ardent abolitionists but more often they were ordinary people of good conscience, often from such religious denominations as the Quakers, Congregationalists, and Reformed Presbyterians.

Because northern states were so half-hearted in enforcing laws requiring the return of escaped slaves, Congress passed the Fugitive Slave Act of 1850 to appease southern slave owners. The act mandated the return of runaways regardless of where they were discovered and prescribed severe punishment for those who disregarded or broke this law. For example, anyone providing food or shelter to a slave was subject to six months in jail and/or a $1,000 fine. Considering that the average working farm was worth less than $1,000, conviction under this law could lead to bankruptcy. Officers or deputies who captured slaves were entitled to a fee and therefore the role of "bounty hunters" or "catchers" became important. One unexpected effect of the law was to consolidate and strengthen the anti-slavery movement in the North.

The small town of Atwater, Ohio, the setting of the novel, is situated in the north-eastern part of the state, about 125 miles south of Cleveland and 50 miles east of Canton.

Principal Characters

Lucinda (Lucy) Spencer, a 16-year-old girl
Mama and Papa, her mother and father
Thomas, her 9-year-old brother
William, her 13-year-old brother
Miranda, her lovable, precocious 5-year-old sister
Jeremiah Strong, a handsome Quaker youth slightly older than Lucy
Charity Strong, Jeremiah's younger sister
Jonathan Clark, Lucy's beau
Rebecca Carter, Lucy's best friend
Widow Mercer (Miss Aurelia), a self-willed reclusive woman
Levi Bowen, a deputy and slave catcher
Clayton Roberts, a Southern slave owner
Mrs. Bessie Smith, a midwife
Emma, a runaway slave with five children
Abraham, Emma's husband
Cass, a pregnant runaway slave with two children

Plot Synopsis

Sixteen-year-old Lucinda (Lucy) Spencer and her devoted Presbyterian family are leading double lives, with the exception of 5-year-old Miranda. Outwardly they are an average farm family living in Atwater, a settled area in northern Ohio. But secretly they are workers on the Underground Railroad actively harboring in their dugout basement runaway slaves who are on their way north across Lake Michigan to freedom in Canada. Besides Lucy and Miranda, the Spencer family consists of liberal-minded, loving Mama and Papa, 13-year-old William, 9-year-old Thomas, and assorted pets including a doe, chicken, duck, and a cat named Brutus. It is January 1, 1851, and Lucy has begun a new journal in which she confides her innermost thoughts and feelings.

Inspired by beliefs in equality and freedom, the family has been helping runaway slaves for years regardless of the risk and possible consequences. Only three nights into the new year, Lucy is awakened by Jeremiah Strong. He is outside her window with two slaves who need shelter. Jeremiah is the oldest son in a Quaker family. Although she has a steady boyfriend in the dependable Jonathan Clark, Lucy is impressed with Jeremiah's gentleness and good looks. Lucy welcomes the slaves and they stay overnight. At church on Sunday, she sees an attractive southern gentleman in the congregation and, after the service, gossips with her best friend Rebecca Carter about the gala party that the Clarks will host in a few days.

When Lucy arrives at the party, she is immediately accosted by Charity Strong, Jeremiah's young sister. She takes Lucy into a deserted room for a secret conversation with Jeremiah. Through coded references, Lucy learns that a group of nine runaways, two women and seven children, has arrived and needs help. A tenth runaway, a man named Abraham, has been captured and is in jail in Canton. A daring scheme has been devised. The refugees are to be hidden in the attic of another activist, the Widow Mercer, a reclusive, strong-willed woman who lives alone in a large house a few miles out of town. To discourage visitors, word has been circulated that the widow has a severe case of measles. Using beet juice for spots and whiskey to produce a flushed face, she has already convinced those who have seen her. However, she needs help and Jeremiah asks Lucy (who has had measles and is therefore immune, providing a good alibi) to volunteer to live with the widow and help her until she "recovers." She consents even though it means a separation from her adoring family.

Their conversation is interrupted by Jonathan Clark. To avert suspicion, Jeremiah feigns a lover's tryst, and kisses Lucy passionately. Jonathan is furious but Lucy secretly enjoys the experience. She moves to the widow's home, isolated both by the quarantine and by heavy snow. Lucy meets the runaways: The adult women are Emma, mother of five and wife of the captured Abraham, and her younger sister Cass, who has two children and is expecting a third in a few days. Cass is very sickly and confined to bed with swollen legs and a heart condition. The runaways are all owned by Clayton Roberts, a married slave owner who Lucy realizes is the stranger she saw in church. He is now in the North searching for the escapees. Lucy is horrified to learn later that Cass has been forced to be Roberts's mistress and that her youngsters, including the unborn one, are his children.

Lucy learns to love her host, the Widow Mercer, whom she now calls Miss Aurelia. The outspoken, independent woman is not really a widow. She and her husband decided to live amicable separate lives: she as an artist and writer for newspapers, and he as a roving frontiersman who has found wealth in California's gold fields, some of which he shares with her.

One day Clayton Roberts and Deputy Levi Bowen appear, demanding to search the farmhouse for the runaways. Through a clever ruse on the part of Tom, Lucy's visiting brother, the two miss the attic and leave empty-handed. Lucy learns that her friend Rebecca is about to be engaged, that Jonathan is still upset about the kissing incident, and Jeremiah and Will, Lucy's other brother, are about to travel to Canton to free Abraham from jail. The rescue is accomplished and Abraham is taken to Cleveland. Plans are made to move the rest of the runaways first to Cleveland to join Abraham and then on to Canada and freedom. However Cass is not well enough to travel and so, after a tearful farewell to her children, she remains behind.

That night Will stashes his precious human cargo in the hidden compartment of his wagon and begins the perilous journey north with Jeremiah. After days of fretful waiting, Jeremiah brings news that the operation was successful and all nine refugees are now in Canada. Meanwhile Lucy and Cass have become close friends. Lucy is making progress teaching her how to write, when the labor pains begin. Lucy rides through a terrible snowstorm to bring the midwife, Mrs. Bessie Smith, a sympathizer of the movement, to Cass's side. A healthy baby arrives and Cass names her Hope. However, in a few days, Cass's illnesses worsen and she dies. Lucy is determined to complete Cass's journey and take Hope to her family in Canada. At her first hotel stop she and the baby are unfortunately intercepted by Clayton Roberts and Levi Bowen. They are suspicious and even when Lucy claims the baby is her own child, born out of wedlock, Roberts is convinced it is his. They hold Lucy prisoner in her hotel room until a doctor can be summoned to examine Lucy and verify her story.

Lucy realizes she is trapped. When the truth is discovered, she and her family face imprisonment and financial ruin for helping runaways. That night, she eludes the sleeping Bowen and makes contact with underground workers in the town. Soon she, like the slaves she has helped, is traveling north via the

Railroad. For several days on the journey, she and Hope escape detection by hiding in a coffin and finally, she boards a steamer to take her to Canada across Lake Erie. She thinks of her family and the dear ones left behind but knows she will be able to make a rewarding life in her new home.

Passages for Booktalking (pagination from the paperback edition)
In the entry dated Saturday, January 4, 1851, Lucy helps save two runaways (pp. 4–6); Jeremiah tells of his plan to help the nine runaways (pp. 23–27); Aurelia introduces herself and explains how she developed the "measles" (pp. 31–34); and Emma talks about her life as a slave (pp. 58–61).

Themes and Subjects
This is a story of courage, sacrifice, and unselfish devotion to a cause. Lucy emerges as a mature, endearing young lady who gallantly forfeits every thing she holds dear to save her loved ones and those less fortunate than herself. The novel gives a fascinating inside look at the workings of the Underground Railroad and the cruelty and injustice of slavery. Some other subjects: friendship, family ties, bravery, Ohio, Canada, independent women, religion, love, death, tragedy, and fortitude.

ERDRICH, LOUISE.
The Birchbark House. Hyperion, 1999, o.p.; pap. $6.99 (978-0-7868-1454-1) (Grades 4–8)

The Game of Silence. Harper, 2005, $15.99 (978-0-06-029789-3); pap. $5.99 (978-0-06-441029-8) (Grades 5–8)

Introduction
Louise Erdrich (1954–) has already written about a dozen highly acclaimed novels for adults in addition to books of nonfiction and poetry. *The Birchbark House* and its sequel *The Game of Silence*, two books for young readers, are the first two volumes in a projected series that deal with important events in her family's history. Ms. Erdrich comes from a racially mixed background (her father was German American and her mother from a French and Ojibwa background) but her Native American birthright and inheritance has been the most powerful influence on her way of life as well as the subject matter of her books, including this series. Born in Minnesota, she grew up in North Dakota where her grandfather, Patrick Gourneau, was the tribal chairman for the Turtle Mountain Band of Chippewa (Ojibwa) Indians. Along with her mother

and sister, the author researched her Ojibwa past and discovered that her ancestors had originally lived on Madeline Island in Lake Superior in Minnesota, the setting of these novels. To bring authenticity to these novels, the author spent time with her children on Madeline Island observing and recording details of this habitat. She has also studied the Ojibwa language, a very complex one that relies heavily on verb formations. Her grandfather was the last in her family to speak the language and then chiefly in his prayers, when he talked to the spirits. The author has said: "In the past few years I've found that I can talk to God only in this language, and that somehow my grandfather's use of the language penetrated. The sound comforts me." Many Ojibwa words and phrases are used in both books. Glossaries give explanations. Both books also contain charming pencil drawings by the author that enhance and complement the text. The books can be read separately but are best if read in proper sequence. This series has already been compared positively to Laura Ingalls Wilder's Little House books. *The Birchbark House* was a finalist for the National Book Award and *The Game of Silence* was the 2006 winner of the Scott O'Dell Award for historical fiction.

Historical Background

The Ojibwa Indians, also known as the Chippewa or Anishinaabe nation, originally lived on the shores of Lake Superior, the setting of these novels. Gradually they expanded their territory across Minnesota and North Dakota to the Turtle Mountains in north-central North Dakota. They were a fairly sedentary people who relied on fishing, hunting, farming (corn and squash), and gathering (berries, nuts, wild rice). They processed maple syrup and smoked much of their meat and fish. At the time of these novels, the late 1840s, the Ojibwa were living in comparative peace with both the white settlers and other Native American tribes. Many engaged in trapping for the fur trade and salting of fish to purchase luxuries like cloth and beads. However, news was spreading among the tribes that the U.S. government was rescinding past agreements and forcing the Ojibwa to relocate farther west into the territory of the Bwaanag, or Dakota and Lakota people. Years later, many settled on reservations in Michigan, Wisconsin, Minnesota, and North Dakota. Today, the Ojibwa number about 100,000, making them one of the most populous Indian groups in the United States.

Smallpox was a highly contagious disease first introduced into the New World by the Spaniards in the 15th century. It remained a problem for the Native American population until the late 19th century when the use of vaccines stopped its progress. From 1837 through 1870 four major smallpox epidemics devastated the population of the western Indian nations. One such epidemic is described in *The Birchbark House*.

Principal Characters

Both novels

Omakayas or Little Frog, an Ojibwa girl (7 years old in *Birchbark*; 9 years old in *Silence*)

Nokomis, her grandmother

Yellow Kettle or Mama, her mother

Mikwam (Ice), her Deydey (father)

Angeline, her lovely older sister

Little Pinch, a pesky, 5-year-old brother

Old Tallow, a reclusive elderly woman

Albert LaPautre, a fat family friend

Auntie Muskrat, his wife

Fishtail, a handsome man, also a family friend

Father Baraga, also known as Black Robe and Soul Stealer, the village Catholic priest

Andeg, a pet crow

Chimookoman, the white setters

Only in *Birchbark*

Neewo, the adorable baby in the family

Ten Snow, Fishtail's beautiful young wife

Only in *Silence*

Miskobines or Red Thunder, a refugee Ojibwa chieftain

Angry One, Miskobines's young son, about Omakayas's age

Animikiins (Little Thunder), an orphaned Indian baby

Twilight, Omakayas's quiet, thoughtful cousin

Little Bee, Omakayas's funny, bold cousin

Two Strike Girl, Omakayas's untamed, wild cousin

Break-Apart Girl (Clarissa) a white girl

Makataywazi, Omakayas's pup

Plot Synopsis of *The Birchbark House*

A brief preface describes how an Ojibwa girl about 2 years old is found on Spirit Island off the coast of Lake Superior. She is the sole survivor of a small-pox epidemic. She is given to an elderly lady, Old Tallow, on neighboring Madeline Island, who allows a loving Ojibwa family to adopt the child.

The body of the novel takes place about five years later, in the late 1840s, and is divided into four parts: Neebin (Summer), Dagwaging (Fall), Biboon (Winter), and Zeewun (Spring). As summer approaches, Omakayas, a thoughtful 7-year-old Ojibwa girl whose name means Little Frog, prepares with the rest of her family to leave their log cabin in the Indian village on Madeline Island (which her people call the Island of the Golden Breasted Woodpecker) for new quarters where they will construct a house made of birch bark. Her mother, Yellow Kettle, and grandmother, Nokomis, do much of the work because father Mikwam is trapping furs for the white traders. Omakayas and her older sister, the beautiful Angeline, help out but their young brother, 5-year-old Little Pinch hinders progress as usual with his attention-getting pranks. In addition to helping cure animal skins, Omakayas is often given a much more desirable task—caring for baby brother Neewo, on whom she dotes like a mother.

One day Omakayas is sent to fetch a pair of scissors from Old Tallow, who has a reputation for being fierce and irascible (she has frightened off three husbands) although, for some unknown reason, she shows great affection toward Omakayas. On the way home, the young girl encounters two baby bear cubs and begins playing with them. Suddenly the mother appears and pins Omakayas to the ground. The girl speaks to the bear. Somehow, in an instant, a mysterious bond is created between the two and instead of harming the girl the bear gathers up her cubs and leaves. For many days later Omakayas wonders about this mystical experience. Suddenly her Deydey (father) returns home and the family is one again. At night, around the fire after the chores have been done, he often tells the family folktales.

While frightening off the crows that are decimating the family's corn patch, Omakayas catches an injured baby crow. She names it Andeg and it becomes her devoted pet, even learning to speak a few words. Deydey, a respected member of the tribe, is often visited by young men seeking advice and counsel. Among them are the pompous, laughable Albert LaPautre, who fancies himself a medicine man, and the handsome, good-natured Fishtail, who has decide to attend the local school to learn the chimookoman (white man's) language. Fishtail has taken as his wife the charming, attractive Ten Snow, who also becomes a friend of the family.

Among the many activities of the fall season is gathering the wild rice that grows on the mainland. Soon the family begins preparations to move into their log cabin for the winter. After the first snow and Old Tallow's appearance in her gaudy winter coat sewn of many pelts, the family knows the time has come and the move is made.

One winter day a sick, feverish stranger arrives in the village and the next day dies. Within days, the whole community is stricken with the terrible plague he has brought—smallpox, known as the scratching or itching disease. The family retreats into its cabin. Mama and Angeline are the first to be stricken. Grandma, Deydey, and Omakayas nurse the sick ones while also caring for Little Pinch and Neewo. Then Deydey and the baby catch the disease.

Neewo becomes Omakayas's personal responsibility and for days she nurses him in her arms, never letting him out of her sight. Unfortunately her care and nurturing are in vain. Although the rest of her family survives (Adeline suffers extreme disfigurement), Neewo dies in her arms. Another victim of the epidemic is Ten Snow, Fishtail's wife. Omakayas is shattered by these losses and she wanders for weeks in a daze, unable to function properly and feeling guilty that she survived unharmed. To add to their misery, the village food supply runs out and starvation seems imminent. Then they spot a young buck deer that Omakayas once saw in the woods and nicknamed One Horn. His death is the salvation of the family.

Soon the ghastly winter is over and spring activities begin. It is maple sugar time. Apart from Pinch receiving painful burns when he accidentally overturns a hot kettle of syrup, the sugaring time goes well. Omakayas is able to ease Pinch's agony through applying herbs she has learned about. One day, when Old Tallow arrives with deer bones, the conversation turns to Omakayas and her continuing grief for her young brother. Old Tallow tells Omakayas of her past. She was found on neighboring Spirit Island five years before, the sole survival of a smallpox epidemic. Being adopted by Deydey and Mama was an act of God. "You were sent here so you could save the others," she said. "Because you'd had the sickness, you were strong enough to nurse them through it. They did a good thing when they took you in, and you saved them for their good act. Now the circle that began when I found you is complete." These words bring comfort to Omakayas. When alone, she feels once more her oneness with nature. As she listens to the voices of the earth, they seem to be joined by another voice, the sound of her little brother Neewo, who has come to help ease her broken heart.

Passages for Booktalking in *The Birchbark House*
Omakayas visits Old Tallow to collect the scissors (pp. 21–24); Omakayas encounters the bears (pp. 26–32); and Omakayas cares for her brother Neewo (pp. 40–46). Three Ojibwa folktales are retold in the text. They are found on pp. 61–68 (Deydey's ghost story), pp. 134–38 (Grandma's ghost story), and pp. 172–175 (Grandma's creation story).

Themes and Subjects in *The Birchbark House*
The Ojibwa belief in their unity and oneness with nature pervades this novel. This pantheism is tinged with an element of fatalism as demonstrated in their acceptance of destiny regardless of how harsh. The daily life and activities of the tribe in the mid-19th century are well depicted, including their diligence, perseverance, and frugality. Their use but not abuse of their environment is clear and their respect for nature and the sanctity of the family is demonstrat-

ed. Some other subjects: epidemics, disease, smallpox, death, disfigurement, family loyalty, Minnesota, Lake Superior, and animals.

Plot Synopsis of *The Game of Silence*

(Like *The Birchbark House*, this novel is divided into four parts: Summer, Fall, Winter, and Spring.)

The tranquility of the summer of 1849 is broken for Omakayas, a 9-year-old Ojibwa girl who lives with her family on Madeline (Golden Breasted Woodpecker) Island on Lake Superior, by the arrival of several frayed canoes filled with Ojibwa Indians of various ages, all in tatters and close to starvation. Among those gathered on the shore to greet this pathetic group are Mikwam and Yellow Kettle—Omakoyas's father (Deydey) and mother, her grandmother Nokomis, her older sister Angeline, her pesky younger brother Pinch, and their neighbor Old Tallow, an outspoken, reclusive crone. Among the refugees are the refugees' chieftain, Miskobines; his taciturn, hostile son who is soon nicknamed Angry One; and an orphan baby who is hovering near death. Over generous portions of stew and dressed in gifts of clothing from the island families, the outcasts tell their story of a brutal attack by Bwaanag (Dakota Indians) who wiped out their village and forced them to flee to safety.

The islanders quickly take in these pathetic homeless people. Chief Miskobines and Angry One go to live in a household that consists of Albert LaPautre, his wife Auntie Muskrat, a handsome widower named Fishtail, who is the chief's nephew, and three youngsters, friends of Omakayas—Twilight, a pensive girl; the amusing Little Bee; and tough, tomboyish Two Strike Girl. Omakayas's family adopts the pathetic orphan. With the help of Nokomis, Mama nurses the orphan baby back to health and names him Animikiins or Little Thunder. Omakayas is thrilled to have a new baby brother.

Whenever the Ojibwa families on the island gather to discuss important tribal subjects, all the children are required to play the game of silence, the object of which is to see who can remain quiet the longest. Prizes are given and, in the meantime, the elders can discuss important family questions in peace. Life has settled down after the refugees' arrival when a new crisis occurs that requires administering the game of silence. It appears that chimookoman (white men) are breaking their territorial agreement with the Ojibwa and are forcing them off their land. Many have tried relocating further west but are encountering violent resistance from the resident Bwaanag tribes. Some men volunteer to leave the island to investigate the situation. Even though it means leaving his girlfriend Angeline, Fishtail courageously volunteers to go into the hostile west. He promises to return by next spring.

When they are not engaged in such household chores as curing animal hides and gutting fish, Omakayas and her girlfriends like to play games in their pine bough shelter. One day mischievous Pinch deliberately destroys it and hides in a tree. Two Strike Girl, the fierce one of the group, gets revenge by chopping down the bough on which Pinch is sitting. He lands in an algae-covered slough. Before the resulting melee is over, even Omakayas and Angry One are covered in mud. Later, even Omakayas feels sorry for Pinch when he accidentally gashes his leg while helping to build a birchbark canoe. The girls also make friends with some of the chimookoman who live in the town of LaPointe, including a young girl who is called the Break-Apart Girl because her corset is so tight her body seems to be in two parts. Shortly afterward, Omakayas and Angeline sell some dried fish in town so that Angeline can make a velvet vest for Fishtail. On this excursion, they meet Father Baraga, the Catholic priest who is nicknamed the Soul Stealer because of his proselytizing, and later they inspect the outside of his church.

Later in the summer, Old Tallow gives Omakayas a puppy from her large menagerie of faithful dogs. She names him Makataywazi. The dog joins Andeg, her pet crow, as a constant companion. During the summer, in a misguided effort to help gathering wild rice, Omakayas and her friend Twilight mistakenly pick rice too green to harvest and ruin some of the plants. Their disgrace is partially forgotten when Two Strike Girl kills a moose with a single arrow shot through the animal's eye. Basking in this glory, Two Strike becomes insufferably bossy and arrogant.

In the fall, plans are made for the winter. Food is stored outdoors in holes in the ground and preparations begin for the move into the cedar cabin for the winter. Two Strike Girl becomes increasingly obnoxious and officious as she organizes some of the village youngsters into her "warrior" band. Omakayas discovers that the group plans to attack Old Tallow's dogs and warns the old woman. As a result, Two Strike Girl's plan misfires, and Omakayas has the satisfaction of seeing Two Strike Girl publicly punished.

Winter passes without any word of Fishtail and the other scouts. As spring approaches and the lake ice begins to crack and melt, Father Baraga asks Deydey to guide him by canoe to a distant settlement to check on his parishioners. After the two have been absent for many days, the family becomes alarmed. Omakayas, who has amazing spiritual powers, dreams about her father and the villagers are able to rescue the two, who had been stranded on an ice floe. Later Nokomis, who is aware of Omakayas's divine gifts, arranges for the girl to undertake a solitary retreat to commune with nature and develop these sacred powers. Omakayas emerges from the experience with an increased reverence for nature.

In the spring, a few of the scouts return. Many died while attempting to collect information. Luckily for Angeline, one of the survivors is Fishtail. The news is devastating. The white man's government has decreed that the Ojibwa must give up their land and move west, to the home of the hostile Bwaanag. Before leaving, Angeline and Fishtail marry.

The families pack their canoes with personal belongings, including seeds to restart their gardens. Omakayas tries at first to hide her puppy in the canoe, but she realizes that his barking and lack of discipline may endanger the tribe and so she tearfully allows Break-Apart Girl to adopt him. The canoes, including one for Old Tallow and her dogs, leave the island for the last time, knowing that on the shoreline await enemies who resent the Ojibwa's arrival.

Passages for Booktalking in *The Game of Silence*
Some important passages are: the refugees arrive and the baby is adopted (pp. 1–11); the game of silence (pp. 12–18); the territorial problem and the volunteering of the scouts (pp. 19 bottom–25); the mud fight (pp. 36–45) and Nokomis tells one of her folk stories (pp. 103–110).

Themes and Subjects in *The Game of Silence*
Many of the themes and subjects of *The Birchbark House* are contained in the sequel. The Ojibwa's respect for nature and the feeling of unity with all forms of life are prominent themes. The daily life of the tribe with its many chores, joys, and hardships is well pictured. The accurate, detailed portrayal of the seasonal activities creates an authentic picture of Indian life. Omakayas's growing oneness with nature and her increased maturity and spiritual growth form important themes as does the graphic description of the sanctity of the family ties and everyday virtues. The perfidy of the white man's actions and attitudes toward Native Americans is well presented. Some other subjects: Minnesota, Lake Superior, animals, friendship, tribal displacement, and adjustment to the seasons.

FLEISCHMAN, SID. *The Giant Rat of Sumatra or Pirates Galore.*
Greenwillow, 2005, $15.99 (978-0-06-074238-6); pap. Harper, $5.99 (978-0-06-074240-9) (Grades 4–7)

Introduction
Sid Fleischman was born in 1920 in Brooklyn, New York, but raised in San Diego, California, the setting of this novel. After years of writing pulp mysteries he turned to books for young readers with a series of humorous historical adventures beginning with *Mr. Mysterious and Co.* (Little, Brown, 1962, o.p.). In 1987, he was awarded the Newbery Medal for the delightful *The Whipping Boy* (Greenwillow, 1986, $16; 0688062164; condensed in *The Newbery/Printz*

Companion), the story of the exploits of Prince Roland, also known as Prince Brat, and Jemmy, his whipping boy. *The Giant Rat of Sumatra* completes a trilogy of books that deal with the chaotic years in Southern California at the time of the War with Mexico and the California Gold Rush (roughly 1846–1850). The first, published in 1983, is *By the Great Horn Spoon* (Little, Brown, pap. $6.99; 0316286125), which tells how 12-year-old Jack Flagg sets out from Boston in 1849 with his aunt's faithful butler, Praiseworthy, to find gold in California and bolster the declining fortune of Aunt Arabella. The second is *Bandit's Moon* (Dell, pap. $5.50; 0440415861), the story of orphaned Annyrose Smith who, at the time of the California Gold Rush, is taken prisoner by a Mexican bandit. Thinking she is a boy, he takes her along during many of his exploits to teach him how to read. The title of the *Giant Rat of Sumatra* comes from a reference to a Sherlock Holmes case in one of Conan Doyle's books. The case was, unfortunately, never written.

Historical Background

San Diego, the setting of the novel is situated on a fine natural harbor. The sea captain Juan Cabrillo claimed it for Spain in 1542. In 1769, a military post, the Presidio of San Diego was founded and in the same year the Mission San Diego was established by Father Juipero Serra. It was the first of a string of missions extending up the coast of California. Eager to gain more territory in the West, the United States declared war on Mexico on May 13, 1846, and invaded its territory from the east, reaching San Diego in December. On July 29, 1846, a marine detachment from the sloop-of-war *Cyane* raised the first American flag in the Plaza of the Old Town. American land forces entered Mexico City in September 1847 and occupied it until June 1848 while diplomats negotiated a peace treaty. A defeated Mexico signed the Treaty of Guadalupe Hidalgo, which ceded a vast tract of land, including present-day California, to the United States. Mexico lost almost half its land but only about 1 percent of its population. As compensation it received a payment of $15 million from General Zachary Taylor, an army leader who became a national hero and won the presidency in 1848. Both Ulysses S. Grant and Robert E. Lee served with distinction during the war.

Principal Characters

Shipwreck, the narrator, a cabin boy who is almost 13 years old
One-Arm Ginger, the first mate, saved with Shipwreck from a sinking whaling ship
Captain Alejandro Gallows, a Mexican and swashbuckling captain of *The Giant Rat of Sumatra*
Jimmy Pukapuka, Trot, and Calcutta, crew members

Ozzie Twitch, a harpooner and conspirator with One-Arm Ginger
Don Simplicio Emilio Charra, a wealthy merchant
Juan Largo, Gallows's ranch manager
Sam'l Spoons, a tavern keeper
Oliviana, an Indian girl Shipwreck befriends
Aunt Mariana, Oliviana's aunt
Candalaria, Gallows's childhood sweetheart
Senorita Wildcat, a female bandit

Plot Synopsis

Early in 1846 a bedraggled sailing ship whose figurehead is a giant rat with sharp ivory teeth and sightless eyes (they once held giant emeralds but these were removed) weighs anchor in San Diego Bay, then part of Mexico. The ship, under the able command of debonair, dashing Captain Gallows is *The Giant Rat of Sumatra*, fresh from pirating in Far Eastern seas and full of plunder. The crew bears such unusual names as Jimmy Pukapuka, Trot, and Calcutta. Two of the more interesting members are One-Arm Ginger and the cabin boy appropriately nicknamed Shipwreck. Both were fished out of the sea, the only survivors of a sinking whaling vessel. One-Arm, who claims to have lost his arm to piranhas, is a shifty type who nevertheless has risen to the rank of first mate. Shipwreck's real name is Edmund Amos Peters. Now almost 13, he was with his new stepfather on a whaling expedition out of Boston when their ship encountered a violent storm off the Philippines.

The boy, a quick, personable lad, is popular with the crew and captain of the *Rat* and he acts as official letter-writer for the men. One-Arm commands Shipwreck to row him to shore to visit the local tavern. The boy senses skullduggery and overhears the first mate plotting with two locals, one a harpooner named Ozzie Twitch, to board the *Rat* and relieve Captain Gallows of his considerable booty. Before the boy can make it back to the ship, he is caught by the innkeeper, Sam'l Spoons, and imprisoned in an outbuilding along with the tavern's dog. Fortunately, the dog knows how to burrow under the earthen floor and Shipwreck gets back to the ship while the robbery is still taking place. He spills a bucket of whale oil on the deck and, when the scoundrels try to leave the ship with their loot they slither off into the water, escaping but leaving the treasure intact.

The captain shows his gratitude by taking a special interest in the boy. He tells Shipwreck that he plans to remain in San Diego, his former home, and leave the *Rat* in the bay. However, he will help the boy get passage back to Boston. This will be difficult because the United States has just declared war against Mexico. The captain explains that as a youngster in San Diego he was the indentured servant of a cruel taskmaster, Don Simplicio Emilio Charra, who beat Gallows regularly until he escaped at the age of 14. Gallows entrusts Shipwreck with part of his treasure, the two huge emeralds that were once the *Rat*'s eyes. The captain sews them into the bottom hem of Shipwreck's baggy coat. Within days, the captain has bought a huge abandoned rancho overlooking the bay and names it El Rancho Candalaria, after an attractive young girl who suffered with him as a slave of Don Simplicio many years ago. He has never forgotten her and hopes to see her again one day. In the abandoned hacienda, Shipwreck encounters two squatters: Oliviana, a young Indian girl, and her Aunt Mariana. Gallows hires them as helpers along with a competent, orderly young man, Juan Largo, who will become his *mayordomo* and get the estate in working order.

Back on the ship, Shipwreck is accosted in his cabin by Ozzie Twitch, who, days before, overheard the captain's conversation about hiding the emeralds. He demands the boy's coat. Although Twitch is frightened off by a passing visitor, Shipwreck knows he will be back and the emeralds are not safe. Thanks to Juan Largo's efficiency, the ranch is made livable within a few weeks and the captain, along with Shipwreck and the loyal crew members, move in. One day, on the trail, Gallows and Shipwreck are waylaid by a group of bandits led by an attractive woman whom Gallows dubs Senorita Wildcat. Far from being upset by the robbery, Gallows is charmed at meeting such a vivacious virago. Back at the ranch, Shipwreck realizes with horror that the emeralds are missing. Fortunately Oliviana had found them after they broke through the coat's lining. She returns his "green marbles."

Don Simplicio, still a merchant dealing in hides, remains a resident of San Diego. Remembering his years of servitude, Gallows devises a scheme to get even. He arranges to have much of the Don's cargo of hides stolen, and when the old man tries to replace them Gallows buys up all the available stock. The Don is brought to bankruptcy and Gallows has his revenge.

Another encounter with Senorita Wildcat—this time the captain bests her in a bizarre duel—increases Gallows's fascination with the woman. An American warship, the *Cyana*, appears in the harbor. Army troops land and the American flag is raised above the town. Hoping the ship will be able to take him home, Shipwreck rides into town to make inquiries. On the trail, he is stopped by One-Arm Ginger and Ozzie Twitch who almost succeed in getting hold of the coat, but Senorita Wildcat appears, rescues Shipwreck, and takes the two ruffians prisoner. She ties them securely and places them in Shipwreck's custody. As she prepares to leave, Shipwreck, on a hunch, calls out "Good-bye, Candalaria." She spins around and glares at Shipwreck. The boy has found his Captain's long-lost love.

After that, events move swiftly. Captain Gallows tries to stage an attack on the Americans. It fails and he resigns himself to being a citizen of the United

States. A ruined Don Simplicio dies and Gallows learns that before his death he tried to make amends to all those he had wronged. He did not realize that Gallows was one of them. Arrangements are made for Shipwreck to sail back to Boston as cabin boy on the American warship but before he does, Gallows is able to locate Candalaria and propose marriage. As a wedding gift, Gallows presents his true love with a pair of earrings made from the large emeralds that were once part of *The Giant Rat of Sumatra*. Shipwreck is saddened to say good-bye to his dear friends, particularly Captain Gallows but he is looking forward to being reunited with his mother in Boston.

Passages for Booktalking

Four exciting passages are: Shipwreck earns his nickname and fits in with the crew (pp. 6–9); One-Arm Ginger plots against the captain (pp. 18–23); Shipwreck is caught at the tavern but escapes (pp. 23–28); and later he foils One-Arm Ginger's plot (pp. 31–35).

Themes and Subjects

This is basically a tale of high adventure on both land and sea. The background events of the Mexican War are nicely woven into the plot. Without being preachy, the author shows a sympathy for the Mexican point of view in the war. The story reveals that even pirates can have admirable qualities. Shipwreck, the narrator, is perceptive and intelligent as well as courageous, loyal, and fair-minded. Other subjects include: treasure, San Diego, ships, sea stories, adventure stories, romance, ranches, friendship, and bandits.

HURST, CAROL OTIS. *Torchlight.* Houghton, 2006, $16 (978-0-618-27601-1) (Grades 4–7)

Introduction

Carol Otis Hurst (1933–2007) was truly a renaissance woman in children's literature. She was a nationally known storyteller, lecturer, columnist, editor, consultant, webmaster, and writer of highly praised children's books. She was born in Springfield, Massachusetts, but spent most of her life in nearby Westfield, the setting of this novel. She began her professional life as a school teacher but her interest in children's literature soon led her to library work and a long association with *Teacher K–8 Magazine*, for which she wrote regular columns. She also wrote numerous books about children's literature and its use in the classroom. In her 60s she began writing books for children and also founded, with her daughter Rebecca Otis, a Web site, Carol Hurst's Children's

Literature Site (http://www.carolhurst.com), which contains information about children's authors and illustrators, reviews of children's books, ideas on how to use children's literature in the classroom, and suggestions for book-related activities.

Her last book was a picture book for the primary grades illustrated by S. D. Schindler. It is *Perfect Storm* (Greenwillow, 2007, $16.99; 0060090014), the story of two grandfathers who grew up together in the hills around Westfield, Massachusetts, and together experienced the massive snow of 1888.

Westfield is also the setting of *Torchlight*, Ms. Hurst's next-to-last book. It takes place during a few months during the year 1854 and deals with an actual incident during which a prominent townsman, Hiram Hull, dissuaded a mob of Protestants from destroying a church that was being built by the town's Irish Catholics. Further details on historic Westfield are given in an Author's Note. Carol Otis Hurst died at age 73 on January 22, 2007.

Historical Background

During the 19th century, a steady stream of Irish immigrants came to the United States. Most were uneducated and forced to take menial jobs in domestic service, the building trades, and factory work. They were largely unrepresented in the professions and were often confined to living in substandard, segregated housing. Job discrimination was rampant and there were reports that advertisements for jobs often stated NINA (No Irish Need Apply). Nativist Americans, known as Yankees, were generally middle- and upper-class Protestants and came from English and Scottish backgrounds. For them, the word Irish became synonymous with drunken behavior, disorderly conduct, and many types of law-breaking. This stereotype of the Irish, combined with fear that they would eventually take jobs away from the Yankees and the concern that American traditions could be undermined by the allegiance Irish Catholics held to their church, Rome, and the Pope, led to a massive anti-Irish feeling by the 1850s. Local nativistic societies were formed to combat these "foreign" influences. Because inquiries about their membership were to be met with "I know nothing" answers, they became known as the Know Nothings. These groups allied themselves with Whigs and supported the campaign of Millard Fillmore in the elections of 1856. Prior to that, they had considerable success in state elections in Massachusetts and Delaware. With the defeat of Fillmore and preoccupation with other national concerns including slavery, the Know Nothing movement lost its momentum.

Westfield, the setting of the novel, is a city in western Massachusetts, close to Springfield. In the 19th century it was a thriving industrial city famous for factories that made bricks, cigars, and buggy whips (it is still known as the "Whip City"). Because of its prosperity, it attracted many Irish immigrants eager for factory work. Even today about 20 percent of the city's population claims Irish descent. Charlotte's original home, Agawam, is a smaller city also located in western Massachusetts.

Principal Characters

Charlotte Hodge, a fifth-grader
Zach Hodge, Charlotte's 14-year-old brother
Maggie (Margaret) Nolan, Charlotte's Irish friend
Aunt Lucy Hull, Charlotte's aunt
Uncle Hiram Hull, Aunt Lucy's husband
Ann Turner, leader of a group of girls hostile to Charlotte
Miss Avery, Charlotte's bigoted teacher
Samuel and Lydia Fowler, married friends of the Hulls

Plot Synopsis

Charlotte Hodge was only 7 years old and enjoying a happy childhood in the town of Agawam in northwestern Massachusetts in the mid-19th century when her world was shattered by her parents' death in a cholera epidemic. She and her older brother, Zach, were promptly adopted by Uncle Hiram and Aunt Lucy Hull and brought to live with them in the neighboring bustling industrial city of Westfield. Uncle Hiram, a liberal, good-hearted man, owns the largest buggy whip factory in town and his wife, though overly class conscious, is basically well intentioned and devoted to such causes as Prohibition and the anti-slavery crusade. It is now four years later and Charlotte, a bright, quiet youngster is entering the fifth grade at the Green District School and Zach, aged 14, is in his first year at the Westfield Academy, a private high school. Charlotte is devoted to her kindly stepparents, so much so that she is fearful of forgetting the looks and behavior of her real parents.

Though outwardly calm and peaceful, Westfield in 1854 is actually seriously divided along economic and religious lines. The "haves" are the prosperous Yankee Protestant middle class who live in relatively posh neighborhoods and the "have nots" are the Irish immigrant laborers, who are Catholic and live in segregated slum areas. Both Charlotte's school and the Academy have recently become integrated, allowing both Protestants and Catholics to be educated together. This has created some controversy among the Protestant majority.

Charlotte is starting school virtually friendless because her two best friends moved away during the summer and the 'in' crowd, led by snobbish Ann Turner, has shunned her in spite of her efforts to be accepted. She therefore welcomes the offer of friendship from another outsider in the class, Irish Catholic Maggie Nolan. Maggie is an outspoken, unpretentious realist. From her, Charlotte becomes aware of the Irish point of view. She often compares her sheltered, affluent life with that of Maggie, who lives in a crowded home where all of her siblings (one only 13 years old) work in factories. Charlotte also becomes aware of forms of discrimination against the Irish. They must, for example, wait in stores like Huntington's Yard Goods until all the Yankees have been served. While Charlotte is becoming more understanding of the Irish situation, her brother Zach, under the influence of some bigoted friends at the Academy, is become increasing intolerant and resentful, particularly of Uncle Hiram's practice of being fair to all.

Charlotte's newfound liberalism is tested one day when she wanders into the Irish district after buying a pound of barley for her aunt. She is suddenly accosted by two young Irish thugs who take the barley from her. She is rescued by an older man, who frightens off the two hooligans and returns the barley. Maggie later identifies Charlotte's savior as Jack O'Malley, a friend of the Nolans. In the meantime, Zach's hatred of the Irish grows after he and a friend fight with two Irish boys and Zach emerges bruised and with a bloodied face. The friendship between Maggie and Charlotte grows as they share experiences and thoughts about their different lifestyles. Zack on the other hand is angry when Uncle Hiram lectures him about staying out late and furious that he has a newly promoted Irishman as his boss at his Saturday job at Uncle Hiram's factory.

Some narrow-minded members of the community are incensed when Samuel Fuller, a respected townsman and friend of the Hulls, sells a piece of his property in town to the Irish to build a Catholic Church. Not long afterward, the Fullers' house is broken into, windows are smashed, and some parts are vandalized. Neighbors, including the Hulls, rally around the Fullers and bring gifts of food and provisions. On one such visit, Charlotte overhears conversations expressing different opinions of the Irish question. Some openly criticize Uncle Hiram for promoting "Micks" at his factory, others want to teach the Irish a lesson, and a few suggest moderation.

One morning, in the school playground, Charlotte is approached by Ann Turner and her friends with an invitation to join them in a game of skip rope. Within minutes she has been tied up and, amid shouts of "Mick lover," pushed into a muddy puddle and left by herself. Maggie finds Charlotte, unties her, and helps her tidy up. When the two arrive late at class, Miss Avery, who in the past has shown signs of prejudice against the Irish, denies them the right to speak and instead punishes them with after-school detention. Even then, she refuses to listen to their story, preferring to believe lies from Ann Turner and the other girls. After dismissing Maggie, Miss Avery lectures Charlotte on her choice of friends and warns her to be more careful in the future. Back at home, Aunt Lucy senses something is wrong and gradually worms the truth out of Charlotte. Both Aunt Lucy and Uncle Hiram reassure her that it is fine having Maggie as a friend. However, they are furious at Miss Avery and vow to take the matter up at next school board meeting.

In fall, every neighborhood in Westfield has its own bonfire night. Charlotte looks forward to the festivities. They begin on a jovial note with singing of old favorites like "Camptown Races" and "Weep No More My Lady" and some energetic square dancing. However, Hiram is summoned to the factory to deal with an emergency and the situation becomes ugly. With tongues loosened by alcohol, several of the immoderates, perhaps members of the Know Nothing Party, begin haranguing the crowd about the Catholic church. Soon a mob with arson in mind decides to march to the new construction. Aunt Lucy and Charlotte race to the factory to alert Uncle Hiram. The emergency—flooding from rain-swollen rivers—requires that he stay a few more minutes at the factory, but he tells the women to run to the Irishmen's bonfire and alert them. The Irish respond quickly and, joining hands, form a ring of protection around the construction site. Angry words are exchanged and violence seems inevitable. Suddenly Uncle Hiram appears and addresses the crowd. In an eloquent speech he reminds the Yankees why they came to this country and says that its riches are sufficient for all. He ends by warning them that the flood waters will soon threaten the entire community. Aunt Lucy is moved to tears. Forgetting their differences, the crowd disperses, most going together to fill sandbags.

Hiram's triumph is tempered by the news that Zach has run away from home. Again Hiram's wisdom prevails—he knows the boy needs some time to sort out his thoughts. Aunt Lucy is convinced that he will return soon. In the meantime, they have a school board meeting to prepare for.

Passages for Booktalking

Each chapter begins with a brief conversation between Charlotte and Maggie. Three interesting ones are: the two girls exchange information about their backgrounds (pp. 1–3); they discuss religion (pp. 23–25); and Maggie describes her home (pp. 34–38). Other important passages are: the incident involving Charlotte walking on Maggie's street (pp. 39–43) and Zach talks about his fight (pp. 49–52).

Themes and Subjects

The social problems presented in this book—and the lessons learned in solving them—remain relevant in this country, where discrimination by race still exists. The corrosive effects of racial prejudice and bigotry and their cumulative destructive power are well depicted. The fallacy of stereotyping a racial group is presented, as is the reality that violence often leads to more violence. A friendship that grows in strength and defies class and religious differences is effectively presented. Charlotte's growth to maturity and Aunt Lucy's increased tolerance for the Irish are important secondary themes. Other subjects include: Massachusetts, factory work, tolerance, religion, small-town life, and the Know Nothing Party.

MOERI, LOUISE. *Save Queen of Sheba.* Dutton, 1981, o.p.; pap. Puffin, $4.99 (978-0-14-037148-2) (Grades 4–7)

Introduction

Louise Moeri was born in Klamath Falls, Oregon, on November 30, 1924. She graduated from the University of California at Berkeley, raised a family, and was a library assistant from 1961 until 1978. On writing she has said, "I consider writing to be one of the hardest jobs in the world, and if I weren't compelled to do it, I'd take up some other line of work. But as difficult, unrewarding, and unnoticed as it often is, there is nothing I can do that is as exciting as watching a story emerge from my pencil onto a piece of paper. No matter how hard it is, I'm going to go right on doing it." She has produced only a handful of books for young people but each is a gem. Another recommended title is *The Forty-Third War* (Houghton, 1989, o.p.; pap. $6.95, 0395669553), which takes place in an unnamed Central America country that is now suffering through its forty-third war in a struggle between the Loyalists and the Rebels. Twelve-year-old Uno, the central character and the only remaining male member of his family in his village, is kidnapped and conscripted at gunpoint into the Rebel Army. During his first eight days of training and battle, he witnesses massacres by the Loyalist forces, who are really only servants of the corrupt upper class. Uno become a supporter of the rebel cause and the novel ends on an optimistic note at the war's end.

Save Queen of Sheba takes place over a period of a few days on the Oregon Trail close to the foothills of the Rockies. The time is probably in the 1850s. Though told in the third person, the story is seen through the eyes of 12-year-old King David.

Historical Background

The two characters in the novel were named after Old Testament figures. In addition to slaying the giant Goliath, King David was a noted warrior and writer of psalms. His son, Solomon, became so famous for his knowledge and wisdom that people came from distant places to confer with him. One was Makeda, the wealthy Queen of Sheba (probably present-day Ethiopia). It is not known if their relationship remained entirely platonic.

The Oregon Trail was one of the chief routes taken by pioneers heading west in the 19th century. It wound more than 2,000 miles through territory that would later become six states (Missouri to Oregon). The first organized wagon train that followed the Oregon Trail set out from Missouri in 1842. The basic route followed river valleys. In the prairies, where the novel takes place, it followed the Platte, North Platte, and Sweetwater Rivers. Pioneers traveled in various conveyances. For a time the huge Conestoga wagon was used; later it was supplanted by the prairie schooner. It was about half the size of the Conestoga and better suited to Oregon Trail conditions. The greatest inducement for the move west was the promise of free land. Fort Laramie, in present-day Wyoming, was the first sign of civilization pioneers saw after about six weeks of traveling. Situated in the foothills of the Rockies, it is about one-third of the way to Willamette. It began as a fur trading post but in 1849 was bought by the U.S. Army to protect pioneers from the increasingly hostile Sioux Indians. In 1854 a simple misunderstanding between the Indians and the Army resulted in an unnecessary massacre of Sioux Indians by U.S. forces. The result was an all-out war that lasted decades. Fort Laramie was never enclosed by a wall or stockade but depended on its location and garrison of troops for security. Pioneers stopped and regrouped at this fort and, in spite of prohibitive prices, patronized its large trading post. After the transcontinental railroad was completed in 1869, the use of the Oregon Trail diminished.

The Sioux, often referred to as Plains Indians, were the second-largest Indian tribe north of Mexico (the Chippewa were the largest tribe). Later, their important leaders included Crazy Horse and Sitting Bull. Fort Laramie, about 200 miles north of Denver, is now an interesting tourist attraction managed by the National Park Service.

Principal Characters

King David, a 12-year-old boy
Queen of Sheba, his 6-year-old sister
Maggie, a horse

Plot Synopsis

The wagon train on the Oregon Trail was just a few days from the safety of Fort Laramie (in present-day Wyoming) when there was a surprise attack by Sioux Indians. Without time to form a protective circle, seven of the wagons were trapped by the attackers while the remaining fourteen were able to flee. Unfortunately, just before the ambush, King David, a 12-year-old boy, and his 6-year-old sister, Queen of Sheba, left their parents' wagon to visit friends in the wagons that were trapped in the ambush.

Hours after the Indians departed, King David awakens to a scene of carnage and destruction. He is surrounded by the dead bodies of his friends and acquaintances and the smoldering remains of wagons and their contents. King David has an aching, open wound across his forehead from a botched scalping attempt. He drags himself painfully from wagon to wagon hoping someone is alive. Miraculously, under some feather bedding, he finds his sister safe and unharmed. For a moment he mistakenly believes there is still life in the body of their guide, Luke Skinner, but his efforts at resuscitation prove fruitless. With dismay, he realizes that he and his little sister are alone on this vast prairie. Their only hope is to follow the tracks of the other wagons westward and to pray for rescue. In spite of his aching head wound, he is able to gather a few supplies that were not stolen by the Indians—a rifle and bullets, some matches, a few apples, and a sack of corn meal. Queen of Sheba doesn't understand their predicament and is a whining, uncooperative nuisance. With great self-control and restraint, King David remains both firm and sympathetic, although at one point he loses his temper and hits her across the hands with a cane when she refuses to eat the raw corn meal.

Their chances of survival improve greatly when they find a horse in a grove near the ambush site. It is Maggie, a mare that belonged to the Stone family. The three head out toward the west, but by sundown King David's head wound, now oozing pus, is so painful that he cannot go on. They stop at a stream and, with his last ounce of strength, King David courageously tears off the loose flap of infected skin and soaks his head in the water. Blood and pus drift away with the current. The next day he feels better and the travelers press on. During a rest stop, King David falls asleep and wakes up to find Little Sheba gone. Eventually he finds her on the banks of a pool, cradling a gnarled piece of wood that looks like a human body. She has found a doll to love. Of greater importance, King David spots a rabbit close by. With a marksman's accuracy, he shoots it. King David rarely lights a fire because he is afraid its smell will be detected by roaming Indians. However, that evening he takes a chance and their dinner offering improves greatly. The next day, they pass through a small valley strewn with the white bones of a herd of buffalo slaughtered by fur traders. King David begins to understand why the Indians hate the white intruders.

As storm clouds approach, the youngsters are lucky enough to find a cave under an overhanging rock before there is a blinding downpour. The rain continues for 24 hours, and both youngsters use this time to rest and regain some strength. As they set out again, King David assesses their dwindling food supplies and wonders if they will last until they are rescued or reach Fort Laramie. The heavy rains have almost obliterated the wagon tracks, but King David trusts his directional instincts. Queen of Sheba usually rides Maggie but King David notices that her legs are bruised and raw from rubbing on the horse's harness. Therefore, he lets her walk behind the horse for a bit. Preoccupied with his own thoughts and apprehensions, King David marches ahead, unaware that Queen of Sheba has lagged behind. When he finally turns to check on her, she has disappeared. He turns back but because she weighs so little, she has left no tracks. King David combs the woods frantically for a sign of his sister. Night falls and he must postpone the search. The next morning, after feeding Maggie, he resumes the hunt. By late afternoon still with no success, King David remembers how Queen of Sheba loved streams and ponds and, on a hunch, begins to search a wooded area where there must be water. By nightfall, he has discovered her two shoes but again must stop until morning light.

The following morning, he finally sees his sister playing by a little pond. Across from her is another child, an Indian boy who is soon joined by his mother. The woman has been gathering roots and is still carrying her knife. When King David raises his rifle to a shooting position, the squaw grabs Queen of Sheba and presses her knife against the girl's throat. King David lowers his rifle, and the woman releases Queen of Sheba. In an instant, King David grabs Queen of Sheba with one hand and Maggie's rope with the other and runs, not stopping until they appear to be out of harm's way.

Once more on the trail, they consume the last of the corn meal. Just as the situation looks hopeless, another miracle occurs. Shapes appear on the skyline and soon horses and their riders can be discerned on the crest of the hill. As they get closer, King David sees that one of the riders is his father. Both King David and Queen of Sheba have been saved.

Passages for Booktalking

King David wakens to a scene of carnage (pp. 1–4); Queen of Sheba proves difficult (pp. 16–29); they start out on the prairie (pp. 21–24); and King David finds Maggie the horse (pp. 28–30).

Themes and Subjects

Like his namesake King David shows unusual courage and fortitude as his confronts his own private Goliath, the will to survive in a hostile environment and save his sister. Through his ordeal, he shows increasing maturity and good judgment. Details of the lives of pioneers on the Oregon Trail are authentic and uncompromising. Although not condoning the Indians' brutal atrocities, the author does present their side of the story and the reasons for their hatred and suspicion of the white man. Other subjects: Fort Laramie, frontier life, survival stories, brother-sister relationships, Sioux Indians, scalping, massacres, wagon trains, death, horses, and the western frontier.

MURPHY, JIM. *Desperate Journey.* Scholastic, 2006, $16.99 (978-0-439-07806-1) (Grades 5–8)

Introduction

Jim Murphy (1947–) was born in a New Jersey community almost overlooking New York City. He received his undergraduate degree in English from Rutgers University and did graduate work at Radcliffe College. From 1970 through 1977, he worked in juvenile publishing and became a managing editor. When his first book was published in 1978, he turned to full-time writing and now has more than thirty books of both fiction and nonfiction (all on American history) to his credit. Many of his titles have won prestigious literary awards and two of his books are Newbery Honor titles. In 2004, *An American Plague: The True Terrifying Story of the Yellow Fever Epidemic of 1793* (Clarion, 2003, $17; 0395776082) was so honored. Prior to that, in 1996, *The Great Fire* (Scholastic, 1995, $16.99, 0590472674) was also an Honor Book. It tells the story of the Chicago fire of 1871, one of the great disasters of the 19th century. This awesome event is chronicled and vividly recreated, drawing on exhaustive research involving original documents, eyewitness accounts, and selective secondary sources.

Desperate Journey is fiction but the same meticulous attention to authentic detail is present. The story takes place on the Erie Canal over a period of approximately two weeks in April 1848. Though told in the third person, the action is seen through the feelings and deeds of the central character, 14-year-old Maggie.

Historical Background

The building of the Erie Canal, often referred to as "Clinton's Ditch," was first proposed in 1699. Almost one hundred years later, in 1798, the Niagara Canal Corporation began preparations, and in 1817 Governor Dewitt Clinton of New York, the chief supporter of the project, convinced the legislature to authorize $7 million for construction. On July 4, 1817, work began at Rome, N.Y., and two years later the first section, 15 miles between Rome and Utica, was opened. Work was completed on October 26, 1825, but the first passage through the canal—from Lake Erie down the Hudson River to New York City—did not take place until November 4, 1825, when a flotilla of boats left Buffalo. In the lead was the *Seneca Chief*, with Governor Clinton on board.

The trip took ten days. On completion of the trip, Clinton symbolically poured two casks of water from Lake Erie into the Hudson in a ceremony known as "The Wedding (or Marriage) of the Waters." The canal rises 566 feet between the Hudson River at Albany, where the canal begins, and Lake Erie and cover adistance of 363 miles. The number of locks was 83 (now 57), each being 90 feet by 15 feet. The canal was 40 feet wide and 4 feet deep. The sides were stone and the bottom clay.

The soil that was removed became a walkway or tow path, about 10 feet wide. Barges were pulled by horses or mules and when a barge needed to pass another barge, the animals would be quickly unhitched and later re-hitched. The canal was often referred as the eighth wonder of the world; it certainly was the greatest engineering marvel of the 19th century. In addition to the creation of a massive trade route, it produced other important social and economic changes in the region. Upper New York State blossomed, and the frontier was pushed further west. It created a surge of immigration to the west and made New York City the most important commercial center in the United States. With the growth of railroads and, later, the emergence of automobiles, the importance of the canal was reduced. The development of the St. Lawrence Seaway in the 20th century caused a further decline. Today it is used primarily by recreational boats rather than cargo carrying barges. The Afterword about the canal's history and a map and glossary of terms all supply valuable background information.

Principal Characters

Maggie Haggarty, a Canal girl, age 14
Eamon, her 9-year-old brother
Tim Haggarty, her father
Anna Haggarty, her mother
Uncle Hen (Henry), Tim Haggarty's younger brother
Jozie Dalrumple, proprietor of a tavern on the canal
Long Fingered John, aka the Canadian, a villainous barge owner
Russell Ackroyd, a worker for Long Fingered John
Sheriff Einhornn, the sheriff of New Boston
Billy Black, a mysterious stranger
Michael Connelly, an attractive young barge worker
Mr. Rivington, Tim's lawyer
Judge Bradley, the judge at Tim's trial

Plot Synopsis

Life is tough for the barge families that navigate the Erie Canal from Albany to Buffalo, New York. In addition to long working hours, cramped living conditions, endless delays at the locks, the hostility of landowners on shore, and problems with caring for their draft animals, they are deprived of a normal social life and the comforts that ordinary people take for granted. It is April 1848, time for the first spring run, and life is particularly hard for the barge-owning Haggarty family, Father and Mother (Tim and Anna), their children—Maggie, age 14 and her 9-year-old brother Eamon, and Tim's brother Henry (Hen). Tim is a fair-minded, much-loved bargeman, respected by everyone up and down the canal, but occasionally, against his will, he is forced into fights to defend the honor of friends and family.

Last fall, Tim lost a wager of more than three hundred dollars on the outcome of a fight with the villainous barge owner Long Fingered John, also called the Canadian. Though a powerful, strong man, who had right on his side, Tim lost and now, unless he can reach Buffalo with his cargo before the due date and collect the bonus money, his loans will be foreclosed and he will lose the barge.

The five family members are now on the *Betty*, a few miles west of Albany heading for Buffalo with their two mule teams—Issachar and James, and Rudy and Tom—and their pet cat, Marcus. Maggie is on the tow path guiding Issacher and James when she and the animals are hit by a barrage of rocks thrown by a gang of young hooligans who shout insults against "canal people." They are frightened off by Uncle Hen but Maggie suffers a painful wound on her cheek. Maggie is a hard-working, sensitive girl and, apart from exchanging insults with her pesky brother, Eamon, she is even-tempered, responsible, and anxious to please her parents.

Life returns to normal on board, with everyone responsible for designated chores. Much to Eamon's annoyance, Papa gives Maggie a chance to steer the boat by managing the sweep, the boat's rudder. All are looking forward to a brief stop at Dalrumple's landing and tavern, run by their dear friend, Jozie Dalrumple. On arrival, they notice that Long Fingered John's barge is already docked and that he and his crew of ruffians are inside. Determined not to fight, Tim ignores taunts from the Canadian but when young Eamon offends one of John's men, Russell Ackroyd, and Russell grabs the boy, Tim intervenes to save his son. This ugly quarrel ends with the Haggartys leaving the tavern to avoid further violence. On the canal later, when an orange-haired barge captain bullies his way into first place in line at a lock, Tim again yields, showing he is determined to avoid any confrontation that could jeopardize getting the bonus money.

However, soon afterward, the barge is stopped by Sheriff Einhornn and his men from New Boston. Russell Ackroyd has been found beaten up and is in a coma. Because of the altercation at Dalrumple's, Tim and Uncle Hen are prime suspects and are placed under arrest. The trial will begin in about a week but the *Betty* is due in Buffalo in four days. Mama, though suffering bouts of stomach problems and fatigue, decides that she, Maggie, and Eamon must somehow get the barge to Buffalo, more than 150 miles away. They bid farewell to the men and start out.

At the Port Byron locks, they discover only the downstream lock is open. When a captain of a barge headed downstream refuses to yield to an upstream vessel, Mama attacks him with such physical force that he acquiesces. When the two barges eventually pass each other, Maggie sees a handsome young deckhand smiling at her. She is smitten and determined to find out who he is. Back on course, the hours are long and the work back-breaking but all three, even Eamon and ailing Mamma, give their best to meet the deadline at all costs. Through clever sleuthing along the way, Maggie learns that the downstream barge was the *Quick City* and the smiling deckhand's name is Michael Connelly.

When the *Betty* approaches Rochester, an odd-looking man with long, scraggly hair begins talking to her from the towpath. He introduces himself as Billy Black and claims, in his strange Irish-Scotch burr, that the good Lord commanded him to seek out the Haggartys and help them in any way possible. Although both Maggie and her mother refuse this strange offer of kindness, they seem unable to rid themselves of Mr. Black's presence. Though rejected, he continues to follow them along the shore. When the death of a horse pulling a packet (passenger vessel) on the canal causes a delay, Mr. Black performs his first act of kindness. He miraculously pounds life into the animal with his fists and the packet continues its voyage, unblocking the canal.

Maggie uses her veterinary skills when the mule Tom becomes lame. She removes a nail lodged in his hoof and, with various ointments, is able to prevent a possible infection. Mamma reveals the cause of her ailments—she is pregnant. Maggie and Eamon are pleased by this news.

At Lockport, the family encounters another disaster. Because of damage to the locks caused by a runaway barge, there are 43 vessels ahead of them. The delay will mean no bonus. Again Billy Black comes to the rescue. He explains the situation to each of the 43 captains and persuades them to let the *Betty* go first. The result? The barge reaches Buffalo on the morning of the appointed day. However, the agreement is that the goods will be unloaded and in place by noon. It is impossible for the three Haggartys to unload 125 stoves and 85 plows. Mr. Black disappears for a time and reappears with a crew of able workers who unload the barge with a half an hour to spare.

News comes that Tim and Henry's trial will be held in New Boston in three days' time. Mr. Black's men stay on board as crew and the *Betty* heads downstream, arriving at New Boston on the day of the trial. The church that substitutes for a courthouse is filled with Tim's well wishers as well as Long Fingered John and his henchmen. Maggie sees Michael in the crowd. After an introduction and a pleasant talk, Maggie feels certain she will be seeing more of this pleasant young man. Mr. Rivington, Tim's lawyer, has little to do because Judge Bradley throws the case out for lack of evidence. Outside the church, Tim is again accosted by Long Fingered John, who resumes his taunts. When he insults Tim's family and his dear friend, Jozie Dalrumple, Tim feels compelled to fight for their honor. Wagers are made that include their barges. Mamma tries to stop her husband but it is too late. They engage in a brutal fight and Tim wins. Instead of the barge he takes money from John before walking back to his vessel in triumph.

Billy Black performs one last miracle. He manages to awaken Russell Ackroyd from his coma. Fully conscious, he declares publicly that neither Tim nor Henry was responsible for his attack. An appreciative family says goodbye to Billy Black. He heads upstream while the Haggartys, now financially secure and happy with the thought that a family addition is near, set off for Albany convinced that guardian angels do exist.

Passages for Booktalking

Some key episodes: the rock attack on Maggie (pp. 8–12); the encounter with the man with orange-colored hair (pp. 50–54); Tim and Henry are arrested (pp. 62–68); and Mamma throws her weight around at the Port Byron locks (pp. 86–89).

Themes and Subjects

As well as a rollicking suspenseful adventure tale, this novel paints an accurate historical and geographical picture of the Erie Canal and the arduous task of shipping goods and equipment on it. The experiences of barge families and the sense of community they produce are well depicted. Maggie is a well-developed character whose growth to maturity, emerging sexuality, and assumption of adult responsibilities are believably presented. Other subjects: New York State, family life, pregnancy, courage, animals, fights, bullying, kindness, courts and lawyers, and villainy.

PAULSEN, GARY. *The Legend of Bass Reeves: Being the True and Fictional Account of the Most Valiant Marshal in the West.* Wendy Lamb Books, 2006, $15.95 (978-0-385-74661-8) (Grades 5–8)

Introduction

After a traumatic childhood and years of drifting from one job to another, Gary Paulsen (1939–) turned to full-time writing for young readers. Some of his nearly forty books are thrilling survival stories, like the five-volume series featuring Brian Robeson that began with *Hatchet* (Atheneum, 1987, $16.95, 0689840926) (condensed in *Classic Teenplots*). Most of his output, however, consists of historical novels that deal with the opening up of the West. Typical of these are the four volumes of Francis Tucket stories beginning with *Mr. Tucket* (Delacorte, 1994, $15.95, 0385311699). Set in 1848, this novel tells how 14-year-old Francis Tucket is kidnapped by Pawnee Indians from a wagon train heading west and how he learns to live in the wild with lessons he learns from a one-armed trapper.

The Legend of Bass Reeves re-creates the courageous life of the African American Wild West hero who lived from 1824 to 1910. The book is described as biographical fiction because little was written about his life and the rest had to be filled in from hearsay and conjecture. About half of this slim volume covers Bass's youth as an African American slave in north Texas, one quarter with his later life with a family of Creek Indians in the Indian Territory, and the last quarter with his career as a U.S. marshal. In the Foreword, the author claims that Reeves "truly qualified as legendary and heroic." The rest of the book proves his point.

Historical Background

Bass Reeves lived through some momentous events in our nation's history. In 1836, when he was 11 and living in Texas, the Alamo was captured by Mexican forces led by Santa Anna. Many of Bass's neighbors volunteered to help avenge this humiliating defeat. The Emancipation Proclamation, issued in 1863 by President Abraham Lincoln, granted freedom to slaves in the southern states. With this, Bass, now 39, became a free man. Much of Bass's life was spent in Indian Territory, the country that included present-day Oklahoma and parts of Kansas and Nebraska. This area was set aside for the Indians by the Indian Intercourse Act of 1834. Before this, the federal government had begun moving the Five Civilized Tribes (including the Creeks with whom Bass stayed) from their ancestral lands to this territory along the shameful "Trail of Tears." Today these events would be described as an early form of genocide.

The arrival of many white settlers brought pressure to abolish the territory. This took place in 1907 (three years before Bass's death) with the entrance of

Oklahoma into the Union. The Comanche Indians, often referred to in the text, were native to the area and resentful of trespassers. They had a reputation as excellent horsemen and for being extremely savage and warlike. According to legend they killed more whites than any other Indian tribe.

Principal Characters

Bass Reeves, a young slave who became a respected marshal in the Old West

Mammy, Bass's mother

Flowers, a slave who is old, silent, and nearly blind

The mister, the owner of Mammy, Bass, and Flowers; his real name is Murphy

Peter, a Creek Indian who cares for Bass

Mary, his wife

Betty Two Shoes, their daughter

Isaac Parker, known as the Hanging Judge, who appointed Bass as a federal marshal

Plot Synopsis

When she was pregnant with Bass, the mister won Mammy in a poker game in Austin and bought her back to his dilapidated ranch in north Texas close to the Indian Territory border. The ranch consists of five crumbling adobe mud huts with sod roofs surrounded by a mesquite fence to keep the mister's mangy herd of Texas longhorns from roaming outside the compound. Bass and his loving Mammy share their hut with a third slave, Flowers, an old, nearly blind man who never speaks. Mammy cooks and cleans for the mister, a reclusive, mean-spirited alcoholic who lives in the best of the huts. As he grows older and enters adolescence, Bass begins assuming adult responsibilities around the ranch, caring for the buildings and the animals. Without rights, money, or property, the three slaves must obey and show complete subservience to the mister. Bass dreams of the day when things will change.

The mister does not allow his slaves the luxury of eating his beef or pork nor does he allow Bass to use any of his guns, so the boy must hunt for meat for his Mammy and Flowers using homemade spears and knives. While on one of these forays, he sees one of the dreaded Comanche Indian warriors on his horse. These Indians are renowned for their cruelty and savagery. Bass knows he should feel terror but instead he admires this painted fighter and the freedom he represents. When the Comanche is joined by others, Bass realizes this raiding party could mean danger for the ranch. He creeps back home and for the next three nights he and his Mammy keep watch. The Indians don't arrive but a group of volunteer soldiers visits the ranch. They include Mr. Garnett from a neighboring ranch. All have heard about the recent fall of the Alamo and are headed south to seek revenge.

Later, Bass spots another Comanche in the area and sees that he is carrying two freshly cut scalps, one yellow and the other red. He tells the mister, who fears they might be those of the Garnett women. The mister demands that Bass accompany him to the Garnett homestead. The sight they come upon causes Bass to vomit—slaughtered livestock, charred buildings, and half-burned corpses. The mister and Bass bury the dead before returning home.

At age 14, Bass accompanies an increasingly infirm mister on one of his trips to Paris, Texas, to buy supplies such as coffee, tobacco, and, of course, liquor. Bass is enchanted by the wild frontier life he sees in this small town.

By the time Bass is 16, he has assumed all of the chores and responsibilities of running the ranch. One day the mister invites Bass to play poker with him. At first the mister loans the ante to Bass but this is soon paid back and Bass continues to win although he tries not to. After many sessions of play, he has won all the mister's money from him. The old man suggests a hand using the freedom of Bass and Mammy as his bid. Bass sees the man hiding aces in his lap and accuses him of cheating. Enraged, the mister pulls a gun on Bass, who defends himself by hitting the mister on the head with a whiskey jug. He falls, unconscious. Mammy tells her son he must flee or face death for striking his master. Hastily, Bass gathers up the master's horse, some provisions, and the money he won at poker. With tears streaming down his cheeks at leaving his beloved Mammy, he heads north into Indian Territory. Bass is now 17.

In the wild and lawless Indian Territory, Bass moves from place to place avoiding people and fearful of being discovered. One day he discovers he is being tracked by two men intent on robbery and murder. He is forced to shoot both to ensure his own safety. Much later, he rescues a young Indian girl who has been attacked by three wolves. He shoots two and frightens the third into retreat but not before he is mauled so badly that he loses consciousness from loss of blood. He awakens in the hut of the Creek Indian family whose daughter he saved. The father is Peter, the mother, Mary, and the girl, Betty Two Shoes.

He lives with the Creeks for 22 years until 1863, the year the Emancipation Proclamation makes him a free man. In 1875, he heeds a recruitment call from Isaac Parker and becomes a federal marshal. Parker is a frontier judge who is intent on cleaning up the lawlessness in the Indian Territory.

Bass's record as a marshal is exemplary. He achieves an exceptional record for bringing murderers, horse thieves, cattle rustlers, rapists, and other criminals to justice. His most difficult assignment comes when he must track down and capture his own son, who is guilty of killing his unfaithful wife. During his career, Bass faces overwhelming odds and arrests thousands of criminals.

Though still largely unsung, Bass Reeves is truly an American hero we should recognize and honor.

Passages for Booktalking

In the Foreword (pp. vii–xii), Gary Paulsen presents his case for recognizing Bass Reeves as a great American hero. Mammy and young Bass talk about slavery and how things must change (pp. 12–15); Bass sees the Comanche warrior (pp. 21–23); Bass and the mister bury the dead settlers (pp. 33–38); and Bass accompanies the mister on his trip to Paris, Texas (pp. 41–46).

Themes and Subjects

The book chronicles the life of a great African American—a man of courage and high principles who overcame enormous obstacles to become a genuine American hero. The book also provides a truthful picture of the American West in the mid-19th century, including a searing depiction of the disgrace of slavery. Other subjects include adventure stories, coming of age, accepting responsibilities, Native American culture, life on the western frontier, the everyday life of slaves, loyalty to family and race, the triumph of duty over personal concerns, the white man's perfidy and promotion of injustice, Indian Territory, Texas, Oklahoma, and United States marshals.

ADDITIONAL SELECTIONS

Barker, M. P. *A Difficult Boy* (Holiday, 2008, $16.95) (Grades 5–9)
Because of family financial difficulties, Ethan's father reluctantly indentures the 9-year-old boy to the wicked, dishonest George Lyman.

Blos, Joan W. *Letters from the Corrugated Castle: A Novel of Gold Rush California, 1850–1852* (Atheneum, 2007, $17.99) (Grades 4–8)
Using an epistolary format, this novel tells how 13-year-old Eldora, an orphan from Massachusetts, finds her long-lost mother, who has become a wealthy woman in the San Francisco of Gold Rush days.

Broyles, Anne. *Priscilla and the Hollyhocks* (Charlesbridge, 2008, $15.95) (Grades 2–4)
Priscilla, a young slave girl, is sold to a Cherokee family and participates in the Trail of Tears of 1838 before she gains her freedom in this richly illustrated book.

Cadnum, Michael. *Blood Gold* (Viking, 2004, $16.99) (Grades 7–10)
Eighteen-year-old William and friend Ben encounter greed, murder, and assorted adventures while taking part in the California Gold Rush.

Dahlberg, Maurine F. *The Story of Jonas* (Farrar, 2007, $16.50) (Grades 4–7)
In the mid-1800s, a slave named Jonas is sent to find gold in the Kansas Territory and realizes that freedom is possible.

DeFelice, Cynthia. *Bringing Ezra Back* (Farrar, 2006, $16) (Grades 5–9)
Set in Ohio in 1840, this continuation of the author's *Weasel* (Macmillan, 1990, $15) tells how Ezra, whose tongue had been cut out by Weasel, is saved from being exhibited as a freak by his loyal friend Nathan Fowler.

Karr, Kathleen. *The Great Turkey Walk* (Farrar, 1998, $17) (Grades 4–8)
In 1860, 15-year-old Simon decides to walk a thousand turkeys from Missouri to Denver, where there is a meat shortage.

Lesourd, Nancy. *The Personal Correspondence of Hannah Brown and Sarah Smith: The Underground Railroad, 1858* (Zondervan, 2003, $9.99) (Grades 4–7)
In letters to each other, two Quaker girls discuss the abolitionist movement and also help a slave escape.

Lester, Julius. *Day of Tears: A Novel in Dialogue* (Hyperion, 2005, $15.99) (Grades 6–9)
Told from a variety of viewpoints, including those of unfortunates about to be sold, their master and families, and brave runaways, this is a re-creation of the largest slave auction in American history, which took place in 1859.

Levine, Ellen. *Henry's Freedom* (Scholastic, 2007, $16.99) (Grades 3–5)
With excellent illustrations by Kadir Nelson, this is the story based on fact of a slave named Henry "Box" Brown whose wife and three children are sold and never seen by him again although, in time, he gains his freedom.

Lyons, Mary E. *Letters from a Slave Boy: The Story of Joseph Jacobs* (Atheneum, 2007, $15.99) (Grades 4–8)
Told in a series of unsent letters, this is the story of a young slave, Jacob, who escapes from his master, poses as a white, and has a series of adventures first as a printer's helper in Boston, then aboard a whaling ship, and later working in California during the Gold Rush, before eventually heading for Australia.

Rinaldi, Ann. *The Ever-After Bird* (Harcourt, 2007, $17) (Grades 5–8)
After CeCe's father dies while helping escaped slaves, she becomes an anti-abolitionist particularly when she is forced to help a freed slave who is pretending to be her slave-servant on their trip into the South.

Torrey, Michele. *Voyage of Ice* (Knopf, 2004, $15.95) (Grades 4–7)
Fifteen-year-old Nick finds life difficult but ultimately rewarding after he signs on to a whaler in 1851.

Wait, Lea. *Finest Kind* (McElderry, 2006, $16.95) (Grades 5–8)
Forced to relocate to the small town of Wiscasset, Maine, in 1837 for financial reasons, Jake and his family have trouble adjusting particularly when they decide to keep the existence of Jake's severely disabled younger brother a secret to avoid ostracism.

Wilson, Diane Lee. *Black Storm Comin'* (Simon, 2005, $16.95) (Grades 7–10)
This adventure story set in the Wild West of 1860 tells of a mixed-race teenager who joins the Pony Express.

CIVIL WAR AND RECONSTRUCTION (1861–1900)

BEATTY, PATRICIA. *Turn Homeward, Hannalee.* Morrow, 1984, o.p.; pap. Harper, $5.99 (978-0-688-16676-2) (Grades 5–8)

Introduction

Patricia Beatty (1922–1991) and her husband John (1922–1975) were prolific writers of historical fiction for young people. Their first book appeared in 1966 and they averaged a book a year until John's death in 1975. After that, Patricia wrote several excellent novels on her own, some dealing with the American West in the late 19th century and others, like *Turn Homeward, Hannalee*, about the Civil War. *Charley Skedaddle* (pap. Troll, $5.50; 08167713170), first published in 1987, is an excellent companion piece to *Hannalee*. It tells of 12-year-old Charley Quinn, who is growing up in the danger-filled streets of the Bowery district of New York in the early 1860s. To escape the threat of an orphanage and to avenge his brother's death at Gettysburg, he joins the Union Army as a drummer boy. In battle he panics and deserts. The remainder of the book describes his life in a Blue Ridge Mountain community until the end of the war.

Of her historical novels, Mrs. Beatty commented in 1989, "I try to make the English and American 'pasts' come to life in order to convince the nine-to-fourteen age group that people of the past were real people with real personalities and real problems and not text-book, dry-as-a-bone beings."

Turn Homeward, Hannalee takes place from the middle of 1864 (the third year of the Civil War) to after the armistice in 1865. It is narrated by 12-year-old Hannalee Reed.

Historical Background

General Philip H. Sheridan (1831–1888), the Union Civil War leader, succeeded Grant in 1864 as leader of the western theater of the war. On July 5, 1864, Northen forces occupied the mill town of Roswell in northern Georgia. They burned the mills that had employed about 400 workers, mostly women, children, and old men. On July 7, General William T. Sherman issued a statement, "I have ordered General Garrard to arrest for treason all owners and employees and send them under guard to Marietta (Georgia), where I will send them North." The flimsy "treason" accusation came because the clothing and rope manufactured in the mills were used by Confederate troops.

The mill workers were transported to Marietta and imprisoned in the Georgia Military Institute there, then loaded into boxcars and sent to Chattanooga, Tennessee, with a stopover in Nashville. The final destination for many was Louisville, Kentucky, though others were sent across the Ohio River into Indiana. The eventual fate of most of the workers remains unknown. As one historian has said, "The mystery of the fate of the Roswell women [and children] is made up of 500 individual tragedies. Most of their stories are lost history."

In July 2000, a memorial monument was unveiled in Roswell to commemorate the cruel deportation. In *Turn Homeward, Hannalee*, Hannalee has an encounter with William Quantrill, the leader of the savage Confederate warriors called bushwhackers. Quantrill was responsible for the Lawrence Massacre in Kansas in 1863, one of the most vicious atrocities of the war. The author's note at the end of the novel supplies extra historical data.

Principal Characters

Hannalee Reed, a bobbin girl growing up in Roswell, Georgia
Davey Reed, her older brother, a sergeant in the Confederate Army
Jem Reed, her younger brother
Mama, Hannalee's loving mother
Rosellen Sanders, a mill worker, who is Davey's fiancée
Aunt Marilla, Rosellen's guardian
Mr. and Mrs. James Fletcher, Hannalee's employers in Louisville
Mrs. Burton, a boardinghouse owner in Cannelton, Indiana
Lucius Carewe, an itinerant peddler

Plot Synopsis

The entire economic life of the close-knit Reed family revolves around the textile mill in the town of Roswell, which is north of Atlanta and 13 miles from Marietta. Before the Civil War and their enlistment in the Roswell Guards, both Papa Reed and his older son Davey worked in the mill. So did Mama Reed, until her fourth pregnancy forced her to quit. Her two other children are employed in the mill—12-year-old Hannalee is a bobbin girl and 10-year-old Jem is a lowly lap boy. The work day starts at five in the morning and extends, with brief breakfast and lunch breaks, until seven in the evening. Since the war began, the mill has produced fabric for Confederate uniforms.

In June of 1864, the Reed family is still recovering from the news that Papa has died of the fever in an army hospital, but they are happy that Davey, now a sergeant, is home on furlough. Davey is engaged to Rosellen Sanders, a beautiful, mature girl who lives with her Aunt Marilla and works at the mill as a drawing girl, setting patterns in fabric. Hannalee greatly admires Rosellen and considers her a mentor. Before Davey returns to his unit, the couple quarrels because Rosellen wants to get married, but Davey—a veteran of such battles as Gettysburg—refuses, fearful that marriage would only leave her a widow.

Within days of Davey's departure, the sounds of battle are heard in the town and on July 5, 1864, the dreaded bluebellies (as the Yankee soldiers are known) enter Roswell. Their commander, General Garrard, orders all mill workers to assemble in the town square. Hannalee's mother gives her a persimmon seed button for remembrance, and Jem and Hannalee meet Rosellen in the square. The group of about 400 (mostly women and children) is kept there for four days while the mills and many town buildings are burned. Their drunken guards become abusive and menacing. Luckily, new Union cavalry troops arrive and whisk the prisoners off to the deserted barracks of a military academy in Marietta. On the way, Hannalee passes her home, now smoldering rubble, and says good-bye to her mother. Their group is to be taken north and given menial jobs as punishment for aiding the South's war effort.

Fearful that the boys and girls will be separated, Hannalee cuts off her braids, sews them onto a bonnet, and dresses Jem in this and one of her petticoats. Jem Reed is now Jemima Reed. Some of the mill workers are dropped off in Nashville and the others—including Jem, Hannalee, and Rosellen—proceed to Louisville, where they are separated. Rosellen is chosen to be a drawing girl in a textile plant owned by Mr. Greenwood and his handsome son, Francis, in Cannelton, Indiana. Jem (whose disguise has been dropped) becomes a household helper on a farm in nearby Hartford, Kentucky, and Hannalee is now the household servant of a Louisville couple, the Fletchers.

Although Mr. Fletcher can be tolerated, Mrs. Fletcher is a cruel tyrant who works Hannalee unmercifully for only three dollars a month plus room and board. Shortly after receiving her first month's pay, Hannalee escapes, disguised as a boy. Now calling herself Hannibal Reed, she decides first to rescue Jem. After a hair-raising experience with the bushwhacker William Quantrill and his men, in which an innocent farmer is murdered, Hannibal reverses her course and heads for Cannelton to find Rosellen. There, she finds Rosellen a changed person. She is doing well at the mill, and has made many friends, including the attentive mill owner's son. Encouraged by Rosellen and kindly boardinghouse owner Mrs. Burton, Hannalee (still disguised as Hannibal) gets a job at the mill as a bobbin boy.

Life in Cannelton is pleasant with the company of beloved Rosellen and the benevolent Mrs. Burton. However, after saving money for two months, Hannalee wants to press on. The South is faring badly, Atlanta has fallen, and Hannalee is needed at home. Not unexpectedly, Rosellen decides to stay in Indiana, so Hannalee again sets out alone. She makes her way to Kentucky and through some clever sleuthing finds the farm where Jem is working. He escapes easily and the two head south to Georgia. In Louisville, they catch a train to Nashville, as far south as they can go in Yankee territory. There they begin walking, always aware that troops are moving around them.

Outside of the town of Franklin, Tennessee, they hide in a sycamore tree while a bloody six-hour battle rages around them. Known as "the bloodiest hours of the Civil War," the battle of Franklin and its scenes of horror and death become imbedded in their minds. When it is safe to leave the tree, the two pick their way through the dead and dying back to the main road. They find a riderless cavalry horse that makes their trip less arduous until the horse is confiscated by Confederate troops. Later they encounter a wise old traveling peddler, Lucius Carewe, who offers them a ride in his cart.

On Christmas Day, they part company only 13 miles from home. When they arrive in Roswell they discover that Mama has moved in with Rosellen's Aunt Marilla and that they have a new baby sister, Paulina. Tenderly, Hannalee returns the persimmon seed button to her mother. Without any source of income, the group almost starves during the long, bleak winter. At one point, they are reduced to gathering corn that falls from horses' feed bags. In April the war ends and Davey miraculously returns, injured but alive. Both he and Aunt Marilla accept Rosellen's decision to remain in the North. With nothing to keep them in Roswell, the Reeds decide to move to Atlanta, where there is work rebuilding. Aunt Marilla stays behind. Hannalee is confident that now that the war is over she and her family will have a bright future.

Passages for Booktalking

Some memorable passages: Jem and Hannalee are sent home from the mill as war approaches (pp. 26–29); the mill workers are ordered to the square (pp. 32–41); Hannalee sees her mother in the ashes of their house (pp. 45–48); and, in Louisville, the three refugees learn their fates and Rosellen is picked as a mill worker (pp. 65–71).

Themes and Subjects

This novel can serve as a great polemic against war. Far from the elite plantation class of *Gone with the Wind*, the characters in this novel are everyday people who suffer unspeakable hardships because of war. Hannalee shows courage and resourcefulness as she matures from a follower to a leader. The strength of family ties and the importance of compassion and understanding are paramount in this novel. Some other subjects: Georgia, Tennessee, Kentucky, brutality, hardship, death, Civil War battles, textile mills, working conditions, General Sherman, William Quantrill, survival, and starvation.

BLACKWOOD, GARY. *Second Sight.* Dutton, 2005, $16.99 (978-0-525-47481-4); pap. Puffin, $6.99 (978-0-14-240747-9) (Grades 5–8)

Introduction

Gary Blackwood was born in Meadville, Pennsylvania on Oct. 25, 1945, and attended a one-room schoolhouse whose library, a few shelves of books, contained the complete series of Dr. Dolittle books. He competed with a friend to be the first to read every one. While in his teens, he began to submit stories to magazines and sold his first story at age 19. He has written more than twenty novels for young people as well as numerous plays (his interest in the theater is evident in this novel). He and his wife live in an old sea captain's house overlooking the ocean in Nova Scotia.

The author describes *Second Sight* as a book of altered history rather than alternate history. An example of the latter is his *The Year of the Hangman* (Dutton, 2002, $16.99; 0525469214). It takes place in 1777, the year after the American Revolution has been crushed by the British. Washington awaits execution and Benjamin Franklin's rebel newspaper, *Liberty Tree*, has gone underground. Creighton Brown, a 15-year-old English lad who has been sent to the colonies against his will, is befriended by Franklin, who gives him a job in his print shop. When the English expect Creighton to become a spy for them, he struggles internally to determine his true allegiances. For more information on Gary Blackwood and his novels see *Shakespeare's Scribe* in Chapter 4.

Second Sight takes place over a period of about eight months—from the fall of 1864 through April 1865—in the city of Washington. It is told in the third person but the author frequently interrupts to make wry comments on the action and the behavior of the characters.

Historical Background

Ford's Theatre today is both a historical monument and a live, working theater. Located on Tenth Street in downtown Washington, D.C., it was a church before being converted into a theater by John T. Ford. The building was destroyed by fire in 1862 and rebuilt as Ford's New Theatre. After Lincoln's assassination it became headquarters for various government agencies and later a government warehouse. Eventually, restoration funding was approved and on February 13, 1968, the restored theater and newly constructed museum were opened to the public.

John Wilkes Booth was one of the children of Junius Brutus Booth, a famous actor who came to America from England in 1821. John Wilkes

Booth was born in Maryland on May 10, 1838. His older brother Edwin, also a famous actor, supervised his childhood. At first he achieved little success as an actor but after he moved to Richmond and joined a stock company, he became popular with audiences and was enamored of the southern life style. During the Civil War, he believed in serving his country—the Confederate States of America. Although he promised his mother never to join the army, he decided to serve in other ways, such as smuggling medical supplies to the south. With friends, including John Surratt, Surratt's mother, and David Herold, he engineered a plan to kidnap Lincoln and hold him as ransom for thousands of Confederate prisoners.

Shortly after this plan failed (Lincoln traveled by a different route than the conspirators expected), Lee surrendered and a more desperate plan was conceived. Booth shot President Lincoln on April 14, 1865, at 10:15 p.m. at Ford's Theatre. On April 26, Booth was shot while hiding in a tobacco shed in Port Royal, Virginia. Mrs. Surratt and Herold were hanged for their part in the conspiracy. John Surratt escaped to Canada and was later captured and tried, but acquitted because of a mistrial.

Thomas "Tad" Lincoln, who was named after his grandfather, was the fourth and last child born to Lincoln and his wife Mary Todd Lincoln. He was 8 years old when his family moved to the White House in 1861. Like his parents, he loved the theater. He was attending a children's play at a different theater when President and Mrs. Lincoln were at Ford's Theatre. In 1868, Mary Todd Lincoln decided to travel to Europe with her son. They remained abroad until 1871. On the return voyage, Tad caught a cold. After arriving in the United States, his health deteriorated and he died at age 18, on July 15, 1871. His death caused great grief to his mother and ultimately bouts of severe depression.

Principal Characters

Joseph Ehrlich, an enterprising boy of about 14 or 15
Nicholas Ehrlich, his father
Carolina Ehrlich, his mother
Margaretta, his dead younger sister
John R. Foley, Joseph's employer
Mrs. McKenna, a boarding house proprietor
El Nino Eddie (Eduardo Montoya), a 12-year-old performer
Patrick Nolan, a bullying Irishman
Cassandra Quinn, his niece
John Wilkes Booth, an actor
Davy Herold, a friend of John Wilkes Booth
Mrs. Surratt, another boarding house proprietor
John Surratt, her son

Honora Fitzpatrick, Cassandra's 18-year-old governess
Abraham Lincoln, the president
Mary Todd Lincoln, his wife
Tad Lincoln, his son
Ward Hill Lamon, chief marshal of Washington, D.C.
James Clarvoe, a U.S. marshal

Plot Synopsis

It is the fall of 1864 in the war-weary city of Washington, D.C. The populace is so sickened by the terrible toll the war has taken that, to spare them further anguish and despair, authorities have decreed that the dead and dying are to be brought into the city only late at night when the townspeople are asleep. During these grim days, people look to the theaters for pleasure and escape. Some of the second-string entertainers employed in the theaters are housed at Mrs. McKenna's boarding house. They include a strong man, the Montoyas (who are tight-rope walkers, clog dancers, and comedians), the Thomson's dog act, and the Ehrlich family. Actually, at present the Ehrlichs are not directly employed in the theater, but father Nicholas, who, in stentorian tones, often claims to have once trod the boards with the famous Junius Booth, is busy perfecting a complicated mind reading act with his son Joseph, a boy of 14 or 15. Some years ago, Nicholas suffered a throat injury (we later learn that it was in a bar room brawl) and he is now unable to act. He makes a meager living giving acting and voice lessons, while Joseph supplements this income as a salesman at John R. Foley's China and Lamp Store. Mrs. Ehrlich, Carolina, has never recovered from the sudden death of her daughter Margaretta some four years before in a horse-drawn omnibus accident. Since then, she has remained depressed, listless, and distant.

Every night after work, a reluctant Joseph and his father rehearse the complicated alphabetical codes that Nicholas has devised so that a blindfolded Joseph can identify objects presented by Joseph's father from audience members. They also must be careful to keep fellow boarders, like the pesky young El Nino Eddie, the youngest member of the tightrope walking act, from discovering and divulging their secrets. El Nino Eddie (real name Eduardo Montoya) is 12 years old but passes for younger to induce sympathy from the audience. He fancies himself as a spy-in-training and is always eavesdropping.

One day at the horse races, Joseph notices that a gruff red-bearded man consults his companion, an attractive girl aged about 11, before he places his bets. The girl reminds Joseph of his dead sister Margaretta and, intrigued, he follows them. When the girl appears to make an error in judgment, the bully starts to hit her and Joseph intervenes. With a warning to Joseph to mind his own business, the man leaves with the girl.

Billed as Professor Godunov and Son, Nicholas gets a booking at the National Theatre where they are an instant success and their engagement is extended. Soon their salaries are sufficient that Joseph can quit his job at Foley's. One night, two strangers move into Mrs. McKenna's boarding house. They are the nasty red-bearded man and young girl from the racetrack. The man is introduced as Patrick Nolan and the girl as his niece Cassandra Quinn. When Joseph gets to know this sad, pensive girl, he realizes that she has a mystical power, the gift of second sight. She can predict what will happen in the future. When circumstances change, however, these prophecies may not come true—as happened at the racetrack weeks before. Cassandra is frightened by this power and tries to conceal her gift.

As their reputation continues to soar, the Ehrlichs move to a lucrative engagement at Ford's Theatre. There, after a particularly successful performance, they are invited by a U.S. Marshal, Ward Hill Lamon, to visit an appreciative President Lincoln, and his wife, Mary Todd Lincoln. Mrs. Lincoln is so impressed that she invites Joseph to attend a séance at the White House.

Later, at the boarding house, Nolan voices outspoken insults about President Lincoln and the northern cause. Mrs. McKenna, a strong supporter of Lincoln, is so incensed at these remarks that she orders Nolan and Cassandra out of her house. Before Joseph can determine their new whereabouts, he and his father go to Baltimore for an engagement.

On their return, Joseph receives a note from Cassandra and traces them to a boarding house run by Mrs. Surratt. There, before going to Cassandra's quarters, he meets three men who are talking together. They are Mrs. Surratt's son Jack, his friend Davy Harold, and the celebrated actor John Wilkes Booth. Joseph also meets Miss Honora Fitzpatrick, an 18-year-old self-possessed girl who is to be Cassandra's governess. Joseph notices that Davy is infatuated with Honora, but that this affection is not reciprocated. When she is alone with Joseph, Cassandra expresses concerns about her visions of the president being abducted. Joseph decides to take this prediction to the White House. There, before meeting with Lamon, he encounters young Tad Lincoln who flatters him by asking for an autograph. Lamon takes Joseph's warning under advisement.

While preparing for a return engagement at Ford's Theatre, Joseph notices that his nemesis, Patrick Nolan, has been hired as a stage hand. He is later told by the ever-vigilant El Nino Eddie that a mysterious stranger in a felt hat with a pock-marked face is following him. Joseph realizes that Eddie is right but is unable to shake his stalker.

The kidnapping of Lincoln does not take place. Now Cassandra has another vision, of Mr. Lincoln being shot in an enclosed box-like place. As Joseph's suspicions of a conspiracy grow, he is confronted by an angry Nolan who, upset with his constant meddling, attacks the boy brutally, breaking several of his ribs. In true theater style, the show goes on, though Joseph is in agony.

Joseph is approached by a love-sick Davy who asks him to intercede on his behalf with Miss Fitzpatrick. He says he will soon show Miss Fitzpatrick how important he is. He shows Joseph a gun Mr. Booth has given him with blank cartridges and blurts out the details of Booth's plan to kill Lincoln. In spite of intense pain, Joseph is able to get to Ford's Theatre. After the president arrives, Joseph tries to enter his theater box but is dragged away by the man who has been stalking him. He hears the report of a small pistol and sees Booth rush out of the theater. Miraculously, Mr. Lincoln emerges unharmed. Outside Joseph discovers why. Davy, realizing that Miss Fitzpatrick would like him more as a savior than an assassin, has secretly switched his pistol with Booth's. Unfortunately, during Booth's escape, Davy is shot and dies.

Joseph's stalker identifies himself as James Clarvoe, a U.S. marshal who, believing that Joseph was part of the conspiracy, prevented him from entering the theater box. However, all works out for the best. Miss Fitzgerald, who is financially secure becomes Cassandra's official protector, Carolina Ehrlich begins to accept Cassandra as a surrogate daughter, Nicholas and Joseph, in true theatrical style, take their show on the road, and, best of all, the president is safe.

Passages for Booktalking

Washington, D.C., in 1864 and young Joseph are both introduced (pp. 4–7); Nicholas demonstrates his mind-reading act with an imaginary audience (pp. 21 bottom–25); Joseph encounters Cassandra and her uncle at the racetrack (pp. 25–33); and Joseph calls on Cassandra and meets John Wilkes Booth, some of his friends, and Miss Fitzpatrick (pp. 142–147).

Themes and Subjects

"What if . . . ?" speculations about historical occurrences are always intriguing and this is no exception. Until the last few pages of this novel, the author has adhered to accurate historical fact. Particularly interesting is the depiction of war-torn Washington, the plight of the country, and opposition to Lincoln and his policies. The show business background adds interest and a touch of the exotic. Joseph is an attractive young hero. His realistic attitude nicely complements his father's flamboyance. The author provides amusing asides on novel writing and techniques of plot and character development. Other subjects include: Civil War, John Wilkes Booth, Abraham Lincoln, clairvoyance, mind-reading fraud, courage, love, father-son relations, death, family stories, vaudeville acts, conspiracies.

————•◦•————

CARBONE, ELISA. *Storm Warriors.* Knopf, 2001, $14.95 (978-0-375-80664-3); pap. Dell, $5.99 (978-0-440-41879-5) (Grades 5–8)

Introduction

Elisa Carbone has said, "I wrote my first book before I learned how to write." At the age of four and a half she announced that she wanted to write a book, and at the end of each work day her father dutifully took dictation. After several weeks, she finished the book. Her mother typed it and Eliza illustrated it. She says, "I felt content that my story was not simply drifting away on the wind, but rather being preserved as a book." She married and had a family at an early age and, when her children were grown, she completed two Master's degrees. In her early thirties, she began writing books for young readers. She is now a full-time writer, an avid reader (6 to 12 books per month), and an enthusiastic outdoors person. She has written about a dozen books, all well received and many of them historical novels.

Storm Warriors, a scrupulously researched book, is narrated by 12-year-old Nathan Williams and takes place over a period of ten months, from December 1895 through October 1896. Although slavery has been abolished, racial prejudice is still rampant. The action occurs primarily on Pea Island, a windswept atoll that is part of the Outer Banks of North Carolina. In addition to actual events, it features many true-life characters including the gallant members of the Pea Island Life Saving Service and their outstanding leader, Richard Etheridge.

Historical Background

In the 18th and 19th centuries, ships in distress off the east coast of the United States usually received little if any help. Some states organized volunteer brigades and built rescue stations. Slowly federal funds were appropriated to fund these operations. In Washington, D.C., Sumner Increase Kimball, a lawyer and administrator in the Marine Division of the Treasury Department, began organizing these stations into a network. In 1878, the network was established as a separate agency of the Treasury Department and named the U.S. Life-Saving Service. About 280 stations were built on the East and West Coasts and the Great Lakes. Full-time crews at these stations usually numbered seven men, each with separate duties and responsibilities. Two means of rescue were used. The most common was the surfboat (thus, the Service's personnel became known as surfmen). It was manned by six oarsmen and launched by dragging the boat to a site near the wreck. If the seas were too rough for boats, another method was used. Using a cannon-like gun, the Lyle gun, a strong hawser (line) was catapulted to the ship. Once the line was secure, a life cart could be pulled back and forth between the ship and the shore. Both methods are described in the novel. Day-to-day routines for the surfmen were rigorous and physically demanding.

Pea Island (the setting of the novel) is in the Outer Banks of North Carolina. The life-saving station on Pea Island in the 1880s was the only one staffed by African Americans. Its leader, known as the keeper, was Captain Richard Etheridge, a black Union Army veteran. He was appointed in 1880 and remained as keeper for twenty years. The motto of the Service was "You have to go out, but you don't have to come back."

In 1915, the U.S. Life-Saving Service and U.S. Revenue Cutter System were united to form the U.S. Coast Guard. The U.S. Life-Saving Heritage Society, founded in 1885 and headquartered in Nantucket, aims to preserve the stations, history, boats, and equipment of the Service. Pea Island, bounded on one side by Pamlico Sound and on the other by the Atlantic Ocean, is now a surfer's paradise and the home of the Pea Island National Wildlife Refuge, a 6,000-acre park that is home to more than 265 species of birds.

Principal Characters

Nathan Williams, the 12-year-old African American narrator
George Williams, Nathan's Daddy, a fisherman
Ulysses Williams, Nathan's Grandpa
Richard Eldridge, the black keeper of the Pea Island Life-Saving Station
Benjamin Bowser, first surfman at the station
Lewis Wescott, George Midgett, L. W. Tillett, Theodore Meekins, and
    Stanley Wise, the other surfmen at the station
William, a 14-year-old friend of Nathan's
Seabright, William's 7-year-old sister
Floyd, almost 11, another of Nathan's friends
Fannie, Floyd's 12-year-old sister

Plot Synopsis

On the night of December 27, 1895, a terrible storm hits the Outer Banks of North Carolina grounding a three-masted schooner on the shoals of Pea Island. Twelve-year-old Nathan Williams and his fisherman father, who live with aging Grandpa in a one-room cabin on the island, are rousted from their sleep to help the seven-man crew of the island's Life-Saving Station drag their equipment to the shore for a rescue operation. At first, station keeper Etheridge and number one surfman Benjamin Bowser plan to fire the Lyle Gun to string a line to the ailing ship but instead they decide to use the surfboat, which resembles a huge rowboat, to effect a stunning rescue. Nathan is in awe of these gallant men who are, like him, African Americans. This incident reaffirms his goal to become a surfman, an ambition his father disapproves of.

Nathan was raised on the mainland in Elizabeth City but when the Klan began terrorizing the black community, Daddy moved the family to the safety of Roanoke Island on Pamlico Sound. There Nathan became an outstanding student at the local school and formed friendships with two other black boys, William and Floyd. However, when Nathan's beloved mother, a schoolteacher, died of diphtheria, Daddy wanted to leave Roanoke Island. It has been several months since Daddy, Nathan, and Grandpa relocated to a small fisherman's cabin on Pea Island close to the Live-Saving Station. Since the move, Nathan, when not helping his father, hangs outs with the surfmen at the station and sometimes becomes the "victim" when the men practice resuscitation techniques.

One day, the three Williams men go to Roanoke Island to buy supplies. While there, Grandpa places an ad in a local newspaper. After emancipation, while he was still a slave, his wife Dahlia had been sold and taken away. Since then, Grandpa has periodically placed advertisements in different North Carolina newspapers hoping in vain to locate her and bring her home. Meantime Nathan spends the day with 11-year-old Floyd, his 12-year-old sister Fannie, William, who is 14, and William's kid sister Seabright. The same group gathers a few days later on Pea Island for an auction of objects salvaged from the sunken schooner. Floyd teases Nathan about his plans to become a surfman. They fight and both suffer injuries before they are parted. Afterward, Grandpa and Daddy explain to Nathan why his hopes are unachievable: white men allow blacks to be employed only at the Pea Island station and, with family nepotism and other factors influencing hiring, the expectation of gaining one of the seven positions on the team is unrealistic. Reluctantly, Nathan has to accept this.

Nathan witnesses an incidence of racial prejudice when a white hunter and his companion refuse first aid from Mr. Bowser after a hunting accident that leaves one of them suffering a severe loss of blood. Mr. Bowser ignores their protestations, applies a tourniquet, and saves the man's life. Nathan becomes so intrigued with emergency doctoring that he "borrows" two books on the subject from the station's bookcase. On a later visit to roanoke Island, Nathan uses his newfound knowledge to help Fannie when she cuts herself. After Mr. Bowser discovers the truth about the lost medical volumes, he quizzes Nathan and is impressed with the vast amount of knowledge the boy has retained. Nathan returns the books, which have become warped from being buried in the sand.

When a government sloop is in distress, Nathan is again asked to help. This time he illicitly assumes the responsibilities of a surfman and causes an accident that leaves him with a fractured skull. After a painful recovery and the humiliation of apologizing to the station's crew, he has learned a lesson about thinking first and avoiding impulsive behavior. This lesson is reinforced when, at a community outing on Roanoke Island, when he lends his friend Fannie a pair of breeches so she can take a forbidden overhead ride on a hawser line set up by the station's crew. Although Fannie loves Nathan for his kindness, Fannie's mother is furious.

Grandpa, who often tells Nathan stories about his life as a slave, suddenly falls ill. Keeper Etheridge helps nurse him but Daddy and Nathan finally take him to visit the doctor on Roanoke Island. It is a recurrence of malaria, which he contracted years before. Back home he rallies after quinine treatments, but the disease returns and he dies. Both Daddy and Nathan grieve for their loss.

In October, the fall storms begin again. A severe nor'easter hits with winds so strong and persistent that Daddy and Nathan are forced to leave their flimsy cabin and take refuge in the station house. At high tide, the waves are so high and powerful that they break the station door and flood the downstairs. At the height of the storm, a flare is seen from a ship in distress. Because the storm is so intense, the men are unable to use either the Lyle gun or the surfboat. A rescue is achieved and Nathan distinguishes himself by using his knowledge of first aid to help many of the victims. The effects of the storm are great. The station, though still standing, has suffered major damage, and the Williams's little house was swept away. Luckily their fishing boat was saved.

Nathan and his father stay at the station and begin the process of rebuilding. The boy has resigned himself to a life fishing with his father. But Fannie has other plans for him. She plants the idea of entering the medical field and soon he is filled with the desire to become a doctor. With the help of his father, the local doctor, and all his friends, Nathan begins studying to take the entrance exams with the hope of eventually entering the Leonard Medical School in Raleigh and becoming the first African American doctor on Roanoke Island.

Passages for Booktalking

Some interesting passages are: the rescue of the men on a shipwrecked schooner (pp. 1–9); background information about Nathan's home in Elizabeth City (pp. 14–17); Nathan becomes a practice victim at the station (bottom of p. 19–22); Grandpa places an advertisement for his wife (pp. 29–31); and Nathan's fight with William (pp. 37–40).

Themes and Subjects

More than an adventure story, this is also a tribute to the brave, sacrificing African Americans who were the surfmen on Pea Island in the late 1880s. It is also the chronicle of a boy's growth to maturity. Nathan evolves from an impulsive, tactless youngster to one who thinks before acting, can accept unpopular truths, and can make wise decisions. His increased ability to postpone gratification of needs is also well presented. The specter of racial prejudice is always present in the novel. Other subjects include: courage, devotion, honor, devotion to duty, family values, friendship, acceptance of responsibility, African Americans, fishermen, Pea Island, North Carolina Grand Banks, slavery, Reconstruction, and the U.S. Life-Saving Service.

COULOUMBIS, AUDREY. *The Misadventures of Maude March, or Trouble Rides a Fast Horse.* Random, 2005. $15.95 (978-0-315-83245-9); pap. Dell, $6.50 (978-0-375-83247-5) (Grades 4–8)

Introduction

Audrey Couloumbis worked at a number of different jobs before becoming a full-time writer of books for young readers. Her first, *Getting Near to Baby* (Putnam, 1999, $17.99; 039923389X) was a Newbery Honor Book in 2000. It is the poignant story of a family torn apart by the loss of Baby, who died after drinking tainted water. Mom can't deal with the tragedy, Dad is away looking for work, and the children, Willa Jo and Little Sister, try to cope while staying with their Aunt Patty. It is a sensitive tale of sorrow, loss, and healing.

In complete contrast, *The Misadventures of Maude March* is a rip-roaring, larger-than-life legend of the Old West. Its tongue-in-cheek humor is telegraphed by the title, surely a takeoff on Saul Bellow's *The Adventures of Augie March*. It's first sequel is *Maude March on the Run, or Trouble Is Her Middle Name* (Random, 2007, $15.99; 0375832467). In it, Maude, now 16, continues to be unjustly accused of hideous crimes. She is arrested but escapes with the help of younger sister Sallie and the notorious Black Hankie Bandit. The two sisters head west into Colorado Territory and many new adventures. Other characters from the first volume, such as the charming con man Marion Hardly and the elusive Uncle Arlen, reappear.

Historical Background

In the novel there are many references to James and the Younger Brothers gang of outlaws. The members of the gang included, at different times, the four Younger brothers, the two James brothers (Frank and Jesse), and other assorted ruffians. They started as a group of Confederate bushwhackers in Missouri during the Civil War and gained their notoriety as fugitive outlaws about 1866. They became legendary for their robberies of banks, trains, and stagecoaches. The gang dissolved in 1876 after the Younger brothers were arrested. Jesse James then formed his own gang. He died in 1882.

Also in the novel, Sallie is addicted (along with thousands of other Americans) to reading dime novels. They came into existence in 1860, were extremely popular, and died out about 1900. In one year—1865—Beadle and Adams, a leading publisher of this genre, sold more than 4 million copies. Most had as their setting the Wild West of the 1840s and 1850s and featured characters like Deadwood Dick and Pawnee Bill. Others were lurid detective and mystery thrillers. A typical first run numbered from 35,000 to 70,000 copies. Their plots were predictable, their characters stereotypes, and their moral was always virtue rewarded. They were mass-produced 10 cent paperbacks of slightly more than a hundred pages each and about 7 by 5 inches in dimension. Today they bring to dealers in rare books the joy they did to a vast reading public years ago!

Principal Characters

Maude March, a clever, resilient 15-year-old girl
Sallie March, the narrator, a tomboy of 11 years of age
Auntie Ruthie, their outspoken schoolteacher aunt
Reverend Peasley, a minister who helps the girls
Mrs. Peasley, his wife
Uncle Arlen, a livery stable owner and the girls' uncle
Mr. Wilburn, an old duffer who wants to marry Maude
Joe Harden, a hero of dime novels
Marion Hardly, a friend who changed his name to Joe Harden
Cleomie Dow, a friend in need
Ben Chaplin, a horse dealer
Mr. and Mrs. Newcomb, innocent bystanders
Willie Griffith, a gang leader

Plot Synopsis

On a hot August day in 1869, no one was more surprised than tough, outspoken Aunt Ruthie when a stray bullet from a local shootout pierced her heart and killed her. This took place in Grand Rapids, Minnesota, when she and her two nieces—15-year-old Maude March and her 11-year-old sister Sallie— were out shopping at the mercantile. Once again the two girls are orphans. Their parents died of the fever six years before, and now their only living relative is a young uncle whom they believe to be living in Independence, Missouri, some 400 miles away. Both girls are spunky and independent and, therefore accept the situation philosophically. Besides, Sallie can retreat into her collection of dime novels (she calls them dimers) for escape, leaving the tough decisions to practical, no-nonsense Maude.

They discover that the bank is about to foreclose on their humble home for overdue mortgage payments. Luckily, the local preacher, the Reverend Peasley, has room for them in his home. As part of the bargain, he commandeers Aunt Ruthie's chickens, cow, and her considerable larder of stored food. Sallie learns that the killer of her aunt has been jailed. His name is Joe Harden, coincidentally the name of her favorite hero from the dimers. Could it be the same man?

Sallie visits the jail and discovers the real Joe Harden is a bald, bearded man in his mid-20s who is far from being her idol. Before she leaves him, he apologizes for the accidental killing of Aunt Ruthie.

Life with the Peasleys is sheer drudgery. Mrs. Peasley is expecting her sixth child and is helpless. As a result, Maude and Sallie do all the cooking, baking, cleaning, laundry, and baby sitting, all for only room and board. Mr. Peasley is determined to marry Maude off. The first candidate is a totally unsuitable young fellow. The second, Mr. Wilburn, is an ancient but ardent suitor who won't take no for an answer. The only solution is to run away and try to get to Independence and Uncle Arlen.

One night, the girls cut their hair, don boys' clothes from the church's charity collection, locate a compass, roll up their bedding, and collect provisions from the larder. These, along with a shotgun and rifle from home, are loaded onto the Paisleys' buggy pony, Goldie, and their plow horse, Flora. Filled with apprehension and a sense of adventure, the girls head south, avoiding wagon trails to prevent detection. They have a total of about $30 with them, collected from Aunt Ruthie's household money and their savings.

The first few days on the trail are tough but they are dauntless, and make speedy adjustments. One rainy night, a man suddenly appears at their campsite. Sallie recognizes his as Joe Harden but Maude introduces herself as Johnnie and Sallie as Pete. The following morning, Joe confesses that he recognized Sallie from their encounter at the prison and they exchange confidences. Joe tells them about his escape from jail and a little about himself. His real name is Marion Hardly (a name he found unsuitable in the Wild West) and he has been a drifter for several years. He is now well versed in frontier survival skills but seemingly without direction in his life. The three continue on the trail together, and spend a night in a flophouse in Des Moines where they discover, in the local newspaper, that they are wanted by the police, the girls for stealing horses and he for murder and his prison break.

In the morning they part company, but not for long. Later that day, the girls see his horse in front of a bank and realize that Joe is committing a bank robbery. Onlookers mistakenly take them to be his accomplices. Amid a volley of gunshots, the sisters mount two horses tethered by the bank, and flee the city with only their guns and dwindling cash to their name. To their impressive police record, bank robbery has now been added. Back on the road, they spend the night in an abandoned log cabin where Maude saves the life of a young goat by shooting the head off a rattler. After another brief encounter with Marion (Maude is increasingly hostile to him—is she fighting a hidden attraction?), the girls press on. When they stop at a seemingly deserted cabin in the woods, they find an elderly woman desperately ill with influenza. They spend days nursing her back to health. Her name is Cleomie Dow and she is a feisty pioneer lady.

When the police begin snooping around inquiring about the two strange horses in the paddock, the girls tell all to sympathetic Cleomie, who reluctantly sends them on their way on her mule with instructions to trade it for a horse with her friend, Ben Chaplin, a horse trader who live several miles south. On the way they encounter a violent snow storm, the first of the season. Frostbitten and exhausted, they arrive at Ben Chaplin's cabin, where other guests, Mr. and Mrs. Newcomb, have also taken shelter.

After a short period of peaceful recovery, another calamity occurs. The cabin is stormed by three gun-toting bandits intent on robbery and other mischief. They take the inhabitants prisoner. Soon they are joined by a fourth man— Joe Harden (now named Dusty)! The gang leader is a braggart named Willie, who swaggers and bullies. It soon becomes apparent that Joe is a reluctant member of the gang and is trying to help the prisoners. In a dramatic turn of the tables, Sallie shoots Willie. With Joe's help, the other two gang members are overpowered and taken prisoner.

Order may have been restored, but murder has now been added to the girls' rap sheet. Maude and Sallie hit the road again and, with great relief, finally reach Independence, where Maude exchanges her breeches for a dress and gets a job as a waitress while Sallie combs the city for long-lost Uncle Arlen. Joe reappears and helps them in their search.

Still disguised as a boy, Sallie takes a job in a livery stable and is astonished to learn that the owner is none other than Uncle Arlen. A joyful reunion takes place. The sisters have a new home and Joe settles down (at least temporarily) when Uncle Arlen offers him a job. It seems like a happily-ever-after situation but one wonders if the law will ever catch up with the notorious "Mad" Maude March and her gang.

Passages for Booktalking

A few incidents to stimulate reading (with paperback pagination) are: Aunt Ruthie gets shot (pp. 1–6); the girls prepare to leave the Peasleys (pp. 41–46); their first hours on the trail (pp. 52–56); and the incident with the rattlesnake (pp. 131–134).

Themes and Subjects

One critic called this novel "like Lemony Snicket on horseback." It is essentially a fast-paced, laugh-out-loud junket that is fun for all. The author includes many authentic details of life in frontier America in the 1860s. The girls are portrayed as resourceful, quick-witted sisters who are always loyal and faithful to each other. The humor is often outlandish but not offensive. The character of Marion Hardly gives a new dimension to the term "confidence man." Subjects include Grand Rapids, Independence (Missouri), pioneer life, cowboys, outlaws, murder, robberies, friendship, and horse trading.

HAHN, MARY DOWNING. *Hear the Wind Blow.* Clarion, 2003, $16 (978-0-618-18190-2) (Grades 5–9)

Introduction

Mary Downing Hahn (1937–) was born and raised in College Park, Maryland, and at an early age began writing and illustrating comic-book-like stories. In high school she specialized in short stories and dreamed of being published in the *New Yorker*. Much later in life, while she was still a children's librarian, she began writing in earnest and had her first book published when she was 41 in 1979. It was *The Sara Summer* (Clarion, 1979, o.p.), the story of a far-from-perfect young girl who proves to be a true friend. Since then she has averaged a book a year. Among her most famous is another historical novel, *Stepping on the Cracks* (Houghton, 1991, o.p.; pap. Harper, $5.99; 0380719002), which is set on the homefront during World War II and involves 11-year-old Margaret and her friend Elizabeth. While spying on hated Gordy and his friends, who hang out in a secluded shack in the woods, the girls encounter a mystery man, a pacifist deserter, and must make a painful decision about his fate.

Hear the Wind Blow is set entirely in northern Virginia and takes place over roughly a six-month period—the last four months of the Civil War and the first two after the armistice. The title is taken from a line in the ballad "Down in the Valley"—"Hear the wind blow, dear, hear the wind blow."

Historical Background

By 1864 it was apparent that the Civil War was going badly for the South. In late 1864, General Sheridan and his men rampaged through the "Confederate Breadbasket" of the Shenandoah Valley in northern Virginia leaving a path of destruction and death. A thorn in their side was the guerrilla warfare of John Singleton Mosby and his Raiders, also known as Bushwhackers. They were so noted for their lightning raids on the Yankee forces that General Grant told Sheridan, "When any of Mosby's men are caught, hang them without a trial." Ironically, after the war, Mosby was campaign manager for Grant in Virginia.

In late June 1864, the Union forces laid siege to the city of Petersburg (where Haswell's brother is stationed in the novel) after the Battle of the Crater. Grant lost 8,000 men during the siege but was unable to take the city until April 2, 1865, when Grant's army broke through Lee's defenses. Lee abandoned Petersburg and regrouped at nearby Farmville to get rations and feed his soldiers. It proved to be the scene of the Confederate Army's last stand. In spite of their heroic efforts they were stopped by the arrival of Sheridan and the Union forces. Soon Lee found himself surrounded. The fighting ended and a surrender took place at Appomattox Court House, a few miles away, on April 19, 1865.

Principal Characters

Haswell Colby Magruder, the 13-year-old narrator
Rachel, his 7-year-old sister
Avery, his 16-year-old brother
Mama (formerly Rebecca Colby), his mother
James Marshall, one of Mosby's Raiders
Captain Powell, a Union officer
Otis Hicks, one of Captain Powell's men
Grandma Colby, Mama's mother
Uncle Cornelius Colby, Mama's brother
Aunt Hester and Aunt Esther Colby, Mama's spinster sisters
Major Dennison, a Union army officer stationed at the Colby house
Mr. and Mrs. Caples, a couple who befriend Haswell
Polly and Henry O'Brien, a brother and sister who help Haswell
Widow Ransom, a neighbor of the O'Briens

Plot Synopsis

During the winter of 1864–1865, 13-year-old Haswell Magruder finds he has become the only man in his household. His beloved, gentle father, a Confederate Army soldier, died in a Richmond, Virginia, hospital of dysentery a year before and his only brother Avery, though just 16, has recently joined the Confederate forces and is rumored to be serving at Petersburg, a city south of Richmond under siege by the Union forces. Haswell, along with his gentle, sensitive Mama and precocious, outspoken younger sister, 7-year-old Rachel, are living on the family horse farm in a remote part of the Shenandoah Valley in northern Virginia, close to the West Virginia border. One day, a severely wounded Confederate soldier appears on horseback. Fearful of the possible consequences but not wishing to have a death on her hands, Mama reluctantly allows the soldier into the house after Haswell hid him in the barn for the night. The soldier's name is James Marshall. He is about 18 years old and a member of Mosby's Confederate raiders. He charms the family and under their tender care and with Mama's home remedies, he begins to improve. However, he gives Haswell a letter to send to his family should he die of his wounds.

Their good times together end suddenly with the arrival of a troop of Yankee cavalry led by Captain Powell. They are searching for Marshall. He escapes through an open window and Powell sends his men, including a scared young soldier named Hicks, in hot pursuit. Powell drags Mama to an upstairs bedroom. A gunshot is heard and Mama, spattered with blood, appears with her husband's revolver in her hands. She has killed her would-be rapist. Haswell leads Powell's horse away from the house and the Magruders hide in a nearby gully. There they see Powell's men return with the body of James Marshall, which they hang from a maple tree in the yard. Thinking Powell has gone on ahead, his men leave but not before killing the livestock and burning both the farmhouse and barn.

The Magruders emerge to a scene of total destruction. Under the strain of these events, Mama loses contact with reality and sinks into dementia. Haswell must take charge. He retrieves Powell's horse, hides Marshall's body in the springhouse, and moves the family into the spacious root cellar. But Mama develops a fever and dies within days. Haswell and Rachel placed her body beside Marshall's and, armed with Papa's revolver retrieved from the ruins, they mount Powell's horse, now named Ranger. They head for the home of Mama's family, the Colby farm, about 20 miles away near Winchester. Adding a postscript giving details of his death, Haswell posts Marshall's letter to his parents.

Haswell and Rachel pass scenes of complete devastation, the result of General Sheridan's scorched earth policy. The Colby farm has not been spared. It lies deserted and ravaged. The two continue into the town of Winchester, to the home of Mama's brother, a curmudgeonly widower named Cornelius. They find the town occupied by Yankees. They are greeted by their uncle and by Grandma Colby, a cranky, domineering woman, and two fluttering, well-meaning aunts, Hester and Esther. There is also a stranger in the house—Major Thomas Dennison, a mean-spirited Yankee officer who has been billeted there. From the beginning, Dennison is suspicious of Haswell. He conducts an investigation and Hicks, who participated in the Magruder raid, soon identifies Ranger as Powell's horse. Haswell is thrown in jail, facing charges that might lead to the death penalty.

Fortunately Hicks comes to his rescue. Sickened by the war and remembering his part in the torching of the Magruder property, the young man decides to desert and free Haswell at the same time. That night, with Hicks's help, Haswell escapes from jail, retrieves Ranger, and heads south to find his brother Avery at Petersburg. He passes a Union encampment and hearing a soldier singing "Tenting on the Old Camp Ground" he bursts into tears, mourning the deaths of his parents and James Marshall, and the loss of his home.

After a week of wandering, Haswell is fortunate enough to meet Mr. and Mrs. Caples, a couple who have already lost two of their three sons in the war. They feed Haswell and give him a room for the night. In the morning, he sets off and is soon enveloped in a blinding rain storm. He develops a severe cold and fever. Near death, he discovers a cabin and is taken in by its inhabitants, two freckle-faced youngsters, 15-year-old Polly O'Brien and her brother Henry, who is 11. The two nurse Haswell back to health. He learns that their mother is dead and their father off to war. Meanwhile, they live off the land and by doing chores for their neighbor, the Widow Ransom. Haswell learns that the siege of Petersburg has ended and that the Union and Confederate forces are converging for a final battle at the town of Farmville only a few miles away.

Suddenly the countryside becomes a battleground, with sounds of conflict everywhere and the landscape filled with the dead and dying. The cabin is in the line of fire, so the O'Briens and Haswell flee to the Widow Ransom's house. After the battle, the triumphant Yankees turn it into a hospital and the Widow, Henry, and Polly become helpers. Meanwhile Haswell begins a search among the wounded for his brother Avery. Through good fortune, he finds Avery, more dead than alive. He forces Avery onto the back of Ranger, bids the O'Briens a tearful farewell, and heads back north. The armistice has been signed and the fear of capture is over.

After a long, tiring journey, they arrive in Winchester at Uncle Cornelius's house. Haswell is overjoyed to be reunited with his adored Rachel. The two brothers stay in Winchester for a month while Avery regains his strength. Then they set out with Rachel for the family farm and the process of rebuilding the ruins of their property. They discover that the springhouse is empty and at the family burial ground they find Mama's name on a new marker beside their father's grave. The Marshalls had retrieved their son's body and, in an act of kindness, buried Mama. The three return to the site of their old house hoping to gather enough unburned timber to build a new cabin and start life afresh.

Passages for Booktalking

Some exciting passages from the book are: James Marshall is taken in by the Magruders (pp. 1–6); James Marshall settles in and Captain Powell arrives (pp. 27–33); Mama kills Powell (pp. 34–38); and Haswell abandons the idea of burying Powell (pp. 42–47).

Themes and Subjects

Because one sees this story through the eyes of a Confederate lad, the reader feels particular sympathy for the defeated, abused Southerners, but the real villain of the novel is the war itself, which turns otherwise decent people into barbarians. The horrors of war are vividly depicted and never glorified and the terrible consequences of following orders without question are detailed well. Haswell's transition from boy to man is convincing. Other subjects are: family life, love, courage, compassion, loyalty, determination, the Civil War, Mosby's Raiders, the Battle of Farmville, the siege of Petersburg, Appomattox Court House, Virginia, the Confederate and Union Armies and their leaders, and the Shenandoah Valley.

HOLM, JENNIFER L. *Boston Jane: An Adventure.* Harper, 2001, $12.95 (978-0-06-028739-9); pap. $6.99 (978-0-06-440849-3) (Grades 5–8)

Introduction

After graduating from college, Jennifer Holm moved to New York City and began working as a producer of television commercials. Her father told her intriguing stories about his life on a farm in Washington State. Later she gained possession of her great-aunt's diary about the same region. From this came her first book for young readers, *Our Only May Amelia* (Harper, 1999, $18.99; 0060278226), which was one of the Newbery Honor Books in 2000. Later she wrote the Boston Jane trilogy, which begins with *Boston Jane: An Adventure.* The two sequels are now unfortunately out of print but are still available through book dealers and in libraries. The first, *Boston Jane: Frontier Days* (Harper, 2002, o.p.) begins where *An Adventure* ends. Jane is about to board a ship to take her back to Philadelphia when she receives word that her beloved father has died. With no family to return to, she decides to stay in Shoalwater Bay, Washington Territory. Events in this volume also include helping in a manhunt, trekking through the wilds to participate in the Stevens negotiations involving the fate of the Chinook Indians, and continuing the budding romance with Jehu. In the third volume, *Boston Jane: The Claim* (Harper, 2004, o.p.), the settlement on the bay has become a thriving town, and Jane gets a job as a concierge in the local hotel. The appearance of her nemesis, Sally Biddle, causes problems along with William's challenge to Jane's land claim, but all is nicely resolved and Jane marries Jehu.

Historical Background

The Chinook Indians lived near the Columbia River in the Cascade region of what is now Oregon and Washington. They were first contacted by Lewis and Clark in 1805. They lived in cedar plank longhouses and traveled the rivers in canoes, some as long as 40 feet. Noted as a peaceful people, they gained their livelihood from hunting, fishing, and trading in furs, fish, and slaves. They were known as extensive traders who developed a language that combined elements from several others. It is known as Chinook Jargon. Eventually the Chinooks were taken from their land and moved to reservations.

Washington Territory came into being in 1853 and included Washington, northern Idaho, and western Montana. Its first governor was Isaac Stevens, who made his capital at Olympia. Washington became a separate state in 1889. Shoalwater Bay is now know as Willapa Bay and is located on the southern coast of Washington just north of the mouth of the Columbia River. A cape on the northern part of the bay is still named Cape Shoalwater.

At the end of the novel the author gives extensive notes on background material and the sources she used. Some of the characters are based on real people. For example, James G. Swan, an adventurer, actually left his family in Boston and came to Shoalwater Bay in 1852 to study the Northwest and the Chinook Indians. His book on the subject was published in 1857 and is one of the sources used by Ms. Holm.

Principal Characters

Jane Peck, the narrator, who is 11 in 1849
Dr. Peck, her loving father
Sally Biddle, age 13, a spiteful girl
William Baldt, a 19-year-old medical student, later Jane's fiancé
Jebediah Parker, Jane's playmate
Miss Hepplewhite, headmistress of a finishing school for young girls
Mrs. Parker, the Pecks' housekeeper
Mary Hearn, a servant, two years older than Jane
Jehu Scudder, first mate on the *Lady Luck*
Father Joseph, a passenger on the *Lady Luck*
James G. Swan, a chronicler of the Chinooks
Mr. Russell, the trading post owner in Shoalwater Bay
Chief Toke, the chief or *tyee* of the Chinooks
Suis, Chief Toke's wife
Sootie, their daughter
Dolly, their slave

Handsome Jim, an attractive Indian later named Keer-ukso

Yelloh, a Chinook sent to find William

Plot Synopsis

It is the summer of 1894, and 16-year-old Jane Peck—along with Mary Hearn, her servant girl, who is two years older than Jane—is suffering acute sea sickness among other ailments aboard a ship inappropriately named the *Lady Luck*, on a journey from Philadelphia to Shoalwater Bay in the newly founded Washington Territory. Jane is a spunky, independent type, the only daughter of widower Dr. Peck, a surgeon who has allowed Jane great freedom in life.

When she was 11, for example, one of her great joys—in addition to eating cherry pies made by housekeeper Mrs. Parker—was playing with Jebediah, Mrs. Parker's son, and flinging rotten apples and dollops of horse manure at passing carriages and inanimate objects (never at people). Jane's tomboy ways were ridiculed by snobbish 13-year-old Sally Biddle and her gang of uppity would-be debutantes who attended a fashionable finishing school, Miss Hepplewhite's Young Ladies Academy.

When handsome, well-groomed William Baldt, a medical student, came to live with the Pecks to complete his internship, Jane developed a crush on this 19-year-old Adonis and decided she should change her habits and become a lady. Dr. Peck, who preferred his daughter without frills, reluctantly gave permission for Jane to study at Miss Hepplewhite's. There she learned the niceties of life—etiquette, embroidery, and French conversation—and treasured their textbook, *The Young Lady's Confidante*. Soon she became one of Miss Hepplewhite's star pupils, much to the annoyance of Miss Sally Biddle. She was also becoming an insufferable, class-conscious snob.

William completed his studies and decided to try his luck on the West Coast in a small settlement at Shoalwater Bay on the Pacific Coast of Washington Territory. He and Jane began an increasingly personal correspondence, although letters took about four months to arrive.

Three years passed, then—by letter—William proposed marriage. Jane was determined to go west and Dr. Peck grudgingly consented. Intricate preparations, including sewing a beautiful wedding dress, delayed their departure beyond the date promised.

The voyage is a nightmare but Jane makes the acquaintance of several people including the attentive first mate, Jehu Scudder, and pompous Father Joseph, who is going to found a church at Shoalwater Bay. Mary develops a high fever and during a violent storm she suffers a concussion when she falls from her bunk. Mary dies and Jane is distraught at the loss of her dear friend. After 180 days at sea, the boat enters Shoalwater Bay.

At the settlement Jane meets a new cast of characters including scholarly Mr. Swan, who is studying the environment and the Indians; Mr. Russell, the ill-mannered, tobacco-spitting trading post proprietor; some friendly Chinook Indians—Chief Toke, his wife Suis, their daughter Sootie, their slave Dolly, and the appropriately named Handsome Jim. Because the Indians think everyone in the East comes from Boston, she is introduced as Boston Jane.

However, there is no William. Jane is told that he believed she wasn't coming and accepted a commission from Governor Stevens to survey the Indian population. Nor is there a house for Jane and after trying to sleep outdoors she is forced to sleep in the company of several snoring men on the floor of Mr. Russell's trading post. One by one, Miss Hepplewhite's rules of proper behavior and decorum are tested and discarded. Mr. Russell's cow chews up all Jane's dresses except her wedding dress and she must barter with Suis for one of her immodest gingham shifts.

Mr. Russell demands that Jane earn her keep by cooking for the men. Some of her efforts are pathetic but she finds some recipes among Mary's effects and things improve somewhat. Her salmonberry pie, for example, is a big hit. Mr. Swan and Jehu Scudder, whose ship is still in port waiting for a cargo of lumber, are a constant source of kindness. Mr. Swan, far from a handyman, has somehow managed to build a stone chimney in a dwelling the Indians have leased to him. He invites Jane to stay with him. She accepts and diligently makes the house livable, but during a violent storm the chimney collapses, destroying the house and Jane's hope of escaping from the trading post.

As she has still received no word about William, Jane hires a Chinook, Yelloh, to search for him in the wilderness. Weeks go by and Yelloh finally returns without news. Using the last of her money, she sends him out again. Jehu says she is foolish to wait any longer and declares his love for her. Confused, Jane rejects his proposal. In her troubled state, Jane is further confused by the appearance of what she thinks is the ghost of Mary Hearn. During another violent storm Jane tries unsuccessfully to save Mr. Swan's canoe, which has been cast adrift. Without the means to gather oysters, he faces economic ruin.

Jane comes to the rescue by trading with Suis the last of her possessions (except the wedding dress) for an Indian canoe. Together the two garner a prize crop of oysters to be shipped to San Francisco.

Jane suffers a bout of extreme loneliness when Jehu's ship leaves and Mr. Swan, Mr. Russell, and Chief Toke go to Astoria on business. After an unhealthy-looking stranger visits their camp briefly, a case of smallpox is reported. Father Joseph and Mary, who has been inoculated, heroically nurse the victims, who include Suis, her daughter Sootie, and Handsome Jim. In spite of Jane's tender care, Suis dies. Dolly, their slave, uses this opportunity to break for freedom. In a gesture of great sacrifice, Jane clothes Suis in her wedding dress before burying her. Handsome Jim recovers and, to show his appreciation to his gods, changes his name to Keer-ukso. Mr. Swan and his friends return, bringing William with them.

Jane senses a change in William. He is more demanding and less the dashing figure she remembers. She also notices that he is being followed by an Indian woman. In a tense confrontation, he confesses that he married the woman, a half-breed, at Governor Stevens's suggestion. Full land grants are available only to married men. He vows to send the Indian girl away but, considering the circumstances, Jane refuses to go through with the marriage. Instead, she decides to pack up and return to Philadelphia on the next boat. By coincidence, her boat has a new captain, Jehu Scudder. Jehu rows ashore to take Jane to the ship. Their eyes meet and they smile.

Passages for Booktalking
Some interesting passages about Jane's life in Philadelphia are: Jane throws a missile and hits Sally Biddle (pp. 5–8); Jane and Sally meet William (pp. 15–19); Jane enrolls in Miss Hepplewhite's Academy (pp. 20–22); and Jane is insulted by Sally and comforted by William (pp. 31–34).

Themes and Subjects
The author has produced a realistic, authentic picture of frontier life in the Pacific Northwest in the 1850s. The customs, culture, and social organization of the Chinook Indians are portrayed without glossing over such aspects as the ownership of slaves. Jane is a most likable, outspoken, and self-reliant young lady. The reader experiences her transition from a feisty tomboy through an adolescent searching for values to maturity as a young woman secure in her principles and ready to fight for them. The grim details of shipboard life in the mid-19th century are well presented. Other subjects include: Washington Territory, love stories, marriage, frontier medicine, courage, ghosts, religion, smallpox, humor, 1850s manners and etiquette, and self-perception.

HUNT, IRENE. *Across Five Aprils.* Follett, 1964, o.p.; pap. Berkley, $4.99 (978-0-425-18278-9) (Grades 5–9)

Introduction
Irene Hunt (May 18, 1907–May 18, 2001) was born in Pontiac, Illinois, and, after her father's death when she was 7, moved to Newton (the setting of some scenes in *Across Five Aprils*). She listened to many stories her grandfather told about the Civil War and incorporated some of them into her book.

He, like Jethro—the central character of the novel—was a 9-year-old farm boy when the war broke out. After obtaining two university degrees, Irene Hunt devoted the next 39 years to a teaching career, including 15 years teaching English and French in the Oak Park schools and several years teaching at the college level. During that period, she realized that children learned history better from literature than from textbooks. After retiring, she devoted her life to writing.

Across Five Aprils was her first novel. It was a Newbery Honor Book in 1965 and winner of both the Dorothy Canfield Fisher and Lewis Carroll Shelf Awards. Her second book, the Newbery winner in 1967, was *Up a Road Slowly* (pap. Scholastic, $2.95; 0590031716) (condensed in *The Newbery/Printz Companion*). It covers ten years in the life of Julie Trelling, from age 7 when she was sent to live with her strict but loving Aunt Cordelia to her graduation from high school. Concerning the function of children's books, the author wrote "great books do not have to preach. But they do speak to the conscience, the imagination, and the heart of many a child." *Across Five Aprils* covers the four years of the Civil War and, though told in the third person, is seen primarily through the eyes of Jethro Creighton.

Historical Background

The author has incorporated her own historical background into the novel. The newspaper accounts that Jethro reads and the firsthand reports of his brothers and their friends introduce the major personnel and battles of the Civil War. Particularly interesting are the brief but telling portraits of many of the key players in this drama, among them Lincoln, Grant, McClellan, Farragut, Bragg, Hood, and Longstreet. Some of the battles discussed are Fort Sumter, Bull Run (I and II), Wilson's Creek (close to the novel's setting), Pea Ridge, Shiloh, Antietam, Fredericksburg, Chancellorsville, Gettysburg, Vicksburg, and the Battle of the Wilderness. The author is so intent on telling the story of the Civil War that occasionally the novel reads like a history lesson rather than a moving story of the war's effects on one family, but this rarely detracts from the power of the novel.

Principal Characters (ages at beginning of novel)

Jethro Creighton, a 9-year-old boy
Ellen Creighton, his mother
Matthew (Matt) Creighton, his father
Shadrach (Shad) Yale, a 21-year-old schoolteacher
Tom Creighton, Jethro's brother
Eb Carron, Matt's 18-year-old nephew
Jenny, Jethro's 14-year-old sister

John, his 24-year-old brother
Nancy, John's wife
Bill, Jethro's 23-year-old brother
Wilse Graham, a cousin from Kentucky
Dave Burdow, a neighbor
Travis Burdow, his son
Jake Roscoe, owner of a grocery store
Ross Milton, the crippled editor of the local newspaper
Guy Wortman, a local redneck
Israel Thomas and Ed Turner, two helpful neighbors
Aunt Victoria, Shad's relative in Washington

Plot Synopsis

On a warm April day in 1861, 9-year-old Jethro and his mother, Ellen, are working in the fields of their southern Illinois farm. To keep his mother from worrying about the possibility of a war between the states, Jethro tells her a story about Copernicus and the solar system that he has learned from his much-respected schoolteacher, Shadrach Yale. Shad is sweet on Jethro's 14-year-old sister Jenny, but Mr. and Mrs. Creighton, though fond of Shad, don't want them to marry until Jenny is older. Kentucky-born Ellen is appalled at the thought of a civil war but some in the household, like 18-year-old Tom and Eb Carron—an orphaned relative, also 18, who lives with the Creightons—think the prospect of war is exciting.

The family also consists of the father, Matthew Creighton, a highly principled, well-liked pillar of their farming community; and Jethro's two other brothers—John, who lives nearby with his wife Nancy and his two young children, and Bill, a bookish, sensitive young man. John, now 24 and Bill, only one year younger, grew up together and even now are inseparable. A middle sister, Mary, was killed a few years before in an accident caused by a drunken, irresponsible young neighbor, Travis Burdow. Matthew, though desolated by the death of his daughter, disbanded a posse intent on lynching Travis. Matt continues to disapprove of violence and joins his wife in fearing that war may come.

Because he helped so diligently with the planting, Jethro is allowed to sit at the adult table when dinner is served. The family is enjoying a visit from a Kentucky cousin, Wilse Graham. The discussion becomes heated when the topic of slavery in the South is introduced. Wilse maintains that conditions in the South are no worse than those in the North where industrialization has produced inhuman working conditions for the common man. Wilse is not the only person to defend the South—surprisingly Bill joins in. Mrs. Creighton's attempts to restore calm are interrupted by the arrival of Shad, who brings news that Fort Sumter has been attacked. Jethro goes to bed and hears the adults' conversation well into the night.

By summertime, the war has become a full-scale conflict and there is a skirmish nearby at Wilson's Creek. Tom and Eb leave for the Union Army in August. John and Shadrach join the Northern forces later after John has helped with the harvest and Shad has completed the school year. A tormented Bill tells Jethro of his inner struggle and of the difficult decision that leads him to steal away to join the Southern forces. Even though the family is now divided in its loyalties, Matt and Ellen respect Bill's right to make his own choice.

With his brothers away at war, Jethro must assume many adult chores. One day when he is in town buying supplies at the local store operated by Jake Roscoe, he is accosted by an uncouth, belligerent farmer, Guy Wortman, who accuses the Creightons of being Southern sympathizers. He calls them "Copperheads" and threatens vengeance. This confrontation is witnessed by Dave Burdow, father of the scoundrel Travis and, eventually terminated by the intervention of Ross Milton, the crippled editor of the local newspaper. On the way home, Travis is saved by Dave Travis from an ambush by Wortman. Jethro realizes that this was Burlow's way of saying "thank you" to his father.

Several tragic events occur during the early spring: Matt Creighton suffers a debilitating heart attack, Wortman and his gang burn their barn, and news comes of Tom's death in battle. The war has becomes a fearful reality and things look black for the Creightons. Their hope and faith are restored when neighbors led by Good Samaritans Israel Thomas and Ed Turner bring their labor and materials to rebuild the barn. Later, in a kind of poetic justice, they learn that Wortman got a load of buckshot in his pants when he tried to rob Roscoe's grocery story.

As 1863 begins, large numbers of deserters from the Union Army begin to camp near the Creighton farm. One afternoon while he is out plowing, Jethro discovers that one of them is Eb, who, sickened by the carnage, has run away from his troop. He now regrets his action but knows that returning to his unit would mean facing the firing squad. Jethro writes a letter to President Lincoln pleading for mercy. In the meantime, Jenny goes east to care for a seriously wounded Shad, who is recuperating at his Aunt Victoria's home in Washington. When he recovers, he and Jenny are married. Jenny realizes that she is now 16, the age at which her mother married. Jethro receives a reply from the President in which he announces that he is giving the deserters a general amnesty. Eb can now return to his unit.

Jethro follows the progress of the war through letters the family receives and accounts in Mr. Milton's newspaper. When John writes telling them that he has seen Bill, who has been wounded and is now a prisoner of war, the family is grateful to know that at least he is alive. While everyone in the North awaits an imminent victory after President Lincoln's reelection in 1864, the war drags on, with Sherman's army apparently lost in its sweep through the South. Jethro thinks peace will be wonderful, but Mr. Milton explains philosophically that Jethro is expecting too much from peace, just as he has from war.

When another April arrives and the war ends, it proves to be the cruelest April of them all because it brings the assassination of Lincoln. Jethro and his family are stunned by the tragedy, but gradually life resumes its normal pace as the boys return from the service and the process of rebuilding begins. Jenny and Shad also come back. Shad is intent on continuing his studies at the university and both he and Jenny plan on taking Jethro with them so that he, too, can continue his schooling. War and time have changed the family. Across the five Aprils of Jethro's adolescence he has done a man's work, learned a man's lesson, and is now looking to a brighter future.

Passages for Booktalking

Some interesting incidents: talk of war around the Creighton table (pp. 24–30); Shad brings news of Fort Sumter (pp. 30–34); Bill talks to Jethro about his feelings about the war (pp. 38–41); and Shadrach and Jethro talk about the boy's future (pp. 61–64).

Themes and Subjects

Jethro's rapid growth to manhood is believably presented, as are the ravaging effects of the war on one family. Many aspects of war are covered, including how it unleashes the best and worst in people. The terrible horror and waste of warfare is an important theme as is the depiction of strong family loyalty and devotion and the emphasis on the importance of education. Details of every-day life on a 19th-century farm are interesting. Mr. Creighton represents the best in American values: strength, courage, tolerance, fairness, ethical behavior, family ideals, hard work, compassion, neighborliness, and perseverance. Some other subjects: Civil War battles, Civil War personalities, army life, deserters, death, friendship, bigotry, love, and marriage.

NAPOLI, DONNA JO. *The King of Mulberry Street.* Random, $15.95 (978-0-385-74653-3); pap. $6.50 (978-0-553-49416-7) (Grades 5–8)

Introduction

Donna Jo Napoli is an accomplished linguist and author who has written books for all ages, from picture books for the very young to young adult novels for more mature readers. In the latter area, her favorite is *Breath* (Atheneum,

2003, $17.95; 0689861745) for a slightly older group of readers than *Mulberry Street*, (for grades eight and up). It is set in the German town of Hamelin in 1284 and tells of a lame boy, Salz, who also suffers from painful coughing fits (in the author's Afterword it is diagnosed as cystic fibrosis). He lives with his older brothers, father, and grandmother on the outskirts of a town that is beset with huge problems including torrential rains, a severe rat infestation, diseased cattle, and unusual human maladies. Salz hopes that a piper he has met can help.

The King of Mulberry Street, though filled with painfully realistic details, is not as gruesome as *Breath*. It is set principally in the Five Points section of New York City in 1892 and takes place over a period of about nine months. In a brief postscript, the author gives some details about her family history. The experiences of the book's narrator are based loosely on the early life of her paternal grandfather, who supposedly migrated to the United States at the age of 5 and earned his living at one time reselling sandwiches at a higher price in the Wall Street area.

Historical Background

The Five Points section of Manhattan was located at the intersection of Park (now Mosco), Worth, and Baxter Streets, an area that presently houses many city and state administrative and court buildings and is called the Foley Square District. In the 19th century it was a thriving working class area and slum notorious for its vice and debauchery. After a visit in 1842, Dickens wrote, "This is a place . . . reeking every where with dirt and filth . . . Debauchery has made the very houses prematurely old. Many pigs live here. Do they wonder why their masters walk upright in lieu of going on all-fours? And why they talk instead of grunting?" It was the home of many minorities, first blacks and the Irish, then Italians and Jews. Martin Scorsese used this setting for his 2002 movie *Gangs of New York*. To the north, Mulberry Street is still the center of Little Italy and houses many fine Italian restaurants. It is a short street, running north and south from Spring to Canal Streets. Old St. Patrick's Cathedral still stands on the corner of Prince and Mulberry. Built in 1809–1815 and restored in 1868, it is the oldest Roman Catholic church building in New York.

Many New Yorkers in the 18th century, including William Cullen Bryant, advocated building a park in New York City similar to Hyde Park in London. It took many years to complete New York's Central Park. In 1857 the existing residents were relocated, but the site didn't officially open until 1873. The design was by landscape designer Frederick Law Olmsted and architect Calvert Vaux, both of whom later collaborated on Prospect Park in Brooklyn.

Principal Characters

    Beniamino (later Dom Napoli), a 9-year-old Neapolitan refugee
    Mamma, his mother
    Nonna, his grandmother
    Gaetano, a 12-year-old street waif
    Tin Pan Alley, or Pietro, a pathetic young beggar
    Padrone, Pietro's hated owner
    Mr. Grandinetti, a fruit store owner in Five Points
    Signora Esposito, an apartment dweller who takes in boarders

Plot Synopsis

Although there are many material comforts lacking in 9-year-old Beniamino's life, there is no absence of love. The year is 1892 and the boy is growing up in a small apartment where ten people live in the slums of Naples. Along with beloved Mamma, his unmarried mother, and his grandmother Nonna, Beniamino is surrounded by several aunts and uncles and their children. The apartment is so crowded that he sleeps on two chairs pushed together.

Suddenly his mother suggests that he visit his favorite places in Naples instead of doing chores. This includes a stopover with his Uncle Aurelio in the stables where he works, another with Aunt Rebecca in the mansion where she is a servant, and then time with sisters at the local convent. Although Beniamino is a Jew in a household where a kosher kitchen is maintained, he enjoys doing errands for the nuns such as bringing wine from their grotto. This time it is not so pleasant—he sees a decaying human body floating in the nearby river.

That night, when everyone is asleep, his mother dresses him in his synagogue pants and shirt, his first shoes and socks, and his yarmulke and takes him to a freighter in the harbor. She learns from a sailor on guard that the man to whom she paid passage money for Beniamino is not aboard. Desperate to get her son on the ship, she offers herself to the watchman as payment. Thinking his mother will accompany him, the boy goes to a hiding place below deck. When the ship is safely out at sea he emerges and is heartbroken to learn that his mother is not on the ship. There is one other stowaway, a man so sick with cholera that he dies within hours and is buried at sea.

Beniamino gets along well with the crew members who feed him and give him the name Dom Napoli. He discovers that his mother has carefully placed four tassels from his grandfather's prayer shawl in his new shoes.

After the ship arrives in New York, Dom hides on board, determined to return home to Naples. But he is discovered just as the boat is about to depart and thrown overboard. He swims to a dock where a passenger ship, full of immigrants from Italy has just moored. Mistaken for a passenger who has accidentally fallen in the water, he is fished out. Unfortunately his socks, along with the much-loved tassels, are stolen. The following day, he and the other people from steerage are ferried to Ellis Island where they endure the various indignities involved in becoming a landed immigrant. One man wants to claim him as his "uncle" and others think he should he sent to an orphanage. Dom eludes them all and, after getting immigration papers, makes his way to Manhattan.

On a street corner, he meets a slightly older boy begging while playing a triangle and whistling. When he tells Dom that one of his songs came from Tin Pan Alley, Dom immediately decides to call him by that name. Tin Pan Alley explains that he works for a "padrone," a pimp-like older man who controls him like a slave and binds him every night to a bedpost. This servitude supposedly will end when he has paid back his passage money to the United States.

Later that day, Dom meets a street-smart boy three years his senior named Gaetano, who begins to show him around his part of town, the slum area known as Five Points. Gaetano shows Dom ways to survive in this barbarous environment. They wander around Mulberry Street, an Italian neighborhood, and Dom ventures further north by himself and visits Central Park. At night, Dom sleeps in a barrel in a filthy alley, but during the day he helps out in a greengrocer's shop run by Mr. Grandinetti and watches the ships, hoping to find a way to get back to Italy.

Dom is a clever boy, wily and sharp but also generous and fair-minded. Gaetano steals Dom's immigration papers and sells them. Although Dom forgives Gaetano he feels increasingly trapped without these documents. The barrel in which he has been sleeping disappears and he is forced to move to Central Park. Dom notices that in the affluent areas, like Wall Street, where Tin Pan Alley begs, merchandise sells for much more than in Five Points. A born entrepreneur, he has a brilliant idea—buy one of the long, 25 cent sandwiches at Luigi Pierano's store on slummy Park Street, cut it into four parts, wrap them separately, and sell each for 25 cents on fashionable Wall Street. The plan is a big success and the three go into business together although Tin Pan Alley's participation is limited somewhat by having to watch for his vengeful padrone.

Each day Dom makes sure that Tin Pan Alley's tin cap contains the expected amount (81 cents) before the boy reports to his master. Soon sandwich sales double, triple, and more, but this bonanza is not without problems. In rainy weather the sandwiches get soggy. Neighborhood kids sometimes mug Dom and steal his money and sandwiches. The former problem is solved by buying coverings and the second by securing "protection" from Gaetano's older brother.

During all this, Dom remains loyal to his faith without revealing that he is Jewish. He refuses to work on Saturdays, the Sabbath, or to eat the salami in sandwiches that also contain cheese. Later, he discovers a synagogue nearby and begins attending religious services. Dom saves all his money to pay for his return to Naples but Mr. Grandinetti insists that Gaetano and Dom, both street dwellers, spend a little money on proper sleeping accommodations. He suggests seeing Signora Esposito who has a single room available in her apartment. A deal is made: the two sleep in her three-bedded extra room and have dinner for two dollars each per week! In these comfortable surroundings, with a bed of his own, Dom feels like the king of Mulberry Street. Signora Esposito has a gruff, severe exterior but, the boys discover that this hides a sympathetic, caring interior.

Because business is flourishing, Dom branches into other foods, including kosher sandwiches. Dom's next project is to rescue Tin Pan Alley (his real name is Pietro). Dom convinces him to run away, disguise himself (as a girl for a time), and take the extra bed at Signora Esposito's. Pietro is frightened but agrees. When he learns that he has actually paid back to his padrone his passage money—many times over—he is so incensed that he decides return to the padrone's apartment and alert the other boys to this injustice.

When he doesn't return, Dom goes looking for him. It takes clever sleuthing to find the apartment and when he does the padrone is not there. But one of the imprisoned boys says that Pietro has been beaten to death by his enraged padrone. The padrone returns, discovers Dom, and beats him severely before tying him to the floor. Dom manages to escape but it takes two weeks before he recovers from his wounds sufficiently to get back to work. On the eve of his 10th birthday Dom reflects on how much he has matured in the past few months. He now realizes that America is his permanent home and truly a land of opportunity. Who knows, maybe he will become the king of Mulberry Street one day.

Passages for Booktalking

Here are some interesting passages: Beniamino visits his favorite places in Naples including the convent (pp. 7–14); Mamma and Beniamino board the ship (pp. 20–25); the boy encounters the sick stowaway and looks for Mamma (pp. 26–30); and the sailors welcome Beniamino and there is a burial at sea (pp. 32–38).

Themes and Subjects

This is a masterful portrait of life at different levels in the late 19th century in New York City, told by a wonderful prose writer. History truly comes to vibrant life in this tale of survival where little human kindness is present. The contrast between a loving family life in Naples and the brutality and violence of slum life in New York is well presented. Dom's blossoming career is a lesson in resourcefulness, ingenuity, and perseverance. Part of his strength comes from his generosity, courage, and enduring faith in others. He also learns from his experiences and matures. Other subjects are: religion, Jews, Italian Americans, Five Points, Central Park, Naples, sea stories, death, the "padrone" system, entrepreneurship, friendship, loyalty, slum life, beggars, death, immigration, Ellis Island, family life, and poverty.

ADDITIONAL SELECTIONS

Avi. *Iron Thunder* (Hyperion, 2007, $14.99) (Grades 5–8)
> Told through the eyes of 13-year-old Tom, this is the story of the construction of the *Monitor* and its eventual cataclysmic battle with the *Merrimack*.

Bildner, Phil, and Long, Loren. *The Barnstormers: Tales of Travelin' Nine Game 1* (Simon, 2007, $9.99) (Grades 4–7)
> Lots of family secrets are revealed when a family of baseball players, known as the Travelin' Nine, go to Cincinnati in 1899 to play ball.

Brown, Don. *The Notorious Isey Fink* (Roaring Brook, 2006, $16.95) (Grades 6–9)
> This is a novel of the difficult struggle for survival of immigrants and their children who lived on the East Side of Manhattan during the 1890s.

Bruchac, Joseph. *March Toward the Thunder* (Dial, 2008, $16.99) (Grades 7–10)
> In 1864, Louis, a 15-year-old Abenaki Indian from Canada enlists in the Union forces and experiences the grim realities of war from the battlefields to field hospitals.

Denslow, Sharon Phillips. *All Their Names Were Courage* (Greenwillow, 2003, $15.99) (Grades 4–6)
> In a series of letters chiefly to her brother, a Union soldier, 11-year-old Sallie describes her project in which she writes to Civil War generals asking them to name their most courageous horses.

Durrant, Lynda. *My Last Skirt* (Clarion, 2006, $16.) (Grades 5–8)
> In this novel based on truth, Jennie Hodges, who has grown accustomed to wearing trousers, becomes Albert Cashier and joins the Union Army.

Ernst, Kathleen. *Hearts of Stone* (Dutton, 2006, $16.99) (Grades 6–9)
> After her father joins the Union Army and her mother dies suddenly, Hannah and her siblings venture from their east Tennessee home to Nashville where, they hope, they can live with an aunt.

Gray, Dianne E. *Tomorrow the River* (Houghton, 2006, $16.) (Grades 4–8)
> In 1896, 14-year-old Megan spends an eventful summer traveling up the Mississippi River on her married sister's steamboat.

Hart, Alison. *Gabriel's Horses* (Peachtree, 2007, $14.95) (Grades 6–9)
> During the Civil War, 12-year-old Gabriel Alexander, a slave growing up on a Kentucky plantation, dreams of becoming a jockey and also of going to war like his

Dad, who is fighting for the Yankees. *Gabriel's Triumph* (Peachtree, 2007, $14.95) tells how Gabriel is freed after the war and becomes a famous jockey.

Hite, Sid. *Stick and Whittle* (Scholastic, 2000, $16.95) (Grades 5–9)
An orphan on the run and a Civil War veteran who is searching for his true love team up and make an unusual pair.

LaFaye, A. *Worth* (Simon, 2004, $15.95) (Grades 3–7)
In Nebraska during pioneer days, 11-year-old Nathaniel feels threatened by the arrival of John Worth, who is joining Nate's family from the Orphan Train.

Lyons, Mary E., and Muriel M. Branch. *Dear Ellen Bee: A Civil War Scrapbook of Two Union Spies* (Atheneum, 2000, $17) (Grades 5–9)
Based on journals and letters of a Southern woman and her freed slave, this is an exciting story of espionage during the Civil War.

McCaughrean, Geraldine. *Stop the Train!* (HarperCollins, 2003, $15.99)
In this rollicking adventure set in 1893, Cissy and her family arrive as new settlers in a town in Oklahoma and find there is nothing there. (Grades 5–8)

McGowen, Tome. *Jesse Bowman: A Union Boy's War Story* (Enslow, 2008, $20.95) (Grades 5–8)
Looking for excitement, 15-year-old Jesse joins the Union Army and finds instead a lifetime's worth of deprivation, death, and misery.

McKissack, Patricia C. *Away West* (Viking, 2006, $14.99) (Grades 3–6)
The contributions of African Americans to the Civil War and to the westward movement are revealed in this story of Everett Turner, a black man who won a medal during the Civil War and later moved west to Kansas.

McMullan, Margaret. *When I Cross No-Bob* (Houghton, 2007, $16) (Grades 4–8)
In post-Civil War America, Addy O'Donnell, who has grown up in squalor and violence, hopes for a brighter future at a time when local Native Americans are being relocated and the Klan is gaining power.

Murphy, Jim. *The Journal of James Edmond Pease: A Civil War Soldier, Virginia, 1863* (Scholastic, 1998, $9.95) (Grades 5–8)
In the form of a journal, this novel follows a 16-year-old private in the New York Volunteers during the Civil War including a time spent behind enemy lines.

Oatman, Eric. *Cowboys on the Western Trail: The Cattle Drive Adventures of Josh McNabb and Davy Bartlett* (National Geographic, 2004, pap. $6.99) (Grades 4–7)
This heavily illustrated paperback tells how two young teenagers participate in a cattle drive from southern Texas to Nebraska in 1887.

Rinaldi, Ann. *Juliet's Moon* (Harcourt, 2008, $17) (Grades 5–8)
During the Civil War in the South 12-year-old Juliet loses her father, suffers the destruction of her home, and later is imprisoned for aiding some anti-Yankee guerrillas.

Siegelson, Kim. *Trembling Earth* (Putnam, 2004, $17.95) (Grades 7–12)
This Civil War story set in the Okefenokee Swamp area tells how a poor 12-year-old white boy sets out to track down a runaway slave to collect a bounty.

Spain, Susan Rosson. *The Deep Cut* (Marshall Cavendish, 2006, $16.99) (Grades 5–8)

Based on fact, this is the story of the tragedy that the Civil War brought to a small Virginia village and, in particular to the family of the sensitive Lonzo, many of whose members fought on the Confederate side.

Taylor, Theodore. *Billy the Kid* (Harcourt, 2005, $17) (Grades 6–9)

In this retelling of a segment of Billy the Kid's career, the outlaw is 19 and discovers that his best friend from childhood is the local sheriff.

Wells, Rosemary. *Red Moon at Sharpsburg* (Viking, 2007, $16.99) (Grades 6–10)

As the Civil War rages around her in northern Virginia, India Moody, who sees her family march off to war and witnesses death and destruction in her own settlement, still hopes one day to pursue her education.

Wyss, Thelma Hatch. *A Tale of Gold* (Simon, 2007, $15.99) (Grades 4–6)

In 1897, while journeying to Alaska in search of gold, 14-year-old James encounters many unusual people including a young girl disguised as a boy.

TWENTIETH CENTURY

CHOLDENKO, GENNIFER. *Al Capone Does My Shirts.* Putnam, 2004, $18 (978-0-399-23861-1); pap. Puffin, $6.99 (978-0-14-240370-9) (Grades 5–8)

Introduction

Like this novel's hero, Moose Flanagan, author Gennifer Choldenko hails from Santa Monica, California, where she was born in 1957. She later moved to San Francisco, her present home. At the age of 6, she decided to become a writer and was encouraged in this goal by her father, who loved books and reading. She spent time during her childhood riding horses and exploring the hills of Southern California. After college she worked as a copywriter at an ad agency but decided to hone her skills as an illustrator by attending the Rhode Island School of Design, where her teachers included the famous illustrators Chris Van Allsburg and David Macaulay. Soon, however, her writing skill surpassed her ability as an illustrator and for her first published book, a picture book, she wrote the text only. Choldenko claims to be an intuitive writer and has said, "I have to trust my intuition. It's all I have." She lives through her characters. For example, she was saddened after finishing the Capone novel (which takes place in 1935) to realize that Moose would probably have to fight in World War II. She spends years doing research for her books. *Al Capone Does My Shirts* required months of exploration of such topics as life on the island of Alcatraz (both outside and inside the prison), baseball, autism, and gangsters. At one point Choldenko even served as a guide on Alcatraz Island. *Al Capone Does My Shirts* is narrated by 12-year-old Moose Flanagan and takes place over the six-month period from January 1935 through June of that year.

Historical Background

An eight-page Author's Note separates fact from fiction and gives interesting details about life on Alcatraz Island. She also discusses autism and the prison life of Al Capone.

Alcatraz Island (also known as "the Rock") is a 12-acre island in the middle of San Francisco Bay. Discovered in 1775 by a Spanish explorer, it was named the Island of the Pelicans (*Alcatraces*). After sea traffic dramatically increased as a result of the California Gold Rush of 1848, a lighthouse was built in 1853. A military outpost and detention center were also constructed on the island and served various purposes. During the Civil War, Confederate sympathizers were housed there. In 1909 the lighthouse and other buildings were torn down to make room for a new military prison. It became the official military prison for the western United States. Prohibition in the 1920s and 1930s bought a rise in crime and the need for a federal maximum-security prison at Alcatraz. This facility opened on January 1, 1934, and closed on March 21, 1963, to become a recreational area administered by the National Park Service as part of the Golden Gate National Recreational Area. It is now a major tourist attraction in the Bay Area and is visited by thousands of tourists each year. The Rock had many famous inmates. One was Robert Stroud, also known as the Birdman of Alcatraz. He arrived in 1942 and in 1959 was transferred to a medical center on shore. His career taming birds was the subject of a book and movie. The racketeer Al Capone arrived in 1934 and spent four and a half years on the island. Born in Brooklyn in January 1899, Alphonse Capone began a life of serious crime as a teenager after he was expelled from school at the age of 14. He shifted operations to Chicago, where he became head of a gang known as the Chicago Outfit. Engaged in all sorts of rackets associated with Prohibition, the gang took in about $10 million a year. Capone acquired some gruesome-looking facial scars as a result of a fight and became known as "Scarface." Gang rivalry led to the vicious killings known as the St. Valentine's Day Massacre of 1929, in which seven people were gunned down. Capone engineered the massacre but it was for tax evasion that Capone was sent to prison in 1932. When it was discovered that he continued to organize crime from his cell, he was transferred to Alcatraz, then a maximum-security prison, in 1934. He completed his term in 1939 but was sent to another prison on a misdemeanor charge for one year. Broken both mentally and physically from syphilis that he contracted as a young man, he retired to his Florida home when released and died there on January 22, 1947.

Machine Gun Kelly (also mentioned in the novel) was born George Barnes in Memphis, Tennessee, in 1895. To protect his family, he changed his name to Kelly after several brushes with the law. During the 1920s, he became involved with organized crime and bootlegging. After spending time in Leavenworth Prison, he married a woman who encouraged his criminal activities and bought him a machine gun.

They were caught in 1933 after a failed kidnapping plot was exposed and each sentenced to life in prison. His wife was released in 1958, but George spent the remaining twenty-one years of his life in jail, much of it on Alcatraz Island, where he was nicknamed "Pop Gun Kelly."

Mention is made of the building of the Golden Gate Bridge. Construction, at a cost of $27 million, began in 1933 and the bridge was opened on May 27, 1937.

Moose's sister suffers from a severe neurological disorder that, since 1943, has been classified as autism. It is a complex developmental disability that occurs in the brain and affects an estimated 1 in 150 births or an estimated 1.5 million people in the United States. Symptoms usually appear before a child reaches age 3 and the severity of the condition varies greatly. Early intervention can help improve the condition but there is no cure. The exact causes are not known although genetic factors may be important. Autism is characterized by difficulties in verbal and nonverbal communication, impaired social activities, unusual leisure and play activities, and repetitive actions. The ratio of affliction is four boys to one girl and its frequency is rising at the rate of 10 percent to 17 percent each year.

Principal Characters

Moose (Matthew) Flanagan, the 12-year-old narrator
Cam Flanagan, his father
Helen Flanagan, his mother
Natalie, their 15-year-old autistic daughter
Theresa Mattaman, a 7-year-old girl
Jimmy Mattaman, her 12-year-old brother
Annie Bomini, a 12-year-old girl
Mr. Williams, the warden
Piper Williams, his 12-year-old daughter
Scout McIlvey, Moose's baseball-playing friend
Miss Bimp, Moose's teacher
Del Peabody, a classmate
Onion, a prison inmate
Al Capone, another prison inmate
Mr. Purdy, headmaster of the Esther P. Marinoff School

Carrie Kelly, Natalie's teacher

Plot Synopsis

It is January 1935, and the Flanagans have just moved from Santa Monica, California, to the prison on Alcatraz Island, where Cam, the father, has taken a position as guard/electrician. In addition to Cam, the family consists of his wife, Helen, and two children: 15-year-old Natalie and 12-year-old Matthew, known as Moose. At first impression, the Flanagans appear to be an ideal American family filled with love, understanding, and closeness, but they face a problem: Natalie suffers from a developmental brain disorder (now known as autism) and requires constant attention. The main reason for their move is news about the Esther P. Marinoff School in San Francisco, which treats this disorder. Mrs. Flanagan is determined to get Natalie admitted regardless of the cost or effort. Although Natalie is 15, Mom insists she is only 10 to fool people into thinking she is still a child and also to meet the admission requirements of the school. Moose understands that helping Natalie is the family's first priority and instead of feeling resentment, he loves his sister and respects his parents' dedication, even though it means always being in second place. Though he is only 12, Moose is entering adolescence and has shot up to almost 6 feet, a height that is helping him in his passion for baseball. He is fiercely protective of Natalie and likes to show off her remarkable calculating ability to his new friends on the island. They include the Mattaman kids, 12-year-old Jimmy and precocious Theresa, age 7; always-supportive Annie Bomini, also 12; and (sometimes) the warden's daughter, Piper Williams, another 12-year-old. Piper can be irritating with her bossy, domineering ways and her feelings of privilege because of her father's position.

One day, Moose is summoned to Mr. Williams's office where he is sternly oriented to the dos and don'ts of civilian life on the island, which is also home to convicts such as Al Capone. Moose and Piper are in the same grade in school on the mainland and there, in Miss Bimp's class, Moose makes other acquaintances including Del Peabody and another baseball fanatic, Scout McIlvey. After his first day at school, Moose hears Piper outlining a scheme to make quick money. The prison inmates do the washing for all the island's residents and, for a price, she will add her classmates' clothing to the laundry. Imagine being able to say to your friends, "Al Capone did my shirts." She begins collecting items and to avoid suspicion about such a large amount of laundry coming from one family, she divides them up among Jimmy, Annie, and herself. Moose is aware of the scheme but does not participate. The enterprise seems to be working and the money pouring in when disaster strikes. Del Peabody's mother learns about the scheme and writes an indignant letter to Mr. Williams, who summons the kids, including Moose, to his office where they are severely chastised. As punishment Piper is sent off the island to her grandmother's for two months and Moose, though innocent, is grounded by his parents.

In the meantime, Natalie's admission to the Esther P. Marinoff School is a dismal failure. She is completely uncooperative and has terrible screaming fits. Mr. Purdy, the headmaster, sends her home with a "Not Ready for Admission" report. At Mr. Purdy's bidding, the family hires Mrs. Carrie Kelly, a specialist, to work with Natalie. To help with this expense, Mom begins giving music lessons on the mainland and Moose must look after Natalie after school. No more baseball with Scout, who stops being Moose's friend because of the constant cancellations. Scout has heard that during prison games, baseballs sometimes land outside the walls of the game area. He longs to have one of these baseballs as a souvenir, so to restore their friendship Moose and Natalie spend hours scouring the outside areas looking for one of these elusive mementos.

Sometimes he must leave Natalie alone while he searches in inaccessible places. Unknown to Moose, Natalie has met a convict who is on garden duty. One day, a horrified Moose sees Natalie talking to the convict, who turns out to be a gentle person named Onion who is nearing parole. When he learns of Moose's quest, he gives Natalie a baseball from the prison compound. Unfortunately, Piper, fresh from her mainland stay, intervenes and Natalie gives her the ball instead, with the result that Scout gets his precious gift not from Moose but from Piper. However, Moose and Scout later resume their friendship.

Through examining the prisoner's mail, Piper learns that Mrs. Capone, Al's mother, is planning to visit her son. Piper again seeks her friends' help to get an interview during the old lady's ferry ride to the island. The gang—which includes Piper, Moose, Annie, Theresa, Jimmy, and their new baby brother, Rocky—boards the ferry along with Mama Capone. Mrs. Capone ignores Piper's continual efforts at conversation and instead quiets a crying Rocky by rocking him to sleep. Another failure for Piper.

In the meantime, Mrs. Kelly is making such progress with Natalie that she suggests the Flanagans try once more to get Natalie into Mr. Purdy's school. Hopes are high and the tension causes differences and arguments in the usually peaceful Flanagan household. Unfortunately Natalie is again refused admission. This time, they realize, it is because the school has found out her real age. Moose and his parents are devastated by the news and Moose decides he must pressure Mr. Purdy to change his mind. The only person he knows who has that much money and influence is Al Capone. With Piper's help, he smuggles a note to the convict explaining the situation and asking for his help. For days there is no word, then a message comes from Mr. Purdy's office stating that a new facility for older children is being opened and Natalie will be the first to be admitted. Later, when Moose puts on a shirt fresh from the prison laundry, he finds a one-word note in the breast pocket: "Done."

Passages for Booktalking

Theresa introduces Moose and Natalie to Piper (pp. 27–29); Moose is given a lecture by the warden (pp. 35–41); Moose's first day at school and Piper's laundry project (pp. 42–47); and Al Capone's mama visits and the gang attempts to meet her (pp. 128–134).

Themes and Subjects

This is a strong, poignant story of a family torn by the pressures and conflicts of having a disabled child in the household. It is also a story of love and hope. The author has created some wonderful characters (reminiscent of the much later "Peanuts" gang with Piper being Lucy's counterpart). The youngsters' dialogue has a truthful ring of youth and innocence. The portrait of an autistic girl is accurate and at times wrenching. Moose is a wonderful creation, a noble well-intentioned boy beset by conflicts, responsibilities, and problems beyond his years. His relationship with his sister is beautifully portrayed. Other subjects include: prison life, Alcatraz, Al Capone, schools, baseball, friendship, and humor.

CUSHMAN, KAREN. *The Loud Silence of Francine Green.* Clarion, 2006, $16 (978-0-618-50455-8) (Grades 5–9)

Introduction

This is Karen Cushman's sixth historical novel for young readers (see also *Matilda Bone* in Chapter 4). The first three take place in Europe during the Middle Ages and the last three in the United States. Probably the most famous of the first group is *The Midwife's Apprentice* (Clarion, 1995, $10.95; 0395692296) (condensed in *The Newbery/Printz Companion*), which won the Newbery Medal in 1996.

The Loud Silence of Francine Green takes place in residential Los Angeles in the mid-20th century and is based tangentially on some elements in the author's life. When she was 11, in 1952, her family moved from Chicago, where she was born, to Los Angeles, where she attended a Catholic parochial school that bears some resemblance to the All Saints School for Girls of the story. The narrator of the story, Francine Green, also 11, creates as part of a school exercise on literary imagery an oxymoron, "the loud silence of Francine Green." In the context of the novel, it refers to the consequences of Francine's inability to conquer her fears and speak out against injustice.

Francine reads, for a book report, Thomas Heggen's World War II naval story *Mister Roberts* (which is currently out of print, although many editions of the play on which the novel was based are still available). In it, Ensign Pulver, a character like Francine, manages to summon up the courage to confront the unfair regulations imposed by his captain. Better readers might like to read this inspiring story about the waste of war as a follow-up to this novel.

Historical Background

Enter the world of saddle shoes and pleated skirts, beanies, Archie comic books, the Cold War, backyard bomb shelters, duck-and-cover drills, McCarthyism, and Hollywood blacklisting. In short, enter the world of post-World War II America. The novel covers part of this period, the eighth-grade year (1949–1950) of Francine Green in a parochial school in Los Angeles. In an Afterword, the author outlines the domestic conditions in the United States during the period. The growing fear of Russia, which produced its first atomic bomb in 1949, and of external attacks and subversion from within created insecurity, panic, and growing repression. Riding the crest of this fear, Senator Joseph McCarthy gained and maintained his power through unsubstantiated rumors about communist infiltration. His reign of terror resulted in the ruin of many lives and reputations, particularly of artists working in Hollywood.

The parochial schools of the 1950s were usually much more strict and unyielding than today and humiliation and corporal punishment more freely administered. Many parents of unruly children sent their children to these schools for precisely these reasons. Thus the tyrannical reign of principal Sister Basil the Great, though hardly conceivable today, was not atypical of the period.

Principal Characters

Francine Green, a fearful, imaginative eighth-grade girl who narrates the story

Delores Green, Francine's scatterbrained older sister

Artie Green, Francine's 5-year-old brother

Fred Green, Francine's father, an engineer and a conformist

Lorraine Green, Francine's loving but ineffective mother

Sophie Bowman, Francine's outspoken friend

Harry Bowman, Sophie's liberal father, a screenwriter

Jacob Mandelbaum, an aging character actor

Sister Basil the Great, the tyrannical principal of All Saints School for Girls

Sister Peter Claver, the friendly and understanding librarian at All Saints

Mr. and Mrs. Petrov, local Jewish American storeowners

Plot Synopsis

At the beginning of the school year in 1949, Francine Green, an eighth-grader at All Saints School for Girls in Los Angeles, is amazed to find that her new classmate is her neighbor from down the street, Sophie Bowman. The girls are a study in contrasts. Francine is timid and often fearful but has a fine imagination and a great sense of humor. She has said, "I just want to live my life without any problems, without getting into any trouble." Sophie is exactly the opposite: outspoken, fearless, questioning, and capable of standing up for any cause she feels is just. Sophie has been expelled from the local public school for vandalism (for a cause), and her father, a widowed screenwriter, hopes Sophie will profit from a stricter environment. This is not fated to be.

On the first day of school, Sophie clashes with Sister Basil the Great, the principal and eighth-grade teacher at All Saints, by questioning the suitability of including the school's volleyball team in their classroom prayers. Sophie suffers Sister Basil's favorite punishment, the humiliation of standing in the class wastebasket.

The girls' opposite natures seem to attract and soon they become fast friends. Sophie meets Francine's family: bean-brained, boy-crazy older sister Delores, her lovable 5-year-old brother Artie, and her parents—Mr. Green, a conservative, hard-working building engineer from whom Francine seems to have inherited her conformist nature, and Mrs. Green, a caring, cautious person who is dominated by her husband's conventional thinking. In turn, Francine meets Sophie's father, whom Sophie calls by his first name, Harry. Mr. Bowman is a liberal, affectionate Hollywood scriptwriter who, unlike her own family, always makes Francine feel she is particular and unique. Together and separately, the two friends share many adventures and misadventures typical of preteens.

On a shopping outing with Francine, Artie gets lost and explores the wonders of a new Piggly Wiggly supermarket. On the way home, Francine learns from the Petrovs, an elderly Russian Jewish emigrant couple who run a small store, that they are being harassed by local anti-Russian ruffians. After school, Francine volunteers in the school library where she meets Sister Peter Claver, a kinder version of Sister Basil, and, on anther occasion, the two friends drool over the new soda jerk at Riley's drugstore. Under Delores's misguidance, Francine ruins her hair using curling irons but regains her composure in time to join the crowd at a movie premiere where her idol, Montgomery Clift, makes an appearance. Sophie astounds everyone, including Sister Basil, by winning a city-wide speech contest on the topic, "What Today's Youth Can Learn from Yesterday's Saints," and one day the two girls skip school to go to a stage show starring Dean Martin and Jerry Lewis. Other events in their everyday lives involve Francine's first period, her attempts to teach Sophie to dance and Delores to act, and watching Mr. Green, reacting to the growing Red scare, begin digging a bomb shelter in the back yard.

Francine gets to know a friend of Mr. Bowman, Jacob Mandelbaum, an aging character actor who has a phenomenal knowledge of baseball. Mr. Mandelbaum (screen name Mann) lauds the ideals of the communists while condemning their practices. This liberal attitude soon gets Mr. Mandelbaum into trouble and Francine later learns he has been blacklisted and can no longer work in Hollywood.

The political situation continues to encroach tragically on Francine's life. Because Mr. Bowman has organized some benefits to help his friend Mr. Mandelbaum, he too has fallen under suspicion and could be blacklisted. Unable to withstand the persecution they have suffered, the Petrovs board up their shop and move. Mr. Mandelbaum collapses under the constant unjust stress and commits suicide. Sophie, who tries to moderate some of Sister's rants against the pagan Russians by organizing a Ban the Bomb club, suffers first the indignity of the wastebasket treatment and later expulsion from school. Francine feels miserable that she did not come to her friend's defense.

In spite of her father's ban on communication, Francine tries to keep in touch with the Bowmans. But no one answers their phone and the house seems deserted. Finally, Sophie calls Francine for a tearful farewell. Her father has become a target for the "red-baiters" and they must move to a destination she cannot reveal.

Francine is so filled with outrage she knows she must openly stand up for justice and her beliefs. One evening she returns to school. In Sister Basil's room, she grabs the wastebasket, and after twisting it out of shape throws it into the school incinerator. Outside, she sees a light in Sister Basil's room. She goes back into the school, intent on telling Sister Basil how she feels about injustice and oppressors. She has her speech ready. It ends with "Sister Basil the Great, I think you are a bully. And I think you should stop it."

Passages for Booktalking

This story has a wealth of incidents that are suitable for booktalking Some are: Francine learns that Sophie is going to attend All Saints School (pp. 1–8); Sophie is confined to the wastebasket for the first time (pp. 9–14); Sophie and Francine go for ice floats at Riley's (pp. 44–45); and Francine's use of a hair curling iron ends in disaster (pp. 46–51).

Themes and Subjects

On the dedication page, the author includes a quotation from Graham Greene: "Sooner or later one has to take sides if one is to remain human." This is the principal theme of this novel. It traces the evolution of Francine from a timid, obedient conformist to a person willing to speak for her ideals and beliefs. As well as being a coming-of-age story in which the heroine gains courage, commitment, and self -confidence, this novel is about bullying at different levels: nationally, locally, and within the family. Additional topics include the Cold War, atomic warfare, conformity, red-baiting, friendship, family commitments, liberalism, communism, Hollywood, challenging authority, and the meaning of democracy.

KADOHATA, CYNTHIA. *Weedflower.* Atheneum, 2006, $16.95 (978-0-689-86574-9) (Grades 5–8)

Introduction

Cynthia Kadohata was born in Chicago in 1956. Her father's family came to the United States in the 1920s and her mother was a Japanese American from Southern California. Her first novel for young readers (she had previously written three adult novels) was *Kira-Kira* (Atheneum, 2004, $14.95; 06898563930). Condensed in *The Newbery/Printz Companion*, *Kira-Kira* was the winner of the 2004 Newbery Medal. It is the story of Katie, growing up in Georgia during the late 1950s in a poor Japanese American family of poultry workers. It also tells of the enduring bond between her and her older sister Lynn that survives Lynn's death from lymphoma. The title comes from the Japanese word meaning "shining" or "glittering." The author has drawn on many autobiographical elements for *Kira-Kira* and *Weedflower*. For example, the incarceration of the author's father during World War II at the Poston Internment Center in Arizona was the stimulus for writing *Weedflower*. The title is the name of a fragrant plant cultivated by many Japanese flower growers in Southern California. The story is told from the point of view of its 12-year-old heroine, Sumiko Matsuda, a bright, sensitive girl who matures into a responsible but still vulnerable young woman during the novel. The author captures Sumiko's thoughts and feelings brilliantly. The story takes place from December 1941 to the middle of 1943.

Historical Background

When they first began to immigrate to America around 1890, the Issei (first-generation Japanese Americans) faced racism and discrimination. For example, the Supreme Court in 1922 designated them "aliens, ineligible for citizenship." When the attack on Pearl Harbor occurred on December 7, 1941, there were about 125,000 Japanese Americans in the United States, about 65 percent of them native-born from second-generation (Nisei) or third-generation (Sansei) families. Following the attack, much hysteria and fear was directed at Japanese Americans. Though there was no proof of any disloyalty, President Roosevelt, responding to public pressure, established the War Relocation Authority on March 18, 1942, designed to remove people considered "risky" from any "military zone." That was, essentially, the West Coast. About 110,000 Japanese Americans were rounded up and placed in temporary "assembly centers." They were later transferred inland to ten concentration camps. Conditions varied from camp to camp, but in general personal liberties were suspended, living conditions were substandard, and schools for the children inferior. Most of the detainees suffered loss of property, personal possessions, livelihood, and accumulated savings (German and Italian non-citizens, though also "enemy aliens," did not suffer these losses and were not interned). In spite of these deprivations, more than 25,000 Japanese Americans served in the armed forces during the war. Likewise, large numbers of Native Americans (who suffered similar injustices) enlisted. In 1988, the United States government formally apologized to the Japanese American population and appropriated $38 million to settle all claims by the survivors. This amounted to $20,000 per person, although the Federal Reserve Board estimated the total loss in excess of $400 million. Asians were given the right of naturalization in 1952.

Principal Characters

Sumiko Matsuda, a 12-year-old sixth-grader who is Japanese American
Tak-Tak (Takeo), her brother who is almost 6
Juchan (Masanori Matsuda), her grandfather
Aunt and Uncle Hatsumi, Sumiko's surrogate parents, in their late 40s
Ichiro, the Hatsumis' older son, age 23
Bull, the Hatsumis' younger son, age 19
Baba, the family's pet horse
Mr. Moto, Sumiko's neighbor at Poston
Sachi Shibata, Sumiko's friend
Frank, a Mohave boy a little older than Sumiko
Miss Kelly, Sumiko's teacher
Joseph, Frank's brother

Plot Synopsis

The life of 12-year-old Sumiko, a Japanese American girl growing up in Southern California, could be divided into two parts: before Pearl Harbor and after. Ever since Sumiko's parents died in an automobile accident, she and her 5-year-old brother, Tak-Tak, have lived with her aunt and uncle, who operate a small flower-growing business. Their sons are Ichiro (something of the family Lothario) and earnest, hard-working Bull, age 19. Their beloved grandfather,

Juchan, and pet horse, Baba, round out the family. Sumiko, a thoughtful, insightful girl, loves all her family, particularly her young brother, her grandfather, and Bull, all three of whom seem to notice her more than the others. She is conscientious about her chores, such as tending to the family's bathwater, deadheading flowers, and grading the blossoms when they have been picked. At school she is a good student but is a social outcast, teased because she is the only Asian. Therefore, she is surprised and thrilled when she, along with the rest of her class, is invited to the birthday party of Marsha Melrose, to take place on December 6, 1941. For days she can't decide which of her two dresses to wear and her excitement grows when her uncle purchases a lovely silk scarf she can take as a present. When she arrives at the Melroses' home, however, Marsha's mother quickly turns her away after condescendingly giving her a piece of birthday cake to take home. Sumiko has enough presence of mind to ask for her gift back but her feelings of humiliation and rejection leave her inconsolable.

The next day, news arrives that the Japanese have bombed Pearl Harbor. Uneasiness and alarm fill the Japanese community. Everyone worries about the future. Even Tak-Tak wonders if they will all be killed. Reports of violence against Japanese civilians and fear of sabotage reach the family, who take precautions by burning any possession that reveals their Japanese heritage. But within days police officers take Uncle and Juchan, the two first-generation Japanese in the household, into custody and send them to a prison camp in North Dakota.

Later news arrives that in one week the rest of the Japanese community will be relocated. Tearfully the family disposes of personal possessions and furniture, selling them for a fraction of their value. Tak-Tak and Sumiko are brokenhearted where they are forced to sell their beloved Baba. Army trucks take the family to the deserted San Carlos Racetrack, where they are housed in the stables. Each person is given a bag to fill with straw for a mattress and meals are served soup-kitchen style. After a few days of this, the residents are notified that permanent relocations will occur soon, with several hundred people to be shipped out at a time. Sumiko and her family are taken by train to the Poston Internment Camp in Arizona—hot, dusty, newly constructed barracks in the desert. They discover that the property has been appropriated by the government and is actually part of an Indian reservation. The accommodations are primitive and the food sometimes inedible, but family realizes that for some time this will be home. As the detainees settle in and learn to endure the oppressive heat and dust, a sense of community emerges and, true to their industrious and accommodating nature, they begin farming and raising poultry.

Sumiko is befriended by a girl her age named Sachi and an elderly, wise neighbor, Mr. Moto, who gives her bits of tasty rattlesnake he has smoked.

Together, Mr. Moto and she begin a small garden, aided by Sumiko's knowledge of plants and how they grow. They carry water from the latrine, collect chicken droppings for fertilizer, and protect fledgling plants by covering them with cheesecloth. Their efforts pay off and their garden wins third prize at an encampment competition. Both Tak-Tak and Sumiko attend school. Sumiko's teacher is the well-meaning Miss Kelly, whose best efforts are thwarted by a complete lack of textbooks and supplies. Boredom and disillusion are rampant in the camp and many of the young people turn to gambling, stealing, and other rebellious behavior.

One day while wandering the bean fields outside the camp, Sumiko meets Frank, an Indian boy about her age. They form a tentative friendship, both hesitant and suspicious of the other. Frank confesses that his people feel resentment toward the detainees because their barracks were built on Indian land. Also, the detainees have been provided electricity and water for irrigation, two basics that the Indians lack. Sumiko and Frank gradually become friends. Because Indians are forbidden to enter the detention area, their meetings are infrequent but Sumiko, at Frank's bidding, is able to arrange a meeting between Bull and Frank's brother Joseph to discuss irrigation of the Indian lands in the future.

After more than a year in the camp, official word comes down that every man and woman over the age of 17 can be drafted into the armed forces if they wish. There is much debate within the group, but both Bull and Ichiro decide to enlist. Regulations are also relaxed to allow others to leave the camp for employment outside the coastal areas. Realizing she will be without her two sons, Aunt decides to take a job in a sewing factory near Chicago. Sumiko has grown to feel secure in the barracks, and at first refuses to leave with her aunt. Gradually she realizes that she has no alternative and, true to her resilient nature, determines to make the best of still another move. She says good-bye to her friends, including Mr. Moto. Just before the bus leaves, Frank appears. They exchange addresses, promise to remain friends though apart, and say a bittersweet good-bye.

Passages for Booktalking

Some memorable passages: life within Sumiko's family and her anticipation of the birthday party (pp. 14–22); the party and Sumiko's humiliation (pp. 33–39); news of Pearl Harbor and the family's reaction (pp. 44–53); and Juchan and Uncle are taken away (pp. 54–60).

Themes and Subjects

This dark time in American history is told in human terms in a compelling narrative. The story portrays expressively and without undue moralizing the fate of two disenfranchised groups (Japanese Americans and American Indians) suffering unfair discrimination and hardship because of public ignorance. Family unity, love, and respect are beautifully portrayed. Readers will be inspired by Sumiko's determination to survive and her ability to make the best of her fate. Coping with rejection, loneliness, and isolation and finding salvation through hard work and dedication (in Sumiko's case, in the garden) are important themes. Her growing maturation and ability to act independently are well depicted. Other subjects: World War II, Pearl Harbor, California, Arizona, Japanese Americans, Native Americans, desert life, denial of civil rights, boredom, loss of dignity, and social cruelty.

———⋅•⋅———

PATERSON, KATHERINE. *Bread and Roses, Too.* Clarion, 2006, $16 (978-0-618-65479-6) (Grades 5–9)

Introduction

Katherine Paterson (1932–) is one of the most respected and appreciated writers of books for young readers. She is also one of the few authors to have won the Newbery Medal twice. In 1978 it was awarded to *Bridge to Terabithia* (Crowell, 1977, $15.95; 0690013590) and in 1981 to *Jacob Have I Loved* (Crowell, 1980, $14.95; 0690040784) (both condensed in *The Newbery/Printz Companion*). *Bread and Roses, Too* is set in New England in 1912 during the Lawrence, Massachusetts, textile workers' strike (also known as the bread and roses strike) from January 12 through March 12. Two of Paterson's other historical novels are also set in New England. *Lyddie* (Dutton, 1991, $17.99; 0525673385) takes place in 1843 when young Lyddie, in a futile effort to save her family's debt-ridden farm, takes a job in a textile mill in Lowell, Massachusetts. She endures deplorable working conditions but eventually is fired when she saves a young girl at the mill from an attack by a supervisor. Undaunted, she decides to journey to Ohio where she hopes to enter a college that will accept women. In *Preacher's Boy* (Houghton, 1999, $15.95; 00395838975), set in a rural Vermont community in 1899, minister's son Robbie Hewitt faces the coming of the new century with fear and apprehension (some say the end is near). The growing conflict between his rebellious nature and community expectations produces a fascinating tale of a boy struggling with his conscience.

Historical Background

Founded in the early 19th century, Massachusetts mill towns such as Lowell and Lawrence (named after Frances C. Lowell and Abbott Lawrence, respectively) at first treated their employees paternalistically, but these conditions soon changed and the mills evolved into sweatshops with deplorable working and living conditions. A work week was often six ten-hour days and the average wage was less than $9 per week. When, in 1912, the legal work week was reduced from fifty-six hours to fifty-four hours by the state legislature, the mill owners retaliated by cutting wages proportionally. The result: About 20,000 workers from the mills in Lawrence (a town on the Merrimack River about 26 miles northeast of Boston) went on strike and took to the streets. Many were women and children and most were new immigrants from Italy, Lithuania, Poland, and Russia (by this time, the Irish had moved upward into managerial positions). The Lawrence textile workers' strike is also known as the bread and roses strike because of a banner carried by striking women calling for "bread and roses:" that is, respect and better living conditions as well as better pay. The origin of the "Bread and Roses, Too" banner is given a fictitious but plausible explanation in the novel. Although some of the strikers were members of the union Industrial Workers of the World (IWW or Wobblies) and others belonged to United Textile Workers, most were unorganized. Nationally known union supporters arrived in Lawrence to help organize the strikers. Some mentioned in the novel are J. J. Ettor and Arturo Giovannitti. After these two were arrested on trumped-up murder charges (but later acquitted), William D. Haywood and his helper, Mrs. Elizabeth Gurley Flynn, took over.

Support and aid for the strikers poured in from around the nation and, as the violence grew, the residents of many towns and cities volunteered to temporarily "adopt" children from the town to prevent them from being harmed. One of these towns was Barre, Vermont, about 100 miles north of the Massachusetts border. The strike lasted about two months and was settled when management surrendered and met the workers' demands, including overtime pay, wage increases and an end to discrimination. Other details of the strike are given in the author's historical note at the end of the novel.

Principal Characters

Rosa Serutti, a 12-year-old sixth grader
Alma Serutti, her mother
Anna, Rosa's older sister
Ricci, Rosa's 1-year-old brother
Miss Finch, Rosa's sixth-grade teacher
Jake Beale, a 14-year-old illiterate mill worker
Granny Jarusalis, the Seruttis' Lithuanian tenant
Mrs. Jarusalis (called Mrs. J.), Granny's daughter
Marija, Mrs. J.'s daughter
Joe Ettor and Arturo Giovannitti, two labor organizers

Big Bill Haywood, another labor organizer
Mrs. Elizabeth Gurley Flynn, Haywood's co-worker
Mr. Gerbati, owner of a granite mill in Barre, Vermont
Mrs. Gerbati, his loving wife

Plot Synopsis

Two young people, Rosa Serutti and Jake Beale, are the principal characters in this novel. They are growing up in the textile mill town of Lawrence, Massachusetts, in 1912. Since the death of her father in a mill accident, 12-year-old Rosa and her Italian American family have fallen on terrible financial times. Mrs. Serutti faces a weekly rent bill of $6 though her wages at the mill are only $6.50. To make ends meet, 14-year-old daughter Anna also works in the mills and Mrs. Serutti has rented out space in her small apartment to a Lithuanian American family, the Jarusalises: Granny, her daughter known as Mrs. J., and Mrs. J.'s daughter Marija and two young sons. Mrs. J. and Marija also work in the mills. Rosa, who has to share a bed with Granny Jarusalis, is in the sixth grade. Her teacher, Miss Finch, frequently editorializes on the many virtues of the mill owners and the ingratitude of the complaining workers. Miss Finch is a Protestant and Rosa, a devoted Catholic.

Fourteen-year-old Jake Beale's circumstances are, if possible, even more difficult. He has never been to school, works long hours at the mill, and lives in a squalid shanty where he supports a drunken, physically abusive father. Rosa and he meet in an unusual way. Rosa is searching through a pile of trash trying to retrieve a pair of shoes she had thrown away thinking she was getting a new pair when she disturbs Jake, who is settling into the pile to sleep after being beaten by his father. Rosa suggests that Jake sleep on her kitchen floor. He does and in the morning, after stealing the Seruttis' meager bread supply, he leaves without making himself known to Rosa's family.

After mill management cuts the workers' pay, "strike fever" grips the town. Workers march daily through the streets and hold rallies in the many ethnic community halls in town. Even Mrs. Serutti hosts morning meetings in her kitchen with other female strikers. In no time the situation becomes ugly and people are afraid of violence. Rosa, a timid, fearful girl, is concerned for the welfare of her mother and sister, who are becoming militant workers for the strike. The unions send in professional organizers including the well-known Joe Ettor and Arturo Giovannitti. Because their money has run out, the Serutti and Jarusalis families rely on food from soup kitchens that are financed by donations from strike supporters. Jake's situation is particularly desperate. He resorts to stealing from church poor boxes and on one occasion is apprehended by a priest. The priest takes pity on Jake and instead of punishing him gives him a bath, new clothes, and a silver half dollar. Jake uses most of the money to buy whiskey, which he leaves by the bed of his comatose father. A female striker is killed and, on trumped-up charges, Ettor and Giovannitti are accused of her murder and arrested. The leadership vacuum is filled by two other union personnel, Big Bill Haywood and Mrs. Elizabeth Gurley Flynn. Jake is impressed by this charismatic duo, particularly the glamorous Mrs. Flynn, whom he follows from rally to rally.

Fearing bloodshed in the streets, Mrs. Serutti keeps Rosa out of school. At one of her mother's kitchen meetings, Rosa, a fine speller, is dragooned into making posters for an upcoming march. It is she who creates the famous poster that reads, "We Want Bread and Roses, Too."

Jake's father dies of alcohol poisoning and the boy is afraid he will be accused of murder. Desperate to leave town before his father's body is discovered, Jake learns from Rosa that children are being evacuated the next day to be placed with friendly families in neighboring towns and cities. He decides this is an opportunity to escape. Thinking he is heading for New York City, Jake stows away on the train carrying Rosa and thirty-four other children. Their destination is actually Barre, a town in central Vermont. Posing as Rosa's older brother, Jake, along with Rosa, is taken into the home of an elderly Italian American couple, Mr. and Mrs. Gerbati. Mrs. Gerbati is not prepared for a second visitor, so she gives Jake (who calls himself Sal) clothes that had belonged to their only son, who died many years before. Mr. Gerbati is furious when he sees this and demands that Jake take off the clothes. The next day Jake is outfitted in new clothes. Rosa is terribly homesick and worried about the fate of her family but easily adjusts to her new surroundings and quickly grows to love her foster parents. By contrast, Jake is restless and looks for ways to get to New York City. Rosa starts school but Jake, who cannot read, is unable to face being placed in the first grade with children half his age and begs not to go. Instead, Mr. Gerbati suggests that the boy accompany him to his workplace the following morning. Jake is surprised to learn that Mr. Gerbati is the owner of a prosperous granite workshop that specializes in making elaborate monuments and gravestones. Determined to raise money to travel to New York, Jake returns to the workshop after hours to crack open the office safe. He is caught in the act by Mr. Gerbati who, instead of turning the boy over to the police, questions Jake about his motives and his past. The boy reveals his background, his true identity, and the circumstances surrounding his father's death. He apologizes for his behavior and asks for forgiveness. Mr. Gerbati responds by suggesting that Jake stay in Barre and learn to become a granite cutter. When news comes that the strike has been settled in favor of the mill workers, Rosa bids farewell to the couple she now loves and returns home. Jake remains behind, secure in his new family and looking forward to a stable future.

Passages for Booktalking

Jake and Rosa meet in the trash pile (pp. 1–5); the workers go on strike (pp. 6–9); Miss Finch's classroom and her opinion of the strikers (pp. 17–21); Rose and the creation of the Bread and Roses poster (pp. 80–84).

Themes and Subjects

For young readers, this novel will supply a revelatory glimpse into labor conditions and practices in early 20th-century America. It is also a chronicle of labor's struggle for basic rights including the right to organize to achieve better wages and working conditions. The account shows that victories can be won through sacrifice, solidarity, and unity of purpose. Conflicting attitudes and practices within the Roman Catholic clergy are depicted. This novel is also the story of two youngsters who face adult problems and mature through the experience. Other subjects include: the Lawrence textile workers strike, labor unions, labor-management conflicts, New England, Massachusetts, Vermont, family relations, foster parents, Italian Americans, Lithuanian Americans, coming of age, poverty, factory conditions, perseverance, and courage.

PECK, RICHARD. *The Teacher's Funeral: A Comedy in Three Parts.*

Dial, 2004, $16 (978-0-8037-2736-6); pap. Puffin, $6.99 (978-0-14-240507-9) (Grades 5–9)

Introduction

Richard Peck was born in Decatur, Illinois, in 1934. After college and a stint in the army, he taught English in high schools from 1958 to 1971, when he began writing full time. His thirty-plus novels for young people began with a series that depicted teenage problems such as loneliness, family conflicts, rape, pregnancy, and suicide. More recently, he has turned to an examination of rural America's past, particularly in the first half of the 20th century. Two of these deal—in a humorous, sentimental way—with Mary Alice, her older brother Joey, and their remarkable Grandma Dowdel, who lives in a sleepy small town in Illinois. The first, a Newbery Honor Book in 1999, is *A Long Way from Chicago* (Dial, 1998, $19.99; 0803722907). It covers the summer visits that Mary Alice and Joey made to their eccentric but wise grandmother during the years 1929 to 1935. The second, *A Year Down Yonder* (Dial, 2000, $16.99; 0803746183) (condensed in *The Newbery/Printz Companion*), won the Newbery Medal in 2001. This sequel opens in 1937, while the country in still wracked by the Great Depression. Mary Alice, 15, is sent to spend a year with her Grandma while her father looks for work. Although Mary Alice relates the events of the year, the star of the novel remains the feisty, resourceful, indomitable, and unscrupulous Grandma Dowdel.

The Teacher's Funeral takes place over a period of about four months in 1904 in a small rural farming community in Indiana. It is narrated by 15-year-old Russell and captures the flavor of a gentler, more hospitable time in American history.

Historical Background

In America in 1904 the average life expectancy was forty-seven. Fourteen percent of homes had bathtubs and 8 percent had telephones; there were only 8,000 cars in the country and 144 miles of paved roads; the average wage was 22 cents an hour, sugar was 4 cents a pound, and coffee 15 cents a pound. The United States had forty-five states, and one in ten Americans could not read or write. Some important events of the year included:

+ Feb. 8. With a surprise attack by the Japanese on the Russian city of Port Arthur, the Russo-Japanese War began over Korea and Manchuria and lasted into 1905.
+ April 8. Longacre Square in New York City was renamed Times Square in honor of the *New York Times*.
+ July 23. The ice cream cone was invented in Saint Louis, Missouri.
+ Oct. 27. The first subway in New York City opened.
+ Nov. 8. Theodore Roosevelt defeated Alton B. Parker for the presidency.
+ Dec. 27. The stage play *Peter Pan* opened in London.

Construction of the Panama Canal began that year and the teddy bear was named after President Theodore Roosevelt. The composer Antonin Dvorak and the explorer Henry Morton Stanley died and Cary Grant, George Balanchine, Glenn Miller, and Cecil Day-Lewis were born.

Principal Characters

    Russell Culver, the 15-year-old narrator
    Lloyd, his 10-year-old brother
    Tansy, his 17-year-old sister
    Dad Culver, Russell's father
    Maud Singleterry, his aunt
    Charlie Parr, Russell's best friend
    Eugene Hammond, an automobile industry executive
    Miss Myrt Arbuckle, the deceased school teacher
    Flopears (Floyd Lumley), a thick-headed student
    Lester Kriegbaum, another student
    Pearl Nearing, a sassy student
    Little Britches (Beulah Bradley), a 6-year-old student

Glenn Tarbox, another student
Aunt Fanny Hamline, a crotchety neighbor
Mr. George Keating, the postman

Plot Synopsis

In August 1904, in a tiny rural farming community in Sycamore Township, Indiana, late-summer activities are proceeding as usual when the unexpected occurs. Just a few days before the scheduled reopening of the one-room Hominy Ridge School, Miss Myrt Arbuckle, its tyrannical, universally feared and hated teacher, shuffles off this mortal coil. For 15-year-old Russell Culver, this is a double blessing. Not only is he rid of his arch-oppressor but he has another reason to fulfill his dream of leaving home with his older friend, minister's son Charlie Parr, to seek his fortune as a farm hand in the Dakotas.

In the meantime, life at the Culvers proceeds as usual. The family consists of Dad, Russell, 10-year-old Lloyd, 17-year-old Tansy—who is about to leave the farm to complete her last year in high school in town—and the matriarch, Aunt Maud Singleterry, probably the worst cook in the county. Aunt Maud, a feisty and well-intentioned woman, lives alone in her house down the road, having eschewed Mr. Culver's offer of marriage after her sister, the first Mrs. Culver, died giving birth to Lloyd. Nevertheless, she supervises all activities at the Culver household. Before the day of the teacher's funeral, Lloyd, Charlie, and Russell begin their annual overnight camping trip at the creek. As darkness falls, Russell tells Lloyd about ghosts and the restless spirit of Old Man Lichtenberger, recently interred in a nearby cemetery. Suddenly a specter-like figure appears. Lloyd is so scared that he runs into the creek. The "ghost" is only Charlie, playing a prearranged trick on the young boy. Later the tables are turned when another ghostly figure of the dead Miss Myrt appears. This time, it is Russell's turn to panic and plunge into the stream. The spirit is revealed to be Tansy who engineered the second supposed ghostly visitation with Russell.

At the church on the day of the teacher's funeral, everyone is dressed in his best bib and tucker. After inspecting the body in the coffin, they listen to Reverend Parr, a hellfire and brimstone adherent, who delivers a Bible-thumping eulogy. He blames the unruly students for Miss Myrt's untimely death (others think she was just too mean to last). The service ends with Reverend Parr reading a poem on Miss Myrt's death written by the anonymous "Sweet Singer of Sycamore Township." On the journey home in the Culver buggy they narrowly miss a collision with a vehicle rarely seen in the area—an automobile. The driver, a handsome, affable young man named Eugene Hammond, apologizes profusely for the near-accident, which left Aunt Maud in a ditch and a hole in Tansy's new hat. Before a cordial leave-taking, Mr. Hammond, an automobile industry executive, pays particular attention to the attractive Tansy.

Later, a poem by the mysterious Sweet Singer immortalizing the accident appears in the local paper.

When the school board calls an emergency meeting to deal with the teacher crisis, Tansy mystifies Russell by attending the meeting and, later, dumbfounds him when he learns that not only has she applied for the job but also that she has been hired on an interim basis. His sister will be his teacher! Ugh! Tansy soon makes it clear she will be as firm with her brothers as she is with the other pupils. On the first day of school, Russell, as a practical joke, ties a sheet around the clapper of the school bell in the steeple, but Tansy has been tipped off by Dad and foils the plot by summoning the pupils with a cowbell she has brought from home.

The pupils number only six: the two Culver boys, Charlie, thick-headed Flopears (Floyd Lumley), bossy Pearl Nearing, and bright Lester Kriegbaum. A seventh is found hiding in the girls' privy. She is 6-year-old Beulah Bradley, nicknamed Little Britches, who is made welcome when quick-thinking Tansy lets her sit in the teacher's chair. Tansy proves to be an inventive, inspiring teacher. She makes up for the lack of supplies, improvising brilliantly. For example, for geography classes the students bring in the maps of the United States found on the shipping instructions pages of the Monty Ward catalog. Help arrives in the form of boxes of materials that contain items such as notepads, a bust of Lincoln, and a new hat, all from the Overland Automobile Company, Mr. Hammond's employer.

When it is learned that the school must have a minimum of eight pupils to remain open, Russell's dreams of skedaddling off to the Dakotas are rekindled. Ever-resourceful Tansy, Russell, and the family dog J. W. visit the Tarbox home on the outskirts of town. Not one of the dirt-poor Tarbox children attends school. Tansy is ordered off the property by bad-tempered Mrs. Tarbox. Before leaving, J. W. has an unfortunate encounter with a porcupine but the quills are safely removed by Glenn Tarbox, an attractive boy not much younger than Tansy. Within days, the eighth pupil arrives at school. It is Glenn Tarbox, who has defied his family and wants to learn to read and write.

A couple of strange mishaps occur at the school. A puff adder is found in Tansy's desk, and the plank over the ditch at the school's entrance is sawed partway through. The latter event coincides with a visit from fat, fierce, disliked Aunt Fanny Hamline, who is intent on complaining that someone is trespassing on her property on the way to school. Before the complaint can be lodged, Aunt Fanny must be hoisted out of the ditch with the help of postman Mr. George Keating.

Charlie and Glenn become rivals for Tansy's attention. This leads to a schoolyard brawl in which Charlie's hand is broken. Now deprived of a traveling companion, Russell gives up his plans to leave for the Dakotas.

One day, the county school inspectors arrive to test Tansy's competence. With her customary aplomb and the support of her students, she passes with flying colors. She later confesses to Russell that she took the teaching position to keep Russell from ruining his future by quitting school. It is discovered that the spiteful Tarbox clan is responsible for the school "accidents." Their plan to deter Glenn's attendance backfires and instead Glenn leaves home and moves into Aunt Fanny's house as her handyman. Another mystery is solved when, years later, after her death, it is discovered that Aunt Maud was the elusive Sweet Singer of Sycamore County. Tansy continues to be an inspiring teacher and life goes on in Sycamore Township.

Passages for Booktalking

On the camping trip, Lloyd and Russell are visited by the ghost of Old Man Lichtenberger (pp. 16–21); and later by the ghost of Miss Myrt (pp. 26–28); Reverend Parr's sermon at the funeral (pp. 37–41); and the mishap between the automobile and the buggy (pp. 47–52).

Themes and Subjects

This book gives a realistic, sympathetic and often humorous picture of farm life in America in the early 20th century. It speaks of family values, children's innocent fun and pranks, harsh schoolteachers, and neighborliness: aspects of life in a distant, gentler time. This time, characterized by party telephone lines, buggy rides, one-room schoolhouses, and the novelty of automobiles, is accurately re-created. The novel pokes quiet fun at old-fashioned ideas of propriety, superstition, and puritanical, Bible-thumping religion. The value of education is well presented. Many of the characters are unforgettable, including the stalwart, enterprising Tansy. Other subjects are: Indiana, farm life, death, funerals, corporal punishment, teaching, poverty, camping, automobiles, small-town life, and family solidarity.

SALISBURY, GRAHAM. *Eyes of the Emperor.* Wendy Lamb, 2005, $15.95 (978-0-385-72971-0); pap. Dell, $7.50 (978-0-440-22956-8) (Grades 6–10)

Introduction

Graham Salisbury has lived an interesting and exciting life. He was born into a family of newspapermen and grew up in Hawaii. He did his undergraduate work at California State University at Northridge and took a master's degree at Vermont College of Norwich University. In the late 1960s, he became a songwriter and musician for rock-and-roll bands before beginning a solo career in music. His first album remained unreleased for thirty years. Before turning to writing, he held several other jobs, including as skipper on a glass-bottomed boat and teacher in a Montessori elementary school. Another of his novels, *Under the Blood-Red Sun* (pap. Dell, $6.50; 0553494872) takes place in Hawaii at the time of the Pearl Harbor attack. Its hero is 13-year-old Tomikazu Nakaji, who must assume responsibility for the welfare of his family after his father and grandfather, both Japanese Americans, are arrested and taken to concentration camps at the same time his mother loses her job because of her race. In time, Tomikazu risks his life to visit his father. Salisbury has said of his writing, "If my stories show characters choosing life options, and the possible consequences of having chosen those options, then I will have done something worthwhile." One such life choice is made in *Eyes of the Emperor*. The novel takes place over a period of about one year and is narrated by 16-year-old Eddy Okubo.

Historical Background

By September 1941, the Japanese had completed plans for an assault on Malaya, the Philippines, and the Netherlands East Indies. To ensure success, they had to minimize the threat of American retaliation by destroying the eastern fleet docked at Pearl Harbor in Hawaii. A surprise attack on the naval base took place on the morning of December 7, 1941. Two main attacks involved 353 airplanes launched from six aircraft carriers. Japanese losses were light—just 29 planes and 5 midget submarines—but for the United States, with 95 vessels in port, it was a major defeat. Eighteen ships were sunk or destroyed, including battleships, minelayers, and destroyers. Others were severely damaged. More than 2,300 people died and approximately 1,000 were wounded. President Roosevelt called December 7 "a date which will live in infamy." On December 8, 1941, the United States declared war on Japan. Four days later, Germany and Italy (Japan's allies in the three-country Axis) declared war on the United States. Immediately after, the U.S. Congress passed a duplicate declaration.

Shortly after the tragedy of Pearl Harbor, the American Kennel Club and an organization called Dogs for Defense organized a campaign to recruit dogs for wartime duty. This unit became known as the K-9 Corps. Thousands people volunteered their dogs for duty. At first, thirty breeds were accepted. This was later narrowed to six including German shepherds, Doberman pinschers, and farm collies. The first training center was at Front Royal, Virginia, followed by a second operated by the K-9 Quartermaster Corps at Fort Robinson, Nebraska.

Training took about twelve weeks. After basic training, dogs were specialized. They could become sentry dogs, who were taught to alert military guards of strangers; scout or patrol dogs, used to detect snipers and ambushes; messenger dogs, used to carry messages in pouches around their necks; or mine dogs, who could detect trip wires, booby traps, and mines. Attack dogs (featured in the novel) were given further training. These dogs were taught to attack and destroy.

During World War II, Cat Island, Mississippi, became the headquarters for the Cat Island War Dog Reception and Training Center. This T-shaped island is off the Gulf Coast of the United States, opposite Long Beach and Gulfport on the mainland. Named by explorers who mistook its native raccoons for cats, the island contains dense forests of slash pines and oak. Alligators and poisonous snakes live in and around its bayous and swamps.

Close by is Ship Island, where Eddy and his mates were stationed. After Hurricane Camille in 1969, this island was split into two and is now known as West and East Ship Island. In its early history, the island flew, in chronological order, the French, Spanish, British, Confederate, and Union flags. It was used as a launching point by the British during the Battle of New Orleans in the War of 1812 but in 1858, the jurisdiction of the islands was turned over to the United States government and construction of Fort Mississippi began. During the Civil War, it was a prison for Confederate soldiers and in 1880 became the country's first quarantine station. This was closed in 1903. During World War II it served various purposes and, in 1942, became a military recreation center. Today, tourist excursions from Gulfport, 12 miles away, take visitors to view West Island and its historic buildings.

Principal Characters

Eddy Okubo, a 16-year-old Japanese American, the narrator
Herbie Okubo, his 13-year-old brother
Koji Okubo, his father
Ma Okubo, his mother
Nick (Chik) Matsumaru, Eddy's friend
Takeo (Cobra) Uchara, another friend
Lieutenant Sweet, Eddy's officer
Captain Parrish, Eddy's commanding officer
Sakamaki, a Japanese prisoner
Lieutenant Ricky Konda, Hot Dog, Golden Boy, and Pee Wee, Eddy's army
    buddies
Franz, a civilian dog trainer
Smith, an army dog trainer
Leroy, a boat captain

Plot Synopsis

If 16-year-old Eddy Okubo could be granted a single wish, it would be to become 18 so he could join the U.S. Army and be with his two older best buddies, Chik Matsumaru and Cobra Uchara. It is August 1941, in a suburb of Honolulu, Hawaii, and Eddy has just graduated from high school as an accelerated student. He and his 13-year-old brother, Herbie, are spending the summer helping their father complete work on a beautiful boat called the *Red Hibiscus*, which they are building for a rich white man. Eddy's father and mother emigrated from Japan to Hawaii in 1921 and have prospered through hard work and diligence. Eddy loves his mother and admires his father deeply in spite of fact that his dad is often sullen and uncommunicative. Eddy also questions some of his father's old-fashioned Japanese ideals involving family honor, saving face, and integrity.

Relations between Japan and the United States have deteriorated. There is talk of war, and some whites on the islands now regard their Japanese American neighbors with suspicion and fear. When the *Red Hibiscus* mysteriously catches fire shortly after it is launched, Eddy wonders if it was an accident or an act of sabotage. There are no clues either way. In any case, the family fortune has been wiped out, giving Eddy another reason to join the army—to earn a regular paycheck for the family.

After weeks of agonizing indecision, Eddy finally marches to the recruitment center armed with a birth certificate that he has cleverly altered to make his birth date of 1925 look like 1923. He is accepted without a problem but faces the chore of telling his parents. His mother sorrowfully accepts the news but his father turns his back and refuses to speak to his son. Eddy is sent to Schofield Barracks in Honolulu, where he is reunited with Chik and Cobra and enters basic training in a Japanese American unit of twenty-five men under the command of surly, arrogant Lieutenant Sweet. The commanding officer is Eddy's old shop teacher, amiable Captain Parrish. After seven weeks, Eddy and his friends are given home leaves. It is now early December.

On their first Sunday home, the Japanese strike Pearl Harbor. This terrible tragedy makes Pop Okubo realize the importance of his son's enlistment and, as Eddy rushes off to return to the barracks, he wishes him well. Because there is fear of an invasion, Eddy's squad, called "the Japs" by Lieutenant Sweet, is sent to a beach to build machine-gun placements. There they see a Japanese midget submarine stranded on the rocks. One crew member is dead, but they rescue the other, whose name is Sakamaki, and take him prisoner. When he begs to be shot to rather then endure the disgrace of capture, Eddy is reminded of his father and his values. One day, Eddy openly questions Sweet's calling his corps "Japs" and in reply is knocked to the ground. He learns another lesson in accepting authority.

June arrives and the company is sent stateside. Before leaving, Eddy spends time at home, where the situation has calmed considerably. His brother Herbie gives him a lapis stone as a good-luck charm. In the States, the unit is sent first to Camp McCoy in Wisconsin and then, inexplicably, to Cat Island, Mississippi. The group has now become like a family. As well as Chik and Cobra, Eddy is chums with other guys with names like Hot Dog, Pee Wee, Golden Boy, and Ricky (who later becomes Lieutenant Kondo). On the island, Captain Parrish and a civilian named Franz explain the nature of their special mission. As part of a K-9 corps, an army dog training program, the soldiers are to represent the Japanese enemy. As Captain Parrish says, "We're going to train the dogs to find you by your Japanese scent. You're not the trainers, you're the bait. We are going to teach them to smell you, track you down, and attack you." Eddy and the rest are horrified at being dog bait and mystified by the concept that Japanese exude a telltale scent.

The group is billeted at nearby Ship Island and ferried between the islands by a disreputable, scruffy old boat captain named Leroy. Ship Island is a pleasant place with sandy beaches, good fishing, and deserted old buildings to explore. On Cat Island, each unit member is assigned to a different dog and its trainer. Eddy is assigned to a taciturn young soldier named Smith and a dog named Gooch, a beautiful German shepherd. At first, Gooch is trained to locate Eddy in the jungle and eat raw meat off his neck. Slowly, the training routine changes: the dog must grow to hate Eddy. First, Eddy must hit Gooch with rocks from a slingshot. Then come more severe measures, culminating in Eddy beating the dog with a burlap sack. Eddy is disgusted and sickened by these procedures but cannot disobey his superiors. Eventually when he sees Eddy, Gooch bares his fangs and tries to break his leash to attack him. As a final exercise, Gooch is to be set free to locate Eddy, who is hiding in the jungle a mile away clad in a padded suit. Smith follows close behind to call the dog off if he does attack Eddy. The dog not only finds Eddy but attacks him mercilessly, cutting through the padding and biting him savagely. Angry about Smith's delay in stopping the dog, Eddy jumps on Smith. They fight on the ground while being attacked by Gooch. Finally Smith is able to call the dog off. Silently the two return to camp. Each is wounded and in pain, but unwilling to discuss the matter further.

A few days later, the island is abuzz with news that Captain Parrish and some top brass from Washington are coming to assess the attack-dog program. To test its effectiveness, both Caucasian soldiers and the Japanese American corps, including Eddy, are sent to hide in the jungle to see if the dogs can distinguish between the two by scent. By army standards the test is a complete failure—the dogs sniff out the soldiers regardless of race. But for Eddy and his pals, it is a great success: Japanese smell like the rest of mankind. The experiment is closed down and Eddy and his friends are free to do the job they have been trained for: winning the war.

Passages for Booktalking

Eddy talks to Chik and Cobra about joining up (pp. 6–11); the *Red Hibiscus* burns (pp. 11–16); Eddy tells Ma and Pop that he is in the Army (pp. 26–30); and the family's reaction to the bombing of Pearl Harbor (pp. 37–43).

Themes and Subjects

Eddy decides to enlist in spite of opposition from family and friends. His ability to accept the consequences of this decision and to profit from them is an important theme. The necessity of sometimes accepting authority even though it is arbitrary and unjust (as in the armed forces) is stressed. The damaging effects of racial prejudice and the injustices that it produces are vividly portrayed. Intergenerational conflicts about behavior and values are shown in Eddy's relations with his father. Traditional Japanese ideals and standards are realistically portrayed. The fallibility of science is depicted in the misguided attack-dog experiment. Other subjects are: World War II, Pearl Harbor, Japan, Japanese Americans, family stories, friendship, dogs, the U.S. Army, the K-9 Corps, Mississippi, and boat building.

SCHMIDT, GARY D. *Lizzie Bright and the Buckminster Boy.* Clarion, 2004, $15 (978-0-618-43929-4); pap. Dell, $6.50 (978-0-553-49495-2) (Grades 5–8)

Introduction

Gary Schmidt was born in 1957 and is currently a professor of English at Calvin College in Grand Rapids, Michigan. According to the dust jacket of *Lizzie Bright and the Buckminster Boy*, Schmidt lives with his wife and six children on a farm in Alto, Michigan, where he "splits wood, plants gardens, writes, feeds the wild cats that drop by and wishes that sometimes the breeze came this far inland." (Sea breezes play an important role in creating atmosphere in this novel.) Of Schmidt's writing, a colleague has said, "Our individual life stories reveal underlying patterns that Gary Schmidt believes to be universal and transpersonal, binding us together as human beings trying to make sense of the ups and downs of life." This theme is also found in his book *The Wednesday Wars* (Clarion, 2007, $16; -618724833), which is set on Long Island during the Vietnam War. In the novel, seventh-grader Holling Hood-wood, the only Presbyterian in his class, must spend his Wednesday afternoons alone with his teacher while his classmates attend religious instruction. At first he thinks the teacher, Mrs. Baker, dislikes him but as they begin analyzing Shakespeare's plays a friendship emerges. Mrs. Baker helps Holling in a variety of ways, including arranging a meeting with the New York Yankees.

Lizzie Bright and the Buckminster Boy is a third-person narrative that takes places over a period of a year (1912–1913).

Historical Background

The setting of this novel is the town of Phippsburg, Maine, at the mouth of the New Meadows River. Action also takes place on the mainland and adjacent Malaga Island, where in the 19th and early 20th centuries there was a small black community. The 41-acre island was probably named in the late 18th century by Captain Darling, whose brig loaded with timber from Malaga, Spain, sank in the area. In its early history it was dubbed a "maroon society" because of the racial mix of the small community. In time the mainlanders came to resent the presence of the "squatters" on the island and hoped to rid themselves of the shantytown in order to develop the island as a tourist attraction. They posted eviction notices. Some residents dismantled their homes, placed them on rafts, and floated them to other more hospitable locations, but a few residents remained.

One dark night in 1912 some townspeople invaded the island. One account reads "When three men stood before each house, they lit great torches, and threw open the cottage doors, shouting and dragging our men and women and children, too." Some were dispersed to various communities but others were sent to the Maine School for the Feeble-Minded in Pownal. The bodies buried in the island cemetery were disinterred and also sent to Pownal. The irony of this shameful act is that no buildings were ever constructed on the island and today it remains uninhabited and desolate.

Turner Buckminster, the young hero of *Lizzie Bright and the Buckminster Boy*, must translate the *Aeneid* as well as read the religious writings of Robert Barkley (1648–1690). Born in Scotland, Barkley was a Quaker who emigrated to the New World where, in addition to being an important theologian, he became the governor of the East Jersey Colony in the 1680s. His *Apology for the True Christian Divinity*, which Turner studies in the novel, was published originally in Latin in Amsterdam in 1676 and explains the grounds for holding certain fundamental religious positions. It was translated into English in 1678 and has been called "one of the most important theological writings of the century." In short, a weighty and learned book.

At baseball games in the novel, people drink Moxie, one of the first mass-produced soft drinks in America. It was originally marketed for medicinal purposes. If a person is said to be "full of Moxie," he or she is high-spirited. The drink is still consumed in New England and in 2005 it became the official soft drink of Maine.

A few important events that occurred in 1912: Arizona became the forty-eighth state, the Girl Scouts were founded, the *Titanic* sank, Fenwick Park in Chicago opened, and Wilson won the presidency over Taft and Teddy Roosevelt. Among the famous people born that year were Pat Nixon, Lady Bird Johnson, Perry Como, Julia Child, and Jackson Pollock.

Principal Characters

Turner Buckminster, a 13-year-old preacher's son
Reverend Buckminster, Turner's father
Mrs. Buckminster, Turner's mother
Deacon Hurd, a townsperson
Willis Hurd, his son
Mrs. Eliza Hurd, the deacon's mother
Lizzie Bright Griffin, a black girl
Preacher Griffin, Lizzie's father
Mrs. Cobb, a neighbor of the Buckminsters
Mr. Stonecrop, a wealthy townsperson
Sheriff Elwell, the town's lawman
The Tripps, an island family
Mr. Newton, a grocer

Plot Synopsis

Although Boston isn't too far geographically from the coastal town of Phippsburg, Maine, for 13-year-old Turner Buckminster the distance between the two is enormous. It is 1912, and he, with his father and mother, has just moved to Phippsburg where his father has become the pastor of the First Congregational Church. Small-town life—with its petty intrigues and narrow viewpoints—disturbs the sensitive, bright Turner. He also gets off on the wrong foot. First, he is the only kid to strike out during the baseball game at a town picnic. (Mr. Hurd, the church deacon, is umpire and his son, the obnoxious Willis Hurd, is pitcher.) Next, Turner is branded a coward when he goes swimming with the gang but lacks the nerve to join the others in jumping off a cliff into the cold Atlantic. He also incurs the wrath of Mrs. Cobb, a crusty neighbor, when, after the swimming fiasco, he walks past her house idly throwing stones, one of which hits her white picket fence. However, the slightly dotty Mrs. Hurd, the deacon's mother, who lives alone across the street, comes to his defense.

Reverend Buckminster is a strict but open-minded man who believes that his son must be a shining example of behavior and dress (including starched shirts and collars) to all the other children in town. This causes some tensions in the household and Mrs. Buckminster, Turner's understanding mother, sometimes intervenes on Turner's behalf. Is it any wonder that Turner often dreams of running off to the Territories? As punishment for disturbing Mrs. Cobb, Turner is sent to read to her. In addition to being cranky, the old lady is obsessed with death and wants Turner to record her last words if he is present at her demise.

Outside Mrs. Cobb's home, Turner is taunted by Willis Hurd and the two fight. Turner lands a slammer on Willis's nose, but is knocked to the ground. Covered with blood, he washes his clothes at Mrs. Cobb's and she catches him nearly naked in her kitchen. More trouble for Turner.

In the meantime, some of the prominent townspeople—led by Sheriff Elwell, Deacon Hurd, and Mr. Stonecrop, a wealthy shipbuilder—are hatching a scheme. They want to evict the ragtag black population of Malaga Island across the bay and turn it into a lucrative resort. Without legal right to the land, the population of squatters is vulnerable. They look for guidance to their leader, the aging Pastor Griffin, who lives alone with his 13-year-old daughter Lizzie Bright. But the old man realizes they are helpless before the law. Eviction notices are posted and, in no time, some begin leaving. On a deserted part of the mainland beach where Lizzie often goes clamming, she and Turner meet. She is the first black person Turner has ever spoken to. He is attracted to her direct, sassy attitude and speech and the two soon become friends. When Lizzie accidentally beans him with a rock, she makes amends by teaching him the proper way to bat rocks with a stick.

One day, Lizzie rows Turner to the island in her dory and he meets her gentle, religious father and some of the Tripps, a neighboring family. When Mr. Stonecrop hears of this visit, he persuades Reverend Buckminster to forbid Turner to go to the island. But Turner continues to see Lizzie when she comes to the mainland. On one of these occasions, Lizzie falls and cut her head. Turner realizes he must get her home and a semi-conscious Lizzie and Turner set out on the dory. Unfortunately Turner does not know how to row and soon they are way off course. They drift for hours and Turner has a near-religious experience when whales surface around him. One comes so close that he can look directly into his eye. The two are finally rescued. Lizzie gets help from a mainland doctor and, as punishment, the Reverend forbids Turner to see Lizzie again. Lizzie nevertheless visits Mrs. Cobb while Turner is making his daily visit—now to play hymns on her organ. Mrs. Cobb proves to be far from the ogress she seemed to be and the three become great friends. When school begins, Turner is home-taught by his father and spends time translating the *Aeneid* and paraphrasing the religious writings of Robert Barkley. For recreation he reads books by Charles Darwin (recommended by his father).

One day, in the middle of their hymn-sing, Mrs. Cobb suffers a seizure. Her last words, duly recorded by Turner, were "Oh hell, it's warm here. Get me a ginger ale." Instead of willing her house to the town as expected, she leaves it to Turner. Mr. Stonecrop and Deacon Hurd try to get Turner to sell it and give part of the proceeds to the town. Turner, with the support of his father, refuses. To everyone's consternation, he proposes moving Lizzie and her father into the house but even Lizzie knows that black people could not live in Phippsburg.

In order to get possession of his mother's house, money-hungry Deacon Hurd has her committed to an asylum. His son Willis opposes his father's actions, bringing Turner onto his side. Slowly, the two former enemies become friends. Lizzie's beloved father sickens and dies and she buries him on the island. Turner sneaks out of the house and hitches a ride to the island to comfort his dear friend. Willis cryptically warns Turner that trouble is about to strike. Turner thinks it means someone will vandalize Mrs. Cobb's house. It is now winter and freezing cold but, in spite of this, he spends the night in the dark, frigid house. He detects the presence of someone in the attic but before he can identify anyone, the intruder escapes. Outside he sees fires on Malaga Island and encounters Sheriff Elwell, who behaves abusively toward him and tells him to stop interfering in the town's business. As they walk to the cliffs overlooking the island, he says the shacks have been destroyed and that Lizzie, along with her friends, has been sent to the Asylum for the Feeble-Minded in Pownal.

Turner attacks the sheriff in a rage. Reverend Buckminster appears and, while trying to separate the two and save his son, falls off the cliff and is severely injured. Days later, with his father at home near death, Turner attends a church meeting at which Deacon Hurd and his cronies vote to oust their pastor. Only a few supporters, like Mr. Newton, their grocer, come to the Reverend's defense. Shortly afterward, Turner's father dies and is buried in his churchyard.

When Mr. Newton plans a trip out of town to buy supplies, Turner is able to hitch a ride to Pownal where he discovers that Lizzie died only a week after being sent to the asylum. Turner and his mother move into Mrs. Cobb's house and, as time passes, wounds heal and animosities are forgotten. After Mr. Stonecrop absconds with the shipyard's money, Deacon Hurd faces bankruptcy. In an act of great charity, Mrs. Buckminster offers to take in the family. When this happens, Turner discovers that Willis, now his roommate, is truly a great friend, though no one can take the place of his Lizzie Bright.

Passages for Booktalking

Some interesting episodes are: the picnic and Turner's disastrous baseball game (pp. 2–6); at the swimming spot (pp. 8–11); Turner meets Mrs. Cobb and Mrs. Hurd (pp. 12–15); the fight with Willis and its aftermath (pp. 26–30); and Turner meets Lizzie (pp. 43–49).

Themes and Subjects

As a book that deals with a youngster's relationship with his parents, the process of maturation, and first encounters with racial discrimination, this book stands alongside *To Kill a Mockingbird*. It is also the story of a great friendship that is ended because of man's bigotry and greed. The unity of all nature and the oneness of all life is an important theme. The author describes the atmosphere of northern coastal life and the passing of seasons brilliantly. In lyrical prose often approaching poetry the setting comes alive—even the feel of the sea breezes. It is also the gentle, moving story of a boy's growing strength of character. He conquers his fears, and lives by (and even fights for) sound principles. Other subjects: death, religion, Maine, sports, coastal life, humorous stories, sadness, changing homes, and pre-World War I America.

WOODWORTH, CHRIS. *Georgie's Moon.* Farrar, Straus, 2006, $16 (978-0-374-33306-5) (Grades 5–8)

Introduction

Chris Woodworth, who was born in 1957, now lives with her husband and two children, son Cory and daughter Catie, in rural Indiana next to a nature preserve. She has a part-time job as librarian at the Attica Public Library in Lafayette, Indiana. She has always loved books and when she began reading to her children, she decided to write one. She says she spends as much time thinking about her characters as actually writing about them. It took two years to produce her first book, *When Ratboy Lived Next Door* (Farrar, Straus, 2005, $16; 0374346771), which takes place in 1962 in a small Indiana town. Lydia Carson is disappointed when her new next-door neighbors include Willis Merrill, whom she nicknames Ratboy because of his unusual behavior. Lydia also has serious personal problems at home. Her mother, who has lost both her husband and a son, has withdrawn and is unable to give affection. These problems are gradually resolved in this excellent book. The author's third novel, *Double-Click for Trouble* (Farrar, Straus, 2008, $16; 0374309876), appeared in mid-2008. In it, Eddie McCall is shipped off to his great-uncle

Peavey after his mother learns about the questionable Web sites he has been visiting.

Georgie's Moon takes place over a period of about two months in 1970. It is told from the viewpoint of 12-year-old Georgia (Georgie) Collins.

Historical Background

In the novel Georgie's social studies teacher gives a little information about the Vietnam War, which is sometimes called the Second Indochina War. The first war (1946–1954) was a conflict between the Vietnamese nationals and communist forces and the French colonial government and its supporters. As part of the treaty ending the war, Vietnam was divided in two parts: North Vietnam and South Vietnam. The north was controlled by communists who allied themselves with China and Russia for support. The south, after the departure of the French, relied on support from the United States. Insurgents in the countryside (called offensively the Vietcong) began guerrilla warfare and the United States (fearing that if Vietnam went communist, it would mean a takeover of all South Asia) sent troops. The war began in 1959 and escalated rapidly. After the Tonkin Gulf incident, when U.S. naval ships were fired on by North Vietnam, the United States bombed North Vietnamese targets in a series of air raids that grew in frequency after 1965. Fighting intensified. On January 30, 1968, soon after the Allies ceased fire because of Tet, the Vietnamese New Year, the Vietcong successfully captured new territory, including several important cities, in what became known as the Tet offensive.

In the United States, growing opposition to the war was expressed in demonstrations around the country. The most tragic occurred at Kent State University, in Kent, Ohio, on May 4, 1970, when four students were killed and nine wounded during an anti-war protest. The domestic political quagmire produced by the war resulted first in President Johnson's decision not to run for reelection and then in a victory for Richard Nixon. In October 1972, secret negotiations began between Henry Kissinger and Le Duc Tho of North Vietnam that resulted in the signing of the Paris Peace Accord of January 1973. U.S. troops were withdrawn. Fighting within the country continued, and in late 1974 the North began a major offensive. The Southern forces were routed and Saigon fell on April 30. Vietnam was then reunited under a communist regime and the war officially ended on April 30, 1975. It was the longest war (thus far) in U.S. history. Historian Gabriel Kolko has said of the war, "If we use conventional military criteria, the Americans should have been victorious. They used 15 million tons of munitions (as much as employed in World War II), had a vast military superiority over their enemies . . . and still were defeated." More than 56,000 American troops were killed and another 300,000 wounded. More than a million Vietnam military personnel—and a least twice as many civilians—died.

Principal Characters

Georgia (Georgie) Collins, a 12-year-old seventh-grader
Mrs. Collins, Georgie's mother
Major Collins, Georgie's father
Mrs. Donovan, a guidance counselor
John, a 3-year-old boy
Lisa Loutzenhiser, another seventh-grader
Carla, her sister at college
Denny, her pesky 10-year-old brother
Alan, her absent older brother
Craig Evans, a seventh-grade boy
Miss Horton, Georgie's homeroom teacher
Principal Gordon
Mr. Hennessy, a social studies teacher
Kathy Newman, another seventh-grader
Angel, her friend
Mrs. Sophie Albertson, a nursing home resident
Aggy Jensen, another resident
Jack, an Air Force friend of Georgie's dad

Plot Synopsis

Twelve-year-old Georgie Collins is developing into a dislikable person. She is so filled with anger and hostility that she has become impertinent, disdainful of others, and sometimes cruel. Her attitude is partly due to the many moves she and her parents have had to make because her father is an Air Force officer. Each move requires an adjustment to new quarters, a different school, and the need to make a new set of friends. Her problems are also related to her anxiety over her father. It is 1970, the Vietnam War (and opposition to it) is intense, and for the last few months her dad has been stationed in Vietnam. Georgie loves her mother, but she *adores* her father. Every night she looks at the moon knowing that her father, hours earlier, has stared at the same moon and thought about her. She also watches the TV news every night hoping for a glimpse of her dad. Other children have sometimes been nasty to her, and her father gave her military-style advice, which she has followed ever since: Never retreat and always be on the offensive.

Georgie and her mother are living in Glendale, Indiana, a town that has just merged with neighboring North Ridge. The merger has produced a new middle school where Georgie will enter the seventh grade and students from the two towns will mix for the first time. Mom, who is busy during the day with her baby-sitting service, is concerned about Georgie and makes an appointment before school opens for her to see Mrs. Donovan, the school's guidance counselor. During the meeting, Georgie is her usual taciturn, uncooperative self. She notices a model ship in a bottle and learns that Mrs. Donovan's late father made it. While Mrs. Donovan is out of the room, Georgie pushes a letter-opener into the bottle, breaking the mast off the ship.

On Labor Day, Georgie and her mother—along with her mother's charges, whom Georgie calls the "brat brigade"—attend a town picnic. Georgie is particularly fond of tormenting 3-year-old John, who tries unsuccessfully to please her. Georgie notices that a girl her age has wandered away from her family and is sitting alone. The girl is Lisa Loutzenhiser, and she tells Georgia about her family: Mom and Dad, older sister Carla who is entering college, and bratty 10-year-old brother Denny. She mentions a still-older brother, Alan, whom she says is "away." Lisa is also entering the seventh grade and, in a further coincidence, she and Georgie are in the same homeroom, with Miss Horton. Also in the class are dreamboat Craig Evans; Kathy Newman, Lisa's former friend; and Kathy's new buddy, Angel. During the first social studies class, the teacher, Mr. Hennessy, discusses the Vietnam War and, when Craig voices belligerent "peacenik" sentiments, Georgie becomes so agitated that the teacher changes the subject.

For a term project, students are to sign up in pairs to perform community services. Georgie persuades the sensitive, quiet Lisa to work with her. On the sign-up sheets, Georgie writes that her partner will be Richard Starkey (Ringo Starr's real name) and Lisa's, Simon Garfunkel. This lands both of them in the office of Principal Gordon who assigns them to six Saturday visits with Mrs. Sophia Albertson at the Sunset Home for the Aged. On the first visit Georgie is her usual wisecracking, cynical self, but after a couple of meetings she becomes quite attached to Sophie and Aggy Jensen, who has been a pal of Sophie's for years. Georgie is also warming up to Mrs. Donovan, whom she visits regularly in the guidance office. She notices that there is an empty spot on the shelf where the ship in the bottle had been.

Lisa tries hard to break down Georgie's defensive behavior and tells Georgie her secrets, including her private poems. Georgie reads one that expresses Lisa's deep feeling of loneliness. Georgie seems indifferent but asks to take the poem home to copy it. Georgie learns that Lisa's family has been ripped apart by the war: Mr. Loutzenhiser is a strong supporter of the war, and daughter Carla has been ostracized because of her anti-war feelings. No one mentions the absent Alan, whom Lisa insists is living in Chicago. At school, Georgie is shaken when she learns that Kathy Herman's brother has been killed in Vietnam and, when Craig again voices his pacifist feelings, Georgie physically attacks him. Another classmate says that if he were called up for service, he would burn his draft card "just like Alan Loutzenhiser and move to Canada." Georgie is stunned by the news and feels she has been lied to and betrayed by her only friend. Seeking revenge, she gives Kathy a copy of Lisa's poem. But Georgie's attempts to make friends with Kathy and Angel are rebuffed and she is shocked when the two put a copy of the poem in Lisa's gym sneakers for all to see. Lisa, hurt and humiliated, refuses to speak to Georgie.

The visits to the nursing home become tense, but Sophie and Aggy are oblivious to the girls' strained relationship. After the last visit, Georgie returns home to find her father's Air Force friend Jack in the living room. Knowing what his news will be, she runs out of the house but is caught and brought back. Jack confirms what Georgie has been unable to accept after she learned in July that her father was missing in action. Jack, who was part of the operation in which her father's plane was shot down, has come to tell them that there is no chance that he survived.

He brings Georgie a final letter from her father, which he wrote before the mission. It ends "Always remember that my love for you is bigger than life, Georgie. A little thing like dying isn't going to stop it." Georgie is now able to accept the truth and with this catharsis, the anger and resentment she has felt vanish. She realizes she has some fence-mending to do. First she apologizes to Lisa who tells her that, because of the family's differences about the war, her father has left home. Georgie finds him in his paint store and talks to him about her father's death and how she can now accept the fact that Alan and others have refused to fight. She urges him to do the same and, a few days later, she learns he has returned home. Lisa and Georgie write a joint report on their community service project and decide they will continue their visits to their dear friends at Sunset. In a last gesture of reconciliation, Georgie gives her father's Distinguished Flying Cross medal to Mrs. Donovan, who places it on the shelf in the exact spot where the model ship had been.

Passages for Booktalking

Georgie, Mrs. Donovan, and the destruction of the ship in a bottle (pp. 3–7); Georgie's first day at school and the term project (pp. 18–23); Georgie and Lisa choose partners (pp. 24–27) and suffer the consequences (pp. 47–49); and Georgie's father works out a survival plan for her (pp. 47–49).

Themes and Subjects

All wars are tragic and destructive but particularly devastating are those in which countries, factions, and even families have different loyalties. In American history examples of these wars are the Civil War, the Vietnam War, and the Iraq War. Members of Georgie's class and Lisa's family have different opinions about America's presence in Vietnam. Both sides of the debate are fairly presented. Georgie's constant emotional turmoil, her inner fragility, and the acceptance of her father's death and the resolution this brings are poignantly depicted. Lisa also grows emotionally and, like Georgie, becomes increasingly mature and able to accept reality. Other subjects include: baby-sitting, the U.S. Air Force, friendship, Indiana, schools, teachers, guidance counselors, and nursing homes.

ADDITIONAL SELECTIONS

Adler, David A. *Don't Talk to Me About the War* (Viking, 2008, $15.99) (Grades 4–7)

It is 1940 in the Bronx, and though he tries to ignore the facts, the realities of what will be World War II invade the isolated world of 13-year-old Tommy.

Arato, Rose. *Ice Cream Town* (Fitzhenry and Whiteside, 2007, pap. $11.95) (Grades 5–6)

Young Sammy, who is growing up in squalor on the Lower East Side of New York in the early 1900s, wonders why his orthodox Jewish family emigrated from Poland to live in this misery.

Blume, Lesley M. M. *The Rising Star of Rusty Nail* (Knopf, 2007, $15.99) (Grades 4–6)

Beginning in the 1950s, the Red Scare gripped America, including 10-year-old Franny who is afraid that her new music teacher is a Commie.

Blume, Lesley M. M. *Tennyson* (Knopf, 2008, $18) (Grades 4–6)

When 11-year-old Tennyson and her younger sister go to live their Aunt and Uncle in a crumbling southern plantation in 1932, she begins to explore her Civil War ancestors.

Boling, Katherine. *January, 1905* (Harcourt, 2004, $16) (Grades 4–7)

Set in 1905 when exploitation of child labor was common, this is the story of 11-year-old twins Pauline and Arlen, one of whom works long hours in a mill and the other who stays home because of a deformed foot.

Borden, Louise. *Across the Blue Pacific* (Houghton, 2006, $17) (Grades 3–6)

During World War II, young Molly has grown to love and admire her older neighbor, Lieutenant Ted Walker, who plays with her during his leave from the navy and she is crushed when she learns of his death on a submarine in the Pacific.

Brown, Don. *The Train Jumper* (Roaring Brook, 2007, $16.95) (Grades 6–9)

During the Depression, 14-year-old Collie leaves his Wisconsin home and hits the rails looking for his older brother.

Bruchac, Joseph. *Code Talker* (Dial, 2005, $16.99) (Grades 6–9)
In novel format, this is the story of the Native Americans who used their native language for sending secret coded messages during World War II, as retold by Ned Begay, who was only 16 at the time.

Bryant, Jen. *Ringside, 1925: Views from the Scopes Trial* (Knopf, 2008, $15.99) (Grades 5–8)
Told from various points of view—of students who represent both sides, merchants, a reporter, and others—this is an account of the famous Tennessee trial concerning evolution that pitted Darrow against Bryant.

Burg, Shana. *A Thousand Never Evers* (Delacorte, 2008, $15.99) (Grades 7–12)
As she enters her segregated Mississippi junior high school in 1963, Addie experiences many forms of prejudice including her brother's narrow escape from the Klan.

Carter, Dorothy. *Grandma's General Store: The Ark* (Farrar, 2005, $16) (Grades 3–5)
African American life in the South during the Depression is depicted in this story about Pearl and her younger brother, who are living with their grandmother in Florida at a time of segregation and an active Klan.

Carwell, Marlene. *Sweetgrass Basket* (Dutton, 2005, $15.99) (Grades 7–10)
In this novel set at the turn of the last century, two Mohawk sisters, Marie and Sarah, suffer cruel abuse while kept in Pennsylvania's Carlisle Indian Boarding School.

Cheney, J. B. *My Friend the Enemy* (Knopf, 2005, $15.95) (Grades 5–8)
Growing up on an Oregon farm during World War II, 11-year-old Hazel is worried about the fate of her dear friend Sogoji, an orphaned Japanese American boy who lives and works on the farm.

Coleman, Evelyn. *Freedom Train* (Simon, 2008, $15.99) (Grades 5–8)
In Atlanta in 1947, 12-year-old Clyde, whose family is "poor white trash," objects to his father's racial prejudice aimed at a black doctor and his family.

Crum, Shutta. *Spitting Image* (Clarion, 2003, $15) (Grades 5–9)
It is the mid-1960s and, while her town is coping with President Johnson's War on Poverty, 12-year-old Jessie Kay searches for her father.

Currier, Katrina Saltonstall. *Kai's Journey to Gold Mountain* (Angel Island, 2004, $16.95) (Grades 4–6)
This is a well-illustrated story, based on fact, of a 12-year-old Chinese boy's journey to live with his father in San Francisco and of his detention on Angel Island.

Dowell, Frances O'Roark. *Shooting the Moon* (Atheneum, 2008, $16.99) (Grades 5–8)
It is 1969, and the horrors of the Vietnam War come to 12-year-old Jamie, a colonel's daughter, through roles of film sent by her older brother who is serving in Vietnam.

Gaeddert, Louann. *Friends and Enemies* (Atheneum, 2000, $16) (Grades 5–8)
In World War II Kansas, a patriotic young boy must come to terms with his friend's pacifist beliefs.

Graff, Nancy Price. *Taking Wing* (Clarion, 2005, $15) (Grades 5–8)
In 1942 while staying on his grandfather's farm, 13-year-old Gus makes friends with the daughter of French Canadian immigrants and witnesses the intolerance and prejudice heaped on these people because of their poverty, lifestyle, and religion.

Haddix, Margaret. *Uprising* (Simon, 2007, $16.99) (Grades 5–8)
Told from three points of view—those of an immigrant Italian girl, a young Jewish American girl, and the daughter of a wealthy businessman—this is the story of the 1910 garment workers strike in New York and of the Triangle Shirtwaist fire 13 months later.

Hale, Marian. *Dark Water Rising* (Holt, 2006, $16.95) (Grades 5–8)
Set in 1900 during the storm that destroyed Galveston, Texas, this is the story of one survivor, 16-year-old Seth.

Hobbs, Valerie. *Sonny's War* (Farrar, 2002, $16) (Grades 7–10)
Cory's life is in conflict when she joins a peace movement at the urging of her teacher although her beloved brother Sonny is fighting in Vietnam.

Holm, Jennifer L. *Penny from Heaven* (Random, 2006, $15.95) (Grades 5–8)
It is the summer of 1953, and while rooting for the Brooklyn Dodgers and hanging out with a scheming cousin 11-year-old Penny discovers some amazing secrets about her Italian American family.

Holt, Kimberley Willis. *Part of Me: Stories of a Louisiana Family* (Holt, 2006, $16.95) (Grades 5–8)
In this intergenerational novel set in 1939, to help her family financially, 14-year-old Rose must lie about her age to get a job on a bookmobile that stops at small bayou towns.

Jennings, Patrick. *Wish Riders* (Hyperion, 2006, $15.99) (Grades 5–10)
Set in a West Coast logging camp during the Depression, this variation on the Cinderella story involves a poor orphan named Edith who works as a flunkey at the camp.

Johnston, Tony. *Bone by Bone by Bone* (Roaring Brook, 2007, $16.95) (Grades 6–9)
In a small Tennessee town in the 1950s, David, a white boy whose best friend is a black boy named Malcolm, is afraid that his father is an active member of the Klan.

Joselyn, Marthe. *How It Happened in Peach Hill* (Lamb/Random, 2007, $15.99) (Grades 6–10)
While the country is recovering from two great tragedies, World War I and the 1918 influenza epidemic, Madame Caterina, a medium and con artist, is duping gullible customers with the help of daughter Annie, age 15.

Karwoski, Gail. *Quake! Disaster in San Francisco* (Peachtree, 2004, $14.95) (Grades 4–6)
A reenactment of the 1906 San Francisco earthquake as seen by 13-year-old Jacob Kaufman, who lives there with his father and young sister.

Kerr, M. E. *Slap Your Sides* (HarperCollins, 2001, $15.89) (Grades 7–10)
Teenage Jubel, a Quaker and pacifist, finds oppositions to his beliefs in his small Pennsylvania town during World War II.

Kidd, Ronald. *Monkey Town: The Summer of the Scopes Trial* (Simon, 2006, $15.95) (Grades 5–10)
It is 1925 in Dayton, Tennessee, and 15-year-old Frances's biology teacher, on whom she has a great crush, is on trial for teaching evolution.

Klages, Ellen. *The Green Glass Sea* (Viking, 2006, $16.99) (Grades 4–8)
During World War II, 10-year-old Dewey moves to Loa Alamos where her father is working on a top-secret government project.

Krisher, Trudy. *Fallout* (Holiday, 2006, $17.95) (Grades 7–10)
In her small South Carolina town, which is still recovering from the destructive hurricane of 1954, 14-year-old Genevieve's beliefs and opinions are challenged when an unconventional, free-thinking girl and her family move into town.

Kwasney, Michelle D. *Itch* (Holt, 2008, $16.99) (Grades 5–8)
Sixth-grader Delores, nicknamed Itch, moves in the 1960s to Ohio and notices that her new friend Wendy hides bruises; Itch finally summons up the courage to speak up against child abuse.

Larson, Kirby. *Hattie Big Sky* (Delacorte, 2006, $15.95) (Grades 7–10)
This is the heartwarming story of a 16-year-old orphan, Hattie, and her struggle to keep her new homestead in Montana during 1918.

Lawrence, Iain. *Gemini Summer* (Delacorte, 2006, $15.95) (Grades 4–6)
In 1965, 9-year-old Danny Rivers is so traumatized by the death of his older brother that he begins to believe that his spirit exists inside their pet dog Rocket. Astronaut Gus Grissom plays an important part in the novel's satisfying conclusion.

Lemma, Don. *When the Sergeant Came Marching Home* (Holiday, 2008, $16.95) (Grades 4–7)
Ten-year-old Donald is delighted when his father comes back from war in 1946 unharmed, but dismayed when the family, under his father's direction, moves from the city to a farm in Montana.

Levine, Ellen. *Catch a Tiger by the Toe* (Viking, 2005, $15.99) (Grades 5–8)
During the Red scare, Jamie's dad loses his job because he is accused of being a communist and she is afraid that he will name names to save himself and his family.

Lisle, Janet Taylor. *The Art of Keeping Cool* (Simon, 2000, $17) (Grades 5–8)
During World War II in his Rhode Island town, Robert wonders if the outcast German painter his cousin is helping is really a spy.

Lisle, Janet Taylor. *Black Duck* (Philomel, 2006, $15.99) (Grades 4–8)
    Through a flashback, Ruben Hart recalls when he was 14 in 1929 and he and his best friend Jeddy, the police chief's son, found a body on the shore in coastal Rhode Island.

Loizeaux, William. *Wings* (Farrar, 2006, $16) (Grades 4–7)
    In the quiet summer of 1960, Nick learns that his dad died in the Korean War, makes a new friend of the family's handyman, and nurtures a young mockingbird he names Marcy.

Lowry, Lois. *The Silent Boy* (Houghton, 2003, $15) (Grades 6–10)
    Set in New England at the beginning of the 20th century, this is the story of young Katy, the daughter of a local doctor, and her friendship with a mentally backward boy.

Lyon, George. *Sonny's House of Spies* (Atheneum, 2004, $16.95) (Grades 6–10)
    Family secrets abound in this humorous look at the 1950s coming-of-age—in Mozier, Alabama—of 13-year-old Sonny, which also contains a serious message about segregation.

McKissack, Patricia C. *Abby Takes a Stand* (Viking, 2005, $14.99) (Grades 2–4)
    In this picture book, Abby, also known as Grandma Gee, recalls incidents in Nashville in 1960 when she was only 10 and everyday segregation produced both humiliation and anger.

McKissack, Patricia C. *A Friendship for Today* (Scholastic, 2007, $16.99) (Grades 4–7)
    In the fall of 1955 in suburban St. Louis, school segregation ends and Rosemary becomes the lone black student in her sixth-grade class.

Martinez, Arturo O. *Pedrito's World* (Texas Tech University, 2007, $16.95) (Grades 5–7)
    This gently first-person narrative set in rural south Texas is the story of a boy growing up in 1941 in a loving Mexican American family.

Mazer, Harry. *Heroes Don't Run: A Novel of the Pacific War* (Simon, 2005, $15.95) (Grades 6–10)
    In this, the last of the trilogy about Adam Pelko and World War II, he is now 17 and, through lying about his age, joins the Marines. The other titles are *A Boy at War* (Simon, 2001, $15.95) and *A Boy No More* (Simon, 2004, $15.95).

Mazer, Harry. *Tough Times* (Clarion, 2007, $16) (Grades 5–8)
    In Depression era America, poverty forces high school senior Joey Singer to leave his family and join the thousands of homeless young people who are riding the rails.

Miller, Sarah. *Miss Spitfire: Reaching Helen Keller* (Atheneum, 2007, $16.99) (Grades 7–10)
    Using a fictional format, the author re-creates the struggles and triumphs involved in the relationship between Helen Keller and Annie Sullivan.

Myers, Walter Dean. *Harlem Summer* (Scholastic, 2007, $16.99) (Grades 5–8)
   Historical characters such as Fats Waller and Dutch Schultz appear in this novel
   set in 1925 during the Harlem Renaissance that features a teenage sax player who
   hopes to break into the world of jazz.

Nolan, Han. *A Summer of Kings* (Harcourt, 2006, $17) (Grades 6–9)
   Various forms of racial prejudice emerge when, in 1963, the parents of 14-year-old
   Esther invite into their home an 18-year-old African American who is the victim of
   southern racial violence.

Noonan, Brandon. *Plenty Porter* (Abrams, 2006, $16.95) (Grades 7–10)
   Twelve-year-old Plenty is the youngest of eleven children in a poor sharecropper's
   family that is combating poverty and prejudice in America during the 1950s.

Nuzum, K. A. *A Small White Scar* (HarperCollins, 2006, $15.99) (Grades 6–8)
   In 1940, 15-year-old Will leaves home to begin working as a cowboy in Colorado
   and finds he has been followed by his brother who has Down syndrome.

Park, Linda Sue. *Keeping Score* (Clarion, 2008, $16) (Grades 4–7)
   Young Maggie hopes their ties of friendship and mutual love of baseball will help
   her nurse Jim back to health after he returns traumatized from the Korean War.

Parker, Robert B. *Edenville Owls* (Philomel, 2007, $17.99) (Grades 4–7)
   After the end of World War II in a small, placid Massachusetts town, Bobby
   Murphy, an average boy with average interests, discovers a dark secret about his
   teacher, Miss Delaney.

Paterson, Katherine. *Park's Quest* (Penguin, 1988, pap. $5.99) (Grades 5–8)
   Park's mother refuses to talk about his father, who was killed in Vietnam, until he
   learns about his father's past after meeting his half-sister Thanh.

Paulsen, Gary. *The Quilt* (Random, 2004, $17.99) (Grades 3–6)
   A gentle story set during World War II, about a 6-year-old boy who lives with his
   grandmother in a Norwegian American community in Minnesota.

Peck, Richard. *On the Wings of Heroes* (Dial, 2007, $16.99) (Grades 6–9)
   While older family members and friends go to fight in World War II, young Davy
   helps by collecting scrap metal while fixing up an old car and coping with a new
   teacher.

Porter, Tracey. *Billy Creekmore* (HarperCollins, 2006, $17.99) (Grades 5–8)
   Set in the early 20th century, this story tells of 12-year-old Billy, whose quest for
   his father takes him from his orphanage to a coal mine and later to a traveling circus.

Ray, Delia. *Singing Hands* (Clarion, 2006, $16) (Grades 5–8)
   This story set in Alabama in 1948, tells how Gussie, one of three hearing daughters of deaf parents, matures from a troublesome rebellious child to a caring mature
   young lady.

Rodman, Mary Ann. *Jimmy's Stars* (Farrar, 2007, $16.95) (Grades 4–7)
   World War II becomes a reality for 11-year-old Ellie, who lives in a working-class
   neighborhood in Pittsburgh, when her brother is sent off to war.

Rostkowski, Margaret. *Best of Friends* (HarperCollins, 1989, $12.95) (Grades 7–10)
Set in the 1960s, this coming-of-age novel involves three teenage friends who are torn apart by their attitudes toward the Vietnam War and draft resistance.

Salisbury, Graham. *House of the Red Fish* (Random, 2006, $16.99) (Grades 5–8)
In Hawaii after Pearl Harbor, a young Japanese American combats prejudice and poverty when his father is deported to an internment camp.

Salisbury, Graham. *Night of the Howling Dogs* (Lamb/Random, 2007, $16.99) (Grades 4–9)
This novel takes place on Hawaii's Big Island when a group of Boy Scouts become involved in the giant earthquake and resulting tsunami that occurred in 1975.

Schlitz, Laura Amy. *A Drowned Maiden's Hair* (Candlewick, 2006, $15.99) (Grades 4–7)
Set in the early 20th century, this novel deals with the fraudulent Hawthorne sisters, who adopt a young orphan Maud to assist them in their sham séances where she will appear as an apparition of a victim's dead child.

Schmidt, Gary D. *Trouble* (Clarion, 2008, $16) (Grades 5–10)
In the 1970s in a Boston suburb, a tragic car accident has lasting effects on the victim's family and the driver, a young Cambodian immigrant.

Schmidt, Gary D. *The Wednesday Wars* (Clarion, 2007, $16) (Grades 4–9)
During the Vietnam War, seventh-grader Holling Hoodwoodoodhood, forms an unusual friendship with forms an unusual friendship with his teacher, Mrs. Baker, whose husband is missing in action.

Sturm, James. *Satchel Paige: Striking Out Jim Crow* (Hyperion, 2007, $16.99) (Grades 6–12)
Baseball and racism are featured in this novel set in the 1940s about a fictional ballplayer Emmett Wilson and his encounter with Satchel Paige.

Sullivan, Jacqueline Levering. *Annie's War* (Eerdmans, 2007, $15) (Grades 4–7)
In 1946, Annie and her family in Walla Walla, Washington, are still recovering from the loss and disruption caused by World War II when they confront racism after accepting an African American as a lodger.

Tate, Eleanora E. *Celeste's Harlem Renaissance* (Little, Brown, 2007, $15.99) (Grades 5–8)
At the height of the Harlem Renaissance, 13-year-old Celeste moves from North Carolina to live with her aunt, a Broadway singer, in this novel that features such notables as Duke Ellington and James Weldon Johnson.

Tocher, Timothy. *Chief Sunrise, John McGraw and Me* (Cricket, 2004, $13.95) (Grades 6–9)
In 1919, while Herb Cobb, age 15, is running away from home and an abusive father, he meets Chief Sunrise, a great baseball player who wants to find the New York Giants' manager John McGraw and get a chance at the majors.

Vollmar, Rob. *The Castaways* (Comic/Lit, 2007, $17.95) (Grades 6–9)
   In this graphic novel set in the Great Depression, a 13-year-old white boy finds help in his friendship with an old black tramp.

Whelan, Gloria. *Summer of the War* (HarperCollins, 2006, $15.99) (Grades 6–9)
   It is 1942 but the war seems far off on tiny Turtle Island in Lake Huron where 14-year-old Mirabelle is spending a summer with her grandparents that is peaceful until her sophisticated 15-year-old cousin Carrie arrives.

White, Ruth. *Tadpole* (Farrar, 2003, $16) (Grades 5–8)
   In the summer of 1955, a 13-year-old orphan comes to visit his aunt and his four girl cousins and nothing will be the same again.

White, Ruth. *Way Down Deep* (Farrar, 2007, $16) (Grades 4–7)
   This tender story of Ruby and her search for a family is set in Appalachia in the 1950s.

Whittenberg, Allison. *Sweet Thang* (Delacorte, 2006, $15.95) (Grades 5–8)
   Along with all the problems of growing up in a middle-class black community in Philadelphia in the 1970s, 14-year-old Charmaine must adjust to a new member of the household, a young cousin named Tracy John.

Woodson, Jacqueline. *Feathers* (Penguin, 2007, $15.99) (Grades 4–6)
   Various facets of racial prejudice are revealed when a lone white boy enrolls in Frannie's all-black sixth-grade class in this novel set in 1971.

Yep, Laurence. *The Earth Dragon Awakes: The San Francisco Earthquake of 1904* (HarperCollins, 2006, $14.99) (Grades 3–7)
   Told in alternating chapters from the viewpoint of two families—that of 8-year-old Henry Travis and that of a Chinese immigrant boy, Chin—the horror and heroism surrounding the San Francisco earthquake is re-created.

Author Index

This index lists authors of historical novels mentioned in Chapters 4 through 8.

Title Index

This index lists titles of historical novels mentioned in Chapters 4 through 8.

Subject Index

This index provides subject access to the 81 main-entry titles included in Chapters 4 through 8.

About the Author

JOHN T. GILLESPIE, former Dean and Instructor of Library Science, Long Island University, N.Y., has authored numerous books in the areas of library management, school libraries, and children's and young adult literature.